Sources of Anglo-Saxon Literary Culture

Volume One

dedicated to the memory of
J. E. Cross

The following wrote or contributed to entries in this volume:

Frederick M. Biggs
Alan Brown
Mary C. Clayton
†J. E. Cross
Thomas N. Hall
Joyce Hill
Patrizia Lendinara
Hugh Magennis
Gavin Richardson
E. Gordon Whatley
Charles Wright

Sources of Anglo-Saxon Literary Culture

Volume One

Abbo of Fleury, Abbo of Saint-Germain-des-Prés, and Acta Sanctorum

Edited by

Frederick M. Biggs

Thomas D. Hill

Paul E. Szarmach

E. Gordon Whatley

all with the assistance of Deborah A. Oosterhouse

Medieval Institute Publications
WESTERN MICHIGAN UNIVERSITY

Kalamazoo, MI — 2001

Library of Congress Cataloging-in-Publication Data

Abbo of Fleury, Abbo of Saint-Germain-des-Prés, and Acta Sanctorum / edited by Frederick M. Biggs, Thomas D. Hill, Paul E. Szarmach. Acta Sanctorum edited and written in major part by E. Gordon Whatley ; all with the assistance of Deborah A. Oosterhouse.
    p. cm. -- (Sources of Anglo-Saxon literary culture ; v. 1)
    Includes bibliographical references.
    ISBN 1-58044-072-X (casebound : alk. paper) -- ISBN 1-58044-073-8 (pbk. : alk. paper)
    1. English literature--Old English, ca. 450-1100--Sources. 2. England--Civilization--To 1066--Sources. 3. Transmission of texts. I. Biggs, Frederick M. II. Hill, Thomas D., 1940- . III. Szarmach, Paul E. IV. Whatley, E. Gordon, 1944- V. Series.

  PR182 .A28 2001
  829.09--dc21   2001030235

ISBN   1-58044-072-X (casebound)
           1-58044-073-8 (paperbound)

© Copyright 2001 by the Board of The Medieval Institute

Printed in the United States of America

Cover design by Linda K. Judy

Contents

FOREWORD   vii
    Paul E. Szarmach

INTRODUCTION   xv
    Thomas D. Hill

GUIDE FOR READERS   xxxv
    Frederick M. Biggs

Abbo of Fleury   1
    Patrizia Lendinara

Abbo of Saint-Germain-des-Prés   15
    Alan Brown, †J. E. Cross, Patrizia Lendinara

Acta Sanctorum   22
    E. Gordon Whatley *et multi*

BIBLIOGRAPHY   487

Foreword

The dear and gentle reader who peruses this *lytel tretys* may suddenly be seized with a fear and loathing at the looming prospect that a Borgesian enterprise is at hand: a band of hardy scholars works years to produce a reference work whose first volume contains but three entries in some 600 pages, its alpha ordering system portending for groaning shelves large volumes that number in the scores, whether the Old English alphabet or the Modern English alphabet holds sway. And the reader will be prompted to ask if the series will show its Borgesian roots with this exuberant first volume and then, as the alphabet stretches on and the scholars falter in graying step, successor volumes say increasingly less, letters get combined, and volumes become lithe and svelt? Prophecy is a dead art, but it is true that this first volume introducing *Sources of Anglo-Saxon Literary Culture* [*SASLC*] is atypical in the considered decision to incorporate Acta Sanctorum as one large, book-length entry rather than a series of many smaller entries tucked away in a vast body of reference material. The focus of Acta Sanctorum has furthermore created its own special reason to be, given the original mandate to E. Gordon Whatley and the several scholars who have assisted him. The present readiness of the entry, as well as its patent importance for a central field in Anglo-Saxon Studies that cuts across the subdisciplines, further confirmed the need for an alphabetic treatment under Acta and in this first volume. When these considerations joined with the propensity of Anglo-Saxons to indulge themselves with names beginning with *A* or *Æ*, it became obvious that the first three volumes would have to concern themselves with the first letter of the alphabet. Originally, the *SASLC* committee had serious plans to issue only three volumes for the whole project.

In fact, much has changed in the planning and procedures of this project over the first half generation of it. At one time early on there was strong sentiment among the project participants that a mere correction of J. D. A. Ogilvy's pioneering *Books Known to the English, 597–1066* (Cambridge, Mass., 1967) would be a sufficient task and that diskette and loose-leaf binder would be two forms of issue in addition to a codex book of this sort. Work on *A Trial Version* (Binghamton, 1990) confirmed what the late 1980's had begun to teach the project, viz., that correction of *Books Known* would be an insufficient response to the vast knowledge that had been developed to that point and that a new format, which *A Trial Version* presented, would be necessary. The experience of *A Trial Version* also demonstrated that there could be no "quick and dirty" publication of project results. At many a point contributors found new information and new research discoveries or, alternatively, unexpected nuances that a project format, suitable in one area, might be misleading or insufficient in another. At almost every point contributors saw that mere accumulation of information or data, however wide-ranging, was no substitute for weighing and evaluating evidence. Sometimes the border between reference work and creative deduction was less than minimal, and many a time a contributor asked for a variance from procedure for "the special case." The appearance of two Old English Newsletter *Subsidia* volumes, *The Liturgical Books of Anglo-Saxon England* (1995) and *Ambrose in Anglo-Saxon England with Pseudo-Ambrose and Ambrosiaster* (1997), sought in part to address special areas and to capitalize on expertise available for those areas at the time. The mention above of a loose-leaf binder can now only inspire mirth, but the technical side of *SASLC* has seen no less a change, if not a revolution, in the life of this project. Computer applications for the humanities were in their infancy when *SASLC* was first discussed, just as the hardware and the software of that era had remarkable limitations such as the absence of Old English characters. The computer, its pomps, and its works have made much possible and easy, while requiring and demanding other responses such as apparent continual retraining, reconfiguring data for new software, and reinfusion of financial support to keep up with the cunning churn of new equipment as vendors rendered the last great advance dead within a very brief shelflife. The production of *A Trial Version*, for example, depended on a computerized system of bookmaking soon obsolete after publication and untranslatable to other formats with the result that there could be no repeat applicability of stored input. All would have to be rekeyed, and so it was! *Ubi sunt qui ante nos fuerunt*: Kaypro, MAC SE, Wordperfect 4.0, Wordstar? There was as well no WorldWideWeb and no futuristic vision that allowed it to dazzle the imagination and offer to repeat the same Heraclitean dynamic of change, contingency, and shuffle.

The planning for *SASLC* began then in the antediluvian year of 1982 with the writing of a successful grant application to the National Endowment for the Humanities for a Symposium on the Sources of Anglo-Saxon Culture, which took place in 1983 as part of the Congress of Medieval Studies at Western Michigan University, thanks to the generosity of Otto Gründler, then Director of the Medieval Institute. The many hands who contributed to the proposal created a program of international scholars that focused on three subfields in Anglo-Saxon studies: literary culture, iconography, and archaeology, with special emphasis on new directions. The proceedings of this first Symposium appeared as *Sources of Anglo-Saxon Culture*, Studies in Medieval Culture 20 (Kalamazoo, Mich., 1986), which sold out a few years ago and will not be reissued. This first Symposium proved fruitful in a number of ways. Though any administrator would consider it a blunder to end a grant with a surplus, the flexibility of the NEH allowed the convenors to fund in part the second Symposium. The enthusiasm for source study through this public forum has remained steady thereafter, as the Symposium moves on to its twentieth anniversary, now under the able direction of Thomas N. Hall. The strong consensus for a successor publication to Ogilvy's *Books Known* metamorphosed into a successful major grant application to the NEH (1987–89) and a renewal (1990–92). Under these grants *SASLC* became a possibility and then an experimental reality with *A Trial Version*. Based in these years at the State University of New York at Binghamton, where the Center for Medieval and Early Renaissance Studies and the State University of New York Research Foundation gave it intellectual and budgetary homes, respectively, *SASLC* received further support from Cornell University, Brigham Young University, the University of Connecticut, the University of Illinois at Urbana-Champaign, and Queens College of the City University of New York. Crucial to the early development of

SASLC was Medieval and Renaissance Texts and Studies, the publishing program developed at Binghamton by Mario A. DiCesare, its Director and General Editor, whose vision that scholars should take control of the means of the production of their own work and could harness the computer to the task of humane learning proved practical and effective. More than a score of scholars in Anglo-Saxon England and related fields gave counsel and wrote entries—and rewrote them as format changes occurred. *SASLC* has never had a full-time employee in its history, relying, as is customary in the humanities, on the scholarly kindness of voluntary contributors. In 1994–95 *SASLC* moved back to where it began, the Medieval Institute at Western Michigan University, and to a new entity, the Richard Rawlinson Center for Anglo-Saxon Studies and Manuscript Research, established through the generosity of Georgian Rawlinson Tashjian and David Reitler Tashjian. The move, while reaffirming the connection with the annual Symposium, more importantly established a relationship with Medieval Institute Publications, which will publish future *SASLC* volumes under contractual arrangement.

The first Symposium also stimulated interest and activity in Great Britain, where in March 1984 Joyce Hill and J. E. Cross organized a conference at Leeds University. It was Cross who had first energized his North American colleagues to organize the WMU Symposium, after all. The British conference was the forerunner of *Fontes Anglo-Saxonici*, which is a register of sources used in the creation of works produced in Anglo-Saxon England. Directed successively by Peter Clemoes, Malcolm Godden, and now Joyce Hill, *Fontes* is now in the process of producing a database, managed by Dr. Rohini Jayatilaka, available online at http://fontes.english.ox.ac.uk. Both projects have sustained each other over time, and their development has been similar in structure. *Fontes* likewise supports an annual public meeting, held at King's College London in March and organized by Jane Roberts. The management committee meets regularly, apart from the public meeting. From the beginning the *Fontes* and *SASLC* committees have had partial, overlapping membership, and they have encouraged cross-participation in their respective programs and publications. An early witness to the spirit of cooperation was the joint sponsorship of Michael Lapidge's *Abbreviations for Sources and Specification of Standard Editions for Sources* (Binghamton, 1988), a working document that assisted both projects at their formation. Perhaps most important of all, both projects have reaffirmed the significance of source study in the post-modern age and its power to receive the resisting reality of Anglo-Saxon England on solid foundation.

SASLC and its Symposium have assisted the development of other, related projects. The J. Paul Getty Trust supported the photographic acquisition phase of the *Corpus of Insular and Anglo-Saxon Manuscripts*, a scholarly collaboration begun at the 1983 Symposium. Directed by Thomas Ohlgren, the project published a hard-copy catalog of manuscripts (1986), a revised electronic database, and a photographic supplement. The Symposium assisted *Anglo-Saxon Manuscripts in Microfiche Facsimile* in that project's early stages and similarly the *Directory of Individual Liturgical Sources*. The "warming effect" of *SASLC* continues, particularly through the Symposium, which offers a forum for younger scholars, their articles, and their book projects. A working group on Old English saints' lives is among the most recent spin-offs from the main project.

My role in this volume has been to serve as coordinating editor by expediting the substantial editing efforts of E. Gordon Whatley and Frederick M. Biggs through the new publisher, Medieval Institute Publications [MIP]. Quite obviously, much of this book comes from the efforts of Whatley and his several contributors to Acta Sanctorum. We are equally grateful to Patrizia Lendinara for her work on Abbo of Fleury and Abbo of Saint-German-des-Prés, which, joined with the work of Alan Brown and the late J. E. Cross, round out this first volume. I have had the steady support of Thomas D. Hill, whose public contribution is the "Introduction," which gives the intellectual and theoretical rationale for *SASLC*, and whose help and support behind the scenes have been equally important. Messrs. Whatley, Biggs, and Szarmach have in turn received the day-to-day editorial assisance of Ms. Deborah A. Oosterhouse, whose careful work has assisted the progress of many an MIP book. Thomas Seiler, Director of MIP, made publication of *SASLC* possible in the first instance by a commitment to publish its first five volumes. Behind this first book are more than fifteen years of international, interdisciplinary, collegial cooperation. *SASLC* has not operated in recent years under a tight administrative structure, as it had in the beginning. Accordingly, what follows now is not quite a history of the personnel involved in the project nor an indication of their full contributions, but rather an acknowledgment of those who actively continue to support *SASLC* as a project:

Administrative Committee:	Frederick M. Biggs
	Thomas D. Hill
	Paul E. Szarmach
Editors:	Thomas N. Hall
	David Johnson
	Patrick O'Neill
	Richard W. Pfaff
	Joseph Wittig
	Charles D. Wright
Webmaster:	William Schipper
Project Committee:	Janet M. Bately
	George H. Brown
	Sarah Larratt Keefer
	Thomas W. Mackay
	Donald G. Scragg
	Elizabeth Teviotdale
Graduate Support Staff:	Larry Swain
	Joshua Westgard

The current working plan is for the editors to produce the following additional volumes:

from Adalbero of Laon to Augustine:	ed. Biggs
from Augustine to Alcimus Avitus:	ed. Biggs
"B" authors:	ed. Johnson
"C" authors:	ed. Hall
"DEF" authors	TBA
"GHIJ" authors	ed. O'Neill and Wittig

At this time there are plans-in-progress to develop the *SASLC* website further beyond the initial experiments with Ambrose, Pseudo-Ambrose, and Ambrosiaster. It is expected that select and limited parts of this volume and subsequent volumes will appear online. There are no plans as yet to develop a *SASLC* CD-ROM.

It was J. E. Cross who energized this project at its start. His winning enthusiasm and his own substantial contributions served as personal examples to so many over so long a time. Even well into retirement Prof. Cross continued his own work and inspired others to follow his *swæð*. *Dulce et decorum est* to dedicate this first volume of *SASLC* to his memory.

Paul E. Szarmach,
Project Director
Western Michigan University

Sources of Anglo-Saxon Literary Culture: A Bibliography

BOOKS

Bankert, Dabney Anderson, Jessica Wegmann, and Charles D. Wright, eds. *Ambrose in Anglo-Saxon England with Pseudo-Ambrose and Ambrosiaster.* Old English Newsletter *Subsidia* 25 (1997). Website under construction: http://www.mun.ca/Ansaxdat/ambrose (created with William Schipper and Larry Swain)

Biggs, Frederick M., Thomas D. Hill, and Paul E. Szarmach, eds. *Sources of Anglo-Saxon Literary Culture: A Trial Version.* Medieval and Renaissance Texts and Studies 74. Binghamton, 1990. [Distributed free to *OEN* subscribers; now out of print.]

Pfaff, Richard W., ed. *The Liturgical Books of Anglo-Saxon England.* Old English Newsletter *Subsidia* 23 (1995).

ARTICLES

"St. Jerome at UNC:" " I. An Introduction," Theodore H. Leinbaugh; "II. St. Jerome and *Sources of Anglo-Saxon Literary Culture (SASLC)*: Traces of Jerome in Old English Literature," Debra Best, John Brinegar, and John Black. *Old English Newsletter* 29/3 (Spring, 1996): 17–24.

Wegmann, Jessica, and Dabney Anderson Bankert. "Ambrose in *Sources of Anglo-Saxon Literary Culture.*" *Old English Newsletter* 27/1 (Fall, 1993): 30–34.

Whatley, E. Gordon. "Hagiography in Anglo-Saxon England: A Preliminary View from S*ASLC.*" *Old English Newsletter* 23/2 (Spring, 1990): 36–46.

Wright, Charles D. "Hiberno-Latin Writings in *Sources of Anglo-Saxon Literary Culture.*" *Old English Newsletter* 25/3 (Spring, 1992): 21–23.

PAMPHLETS

[NOTE: An asterisk marks joint publication with *Fontes Anglo-Saxonici.*]

*Bately, Janet, comp. *Anonymous Old English Homilies: A Preliminary Bibliography of Source Studies*. Binghamton, 1993. [Distributed free to *OEN* subscribers.] The bibliography is now available at: http://www.wmich.edu/medieval/rawl/bately1/

*Lapidge, Michael, comp. *Abbreviations for Sources and Specification of Standard Editions for Sources*. Binghamton, 1988. [Distributed to *SASLC* contributors.]

[Szarmach, Paul E., comp.] *Symposium on the Sources of Anglo-Saxon Culture*. Binghamton, 1992. Rev. and updated, Kalamazoo, Mich., 1997.

REPORTS

Old English Newsletter has regularly printed announcements of the Sources Symposium and *SASLC*, since vol. 15/2 (Spring, 1982) and vol. 27/1 (Fall, 1987), respectively. Every Spring issue since vol. 19/2 (Spring, 1986) *OEN* has printed the annual report of *Fontes Anglo-Saxonici*.

REVIEWS/NOTICES of Biggs, Hill, and Szarmach, *Sources of Anglo-Saxon Literary Culture: A Trial Version*.

by Robert Godding, *Analecta Bollandiana* 111 (1993): 460–61

by Fred C. Robinson, *Speculum* 68 (1993): 1065–67

WEBSITE: http://www.wmich.edu/medieval/rawl

Flyers marking project development at various stages are not noted here, nor are internal documents that may have achieved wide circulation.

Introduction

The predecessor and inspiration for our present volume is J. D. A. Ogilvy's *Books Known to the English, 597–1066*, whose title neatly synopsized the aims of his collection. Our title is vaguer and more amorphous—in part because it was composed by a committee and in part because our goals are less easily defined. Ogilvy was concerned simply with "books"—with Latin texts transcribed and transmitted in the Anglo-Saxon period—whereas we are interested more broadly in "sources," including oral traditional literature as well as written texts, and in written texts such as charters, medical recipes, and charms, which can only be loosely described as books. These concerns necessitated a new, somewhat more inclusive title, and it was necessary to distinguish our project from his in any case; but we have lost something in the change. Since our title no longer speaks for itself with the brisk assurance of Ogilvy's, and since the user of this guide needs some general orientation in any case, this essay is intended to serve as an introduction to the entries gathered here. The present reference volume is a collaborative endeavor; it consists of a collection of single entries by numerous scholars and obviously reflects diverse scholarly opinion. This introduction, in contrast, is written by one individual; and it should be emphasized that the views expressed in the introduction—to the degree that they are not merely platitudes—are those of a single individual, who has, however, received enough commentary and criticism over a period of time that he feels it is appropriate to use the editorial first person plural. What we hope to accomplish in this introduction is a definition of certain key terms, a guide and warning to users, and a prospectus concerning the objectives of this particular kind of scholarly inquiry—to put it simply, why we think source scholarship is valid and worth consolidating in a reference work of this kind.

Methodology and Assumptions of Source Scholarship

Since the terms "source" and "influence" are used with a good deal of freedom in literary scholarship, let us begin by defining a literary source and its derivative as a particular mode of textual relationship. The first step in establishing such a relationship is to demonstrate parallels between two texts that are so striking that to assume they were fortuitous would "outrage probability," to use R. E. Kaske's phrase. Once such parallels have been established, the next step is to evaluate the historical relationship of the two texts and to determine the kind and direction of influence that these parallels imply. In principle, at least, it might be possible to distinguish between a source and a text derived from it on the basis of careful analysis of the idiom, style, and structure of the two texts. But in practice scholars rely on such analyses only when external historical evidence is not available. And our assumptions about the larger historical context in which a given text was composed can affect our interpretation of apparently straightforward evidence. Thus, given textual parallels between some of the homilies of Augustine's *Tractatus in evangelium Ioannis* and certain of Ælfric's homilies, the conclusion that Augustine is the source and Ælfric derivative is determined not by analysis of the texts themselves, but by our knowledge of the historical relationship of the two texts. This example is obviously a very simple one. No one has yet proposed that Ælfric influenced Augustine. But it is important to emphasize at the outset that defining source relationships is not as simple as it might seem; one must always consider questions of historical and literary context. To take a suppositious example, parallels of exactly the same sort as those between Augustine and Ælfric that involved an Anglo-Saxon and a Greek text would not necessarily be accepted as proof that the latter was the source of the former. The probability of some Latin intermediary would seem a more plausible way of accounting for the parallels than the assumption that an Anglo-Saxon author knew Greek. But at the same time the assumption that the Anglo-Saxons were Greekless can become a self-fulfilling prophecy if all parallels between Anglo-Saxon and Greek texts are explained away by hypothesizing lost Latin intermediaries. For a variety of reasons, the current working assumption of most Anglo-Saxonists that the Anglo-Saxons were generally ignorant of Greek seems to us plausible, but source scholars must be sensitive to the fact that this is in fact an assumption, and an assumption that shapes the way they understand the "raw" data of textual relationships.

We have referred to "striking textual parallels," but must concede that defining such parallels is a matter of intuitive judgment and that the range of potential ambiguity and subjectivity is wide. But the fact remains that there are many thousands of such textual relationships that have been adduced in the fields of Old and Middle English scholarship alone, and have never seriously been questioned. The appeal to the *consensus omnium* may not be an elegant or sophisticated mode of scholarly argument, but it has its force. If we were asked to define our working methodology, we would respond that source scholarship involves a kind of dialectical process in which individual scholars propose source relationships on the basis of intuitive judgment, and these judgments are then either confirmed or denied by the general consensus of scholars who take the trouble to evaluate the argument and the supporting evidence. Such a consensus may not be reached quickly if the source relationship is difficult for one reason or another, or if the text involved is obscure. But in principle, once a number of scholars who have no immediate reason to be prejudiced have examined the evidence, a consensus, or at the least an agenda for further research, can be reached.

Implicit in this methodology is the assumption that a "true" definition of a given source relationship is both desirable and in principle attainable, but it must also be clearly acknowledged that, given the limitations of documentation during this period, even the best established and most secure examples of source relationships are provisional and open to correction and modification. If Ælfric drew on Augustine's *Tractatus in evangelium Ioannis*, there remains the question of what version of the text of those homilies was accessible to him, or whether Ælfric's choice of available synonyms in translation was influenced by a previous tradition of glossing; and this list of hypothetical discoveries, which might complicate the apparently simple literary-historical fact that Ælfric used

Augustine on John, could be extended almost indefinitely. Scholars may believe that in certain areas of Anglo-Saxon literary source scholarship the work has been pretty thoroughly done, but there is always the possibility of surprising new finds.

Terminology

Apart from the provisional character of source scholarship in the field of Old English and Anglo-Latin literature, another immediate problem that must concern us is that there is no established terminology to distinguish among the many possible modes of relationship between two or more texts that may obtain in any given case. For practical purposes we propose to stipulate some working definitions. In literary-historical discourse a source can consist of as little as one word or as much as thousands of lines of text. Indeed, many Anglo-Saxon texts are wholly dependent on one specific source and are conventionally defined as translations or versions of an original. But in ordinary usage the term "source" generally refers to a text that provides the antecedent for some significant portion of a derivative (or if one prefers "target")[1] text, while the terms "citation," "quotation," "allusion," or "echo" refer to smaller and more limited instances of similar textual relationships. These less

---

[1] See now Katherine O'Brien O'Keeffe, "Source, Method, Theory, Practice: On Reading Two Old English Verse Texts," *Bulletin of the John Rylands University Library of Manchester* 76 (1994): 51–73 [also printed as the Toller Memorial Lecture, 8 March 1993]. In this paper, which is concerned with the problem of sources, O'Keeffe proposes this alternative phrasing on the grounds that the term "derivative" has negative implications. I would accept this criticism, but I would insist that the statement of a source/derivative relationship is not a value judgment. Most of Shakespeare's plays and Chaucer's tales have sources, but it is the consensus of virtually all critics that in these cases the "derivatives" are aesthetically superior to the "sources." Except, of course, in the case of *Troilus and Cressida*.

extended verbal parallels are sometimes indicated in some explicit fashion comparable to the modern device of using quotation marks. But in both vernacular and Christian-Latin literary tradition the concept of authorial proprietorship was less clearly defined than it is in the modern English literary tradition, and authors would often draw passages from antecedent texts without such acknowledgment. For present purposes a "citation" is defined as a passage that is prefaced or concluded by a reference to the author or text from which the quotation is drawn. A "quotation" by contrast need not include such a reference. In modern English usage such a quotation must be indicated in some formal way, but in early medieval usage verbal borrowings of this sort ordinarily would not be indicated. Even briefer instances of parallel textual relationships are "allusions" or "echoes," the former consisting of words, phrases, or larger units of discourse that purposefully recall some particular antecedent text, and the latter consisting of such parallels that occur simply because one author is so thoroughly familiar with some antecedent text that he echoes it unconsciously and inadvertently. In principle it is possible to distinguish clearly between these various modes of textual relationship, but in practice it can be very difficult to distinguish between a deliberate allusion, intended to call to mind some particular antecedent text, and an echo. For the immediate purposes of this study and in the context of literary-historical discourse, the distinction is not as important as it might seem, since either allusions or echoes reflect the fact that a given author was familiar with a specific source, but readers who consult the various editions and literary handbooks must be aware that there is a good deal of editorial judgment involved in such discriminations.

The Problem of Textual Identity

A further problem involving definition concerns the question of the definition of the text itself, or textual identity. In the modern world the question is a comparatively simple one. An individual author writes a specific text and ultimately "authorizes" its publication in a particular form. The specific form of the text presumably reflects the author's intention—a useful if much debated term—and this particular form of the text is reproduced mechanically and disseminated as widely as the economics of publication permit. Anglo-Saxon literary culture reflects the influence of two originally quite discrete literary traditions—Germanic and Christian-Latin—and the concept of textual identity was rather different from the modern one in both traditions. Germanic literary tradition was in large part an oral one, and without prejudicing the much discussed question of the character and nature of this tradition, it is clear that a "text" that exists in oral tradition exists in a radically different context than in contemporary "literate" tradition.

As far as the Christian-Latin tradition is concerned, the tradition with which we are for the most part concerned in this study, the issue of textual identity is more immediately apprehensible but still raises problems. The Anglo-Saxons knew and understood the concept of textual identity as we understand it—the concept of a text fixed and determined by the intention of an individual author—but the vagaries of early medieval book production, along with scribal practice and the particular circumstances of both vernacular and Anglo-Latin literary culture, frequently complicate the issue of textual identity enormously. A conscientious scholar such as Bede was aware of the problem of textual variation and corruption, and such scholars attempted to correct and correctly identify the texts with which they were dealing. But lesser scholars were less conscientious, and in any case it was necessary to have both good texts and good judgment to correct the faults of one's exemplar. Textual corruption was as a result endemic, and confusion about attribution and canonicity was simply part of the intellectual culture of the period. It could indeed be argued that modern scholarship is still affected by errors deriving from this period. Migne's *Patrologia Latina* is in large part a reprint of sixteenth- and seventeenth-century editions of Christian-Latin authors, and these editions in turn were often simply based on "old," that is, early medieval, manuscripts. The misattributions and textual confusions that have plagued scholars attempting to work with that monumental collection are in part a direct heritage of the scholarship of the Anglo-Saxon period

Thus when one is faced with an apparently simple problem of source scholarship—whether a given Anglo-Saxon author knew a particular classical or patristic text—the first question that must be raised is in what form the text in question might have been circulated. To take a specific example that illustrates something of the complexity of these issues, the Bible was, as it still is, a central text in Catholic Christian culture. Biblical influence is pervasive in the Christian literature of this period. But as one also might expect in a manuscript culture in which every text had to be copied out by hand, there are relatively few manuscripts of the Bible as we would define it—the full text of the Old and New Testaments from beginning to end. Psalters and Gospels, however—texts that could be used in the liturgy—are relatively abundant, and there is a good deal of evidence that Anglo-Saxons would have been especially familiar with the Bible in the form in which it was read in the services. There is also some evidence of the study of specific biblical texts both in Latin and in the vernacular, and interest in the Bible as a historical text, particularly as a record of the earliest events of human history. Again, there is a good deal of biblical legal material transcribed into Anglo-Saxon law. And, finally, there are biblical texts included in sapiential collections, in contexts in which it is very difficult to know whether the collector or scribe recognized the fact that a given maxim or "sentence" was in fact biblical. Certainly the reader would have no way of knowing the difference between a biblical maxim and one drawn from the Fathers or some similar source in such collections. The text of the Bible thus existed not only in formal monumental codices, but also in a variety of other forms as well, and the fact that a given text has a biblical source does not fully answer the more specific question of what particular kind of text a given poet or homilist might have had in front of him.

In one way or another the problem of textual identity has arisen in virtually every entry in this handbook. The problem may be as simple as when and where a given text begins and ends, or it may involve such virtually unresolvable issues as at what point the process of abridgment, alteration, and scribal error creates a "new" text rather than a "version" of a given exemplar. In such matters the authors of specific entries have simply exercised their best judgment; when appropriate they have attempted to warn users of such problems in the body of their entries. In some genres in particular, the problem of textual identity has been particularly difficult. Texts in the wisdom literature tradition, for example, which consist of a series of "wise" and often enigmatic sayings or homilies—particularly the loosely structured homilies of the anonymous tradition—can sometimes be very hard to define in terms of their specific textual identity. In fact it could be argued that such texts should be viewed as improvisations on a theme rather than fixed textual discourse with a clearly defined beginning and end. But for practical purposes the authors of the various entries have had to treat all of these various literary forms as if they were fixed textual entities comparable to a modern text. As long as it is clearly recognized that this is simply a convenient working assumption—that texts such as the *De duodecim abusivis sæculi* or the *Apocalypse of Thomas* did not circulate in a single authorized version, and that an edition of a single version of these texts would misrepresent the way in which most medieval readers had access to them—then the readers of these entries can use the information gathered without serious misapprehension. But it must be emphasized that even in the Christian-Latin tradition various texts existed in quite different modes of textual identity, and that while some of these texts were indeed "books" in Ogilvy's sense and ours, some were not.

The Evidence of the Entries and Their Limitations

A question that must be faced is how the readers of this volume may make use of the evidence that the authors of the various entries have gathered together. The answer is a simple one—with great caution. This caution must extend both to the evidence itself and to what significance to attach to it. As editors and authors, we have made every effort to be accurate, but errors are inevitable in these entries—particularly errors of omission. Ideally the author of any given entry should review the corpus of Anglo-Saxon and Anglo-Latin literature in order to verify that the list of references provided in the entry is as inclusive as possible. In practice we have not been able to accomplish any such effort at verification; and indeed the editorial decision not to include newly discovered source findings has meant that even if a contributor was able to add to our current knowledge of source relationships, he or she could not ordinarily do so in the entry prepared for this volume. Thus errors of omission are inevitable and inevitably common in these entries; in fact one of the goals of this project is to indicate where the lacunae are by presenting the available evidence in summary form. To take a specific example, there is evidence for the availability of the political and sapiential text *De duodecim abusivis sæculi* before the Viking invasions because Alcuin quoted from it, and evidence that it was known in the later period because Ælfric quoted from it and either Ælfric or someone in Ælfric's circle translated an abbreviated version of this treatise. But one naturally wonders whether the text was known in the intervening years—whether the Anglo-Saxons were reading it in the generations between Alcuin and Ælfric. At present we have no clear-cut evidence of the currency of this treatise during this period, and this lacuna is evident in the presentation of our evidence. But the text in question was a popular one, and we expect that further evidence of its use will turn up, and that whoever discovers this evidence will be alerted to its significance by the lacuna in our entry.

Editorial Principles Concerning "New" Source Scholarship

A related issue that requires some discussion is the editorial decision not to include unpublished source discoveries in our entries. In part this decision is motivated by the editorial concern that if we accept and implicitly sanction original source scholarship by our authors, the project may be extended indefinitely. For better or worse all of the entries completed so far have suggested significant new lines of research to their authors and one logical extension of this development is a project without a clear-cut terminus. Another somewhat more principled reason for not including new research is that source scholarship, like any other branch of scholarship, requires a process of review and assimilation. To encourage contributors to present the results of their own scholarship in a reference work without the benefit of this process would weaken rather than strengthen scholarship in this area. There are many journals that publish source scholarship in Anglo-Saxon and Anglo-Latin literature, and we therefore see no need to make the present volume a vehicle for new research. While this principle governs the guidelines for authors of entries, we have made exceptions on occasion, and scholars have been generous in communicating to us the results of research that have been accepted for publication but are not yet in print.

Paleographical and Codicological Issues

Another problem that the users of this volume must consider is that while the format of the entries we have chosen gives a certain prominence to the manuscript evidence, and that while this is of course a very important kind of evidence, there are certain immediate problems with the witness of the manuscripts in themselves. The first is that interpreting it depends upon the judgment of paleographers, a judgment that is potentially as subjective and fallible as that of scholars in any other discipline. In the present volume we have simply accepted the dating and locations suggested by the paleographers and cataloguers of the major collections. It is important to bear in mind that while we have reproduced this information and have in some instances based our discussions upon it, we have not ordinarily independently verified it. The Gneuss list of Anglo-Saxon and Anglo-Latin manuscripts, for example, which is one of our fundamental reference tools, was not and could not be based on an actual reexamination of the manuscripts themselves.[2] Although all of the members of the editorial board have at least some experience of working with manuscripts, no member is a paleographer in terms of scholarly specialization. Here as elsewhere we have been concerned not with attempting to provide new information for the present volume, but rather with codifying and gathering received scholarly opinion as of the time of publication. What this means in practical terms is that when users of this volume notice that the evidence for the currency of a certain work is dependent on limited or ambiguous paleographical evidence, then it is important that they examine the evidence and the argumentation for themselves. Error or unwarranted dogmatism on the part of the paleographers we have quoted are, of course, obvious problems; but a more subtle source of confusion is that scholarly qualifications and hesitations tend to be suppressed in transition from one scholarly work to another. If a paleographer discusses a problem of dating at some length and in the end with some reluctance opts for a particular date, the hesitations and in particular the

---

[2]Helmut Gneuss, "A Preliminary List of Manuscripts Written or Owned in England up to 1100," *Anglo-Saxon England* 9 (1981): 1–60.

degree of hesitation he or she may have about assigning a particular date are not adequately expressed in the conventional notation we have accepted from our predecessors. Thus a notation like "10c Worcester ?" can mean anything from "this is the paleographer's opinion but he is not absolutely certain" to "if forced to hazard an opinion, the paleographer would desperately offer the above-mentioned." As in other areas of scholarship, part of the object of the present volume is to focus attention on possible areas of fruitful scholarly investigation, and the numerous occasions of reticence and the question marks that adorn our entries can at least illustrate the limitations of our knowledge with graphic clarity.[3]

The Relevance of Literary History

Even when the paleographers agree about the place and the date—or, as more often happens, about a range of possible places and dates that would accord with the evidence of a manuscript—it is still necessary to interpret the evidence of the manuscript in specifically literary terms. If we have, for example, a manuscript of Vergil's *Aeneid* that appears to have been copied by an Anglo-Saxon scribe, does the format and the presentation of the text suggest that the scribe understood what he was copying? Is there evidence that the text was read? And if so by whom? Such issues might seem narrowly codicological, but as soon as one raises the question of who ordered a manuscript to be written, for whom, and for what purpose, one is dealing with issues that pertain to literary and intellectual history. And once a scholar is dealing with these issues, he or she is very quickly involved with issues of literary criticism as well. For example, if the putative Vergil manuscript was glossed by an Anglo-Saxon scribe, these glosses would provide evidence that some Anglo-

---

[3]These paragraphs have occasioned some comments from friendly paleographers. I intend no disrespect for the scholarly discipline of paleography, but simply wish to emphasize that the paleogaphical information included in these volumes is ordinarily derivative and is not based on any new examinations of the manuscripts.

Saxon was concerned enough to attempt to read and gloss Vergil's poetry. This inference, however, would depend upon the assumption that these glosses were in fact available in Anglo-Saxon England or at least were an intelligent copy of some Continental or Irish precursor. To say the least, these are not simple and straightforward questions, and the answer one arrives at would depend upon one's own interpretation of Vergil's poetry and one's knowledge and understanding of the tradition of commentary on the *Aeneid*. Even if the glosses in question were clearly wrong and inappropriate, the kind of error they reflected might tell us something about the study of classical texts during this period and the level of education of the scribe or scholar who was responsible for them. The point is that there is no escaping the necessity of literary and historical judgment.

One final warning for the user of this volume concerns the complexity of the issues related to source relationships. When one considers the relationship of a given Anglo-Saxon or Anglo-Latin text to its sources, the more closely one examines the relevant texts, the more problems of detail emerge. Even if certain broad patterns can be discerned and clarified, there remain anomalies of detail, problems concerning word choice, omissions, relevant aspects of textual criticism, and so on. One of the ongoing problems in this field is that scholarly attention has focused on certain texts almost to the exclusion of others. And those texts that have been studied in detail are the monuments of the native Germanic literary tradition whose sources must be reconstructed. Detailed source study of those texts that actually draw on known Christian-Latin literary sources is very much an ongoing project in modern Anglo-Saxon scholarship. As a result there are relatively few texts from this period that have been studied in detail in terms of their sources, and none that might not be profitably studied further. As this mode of study proceeds, it opens up new questions even as it resolves outstanding ones.

The Form and the Scope of the Entries

Given these various warnings and qualifications, it might seem that we have qualified our project out of existence; some positive statement of our goals may therefore be appropriate. The first point to emphasize is that each entry is the work of an individual scholar who is ultimately responsible for its content, and that therefore each entry is to a significant degree an individual statement. But while we emphasize the individual responsibility of our contributors and have allowed them to shape their entries in many ways, the definition of our common purpose is that each entry is intended to provide a succinct and authoritative summary of what evidence exists for the currency of a given text in Anglo-Saxon literary culture as a whole. Each contributor has had to balance the demand for a comprehensive and judicious presentation of the evidence on the one hand and the necessity for succinctness and clarity on the other. In the present volume our aim has been to be relatively brief. Our model has been Ogilvy's volume of approximately 300 pages, and we are very much aware of the larger project based in England, the *Fontes Anglo-Saxonici*—a project that will not merely summarize the evidence as ours does, but will present the evidence itself in some detail. The existence of this project has freed us from the responsibility of presenting evidence or from reviewing in any detail argumentation concerning the currency and use of a given source. We do hope however that the bibliographical information we have gathered will permit the users to review the argumentation and available evidence for themselves relatively quickly.

We have construed "literary culture" broadly to include legal, historical, and religious literature as well as the imaginative literature with which literary scholars are conventionally concerned. In this field such a broad definition of literature is a necessary response to the fact that the literary culture of the Anglo-Saxons is fragmentarily preserved; and in any case the distinction between "imaginative" literature and other modes of literature is one that is very much a product of modern literary fashion. Even in the context of contemporary literary culture, the distinction is hard to draw, and in the literature of the Anglo-Saxon period, the distinction between literary and extra-literary genres and works would be both pointless and destructive. This is not to say that aesthetic and literary discriminations cannot and should not be made, but simply that for the literary historian or the historian concerned with intellectual or religious culture, all of the available evidence is precious.

In the present volume the range of our concerns is quite wide. We are potentially concerned with the entire corpus of Anglo-Saxon and Anglo-

Latin written literature and with oral literature and oral genres as well. Our treatment of some of the larger topics is very succinct indeed, and one problem that does not admit of any easy solution is that it is much easier to present the evidence for the knowledge of an obscure or little known work than for a much used text. Here again, the authors of individual entries have exercised their best judgment and have indicated the scope of their discussion in their articles.

Apologia

In the final portion of this essay we would like to offer a prospectus concerning this kind of research and to try to make explicit the rationale for source work in the field of Anglo-Saxon and Anglo-Latin literary culture. The first point to emphasize is that Old English is a deciphered language. The ability to read Old English accurately was lost for a long time and was not fully recovered with philological accuracy until the nineteenth century. The process of recovery took place over a period of centuries and was immensely facilitated by the fact that a significant portion of the corpus of Old English literature is based upon readily accessible Latin sources. These texts remain the most important source of information about what Old English words mean and about what given syntactical devices imply; and the task of Anglo-Saxon lexicography was begun by Anglo-Saxon scribes who glossed difficult Latin words with vernacular equivalents. Any extended study of Old English language or literature that does not consider the problem of sources is in a sense rootless, since our knowledge of the language is so heavily dependent on the cultural interweaving of Latin and Anglo-Saxon in this period. From the perspective of the literary critic and the literary historian, those texts that are most heavily dependent on Latin sources are usually of least intellectual and aesthetic merit; but from that of the linguist or the Anglo-Saxonist of any scholarly persuasion who is attempting to explain a difficult word or locution, those Anglo-Saxon texts that have a known Latin source are a crucial linguistic resource without which our knowledge of the language would be much less assured than it is. And obviously the linguist or historian who cites the Latin *Vorlage* of a given Old English text is either using the source scholarship of some predecessor or offering his or her own.

If the most immediate value of source scholarship is to enable us to understand Old English as a language, the further value of such scholarship for the intellectual and literary historian is no less fundamental. The immediate questions of literary and intellectual history—what the Anglo-Saxons knew and believed about themselves and their world—can best be addressed by detailed study of those texts that the Anglo-Saxons composed or compiled or copied. And in studying such texts it is impossible to proceed very far without facing issues of source scholarship. Tracing the filiations of one text with another is often laborious, but it can be very enlightening. Even the disjunctions, the gaps where one might expect a relationship, can be suggestive, and the larger patterns that emerge when one traces the relationship of one text with its sources can be strikingly revealing. J. E. Cross has spoken of "going close" to one's text, and there are moments in source study when one has the eerie sense of almost eavesdropping on the thoughts and hesitations of an author who may be nameless and has been dead for many hundred years, but whose characteristic voice and intellectual preferences are gradually becoming clear.

In considering scholarly and critical discourse about Anglo-Saxon and Anglo-Latin literary culture in relationship to its sources, it is possible to discern two positions that, with some polemical exaggeration, we will call "maximalist" and "minimalist." The maximalists tend to accentuate the depth and the breadth of Anglo-Saxon and Anglo-Latin literary culture, to take for granted a relatively wide degree of literary Christian-Latin culture and acquaintance with Classical culture. For better or worse, Ogilvy with his concern for libraries and Latin manuscripts was a maximalist, and many of the great Anglo-Saxonists of the first generations of Old English literary scholarship tended toward this position. One thinks of A. S. Cook or Fr. Klaeber, who never hesitated in their belief that the Anglo-Saxons were a deeply literate and literary people. By contrast (and in part in reaction to such assumptions) other scholars have emphasized the enormous obstacles that the Anglo-Saxons faced in attempting to perpetuate a literary culture and have focused on the very substantial evidence that exists to show the sharp limitations on Anglo-Saxon learning. One eminent and authoritative contemporary Anglo-Saxonist has recently argued, for example, that we must take Alfred quite literally when he says that there were no literate persons, lay or clergy, in large portions of Anglo-Saxon England in his youth. This "minimalism" is, for the literary scholar at least, a less congenial view of the literary culture of the period, but precisely because it is less congenial its implications must be faced directly.

The debate between these two perspectives is an ongoing one, and there is no reason to believe it will be concluded any time in the immediate future. At the risk of seeming to lack zeal for controversy, we would like to suggest a *via media* that grants a certain cogency to both perspectives, and that we would call "particularist." We would begin by granting the enormous problems that the Anglo-Saxons faced in acquiring, disseminating, and transmitting literary culture whether in Latin or the vernacular. The Anglo-Saxons were presumably generally illiterate before they were converted to Christianity; there is some truth in the old and nationalistic saying that the Irish taught the English to write. After the conversion, the Anglo-Saxons could acquire literary skills and literary culture, but it is difficult to know how many of them chose to do so. The literacy rate in Anglo-Saxon England is unknown and unknowable; but lay literacy is often associated with mercantile culture, and the urban population of Anglo-Saxon England was relatively small. The presumption must be that only a minority of Anglo-Saxons were ever literate even in their own language. And if Latin was a learned language everywhere in Europe, Anglo-Saxons were handicapped in comparison with the speakers of the various romance vernaculars in that their mother tongue was quite different from Latin. In addition to the immediate practical difficulties of learning Latin and copying and disseminating Latin manuscripts in the Anglo-Saxon speaking world, Anglo-Saxons concerned with literary culture faced an even larger problem in that learning was threatened by constant internal warfare and after 793 by the threat of pagan Viking raiders who had no scruples about destroying churches and monasteries.

The list of potential threats to Anglo-Saxon literary culture could be prolonged, and it is certainly easy to find evidence for ignorance and barbarism in the written records of the Anglo-Saxons. There is, however, one immediate counter-argument so salient that it is sometimes overlooked. Christianity is for better or worse a religion of the book. Without a certain degree of literary culture, Christianity, at least Latin Catholic

Christianity, could not continue to exist. It is possible to imagine an illiterate or semi-literate priest who fulfilled the functions expected of him by memorizing the Latin words of the canon of the mass and the other most important liturgical texts by rote with only a minimal understanding of what he was saying. But it is very difficult to imagine how such a priest could train a successor. It would therefore follow that an aspirant to the clergy would have good reason to seek out a more learned cleric for his education. It is of course true that a priest or monk need not be an intellectual or a particularly learned man in order to fulfill his office. But Christian education and the continual necessity of training younger generations of clergy demanded a certain degree of Latin and vernacular literary culture. Christianity did not take root everywhere in the early Middle Ages; there were numerous missions that failed, and it is perfectly imaginable that the pagan Anglo-Saxons newly converted to Christianity might have relapsed into the non-literate pagan Germanic culture that they traditionally had practiced. But for the most part they did not. Anglo-Saxon England converted to Christianity and remained Christian, and the consequence was that there existed a milieu, clerical for the most part but to some degree lay, in which literary culture could exist and in which, at the least, there was a tradition of respect for learning and an interest in the transmission of texts. In considering barbarian Anglo-Saxon England from such a perspective, the continued existence of any native literary culture at all either in Latin or Old English represents a substantial achievement, and instances of error and naive ignorance are much more understandable. The Anglo-Saxons, however, did not simply acquire sufficient literacy for a native Christian tradition to exist and perpetuate itself. Within three generations of the conversions there were Anglo-Saxon Christians whose learning and knowledge of Latin were comparable to those of any scholar in Europe. The achievement of Bede would be remarkable in any age, but when one remembers that his grandparents were probably born before the coming of Christianity to Northumbria, it brings his achievement into sharper focus. It is thus a matter of historical fact that some Anglo-Saxons attained a very high level of Latin literary culture in places and times in which one might not have expected it. It is also of course true that the Anglo-Saxons faced formidable problems in acquiring and transmitting literary culture; and we, as particularists, would argue that every Anglo-Saxon text be approached individually and as far as possible without preconceptions—either maximalist or minimalist. As a practical matter, Anglo-Saxonists will have to be practicing maximalists when they first approach an Anglo-Saxon literary text in that one must test every possible hypothesis about sources and influence before dismissing it; but in deference to the minimalist position we must remind readers that no single library in Anglo-Saxon England possessed all of the books listed in our present volume. Indeed, the fact that an author is mentioned and an entry listed in the present volume does not necessarily mean that "this book was known to the Anglo-Saxons," but rather that there is evidence of at least one Anglo-Saxon's having known it, either directly or indirectly—a much more limited and localized proposition. It may also be mentioned in passing that our silence does not prove a given text was not known, but simply that we did not know of any evidence for it.

A prospectus ordinarily includes an invitation to the public at large, and we would like to make such an invitation in pointing out that the work of tracing the sources of Anglo-Saxon literary culture is very much in progress and that there is much to be done. We hope to be able to publish ongoing revisions of these entries under the auspices of the *Old English Newsletter*, and we hope the more obvious deficiencies of our volume will be corrected in an ongoing process of correction and revision that will extend beyond the date of formal publication.

A question that historians enjoy debating is whether the advent of the Norman conquest involved a radical break with Anglo-Saxon culture and political institutions—whether one defines the relationship between the Anglo-Saxon and Anglo-Norman eras in terms of rupture or continuity. Even accepting the most radical account of the changes that William and his successors worked, however, these changes are trivial in comparison with those that had already occurred in the development of Anglo-Saxon culture and the Anglo-Saxon polity. A scattered and fragmented group of tribes had been joined together to form one nation; these Germanic peoples had become Christian and as a result literate. Any story must have a beginning, and the beginning of the history of England and the English-speaking nations begins with the Anglo-Saxons. For better or worse, "England" became inhabited by the "English," the "English" became

Christian during our period, and the consequences of these events are still being felt. The study of the sources of Anglo-Saxon literary culture may sometimes seem pedestrian and is often difficult, but this kind of scholarship can provide genuine insight into the intelligence and aspirations of men and women who lived a millennium ago, spoke our language, and created the foundations of our culture. And this is no small reward.

Thomas D. Hill
Cornell University

Guide for Readers

As discussed in the introduction, a variety of problems arises in an effort to survey the sources of Anglo-Saxon literary culture; the aim of this guide is to indicate how these bear on the organization of this reference work. Had all of the sources survived in written form, and had each been the sole work of a known writer, a series of entries on individual works arranged alphabetically by author would have sufficed. While the reality is more complicated, this model reveals two principles that control our presentation when possible: an individual entry treats a specific work, and the main entries are arranged alphabetically by author.

Entries

Many authors surveyed in *SASLC* are responsible for more than one work, and so their individual entries are gathered into major-author entries; for example, under **AMBROSE** appear entries on **HEXAMERON** and **DE FIDE** (more in a moment on cross-references). Similarly, numerous anonymous works can be considered more effectively when gathered into generic entries such as **ACTA SANCTORUM** or **LITURGY**. Authors take precedence: **ALCUIN**'s hagiographic works, for example, appear in his entry, and not in Acta Sanctorum (although generic entries may include a single work by a named author if this is the only work by the author known in Anglo-Saxon England).[1] It is also important to note

---

[1] See the introduction to Acta Sanctorum for a further qualification.

that individual entries within major-author or generic entries are not necessarily structured alphabetically: readers must consult the introduction of each to determine its order.

Major-author and generic entries are listed in alphabetical sequence along with authors of single works and titles of anonymous works (alphabetized by the first word other than a preposition). Works, however, that modern scholars conventionally identify as by, for example, **PSEUDO-BEDE**, follow the author in question (**BEDE**) and are in turn followed, when there is significant evidence, by entries on Old English translations of the work (**OLD ENGLISH BEDE**). Further exceptions are handled by cross-references.

Titles and Their Abbreviations; Designated Editions

In general, individual entries, whether free-standing or part of larger groups, discuss particular works; exceptions include cases where a written source has not survived, or instances when the writer of the entry must decide if, for example, Ambrose's **EPISTULAE** are better treated as one work or many. When the subject of an entry is a surviving written work, its title is followed by an abbreviation,[2] drawn in the case of Latin works from Michael Lapidge's *Abbreviations for Sources and Specification of Standard Editions for Sources* (Binghamton, 1988) and in the case of Old English from the *Microfiche Concordance to Old English* [*MCOE*].[3] The title (and abbreviation) may then be followed by references to standard

---

[2]Because these abbreviations are expanded in the title that precedes them, they are not included in our list of abbreviations. They appear at the start of each entry because they tie our work to *Fontes Anglo-Saxonici* and to the Toronto *Dictionary of Old English*; indeed they may become more useful to our readers as our project progresses and entries are linked electronically.

[3]See below, Standard Research Tools, Standard Editions, and Bibliography, for the system used in *SASLC* to refer to other works.

research tools, such as the *Clavis Patrum Latinorum* [*CPL*], to which the reader may turn to learn more about the source itself. When the source has been edited, the next line of the entry designates the specific edition to which the writer of the entry refers, usually following Lapidge (1988) or the *MCOE*.

Headnote

It is often possible to present in a headnote five kinds of information that indicate that a work was available in Anglo-Saxon England: manuscripts, booklists, Anglo-Saxon versions, quotations or citations, and references. Each category of evidence requires some comment.

MSS *Manuscripts.* The inclusion of a work in a relevant manuscript provides firm physical evidence for its presence in Anglo-Saxon England. Helmut Gneuss's "Preliminary List of Manuscripts Written or Owned in England up to 1100" [HG] provides the basis for this category of evidence, and Professor Gneuss has kindly shared a revised, second draft of the work with us, which considerably expands on the lists of manuscript contents. Contributors have, of course, consulted other sources as needed, and have also been encouraged to include Continental manuscripts, by definition outside of Gneuss's concern, that provide evidence (such as Anglo-Saxon script or Old English glosses) that a work was known in Anglo-Saxon circles. Manuscripts not in Gneuss's list are preceded by a question mark in the headnote and are discussed in the body of the entry.

Lists *Booklists.* Although less informative than a surviving manuscript, the mention of a work in wills, lists of donations, or inventories of libraries from our period provides a good indication that it was known. In "Surviving Booklists from Anglo-Saxon England" [ML] Michael Lapidge edits the remaining catalogues of manuscripts from our period and identifies, whenever possible, the work in question. The following shortened titles are used to refer to these lists: 1. Alcuin; 2. King Athelstan; 3. Athelstan (grammarian); 4. Æthelwold; 5. Ælfwold; 6. Sherburn-in-Elmet; 7. Bury St Edmunds I; 8. Sæwold; 9. Worcester I; 10. Leofric;

11. Worcester II; 12. Bury St Edmunds II; and 13. Peterborough. For a discussion of these lists—and specifically on the localizing of the second list associated with Worcester and the Peterborough list—see ML.

A-S Vers   *Anglo-Saxon Versions.* Like the manuscript evidence, an Anglo-Saxon translation into Old English, or adaptation into Anglo-Latin, indicates that the source was known to the English at some time during the Anglo-Saxon period. The abbreviations for Old English texts are from the *MCOE*, and those for Anglo-Latin from Lapidge (1988); in order to make our work self-contained, these abbreviations are expanded later in the bodies of the entries where they occur and the designated editions specified. Writers of individual entries have, of course, exercised judgment in how to represent the information when a translation or adaptation is quite loose, or when the use of a source is so limited that it is better considered a quotation.

Quots/Cits   *Quotations or Citations.* The source notes of modern critical editions can make it clear that Anglo-Saxon writers knew a work in full or in some shortened form. A citation, including both the name and the words of an author, is sometimes significant since it shows the knowledge of the origin of an idea or phrase. Writers of entries have used their judgment in determining which quotations and citations significantly further the evidence for the knowledge of a work during our period. For example, listing each use by Bede of **AUGUSTINE**'s **DE GENESI AD LITTERAM** may well be less significant for our purposes than indicating a single, anonymous use of a more obscure work.[4]

In itemizing quotations and citations, the abbreviation for the source (perhaps in a shortened form) is followed by a reference to the edition specified at the beginning of the entry. These references to specific passages may take three forms, depending on the lineation of the edition cited: when a text is line numbered as a unit, only line numbers are used; when its sections (such as books or chapters) are line numbered separately, sectional divisions are in roman (upper case for larger divisions

---

[4]The full listing of such relationships is the task of *Fontes Anglo-Saxonici.*

such as books, lower case for smaller ones such as chapters) followed by line numbers (for example, II.xx.3–4); and when it is line numbered by page (or column) or not provided with line numbers, page (or column) and line numbers are used (for example, 26.1–15 or 37.6–42.4).[5] Following a colon, the Anglo-Saxon work in which the specified source passage is quoted or cited is given in abbreviated form. These abbreviations are again drawn from Lapidge (1988) and the *MCOE* and usually refer to the editions designated in them; however, in order to keep our volume self-contained, these abbreviations are expanded in the bodies of the entries in which they occur and the designated editions identified. References to specific passages in Anglo-Saxon texts follow the numbering system explained above.

If the quotation or citation is noted in the specified edition of the Anglo-Saxon work, no further reference need be provided. If not, the source of the identification is mentioned in the body of the entry. Entries have not reproduced information gathered for the database of *Fontes Anglo-Saxonici*.

Refs *References*. Although always open to interpretation, a specific reference by an Anglo-Saxon writer to a work may indicate its presence in England during our period. The letters of **BONIFACE** and his circle provide good examples of this kind of evidence. Line numbers are referred to in the same way as specified above under Quotations or Citations.

Body

The body of the entry discusses any information in the headnote that requires clarification or amplification, and then introduces other kinds of evidence for the knowledge of a work in Anglo-Saxon England, such as allusions in literary texts or distinctive iconographic motifs from the visual arts. One kind of evidence that may be considered in this section—

---

[5]If the columns are not numbered, letters are added; for example, *AS* Oct. 13.794a.1–10.

and that requires some specific comment here—is the presence of echoes in hexametrical poetry. Within this poetic tradition, the terms "quotation" and "citation" are restricted either to entire lines taken from a previous work or to situations in which the Anglo-Saxon author calls attention to the source with a phrase such as "as the poet says": these quotations and citations are included in the headnote. In contrast, an "echo" in hexametrical poetry consists of at least two words occurring in the same metrical feet (but not necessarily in the same grammatical form) in both the source and the Anglo-Saxon text: these are discussed in the body. A similar distinction between "quotations and citations" and "echoes" may be preserved in the case of some prose writers. The body of an entry may also consider other questions, such as the temporal and geographical extent of the use of a work, and often concludes with a discussion of bibliography and suggestions about work in progress or desiderata.

Cross-references

Readers are directed to other entries (written or projected) in *SASLC* by names in bold: large capitals are used for names that figure into the alphabetical scheme of the project as a whole (that is, known authors and the names of generic entries, as well as the titles of anonymous works not gathered into generic entries); small capitals for any division of a major-author or generic entry. Thus **AMBROSE** and **DE FIDE**. Names in small bold capitals need not, however, always refer to individual works since some major-author and generic entries are further divided into sections (for example, **OLD TESTAMENT APOCRYPHA** in **APOCRYPHA**). A name is placed in bold the first time (and only the first time) it appears in an individual entry or in a section of a major-author or generic entry.

Standard Research Tools, Standard Editions, and Bibliography

Some research tools and editions (listed below) are referred to by abbreviations without further bibliographical elaboration. When items in a research tool are numbered individually, references are to items (or to volume and item; e.g., *CLA* 2.139); otherwise, references are to pages (or to volume and page; e.g., *OTP* 2.249–95). When necessary, particular passages are identified by the system explained above under Quots/Cits. Other bibliographical references are by author and date; full information appears in the bibliography at the end of each volume.

References to the Bible are to the *Biblia sacra iuxta Vulgatam versionem*, 2nd ed., ed. R. Weber (Stuttgart, 1975).

ABBREVIATIONS

AC = Angus Cameron, "A List of Old English Texts," in *A Plan for the Dictionary of Old English*, ed. Roberta Frank and Cameron (Toronto, 1973), pp. 27–306.

AH = *Analecta Hymnica Medii Aevi*, 55 vols., ed. Guido Maria Dreves and Clemens Blume (Leipzig, 1886–1922).

AS = *Acta Sanctorum*, 68 vols., ed. J. Bollandus et al. (1643–1940): Ian.–Oct., 60 vols. (repr. Brussels, 1965–70); Auctaria Oct. (Paris, 1875); Propylaeum ad Nov. (Brussels, 1902); Nov. 1 (Paris, 1887); Nov. 2/1 (Brussels, 1894); Nov. 2/2 (Brussels, 1931); Nov. 3 (Brussels, 1910); Nov. 4 (Brussels, 1925); and Propylaeum ad Dec. (Brussels, 1940).

ASPR = *Anglo-Saxon Poetic Records*, 6 vols., ed. G. P. Krapp and E. V. K. Dobbie (New York, 1931–53).

BaP = *Bibliothek der angelsächsischen Prosa*, 13 vols., ed. Christian W. M. Grein, Richard P. Wülker, and Hans Hecht (Kassel, 1872–1933).

BCLL = *Bibliography of Celtic-Latin Literature 400–1200*, Michael Lapidge and Richard Sharpe (Dublin, 1985).

BEASE = *The Blackwell Encyclopaedia for Anglo-Saxon England*, ed. Michael Lapidge, John Blair, Simon Keynes, and Donald Scragg (Oxford, 1999).

BEH = *Bibliography of English History to 1485*, ed. Edgar B. Graves (Oxford, 1975).

BHG = *Bibliotheca Hagiographica Graeca*, 3rd ed., François Halkin (Brussels, 1951; *Subsidia hagiographica* 8a).

BHG^a = *Auctarium Bibliothecae Hagiographicae Graecae*, François Halkin (Brussels, 1969; *Subsidia hagiographica* 47).

BHG^{na}= *Novum Auctarium Bibliothecae Hagiographicae Graecae*, François Halkin (Brussels, 1984; *Subsidia hagiographica* 65).

BHL = *Bibliotheca Hagiographica Latina*, 2 vols. (Brussels 1898–1901; *Subsidia hagiographica* 6).

BHL NS = *Bibliotheca Hagiographica Latina Novum Supplementum*, ed. H. Fros (Brussels, 1986; *Subsidia hagiographica* 70).

BHM = *Bibliotheca Hieronymiana Manuscripta*, 4 vols. in 7 parts, Bernard Lambert (Steenbrugge, 1969–72; *Instrumenta Patristica* 4).

BKE = *Books Known to the English, 597–1066*, J. D. A. Ogilvy (Cambridge, Mass., 1967); with addenda and corrigenda in *Mediaevalia* 7 (1984 for 1981): 281–325, also in Old English Newsletter *Subsidia* 11 (1985).

BLS = *Butler's Lives of the Saints*, 4 vols., ed. Herbert Thurston and Donald Attwater (New York, 1963).

BSS = *Bibliotheca Sanctorum*, 13 vols. (Rome, 1961–70).

CCSL = *Corpus Christianorum, Series Latina* (Turnhout, 1953–).

CCCM = *Corpus Christianorum, Continuatio Mediaevalis* (Turnhout, 1966–).

CCSA = *Corpus Christianorum, Series Apocryphorum* (Turnhout, 1983–).

CLA = *Codices Latini Antiquiores*, 11 vols., E. A. Lowe (Oxford, 1934–66); with a supplement (1971); 2nd ed. of vol. 2 (1972).

CPG = *Clavis Patrum Graecorum*, 5 vols., M. Geerard and F. Glorie (Turnhout, 1974–87).

CPL = *Clavis Patrum Latinorum*, 3rd ed., E. Dekkers and A. Gaar (Steenbrugge, 1995).

CPPM = *Clavis Patristica Pseudepigraphorum Medii Aevi*, J. Machielsen, IA–B: *Homiletica* (Turnhout, 1990); IIA: *Theologica, Exegetica* (Turnhout, 1994); IIB: *Ascetica, Monastica* (Turnhout, 1994).

CSEL = *Corpus Scriptorum Ecclesiasticorum Latinorum* (Vienna, 1866–).

CSLMA AG = *Clavis Scriptorum Latinorum Medii Aevi. Auctores Galliae 735-987. Tomus I. Abbo Sangermanensis–Ermoldus Nigellus*, Marie Hélène Jullien and Françoise Perelman (Turnhout, 1994).

DACL = *Dictionnaire d'archéologie chrétienne et de liturgie*, 15 vols., ed. F. Cabrol (Paris, 1907–53).

DB = *Dictionary of the Bible*, 4 vols. and an extra vol., ed. James Hastings (New York, 1900–05).

DHGE = *Dictionnaire d'histoire et de géographie ecclésiastiques*, ed. A. Baudrillart, A. de Meyer, É. Van Cauwenbergh, and R. Aubert (Paris, 1912–).

DMA = *Dictionary of the Middle Ages*, 12 vols., ed. Joseph R. Strayer (New York, 1982–89).

DS = *Dictionnaire de Spiritualité*, 16 vols. in 22 and Tables générales, ed. Marcel Viller et al. (Paris, 1937–95).

DTC = *Dictionnaire de théologie catholique*, 15 vols., ed. A. Vacant, E. Mangenot, and E. Amann (Paris, 1908–50).

DTC^g = *Dictionnaire de théologie catholique. Tables générales*, ed. B. Loth and A. Michel (Paris, 1953–72).

EEMF = *Early English Manuscripts in Facsimile* (Copenhagen, 1951–).

EETS = *Early English Texts Society*.
   ES = Extra Series.
   OS = Original Series.
   SS = Supplementary Series.

EHD = *English Historical Documents: Volume 1 c. 500–1042*, 2nd ed., ed. Dorothy Whitelock (London, 1979).

GCS = *Die griechischen christlichen Schriftsteller der ersten drei Jahrhunderte* (Leipzig, 1897–).

GL = *Grammatici Latini*, 8 vols., ed. H. Keil (Leipzig, 1857–80).

HBS = *Henry Bradshaw Society* (London, 1891–).

HG = Helmut Gneuss "A Preliminary List of Manuscripts Written or Owned in England up to 1100," *Anglo-Saxon England* 9 (1981): 1–60.

HLW = *A Handlist of the Latin Writers of Great Britain and Ireland before 1540*, Richard Sharpe (Turnhout, 1997; Publications of the Journal of Medieval Latin 1).

IASIM = *Insular and Anglo-Saxon Illuminated Manuscripts. An Iconographic Catalogue*, Thomas H. Ohlgren (New York, 1986).

ICL = *Initia Carminum Latinorum saeculo undecimo Antiquiorum*, D. Schaller and E. Könsgen (Göttingen, 1977).

ICVL = *Initia Carminum ac Versuum medii aevi posterioris Latinorum*, Hans Walther (Göttingen, 1959; Carmina medii aevi posterioris latina I); *Ergänzungen und Berichtigung* (Göttingen, 1969; Carmina medii aevi posterioris latina I/1).

ISLMAH = *Index Scriptorum Latinorum Medii Aevi Hispanorum*, Manuel C. Díaz y Díaz (Madrid, 1959).

KVS = *Kirchenschriftsteller. Verzeichnis und Sigel*, 4th ed., Hermann Josef Frede (Freiburg, 1995; Vetus Latina 1/1).

LTK = *Lexikon für Theologie und Kirche*, 2nd ed., 10 vols. and an index, ed. Josef Höfer and Karl Rahner (Freiburg i.B., 1957–67).

MCOE = *A Microfiche Concordance to Old English: The List of Texts and Index of Editions*, comp. Antonette diPaolo Healey and Richard L. Venezky (Toronto, 1980).

MGH = *Monumenta Germaniae Historica.*
  AA = Auctores antiquissimi.
  CAC = Concilia aeui carolini.
  ECA = Epistolae carolini aeui.
  ES = Epistolae selectae.
  PLAC = Poetae latini aeui carolini.
  SRM = Scriptores rerum merovingicarum.

ML = Michael Lapidge, "Surviving Booklists from Anglo-Saxon England," in *Learning and Literature in Anglo-Saxon England*, ed. Lapidge and Helmut Gneuss (Cambridge, 1985), pp. 33–89.

NCE = *New Catholic Encyclopedia*, 17 vols., ed. William J. McDonald et al. (New York, 1967–79).

NRK = N. R. Ker, *Catalogue of Manuscripts Containing Anglo-Saxon* (1957; repr. Oxford, 1990).

NTA = *New Testament Apocrypha*, Edgar Hennecke, 2 vols., ed. Wilhelm Schneemelcher and trans. R. McL. Wilson (Philadelphia, 1963–65).

OCD = *Oxford Classical Dictionary*, 3rd ed., ed. Simon Hornblower and Antony Spawforth (Oxford, 1996).

ODCC = *Oxford Dictionary of the Christian Church*, 3rd ed., ed. E. A. Livingstone (London, 1997).

OTP = *Old Testament Pseudepigrapha*, 2 vols., ed. James H. Charlesworth (London, 1983–85).

Pat. = *Patrology*, 4 vols.; vols. 1–3, ed. Johannes Quasten (Westminster, Md., 1950–60); vol. 4, ed. Angelo di Berardino, trans. Placid Solari (Westminster, Md., 1986).

PG = *Patrologia Graeca*, 161 vols., ed. J.-P. Migne (Paris, 1857–66).

PL = *Patrologia Latina*, 221 vols., ed. J.-P. Migne (Paris, 1844–64).

PLS = *Patrologiae Latinae Supplementum*, 5 vols., ed. A. Hamman (Paris, 1958–74).

RBMA = *Repertorium Biblicum Medii Aevi*, 11 vols., F. Stegmüller (Madrid, 1950–80).

RFHMA = *Repertorium fontium historiae Medii Aevi primum ab Augusto Potthast digestum, nunc cura collegii historicorum e pluribus nationibus emendatum et auctum* (Rome, 1962–).

RS = "Rolls Series"; *Rerum Britannicarum Medii Aevi Scriptores* (London, 1858–96).

SC = *A Summary Catalogue of Western Manuscripts in the Bodleian Library at Oxford*, 7 vols., Falconer Madan and H. H. E. Craster (Oxford, 1895–1953).

SChr = *Sources chrétiennes* (Paris, 1940–).

SEHI = *Sources for the Early History of Ireland: Ecclesiastical*, James F. Kenney (1929; repr. New York, 1966 with addenda by L. Beiler).

SS = *The Publications of the Surtees Society* (London, 1835–).

TU = *Texte und Untersuchungen zur Geschichte der altchristlichen Literatur. Archiv für die griechisch-christlichen Schriftsteller der ersten drei Jahrhunderte* (Leipzig/Berlin, 1882–).

Frederick M. Biggs
University of Connecticut

ABBO OF FLEURY

According to the life written by Aimoin (*PL* 139.387–414; *BHL* 3), Abbo, born in the Orléanais ca. 945, was an oblate at Fleury (Saint-Benoît-sur-Loire) and later studied in Rheims and Paris. He may have been present at the synod of Winchester (ca. 973; see Knowles 1963 p 46 note 3 and the **REGULARIS CONCORDIA**, ed. Symons and Spath 1984 p 72). He became master of the monastic school at Fleury, but, apparently disappointed by the selection of another to be abbot (Mostert 1986), he accepted an invitation to teach at the recently established abbey of Ramsey; he remained in England from late 985 to the autumn of 987. He returned to Fleury to become abbot in 988, proving to be an active supporter of the Cluniac reform and opposed to the power of the bishops. He was killed at La Réole (Gascony) in 1004. An epitaph survives (*MGH* PLAC III.344; *ICL* 5795), and he was venerated as a martyr during the Middle Ages. For further discussion of his life, see Cousin (1954), Mostert (1987 pp 40–64), Engelen (1993 pp 3–4), Schupp (1997 pp xi–xviii), *BEASE* p 3, and *DMA* 1.12–13. On the importance of Fleury at this time, see, for example, Pellegrin (1984–85). On his influence on **DUNSTAN**, **ÆLFRIC**, and **BYRHTFERTH**, this last his pupil at Ramsey, see John (1983 pp 300–06) and Baker and Lapidge (*EETS* SS 15 pp xx–xxiii and xliii–xlv). For further evidence of the cultural traffic between Fleury and English abbeys, see Vezin (1977), Gransden (1995 p 23 note 25), and *BEASE* pp 187–88.

Setting out Abbo's works is complicated by several related problems. Some, most notably the **COMPUTUS**, lack critical editions while others remain unedited. Moreover, since some are quite brief yet on related topics, it can be difficult to determine which should stand alone. These problems are further complicated by the differing titles that appear in the manuscripts and thus in the scholarship: the more common, but not all, of these variant titles are listed with cross-references.

The individual entries below begin with two works closely associated with Abbo's time in England, the **PASSIO EADMUNDI** and the

QUAESTIONES GRAMMATICALES, and then turn to the *Computus* that he would have brought with him to Ramsey. Following these entries are sections, with individual entries arranged alphabetically, on his other MATHEMATICAL AND ASTRONOMICAL TRACTATES and his POEMS. The only letter by him known in Anglo-Saxon England is the one to Dunstan at the beginning of the *Passio Eadmundi*. While many questions about the chronology of Abbo's works remain (see Evans and Peden 1985 pp 109–10), it appears that during the period of his abbacy his interests shifted from scientific to political matters; these later works, set out by Sharpe (*HLW* 1–4), are not currently known to have circulated in Anglo-Saxon England. The request of abbot **WULFRIC** of St Augustine's (ed. *RS* 63.409; see Van de Vyver 1935 p 165 note 1) for a verse counterpart to a prose work on Dunstan (B's *Vita Dunstani*: see **ACTA SANCTORUM, DUNSTANUS**) may serve as a reminder not only of continued interest in the *opus geminatum* in England, but also of the continued contact between Abbo and the Anglo-Saxons, which could have led to knowledge of his later works.

Finally, since much uncertainty about Abbo's actual *oeuvre*—particularly his poems and shorter tracts—remains, it seems premature to create a separate section for Pseudo Abbo. There are, therefore, entries here on two poems, **IN PATRIS NATIQUE SUI** and **TERMINAT HYGINUS**, that Lapidge and Baker (1997 p 10) consider to be by a follower. An entry on **DE QUINQUE ZONAE CAELI** is also included with other astronomical tracts because Bober (1956–57 pp 67 and 93) considers it "Abbonian." For other works associated with Abbo but not individually catalogued by Sharpe (*HLW* 1–4), see the introductory remarks to the two sections below.

Passio Eadmundi [ABBO.FLOR.Pass.Eadmund.]: *BHL* 2392; *BLS* 4.394–96; *BSS* 4.917–20; *DHGE* 14.1439–41; Farmer (1987) pp 131–32.
　ed.: Winterbottom 1972 pp 67–87.

MSS　1. Copenhagen, Kongelige Bibliotek G.K.S. 1588 (4°): HG 813.
　2. London, BL Cotton Tiberius B. ii: HG 371.
　3. London, Lambeth Palace 362: HG 514.
　4. Paris, Bibliothèque Nationale lat. 5362: HG 885.3.

Lists Bury St Edmunds: ML 7.7.
A-S Vers *ÆLS* Edmund (B1.3.31).
Quots/Cits see below.
Refs *ÆLS* Edmund 7–8.

The major work arising from Abbo's English period and perhaps written there (Gransden 1995 pp 47–56), the *Passio Eadmundi* was composed at the request of the Ramsey monks. It begins with a letter to **DUNSTAN** (ed. Winterbottom 1972 pp 67–68; previously edited in *RS* 63.378–80). Dunstan may also have influenced its style, which differs from Abbo's other works showing several hermeneutic features. In the *Passio*, Abbo transformed the king of the East Angles, Edmund, who had been killed by the Danes in 869–70, into a martyr, which is at variance with the annal for 870 in the **ANGLO-SAXON CHRONICLE** (*ChronA*, B17.1, and *ChronE*, B17.9, ed. Plummer 1892–99; see **CHRONICLES**) and **ASSER**'s life of King Alfred (**DE REBUS GESTIS ÆLFREDI**, ed. W. Stevenson 1904 p 26; see also Keynes and Lapidge 1983 p 78). The cult spread throughout England, Ireland, Scandinavia, and elsewhere (see C. Loomis 1932 and 1933; Whitelock 1970; J. Grant 1978; Ridyard 1988; *RS* 83.42–43; and *RS* 96).

Gransden (1995 pp 63–64) considers the Lambeth manuscript to be the oldest, from before the mid-eleventh century, and thus possibly referred to in the booklist from Bury St Edmunds. She dates the Copenhagen manuscript to the mid-eleventh century or later and the Cotton manuscript to ca. 1100. She does not associate the Paris manuscript with England (p 70 note 303).

Mentioning his source in his opening paragraph, **ÆLFRIC** of Eynsham (not Ælfric, abbot of Malmesbury, as William of Malmesbury claimed, *RS* 52.406–07) translated the *Passio* ca. 998 in his **LIVES OF SAINTS** (*ÆLS*; *EETS* OS 94 and 114, and Needham 1966 pp 43–59), excluding many hagiographic motifs (Woolf 1966b pp 63–64) but otherwise remaining close to the original (Clark 1968; see further Lapidge and Winterbottom 1991 p cl and Benskin 1994). According to Gerould (1924–25), Abbo's *Passio* influenced Ælfric's rhythmic prose.

The text of Ælfric's homily in London, BL Cotton Julius E. vii (HG 339; NRK 162), which was possibly written at Bury, shows several alterations (Needham 1958 p 160), for example in the sentence where Ælfric alludes to the unworthiness of the secular canons who were the guardians of Edmund's shrine until 1020 (lines 255–56, and Winterbottom 1972 p 87 lines 16 and 20–21). In BL Cotton Otho B. x (HG 355; NRK 177A), the antiquarian John Joscelyn has added Abbo's preface to the Latin *Passio* in the margin of the Old English text, declaring that he drew it "e codice Bibliothecae Wigorniensis" (NRK p 227).

There is a couplet in Edmund's honor in the *Metrical Calendar of Ramsey* 116–17 (ed. Lapidge 1984 p 366), and the martyrdom is celebrated in another Ramsey production, the early sections of the *Historia Regum* (ed. *RS* 75/2.76–77) that are now regarded as the work of **BYRHTFERTH** (Lapidge 1982a and Hart 1982).

The influence of the *Passio* is evident in the hymns in honor of Edmund: *Edmundus martyr inclitus* (*AH* 19.196), *Laurea regni* (*AH* 19.197), and *Laus et corona* (*AH* 19.198). All three occur in BL Cotton Vespasian D. xii (HG 391; Gneuss 1968 p 98) and the last two in London, Lambeth Palace 362 (HG 514; Gneuss 1968 p 114). A similar influence is evident in the hymn *O mundi pater unice* of the Psalter and Hymnal from Bury (Gneuss 1968 p 114).

For further discussion of the development of the legend and the manuscripts of the *Passio*, see Gransden (1982, 1985, and 1995); on the historical context of the cult and the *Passio*, see Thacker (1996a pp 249–51) and Folz (1978 and 1984 pp 49–52); and on the *Passio* in the context of Abbo's political theories, see Mostert (1987 pp 40–45) and Head (1990 pp 240–51). There is an English translation of the *Passio* in Hervey's edition (1907 pp 7–61).

Quaestiones grammaticales [ABBO.FLOR.Quaest.gramm.].
 ed.: Guerreau-Jalabert 1982 pp 209–75.

MSS – Refs none.

In this work, perhaps written in England (Guerreau-Jalabert 1982 p 200 and *BEASE* p 3), Abbo answers questions on orthography, morphology, and syntax that had been raised by his pupils at Ramsey. It survives in two manuscripts (Rome, Biblioteca Apostolica Vaticana Reg. lat. 596 and London, BL Additional 10972) from Fleury, but both were copied after Abbo's death (Guerreau-Jalabert 1982 pp 200–01). See Guerreau-Jalabert (1982 p 202) for a fourteenth-century manuscript in Erfurt that contains extracts.

Opposite the Latin text, Guerreau-Jalabert (1982) provides a French translation.

Computus [ABBO.FLOR.Comp.]: see also **ARDUA CONNEXAE LIBAT SACRARIA FORMAE (POEMS)**.
ed.: *PL* 90.727–820: see below.

MSS – Refs none.

Abbo's *Computus*, composed in 978 (Lapidge and Baker 1997 p 1; and see Aimoin, *PL* 139.390), has yet to be adequately edited in part because of the nature of the genre: as a compilation of texts and tables related to the calendar (Abbo's calendar, itself distinctive, is described by Baker and Lapidge *EETS* SS 15 p xliii), a computus is a miscellany drawing on earlier works and itself susceptible to interpolation and selective copying. Lapidge and Baker (1997 p 1) provide a list of manuscripts: the two best, Berlin, Staatsbibliothek 138 (formerly Phillipps 1833) and Bern, Burgerbibliothek 250, are both from Fleury; the English manuscripts are all later than the Anglo-Saxon period. Baker and Lapidge (*EETS* SS 15 pp xliii–xliv) describe its contents with reference to *PL* 90 (see also Jones 1939 pp 59–79, 80, 81, and 90). In spite of the difficulty in establishing this text, Abbo's contribution to the genre should be recognized. According to Baker and Lapidge (*EETS* SS 15 p xlv), he "pruned" earlier computi, which were "unwieldy, redundant and inconsistent," "supplied explanations for both the tables he retained and those he composed, and imposed order on the resulting more tractable collection of materials."

Abbo brought his *Computus* and those of **BEDE** and **HELPERIC OF AUXERRE** (McGurk 1974) and perhaps **HRABANUS MAURUS** (*CCCM* 44.173 note 35) with him to Ramsey. **BYRHTFERTH** drew on these for his own **COMPUTUS** (described in *EETS* SS 15 pp 373–427) and his ENCHIRIDION (*ByrM* 1; B20.20.1; ed. *EETS* SS 15), a commentary in Latin and English on his *Computus*. He acknowledged his debt to Abbo in his *Epilogus* (*EETS* SS 15 pp 375–79), lines 83–86, for his knowledge of the subject (see also Forsey 1928).

Mathematical and Astronomical Tractates

These works, in general, appear to have developed out of Abbo's teaching at Fleury and Ramsey, and are often associated with his COMPUTUS. Two letters on the Dionysian cycle, written in 1003 and 1004 (Van de Vyver 1935 pp 154–58), may serve as a reminder that the dates of individual treatises could vary.

As noted in the general introduction above, DE QUINQUE ZONAE CAELI is included here because Bober (1956–57 pp 67 and 93) considers it "Abbonian." Two other works identified by him, one as "Abbonian" (*De cursu solis et lunae*) and the other as by Abbo (*De ratione bissexti et embolismi*), are not included because there is currently no evidence that they were known in Anglo-Saxon England. Similarly there is no entry on a tract beginning "Karissime frater hoc calculum quod in hoc tuo libro karaxatum habeo" (Saxl and Meier 1953 1.446) identified in the manuscript, Durham, Cathedral Library Hunter 100 (NRK 110), as by Abbo.

Abacus [ABBO.FLOR.Abac.]: Thorndike and Kibre (1963) col 674.
ed.: Bubnov 1899 pp 203–04.

MSS Oxford, St John's College 17: HG 683.
Lists – A-S Vers none.
Quots/Cits see below.
Refs see below.

On folio 35r of the Oxford manuscript are three multiplication tables, the first headed "In hac figura descriptus est numerus infinitus" and the second "Ratio Abbonis supra praefatum numerum." Evans (1979 p 89) claims that they "condense into tabular form" Abbo's COMMENTARIUS IN CALCULUM VICTORII. Baker and Lapidge (*EETS* SS 15 pp 423–24) describe the tables and print the third. The second, fourteen sentences on finger-reckoning, is the source for **BYRHTFERTH**'s ENCHIRIDION (*ByrM* 1; B20.20.1; ed. *EETS* SS 15) IV.i.408–36. Byrhtferth leads into this discussion by recalling his teacher and remarking on the miracles that have followed his death (404–07). The third table, for ferial and lunar calculations, is the source for *Enchiridion* I.ii.73–77.

Commentarius in calculum Victorii [ABBO.FLOR.Comm.calc.Vict.]: Thorndike and Kibre (1963) col 183.
 ed.: see below.

MSS – Refs none.

The preface to this work is printed from one manuscript by Evans and Peden (1985 pp 126–27) and appears in *PL* 139.569–72. Bubnov (1899 pp 199–203) prints extracts from it. Near the end of his **QUAESTIONES GRAMMATICALES**, Abbo refers to this work as "a little book on number, measure, and weight" (Guerreau-Jalabert 1982 p 275), which he identifies as "the three-fold means by which God has ordered creation" (Evans and Peden 1985 p 113, and see further their discussion of its contents and analysis of Abbo's achievement).

Van de Vyver (1935 p 129) speculates that a work on fractions, *De unciarum minutiis* (the relationship of this work to Abbo's *Regulae de minutiis*, Thorndike and Kibre 1963 col 1597, has not been determined), in a manuscript that also contains Abbo's *Quaestiones grammaticales* (London, BL Additional 10972) was written for students perplexed by Abbo's *Commentary* on Victorius's *Calculus*. Evans (1979 p 88) remarks that this "would imply that the abacus commentary was already being studied in England."

De cursu septem planetarum per zodiacum circulum. See DE DIFFERENTIA CIRCULI ET SPHAERAE.

Denique luna totius zodiaci signa. See DE DIFFERENTIA CIRCULI ET SPHAERAE.

De differentia circuli et sphaerae [ABBO.FLOR.Diff.circ.sphaer.]: Thorndike and Kibre (1963) cols 370 and 1530; Saxl and Meier (1953) 1.157 and 198.
    ed.: R. B. Thomson 1985 pp 120–33.
MSS   1. Cambridge, Trinity College R.15.32 (945): HG 186.
    2. London, BL Cotton Vitellius A. xii: HG 398.
    3. London, BL Harley 2506: HG 428.5.
    4. London, BL Royal 13. A. xi: HG 483.
    5. Oxford, St John's College 17: HG 683.
Lists – A-S Vers none.
Quots/Cits see below.
Refs none.

    R. B. Thomson (1985) considers this astronomical treatise (beginning "Studiosis astrologie primo sciendum est per geometricam . . ." and titled "Astronomy" in Thorndike and Kibre 1963 col 1530) to be made up of two separate works, restricting the title used here to the first (which he also refers to as the *Sententia Abbonis de ratione spere*) and identifying the second untitled work by its beginning, *Denique luna totius zodiaci signa*. In his edition, however, he lineates them continuously. He also prints a graph and a table that occur between the sections in more than half of the manuscripts (but not in the Harley or Royal manuscripts listed above). The table, titled *De cursu septem planetarum per zodiacum circulum*, is "of Pliny's planetary latitudes with Abbo's dimension of the zodiacal band added"; the table is "a list of planetary harmonic intervals according to Pliny as well as the distances from the earth to the moon, the moon to the sun and the sun to the stars" (R. B. Thomson 1985 p 115). Following Van de Vyver (1935 p 141), Baker and Lapidge (*EETS* SS 15 p xliv) consider the parts a single work (but see Lapidge and Baker 1997 p 9) and note that it "is found in all Byrhtferthian computi," including the St John's manuscript (see further P. Baker 1982 and Lapidge 1984 pp 348–51) and London, BL Cotton Tiberius C. i (+ BL Harley 3667; written after the Anglo-Saxon period, but see NRK 196), and "in other Abbonian computi" in English manuscripts, all too late for HG.

    The Vitellius manuscript and Exeter, Cathedral Library 3507 provide further hints of the transmission of this text and **DE DUPLICI SIGNORUM**

ORTU VEL OCCASU. According to Stevens (*CCCM* 44.173 note 35), the exemplar of the Exeter manuscript, which contains **HRABANUS MAURUS**'s DE COMPUTO and **ISIDORE**'s DE NATURA RERUM, "was wrapped with two bifolia containing Abbo's *Sententia*, including those composed at Ramsey, when these contents were transcribed into . . . Cotton Vitellius A.xii." Baker and Lapidge (*EETS* SS 15 pp lxxxviii–lxxxix) argue, however, that **BYRHTFERTH** probably did not know a manuscript of this type. On the relationship of these manuscripts, see also Ker and Piper (1969–92 2.813).

Baker and Lapidge (*EETS* SS 15 p xliv) classify the Trinity manuscript as "a computus of Winchester type that has received some Abbonian material." They list but do not comment on the Royal manuscript. The Harley manuscript was probably written at Fleury, but by the early eleventh century it was in England, perhaps Ramsey (Lapidge and Baker 1997 p 8).

In their description of Byrhtferth's *Computus*, Baker and Lapidge (*EETS* SS 15 pp 425–26) print a passage from this work (R. B. Thomson 1985 lines 95–116), identifying it as the source for Byrhtferth's **ENCHIRIDION** (*ByM* 1; B20.20.1; ed. *EETS* SS 15) III.x.186–95. They also note that its accompanying *rota* is the source for figure 21 in the *Enchiridion*.

De duplici signorum ortu vel occasu [ABBO.FLOR.Dupl.sign.ort.]: Thorndike and Kibre (1963) col 372.

ed.: R. B. Thomson 1988 p 673.

MSS 1. Cambridge, Trinity College R.15.32 (945): HG 186.
2. London, BL Cotton Vitellius A. xii: HG 398.
Lists – Refs none.

This brief work, ascribed to Abbo in the Cambridge manuscript, discusses heavenly bodies that sometimes appear in both the evening and the morning sky. It concludes with seven lines from **VIRGIL**'s **GEORGICS** and an excerpt from **SERVIUS**'s **COMMENTARY**, identified in the Cambridge manuscript as a separate work, *De quinque circulis mundi*, by Abbo (see Van de Vyver 1935 p 140).

R. B. Thomson (1988 p 672) accepts that Abbo wrote this work in England (see Van de Vyver 1935 p 147), but it is surprising that **BYRHTFERTH** did not use it (*EETS* SS 15 pp lxxxviii–lxxxix; see the comments on the Vitellius manuscript in DE DIFFERENTIA CIRCULI ET SPHAERAE). Thomson edits it from six manuscripts, five of which he notes are English. The sixth, Rome, Biblioteca Apostolica Vaticana Reg. lat. 596, also contains Abbo's QUAESTIONES GRAMMATICALES, and the other manuscript of this work, London, BL Additional 10972, includes *De duplici signorum ortu vel occasu* but without passages from Virgil and Servius.

Excerptio ex Hygino de figuratione signorum [ABBO.FLOR.Excerp. Hyg.]: Thorndike and Kibre (1963) col 400; Saxl and Meier (1953) 1.197.
   ed.: unedited.

MSS 1. Cambridge, Trinity College R.15.32 (945): HG 186.
      2. London, BL Royal 13. A. xi: HG 483.
Lists – Refs none.

Abbo compiled a catalogue of stars (beginning "Denique, ut dicit Plinius, inter omnia LXXII sunt signa . . .") summarizing the third book of HYGINUS's ASTRONOMICA. Van de Vyver (1935 pp 140–41, 147–49) argues it is his first work and that he brought it with him to England.

Quadratus hic equilaterus. See ARDUA CONNEXAE LIBAT SACRARIA FORMAE (POEMS).

De quinque circulis mundi. See DE DUPLICI SIGNORUM ORTU VEL OCCASU.

De quinque zonae caeli [ANON.Quin.zon.cael.].
   ed.: Silk 1935 p 326 lines 10–21.

MSS Oxford, St John's College 17: HG 683.
Lists – Refs none.

In his discussion of a thirteenth-century French manuscript now in the Walters Art Gallery, Bober (1956–57 pp 67 and 93) designates this work, beginning "Iginus et alii astrologi ferunt quod quinque sunt zone celi," as "Abbonian." Baker and Lapidge (*EETS* SS 15 p 426) identify it, without reference to Abbo, as "from a gloss to Remigius of Auxerre's

Commentary on Boethius, *De consolatione philosophie* ii pr. 7" as edited by Silk (1935). Saxl and Meier (1953 1.131) note its presence in London, BL Cotton Tiberius C. i, again without associating it with Abbo.

Quoniam brevitatem. See ARDUA CONNEXAE LIBAT SACRARIA FORMAE (POEMS).

Ratio Abbonis supra praefatum numerum. See ABACUS.

Sententia Abbonis de ratione spere. See DE DIFFERENTIA CIRCULI ET SPHAERAE.

De unciarum minutiis. See COMMENTARIUS IN CALCULUM VICTORII.

Poems

Prominent among Abbo's surviving poems are three—ILLUSTRIS MERITO, O PRAESUL DUNSTANE, and SUMME SACER—addressed to **DUNSTAN**, of which the last two are good examples of the acrostic genre, following the conventions set by **OPTATIANUS PORPHYRIUS**. They ostensibly influenced Dunstan's own acrostic poem, O PATER OMNIPOTENS (*ICL* 10972; ed. Lapidge 1975a pp 108–11). Dunstan liked the acrostic genre and he might owe to Abbo his knowledge of **HRABANUS MAURUS**'s *versus intextus* (from DE LAUDIBUS SANCTAE CRUCIS, figure 28; *CCCM* 100.216), which Dunstan himself adapted and copied into a full-page drawing on folio 1r of Oxford, Bodleian Library Auct. F.4.32 (*SC* 2176; HG 538; see Gneuss 1978 p 148 and Lapidge 1975a p 108).

As noted in the general introduction above, much remains uncertain about Abbo's verse compositions. Although not given separate entries here because we have no knowledge that they were known in Anglo-Saxon England, the following works deserve mention because they are not separately listed by Sharpe (*HLW* 1–4). First are twelve calendarial verses (*ICL* 394, 4551, 4970, 5388, 8348, 8528, 8600, 9354, 9565, 11154, 11254, and 12100) and an additional poem (*ICL* 13555), all by Abbo, that circulated with his computistica and can now be found in *PL* 90. His

Syllogismorum Categoricorum et Hypotheticorum Enodatio (ed. Van de Vyver 1966; see also Schupp 1997) contains two longer poems (*ICL* 15186a and 11877a; ed. Van de Vyver 1966 pp 30–31 and 58) and other verses (*ICL* 5799a, 5658a, and 9467a; ed. Van de Vyver 1966 pp 40 and 46), and another poem (*ICL* 4946; *PL* 139.423) for Pope Gregory V appears at the conclusion of one of his letters. A sequence, "Valde lumen" (ed. *AH* 7.161; *ICL* 16976), and three verses found in one manuscript of his **COMMENTARIUS IN CALCULUM VICTORII** (*ICL* 10749; ed. Bubnov 1899 p 203) have been associated with him. On the verses in an Erfurt manuscript mentioned by Van de Vyver (1935 p 165 note 1), see Lendinara (1989), who identifies them as excerpts from the poem *Quid suum virtutis*.

Ardua connexae libat sacraria formae [ABBO.FLOR.Ard.conn.]: *ICL* 1006; Thorndike and Kibre (1963) col 127.

ed.: Lapidge and Baker 1997 pp 12 and 14.

MSS Oxford, St John's College 17: HG 683.
Lists – Refs none.

This acrostic poem, modeled on **OPTATIANUS PORPHYRIUS**'s **CARMEN XXV**, is the first item in Abbo's **COMPUTUS**, and so appears in manuscripts of this work, as well as those influenced by it, such as **BYRHTFERTH**'s **COMPUTUS**, represented by the Oxford manuscript. Baker and Lapidge (*EETS* SS 15 pp xliii–xliv), who refer to it as "an elaborate arithmetical and astronomical table in verse," note that it is usually accompanied by one of two explanations: *Quadratus hic equilaterus* (ed. Lapidge and Baker 1997 p 16; Thorndike and Kibre 1963 col 1157) in Continental manuscripts of the *Computus*; and *Quoniam brevitatem* (ed. Lapidge and Baker 1997 pp 18–19) in English manuscripts. It also circulated independent of the *Computus*; for the manuscripts, see Lapidge and Baker 1997 p 3.

Illustris merito [ABBO.FLOR.Illust.]: *ICL* 7744.
ed.: *RS* 71/1.462.

MSS London, BL Cotton Nero E. i: HG 344.
Lists – Refs none.

Addressed to **DUNSTAN**, this poem is preserved in chapter 5 of **BYRHTFERTH**'s VITA OSWALDI (see also OSWALDUS WIGORNIENSIS in **ACTA SANCTORUM**; Crawford 1929; and Lapidge 1975a p 91) preserved in the London manuscript. In addition to Raine's edition (*RS* 71/1.462), it was printed by Stubbs (*RS* 63.412).

O decus et cui vernat honor [ANON.O.decus.].
   ed.: Lapidge and Baker 1997 pp 22–23.

MSS – Lists none.

Preserved in a manuscript of **BYRHTFERTH**'s COMPUTUS (London, BL Harley 3667) is a complex acrostic poem that Lapidge and Baker (1997 p 6) attribute to Abbo. The identity of the addressee, possibly an Anglo-Saxon, is still an open question.

O praesul Dunstane [ABBO.FLOR.O.praes.]: *ICL* 10897.
   ed.: Gwara 1992 pp 222 and 226.

MSS London, BL Cotton Nero E. i: HG 344.
Lists – Refs none.

This acrostic poem was composed by Abbo just before his departure from England in 987. It survives in **BYRHTFERTH**'s VITA OSWALDI (see ILLUSTRIS MERITO). In addition to editing the text from the London manuscript, Gwara provides a reconstruction of the *figura* along with the Latin prose exposition (p 224) and an English translation. Earlier editions are those of Raine (*RS* 71/1.461) and Stubbs (*RS* 63.411).

O Ramesiga cohors [ABBO.FLOR.O.Ramesi.]: *ICL* 11013.
   ed.: *RS* 71/1.431–32.

MSS London, BL Cotton Nero E. i: HG 344.
Lists – Refs none.

Abbo's poem on Ramsey Abbey is incorporated into chapter 3 of **BYRHTFERTH**'s VITA OSWALDI, as preserved in the London manuscript, from which it was printed by Raine (*RS* 71/1.431–32). It was also included by Andrew of Fleury in the *Vita Gauzlini* (ed. Bautier 1969 pp 94–97), and it appears in London, BL Additional 10792 following Abbo's QUAESTIONES GRAMMATICALES (this manuscript was used by Mabillon for his edition that is reprinted in *PL* 39.534). The last line varies, appearing in the *Vita Oswaldi* as "Quos Christus semper salvet, honoret, amet," and in the *Vita Gauzlini* as "Quos, Benedicte pater, iure tuere pares." The Oxford manuscript agrees with the *Vita Gauzlini*, and the line was written by P. Daniel (see Bautier 1969 p 96 note 3 and Van de Vyver 1935 p 124 note 5). The poem also occurs in the fourteenth-century Erfurt manuscript that contains extracts of the *Quaestiones grammaticales* (Guerreau-Jalabert 1992 p 202).

In patris natique sui [ANON.Patr.nati.sui].
ed.: Lapidge and Baker 1997 p 24.

MSS London, BL Harley 2506.
Lists – Refs none.

Two acrostic poems (this and TERMINAT HYGINUS) frame HYGINUS's ASTRONOMICA in the Harley manuscript. Lapidge and Baker (1997 p 9) argue that the manuscript was "compiled for Abbo's use at Fleury and subsequently taken by him to Ramsey." Because of some metrical awkwardness, they conclude that the poems are the work of "a less proficient follower" of Abbo (p 10).

Summe sacer [ABBO.FLOR.Sum.sac.]: *ICL* 14822.
ed.: Gwara 1992 pp 215–16.

MSS 1. London, BL Cotton Nero E. i: HG 344.
2. Oxford, St John's College 17: HG 683.
Lists – Refs none.

"Summe sacer," a triple acrostic, was written after Abbo's arrival in England. The poem appears on folio 3r of the Oxford manuscript (Hart 1970 p 31), where its original layout is preserved, but, as pointed out by Gwara (1992 p 205 note 13), the Worcester scribe of the London manuscript was not capable of reproducing the acrostic form of either this poem or **O PRAESUL DUNSTANE**. **BYRHTFERTH** incorporated it into chapter 5 of his **VITA OSWALDI** (see **ILLUSTRIS MERITO**). The Oxford manuscript contains Byrhtferth's **COMPUTUS** (P. Baker 1982).

Gwara's edition, based on both manuscripts, is accompanied by an English translation (p 217). Raine's edition (*RS* 71/1.460) prints the poem as part of the *Vita Oswaldi*. An earlier edition is that of Stubbs (*RS* 63.410).

Terminat Hyginus [ANON.Term.Hygin.].
   ed.: Lapidge and Baker 1997 p 25.

MSS London, BL Harley 2506.
Lists – Refs none.

   See **IN PATRIS NATIQUE SUI**.

Patrizia Lendinara

ABBO OF SAINT-GERMAIN-DES-PRÉS

Abbo, a native of Neustria and a pupil of Aimoin, was a monk of Saint-Germain-des-Prés; he died on 9 March sometime after 921. He is known for two works, the **BELLA PARISIACAE URBIS** and a collection of **SERMONS**. The first is divided here into two entries because, although there is some evidence that the entire work was known to the Anglo-Saxons, most of our information concerns only Book III, which circulated independently of the first two books. For a discussion of the little known about his life, see Önnerfors (1985 pp 16–18). For further bibliography, see *CSLMA AG* 1.3–7.

Bella Parisiacae urbis [ABBO.ST.GERM.Bell.Par.urb.].
   ed.: *MGH* PLAC 4.77–122.

MSS none.
Lists Æthelwold: ML 4.10.
A-S Vers – Refs none.

This poem, completed by 896–97 (see Lendinara 1986 p 74 note 4), consists of three books: the first two describe the siege of Paris by the Vikings (885–86) and some of the following events up to 896; and the much shorter third book (see below) pretends to offer moral advice to young clerics. The entry in the Æthelwold booklist, "Descidia Parisiace polis," indicates that the entire work was known in Anglo-Saxon England since the siege is not mentioned in Book III (Lendinara 1986 p 73). Lendinara (1990 p 139) speculates that it may have been introduced into England by Oda, archbishop of Canterbury (941–58), or by Dunstan. The fifteenth-century Peterborough *Matricularium* (ed. James 1926 nos. 125, 133, and 136) lists three volumes said to contain "Versus Abonis," but in this case there is no way of deciding whether they refer to a work by this or some other Abbo, perhaps **ABBO OF FLEURY**.

Book III of the *Bella Parisiacae urbis*.
  ed.: *MGH* PLAC 4.116–22.
MSS 1. Cambridge, University Library Gg.5.35: HG 12.
  2. Cambridge, Corpus Christi College 326: HG 93.
  3. Edinburgh, National Library of Scotland, Advocates 18.6.12: HG 252.
  4. London, BL Harley 3271: HG 435.
  5. London, BL Harley 3826: HG 438.
Lists see above.
A-S Vers – Refs none.

Consisting of 115 lines, this book differs in subject matter, tone, and diction from the previous two books. For example, one of the precepts that it offers to the cleric (addressed as "cleronomus") is "Prodigus, obliqus, monotalmus, subdolus haud sis" (III.35). By writing such lines, Abbo meant to mock the Greek vogue of his time, that is, the penchant for grecisms and rare words in general. Many of the unusual words have counterparts in bilingual or monolingual glossaries such as the *Liber glossarum* (see **GLOSSARIES**; about 150 of the words that begin mostly with the letters A through E were drawn from this source). Another source, identified by Laistner (1924), were the **SCHOLICA GRAECARUM**

17 ABBO OF SAINT-GERMAIN

GLOSSARUM (see Glossaries). It is from such compilations that Abbo drew not only his "difficult" vocabulary, but also the interlinear glosses that he himself provided for about half of the words in this book.

It was this vocabulary, especially the Greek loanwords, that was responsible for the popularity of this book in Anglo-Saxon England (see Lendinara 1990 p 133). It entered the curriculum of the English schools of the tenth and eleventh centuries, and it provided a sourcebook of "hermeneutic" vocabulary for many Anglo-Latin authors (see also Lapidge 1975a pp 71–72, 75–76, 78, 101, and 123). Lendinara (1990 p 139) suggests that it was most likely at Canterbury where this study began, calling attention to a previously unprinted glossary in Cotton Domitian i, from St Augustine's, Canterbury (ed. Lendinara 1990 pp 144–49). The first 199 lemmata (followed by one or more *interpretamenta*) are identical with words and glosses of this book. (See Lendinara 1996 for a discussion of the glossary in a thirteenth-century British Library manuscript, Royal 7. D. ii, which also contains batches of entries drawn from this book.) The two other Cambridge manuscripts of the work are also from Canterbury; the copy in Corpus Christi College contains only the first seventeen lines.

In addition to Book III with interlinear Latin glosses (fols 118v–120r), Harley 3271 contains a Latin prose version with Old English contextual glosses. These glosses have been edited by both Zupitza (1887 pp 1–27) and Stevenson and Lindsay (1929 no. 7, pp 103–12); the *MCOE* is thus misleading in distinguishing Abbo 1 (C1.1) and Abbo 2 (C1.2) on the basis of these editions, and the *Dictionary of Old English* now has only the short title Abbo, which refers to the text in Harley 3271 and variants, when they occur, from Oxford, St John's College 154. Lapidge (1975a p 75) argues that the manuscript arrangement in Harley 3271 reflects the way students approached the text, first through the prose with its vernacular glosses. This prose version, also with interlinear Old English glosses, appears on the last folios (221v–22r) in St John's College 154, breaking off with "esto memor tui gallonis" (compare III.53, and see Lendinara 1986 p 85). The Old English glosses of these two manuscripts have several phonological and morphological differences, and the Latin versions are marked by independent omissions of the original text, although they possibly derive from the same original. The language of the glosses is clearly late West Saxon, but their vocabulary shows non-West Saxon traces; the presence of *ælfremed* (if it was already in the original gloss) would date the Old English gloss after the middle of the tenth century (see Hofstetter 1987 no. 210).

Patrizia Lendinara

Sermons

There remains some uncertainty about the original shape of Abbo's collection and about the form in which his sermons were known in Anglo-Saxon England. The most recent editor, Önnerfors (1985), has published the first twenty-four items (but note 2a, 21a, and 22a) from a twelfth-century Paris manuscript, previously at Saint-Germain-des-Prés, arguing that these, along with the prologue and list of contents with thirty-seven items, should be the starting point for the study of Abbo's collection (p 38). The five sermons printed in the *PL* are included in Önnerfors (7, 13, 10, 9, and 14), as are the eight sermons, treated separately below, preserved in Copenhagen, Kongelige Bibliotek G.K.S 1595 (4°) (HG 814), identified by Cross and Tunberg (1993 p 13), as copied at the order of **WULFSTAN OF YORK**. Thus the numbering used here follows Önnerfors (1985). Cross and Brown (1993 p 78), however, speculate that the rubric of one of the items in the Copenhagen manuscript (5, the first of the material drawn from Abbo), which retains a reference to chapter 36, may indicate that Wulfstan had access to a full collection of Abbo's sermons; their connections between **SERMO 1** and Wulfstan's *Homily* 3 (ed. Bethurum 1971 pp 123–27) would support this claim.

The relationship of three sermons by Abbo (10, 12, and 13) to the writings of Wulfstan requires additional comment. All three appear in an abbreviated form in Cambridge, Corpus Christi College 190, a manuscript of Wulfstan's "Commonplace Book"; the abbreviated forms of 10 and 13 also appear in two manuscripts in the British Library, Cotton Nero A. i and Cotton Vitellius A. vii. Bethurum (1971 pp 345–46) identifies the shortened version of 13 as the source for Wulfstan's *Homily* 15 (pp 236–38; see the entry below for a reference to a second Old English translation of this adaptation) and notes that it is "quite likely" that Wulfstan himself had made the Latin abridgment as well. Cross and Brown (1993 p 72) agree and provide further reasons to believe that Wulfstan was responsible for all three Latin abridgments.

Sermo 1 [ABBO.ST.GERM.Serm.1].
  ed.: Önnerfors 1985 pp 66–71.

MSS – A-S Vers none.
Quots/Cits 1. 67.2–4: WHom 3.45–48.
  2. 67.11–14: WHom 3.48–49.
  3. 67.18–21: WHom 3.50–52.
Refs none.

This sermon, which treats the end of time, is drawn largely from **HAYMO OF AUXERRE, HOMILIA DE TEMPORE** 2 (*PL* 118.17–25). Cross and Brown (1993 pp 79–80), however, note the three quotations above that indicate that in his third *Homily*, **WULFSTAN OF YORK** (ed. Bethurum 1971 pp 123–27) followed elaborations in Abbo. They also provide four examples of places where Wulfstan follows Abbo in providing additional passages from scripture, including two cases in which he uses Abbo's adaptations of the biblical verses.

Sermo 6 [ABBO.ST.GERM.Serm.6].
  ed.: Önnerfors 1985 pp 94–99.

MSS Copenhagen, Kongelige Bibliotek G.K.S. 1595 (4°): HG 814.
Lists – A-S Vers none.
Quots/Cits see below.
Refs none.

Cross and Brown (1993) note the similarities in theme between this sermon, which exhorts its "listeners and readers to *justum bellum* in defence of their own land against not only attackers but enemies of God" (p 280), and **WULFSTAN OF YORK**'s *Sermo Lupi ad Anglos* (WHom 20, B2.4.2; 3 versions ed. Bethurum 1971 pp 255–75). Whitelock (1963 p 37) notes a probable influence on Wulfstan's sermon from a passage in a manuscript of his "Commonplace Book," Corpus Christi College 190.

Cross and Tunburg (1993 p 18) identify Abbo's sermon as a source for this passage and indeed for two others in the same section of the Corpus manuscript, one of which, as Bethurum notes (1971 pp 297–98), was used by Wulfstan in *Homily* 6, lines 115–21. Cross and Brown (1989) conclude: "No doubt Wulfstan was impressed by Abbo's verve and, directly through the sermon or indirectly through the Corpus extracts, was incited to produce his own sermon with appropriate contemporary reference but with the same purpose" (p 280).

The text is also edited in Cross and Brown (1989 pp 281–84) from the Copenhagen manuscript and is translated (pp 285–87).

Sermo 7 [ABBO.ST.GERM.Serm.7].
  ed.: Önnerfors 1985 pp 100–03.

MSS Copenhagen, Kongelige Bibliotek G.K.S. 1595 (4°): HG 814.
Lists – Refs none.

Abbo's topic is the Lord's supper. The sermon is also printed in *PL* 132.763–64.

Sermo 8 [ABBO.ST.GERM.Serm.8].
  ed.: Önnerfors 1985 pp 104–07.

MSS Copenhagen, Kongelige Bibliotek G.K.S. 1595 (4°): HG 814.
Lists – Refs none.

Abbo's topic is again the Lord's supper, "ad penitentes reconciliandos"; the title in the Copenhagen manuscript is "sermo ad populum."

Sermo 9 [ABBO.ST.GERM.Serm.9].
  ed.: Önnerfors 1985 pp 108–09.

MSS Copenhagen, Kongelige Bibliotek G.K.S. 1595 (4°): HG 814.
Lists – Refs none.

Abbo's topic is again the Lord's supper, "ad penitentes reconciliatos"; the Copenhagen manuscript adds "aecclesiae."

This sermon is also printed in *PL* 132.770.

21 ABBO OF SAINT-GERMAIN

Sermo 10 [ABBO.ST.GERM.Serm.10].
ed.: Önnerfors 1985 pp 110–12.

MSS Copenhagen, Kongelige Bibliotek G.K.S. 1595 (4°): HG 814.
Lists none.
A-S Vers see below.
Quots/Cits – Refs none.

This sermon is addressed to penitents not yet reconciled to the Church. As noted above (**SERMONS**), this is one of three sermons abridged possibly by **WULFSTAN OF YORK** and preserved in Cambridge, Corpus Christi College 190 and in two British Library manuscripts, Cotton Nero A. i and Cotton Vitellius A. vii. The abridged version is translated in the second part of Corpus Christi 190 (B.3.2.9; unpublished).

The sermon is also printed in *PL* 132.769–70.

Sermo 11 [ABBO.ST.GERM.Serm.11].
ed.: Önnerfors 1985 pp 113–17.

MSS Copenhagen, Kongelige Bibliotek G.K.S. 1595 (4°): HG 814.
Lists – Refs none.

This sermon condemns those who steal from the poor since such sins make the nation vunerable to attack from outside.

Sermo 12 [ABBO.ST.GERM.Serm.12].
ed.: Önnerfors 1985 pp 118–22.

MSS Copenhagen, Kongelige Bibliotek G.K.S. 1595 (4°): HG 814.
Lists none.
A-S Vers see below.
Quots/Cits – Refs none.

This sermon stresses the importance of humility and obedience to God's laws. As noted above (**SERMONS**), this is one of three sermons abridged possibly by **WULFSTAN OF YORK** and preserved in Cambridge, Corpus Christi College 190.

Sermo 13 [ABBO.ST.GERM.Serm.13].
ed.: Önnerfors 1985 pp 123–32.
MSS Copenhagen, Kongelige Bibliotek G.K.S. 1595 (4°): HG 814.
Lists none.
A-S Vers see below.
Quots/Cits – Refs none.

Abbo develops his topic, the Lord's supper, by discussing Adam and the ways to salvation. As noted above (**SERMONS**), this is one of three sermons abridged possibly by **WULFSTAN OF YORK** and preserved in Cambridge, Corpus Christi College 190 and in two British Library manuscripts, Cotton Nero A. i and Cotton Vitellius A. vii. The abridged version is the source for Wulfstan's *Homily* 15 (ed. Bethurum 1971 pp 236–38). Bethurum suggests that Wulfstan may also have relied on a closely translated Old English version of the abridgment also preserved in the Cambridge manuscript, but Clemoes (1960 p 272) and Cross and Brown (1993 p 72) disagree.

The sermon is also printed in *PL* 132.764–68.

J. E. Cross and Alan Brown

ACTA SANCTORUM: INTRODUCTION AND ACKNOWLEDGMENTS[1]

From the evidence available, it seems that the Anglo-Saxons before the Norman Conquest did not produce as much Latin hagiographic literature as their Merovingian, Carolingian, and Ottonian contemporaries on the Continent. Hagiographic texts are relatively rare among extant Latin manuscripts of Anglo-Saxon provenance. It is well known that in later Anglo-Saxon England, after the monastic decline and Viking inroads of

---

[1] An earlier version of this introduction, and of several entries, appeared in Biggs, Hill, and Szarmach (1990 pp 1–16).

the ninth century, *latinitas* was generally poor and saw improvement only in a few centers of the ecclesiastical reform. Apparently as a result of this, half of the native English saints' *vitae* from the tenth and eleventh centuries were written by foreigners (see **DUNSTANUS, EADMUNDUS, SWITHUNUS,** and **WILFRIDUS**). Nonetheless, it is clear that hagiography was an important genre in Anglo-Saxon England. Major writers in the early period, such as **BEDE, ALDHELM,** and **ALCUIN,** and in the later period, such as **ÆLFRIC** and **BYRHTFERTH,** devoted significant efforts to one or another form of hagiographic writing. Bede not only wrote several individual saints' lives, but his **MARTYROLOGIUM** is well known as the first "narrative" martyrology in the West and as the lineal ancestor of the most important and influential Continental martyrologies of the Carolingian age and beyond. The ninth-century **OLD ENGLISH MARTYROLOGY,** on the other hand, while apparently without any impact outside England, is becoming recognized (thanks to the work of the late J. E. Cross and Günter Kotzor) as a unique specimen of the martyrologist's art. Finally, although the rhthymic Old English saints' lives of Ælfric alone would constitute an important achievement in the history of Western hagiography, they survive alongside several thousand lines of justly celebrated Old English poetic saints' lives and numerous anonymous hagiographies in vernacular prose.

Although valuable studies have been and are being done on individual hagiographic works and authors of pre-Conquest England, and on the saints' cults themselves, there is as yet no comprehensive treatment of the Anglo-Saxons' hagiographic writing or of their reception and adaptation of the early Christian and early medieval hagiographic traditions, both Western and Eastern, by which their own narrative compositions were undoubtedly influenced. (The first few chapters of the pioneer surveys by Gerould 1916 and Wolpers 1964, and the well-known articles by Kurtz 1926 and Colgrave 1958, focus on the early period, as do more recent discussions in Berschin 1986–91, vol 2, and Goffart 1988.) The materials for pursuing a more broad-based approach to Anglo-Saxon hagiography and hagiology have not been readily available. Hardy's *Descriptive Catalogue*, in the Rolls Series (*RS* 26), although still a valuable guide to the manuscripts of insular history, biography, and hagiography, is outdated and incomplete in various ways and deals primarily with texts on insular saints. Moreover, the Bollandists' roster of indispensable catalogues of hagiographic manuscripts unfortunately does not include any volumes devoted to the major libraries of England, except for one on Greek texts. And while Levison's *Conspectus* of important hagiographic manuscripts (*MGH* SRM 7.529–706) analyzes the contents of some English libraries, he is highly selective as to which saints' lives he itemizes, focusing mainly on Gallic, Merovingian, and Carolingian historical figures whose lives are relevant to the *Monumenta Germaniae Historica* series, especially to *Scriptores rerum merovingicarum*. This lack of hagiographic research tools in the Anglo-Saxon field has been matched by the lack of scholarly attention to the English hagiographic manuscripts themselves, which have only recently begun to be studied with the close attention they deserve.

Building on the preliminary list of hagiographic references supplied by Ogilvy (*BKE* pp 44–52), the present Acta Sanctorum, along with certain author entries in *SASLC*, attempts to collect in one place the basic materials for studying hagiography in Anglo-Saxon England, both what was written and what was available to be read. The entries that follow contain a digest of published information about the texts and textual traditions of all the anonymous *vitae, passiones*, and *miracula* that the Anglo-Saxons seem to have known. It is hoped that the entries will be of service not only to Anglo-Saxonists, Celticists, and students of medieval English culture in general, for exploring the hagiographic writing and reading of the Anglo-Saxons, but also to scholars outside the insular sphere, who need information about Anglo-Saxon copies and versions of particular hagiographic texts and about their reception in early England. (Continental scholars neglect English hagiographic sources at their peril, and vice versa.) It is also hoped that Acta Sanctorum will help in general to further stimulate and support the scholarly work undertaken in recent years on hagiography and the cults of the saints in England up to the year 1100.

Criteria of Selection

The bulk of the entries in Acta Sanctorum concerns individual saints' lives (*vitae*) or martyrdom narratives (*passiones*) by unknown authors. Each entry normally treats of one hagiographic work, to which a specific classification number has been assigned by the Bollandists in their fundamental *Bibliotheca Hagiographica Latina* (*BHL*) and its supplements (see below). A work by a known author, on the other hand, particularly a major author such as Bede or **GREGORY THE GREAT**, is not usually the subject of an entry here but is cited by the saint's name and cross-referenced to the *SASLC* author-entry. But when an author is known only, or chiefly, through a single hagiographic work, this is usually dealt with here under the saint's name, not that of the author: for example, Adrevald of Fleury (**BENEDICTUS CASINENSIS**), Stephen of Ripon (see Wilfridus), Felix (**GUTHLACUS**), Bili (**MACHUTUS**), and the deacons John (**GREGORIUS MAGNUS**) and Paul (**MARIA AEGYPTIACA, THEOPHILUS**). Sometimes, however, it has seemed appropriate and helpful, even at the risk of some minor duplication, to devote an entry in Acta Sanctorum to a hagiographic work or works by an author (e.g., **JEROME** or **VENANTIUS FORTUNATUS**) who is the subject of an author-entry elsewhere in *SASLC*. (One reason for such entries is to provide more hagiographic information than would be convenient in the main author-entry.)

The stories of some quite important saints, such as **ABDON ET SENNEN**, **CHRYSOGONUS**, and **VALERIANUS ET TIBURTIUS**, as well as some lesser saints, such as **CYRILLA** or the **QUADRAGINTA SEX MILITES**, are not the subject of *vitae* or *passiones* of their own, but rather their stories survive as episodes in the longer "epic" legends of major saints such as **ANASTASIA, CAECILIA, LAURENTIUS, MARCELLUS PAPA**, and **SEBASTIANUS**. Frequently, however, these episodes occur as separate extracts in the manuscripts, or they receive separate notices in Bede's *Martyrologium* and the *Old English Martyrology*, as well as in calendars. Where such saints are featured in two or more Anglo-Saxon narrative sources, they are discussed in a separate brief entry here, usually without full headnotes and with limited information and commentary, referring the reader to the entry for the relevant major saint for information about manuscripts and textual traditions. In other instances, where a minor saint features separately in only one Anglo-Saxon source (e.g., **ZOE** from the Sebastianus legend), we have not provided a separate entry but simply refer the reader, for all pertinent information, to the entry for the relevant major saint.

Saints, such as the **SEBASTENI**, possessing alternative names (**QUADRAGINTA MARTYRES [MILITES]**) are appropriately cross-referenced.

As the number of entries in Acta Sanctorum indicates, there is evidence for the circulation in England, before 1100, of about three hundred works celebrating individual saints. Many more saints, however, became known to the Anglo-Saxons through service books and martyrologies like that of **USUARD** and through widely circulated "collective" hagiographies such as Gregory the Great's **DIALOGI**, **PRUDENTIUS**'s **PERISTEPHANON**, the various works that came to be subsumed under the heading **VITAE PATRUM**, the **LIBER PONTIFICALIS**, and also Bede's **HISTORIA ECCLESIASTICA**: such compilations as these are not systematically analyzed here but will be treated elsewhere in the main entries of *SASLC*. In Acta Sanctorum such works are cross-referenced where appropriate (e.g., treatment of the life of **BENEDICT OF NURSIA**, which is the second book of Gregory's *Dialogi* II, is reserved for the main entry on Gregory the Great, but Benedict's separate *miracula* and *translatio*, composed by later authors, are the subject of entries here). The few exceptions to this general rule include some of the *Vitae patrum* saints to whom Anglo-Saxon writers gave special attention (e.g., **AMOS NITRIAE, APOLLONIUS, IOHANNES EREMITA, MACARIUS AEGYPTIUS**). Also, for various reasons, separate entries are devoted to some of the so-called "Vitae maiores" printed among the *Vitae patrum* by Rosweyde (1615) or in volume 73 of Migne's *Patrologia Latina* (**ABRAHAM ET MARIA, ANTONIUS, BASILIUS, EUGENIA, HILARION, MALCHUS**, Maria Aegyptiaca, **PAULUS THEBAEUS, PELAGIA**, and **THAIS**), most of which circulated independently of the early medieval manuscripts of the *Vitae patrum*.

Most Acta Sanctorum entries, however, deal with individual hagiographic works concerning both native English and non-English saints. The latter far outnumber the former. While there are known to have been very many native saints with genuine cults in Anglo-Saxon England (see Rollason 1978), surviving calendars and service books, mainly representing the monastic practices of the tenth and eleventh centuries, devote the great majority of their feasts of rank to the saints of the Roman and Gallican traditions, and the long list of relics from Exeter, for example, reflects this situation (Conner 1993a pp 141–209). These mainly non-native feasts are those for which, presumably, narrative lections would be required for the monastic office in important centers such as Canterbury, Winchester, and Worcester, and abbeys such as Glastonbury, Bury, and Ramsey. It is not surprising therefore that these are the saints whose lives and martyrdoms are encountered in greatest numbers in the surviving records, and in the following pages. Note, however, that most of the early Christian narratives concerning the apostles and the Virgin Mary are not discussed in Acta Sanctorum entries: at the appropriate alphabetical locations they are listed by name, with a cross-reference to their proper entries among the **APOCRYPHA**.

As for the native English saints, a relatively small number of works about them are extant from our pre-1100 period, a fact lamented by William of Malmesbury among others (*RS* 52.144). Individual Latin or vernacular hagiographies concerning a few Anglo-Saxon saints survive from clearly marked periods (**ÆTHELWOLDUS, ÆTHELDRYTHA, BENEDICTUS BISCOPUS, CEOLFRIDUS, CEADDA, CUTHBERTUS,** Dunstanus, **EGWINUS,** Eadmundus, Guthlacus, **OSWALDUS REX, OSWALDUS WIGORNIENSIS,** Swithunus, and Wilfridus); and there is evidence, varying in cogency, that other Anglo-Saxon lives were once current either in Latin or Old English but did not long survive the demise of Anglo-Saxon culture. They were either rewritten or embedded, or otherwise subsumed, in later texts after the Norman Conquest, or simply lost (e.g., those of **ÆTHELBURGA, ÆTHELREDUS ET ÆTHELBERHTUS, AUGUSTINUS CANTUARIENSIS, BOTOLPHUS, EDBURGA, EDITHA, EDWARDUS MARTYR, ERKENWALDUS, HILDA, INDRACTUS, IVO, KENELMUS, MILDREDA, SEXBURGA, WERBURGA, WISTANUS,** and **WULFSTANUS II**). Still others (**AIDANUS, BEDA, BIRINUS,** and **NEOTUS**) survive only in post-Conquest manuscripts and are difficult to date. All of these native saints have entries here, however sketchy, although in most cases lack of pre-Conquest textual evidence has necessitated a modified format, without headnotes.

The written lives of more shadowy Anglo-Saxon saints, on the other hand, survive only in fourteenth-century collections such as the *Sanctilogium* of John of Tynemouth (Horstmann 1901), often misattributed to John Capgrave; the Romsey legendary (see Grosjean 1938 pp 335–39); and the Gotha codex (Grosjean 1940). Works such as these were apparently produced in Anglo-Norman England or later and are not included in Acta Sanctorum. Nor are there systematic entries for the works of the prolific Fleming, Goscelin of Canterbury, or of his fellow hagiographers of the Anglo-Norman era, Folcard, Faricius, and Osbern of Canterbury, although all were active in England before our official cut-off date of 1100. For the most part, texts and authors of the Anglo-Norman era are referred to below only as possible witnesses to pre-Conquest texts. Readers should not expect to find in Acta Sanctorum, therefore, anything resembling a *complete* guide to Anglo-Saxon hagiology or the cults of the saints of Anglo-Saxon England (in lieu of such a guide, see Rollason 1989a and the more specialized work of Ridyard 1988).

Only selective use has been made of the evidence provided by relics lists, calendars, and martyrologies such as those of **ADO** and Usuard. With respect to liturgical sources, some entries include rudimentary liturgical information (especially with regard to calendar evidence for mapping Anglo-Saxon veneration of a particular saint), but the focus is on the saints whose *narrative texts* survive from the Anglo-Saxon period or can at least be conjectured to have existed during that era. No systematic attempt has been made to research all the surviving liturgical material, much of which remains unprinted. See the survey of this material in **LITURGY** (Pfaff 1995).

The sources of information from which the Acta Sanctorum entries have been compiled are many and varied, but those cited with the greatest frequency are listed below, accompanied by their standard abbreviations that *SASLC* shares with *Fontes Anglo-Saxonici* and, for Old English works only, *The Dictionary of Old English*.

Principal Sources I. Early Anglo-Saxon Period (Seventh–Ninth Centuries):
Anglo-Saxon texts:
— Aldhelm's prose and verse DE VIRGINITATE (ALDH.Pros.uirg., ALDH.Carm.uirg.; ed. *MGH* AA 15).
— Bede's *Martyrologium* (BEDA.Mart.; ed. Dubois and Renaud 1976).
— *Old English Martyrology* (*Mart*; ed. Kotzor 1981, vol 2).
Latin manuscripts:
— Paris, Bibliothèque Nationale lat. 10861: HG 898.

The hagiographic sources summarized or quoted in works by Aldhelm and Bede, in the late seventh and early eighth centuries, are identified for Aldhelm by Ehwald in his *MGH* edition and by Lapidge and Herren (1979), and for Bede by Quentin (1908) and others. Readers should note that Aldhelm's *Carmen de uirginitate* is cited below by verses, and the prose *De uirginitate* by pages and line numbers in Ehwald's edition. The *Old English Martyrology*, composed it is thought during the mid- or late ninth century, probably in Mercia or East Anglia, has dozens of notices that condense and select episodes from specific hagiographic sources, as demonstrated in numerous instances by J. E. Cross. The *Martyrology* author appears to have had access to around a hundred and fifty hagiographic texts, which were doubtless contained in miscellaneous English collections no longer extant but similar to the Paris manuscript listed here.[2] This manuscript, the only surviving pre-tenth-century passional of English provenance, containing a mixed collection of nineteen *passiones*, is now accepted as having been written at Canterbury in the early ninth century (M. P. Brown 1986) and may be fairly typical of the hagiographic collections known to and used by Aldhelm and Bede, as well as the author of the *Old English Martyrology*. Attention has recently been drawn to a tenth-century Bobbio manuscript now in Turin (Biblioteca Nazionale F.III.16), part of which, in the opinion of Carmela Franklin (1995), may be a copy of an earlier collection deriving ultimately from Canterbury in the time of Aldhelm and **THEODORE OF CANTERBURY** (see below, ANASTASIUS and ANATOLIA, VICTORIA, ET AUDAX).

Principal Sources II. Later Anglo-Saxon Period (Tenth–Eleventh Centuries):
Anglo-Saxon texts:
— The anonymous Old English lives of saints (*LS*), collectively entitled "Sanctorale" by AC.
— Ælfric's two series of Old English homilies, the so-called **CATHOLIC HOMILIES**, First Series edited by Peter Clemoes (*ÆCHom* I;

---

[2]It is possible that the martyrologist, rather than working from numerous separate sources, had in front of him a Latin martyrology or similar collection. But since no trace of such a Latin collection has ever been found, and given the idiosyncratic nature of most of the *Martyrology* entries, which are unlike those of any other early medieval martyrologies or liturgies, this explanation seems improbable.

EETS SS 17), Second Series edited by Malcolm Godden (*ÆCHom* II; *EETS* SS 5). See now his superb new volume of commentary on the sources of the two sets (*EETS* SS 18, to which it was only possible to refer very briefly in the relevant entries below). Both series were originally edited by Benjamin Thorpe (1844–46) with a facing English translation. Only occasionally relevant to Acta Sanctorum are the supplementary *Homilies of Ælfric*, edited by John Pope (*ÆHom*; *EETS* OS 259–60; see **OTHER HOMILIES**).
— Ælfric's **LIVES OF SAINTS** edited by Walter Skeat (*ÆLS*; *EETS* OS 76, 82, 94, and 114).
Latin manuscripts:
— Cambridge, Corpus Christi College 9: HG 36.
— Dublin, Trinity College 174: HG 215.
— London, BL Harley 3020: HG 433; Cotton Otho A. xiii: HG 351, fragmentary; and Cotton Nero E. i: HG 344.
— Salisbury, Cathedral Library 221: HG 754.5, and 222: HG 754.6, formerly in the Bodleian Library's Fell collection.

The anonymous Old English prose saints' lives form a diverse, scattered group of works, some homiletic, some more obviously "reading" texts, composed variously from the late ninth or early tenth century to the late eleventh or early twelfth, surviving haphazardly and mainly in vernacular **HOMILIARIES** among works by Ælfric and **WULFSTAN OF YORK**. Ælfric's *Catholic Homilies* (mainly for the church feasts of the apostles and a few major saints) survive in numerous manuscripts of the eleventh and twelfth centuries. His *Lives of Saints*, initially composed for private reading, was evidently less well known as a collection. On the manuscripts of the *Lives*, see J. Hill (1996); on Ælfric's hagiography, see Bethurum (1932) and Wolpers (1964); for an introductory survey, and alphabetical lists and sources of the Ælfrician and anonymous Old English lives, see Whatley (1996a; see also 1996b pp 4–9); for detailed surveys of vernacular hagiographic manuscripts, see Nicholls (1993 and 1994) and Scragg (1979 and 1996).

Of the Latin manuscripts in this group, Harley 3020 is the earliest (early eleventh century). It is a composite manuscript, the middle portion of which is a passionary comprising a selection of summer saints, probably from Canterbury (see the recent codicological study by Carley 1994). Corpus Christi College 9 and Cotton Nero E. i, and the two Salisbury Cathedral manuscripts, form two separate but related eleventh-century copies of what has become known to Anglo-Saxonists as the **COTTON-CORPUS LEGENDARY**. Of the two copies, the earlier and more complete (comprising the Cotton and Corpus manuscripts), from Worcester and usually dated mid-eleventh century, contains over 160 hagiographic texts, mainly in calendar order (see Jackson and Lapidge 1996). The Salisbury version has lost a good many of the texts from November and December. Many Anglo-Saxonists now accept that this bulky legendary, of North French origin, was circulating in England by the time of Ælfric, in the late tenth century, as argued initially and most forcibly by Zettel (1979, 1982). While this view is problematic in various respects and has not gone unchallenged (see, e.g., M. Brett 1991 pp 282–83 and note 28, and Morini 1991a, 1993), there is no doubt that the collection was in England by the mid-eleventh century, before the Norman Conquest, and that many, though not all, of the Latin saints' lives evidently known to Ælfric had textual traditions similar to, if not identical with, those of the Cotton-Corpus Legendary (for further discussion, see Whatley 1996a pp 474–82). It is not impossible, however, that many of the hagiographic works in the Legendary may have been unknown to the English until near the very end of the Anglo-Saxon era.

Even less solid is the evidence offered by Dublin, Trinity College 174. This manuscript, according to the recent study by Webber (1992), was written by Salisbury Cathedral scribes working at different periods, some shortly before the end of the eleventh century, others shortly after. The manuscript is dated pre-1100 in Gneuss's list (HG 215) and elsewhere, and numerous entries relying on the Dublin manuscript as a primary source were already sketched out in the Acta Sanctorum database when Webber's work became available. It now appears that the manuscript is perhaps less valuable as a guide to Anglo-Saxon hagiographic traditions than its inclusion in HG might imply. It may best be regarded as a miscellaneous collection put together by several generations of post-Conquest Salisbury scribes to *supplement*, probably from Continental rather than from English exemplars, the Salisbury Cathedral chapter's existing legendaries. The manuscript has not been studied in its own right, however, and it seems safer to include rather than exclude its evidence at this stage.

Even more questionable as witnesses to Anglo-Saxon textual traditions are two other legendaries, included in the HG list but excluded from the main list of Acta Sanctorum sources: Salisbury, Cathedral Library 223 (HG 754.7, formerly Fell 3 in the Bodleian Library), from Salisbury, early twelfth century, the contents of which are itemized with *BHL* numbers by Webber (1992 pp 169–70); and London, British Library Arundel 91 (HG 305), from St Augustine's Abbey, Canterbury, also dated twelfth century by Ker (1964 p 42; its contents are itemized, without *BHL* numbers, in the 1834 catalogue of Arundel manuscripts, *Catalogue of Manuscripts in the British Museum. New Series volume I, Part I, The Arundel Manuscripts* [London, 1834], pp 24–26; another surviving portion of the same legendary is Oxford, Bodleian Library, Fell 2). The texts in these manuscripts, and in another important early-twelfth-century English legendary, London, Gray's Inn 3 (itemized, with *BHL* numbers, by Ker and Piper 1969–92 1.52–55), are excluded for the most part from Acta Sanctorum entries as primary witnesses in the headnotes, but appropriate reference is sometimes made to them, and to other twelfth-century manuscripts, in the commentary provided in the body. For a valuable recent survey of late Anglo-Saxon and post-Conquest Latin legendaries, see Love (1996 pp xi–xxix).

It should be emphasized that little attempt has been made here, as elsewhere in *SASLC*, to pursue original research into manuscripts, sources, and textual problems. Much further work is needed on all the surviving Latin hagiographic collections of Anglo-Saxon England, especially to determine their relationships with contemporary Continental manuscripts. In addition to the arguments of Zettel, M. Brett, and Morini, and other studies mentioned above, among the important recent published contributions to the study of individual Latin hagiographic manuscripts are those of M. P. Brown (1986) on Paris, BN lat. 10861, Carley (1994) on BL Harley 3020, Dumville (1992) on various manuscripts, and Jackson (1992) on Worcester Cathdral F.48. Jackson and Lapidge (1996) have recently published an annotated list of the contents of the Cotton-Corpus Legendary as represented in BL Cotton Nero E. i + Cambridge, Corpus Christi

College 9. Lapidge's published work on Anglo-Saxon saints' lives includes a great deal of authoritative information and insights regarding a variety of Anglo-Latin hagographic manuscripts, while Cross's articles on the *Old English Martyrology* frequently draw attention to early medieval collections of Continental provenance.

For general guidance as to scholarly research resources in the hagiography field, see most recently Dubois and Lemaitre (1993) and Grégoire (1986). For recent introductory essays on the resources for, and critical approaches to, the study of Anglo-Saxon hagiography, see T. Hill (1996) and Whatley (1996b) in a volume devoted otherwise to more specialized studies of Old English prose saints' lives (Szarmach 1996b). Studies on the role of saints' cults and hagiography in Anglo-Saxon society include those of Moloney (1984), Rollason (1989a), Ridyard (1988), and Lapidge (1991a).

Headnotes: Identification and Classification of Works

At the head of each entry, specific hagiographic works are identified by, first, the saint's name, then the genre of the text, then the abbreviated title of the work (following the format devised for *Fontes Anglo-Saxonici*) with, where appropriate, the Bollandists' classification number as listed in their standard guide to Latin hagiographic texts, *BHL*, and its essential *Novum Supplementum, BHL NS* (1986); the abbreviation *BHL* usually refers to both of these, except in some cases where specific reference is made to the supplement volume alone. In the headnotes, *BHL*'s Latin spellings of individual saints' names are adopted (except that native Anglo-Saxon names properly beginning with Æ- are so rendered, not with E- as in *BHL*). On the other hand, in the commentary on such texts (i.e., the "body" of the entry), commonly accepted modern names may be used where appropriate, especially of English and French saints.

Although most of the saints are represented by single entries, implying they were known to the Anglo-Saxons through a single narrative legend, there are many exceptions to this pattern. For example, Benedict of Nursia was known through three distinct works, representing different hagiographic genres: the sixth-century life of Benedict in Gregory the Great's *Dialogi* and its closely translated Old English version (see the main

SASLC entry on Gregory the Great); a collection of posthumous miracles, *Miracula Sancti Benedicti* (*BHL* 1123); and a separate legend concerning the translation of his relics, the so-called *Adventus* or *Translatio Benedicti et Scholastici* (*BHL* 1117). The second and third of these are commonly attributed to the ninth-century monk, Adrevald of Fleury. Accordingly Acta Sanctorum has two entries for Benedict, the first of which, after a general introduction to the saint, has specific information and commentary on Adrevald's book of *Miracula*, while the second entry focuses only on the *Translatio* text.

More complicated is the problem of saints whose stories were known to the Anglo-Saxons in more than one version of the same basic legend. Wherever possible, separate entries are devoted to different versions of a saint's *vita* or *passio*, following the Bollandists' system of classification. This is simple enough where different versions of a legend are attributed to different named authors (as with the two earliest lives of Dunstan), but it is more difficult to distinguish between anonymous works of the same genre and about the same saint. The Bollandists' method in *BHL* is to distinguish significantly different narrative works about a saint by separate numerals. These are in addition to the cumulative classification numbers normally associated with *BHL*. For example, in the first edition of *BHL* there are six separate entries for the Sebasteni, *BHL* 7537–7542, comprising three *passiones*, two sermons, plus a sixth entry listing various epitomes of the *passio*. These six entries are numbered as follows: 1. PASSIO . . . 2. PASSIO . . . 3. PASSIO INTERPRETE IOHANNE DIAC . . . 4. Sermo S. Basilii Magni . . . 5. SERMO S. GAUDENTII . . . 6. EPITOMAE. Some of these larger divisions are further subdivided to represent textual variation. Variant versions of one work are listed under one Arabic numerical heading but distinguished by lower-case letters of the alphabet (e.g., 1. Passio. a., 1. Passio. b., etc.) and further subdivided where necessary by lower-case Greek letters (1. Passio. b . . . *Des.*α) with brief quotations from the variant *Incipit* and/or *Desinit*. Each variant version also has, of course, a separate *BHL* classification number.

It has seemed appropriate to reproduce this system here only in modified form and only in cases where multiple entries are required for a single saint's legend. Only in such cases is *BHL*'s arabic numeral appended to a work's abbreviated title along with any necessary additional markers:

for example, the first entry for **CHRISTOPHORUS** carries the abbreviated title "[ANON.Pas.Christoph.1]: *BHL* 1764" while the second entry is entitled "[ANON.Pas.Christoph.3a]: *BHL* 1766." See also **CHRISTINA** and **COSMAS ET DAMIANUS** for further examples. In a very few cases, such as **GEORGIUS**, other scholarly conventions, besides those of the Bollandists, for marking the different versions of a particular legend have become well known, and we have reproduced these where appropriate alongside those of the Bollandists.

Owing to the instability and proliferation that characterizes many hagiographic textual traditions, there are difficulties and hazards involved in attempting to distinguish and classify variant versions in this way, particularly since many such works have not been thoroughly studied. It is inevitable that future work in the hagiographic field in general, and Anglo-Saxon studies in particular, will necessitate revisions and corrections of the classifications attempted here.

Headnotes: Further Features

A frequent feature of the headnotes in Acta Sanctorum, but not in *SASLC* at large, is the use of the heading *A-S Vers* (*Anglo-Saxon Versions*) to designate not only extensive Anglo-Saxon reworkings (Latin or Old English) of the listed text, but also quite brief summaries. In particular, Aldhelm's *De virginitate*, Bede's *Martyrologium,* and the *Old English Martyrology* frequently contrive to convey the overall scope of a saint's legend, in addition to quoting from it selectively, in only a few lines.

Conversely, Acta Sanctorum makes only sparing use of the heading *Quots/Cits* (*Quotations and Citations*), on the assumption that the detailed tracking and exhaustive listing of smaller borrowings is more the province of the British *Fontes* project. In general, we make use of *Quots/Cits* only to signal clearly identifiable verbal borrowings in works that are not also *A-S Vers*. Normally the headnote will provide only a single *Quot/Cit* for each work so indebted to the source; further quotations or echoes will be briefly mentioned in the body (especially where "see below" is appended to the headnote). Readers can assume, however, unless it is otherwise stated in the body, that works listed under *A-S Vers* usually contain significant verbal parallels with the source text, even when "none" is specified under *Quots/Cits*.

Headnotes usually include citations of some, but not all, the standard reference works. Most frequently cited are *Butler's Lives of the Saints* (*BLS*), which contains useful narrative summaries of legends, and the *Bibliotheca Sanctorum* (*BSS*), the most complete hagiographic encyclopedia, in which the bibliographic information is usually comparable to and often fuller than that in, for example, *LTK*. Regrettably, the valuable *Vie des Saints* by Baudot et al. (1935–54) was not readily accessible during much of my work on this project.

The headnotes also provide, in most cases, a reference to an edition listed in the Bibliography, or to a standard edition such as *MGH* or, most often, the Bollandists' monumental *Acta Sanctorum* (*AS*), which is cited by month and volume, as is customary. *AS* references are to the authoritative first edition, in 65 volumes, comprising the saints of January–November (Antwerp, Paris, Brussels, 1643–1931; reprinted Brussels, 1965–72), rather than to the third edition (Paris, 1863–69), which is cited in Biggs, Hill, and Szarmach (1990 p xxxx).

Commentary

The commentary portion or "body" of each entry provides usually brief information about the saint, his or her early cult, and the origins and transmission of the legend in general, before offering selective commentary, especially references to source studies, regarding the Anglo-Saxon evidence for knowledge of the hagiographic work in question. In some instances the discussion of the legend's transmission outside Anglo-Saxon England may seem disproportionately extensive, but the purpose has been to give readers the means to understand the local Anglo-Saxon textual evidence in relation to that from early medieval Christendom at large.

Acknowledgments

I am grateful to many people for various kinds of help and support during the compilation of Acta Sanctorum, especially to the contributing authors, Mary Clayton, Tom Hall, Joyce Hill, and Hugh Magennis, along with Richard Johnson and Gavin Richardson. Christine Rauer has recently read the numerous entries and bibliography relevant to the sources of the *Old English Martyrology*, generously offering advice, corrections, and encouragement. Fred Biggs, who wrote the *Trial Version* entry for **INVENTIO SANCTAE CRUCIS** (see **IESUS CHRISTUS**) and contributed in detail to several other entries, has provided much patient and persistent editorial guidance and criticism, particularly as regards the format of references and subdividing of entries. I have benefited especially from his reading of the Introduction, the entries for all the "A" saints (Abdon et Sennen through **AUGUSTINUS HIPPONENSIS**), and the entry for **STEPHANUS DIACONUS PROTOMARTYR**. I am also grateful to two other scholars for their help in the early stages of the project: Tom Hill, as one of the supervisory editors of *SASLC*, as a generous and learned host on my visits to Cornell University for research and consultation, and as coordinator of graduate student aides; and the late Jimmy Cross, whose fundamental series of articles on the sources of the *Old English Martyrology* underpins dozens of entries here, and who gave unstintingly and invaluably of his advice, unpublished information, and constructive criticism. Others whom it is also a pleasure to mention gave various kinds of help in the course of the project: Stephan Borgehammar, Martin Brett, James Carley, the late Peter Clemoes, Patrick Conner, Emily Cooney, Alicia Corrêa, Ann DiStefano, David Dumville, Margot Fassler, Ruth Fitzgerald, Carmela Franklin, Katherine German, Helmut Gneuss, Malcolm Godden, Antonia Gransden, Drew Hartzell, Paul Hayward, Peter Jackson, Rosalind Love, Thomas Mackay, Carla Morini, Andy Orchard, Richard Pfaff, J. D. Pheifer, Guy Philippart, Jane Roberts, William Schipper, Elizabeth Teviotdale, David Townsend, Robert Upchurch, Patricia Wallace, Gernot Wieland, Charles Wright, and Richard Zeikowitz.

I am also very grateful to Deborah A. Oosterhouse for her expert and patient copyediting of the final drafts, and especially for her skill in bringing a measure of consistency and accuracy to our system of references and cross-references.

The libraries where most of the research has been done, and to whose staffs I am grateful, are those of Yale University (including the Yale Divinity School), Queens College of the City University of New York (special thanks to Suzanne Katz and Marianne Conti of Interlibrary Loan),

New York Public Library, and, during 1993–94, Cambridge University Library. Other libraries mentioned in the entries below kindly supplied microfilms either directly to me or to my colleagues in the *SASLC* project.

Over half the main draft of Acta Sanctorum was completed in Cambridge during a Fellowship Leave year, 1993–94, for which I am grateful to the President and Trustees of Queens College, Dean Raymond Erickson, and my colleagues in English at Queens and the CUNY Graduate Center. Michael Lapidge, whose inspiring scholarship on Anglo-Latin hagiography is cited and summarized passim in the following pages, was also, as head of the Cambridge University Department of Anglo-Saxon, Norse, and Celtic, a source of much practical help and kindness during my Cambridge stay. Guiding, prodding, and supporting the project from beginning to end, always with cheerful patience and trust, has been the *SASLC* director, Paul Szarmach. Through his resourceful offices, I received some released time from teaching at Queens College, occasional stipendiary support, and some research costs and travel compensation, from the National Endowment for the Humanities via the Center for Medieval and Early Renaissance Studies (CEMERS) at Binghamton University of the State University of New York and the Research Foundation of the City University of New York. As always, I have been wonderfully supported by my wife, Mary Margaret, and our children, Johannah and Will.

Finally, it is a pleasure to acknowledge that this English Acta Sanctorum is deeply indebted to the past and present members of the *Société des Bollandistes*, Brussels, whose tireless scholarship has pioneered and continuously enabled serious study of medieval saints and their texts.

In a work like this, involving hundreds of saints and texts, compiled under less than ideal conditions by an average mortal, it is inevitable that much has been missed or mistaken. As author of most of the entries, and editor of the rest, I accept full responsibility for any imperfections. It should also be made clear that most of the research reflected here was done before 1996–97 and no systematic effort has been made to incorporate scholarship published since then. I would be most grateful if readers who notice significant errors and omissions, or other ways of improving a possible future edition or supplement, would notify me at the following address:

Department of English, Queens College, City University of New York, Flushing NY 11367-1597. email: gwhatley@qc.edu

E. Gordon Whatley
Queens College and the Graduate Center
City University of New York

ACTA SANCTORUM

Abdon et Sennen, passio [ANON.Pas.Abd.Sen.]: *BHL* 6; *BLS* 3.213; *BSS* 1.50–53; *CPL* 2219; *DACL* 1.42–45.
ed.: Delehaye 1933b pp 75–80.
MSS 1. London, BL Harley 3020: HG 433.
2. London, BL Cotton Nero E. i: HG 344.
3. Salisbury, Cathedral Library 222 (formerly Oxford, Bodleian Library Fell 1): HG 754.6.
Lists none.
A-S Vers 1. BEDA.Mart. 138.13–17: see below.
2. *Mart* (B19.fb).
3. *ÆLS* Abdon et Sennes (B1.3.24).
Quots/Cits – Refs none.

Although the Bollandists regard Abdon and Sennen (feast day July 30) as authentic martyrs under Diocletian, with early evidence of cult from the late fourth century (*AS* Nov. 2/2.404), as early as the sixth century their story is told as part II of the **LAURENTIUS** legend, where they are identified as Persian subkings brought to Rome to be martyred for their faith under Decius.

Anglo-Saxon veneration of the two kings and knowledge of their legend is plentiful. The London and Salisbury manuscripts of the eleventh-century **COTTON-CORPUS LEGENDARY** contain a text of the whole Laurence cycle (Zettel 1979 p 23); Harley 3020 (late tenth or early eleventh century, Canterbury: see Carley 1994) contains only parts I and II of the *Passio Laurentii*, namely the *passio* of **POLYCHRONIUS** and that of the two kings. Complete texts of the whole cycle, however, seem to lie behind the notices for Abdon and Sennen in **BEDE**'s **MARTYROLOGIUM** (BEDA.Mart.; ed. Dubois and Renaud 1976, sourced by Quentin 1908 pp 77–81) and in the ninth-century **OLD ENGLISH MARTYROLOGY** (*Mart*; ed. Kotzor 1981 2.136, sourced by Cross 1983a p 204). Both martyrologies contain multiple notices drawn from the whole *Passio Laurentii*.

Two other Persian characters, the noblemen Olympias and Maximus (feast day April 15; see *BSS* 9.77–78), who figure in the Abdon and Sennen portion of the legend, where they are martyred shortly after the two kings have been arrested (ed. Delehaye 1933b pp 76–77), have a separate notice in Bede's *Martyrologium* (ed. Dubois and Renaud 1976 p 62.2–5, sourced by Quentin 1908 p 78). They are passed over, however, by later Anglo-Saxon writers, including **ÆLFRIC** who omits them from his separate rendering of the legend of Abdon and Sennen in **LIVES OF SAINTS** (*ÆLS*; ed. *EETS* OS 94 and 114), sourced by C. Loomis (1931 p 1) and Zettel (1979 pp 227–28), as well as from his homily for Laurence and **SIXTUS II** in **CATHOLIC HOMILIES** I, 29 (see below, the entries for these saints).

Ælfric's decision to compose a separate English legend for the two Persian kings, after treating the cycle's other important figures in his homily for Laurence, may have been due to the liturgical importance of Abdon and Sennen's feast (see F. Wormald 1934 pp 50 and 64). He may also have recognized the lack of narrative connections between the early portions of the cycle (Polychronius, and Abdon and Sennen) and its middle and later portions, where the different episodes are more credibly linked. In addition, and perhaps most important, it is clear that in *Lives of Saints* Ælfric was interested in providing stories about pious kings and noblemen: his brief account of the martyrdom of Abdon and Sennen is followed by the story of **ABGAR**, King of Syria (see **APOCRYPHA**).

Abraham et Maria, vita [ANON.Vit.Abra.Mar.]: *BHL* 12a and 12b; *BLS* 1.605–06; *BSS* 1.113–15; Farmer (1987) p 1.
  ed.: *PL* 73.281–92 and 651–60.

MSS London, Lambeth Palace 173: HG 508.
Lists – Refs none.

The Syrian saint and theologian **EPHRAEM** composed hymns in honor of a hermit Abraham who lived in Kidunaia (Quiduna) near Edessa, Syria, in the mid-fourth century (Beck 1972). The prose life of Abraham, however, traditionally attributed to Ephraem, which survives in very early Syriac, Greek, and Latin manuscripts, is now agreed to have been written in the following century. In the earliest copies, from the fifth and sixth centuries, as well as in later manuscripts, the *vita* is in two parts: the first (in Latin, *BHL* 12a) deals with Abraham's life as a hermit saint, the second (*BHL* 12b), which sometimes occurs separately, focuses on the fall and redemption (through Abraham) of his niece Maria ("Meretrix"). Wilmart (1938a) states that the *vita* of Abraham and Maria had considerable influence on medieval forms of "la vie érémetique, notamment en Angleterre" (p 223 note 3), but unfortunately he does not elaborate. His study of the manuscripts in relation to the early printed editions of the *vita* (including that in Rosweyde's **VITAE PATRUM**, reprinted in *PL* 73.281–94, 651–60) reveals two main recensions of *BHL* 12a–b. The original translation from the Greek is represented only by some fragments from a manuscript possibly of the seventh century (see *CLA* 6.708) and some later medieval copies in Italian libraries. The second recension, a stylistic revision of the first, probably of the Carolingian era, is represented in the overwhelming majority of extant manuscripts and appears to have been dominant outside Italy (Heuclin 1986). Although Rosweyde's printed text (*BHL* 12) is basically that of the revised version, it has an additional six chapters (XII–XVII) at the end of the Maria portion (*PL* 73.659–60) that are not found, apparently, in any of the manuscripts of *BHL* 12a–b and are almost certainly a fifteenth- or sixteenth-century interpolation of material from some other version (see Wilmart 1938a pp 238–39, 244; Heuclin 1986 p 428).

There is no clear evidence of English knowledge of the work before the Lambeth Palace manuscript of the late eleventh century, and neither Abraham nor his niece is commemorated in Anglo-Saxon calendars. The text of the copy in Lambeth Palace 173 breaks off in *Vita Mariae* X, at "et aliquid uestimentorum quid" (*PL* 73.658.10). To judge from Wilmart's findings, it is likely that this represents the so-called "revised" recension. Wilmart does not, however, mention the Lambeth manuscript, and he does not appear to have systematically examined all the manuscripts he lists. His projected parallel edition of *BHL* 12a–b was apparently not completed.

Gradon (1958 pp 21–22) has suggested that Cynewulf's epilogue to *Elene* (*El*, A2.6; ed. *ASPR* 2) and other poems may have been influenced by the similar epilogue that forms chapters XV–XVII of the *Vita Mariae* as printed by Rosweyde. Calder and Allen (1976 pp 68–69) print an English translation of chapters XI–XVII from a possible source of this material, in a Vatican manuscript (*BHL* 12e; ed. Wilmart 1938a pp 238–39); Calder and Allen consider this, however, an analogue to, rather than source of, Cynewulf's poem (pp 59–60, 68–69). See also E. Anderson (1983 pp 17–19) on the "aged author" topos and Bestul (1981) on the scant evidence for Anglo-Saxon knowledge of Ephraem's works, real and spurious.

The story of Abraham and Maria was dramatized by Hrotswitha of Gandersheim in the late tenth century (ed. Homeyer 1970 pp 303–20; trans. Bonfante 1979).

Abundius. See IRENAEUS ET ABUNDIUS.

Acacius et socii 10,000, passio [ANASTAS.BIB.Pas.Acac.]: *BHL* 20; *BSS* 1.134–36; Farmer (1987) p 2.
ed.: *AS* Iun. 4.182–87.

MSS Dublin, Trinity College 174: HG 215.
Lists – Refs none.

Acacius (Achatius), a Roman officer ("primicerius"), is said to have been crucified on Mt. Ararat, Armenia, on the orders of the emperor Hadrian, along with 10,000 (or 1,480) recent converts. The legend includes visions of angels, a victory over Armenian rebels, and various gruesome tortures. The Anglo-Saxons are unlikely to have known of Acacius, unless the Dublin copy of the *passio*, described by Colker (1991 1.326–27), is a late witness to a pre-Conquest manuscript tradition; there is no calendar evidence of an Anglo-Saxon cult. The Bollandists have argued that the work's traditional attribution to the ninth-century translator, Anastasius Bibliothecarius, is groundless, having found no trace of the legend in hagiographical texts, martyrologies, or calendars, in the West or East, before the twelfth century (*AS* Iun. 4.175–77; Delehaye et al. 1940 pp 249–50; see also *BSS* 1.134). This view is contradicted, however, by one modern Bollandist (Devos 1965 p 157) and several German scholars, including Perels and Laehr, who regard the preface to *BHL* 20, and thus the work itself, as genuinely by Anastasius (*MGH* ECA 7.429–30; see Laehr 1928 pp 445–46 for criticism of the older Bollandists' arguments). See also Berschin (1980 pp 200 and 208 note 24) who dates the work 875–76, echoing Siegmund (1949 p 256).

Farmer (1987 p 2) notes the "close resemblance" between this legend and the undoubtedly ancient acts of **MAURITIUS** and the Theban Legion.

The Dublin manuscript (epistle wanting), which was copied at Salisbury Cathedral by Webber's Group II scribes (late eleventh or early twelfth century: see Webber 1992 p 158) is among the earliest extant. For another eleventh-century manuscript, see Siegmund (1949 p 256). A copy formerly in the fourth (supplementary) volume of the early-twelfth-century Chester legendary (London, Gray's Inn 3) has been lost (Ker and Piper 1969–92 1.54–55).

Adrianus. See **HADRIANUS ET NATALIA**.

Aegidius, vita [ANON.Vit.Aegid.]: *BHL* 93; *BLS* 3.457–58; *BSS* 4.958–60; *DHGE* 20.1352–56; Farmer (1987) pp 184–85.
  ed.: E. Jones 1914 pp 99–111.

MSS Dublin, Trinity College 174: HG 215.
Lists none.
A-S Vers *LS* 9 (Giles, B3.3.9).
Quots/Cits – Refs none.

In the later Middle Ages, Aegidius (henceforth Giles; feast day September 1) was one of the most widely venerated saints in England

(Brittain 1928 pp 43–45), but his cult was a late arrival. There may well have been a hermit of this name near Nîmes (Provence) in the sixth century, but his cult seems to have been created in the tenth century at the monastery that adopted the name. What is generally believed to be the earliest version of his legend, falsely attributed in some copies to **FULBERT OF CHARTRES** (who wrote a brief office for the saint, ca. 1023: *PL* 141.343), is likewise dated in the tenth century. Historians attribute the widespread popularity of his later medieval cult, greatly stimulated by the Crusades, to the location of his shrine on pilgrimage routes to Compostella and the Holy Land. Opinion is divided as to how early his cult and *vita* became known in England (see Luiselli Fadda 1982–83, Picard 1980, and Schipper 1986); however, it is likely to be a post-Conquest development following the growth of Giles's cult in northern France (Corbet 1980; Treharne 1997 pp 125–30; see also Ortenberg 1992 pp 227 and 256). The *vita* is significantly absent from the eleventh-century copies of the **COTTON-CORPUS LEGENDARY**. The mass for Giles in the *Leofric Missal* (see **LITURGY, MASSBOOKS**), however, is in the latest of the numerous additions to this complex manuscript, part C, dated to the episcopate of Leofric, 1046–72 (Warren 1883 p 20; Dumville 1992 p 82). The mass set is preceded by a rubric with several biographical details about Giles, suggesting possible knowledge of a *vita* on the part of the scribe or his source.

The Dublin manuscript (Colker 1991 1.323) is among the texts copied by Webber's Salisbury Group II scribes (Webber 1992 p 158) late in the eleventh or early in the twelfth century. It includes the erroneous ascription to Fulbert (see E. Jones 1914 p 96, for five other manuscripts with the same attribution). The Old English prose *Giles* (*LS* 9; ed. Picard 1980), preserved in an early-twelfth-century Rochester manuscript (Cambridge, Corpus Christi College 303; NRK 57), seems not to be much older than its manuscript, despite Luiselli Fadda's ingenious arguments (1982, 1982–83, and 1984) that it predates *BHL* 93 and witnesses to an earlier lost Latin *vita*. That there was another *vita* seems highly likely given Luiselli Fadda's examples of variants, but it has yet to be proven that it was earlier than the tenth century. Treharne, who does not discuss the Dublin manuscript, points to London, BL Cotton Tiberius D. iv (HG

378.5), dated around the turn of the eleventh century, as a close approximation of the source of *Giles* and prints the Latin text from this manuscript (1997 pp 198–206) along with her edition and translation of the Old English text (pp 131–62). Treharne's work came to hand too late for a more thorough account of her findings (see also NICOLAUS, vita).

E. Jones's edition of *BHL* 93, based on a tenth-century manuscript, collated with numerous others, is not the result of a systematic classification of all known manuscripts, but see her valuable lists (pp 95–98). For the Bollandists' older edition, see *AS* Sept. 1.299–303. For a recent brief discussion of the Old English *Giles* as a post-Conquest composition, and for further references, see Scragg and Treharne (1996).

Ælfegus: *BLS* 2.129–31; *BSS* 4.1017–18; *DHGE* 15.267–69; Farmer (1987) p 15.

Apart from several important annals in the ANGLO-SAXON CHRONICLE (see **CHRONICLES**), which may in turn rest on a longer lost account, there seem to be no pre-Conquest Anglo-Saxon literary memorials to Ælfheah (variously Ælfegus, Ælphegus, Elphegus, Alphege, etc.), Archbishop of Canterbury from 1006–12 (not to be confused with the earlier Ælfheah, bishop of Winchester, 934–51). The archbishop was brutally executed in April 1012 by the Danish army at Greenwich, apparently for failing to pay ransom. His body was initially taken to St Paul's, London, but with the help of King Cnut the relics were translated to Canterbury in 1023. The main historical account of his martyrdom, the annals for 1011–12 in the E text of the *Anglo-Saxon Chronicle*, includes a passage in rough Old English verse (*ChronE*, B17.9; ed. Plummer 1892–99; see *EHD* 244–46) that may be from a longer poem, now lost. For the translation to Canterbury, see *Chronicle D* 1023 (*ChronD*, B17.8; ed. Classen and Harmer 1926; see *EHD* 253). Ælfheah's cult was widespread in eleventh-century England, but the first known hagiographic text (ca. 1080) is the *Vita Ælfegi* (*BHL* 2518, ed. *AS* Apr. 2.631–41) by Osbern, precentor of Christ Church, Canterbury, under Lanfranc. Osbern indicates in his prologue that he has been forced to rely mainly on oral tradition, except for some unspecified writings ("aliqua . . . de his rebus non incommode scripta") from which he has culled passages at the appropriate places (*AS* Apr. 2.628b.31–32). His phrasing, however, need not imply a pre-existing life of Ælfheah himself: he could be alluding to his use of other hagiographic works, especially those concerning ÆTHEL-WOLDUS, DUNSTANUS, and LAURENTIUS.

Osbern's work has been little studied (but see Southern 1963 pp 248–52; Rubenstein 1995). For the famous debate between Lanfranc and Anselm regarding Ælfheah's status as martyr, see Eadmer's life of Anselm (Southern 1963 pp 50–54). For a recent discussion of Osbern's literary method in its cultural context, see Townsend (1991 pp 403–12). On the martyrdom and its foreign accounts, see Brooks (1984 pp 282–85).

Æthelberhtus: *BLS* 2.358–69; Farmer (1987) p 147.

Æthelberht (Ethelbert), king of East Anglia, titular saint of Hereford Cathedral (feast day May 20), was the victim of an assassination plot orchestrated in Herefordshire in 794 by Offa, king of Mercia, and perhaps his wife, Cynethryth. By the tenth century, a martyr's cult had developed around the body, which was moved to Hereford itself, and he was also venerated in East Anglia (Thacker 1985 p 17). As with several other pre-Conquest royal saints, Æthelbert's hagiography survives only in late recensions, the earliest of which (preserved in a twelfth-century manuscript) is the *passio* (*BHL* 2627; ed. James 1917 pp 236–44) attributed to Osbert of Clare in *BHL*, but the author is unknown and of uncertain date. Some scholars regard this *passio* as incorporating a pre-Conquest text, while others are less sure, although pre-Conquest traditions from the West Midlands are almost certainly involved. The extant work, however, appears to have been composed in the later eleventh or early twelfth century. See James (1917 pp 218–20), Wilson (1970 pp 97–99), Rollason (1983 p 9), Thacker (1985 pp 16–18), and Hayward (1993 pp 90–91).

Æthelburga, miracula: *BLS* 4.95–96.

MSS – Lists none.
A-S Vers BEDA.Hist.eccles. 354–68.

Quots/Cits none.
Refs BEDA.Hist.eccles. 356.8–9, 364.7, 25–26.

Æthelburh (also Ædilburga and Ethelburga), sister of **ERKENWALDUS** of London, was the first abbess of Barking in the 660s and 670s (feast day October 11). In his long account in **HISTORIA ECCLESIASTICA** IV.vi–ix (BEDA.Hist.eccles.; ed. Colgrave and Mynors 1969) of miracles associated with the regime of Æthelburh and her successor Hildelith, to which *BHL* assigns no separate number, **BEDE** says he is drawing on a "libellus," which also included material on King Sebbi of the East Saxons. Plummer (1896 2.218) considers the style of the Barking stories "very like" Bede's, implying substantial reworking rather than verbatim transcription. Bede says the work was well-known and that many people had copies of it, making it all the more surprising that the *libellus* seems to have disappeared from British and Continental libraries and that later writers show no proven knowledge of it. The notice for Æthelburh in the **OLD ENGLISH MARTYROLOGY** (*Mart*, B19.hw; ed. Kotzor 1981 2.228, sourced 2.361) is based solely on Bede (Cross 1982d pp 24–25). In his *Vita S. Ethelburgae* (*BHL* 2630b, ca. 1087; ed. Colker 1965 pp 398–417), Goscelin of Canterbury shows no sign of having known the *libellus* other than through Bede's version. As in the case of her brother, Æthelburh's historical origins are described somewhat erratically in the standard modern reference works. See the more reliable treatments by Hart (1953 and 1966) and Yorke (1990 pp 45–57). For some analysis of the Barking stories in Bede, focusing mainly on Æthelburh's successor, Hildelith, see Hollis (1992 pp 111–12 and 258–61).

Æthelburh of Barking is mistakenly conflated with Æthelburh, abbess of Brie, daughter of King Anna of East Anglia (635–54), by Colgrave and Mynors in their index (1969 p 597; cf. p 234 note 1).

Ætheldrytha: *BLS* 2.620–21; *BSS* 5.121–22; *DHGE* 15.1160–62; Farmer (1987) pp 148–49.

Although more than one lost work is at issue here, it is not yet possible to treat them under separate headings given the lateness of the evidence, the uncertain number and character of lost sources, and the incomplete state of modern research. Æthelthryth (Etheldreda, Audrey; feast day June 23), daughter of Anna, king of the East Angles (635–54), was married first to Tonbert, prince of the South Gyrwe, and then to King Ecgfrith of Northumbria. She managed to avoid consummating either marriage and eventually was allowed to become a nun, first at Coldingham, and then as abbess of her own new community at Ely (673), where her cult was established some years after her death in 680 by her sister Sexburh (SEXBURGA). BEDE provides the primary account (*BHL* 2632) in his HISTORIA ECCLESIASTICA IV.xix (ed. Colgrave and Mynors 1969 pp 390–96), to which he appends (IV.xix) a hymn celebrating Æthelthryth's virginity (pp 396–400; *BHL* 2633). The brief notice in his MARTYROLOGIUM (ed. Dubois and Renaud 1976 p 113.3–5; see Quentin 1908 p 106), the quite lengthy account in the OLD ENGLISH MARTYROLOGY (*Mart*, B19.du; ed. Kotzor 1981 2.127–29, sourced 2.322), and ÆLFRIC's version in LIVES OF SAINTS (*ÆLS*, B1.3.21; ed. *EETS* OS 76, 82) all derive directly from Bede's account (Cross 1982d pp 25–27; Ott 1892 pp 46–47).

There appear, however, to have been other Anglo-Saxon narratives concerning Æthelthryth, to which the *Liber Eliensis* is a late witness. Richard of Ely (third quarter of twelfth century) reveals that in compiling Book I (his life of Æthelthryth, *BHL* 2634), he drew inter alia on an English vernacular life ("libellum de vita eius conscriptum Anglice") in which there were detailed accounts of episodes treated only in brief in *Liber Eliensis* (Blake 1962 p 6; Wilson 1970 pp 88–89). This Old English life was most probably composed after the refoundation of Ely under ÆTHELWOLD of Winchester (ÆTHELWOLDUS). It is unlikely that Richard is referring here to Ælfric's version in *Lives of Saints* since this is itself a somewhat abbreviated version of Bede's account, on which Richard also draws copiously. No attempt has yet been made to reconstruct the work to which Richard alludes. Presumably such a reconstruction would involve a detailed comparative analysis of Bede's and Ælfric's accounts not only with the Æthelthryth portions of *Liber Eliensis* but also with some unpublished, twelfth-century redactions of a lost Latin *Vita Etheldredae* (*BHL* 2636d, probably from the late eleventh or early twelfth century). See Blake (1962 pp xxx–xxxi and note 6), Hardy (*RS* 26/1.264 and 282–84), and Ridyard (1988 p 56 note 186).

Similarly, a group of the posthumous miracles included in *Liber Eliensis* I.xliii–xlix (Blake 1962 pp 57–61) appears to be based on a miracle collection from the tenth century, specifically the narrative purportedly written by the priest Alfhelm during the reign of King Eadred, 946–55 (see Ridyard 1988 p 183). It is unclear whether the original of these chapters was in Latin or English, or why Ælfric made no use of it.

Hollis (1992 pp 67–74) critically analyzes Bede's account of Æthelthryth in the light of **THEODORE OF CANTERBURY**'s penitentials (IUDICIA). See also P. Thompson (1996) on the historicity of Bede's account (I am grateful to Peter Jackson for this reference). Ælfric's version is analyzed by Garrison (1990) and Jackson (2000), who provides copious references to other recent scholarship on Æthelthryth.

Æthelredus et Æthelberhtus: Farmer (1987) p 150.

Among the great-grandchildren of Æthelberht (Ethelbert) of Kent, the earliest English Christian king (died 616), were the princes Æthelberht and Æthelred (feast day October 17). They were murdered during the reign of their somewhat older cousin, King Egbert (664–73), either by his counselor, Thunor, or by Egbert himself, doubtless for reasons connected with the succession to the throne (Whitney 1984). According to the legend, a miraculous light revealed their burial place (under the royal throne!), and Egbert provided compensation to the murdered princes' sister, Domne Eafe (Domneva, alias Ermenburga), in the form of land for a new monastery, Minster-in-Thanet, of which Domne Eafe became first abbess and her daughter, Mildrith (**MILDREDA**), second. The earliest surviving account of the princes' murder, *BHL* 2643, is preserved in the first section, comprising nine chapters, of the twelfth-century historical miscellany, *Historia Regum* (*RS* 75/2.3–13) attributed to Simeon of Durham. Lapidge (1982a) has argued that this *passio* (which with the four following sections of the *Historia* has been accepted by previous scholars as a separate pre-Conquest work) should be attributed to **BYRHTFERTH**. In Rollason's opinion this *passio* in turn may well have been based on an earlier *passio*, now lost, of the second quarter of the eighth century, from an obscure "monasterium Wacrinense" (possibly represented in the place-names of Great and Little Wakering in Essex), which possessed the relics of the princes from soon after the murder until 978–92, during which time they were translated to Ramsey Abbey (Rollason 1982), possibly in response to the murder (978) of Edward the Martyr (EDWARDUS MARTYR; Thacker 1996a pp 247–49; see also EADMUNDUS). For another version of the legend (*BHL* 2461–62), more closely associated with Canterbury, see Mildreda. On other possible earlier versions, reflected in the fourteenth-century Gotha manuscript, see Rollason (1982 pp 21–25), Colker (1977), and Grosjean (1940). Whitney (1984) discusses the seventh-century historical background, and comments on **BEDE**'s quite different perspective on the events in question (pp 6 and 18). See also Hayward's contextual study (1993) of this and other similar accounts of "innocent martyrdom."

Æthelwaldus. See OETHELWALDUS.

Æthelwoldus: *BLS* 3.240–41; *BSS* 1.129–30; Farmer (1987) pp 150–52.

ÆTHELWOLD (feast day August 1), bishop of Winchester 963–84, former abbot of Abingdon, was one of the leaders of the Benedictine reform movement in the second half of the tenth century. For discussions of various aspects of his life and time, see Yorke (1988). His hagiographers, **WULFSTAN OF WINCHESTER** ("the Cantor") and **ÆLFRIC**, abbot of Eynsham, were both his students at Winchester. Ælfric's Latin life of Æthelwold (*BHL* 2646, ed. Winterbottom 1972 pp 17–29; Lapidge and Winterbottom 1991 pp 70–80, translated in *EHD* pp 903–11), formerly considered the earlier work, is now believed to be an epitome of Wulfstan's more elaborate work (ed. Winterbottom 1972 pp 33–63; Lapidge and Winterbottom 1991 pp 2–68; with English translation pp 3–69). For a full discussion and survey of the eleventh- and twelfth-century examples of the literary influence of Wulfstan's work, see the introduction to the recent edition by Lapidge and Winterbottom (1991).

Afra, passio [ANON.Pas.Afr.]: *BHL* 108–09 and 111; *BLS* 3.267–68; *BSS* 1.283–87; *CPL* 2077; *NCE* 1.171–72.
ed.: *MGH* SRM 3.51–52 and 55–64.
MSS 1. Paris, Bibliothèque Nationale lat. 10861: HG 898.
2. Dublin, Trinity College 174: HG 215.
Lists none.
A-S Vers Mart (B19.fn).
Quots/Cits – Refs none.

There is early evidence for the cult of Afra (feast day August 8) at Augsburg (her shrine is mentioned by **VENANTIUS FORTUNATUS**; on the archeological evidence, see Prinz 1981 p 211). Narrative sources, however, for the legend of the reformed prostitute, supposedly martyred under Diocletian, are much later. The earliest recension (*BHL* 107b) of the *passio* is believed to be of the seventh century, most likely during the establishment of the bishopric of Augsburg under Dagobert I, 629–39 (Berschin 1974 p 127; 1981 pp 217–21; Prinz 1981 pp 213–14). This short work was then expanded, early in or shortly before the Carolingian period, into a more developed *passio* (*BHL* 109), and the story of Afra's conversion by a Bishop Narcissus of Narbonne was added to the beginning (*BHL* 108).

This later, less-studied version (*BHL* 108–09) was known to the Anglo-Saxons at least by the early ninth century, the date of the copy in the Canterbury passional (Paris, Bibliothèque Nationale lat. 10861, classified A2 in the *MGH* edition). This manuscript also contains *BHL* 111, an "additamentum" on Saint Quiriacus and other characters in the legend (*MGH* SRM 3.51–52). Misbinding is responsible for confusion in the order of folios and text, indicated by the Bollandists' foliation of the *passio*: fols 110r–112v, 101r–104v (Bollandists 1889–93 2.606). M. P. Brown (1986) says the *passio* occupies fols 102r–108v, perhaps to indicate what would be the corrected foliation (J. E. Cross, personal communication).

The notice for Afra in the **OLD ENGLISH MARTYROLOGY** (*Mart*; ed. Kotzor 1981 2.73–75) appears to draw on *BHL* 108–09 (*EETS* OS 116.xl), attributing her conversion to Narcissus and echoing some of the wording of *BHL* 109 rather than *BHL* 107b. A more precise sourcing is needed.

Afra's legend does not appear in the mid-eleventh-century **COTTON-CORPUS LEGENDARY**, and her feast day is recorded in only one extant Anglo-Saxon calendar (F. Wormald 1934 p 51). The only exception to this later Anglo-Saxon lack of interest in Afra is the Dublin manuscript (late eleventh century, Salisbury), which contains *BHL* 108–09 in a text of unknown affiliations (not listed in the *MGH* edition). On the manuscript's contents, see Colker (1991 1.322). The text was copied by one of Webber's Group I scribes (Webber 1992 p 142).

For a recent overview of the legend, see Berschin (1986–91 2.82–87).

Agape, Chionia, et Irene, passio [ANON.Pas.Agap.]: *BHL* 118; *BLS* 2.19–21; *BSS* 1.303; *CPL* 2163.
ed.: Delehaye 1936 pp 228–35.
MSS Cambridge, Corpus Christi College 9: HG 36.
Lists none.
A-S Vers 1. ALDH.Carm.uirg. 2194–278.
2. ALDH.Pros.uirg. 305–07.
3. BEDA.Mart. 57.2–5 and 58.15–18.
4. *Mart* (B19.br and bt).
Quots/Cits – Refs none.

Agape, Chionia (feast day April 3), and Irene (April 5) were young Christian women of Salonika martyred under Diocletian. The simple story told in their original Greek *acta* (*BHG* 34), which is considered historically genuine by modern scholars (Delehaye 1936 pp 103–04), was later drastically rewritten to include, for example, the slapstick episode of Dulcitius making love to some kitchen utensils. In this form it was incorporated in the epic *passio* of **ANASTASIA** (*BHL* 1795, 118, 8093, 401), which was known in both early and late Anglo-Saxon England.

BEDE's account in his **MARTYROLOGIUM** (BEDA.Mart.; ed. Dubois and Renaud 1976), despite some discrepancies over feast days (Quentin 1908 pp 58–59), is clearly based on this work, as are **ALDHELM**'s much longer, boisterous epitomes in the verse and prose DE VIRGINITATE (ALDH.Carm.uirg. and Pros.uirg.; ed. *MGH* AA 15) in which the humorous Dulcitius episode is prominent.

Cross (1985b p 231 note 21) follows Herzfeld (*EETS* OS 116.228) in pointing out that the **OLD ENGLISH MARTYROLOGY** (*Mart*; ed. Kotzor 1981 2.49) draws on Aldhelm's *Carmen de uirginitate* (to which the martyrologist refers, Kotzor 1981 2.49.4–5) for some particulars of the account of Agape and her sister. The borrowing incorporates a gloss on one of Aldhelm's arcane words, "larva" (*Carmen* 2244); see also Kotzor's note on "larbo . . . egesgrima" (1981 2.300; and see 1.257). Some of the wording of the *Martyrology* notice, however, derives not from Aldhelm but from *BHL* 118 (Cross 1986b p 281). In addition, some narrative details common to the *Martyrology* and the *passio* do not appear in either of Aldhelm's texts (e.g., the fact that the clothes and bodies of Agape and Chione are undamaged by the fire; admittedly this is a hagiographic commonplace). Surprisingly, in the separate *Martyrology* notice for Irene, there is no mention of her being killed by one of Sissinius's bowmen, a detail common to all the Latin versions.

In the later Anglo-Saxon period, Agape and her sister are not represented separately from Anastasia (for a lone calendar entry, from the later eleventh century, see F. Wormald 1934 p 102).

For the original Greek *acta* with an English translation, see Musurillo (1972 pp xlii–xliii and 280–93). Cross (1986b pp 296–97 note 39) identifies ninth-century manuscripts containing *BHL* 118. For the tenth-century Latin comedy (*BHL* 120) by Hrotswitha of Gandersheim, see Homeyer (1970 pp 268–77).

Agapitus Praeneste, passio [ANON.pas.Agapit.]: *BHL* 125; *BLS* 3.345; *BSS* 1.313–15.
   ed.: Mombritius 1910 2.35–37 and 619.

MSS   1. London, BL Harley 3020: HG 433.
   2. London, BL Cotton Nero E. i: HG 344.
   3. Salisbury, Cathedral Library 222 (formerly Oxford, Bodleian Library Fell 1): HG 754.6.
Lists – Refs   none.

There is archaeological as well as liturgical evidence for the early cult of a martyr Agapitus (feast day August 18) at Praeneste (Palestrina). The *passio*, however, in which he is said to have been martyred as a boy under the emperor Aurelian (270–75), is spurious. Kellner (1930 p 410) dates its composition sixth/seventh century. There is a simple entry for the saint's feast, August 18, in the "second family" of BEDE's MARTYROLOGIUM (ed. Dubois and Renaud 1976 p 152.2), but it may also have been in the "first family" since the short entries of the latter are missing after July 25. The earliest indisputable evidence for knowledge of Agapitus in Anglo-Saxon England is the ninth-century OLD ENGLISH MARTYROLOGY (*Mart*, B19.fx; ed. Kotzor 1981 2.183), but the notice is a simple liturgical commemoration, not a narrative (see 1.282–83, 207–08, on Agapitus in the other martyrologies). Service books of the Gregorian type have a proper mass for this saint and it is not surprising therefore that Agapitus's feast day is noted in several of the tenth- and eleventh-century Anglo-Saxon calendars printed by F. Wormald (1934); there is also a proper mass in the early-eleventh-century *Missal of Robert of Jumièges* (see LITURGY, MASSBOOKS).

The copies of the *Passio Agapiti* in the three eleventh-century manuscripts listed above have *incipit*s and *explicit*s identical with those of *BHL* 125e, but the text in the Cotton and Salisbury manuscripts is somewhat abridged in comparison with the older Harley manuscript (probably from Canterbury, early eleventh century: see Carley 1994).

Agatha, passio [ANON.Pas.Agath.1]: *BHL* 133; *BLS* 1.255–56; *BSS* 1.320–35; *CPL* 2158.
ed.: *AS* Feb. 1.615–18.
MSS 1. London, BL Cotton Nero E. i: HG 344.
2. Salisbury, Cathedral Library 221 (formerly Oxford, Bodleian Library Fell 4): HG 754.5.
Lists – Refs none.

Agatha's cult (feast day February 5), which quickly became one of the most important in the late Roman world, originated apparently in Catania, Sicily, where, according to her legend, she was martyred as much for her heroic chastity as for her Christianity, under the persecution of Decius

(*BHL* 133) or Diocletian (*BHL* 134; next entry). The Latin *passio* survives in several slightly varying forms, *BHL* 133–36, none of which appears to represent the original exactly and which differ mainly as to their *incipit*s and chronological details, except that *BHL* 135 (see the third Agatha entry below) is somewhat amplified, though verbally still very like the others. Brusa (1959) argues for a lost original from which derive independently all the surviving versions: the Latin *passio*, an anonymous Greek *passio* (*BHG* 36), and one by Metaphrastes (*BHG* 37). She does not indicate whether the original was more likely to have been Latin or Greek, but considers that of Metaphrastes to be closest to it (p 345). The composition date of the putative original is uncertain (possibly sixth century: *CPL* 2158).

The earliest English copies of *BHL* 133 are in the eleventh-century manuscripts of the **COTTON-CORPUS LEGENDARY** (Morini 1993 p 79; Jackson and Lapidge 1996 p 136).

There is no critical edition of the Latin *passio*. The most important recent work on the manuscripts is that of Morini (1993 pp 79–86, to whom I am very grateful for sending me a copy of her important monograph and several offprints); see also D'Arrigo's master list of 171 manuscripts (1988 1.374–481) and Morini's useful appendix of Latin and vernacular versions from England and Scandinavia (1993 pp 645–56).

Agatha, passio [ANON.Pas.Agath.1α]: *BHL* 134.
  ed.: D'Arrigo 1988 1.379–87.

MSS Paris, Bibliothèque Nationale lat. 10861: HG 898.
Lists none.
A-S Vers 1. ALDH.Carm.uirg. 1736–85.
  2. ALDH.Pros.uirg. 293.1–14.
  3. BEDA.Mart. 30.2–7.
Quots/Cits – Refs none.

Among the earliest Latin manuscript versions of the *Passio Agathae* is a copy in the Canterbury passional, now Paris Bibliothèque Nationale lat. 10861, representing *BHL* 134 (M. P. Brown 1986 p 122; Morini 1993 p 58).

BEDE's familiarity with the legend is evidenced by his epitome in the MARTYROLOGIUM (BEDA.Mart.; ed. Dubois and Renaud 1976), sourced by Quentin (1908 p 57); ALDHELM's by his eulogies in the verse and prose DE VIRGINITATE (ALDH.Carm.uirg. and Pros.uirg.; ed. *MGH* AA 15; sourced 15.293, 425). Brusa (1959 pp 361–63) offers textual evidence for Aldhelm's use of something close to the lost original, citing passages where Aldhelm has language in common with the earlier of the two Greek versions, rather than the Latin *passio*. Unfortunately, her arguments in this and other parts of her study cannot be considered conclusive since she does not consult manuscript variants and relies on the Bollandists' Latin translation of the earlier Greek text and on Consoli's Italian translation of Metaphrastes for close verbal comparisons of the Latin and Greek versions. Morini (1993 pp 44–47, 57–58; see D'Arrigo 1988 1.49 and 52) points out that both Bede and Aldhelm used texts containing the "Diocletian" *incipit* characteristic of *BHL* 134 and that this variant version, which may have originated with Aldhelm himself, is found in other early manuscripts with Anglo-Saxon associations. The Bollandists classify Aldhelm's verse epitome itself as *BHL* 137.

The **OLD ENGLISH MARTYROLOGY** would, most likely, have contained a notice for Agatha, but it has been lost, along with those of other January–February saints.

D'Arrigo's edition of the *passio* is simply a transcription of a late-eighth- or early-ninth-century Würzburg manuscript, apparently the oldest witness, collated with Mombritius's edition (1910 1.37–40; *BHL* 136). Morini (in D'Arrigo 1988 1.650–52) provides a partial transcription of the Paris manuscript listed here, to permit comparison with the Würzburg text. In his catalogue of Karlsruhe manuscripts, Holder (1914 pp 475–83) prints an incomplete ninth-century Reichenau copy.

Agatha, passio: see below.
ed.: Morini 1991b pp 320–29.
MSS – Lists none.
A-S Vers ÆLS Agatha (B1.3.9).
Quots/Cits – Refs none.

The fullest reworking of the *Passio Agathae* by an Anglo-Saxon is that of ÆLFRIC in LIVES OF SAINTS (*ÆLS*; ed. *EETS* OS 76 and 82), first sourced by Ott (1892 pp 29–31) with reference to *BHL* 133 and the *AS* edition, and later Zettel (1979 pp 151–52, 215–17), who argues that Ælfric's Agatha is based on a text closely resembling that in the **COTTON-CORPUS LEGENDARY** (see the above entry on *BHL* 133). Recent, more detailed work by Morini (1991a pp 88–92), however, discounts Zettel's findings and points to several readings that Ælfric's version shares with another variant recension, *BHL* 135, originating in Spain probably in the ninth century and surviving in the Spanish passional (Fábrega Grau 1953–55 pp 220–26). Morini (1993) has concluded that Ælfric's source was a hybrid text, based on *BHL* 135 but contaminated or conflated with readings from *BHL* 133. This hybrid text, unclassified by the Bollandists, is preserved in a three-volume twelfth-century Cistercian legendary, which she believes to be based on a collection brought from southwest England by the Cistercian founder, Stephen Harding. See her 1993 edition, especially pp 61–76 (on the Cistercian recension) and 95–124 (on Ælfric's relation to the Latin texts). For her text of Ælfric's Agatha, see pp 183–237 (right hand pages), and for parallel texts of the Cistercian redaction and *BHL* 133 (reprinted from *AS* Febr. 1.615–18), see pp 182–236.

Agaunenses. See **MAURITIUS**.

Agnes, passio [ANON.Pas.Agnet./PS.AMBR.]: *BHL* 156; *BLS* 1.133–37; *BSS* 1.382–407; *CPL* 2159; *CPPM* IIA.28a; *DACL* 1.905–65.
   ed.: *PL* 17.735–43.

MSS 1. London, BL Cotton Nero E. i: HG 344.
    2. Paris, Bibliothèque Nationale lat. 10861: HG 898.
    3. Salisbury, Cathedral Library 221 (formerly Oxford, Bodleian Library Fell 4): HG 754.5.
Lists none.
A-S Vers 1. ALDH.Carm.uirg. 1925–74.
    2. ALDH.Pros.uirg. 298.12–299.17.

3. BEDA.Mart. 18.2–4.
4. *Mart* (B19.ai).
5. *ÆLS* Agnes (B1.3.8).
Quots/Cits   see below.
Refs   *ÆLS* Agnes (B1.3.8) 1–5.

The cult of Agnes (feast days January 21, 28) was prominent in Rome by the mid-fourth century, when a basilica was built in her honor by CONSTANTINA, daughter of Constantine. Her name and some aspects of her martyrdom were also popularized by **AMBROSE** (**DE VIRGINIBUS** I.v–ix; ed. Cazzaniga 1948) ca. 377, and somewhat later by **PRUDENTIUS** (**PERISTEPHANON** XIV; ed. *CCSL* 126.386–89) and other writers equally well-known to the Anglo-Saxons, such as **AUGUSTINE** and **GREGORY THE GREAT** (see *BSS* for references); the sermon on Agnes often attributed to **MAXIMUS OF TURIN** (*BHL* 158, ed. *PL* 57.643–48) is now rejected as spurious.

The anonymous *passio* (*BHL* 156), whose author poses as Ambrose himself, is a synthesis of the various earlier literary and oral traditions. Dated ca. 415–23 by some (Jubaru 1907, Denomy 1938), by others in the sixth and seventh centuries (Franchi de' Cavalieri 1899 pp 53–67), it may have been composed by the author of the legends of **EUGENIA** and **SEBASTIANUS** (Jubaru 1907 pp 124–33). Unlike many such legends, its textual tradition seems to show little variety. Three Anglo-Saxon copies survive, one from early-ninth-century Canterbury (the Paris manuscript above: M. P. Brown 1986 p 122) and two in the eleventh-century recensions of the **COTTON-CORPUS LEGENDARY**.

Among the early Anglo-Saxons, the text was used by **BEDE** in his **MARTYROLOGIUM** (BEDA.Mart.; ed. Dubois and Renaud 1976) for notices on both Agnes and Emerentiana (Quentin 1908 p 57). It was summarized by **ALDHELM** in the **DE VIRGINITATE** (ALDH.Carm.uirg. and Pros.uirg.; ed. *MGH* AA 15), and in the **OLD ENGLISH MARTYROLOGY** (*Mart*; ed. Kotzor 1981 2.22–23). Cross (1982d pp 31–32) points to the influence of Aldhelm's version on the *Martyrology* in one intriguing phrase, but otherwise the *passio* appears to be the martyrologist's main source (*EETS* OS 116.226).

The *passio* was later translated by **ÆLFRIC**, in **LIVES OF SAINTS** (*ÆLS*; ed. *EETS* OS 76 and 82), who refers to his source as the work of

Ambrose (see Ott 1892 pp 24–26 and Denomy 1938 pp 134–37). According to Zettel (1979 p 213), Ælfric's version is closer in some details to that in the Cotton-Corpus Legendary than in *PL* (for a caveat, see Whatley 1996a p 481). For the *Alia Sententia* that Ælfric appended to his account of Agnes, see **IOHANNES ET PAULUS** and **GALLICANUS** (*BHL* 3236 and 3238).

There are several verbal echoes of the *passio* among prayers (possibly composed in England) for Agnes's feast days in the eleventh-century *Canterbury Benedictional* (*HBS* 51.79) and in the early-eleventh-century *Samson Pontifical* (Cambridge, Corpus Christi College 146 [HG 46] p 242: see Dumville 1992 pp 72–73); this manuscript was kindly brought to my attention by Alicia Corrêa. See **LITURGY, PONTIFICALS AND BENEDICTIONALS**. See also Ortenberg (1992 p 177).

Some verses in Agnes's honor attributed to Pope **DAMASUS** (but now rejected as spurious: De Rossi and Ferrua 1983 pp 12–13), along with an acrostic inscription attributed to Constantina, are preserved in Cambridge, Corpus Christi College 23 (HG 38, ca. 1000, at Malmesbury by the eleventh century), after the end of the text of Prudentius's *Peristephanon* XIV. These sets of verses on Agnes (printed by De Rossi and Ferrua 1983 pp 12–13) commonly occur in Prudentius manuscripts; see Jubaru (1907 pp 38–61 and 246–67).

Most of the scholarship on Agnes has been devoted to the early history of the cult and the martyr's authenticity; for earlier scholarship, see Denomy (1938 pp 3–37), who also discusses the legend's influence on vernacular, especially French, literature. Agnes's place in Anglo-Saxon culture has not been the subject of special study. There is no critical edition of the *passio*, only separate editions of individual manuscripts (see *BHL NS* p 22: some of the most important early manuscripts are listed by Cross 1982d p 42 note 82). For a brief literary appreciation of the Latin work in the context of others like it such as Eugenia, Sebastianus, and **LAURENTIUS**, see Berschin (1986–91 1.85–87), who dates the earliest form of the work in the late fourth century. Villamor's (1980) overview of the cult bypasses the English sources.

The edition in *PL* differs only in minor ways from that in *AS* Ian. 2.715–18.

Aichardus, vita [ANON.Vit.Aichard.]: *BHL* 181; *BLS* 3.556–57; *BSS* 1.147–48; *DHGE* 1.307.
  ed.: *AS* Sept. 5.85–99.

MSS 1. Arras, Bibliothèque Municipale 1029 (812): HG 781.
  2. Boulogne, Bibliothèque Municipale 106: HG 804.
Lists Saewold: ML 8.19.
A-S Vers – *Refs* none.

Aichardus (Aichadrus, Achart), though a Poitevin by birth, ended his life ca. 687 (feast day September 15) as abbot of Jumièges, where he succeeded Filibert (**PHILIBERTUS**) on the latter's retirement. He does not appear to have had any cult in England, except for a time in the tenth and eleventh centuries at St Peter's, Bath, where a party of Flemish monks, fleeing the reforms of Saint Gérard, settled in 944 at the invitation of King Athelstan (Grierson 1940 pp 103–04; Ortenberg 1992 pp 24–25). Aichard's *vita* is preserved in two manuscripts associated with Bath and Flanders. Arras 1029, from the late tenth or early eleventh century, was donated ca. 1070 to the abbey of Saint-Vaast by the exiled Abbot Saewold of Bath, among a substantial collection of books presumably from Bath itself. This copy is imperfect, beginning in paragraph seven of the *AS* edition (Van der Straeten 1971 p 63). Boulogne 106, a composite manuscript of the tenth/eleventh century (Van der Straeten 1971 p 137), was at Saint-Bertin in the Middle Ages and contains a block of four texts apparently of Anglo-Saxon provenance (HG 804). One of these, *Vita Filiberti* (*BHL* 6805), is textually close to the copy of the same life in Arras 1029 (see *MGH* SRM 5.575: manuscripts B 1.a and B 1.b). Both manuscripts also contain closely related copies of Felix's life of **GUTHLACUS** (Colgrave 1956 pp 35–36). It is therefore likely that the Boulogne copy is also a product of the Bath scriptorium around the turn of the eleventh century (Colgrave 1956 pp 36, 39) and that the ultimate exemplar of both was a Flemish legendary brought to Bath by the exiles from Saint-Bertin.

Aidanus, vita [ANON.Vit.Aidan.]: *BHL* 190; *BLS* 3.451–52; *BSS* 1.625–27; Farmer (1987) pp 7–8.
  ed.: Horstmann 1901 1.23–27.

MSS Oxford, Bodleian Library Digby 175 (*SC* 1776): HG 614.
Lists – A-S Vers none.
Quots/Cits see below.
Refs none.

Aidan (also Aedhan, Aidus; died 651, feast day August 31), an Irish monk of Iona invited to Northumbrian Bernicia in 635 by King Oswald (**OSWALDUS REX**), was the first bishop of Lindisfarne and one of **BEDE**'s heroes of the early Northumbrian church (**HISTORIA ECCLESIASTICA** III.iii–vi, xv–xvii, and xxvi; ed. Colgrave and Mynors 1969 pp 218–20, 226–28, 258–67). Aidan's cult developed at Lindisfarne, the first home of his relics. In later Anglo-Saxon England, however, Glastonbury claimed to have acquired them (Rollason 1989a p 152), as is reflected in a tenth–eleventh century list of English saints' shrines (Rollason 1978 pp 66, 92) and in a handful of calendars with southwestern links (F. Wormald 1934 pp 23, 51, and 65).

The brief account of Aidan in the ninth-century **OLD ENGLISH MARTYROLOGY** (*Mart*, B19.gk; ed. Kotzor 1981 2.195–96) draws on Bede's *Historia* and, for one narrative detail, as Cross (1982d p 27) indicates, on his prose **VITA CUTHBERTI** (ed. Colgrave 1940 pp 164–67; see also **CUTHBERTUS**). The different recensions of the *Old English Martyrology* disagree, however, as to the location of the relics, one manuscript pointing to Lindisfarne, the other to Glastonbury. Kotzor and Cross remark (following Herzfeld, *EETS* OS 116.xxx–xxxi) that this discrepancy may be explained as an instance of Glastonbury forgery (Kotzor 1981 2.344; Cross 1982d pp 27–28).

It is possible that the *Martyrology* author had access to a life of Aidan, such as that in question here, based mainly on Bede's *Historia* but also including material, in abbreviated form, from other sources. The structure of one sentence in the *Martyrology* ("þaes saule geseah Sancte Cuthberhtus on middeniht englas laeddan micle leohte to heofonum," "whose soul Saint Cuthbert saw angels leading towards heaven amidst great light, in the middle of the night"; Kotzor 1981 2.195.8–10) is closer to the equivalent passage of this life of Aidan ("Cuius animam ab angelorum choris in celum eleuatam sanctus Cuthbertus . . . intempeste noctis silenti . . . videre meruit," ed. Horstmann 1901 1.26.1–4) than to that of Bede's

Vita Cuthberti (ed. Colgrave 1940 pp 164.21–166.1), although the *Martyrology*'s "micle leohte" echoes Bede rather than the anonymous life of Aidan.

The earliest manuscript copy, the Digby manuscript, is late eleventh century, probably from Durham (Colgrave 1940 pp 22 and 24). It ends imperfect at "laudans atque ad" (cf. Bede's *Historia*, ed. Colgrave and Mynors 1969 p 266.10). Later copies are noted by Colgrave (1940 pp 22, 24, and 26). See also the entry for Cuthbertus (vita) for further evidence of the apparent existence of composite or hybrid Anglo-Saxon texts of the lives of the northern saints.

Aidus. See AIDANUS.

Albanus, passio [ANON.Pas.Alban.]: *BHL* 211a; *BLS* 2.612–14; *BSS* 1.656–58; *CPL* 2079.
ed.: W. Meyer 1904 pp 37–47.

MSS – Lists none.
A-S Vers BEDA.Hist.eccl. 28–34 and 58–60.
Quots/Cits – Refs none.

The fifth-century life of Germanus of Auxerre (GERMANUS AUTISIODORENSIS) testifies to the early fame of Alban (feast day June 22) of Verulamium (St Albans, Hertfordshire) as Roman Britain's principal martyr (see *Vita Germani*, ed. *MGH* SRM 7.262 and 265). GILDAS, writing in the mid-sixth century, is believed to have known an early *passio* but seems to recall it from memory (Levison 1941 pp 344 and 348–49). Alban's legend was known in the Middle Ages chiefly through BEDE's HISTORIA ECCLESIASTICA (BEDA.Hist.eccles; ed. Colgrave and Mynors 1969), *BHL* 206–10: in some manuscripts this chapter is marked for liturgical reading (Plummer 1896 1.425, note on p 18, line 13). It was also excerpted in legendaries as a separate *passio* (e.g., *RS* 26/1.26 nos. 51–52, and p 28 nos. 60–61).

Bede's account was so successful in supplanting his source (in England as well as elsewhere) that the original *passio* was believed lost until W. Meyer (1904) distinguished and printed three separate recensions of it, usually referred to as Passio 1, 2, 3 in chronological order but numbered by the Bollandists respectively *BHL* 210d, 211a, 211. Levison (1941 pp 348–49) dates Passio 1 ca. 515–40 and points to Auxerre as the place of composition but warns against regarding Meyer's T text (an eighth-century Corbie manuscript now in Turin: see *CLA* 4.446) as the earliest form of the text. Bede's immediate source, Passio 3, formerly regarded as derived from Bede, is an early abridgement of Passio 1. It is preserved in an English legendary, London, Gray's Inn 3 (early twelfth century), along with a recension of the Bedan account (*BHL* 207; Ker and Piper 1969–92 1.54), but Levison (1941 pp 344–45) assumes a Continental origin for this copy "like other texts of the Codex" and like other copies of Passio 2.

Quentin (1908 p 105), who was apparently unaware of Meyer's work, seems correct in regarding Bede's account in the *Historia ecclesiastica* as the source of the summary in his **MARTYROLOGIUM** (ed. Dubois and Renaud 1976 p 112.3–11). Cross (1982d pp 25–26) agrees with Herzfeld that the notice for Alban in the **OLD ENGLISH MARTYROLOGY** (*Mart*, B19.dt; ed. Kotzor 1981 2.126–27) is based solely on Bede's *Historia*.

Alban's June 22 feast day was among the most important in later Anglo-Saxon England, to judge from the *Bosworth Psalter* (**LITURGY, PSALTERS**) and its Canterbury calendar (F. Wormald 1934 p 63, and Hartzell 1975 p 27), but he is not mentioned in the Old English verse *Menologium* (A.14; ed. *ASPR* 6) and **ÆLFRIC** wrote his version of the legend for the more specialized **LIVES OF SAINTS** (*ÆLS* Alban, B1.3.20; ed. *EETS* OS 76 and 82), not for the more widely distributed **CATHOLIC HOMILIES**. Ælfric's main source, which he handles with some freedom, is generally agreed to be Bede's *Historia* (Ott 1892 pp 44–46).

A neumed liturgical office for Alban's feast day at St Albans abbey, believed to have been composed in the late tenth century, survives in a late-eleventh-century manuscript now in New York, which includes a set of eight lessons for matins based on Bede's account; see Hartzell (1975 pp 21, 26–38).

On Alban's martyrdom and the *passio*, see Thomas (1981 pp 48–50). See Biddle (1977) on the shadowy Anglo-Saxon history of the cult site, and for bibliography (pp 138–42). On the later history of the legend, see Levison (1941 pp 350–58). For Continental echoes of the cult, see E. Baker (1937).

Albinus Andegavensis, vita [VEN.FORT.Vit.Albin.]: *BHL* 234; *BLS* 1.452; *BSS* 1.720–21; *CPL* 1040; *DHGE* 5.254–55.
ed.: *MGH* AA 4/2.27–33.

MSS 1. London, BL Cotton Nero E. i: HG 344.
2. Salisbury, Cathedral Library 221 (formerly Oxford, Bodleian Library Fell 4): HG 754.5.
Lists – Refs none.

Albinus, a Breton monk, possibly of British descent, was bishop of Angers 529–50 (feast day March 1). His cult's popularity in France and neighboring countries was aided no doubt by this *vita* by **VENANTIUS FORTUNATUS**. The pre-Conquest English calendars, however, indicate little Anglo-Saxon interest. Copies in the **COTTON-CORPUS LEGENDARY**, which are the only English memorials, omit the prologue and preamble, beginning "igitur Albinus episcopus" (*MGH* AA 4/2.29); the *explicit* is similar to, but not identical with, that in the *MGH*, whose editor, Krusch, does not collate these manuscripts (see pp XII–XV). Levison (*MGH* SRM 7.604 and 632) does not indicate the affiliations of the English manuscripts.

Alcuinus, vita [ANON.Vit.Alcuin.]: *BHL* 242; *BLS* 2.348–49.
ed.: *MGH* SS 15.184–97.

MSS – Refs none.

ALCUIN (ca. 730–804), librarian and teacher at the cathedral school of York under Archbishop Egbert, then head of Charlemagne's palace school at Aachen, and finally abbot of St Martin's, Tours, was not venerated as a saint in the Anglo-Saxon church, although knowledge of his written works was extensive and varied. The only evidence that the

Anglo-Saxons knew the anonymous *Vita Alcuini* (composed 823-29, "probably at Ferrières": Godman 1982 p xxxviii) is a section of **ASSER**'s *Life of King Alfred* (DE REBUS GESTIS ÆLFREDI; chapters 79 and 81, ed. Keynes and Lapidge 1983 pp 93-97), which appears to be modeled on *Vita Alcuini* p 190. The parallel was first indicated by Pierre Chaplais, as noted by Keynes and Lapidge (1983 p 265), who suggest that the *vita* may have come to England in the late ninth century with Continental clerics such as Grimbald.

Alexander papa, passio [ANON.Pas.Alexand.]: *BHL* 266; *BLS* 2.223; *BSS* 1.792-801; *CPL* 2160.
ed.: *AS* Mai. 1.371-75.
MSS   Salisbury, Cathedral Library 221 (formerly Oxford, Bodleian Library Fell 4): HG 754.5.
Lists   none.
A-S Vers   1. BEDA.Mart. 80.5-11.
2. *Mart* (B19.cj and gf).
3. *ÆCHom* II, 18 (B1.2.23) 64-156.
4. *ÆHom* 24 (B1.4.24).
Quots/Cits – Refs   none.

The Roman martyr Alexander (feast day May 3) is identified with the second-century Pope Alexander in his *passio*, but there is no other good evidence for this, and it is likely that the martyr was merely Bishop of Nomentana. For the possible circumstances surrounding the composition of the *passio*, see Llewellyn (1976) who dates it in the fifth century (*CPL* indicates sixth century). The legend and cult were current throughout the Anglo-Saxon period in England, where Alexander's feast day was one of the more important.

The *passio* treated here, and regarded as earliest by the Bollandists, appears to have been in England by the early eighth century. Quentin (1908 p 58) analyzes **BEDE**'s indebtedness to it in his **MARTYROLOGIUM** (BEDA.Mart.; ed. Dubois and Renaud 1976), which has a notice for Alexander. Another character in the *passio*, Hermes of Rome (feast day

August 28), the imperial prefect converted, with a tribune Quirinus, by Alexander's resuscitation of his dead son, has no separate notice in Bede, but his own status as a Roman saint (with a major basilica on the Via Salaria) is recognized in the **OLD ENGLISH MARTYROLOGY**. Here the *Passio Alexandri* is represented by two notices (*Mart*; ed. Kotzor 1981 2.110 and 190–91), respectively for Alexander, with his priests Eventius and Theodolus, and for Hermes, whose feast is widely commemorated, and sometimes graded, in later Anglo-Saxon calendars (e.g., F. Wormald 1934 pp 51 and 65; see also *BHL* 3853–57, *BSS* 5.52–56, and Farmer 1987 pp 204–05). Cross (1979 pp 199–201) develops and corrects the source information provided by Herzfeld (*EETS* OS 116.xxxviii and xl) regarding the *Martyrology* notices, demonstrating that the martyrologist's text of the *passio* was closer in several respects to that printed in *AS* (*BHL* 266) than to that printed by Mombritius (*BHL* 267), which also lacks the story of Hermes.

ÆLFRIC produced two versions of the legend, which are sourced by Förster (1892 pp 38–39), Pope (*EETS* OS 260.734–35 and 737–46), Zettel (1979 pp 187–89), and Godden (*EETS* SS 18.514, 516–19). The earlier version, which forms the second part of **CATHOLIC HOMILIES** II, 18 (*ÆCHom*; ed. *EETS* SS 5.176–79), focuses on the martyrdom of Alexander, Eventius, and Theodolus (part one is devoted to the **INVENTIO SANCTAE CRUCIS** (see **IESUS CHRISTUS**); for a modern translation of the Old English, see Thorpe's edition, 1844–46 2.308–12). Ælfric's second version, *Homilies of Ælfric* 24 (*ÆHom*; ed. *EETS* OS 260.737–46; see **OTHER HOMILIES**), is a later supplement, marked for insertion into the original Alexander homily (at line 69 of Godden's edition, *EETS* SS 5; see also pp liii–liv). Preserved only in one manuscript, from Worcester, it relates episodes from the earlier portions of the *passio*, including Alexander's miracles and the deaths of Hermes and Quirinus.

Pope, in a brief but valuable analysis of the source question (*EETS* OS 260.734), regards Ælfric's two texts, taken together, as "a complete rendering (with some minor abridgements and variations)" of *BHL* 266 as printed in *AS*. Zettel (1979 pp 187–89) corrects Förster's sourcing (1892 pp 38–39) to show that Ælfric used a recension of *BHL* 266 closer to the *AS* edition than that of Mombritius, and one that must have been quite similar, though not identical, to that in the **COTTON-CORPUS LEGENDARY**.

The earliest surviving English copy of the Latin *passio* is that in the Salisbury manuscript of the Legendary (Webber 1992 p 155); an earlier, related copy is listed in the table of contents of BL Cotton Nero E. i, but was lost from the end of the volume (Zettel 1979 p 19 note 49).

Alexandria. See GEORGIUS.

Alexius, vita [ANON.Vit.Alexii]: *BHL* 286; *BLS* 3.123–24; *BSS* 1.814–23; *DHGE* 2.379–81.
ed.: Sprissler 1966 pp 106–53.

MSS 1. New York, Pierpont Morgan Library 926: HG 865.
2. ?Orléans, Bibliothèque Municipale 342 (290): HG 869.
3. Salisbury, Cathedral Library 223 (formerly Oxford, Bodleian Library Fell 3): HG 754.7.

Lists – Refs none.

Alexius (feast day July 17), a young Roman who left his parents and new bride in Rome and lived for the next seventeen years of his life as a beggar (the "man of God," "Mar Riscia" in Syriac) in Edessa, is almost certainly a fiction (Berschin 1986–91 1.167). Despite his later importance in vernacular literature of the later Middle Ages in northwest Europe, there is no trace of the legend in England until, apparently, the end of the Anglo-Saxon period. Although its earliest form has been traced to fifth-century Syria, the legend was not available in the Latin West until late in the tenth century, when one Latin version (*BHL* 289) was produced in Spain (Mölk 1976), and another (*BHL* 286) in Rome at the new Greco-Latin monastery (originally dedicated to **BENEDICT OF NURSIA** [BENEDICTUS CASINENSIS], then to BONIFATIUS TARSI and Alexius) on the Aventine, ca. 980. On the interesting historical context, see Hamilton (1965 especially pp 265–71). Another recension, *BHL* 287, important in later medieval England, appears to derive from Monte Cassino. Either this represents a somewhat expanded version of *BHL* 286, as assumed by Hartzell (1975 p 47), or, as Sprissler implies (1966 pp 106–07) by classifying the Monte Cassino recension as the first of his four families, it is the more original version and *BHL* 286, which is Sprissler's group II, is an abridgement. According to Siegmund (1949 p 256), the Latin versions are based ultimately on one or another of the pre-ninth-century Greek texts (*BHG* 51, etc.).

The version in the Orléans manuscript corresponds, according to Van der Straeten (1982 p 72), to the text printed in *AS* Iul. 4.251–53 and Massmann (1843 pp 167–71), the "Roman" recension (but see Sprissler 1966 p 27). The manuscript was at Fleury by the end of the eleventh century according to Lowe (*CLA* 6.820), but its original provenance is unknown; the script, according to Van der Straeten (1982 p 17), relying on Lowe, is Anglo-Saxon, but Lowe dates it in the eleventh century, Van der Straeten in the tenth. Neither scholar makes clear if the whole manuscript (including the *Vita Alexii*) or merely the first item (*Vita Nicolai*: see **NICOLAUS**) is in the Anglo-Saxon hand.

The Orléans copy of the *Vita Alexii* is defective at the end, lacking roughly the last quarter of the text, from "Ego enim sperabam . . ." (Sprissler 1966 p 142 section 74).

The Morgan manuscript, from St Albans, is dated ca. 1100. The work of Pächt (in Pächt, Dodwell, and Wormald 1960 pp 134–35) and Hartzell (1975 pp 44–47, drawing on unpublished notes by Francis Wormald) suggests that this text derives from one brought to England from Bec, an early center of devotion to Alexius, by Lanfranc himself. Neither Pächt nor Hartzell mentions the Orléans manuscript. Further study is obviously needed to clarify the picture, and to determine whether or not the *Vita Alexii* could have been known in England before Lanfranc. Certainly, it appears that by the end of the eleventh century in England the Monte Cassino version began to displace the Roman recension (Hartzell 1975 p 45).

None of these studies mentions the Salisbury copy, written by one of Webber's Group II scribes at Salisbury around the turn of the eleventh century (Webber 1992 p 170).

Of the several modern editions (see *BHL NS* p 37, "Alexius 1a."), that of Sprissler is the most valuable. He provides a polyglot edition (parallel texts with variants) of four of the principal recensions (*BHL* 286–88, 290), based on nineteen manuscripts of the eleventh century, but not including any of those cited here (see also pp 27–29 on manuscript groups). Berschin (1986–91 1.166–72) provides a narrative summary, critical analysis, and helpful bibliographical notes.

Almachius: *BLS* 1.3–4.

BEDE's brief narrative account in his **MARTYROLOGIUM** (ed. Dubois and Renaud 1976 p 5.3–6, on January 1) of the last words and martyrdom of a Roman martyr Almachius (Alamachus), who attempted to disrupt the gladiatorial combats in the Roman arena, has so far been linked only to the *Martyrologium Hieronymianum* (see Quentin 1908 p 110), and no *passio* of the saint has been discovered.

Amalberga, vita [ANON.Vit.Amalberg.]: *BHL* 323; *BLS* 3.65; *BSS* 1.913–14; *DHGE* 2.924–25.
ed.: *AS* Iul. 3.90–102.
MSS Dublin, Trinity College 174: HG 215.
Lists – Refs none.

According to her eleventh-century life, regarded as "pure romance" by historians, Amalberga the virgin (not to be confused with her namesake the widow, both July 10) took the veil from Saint Willibrord (658–739), spent her life as a nun at Munsterbilzen in Belgium, and was buried at Tamise. Her relics were acquired by St Peter's, Ghent, in the ninth century, but the *vita* was not composed, apparently, until the mid-eleventh century. Although it has been attributed to the Flemish hagiographer, Thierry of Saint-Trond, it may well be the work of another Fleming, Goscelin of Canterbury, who was a monk of Saint-Bertin before moving to England shortly before the Norman Conquest. In another work more firmly attributed to Goscelin, the life of **WERBURGA**, the author refers to the *Vita Amalbergae* as his own work, "quam nostro stylo recudimus" (*PL* 155.105.12–14). A fainter connection to Goscelin may be represented by the copy of the *vita* in the Dublin manuscript (Colker 1991 1.325), written at Salisbury around the turn of the eleventh century, or later, by the Group II scribes (Webber 1992 p 158). Salisbury may have inherited books from Sherborne, which it superseded in 1078, and where Goscelin had first lived when he came to England to join the Lotharingian Bishop Hermann (1058–78). The affiliations of this copy with others are unknown, but it is at least as old as the oldest manuscript known to Poncelet. There is no modern edition.

Neither attribution, to Goscelin or Thierry, is accepted by Poncelet (1912) who believes the life of Amalberga was written at St Peter's, Ghent.

I have seen no other evidence of Anglo-Saxon veneration of Amalberga, although through her cult at St Peter's she may well have been known to English ecclesiasts of the reform era and later.

Amandus, vita [ANON.Vit.Amand.]: *BHL* 332; *BLS* 1.263–64; *CPL* 2080; *DHGE* 2.942–45.
ed.: *MGH* SRM 5.428–49.

MSS 1. London, BL Cotton Nero E. i: HG 344.
2. Salisbury, Cathedral Library 221 (formerly Oxford, Bodleian Library Fell 4): HG 754.5.

Lists – Refs none.

Amand (ca. 584–675) was one of the key figures in the early church of Flanders and N. France and the founder of the principal abbeys of Ghent (St Peter's and St Bavo's) as well as of the community of Saint-Amand itself (Moreau 1949). The *Vita Amandi* is dated ca. 700 by Krusch (in the edition cited here) and others, for example, Berschin (1986–91 2.48–52), although Lesne in *DHGE* suggests that its author was influenced by the later eighth-century lives of Willibrord and the English **BONIFATIUS**. Extant in numerous manuscripts, the work is traditionally attributed to the priest Baudemundus, to whom Amand dictated his will, but evidence is lacking (*MGH* SRM 5.403). Nor is there any evidence that Amand's cult or his *vita* were known in early Anglo-Saxon England, although the expatriate **ALCUIN** draws on the work in some laudatory verses (quoted in *MGH* SRM 5.406: see Dümmler, *MGH* PLAC 1.308).

Given the close cultural links between England and Flanders in the tenth and eleventh centuries (Ortenberg 1992 pp 21–40), it is not surprising that Amand became better known to the English at this time (some calendars of the late tenth and early eleventh century honor him with two feast days, February 6, September 20; see F. Wormald 1934 pp 17, 24; Ortenberg 1992 p 35). Several manuscripts of English provenance are among the more important (if late) copies listed by Krusch, including the eleventh-century manuscripts listed above, written at Worcester and Salisbury respectively (classified as A.3d and A.3f; see *MGH* SRM 5.413).

For an English translation of the *Vita Amandi*, see Hillgarth (1986 pp 139–48).

Amandus, vita [MILO.Vit.Amand.]: *BHL* 333; *DMA* 8.395.
   ed.: *MGH* PLAC 3.561–609.

MSS – A-S Vers none.
Quots/Cits ?Vit.Amand.I.46: FRITH.Breu.Vit.Wilf. 53.
Refs none.

A possible example of the literary stimulus of Amand's cult in Anglo-Saxon England is a phrase from the ninth-century metrical *Vita Amandi* by the monastic poet **MILO** "philosophus," apparently echoed in the **BREVILOQUIUM VITAE WILFRIDI** (FRITH.Breu.Vit.Wilf.; ed. Campbell 1950), a verse life of **WILFRIDUS** written by the Frank **FRITHEGOD** at Canterbury in Oda's time (942–58).

Ambrosius, vita [PAVLIN.Vit.Ambros.]: *BHL* 377; *BLS* 4.509–16; *BSS* 1.945–90; *CPL* 169.
   ed.: Pellegrino 1961 pp 50–128 (left-hand pages).

MSS 1. London, BL Cotton Nero E. i: HG 344.
   2. Salisbury, Cathedral Library 221 (formerly Oxford, Bodleian Library Fell 4): HG 754.5.
Lists none.
A-S Vers 1. ALDH.Carm.uirg. 651–76.
   2. ALDH.Pros.uirg. 260.5–262.7.
   3. ?*Mart* (B19.bs).

Quots/Cits 1. *Vita Ambrosii* XIV.1–11: BEDA.Mart. 110.13–17.
2. ?*Vita Ambrosii* XLV.8–9: CUTHB.ep.ob.Bed. 582.18–20.
Refs ALDH.Pros.uirg. 260.14–15.

The early Anglo-Saxons were naturally interested in and familiar with the life of one of the most important of the Latin fathers, composed ca. 422 by a former member of **AMBROSE**'s *familia*, Paulinus of Milan. **ALDHELM** in both his verse and prose **DE VIRGINITATE** (ALDH. Carm.uirg. and Pros.uirg.; ed. *MGH* AA 15; *BHL* 380–81) draws on the famous episode of the bees entering the infant Ambrose's mouth in the cradle (see *Vita Ambrosii* III.2–14). In his prose version Aldhelm modifies Paulinus's interpretation of the miracle to include the motif of virginity as well as eloquence. In the verse version, however, the emphasis falls on Ambrose's eloquence and achievements as a teacher.

According to Quentin (1908 p 101), **BEDE** summarizes and echoes the *Vita Ambrosii* (and **AUGUSTINE**'s **CONFESSIONES**) in his **MARTYROLOGIUM** (BEDA.Mart.; ed. Dubois and Renaud 1976), in the notice for **GERVASIUS ET PROTASIUS**, to whose *inventio* he also alludes, with less verbal dependence on Paulinus (see *Vita Ambrosii* XIV–XV), in his **CHRONICA MAIORA** (*CCSL* 123B.1514–18, and the editor's note, p 513).

Bede's familiarity with Paulinus's text is evoked by his pupil **CUTHBERT OF JARROW** in the later eighth century in his **EPISTOLA DE OBITU BEDAE** (CUTHB.ep.ob.Bed.; ed. Colgrave and Mynors 1969) telling how Bede would often quote Ambrose's maxim, "Non [ita] vixi. . . ." The verbal discrepancies with the *Vita Ambrosii* imply that Cuthbert did not consult a text but relied on his memory of Bede's memory.

The account of Ambrose in the **OLD ENGLISH MARTYROLOGY** (*Mart*; ed. Kotzor 1981 2.50–51) follows the *vita* for the most part, but is sufficiently different in the treatment of its main anecdote about the war leader (*Vita Ambrosii* LI; cf. **OROSIUS, HISTORIAE ADVERSUM PAGANOS** VII.xxxvi.7–13) for Cross to conclude that the martyrologist knew a version of the *vita* that is now lost (1985b p 248 and note 108).

ÆLFRIC does not appear to have drawn on Paulinus's life directly. His only extended anecdote concerning Ambrose is the lengthy addition, *Homilies of Ælfric* 26 (*ÆHom*, B1.4.27; ed. *EETS* OS 260.762–69; see **OTHER HOMILIES**), to **CATHOLIC HOMILIES** II, 28, *Dominica XII Post Pentecosten* (*ÆCHom*, B1.2.35; ed. *EETS* SS 5.254), on the saint's chastising of the emperor Theodosius. This addition, sourced by Pope (*EETS* OS 260.761 and 763–69), is based on the HISTORIA ECCLESIASTICA TRIPARTITA of EPIPHANIUS (*CSEL* 71.540–46) traditionally attributed to CASSIODORUS. An anonymous ninth-century *Vita Ambrosii* (*BHL* 377d), combining Paulinus's life of Ambrose with passages from the *Historia tripartita* and other sources, includes the same anecdote (ed. Paredi 1964 pp 91.4–101.9; compare also p 69.1–12 with *Homilies of Ælfric* 26, lines 23–27).

According to Pellegrino (1961 pp 27–28, citing Bernard Bischoff), the early-ninth-century Paris manuscript, Bibliothèque Nationale lat. 1771, was originally an Anglo-Saxon book, "begun in England, then completed in Northern France." But more recent scholarship points to Fulda, with its tradition of Anglo-Saxon script, as the book's place of origin, and also to Corbie somewhat later in the ninth century (Avril and Stirnemann 1987 p 9). An insular exemplar may, of course, lie behind the Fulda text.

Pellegrino appears not to have known, or may have discounted, the eleventh-century English manuscripts listed above (from Worcester and Salisbury respectively). His list of manuscripts (1961 pp 27–30) bypasses British libraries, and his edition, lacking a proper classification of manuscripts, offers no means of placing the English copies in the textual tradition of the work. According to R. McClure (1973), Pellegrino's edition, while improving on earlier efforts and valuable for its learned commentary on the historical and literary aspects of Paulinus's work, is textually unreliable and based on only a partial study of the extant manuscripts. Unfortunately the promised critical edition by McClure has not yet appeared and his survey of the manuscripts (1971) remains unpublished. See also Lamirande (1983 pp 27, 32) and the edition of Bastiaensen (1975a).

Ammon. See AMOS NITRIAE.

Amos Nitriae: *BLS* 4.32–33; *BSS* 1.1014–15.

Amos (or Ammon) the hermit, reputed first abbot of the famous Egyptian community of Nitria, who died ca. 350, is the subject of chapter

XXX in HISTORIA MONACHORUM (ed. Schulz-Flügel 1990 pp 375–78), the collection of short lives of desert fathers adapted by **RUFINUS** from an earlier Greek text (for another version of the saint's life, see the similar collection, PARADISUS HERACLIDIS II, a translation of the *Lausiac History* by Palladius, ed. *PL* 74.258–60; both the *Historia* and the *Paradisus* belong to the **VITAE PATRUM**; see also Jackson in Biggs, Hill, and Szarmach 1990 pp 164–65). Amos is one of only three of the desert fathers in the *Vitae patrum* selected by **ALDHELM** for inclusion in his DE VIRGINITATE (*Carmen* 1450–503, *Prosa* 284.18–286.16; ed. *MGH AA* 15); others are **APOLLONIUS** and **IOHANNES EREMITA**. In each case, Aldhelm's source was Rufinus (see Ehwald's notes on Aldhelm's Amos passages in the *MGH* edition; also Lapidge and Herren 1979 p 177). Aldhelm may have been especially interested by the fact that Amos was not only a famous hermit, and the subject of a vision of Saint Antony (**ANTONIUS**), but also one of the select company of virgin spouses (see also IULIANUS ET BASILISSA, CAECILIA, CHRYSANTHUS ET DARIA, and **MALCHUS**). The Nitrian Amos is not to be confused with two other desert saints of the same name who also are commemorated elsewhere in Rufinus's *Historia* (the life of one of whom, Abbot Ammon in Tabenna, Egypt, from *Historia monachorum* III, is separately preserved in Salisbury, Cathedral Library 223, formerly Oxford, Bodleian Library Fell 3, from the turn of the eleventh century: see Webber 1992 p 69).

A copy of the *Historia*, used, if not written, at Worcester in the late eleventh century by Prior Coleman, survives in Worcester, Cathedral Library F.48 (HG 761). For further information on manuscripts and textual traditions, especially at Worcester, see Jackson (1992). On the *Vitae patrum* in English traditions, see also Rosenthal (1936). I am much indebted here and elsewhere to Jackson's published and unpublished work on the *Vitae patrum*. See also his introductory remarks in Biggs, Hill and Szarmach (1990 pp 162–63).

In addition to Schulz-Flügel's edition of the *Historia monachorum*, see also *PL* 21.455–57. For a modern English translation of the Greek life of Amos, see Russell (1980 pp 111–12).

Ananias et Petrus et Septem Milites, passio [ANON.Pas.Anan.]: *BHL* 397; *BSS* 2.1038.
   ed.: *AS* Feb. 3.492–95.

MSS – Lists none.
A-S Vers Mart (B19.ae).
Quots/Cits none.

   According to his legend, Ananias was a Christian priest of Bithynia, martyred after numerous miracles during the Diocletian persecution, along with his erstwhile jailer (Peter) and seven guards, who were converted through the saint's miracles and example and baptized by him. Kotzor does not specify the source text of the quite detailed version in the **OLD ENGLISH MARTYROLOGY** (*Mart*, B19.ae; ed. Kotzor 1981 2.20–21), but J. E. Cross (private communication) suggests, with some reservations, *BHL* 397. See also Cross (1982b p 395; information from Christine Rauer). The feast days given in *BSS* are February 25 and January 27/26, but the *Martyrology* has January 19.

Anastasia, passio [ANON.Pas.Anastasiae]: *BHL* 401; *BLS* 4.613–14; *BSS* 1.1042–46; *CPL* 2163. See also **AGAPE, CHIONIA, ET IRENE**; **CHRYSOGONUS**; and **THEODOTA**.
   ed.: Delehaye 1936 pp 245–49.

MSS Cambridge, Corpus Christi College 9: HG 36.
Lists none.
A-S Vers 1. ALDH.Carm.uirg. 2210–18.
   2. BEDA.Mart. 1.9–22.
   3. *Mart* (B19.b).
Quots/Cits none.
Refs 1. ALDH.Carm.uirg. 2219–21.
   2. BEDA.Mart 142.12 and 213.3–4.

   Historically, Anastasia (feast day December 25) appears to have been a martyr of Sirmium in Pannonia under Diocletian; her relics were translated to Constantinople by the patriarch Gennadius (second half of the fifth century). The Roman cult arose in connection with a church, near the Circus Maximus, bearing the *titulus* of a fourth century foundress by the same name. Anastasia's mass is the second on Christmas Day and she is one of the saints of the Canon. Her own *passio* forms the conclusion of a longer hagiographic cycle or "epic" *passio* that also includes stories of the martyrdoms of Agape and her sisters (*BHL* 118), Chrysogonus (*BHL* 1795), and Theodota (*BHL* 8093, not to be confused with the mother of COSMAS ET DAMIANUS). These the Bollandists classify by means of four distinct numbers, presumably because they sometimes appear separately in the legendaries (see their separate entries for further details). The *passio* is a purely literary attempt to link the eponymous founder of the Roman church with the Sirmian martyr, by representing her as a patrician woman, devoted to caring for imprisoned Christians such as those named above, whose fortunes she followed from Rome into the eastern provinces of the Empire, where she was eventually martyred herself.

BEDE and ALDHELM both seem to have known the epic *passio*. In his MARTYROLOGIUM (BEDA.Mart; ed. Dubois and Renaud 1976) Bede has separate entries for the principal characters in the cycle, in two of which (Chrysogonus, Theodota) he mentions the *Passio Anastasiae* as the source. In his prose DE VIRGINITATE, Aldhelm briefly mentions Anastasia's role in caring for the imprisoned Agape and Chione (ed. *MGH* AA 15.305.11–13); but in his verse eulogy cited above (ALDH.Carm.uirg.), he offers an epitome of her legend and makes elaborate reference to the recitation of her *passio* on her annual feast day.

The OLD ENGLISH MARTYROLOGY likewise provides an epitome of Anastasia's individual *passio* (*Mart*; ed. Kotzor 1981 2.2–3). Whereas Aldhelm, for example, focuses on her liberality with her parents' wealth and her contempt for her husband's patrimony, the *Martyrology* account focuses on the single episode of her sixty-day imprisonment and miraculous feeding by the spirit of Theodota. Cross (1982d pp 32–33) points to one image in the *Martyrology* that cannot be explained from the known source materials. That the martyrologist knew the legends of the other saints in the cycle is evident from his notices for Chrysogonus and Theodota (if not for Agape), but in his sources these may have occurred separately.

The Cambridge manuscript of the **COTTON-CORPUS LEGEND-ARY** (mid-eleventh century, Worcester) has two identical texts of *BHL* 401, the account of Anastasia's own martyrdom. It forms the fourth and final portion of the larger epic *passio* (entitled *Passio S. Chrysogoni*, pp 361–77), then appears again, alone (pp 408–10). See Jackson and Lapidge (1996 pp 142–43). A later English manuscript, now in Oxford, has the same configuration of texts (Zettel 1979 pp 31, 33).

The Latin version of the epic *passio* is almost certainly the original, from which a Greek translation was made in Rome ca. 824 (Delehaye 1936 pp 155–56; see also Siegmund 1949 pp 226–27). Metaphrastes' version (*BHG* 82) derives from the latter and was in turn retranslated into Latin in the sixteenth century.

Anastasius, passio [ANON.Pas.Anastasii.1b]: *BHL* 410b; *BLS* 1.144–46; *BSS* 1.1054–56; *CPL* 2248; *DHGE* 2.1481–82.
   ed.: unpublished.

MSS see below.
Lists none.
A-S Vers BEDA.Pas.Anast.
Quots/Cits none.
Refs BEDA.Hist.eccles. 568.36–570.1.

Anastasius (feast day January 22) was a former Persian magician turned Christian monk who suffered torture and martyrdom at the hands of King Chosroes II in 628. His relics were brought to Jerusalem and a set of Greek *acta* (*BHG* 84) was written, most likely at the request of Modestus, patriarch of Jerusalem, in 630. The Arab invasions of 638 presumably caused Jerusalem monks to bring the saint's head to Rome where, by 645, it had become an object of veneration (Franklin and Meyvaert 1982 pp 383, 396–99). Eventually the monastery "ad Aquas Salvias" (where **THEODORE OF CANTERBURY** may have been a monk, and where the head was kept) took the saint's name, along with that of Vincent (Ferrari 1957 pp 33–48). *BHL* 410b, the crude Latin rendering of the Greek *acta* (*BHG* 84), may have been brought to England by Archbishop Theodore or possibly **BENEDICTUS BISCOPUS** or another English traveler (Franklin and Meyvaert 1982 p 384; Lapidge 1986a p 49), but Franklin

(1995) adduces evidence indicating that Theodore himself was the author of the translation, as an interlinear gloss on the Greek text, and suggests that a tenth-century Bobbio manuscript containing this version (Turin, Biblioteca Nazionale F.III.16) derives from an earlier collection of English origin (see also **ANATOLIA, VICTORIA, ET AUDAX**). Franklin's work on *BHL* 410b and *BHG* 84 is corroborated by that of Flusin (1992 1.30–34).

In any event, *BHL* 410b represents the text that **BEDE** knew and described in his **HISTORIA ECCLESIASTICA** (BEDA.Hist.Eccles.; ed. Colgrave and Mynors 1969 p 568.36–37) as "male de Greco translatum." His exemplar had been corrected, but unskillfully, so he attempted a more correct version himself. Franklin and Meyvaert argue (pp 385–96) that Bede's version is *BHL* 408 (see next entry), a work independent of both *BHL* 410 and 411a, neither of which respects the spirit and words of the original as much as *BHL* 408.

The saint's feast is listed in some of the oldest extant English calendars (Wilmart 1934 pp 57, 65; F. Wormald 1934 pp 2, 16, 44). On other English notices of Anastasius, and the use of Bede's *Passio Anastasii*, see next entry. Superseding the earlier edition of the Greek *passio* (*BHG* 84) is that of Flusin (1992 1.15–91) with French translation and a detailed study of the Persian saint's life and cult in its historical context. I am grateful to Michael Lapidge for this reference.

Anastasius, passio [BEDA.Pas.Anast.]: *BHL* 408. See also **BEDE**.
ed.: Mombritius 1910 1.68–75 and 623.
MSS – Lists none.
A-S Vers BEDA.Chron.mai. 1791–809.
Quots/Cits none.
Refs BEDA.Hist.eccles. 568.36–570.1; ed. Colgrave and Mynors 1969.

The version of the *Passio Anastasii* classified as *BHL* 408, which was the most widely read medieval Latin version of the saint's legend, has now been firmly attributed to Bede, as explained in the previous entry. Lending support to this attribution is the fact that Carolingian Germany, with its early dependence on Insular learning, seems to have been a center for the diffusion of the text (Franklin and Meyvaert 1982 pp 385–86). Bede's version in turn seems to be the basis of his quite full summary of the saint's life in the **CHRONICA MAIORA** (BEDA.Chron.mai.; ed. *CCSL* 123B; see Quentin 1908 p 106), but Bede's shorter notice in his **MARTYROLOGIUM** (ed. Dubois and Renaud 1976 p 20.2-7) appears to be simply an abbreviation of the *Chronica* entry, not an independent use of the *passio*. Similarly the account of Anastasius in the **OLD ENGLISH MARTYROLOGY** (*Mart*, B19.ak; ed. Kotzor 1981 2.24) seems to be drawn from Bede's *Chronica*, but it also contains one piece of information that is in neither, regarding the carrying of the saint's head in Rome (2.24.19–20). This is also mentioned in a posthumous miracle story (*BHL* 412), one copy of which is preserved in the eleventh-century manuscript Orléans, Bibliothèque Municipale 342 (290), listed by Gneuss as of English provenance (HG 869). See Cross (1985b p 239 and note 65). On the manuscript, see **ALEXIUS**.

Anatolia, Victoria, et Audax, passio [ANON.Pas.Anat.Vict.2β]: *BHL* 418a; *BSS* 1.1074–82; *CPL* 2174; *DHGE* 2.1501.
 ed.: Mara 1964 pp 172–200.

MSS see below.
Lists none.
A-S Vers 1. ALDH.Carm.uirg. 2350–445.
 2. ALDH.Pros.uirg. 308.6–310.9.
Quots/Cits – Refs none.

According to their legend, Anatolia (July 10) and her sister **VICTORIA** (December 23) were Christian virgins of the Decian era. After debating with one another, they refused to marry their Roman suitors and were then separately exiled and, after various adventures, martyred. Although the *passio* of Anatolia and Victoria (dated late sixth or early seventh century by Mara 1964 p 166) is only a cento of passages from earlier *passiones*, the cult of Anatolia seems genuine enough, being attested as early as the late fourth century (for example, by Victricius of Rouen, *De laude* *sanctorum*, ed. *PL* 20.453). Anatolia's portrait appears alongside Victoria in the sixth-century Ravenna mosaics (reproduction in *BSS* 1.1075–76).

Until recently, modern scholars could only hypothesize the existence of the original joint *passio* on the basis of the summaries by **ALDHELM** in his verse and prose **DE VIRGINITATE** (ALDH.Carm.uirg., Pros.uirg.; ed. *MGH* AA 15); it was believed lost, except for a partial text concerning only Anatolia and the snake-charmer Audax (see next entry). The original joint *passio* was replaced by two other separate texts: *BHL* 417, the "passio uberior" of Anatolia (*AS* Iul. 2.676–81), which included the first and third parts of the original *passio*, and *BHL* 8591 concerning only Victoria (see her entry). But the most recent editor, Mara (1964), has located the original complete text of the *passio*, as it was apparently known to Aldhelm, in a tenth-century Bobbio manuscript now in Turin (see **ANASTASIUS**). Carmela Franklin (1995) has now presented evidence that the Turin manuscript derives from an Anglo-Saxon exemplar that closely represents a collection known to Aldhelm.

Despite the effusive eulogies by Aldhelm, the later Anglo-Saxons do not seem to have had texts for, or much interest in, Anatolia and Victoria, although Anatolia's July 9 feast day is in the eleventh-century calendar of the female religious community of Nunnaminster, Winchester (F. Wormald 1934 p 36). For detailed analyses of the legend's literary and doctrinal aspects, see Paschini (1919 pp 48–55) and Dufourcq (1900–07 3.256–65). Quentin (1908 pp 95–97) assumes that the two saints were originally unconnected, and early medieval documentary evidence for separate cult sites at Trebula (Victoria) and Tora (Anatolia) is surveyed most recently by Mara (1964 pp 156–58).

Anatolia et Audax, passio [ANON.Pas.Anat.Aud.2α]: *BHL* 418.
  ed.: *AS* Iul. 2.672–73.

MSS – Lists none.
A-S Vers 1. BEDA.Mart. 122.4–19.
  2. ? *Mart* (B19.ek).
Quots/Cits – Refs none.

As Quentin argues (1908 p 96), **BEDE** does not appear to have had access to the original joint *passio* of Anatolia and **VICTORIA** known to **ALDHELM** (see previous entry). In his detailed notices for the two saints in the **MARTYROLOGIUM** (BEDA.Mart.; ed. Dubois and Renaud 1976), Bede keeps them completely separate and appears to know nothing more about Anatolia than is contained in the so-called "Passio brevis" featured here, which concerns only Anatolia and her would-be assassin, the snake-charmer Audax. See the entry for Victoria for Bede's brief treatment of Anatolia's sister. The author of the **OLD ENGLISH MARTYROLOGY** (*Mart*; ed. Kotzor 1981 2.145–46) commemorates only Anatolia and Audax, focusing on Anatolia's healing powers and the snake episode, which he summarizes with some amusing original touches (unless he drew on a version unlike those in print). He appears to have used a text of *BHL* 418 (as represented in the *AS* edition and a mid-ninth-century manuscript collated by Mara 1964 in her edition) as well as Aldhelm's prose and verse **DE VIRGINITATE** (ed. *MGH* AA 15; J. E. Cross, personal communication; see also Cross 1985b p 231 and note 22).

Andochius, passio [ANON.Pas.Andoch.]: *BHL* 424 (*BHL* 4457d–e); *BSS* 1.1093–94; *CPL* 2114; *DHGE* 7.1315.
  ed.: Van der Straeten 1961 pp 447–68.

MSS – Lists none.
A-S Vers 1. BEDA.Mart. 177.3–10.
  2. *Mart* (B19.hk).
Quots/Cits – Refs none.

The martyrdom of Andochius the priest and his deacon Thyrsis (feast day September 24) at Autun, under the emperor Aurelian, is part of a hagiographic cycle of texts composed probably in Dijon in the sixth century and comprising a eulogy of **POLYCARPUS** followed by the *passiones* of Irenaeus of Lyon, Andochius and companions, and **BENIGNUS** of Dijon (*BHL* 4457b–f). Van der Straeten (1961), drawing on important earlier scholarship, argues that the Andochius-Irenaeus-Benignus cycle was originally one continuous text (now preserved uniquely in a ninth-century manuscript) that was subsequently divided into separate texts in calendric legendaries: *BHL* 4458 (Irenaeus), *BHL* 424 (Andochius), *BHL* 1153 (Benignus).

BEDE in his **MARTYROLOGIUM** (BEDA.Mart; ed. Dubois and Renaud 1976) devotes notices to Andochius and Benignus, based on *BHL* 422 and 1153 (Quentin 1908 pp 61–62), but says nothing of Irenaeus of Lyon. His account of Andochius is too brief for useful textual comparisons, but it is clear that his exemplar differed in one instance from Van der Straeten's, namely, the age of the young **SYMPHORIANUS** (fifteen in Van der Straeten, twenty in Bede and the *AS* edition). J. E. Cross (personal communication) says the ninth-century **OLD ENGLISH MARTYROLOGY** notice (*Mart*; ed. Kotzor 1981 2.218) reflects the variant textual tradition preserved in Van der Straeten's manuscript.

Among the later Anglo-Saxons, however, there is no evidence of further interest in Andochius and the other saints of their cycle. Their September 24 feast day coincided with that of the Conception of John the Baptist in all the extant late Anglo-Saxon calendars. Other Burgundian saints known to the Anglo-Saxons include Symphorianus (Autun), **SPEUSIPPUS** (Langres), and **FERREOLUS ET FERRUCIO** (Besançon).

Andrew. See **APOCRYPHA: PSEUDO-ABDIAS, HISTORIAE APOSTOLICAE; ACTA ANDREAE ET MATTHIAE; PASSIO ANDREAE.**

Anianus, vita [ANON.Vit.Anian.]: *BHL* 473; *BLS* 4.367; *BSS* 1.1258–59; *DHGE* 1.1110–11.
ed.: *MGH* SRM 3.108–17 and 4.767–68.

MSS Cambridge, Corpus Christi College 9: HG 36.
Lists – Refs none.

Anianus was a bishop of Orléans in the mid-fifth century, successor to **EVURTIUS**. He is associated in his *vita* with the defence of Orléans against Attila (see also **GREGORY OF TOURS**, HISTORIA FRANCO-RUM II.vii; ed. *MGH* SRM 1/1.48–49 [2nd ed.]). His cult was apparently unknown or disregarded in England until the eleventh century, except that a relic of his body is listed in the copious relics collection supposedly donated by King Athelstan to Exeter in the tenth century (Exeter List of Relics, *Rec* 10.8, B16.10.8; ed. Förster 1943 p 77; Conner 1993a pp 182–83). November 17, his feast day, is devoted to **THECLA** in the earliest calendars of the late Anglo-Saxon era (F. Wormald 1934 pp 3, 26, and 54), but he invariably supplants Thecla in the calendars of the mid- to late eleventh century (pp 41, 125, 139, 167, and 237).

The *Vita Aniani* is preserved in the mid-eleventh-century Cambridge manuscript of the **COTTON-CORPUS LEGENDARY**. This copy, which is not collated in Krusch's *MGH* edition, appears to represent class 3 or 4 in his classification of manuscripts (see Levison, *MGH* SRM 7.573). The *vita* also occurs in later English manuscripts that are affiliated textually with the Cotton-Corpus Legendary: Oxford, Bodleian Library Bodley 354 (*SC* 2432) and Hereford, Cathedral Library P.VII.6 (*BHL* 473a). Recent studies of the legend and cult of Anianus are by Renaud (1978, 1979).

Antoninus Apameae, passio [ANON.Pas.Antonin.]: *BHL* 569; *BSS* 2.79–81; *DHGE* 3.848–51.
 ed.: Cross 1984b pp 21–22.

MSS – Lists none.
A-S Vers ? *Mart* (B19.gp).
Quots/Cits – Refs none.

According to the earliest legend, reconstructed from various Eastern sources, Antoninus was a young stone mason whose zeal for Christianity led him to smash stone idols and build a Christian church at Apamea in Syria before being martyred for his boisterous faith; his body was cut into pieces by his executioners but later was reconstituted miraculously (*AS* Nov. 2/2.484–86; also Delehaye 1935 pp 225–30). The relationship between his legend and that of Antoninus of Pamiers (*Apamia*), near Toulouse, is problematic but according to one view, the Syrian saint's relics must have been brought to southern Gaul in the seventh century and eventually found homes at Pamiers and Saint-Antonin (Tarn et Garonne), where in time the saint's Syrian origins were forgotten and he was venerated as a local martyr. This French Antonin, no longer a stone mason, is a learned priest and healer, but his death and posthumous miracles are similar to those of the Syrian (Delehaye 1935 pp 228–29). *BHL* 568–69 preserves the oriental form of the legend, *BHL* 572–73 the French version.

By some unknown route a version of the legend became familiar to the author of the **OLD ENGLISH MARTYROLOGY** (*Mart*; ed. Kotzor 1981 2.197–98) who describes him as a Syrian and a Christian doctor, "læce" (p 197.4). Cross (1984b pp 18–22) has untangled the sources of the *Martyrology* account in relation to the various versions as extant, and also discusses an image borrowed, via **ALDHELM**, from the life of **HILARION** by **JEROME**. He shows how the *Martyrology*'s account mingles features of both the oriental and French versions and may be based on a (lost) hybrid text.

Cross's edition of the *passio* is based on an early-ninth-century copy from a Vienna manuscript originating at Saint-Amand. Siegmund (1949 p 229) found no pre-tenth-century manuscript copies of the variant version *BHL* 568 (*AS* Sept. 1.354–55), implying perhaps that Cross's version represents the earlier textual tradition.

Antonius, vita [EVAGR.Vit.Anton.]: *BHL* 609; *BLS* 1.104–09; *BSS* 2.106–14; *DHGE* 3.726–34, 16.102–07.
  ed.: *PL* 73.125–70.

MSS ?Worcester, Cathedral Library F.48: HG 761.
Lists none.
A-S Vers Mart (B19.ab).
Quots/Cits 1. Vit.Anton. 125.55–127.4: ANON.Vit.Cuthb. 62.7–13; see below.
  2. Vit.Anton. 125.52–54: FELIX.Vit.Guth. 62.24–27; see below.

3. Vit.Anton. 159.45–46: BEDA.Exp.Act.apost. 28.40–41.
4. Vit.Anton. 150.32: BEDA.Vit.Cuthb.pr. 258.15.
Refs ?ALDH.Pros.uirg. 265.4–5.

ATHANASIUS's famous life of Antony of Egypt, the father of the Christian eremetic tradition (250–356, feast day January 17), composed ca. 357, was translated into Latin ca. 370 by Evagrius (Berschin 1986–91 1.121), friend of JEROME and EUSEBIUS VERCELLENSIS (on the anonymous translation, *BHL* 609e, see below). Despite the immediate success and wide currency of Evagrius's *Vita Antonii*, there is not a great deal of specific evidence for its use by ALDHELM and BEDE. Ehwald (*MGH AA* 15.265 note 1) points out that although Aldhelm refers to it in his DE VIRGINITATE (ALDH.Pros.uirg.; ed. *MGH AA* 15), he could merely have seen it mentioned in the works of RUFINUS or Jerome (see also Lapidge and Herren 1979 p 177). Aldhelm's account of Antony (*BHL* 609m) shows no specific knowledge of the *vita*. Colgrave (1940 pp 16, 350–51, and 355–56) says that it provides the model for portions of Bede's prose VITA CUTHBERTI, *BHL* 2021 (BEDA.Vit.Cuthb.pr.; ed. Colgrave 1940) but he notes only one verbal echo. A more substantial echo, an allusion to Leda's conception of Helen of Troy, occurs in Bede's EXPOSITIO ACTUUM APOSTOLORUM (BEDA.Exp.Act.apost.; ed. *CCSL* 121).

On the other hand, the *Vita Antonii* was definitely used by other early Anglo-Saxons. Several substantial borrowings occur in the anonymous life of CUTHBERTUS, *BHL* 2019 (ANON.Vit.Cuthb.; ed. Colgrave 1940); in addition to the quotation cited above, see the others noted by Colgrave (1940 pp 74, 104, and 106). The same is true of Felix's life of GUTHLACUS, *BHL* 3723 (FELIX.Vit.Guth.; ed. Colgrave 1956); in addition to the quotation cited above, see others noted by Colgrave (1956 pp 64, 86, 110, and 114).

A copy of the Evagrian V*ita Antonii* was almost certainly used at Canterbury under THEODORE OF CANTERBURY and Hadrian in the late seventh century as the basis for the glosses that survive in the eighth-century Leiden Glossary (Lapidge 1986a p 55). On the general influence of the life of Antony on early English hagiography, see the classic essay of Kurtz (1926).

A detailed summary of Antony's life in the ninth-century **OLD ENGLISH MARTYROLOGY** (*Mart*; ed. Kotzor 1981 2.17–18), focusing especially on his temptations, appears to be based closely on the *vita* (see Kotzor 1981 2.285), although one piece of information is drawn from Bede's **CHRONICA MAIORA** (ed. *CCSL* 123B; see Cross 1985b p 240 and note 68).

Although there are several early Anglo-Saxon copies of the life of the saint most closely associated with Antony, Paul the Hermit (**PAULUS THEBAEUS**), this is not the case with the *Vita Antonii* (on the earliest Continental manuscripts, see Siegmund 1949 p 215). That it is also absent from the **COTTON-CORPUS LEGENDARY** is unfortunate but not surprising, since lives of the best-known desert fathers and mothers seem to have circulated generally in separate collections, often with one or other of the collective biographies from the **VITAE PATRUM**, as in the eleventh-century Worcester manuscript listed here. To judge from the Worcester catalogue, this appears to be a complete copy, lacking only the non-Evagrian epilogue of the printed editions (Floyer and Hamilton 1906 pp 22–23), but the make-up of the manuscript is complicated. One portion (fols 105–64, **VERBA SENIORUM**) was definitely written at Worcester in the mid-eleventh century. This, and another portion (fols 49–104v, **HISTORIA MONACHORUM**, eleventh century) originally from the Continent, were corrected and annotated by Prior Coleman towards the end of the eleventh century. But the provenance of the first portion (fols 1–48v), recently dated late eleventh/early twelfth century, which contains Jerome's lives of **HILARION** and Paul the Hermit, and the Evagrian life of Antony, is not yet determined. See Jackson (1992 pp 122–25; also Dumville 1992 p 140 note 324; Gameson 1996 p 225 plate 9).

ÆLFRIC merely refers to Antony as one of several exemplars of chaste living, in his **LETTER TO SIGEFYRTH** 216 (*ÆLet* 5, B1.8.5; ed. *BaP* 3.16).

For bibliography on Athanasius's life of Antony, see *Pat.* 3.39–45. While the anonymous (and relatively uninfluential) pre-Evagrian version of the life of Antony has been the subject of much modern scholarship, the text of the Evagrian life still must be read today in Migne's reprints of the seventeenth-century edition. In addition to that cited here, see also *PG* 26.833–976. For bibliography on the Greek and Latin texts, and discussion of their interrelationships and literary contexts, see most recently Berschin (1986–91 1.113–28).

In the headnotes to this entry, columns and line numbers in the *PL* edition of *Vita Antonii* were provided by F. M. Biggs.

Apollinaris Ravennae, passio [ANON.Pas.Apollinar.]: *BHL* 623; *BLS* 3.167–68; *BSS* 2.239–48; *CPL* 2166.
    ed.: *AS* Iul. 5.344–50.

MSS 1. London, BL Cotton Nero E. i: HG 344.
    2. Salisbury, Cathedral Library 222 (formerly Oxford, Bodleian Library Fell 1): HG 754.6.
Lists none.
A-S Vers 1. BEDA.Mart. 134.4–22.
    2. *Mart* (B19.ew).
    3. *ÆLS* Apollinaris (B1.3.23).
Quots/Cits – Refs none.

Little is known about the historical Apollinaris (feast day July 23), but he is believed to have been the first bishop of Ravenna (second century) and to have suffered persecution; he was honored as a martyr by the mid-fifth century, although he may not have actually experienced literal martyrdom. The *passio*, according to which Apollinaris was a disciple of St Peter from Antioch, is thought to be no earlier than the seventh century, written for Archbishop Maurus, 643–71 (see *CPL* 2166 and the bibliographical references provided by Delehaye 1929 p 6 notes 1 and 2). It is regarded as largely a fabrication. The late-eighth- or early-ninth-century manuscript copy in Basel (*CLA* 7.851) cited by Ogilvy (*BKE* p 45) in a Continental hand, with insular influence, need not represent an Anglo-Saxon original. The earliest copies of English provenance are those in the eleventh-century **COTTON-CORPUS LEGENDARY**, but there is no doubt that the saint was venerated in England throughout the Anglo-Saxon period.

The *passio* was known to **BEDE**, who draws on its tales of Apollinaris's sufferings and exiles for his substantial **MARTYROLOGIUM** notice (BEDA.Mart.; ed. Dubois and Renaud 1976), frequently borrowing words and phrases (sourced by Quentin 1908 p 63). The **OLD ENGLISH MARTYROLOGY** in a brief notice (*Mart*; ed. Kotzor 1981 2.158) likewise makes verbatim use of the *passio* as printed by the Bollandists (sourced by Herzfeld, *EETS* OS 116.xl, confirmed privately by J. E. Cross), although the selection of episodes is much narrower than Bede's.

ÆLFRIC's version in **LIVES OF SAINTS** (*ÆLS*; ed. *EETS* OS 76 and 82; sourced by Ott 1892 pp 54–56 and Zettel 1979 pp 226–27) exhibits numerous verbatim parallels with the *AS* text in the episodes he opts to use, but he omits most of the stories of the saint's enforced travels in exile from Ravenna (Whatley 1997 pp 189–92).

The copy in the Salisbury manuscript is complete, but that in the Cotton manuscript is acephalous, as noted by Jackson and Lapidge (1996 p 139). The Cotton text begins (fol 49r) at "beatus Apollinaris agebat cum discipulis suis" (*Passio Apollinaris* 345.44–45).

Apollonius: *BHL* 646; *BSS* 2.253–57; *DHGE* 3.1000–04.

The life of Apollonius (Apollo; feast day January 21), a fourth-century Egyptian abbot, is told in **RUFINUS**'s **HISTORIA MONACHORUM** VII (ed. Schulz-Flügel 1990 pp 286–307). Like **IOHANNES EREMITA** and **MACARIUS AEGYPTIUS**, but unlike most of the desert saints memorialized in the collective hagiographies that form the **VITAE PATRUM**, Apollonius is dignified with his own *BHL* number, although there is no separate textual tradition among the Anglo-Saxons.

Apollonius is also one of a few desert fathers to receive separate treatment by Anglo-Saxon writers (see also **AMOS NITRIAE**, **ARSENIUS**, Iohannes Eremita, and Macarius Aegyptius). In his **DE VIRGINATE** (*Carmen* 1504–1618; *Prosa* 286.17–291.6; ed. *MGH* AA 15) **ALDHELM** adapts several colorful episodes from Rufinus, including one in which Apollonius miraculously arranges for a multitude of desert ascetics to gorge themselves on a splendid banquet from Easter to Pentecost.

Another episode recounted by Aldhelm, concerning Apollonius and the emperor Julian (*Historia monachorum* VII.58–79, ed. Schulz-Flügel 1990), is adapted by ÆLFRIC for insertion into his *Maccabees* 833–45, in LIVES OF SAINTS (*ÆLS*, B1.3.25; ed. *EETS* OS 94 and 114; see MACHABEI), as an exemplum illustrating the evil of conscripting monks for military service. Apollonius is one of several desert fathers mentioned by Ælfric as exemplars of chastity at the close of his LETTER TO SIGEFYRTH 217 (*ÆLet* 5, B1.8.5; ed. *BaP* 3.16).

The Migne edition of *Historia monachorum* in *PL* 21 is now superseded by the critical edition of Schulz-Flügel 1990. A recent English translation of the Greek text is in Russell and Ward (1980 pp 70–79). For further references, see above, the entry on Amos Nitriae.

Arsenius: *BLS* 3.146–48; *BSS* 2.477–79; *DHGE* 4.745–47.

A Roman by birth (ca. 354), tutor to the sons of the emperor Theodosius in Constantinople (383), Arsenius withdrew to the Egyption desert community of Scete ca. 394, where he stayed almost until his death ca. 450 (feast day July 19). His life and wisdom as one of the greatest of the desert fathers are commemorated in varous anecdotes preserved in the Greek *Apophthegmata patrum*, one of the Latin versions of which was the VERBA SENIORUM attributed to the Roman deacons Pelagius and John (*BHL* 6527–29), and collected in the VITAE PATRUM (see Peter Jackson's introductory remarks in Biggs, Hill, and Szarmach 1990 pp 162–63). It is worth noting here that Arsenius appears to be the only saint from the *Verba seniorum* that BEDE's MARTYROLOGIUM and the OLD ENGLISH MARTYROLOGY have in common, although they offer different anecdotes. Bede (ed. Dubois and Renaud 1976 p 131.2–4) identifies *Verba seniorum* as his source but Quentin (1908 p 99) is undecided as to whether Bede was using the version by Pelagius and John (*PL* 73.860.34–37) or another dubiously attributed to RUFINUS (ed. *PL* 73.790.19–21; *BHL* 715). For the source of the two anecdotes in the *Old English Martyrology* (ed. Kotzor 1981 2.154–55), Jackson points to *PL* 73.865.1–6 and 861.28–30 (private communication).

ÆLFRIC merely mentions Arsenius in his LETTER TO SIGEFYRTH 217-18 (*ÆLet* 5, B1.8.5; ed. *BaP* 3.23).

Artemius. See MARCELLINUS ET PETRUS.

Asclas, passio [ANON.Pas.Ascla.]: *BHL* 722; *BSS* 2.498; *BLS* 1.152; *DHGE* 4.901.
    ed.: *AS* Ian. 2.455–57.
MSS 1. London, BL Cotton Nero E. i: HG 344.
    2. Salisbury, Cathedral Library 222 (formerly Oxford, Bodleian Library Fell 1): HG 754.6.
Lists – Refs none.

The legend of Asclas, according to which he was an Egyptian of the Thebaid, martyred by drowning in the Nile during the fourth-century Diocletian persecution, is extant in Greek, Coptic, and Latin. This Latin version, for which Siegmund (1949 p 229) could find no direct Greek source, was circulating in Europe by the late eighth century. A copy appears in the eleventh-century English **COTTON-CORPUS LEGENDARY** (Zettel 1979 p 17), which is textually almost identical to the Bollandists' edition. The saint's feast (January 23) is not represented in Anglo-Saxon calendars.

Asterius. See CALLISTUS.

Athanasius, vita [ANON.Vit.Athanas.]: *BHL* 730; *BLS* 2.212.16; *BSS* 2.522–40; *DHGE* 4.1313–40.
    ed.: unpublished.
MSS Orléans, Bibliothèque Municipale 342 (290): HG 869.
Lists – Refs none.

The life of the controversial theologian, Athanasius of Alexandria (ca. 296–373, feast day May 2), was known to the early Anglo-Saxons chiefly through **RUFINUS**'s continuation of **EUSEBIUS PAMPHILUS, HISTORIA ECCLESIASTICA** X.xiv–xviii (ed. *GCS* 9/2.979–83; *PL* 21.486–91). **ALDHELM**, for example, draws on this version for his eulogies of Athanasius in **DE VIRGINITATE** (*Carmen* 971–1033, *Prosa* 272.13–274.9; ed. *MGH* AA 15), as does the ninth-century **OLD ENGLISH MARTYROLOGY**'s brief notice (*Mart*, B19.ci: ed. Kotzor 1981 2.74–76) with its anecdote of the child Athanasius baptizing his playmates in the sea. The saint's feast is entered in one late-tenth-century Anglo-Saxon calendar (F. Wormald 1934 p 20) and a few of the eleventh century (pp 48, 118, 132, 160, and 174).

The anonymous *Vita Athanasii* at issue here, in the problematic eleventh-century Orléans manuscript (Van der Straeten 1982 p 72; see above, **ALEXIUS**), is unpublished, as far as I know, and of uncertain affiliation.

Audoenus, vita [ANON.Vit.Audoen.]: *BHL* 750; *BLS* 3.393–94; *BSS* 2.586; *CPL* 2088.
   ed.: *MGH* SRM 5.553–67.

MSS 1. London, BL Cotton Nero E. i: HG 344.
   2. Salisbury, Cathedral Library 222 (formerly Oxford, Bodleian Library Fell 1): HG 754.6.
Lists – Refs none.

Ouen, bishop of Rouen 641–84 (feast day August 24), had been chancellor to the Merovingian kings Dagobert I and Clovis II before he retired from secular life to be ordained, with his long-time colleague, **ELIGIUS** of Noyon, following the example of their older contemporary, Faro. All had met **COLUMBANUS** early in life and all founded monasteries with connections to Luxeuil (Wallace-Hadrill 1983 pp 67–69). Ouen was active in missionary and monastic affairs in west Francia during a period of close relations between Frankish and English patrons of monasticism (see Levison 1946 pp 211–12), but his sanctity left little trace in England until the tenth century when Oda, Archbishop of Canterbury (940–60) apparently acquired some of his relics for Christ Church. **FRITHEGOD** of Canterbury, a Frank in Oda's entourage, wrote a verse life (now lost, but known to John Bale in the sixteenth century), presumably for the reception of the relics in 957–58 (Lapidge 1988a p 48).

The prose *Vita Audoeni* (composed at Rouen, ca. 700: *MGH* SRM 5.543) no doubt became known in England at this time, if not before. Not many copies of this primitive life, designated "Vita I" in the *MGH* edition, survive, owing to the success of the more sophisticated "Vita II," *BHL* 751 (ed. *MGH* SRM 5.544–45), which is not now generally considered to be the work of Frithegod (see Lapidge 1988a p 48 note 19). Among the few copies of Vita I, however, are those listed above, classified by Levison as 4.b.1 and 4.b.2, and linked in his stemma (*MGH* SRM 5.547) with a tradition that includes ninth-century manuscripts from Paris and St Gall. Levison gives variants from the English copies in his apparatus, except for their "mendis . . . peculiaribus."

On the hagiographic context of the *vita*, see Berschin (1986–91 2.63–64). For a recent study of the Merovingian historical context, see Scheibelreiter (1989). On other links between the church of St Ouen in Rouen and Anglo-Saxon England, see Levison (1946 pp 211–12).

Exeter had relics of Ouen among those reputedly donated by King Athelstan in the mid-tenth century (see Exeter List of Relics, *Rec* 10.8, B16.10.8; ed. Förster 1943 p 77; Conner 1993a pp 182–83). Eadmer of Canterbury promoted the cult of Ouen's relics at Canterbury in the early twelfth century (*BHL* 758).

Audomarus, vita [ANON.Vit.Audom.1]: *BHL* 763; *BLS* 3.516–17; *BSS* 2.886–87; Farmer (1987) pp 332–33.
ed.: *MGH* SRM 5.753–64.

MSS – Lists none.
A-S Vers ?*Mart* (B19.gw).
Quots/Cits – Refs none.

Possibly of Saxon stock (Wallace-Hadrill 1983 p 69), Omer (feast day September 9, ca. 690) was a monk of Luxeuil before he went to preach the gospel, with his friend Bertin (**BERTINUS**) and others, among the unconverted in the Pas-de-Calais. Together they founded the abbey of Sithiu, later Saint-Bertin. Omer became bishop of Thérouanne and with Bertin built the cathedral in the city that now bears his name. He was venerated not only in these locales but also in Flemish centers with which English ecclesiasts would come to have close ties in the tenth and eleventh centuries (Ortenberg 1992 pp 21–40, especially p 36).

The earliest version of his Latin life is the first part (chapters I–XVII) of a triptych or composite life (ed. *MGH* SRM 5.753–75) including also the lives of Bertin (chapters XVIII–XXI) and **WINNOCUS** (chapters XXII–XXVIII). It was written ca. 800 according to Levison (1946 p 6 note 4), who points out that it was apparently known in England by the mid-ninth century. The details concerning Omer's death and posthumous miracle recounted in the **OLD ENGLISH MARTYROLOGY** (*Mart*; ed. Kotzor 1981 2.203–04) are closely based on passages from the combined life (p 350), although not necessarily in its pristine form. According to Ortenberg (1992 p 36), the cult of Omer in England reached its "peak" in the late tenth and early eleventh century. There is a proper Mass for him in the so-called *Missal of Robert of Jumièges* (see **LITURGY, MASSBOOKS**).

Audomarus, vita [ANON.Vit.Audom.2]: *BHL* 765.
ed.: unpublished (see below).
MSS 1. London, BL Cotton Nero E. i: HG 344.
2. Salisbury, Cathedral Library 222 (formerly Oxford, Bodleian Library Fell 1): HG 754.6.
Lists – Refs none.

This text of the *Vita Audomari* represents the second redaction, Vita 2, of the original composite life (*BHL* 763: see previous entry). The copies in the eleventh-century London and Salisbury manuscripts of the **COTTON-CORPUS LEGENDARY** (Zettel 1979 p 25) have been studied by Levison who numbers them $4a^{1-2}$ in the *MGH* edition of the composite life (*MGH* SRM 5.742), but $B1b^{1-2}$ with respect to the textual tradition of the *Vita Audomari* alone (pp 744–45). The text occurs separately in both manuscripts, like the lives of BERTINUS and WINNOCUS. This second redaction contains deliberate alterations arising from the ecclesiastical politics of ninth-century Flanders (p 745), and additional posthumous miracles, which Levison prints (pp 776–78) from the manuscripts cited above and another from Cambrai.

Augustinus Cantuariensis: *BLS* 2.407–09; *BSS* 1.426–27; *DHGE* 5.427–32; Farmer (1987) pp 27–28.

Augustine of Canterbury's liturgical feast (May 26) was relatively important in Anglo-Saxon England, especially at Canterbury, but until Goscelin of Canterbury wrote his expansive and creative life of the saint near the end of the eleventh century, there probably was no Latin or English life independent of the chapters devoted to Augustine in BEDE's HISTORIA ECCLESIASTICA I.xxiii–xxxiii, II.ii–iii (ed. Colgrave and Mynors 1969 pp 68–116, 134–44).

As Cross (1982d pp 24–25) makes clear, the author of the OLD ENGLISH MARTYROLOGY depended solely on Bede for his account of Augustine (*Mart*, B19.db; ed. Kotzor 1981 2.109), citing the *Historia* by name. The various lives in Continental manuscripts listed by Hardy (*RS* 26/1.201–02) are probably likewise redactions of Bede. Hardy's reference to a manuscript, "Arras 1012," containing an account of Augustine's "arrival at Fleury" is, disappointingly, an error. The text in question (now Arras, Bibliothèque Municipale 474, eleventh century, from Saint-Vaast) concerns the relics of BENEDICT OF NURSIA (see also BENEDICTUS CASINENSIS, *BHL* 1102).

ÆLFRIC surprises us by not providing a formal life of Augustine, but in his CATHOLIC HOMILIES II, 9, lines 167–253 (*ÆCHom*, B1.2.10; ed. *EETS* SS 5), on GREGORY THE GREAT (see GREGORIUS MAGNUS), he includes a carefully selective account of Augustine's mission to England, based on the usual Bedan chapters, but omitting, for example, any reference to the saint's inglorious attempt to abandon the mission (told in Bede's *Historia* I.xxiii). See now Godden's sourcing (*EETS* SS 18.409–11).

Unfortunately, the eleventh-century fragment of an anonymous Old English homily on the Deposition of Saint Augustine (*LS* 2, B3.3.2; ed. Tristram 1970 p 428), in Cambridge, Corpus Christi College 162 (HG 50), preserves only a rubric and a preface lacking any reference to Augustine himself (see NRK 38, art. 55). The lost narrative portion was most likely based on Bede, like Ælfric's lives of **ÆTHELDRYTHA** and **OSWALDUS REX**, although local traditions unknown to Bede may have been included. Thacker (1992 p 239 and note 119) notes the rubric's epithet for Augustine, "Apostolus Anglorum," and posits St Augustine's, Canterbury, where the epithet was favored, as the homily's place of composition in the early eleventh century. By contrast, Ælfric reserves the epithet "apostle of the English" emphatically for Gregory (*Catholic Homilies* II, 9, lines 1–4).

Augustine's brief roles as baptizer and then ordainer of Saint Livinus (Lievin) of Ghent in the mid-eleventh-century life of this saint (*BHL* 4960) are almost certainly invented (*BSS* 8.74). They are reused, however, later in the century by Goscelin in his *Vita Augustini* (*BHL* 777; ed. *AS* Mai 6.393), which may also be relevant here in preserving traces of possible Anglo-Saxon oral tradition, such as Augustine's purported escapades at Cerne (391–92), but most of these are doubtless as unreliable as the Livinus episodes.

Richard Sharpe is preparing a critical edition of Goscelin's life. See his study (1990b) of the historical context of Goscelin's writings on Augustine and Mildred in Canterbury in the last decade of the eleventh century.

Augustinus Hipponensis, vita [POSSID.Vit.August.]: *BHL* 785; *BLS* 3.426–33; *BSS* 1.430–33; *CPL* 358; *DHGE* 5.441–42.

ed.: Pellegrino 1955 pp 36–196.

MSS 1. London, BL Cotton Nero E. i: HG 344.
2. Oxford, Bodleian Library e Mus. 6 (*SC* 3567): HG 618.

3. Salisbury, Cathedral Library 222 (formerly Oxford, Bodleian Library Fell 1): HG 754.6.
Lists – A-S Vers none.
Quots/Cits 1. Vit.August. XXII.42–43: BEDA.Comm.Prouerb. II.xxiv.97–100.
2. Vit.August. XXVIII.26–27: BEDA.Chron.Mai. 1580–81; see below.
3. Vit.August. XXIX.20–30: BEDA.Vit.Cuth.pr. 280.31–282.9.
Refs none.

The Anglo-Saxons were familiar with many of the writings of **AUGUSTINE** (354–430, feast day August 28), but their interest in him as a saint seems to have been somewhat restrained. The **CONFESSIONES**, for example, was valued by **BEDE** for its exegesis rather than for its biographical information (Joseph F. Kelly in Biggs, Hill, and Szarmach 1990 p 71), but this is not the case with the *Vita Augustini*, which is also much valued by modern scholars (Berschin 1986–91 1.226–27; Saxer 1994 pp 70–71). It was written by Augustine's former disciple and adjunct bishop, Possidius, in the years following the saint's death in 430, before the author himself was forced by Vandal incursions to leave Africa (437).

Bede borrows isolated passages from the *vita* in his commentary **IN PROUERBIA** (BEDA.Comm.Prouerb.; ed. *CCSL* 119B), his prose **VITA CUTHBERTI** (BEDA.Vit.Cuth.pr.; ed. Colgrave 1940), and his **CHRONICA MAIORA** (BEDA.Chron.Mai.; ed. *CCSL* 123B; in addition to the passage above, see also *Chronica* 1584 and 1586, echoing *Vita Augustini* XXIX.11–12 and XXXI.3–4 respectively). He bypasses the *vita*, however, in his **MARTYROLOGIUM** (ed. Dubois and Renaud 1976 p 159.5–8), where he mentions only the translations of Augustine's relics, first to Sardinia and then to Pavia (Ticinum), drawing on the somewhat more detailed notice in his own *Chronica* 2061–66 (see also Quentin 1908 p 109). He probably obtained this information (unsourced in the modern editions) orally. On the importance of Pavia to English travelers, see Ortenberg (1992 pp 100–02).

The ninth-century **OLD ENGLISH MARTYROLOGY** (*Mart*, B19.gg; ed. Kotzor 1981 2.191–92) does not draw directly on the *vita* but closely follows the final notice in Bede's *Chronica* (Cross 1985b pp 239–40).

Regarding the copies of Possidius's *vita* in the **COTTON-CORPUS LEGENDARY** group, Zettel notes (1979 p 24 note 69) that the Salisbury text has two large lacunae and that gaps were also left by the scribe of the Cotton manuscript, but later filled in, indicating that the early exemplars of the Legendary had a defective text of Possidius. The late-eleventh-century Bodleian copy, which was at Bury St Edmunds in the later Middle Ages, is imperfect, owing to the loss of "a leaf or two," according to *SC*. It ends at "clericorum est commune periculum," part way through the letter to Honoratus: *Vita Augustini* XXX.iii.(11).20 (see p 180 of Pellegrino's edition). I found no information on the relation of this manuscript with the other two. Two further Salisbury manuscripts, copied by Webber's Group II scribes (probably early twelfth century) each have chapter XVII of the Possidian *vita* ("Augustinus contra Pascentium hereticum") as a separate extract. See Webber (1992 pp 168–69).

In their lists of manuscripts, neither Pellegrino (1955 p 5 and 1956 pp 198–99) nor Weiskotten (1919 pp 30–32) collates or lists the English copies cited here. Only the Oxford manuscript is listed by Römer in the British volumes of his standard survey of Augustine manuscripts (1972 1.203–04, but see 2.169).

There is a brief but interesting description of Augustine (as author of a thousand books) in the Exeter List of Relics (*Rec* 10.8, B16.10.8; ed. Förster 1943 p 76; Conner 1993a pp 182–83). For recent appreciation of the *Vita Augustini* as hagiography, see Berschin (1986–91 1.226–35). A more recent edition than Pellegrino's is that of Bastiaensen (1975a).

Babylas, passio [ANON.Pas.Babyl.1b]: *BHL* 890; *BLS* 1.160; *BSS* 2.679–80.

ed.: Mombritius 1910 1.127–30 and 627–28.

MSS – Lists none.
A-S Vers 1. ALDH.Carm.uirg. 1034–70.
  2. ALDH.Pros.uirg. 274.10–275.7.

3. *Mart* (B19.an).
Quots/Cits – Refs none.

According to **EUSEBIUS PAMPHILUS**, HISTORIA ECCLESIASTICA VI.xxxix (ed. *GCS* 9/2.595.12–13), Babylas (feast day January 24), bishop of Antioch ca. 240–50, died in captivity under the emperor Decius, but the saint's legend says he was beheaded, along with three of his young pupils, under Numerianus. The Latin *passio*, according to the Bollandists' classification, has three variant versions, two of which (*BHL* 889, 890) are designated Passio 1a and 1b, implying that they are more closely related to one another than to the third and longest (*BHL* 891), which is labeled Passio 2. All three are represented in important early manuscripts (Siegmund 1949 p 229; see also p 209 note 2), but their relationship to the putative Greek source (*BHG* 205) has not been explored, to my knowledge. Among the Anglo-Saxons, *BHL* 890 seems to have been known earlier than *BHL* 891 (see next entry).

BEDE does not seem to have known the *passio* at all, however, or he chose not to use it, since his **MARTYROLOGIUM** has merely a brief obit (ed. Dubois and Renaud 1976 p 21.6–7; Quentin 1908 p 49), similar to that in the *Martyrologium Hieronymianum* (*AS* Nov. 2/2.59) but also mentioning the names of the three pupils (Urbanus, Prilidanus, Epolanus). None of the three versions of the Latin *passio* has the boys' names, and Bede's source may have been **GREGORY OF TOURS**, HISTORIA FRANCORUM I.xxx (ed. *MGH* SRM 1/1.22.11–12 [2nd ed.]). See Cross (1985b p 242 note 1). If so, it is a precious witness to Bede's knowledge of Gregory.

Ehwald, in his edition of **ALDHELM**'s DE VIRGINITATE (*MGH* AA 15.274 note 2), points to *BHL* 889 (*AS* Ian. 2.571–73) as the source of various portions of Aldhelm's eulogy, and notably Babylas's assertion of his virginity (*MGH* AA 15.275.4–5); but in the latter passage, the only one where Aldhelm's phrasing closely resembles that of any of the printed texts, his source definitely seems to be the version in question here (see Mombritius 1910 1.129.45–46). Similarly, Cross (1985b p 242) indicates that the same version is also the source of the notice for Babylas in the **OLD ENGLISH MARTYROLOGY** (*Mart*; ed. Kotzor 1981 2.25), which summarizes two episodes from the *passio* and at the end adds the three boys' names, apparently from Bede (Cross had additional unpublished evidence for the *Martyrology*'s dependence on *BHL* 890).

For John Chrysostom's writings on Babylas, see the edition of M. Schatkin et al. (*SChr* 362).

Babylas, passio [ANON.Pas.Babyl.2]: *BHL* 891.
    ed.: *AS* Ian. 2.573–76.

MSS 1. London, BL Cotton Nero E. i: HG 344.
    2. Salisbury, Cathedral Library 221 (formerly Oxford, Bodleian Library Fell 4): HG 754.5.
Lists – Refs none.

From the later Anglo-Saxon period, the **COTTON-CORPUS LEGENDARY** manuscripts listed here have the long version of the *passio* of Babylas, *BHL* 891 (Zettel 1979 p 17; Webber 1992 p 155), which the Bollandists distinguish as Passio 2.

Balthildis, vita [ANON.Vit.Balthild.]: *BHL* 905; *BLS* 1.204–05; *BSS* 2.971–72; *CPL* 2090; *DHGE* 6.1321–22.
    ed.: *MGH* SRM 2.475–503.

MSS Dublin, Trinity College 174: HG 215.
Lists – Refs none.

Balthild (alias Bathild, Baldhild), originally an Anglo-Saxon slave in the household of the Merovingian mayor, Ercinouald, became Queen of Neustria as the wife of Clovis II (649) and a powerful advocate of monastic Christianity in northwest Francia. She founded the communities of Corbie and Chelles, and she supported the sainted bishops **AUDOENUS** (Ouen) and **LEODEGARIUS** (Léger) before she was "retired" to Chelles (before 673) to lead a life of humble sanctity. She died in 680 (feast day January 30). Her cult, while never popular, was quite widely represented in the liturgies of northern France (Folz 1975).

Balthild and her foundations were certainly known to the English religious aristocracy of her time. The widowed Anglian princess Hereswith, sister-in-law of King Anna of East Anglia, became a nun at Chelles, and her sister Hild, later abbess of Whitby, for a while intended to do the same. Other Anglo-Saxon royal women were abbesses at nearby Faremoutiers (BEDE, HISTORIA ECCLESIASTICA III.viii, IV.xxiii). Balthild appears to have sent monastic personnel and books to England at the request of English royalty (see McNamara and Halborg 1992 p 286 for evidence from the early-eighth-century life of Bertilla). Among early Anglo-Saxon male writers, however, Balthild is not a saint but a dangerous queen. In this connection she is mentioned by Bede, in his *Historia* V.xix (ed. Colgrave and Mynors 1969 p 520), and, with particular animosity, by Stephen of Ripon (Eddius Stephanus) in his life of WILFRIDUS (Colgrave 1927 pp 14.7–25, 154–55). It is not surprising that they do not mention or use the *Vita Balthildis*, although it is said to have been composed before 690 (the "A" version: see Sanders 1982 p 414).

The earliest manuscript copy of English provenance is the late-eleventh-/early-twelfth-century Salisbury manuscript, Trinity College Dublin 174, not collated by Krusch in his *MGH* edition. It is an extract ("capitulum") from the second chapter of the Carolingian "B" redaction (dated 800–33), ending imperfect: "decentessime [sic] conuersata ut honesta eius" (Colker 1991 1.324–25; see *MGH* SRM 2.483.24). The extract was copied by one of Webber's Group II scribes (Webber 1992 p 158; on the scribes, see pp 22–30). Despite the impression given, perhaps unintentionally, by Ortenberg (1992 p 33 and note 61), that Balthild's feast day was a late arrival in Anglo-Saxon England, supplanting that of Aldegund in the later eleventh century, it is commemorated (ungraded) in several quite early calendars (late tenth and early eleventh century: e.g., F. Wormald 1934 pp 30, 58, 115), and a relic of Balthild "þære halgan cwene" is among those in the putative Athelstan donation to Exeter in the mid-tenth century, as recorded in the early-eleventh-century Exeter List of Relics (*Rec* 10.8, B16.10.8; ed. Förster 1943 p 79; Conner 1993a pp 186–87, 197, 205). Moreover, as is well known, monks from Corbie were brought to Abingdon by ÆTHELWOLD (ÆTHELWOLDUS) to train the English monks in liturgical reading and plain-chant (Stenton 1971 p 448). It is thus not unreasonable to suppose, though impossible to prove, that the Salisbury copy had English antecedents. The *vita* is briefly discussed by Berschin (1986–91 2.21–23). For a modern English translation, see McNamara and Halborg (1992 pp 268–78). Recent biographical studies of Balthild are those of Nelson (1978 especially pp 46–52, 60–72) and Laporte (1990).

Barontus, visio [ANON.Vis.Baront.]: *BHL* 997; *BSS* 2.828–29; *CPL* 1313; *DHGE* 6.882–85; *LTK* 2.1; *NCE* 2.106.
ed.: *MGH* SRM 5.377–94.
MSS 1. London, BL Cotton Otho A. xiii: HG 351.
2. London, Lambeth Palace 173: HG 508.
Lists 1. ? Worcester I: ML 9.8.
2. Peterborough: ML 13.51.
A-S Vers see below.
Quots/Cits – Refs none.

The *Visio Baronti* purports to describe the otherworld journey of Barontus, a monk of the Benedictine monastery of St Peter of Longoretus (Lonray, Saint-Cyran-en-Brenne, Berry), during a coma lasting several hours on 26 March, 678 or 679. In the vision, written in the late seventh century in the vicinity of Bourges, two demons battle the archangel Raphael for the soul of Barontus, who is carried off on a tour of hell and heaven, where he beholds the mansions of the saints and the keys of St Peter (illustrated in some manuscripts). He then returns to his body through his mouth and reveals what he has seen to his fellow monks. The *Visio* is remarkable for its elaborate description of the gates of heaven and is believed to be one of the earliest medieval Latin visions conceived as an independent literary text (see also **APOCRYPHA, VISIO SANCTI PAULI**), as opposed to the visions occurring in *vitae* such as those of Fursey (**FURSEUS**) and **GUTHLACUS** or in larger compendia such as **GREGORY THE GREAT**'s **DIALOGI** IV and **BEDE**'s **HISTORIA**

ECCLESIASTICA (III.xix, V.xii–xiii), which were frequently excerpted as separate *visiones* alongside texts like that of Barontus (see below). Of the copy once extant in the badly burnt Cotton manuscript listed here, only a few fragments survive, but enough is legible for Levison to assert in his edition that this copy would have been of great textual importance. He dates the manuscript (which also contained a group of martyrs' passions along with the life of Fursey and the visions of Rotchar and Wettin) in the ninth century but it is dated early eleventh in HG (see *MGH* SRM 5.374–75 and 7.846; see also the list of original contents in Smith 1984 p 67).

Although the complete copy in the later eleventh-century Lambeth manuscript (part 2, fols 192–202) is among the principal texts of the modern edition, numbered 1b (*MGH* SRM 5.372), it is marred by some interpolations and has an altered ending (see 7.846). This collection also includes the Latin visions of Drihthelm, Fulrad, and Wettin, and the life and visions of Fursey.

The Worcester booklist of ca. 1050 includes a reference to a "Barontus" that, in view of the fact that other items in this booklist are said to be in English, may represent a lost Old English translation (ML 9.8, note). The "Baronti uisio" in the Peterborough booklist (ca. 1100) may be identical to the "Visio Baronte Monachi" listed in the fourteenth-century *Matricularium* of Peterborough Abbey Library (James 1926 p 38 [no. 55]; and see p 28).

Levison's *MGH* edition of the *Visio Baronti* has been reprinted twice, once with minimal apparatus in *PLS* 4.2125–38, more recently with an Italian translation and notes by Ciccarese (1987 pp 236–75). For discussion of the work and its relationship to other medieval visions, see Ciccarese (1981–82), Fritzsche (1886 pp 272–74), Laugardière (1951 pp 188–98), and Zaleski (1987 pp 45–46, 50–51, 70–72).

The *vita* of Barontus (*BHL* 976), which identifies the saint with a hermit of Pistoia, is of much later date and undoubtedly a fabrication. Barontus's feast day, 26 March in the new Proper of Bourges, is not commemorated in Anglo-Saxon calendars.

Thomas N. Hall

Bartholomeus. See **APOCRYPHA**: PSEUDO-ABDIAS, HISTORIAE APOSTOLICAE; and PASSIO BARTHOLOMAEI.

Basilides, passio [ANON.Pas.Basilid.]: *BHL* 1019; *BLS* 2.527–28; *BSS* 2.904, 906; *CPL* 2169.
ed.: *AS* Iun. 2.510.
MSS London, BL Cotton Nero E. i: HG 344.
Lists – Refs none.

There probably was a historical Basilides martyred near Rome and venerated at a tomb on the Via Aurelia in the vicinity of the twelfth "milia." This secured his veneration throughout Christian Europe, including Anglo-Saxon England, where his June 12 feast day regularly occurs in extant calendars, but his devotees failed to provide him with a secure history. Several fictitious legends associating the saint with contradictory groups of companions, notably the Milanese saints Nabor and Nazarius, are extant (see the brief accounts and bibliographies in *BSS* and *BLS*). The **COTTON-CORPUS LEGENDARY**, represented here by the Cotton manuscript, preserves the crudely hybrid version in which a portion of the middle of the story is lacking and Basilides is provided with the brothers Tripodis and Mandalis (their names are garbled versions of the African city, Tripolis Magdaletis). The story of the saint's sea journey to Italy seems to borrow certain features from the apocryphal ACTA ANDREAE ET MATTHIAE (see **APOCRYPHA**). There is no martyrdom.

The copy in the Cotton manuscript differs very slightly from the Bollandists' edition (*desinit a*). Another copy, formerly in Salisbury, Cathedral Library 221, is lost (see Webber 1992 p 156 note 65).

It is just possible that the Anglo-Saxons also had the better-known version of Basilides' legend (*BHL* 1018) since in their extant calendars he is always listed with Cirinus (Quirinus), Nabor, and Nazarius. In two such Canterbury calendars of the late tenth century his feast day is graded (F. Wormald 1934 pp 49 and 63), which suggests the need for lections from a *passio*.

Basilissa. See IULIANUS ET BASILISSA.

Basilius, vita [ANON.Vit.Basil/PS.AMPHILOCHIUS, interpr. Euphemius]: *BHL* 1023; *BLS* 2.539–42; *BSS* 2.910–37; *CPG* 3253; *DHGE* 6.1111–26.
ed.: unpublished.
MSS 1. Exeter, Cathedral Library FMS/3: HG 260.
2. London, BL Cotton Nero E. i: HG 344.
3. Salisbury, Cathedral Library 221 (formerly Oxford, Bodleian Library Fell 4): HG 754.5.
Lists none.
A-S Vers *ÆLS* Basil (B1.3.4).
Quots/Cits see below.
Refs. none.

Concerning the life and teaching of **BASIL** the Great of Cappadocia (329–79), bishop of Caesarea, there is an abundance of early and sound biographical material (see Altaner and Stuiber 1980 pp 290–98). Some of this material and portions of Basil's literary works were doubtless passed on to the early Anglo-Saxons by the early missionaries and subsequent visitors from Italy (Ortenberg 1992 pp 114–15, and see the main entry on Basil). According to Lapidge and Herren (1979 p 177) **ALDHELM**'s brief tributes to Basil's chastity and teaching in DE VIRGINITATE (*Carmen* 730–50, *Prosa* 263.11–264.10; ed. *MGH* AA 15) are based on **RUFINUS**'s version of **EUSEBIUS PAMPHILUS**, HISTORIA ECCLESIASTICA XI.ix (ed. *GCS* 9/2.1014.10–1016.19), **JEROME**, DE VIRIS INLUSTRIBUS CXVI (ed. *TU* 14/1a.51.22–26), and **CASSIAN**, DE INSTITUTIS COENOBIORUM VI.xix (ed. *CSEL* 17.125.26–126.3).

Neither Aldhelm nor **BEDE**, however, nor the author of the ninth-century **OLD ENGLISH MARTYROLOGY,** shows any knowledge of the legendary traditions brought together in the apocryphal Greek life (composed eighth century, according to Bardy in *DHGE*) by Pseudo-Amphilochius (*BHG* 247–60aa; *CPG* 3252–53).

The earliest Latin version of the Pseudo-Amphilochian life appears to be that attributed, by Aeneas of Paris (ca. 860), to a certain "Euphemius," surviving in a ninth-century St Gall manuscript and others only somewhat later from France or the Rhineland (Siegmund 1949 p 259). The early currency of Euphemius's version north of the Alps may explain why it, rather than *BHL* 1022 (by Anastasius Bibliothecarius, later ninth century) or *BHL* 1024 (by Ursus), was included in the eleventh-century London and Salisbury copies of the **COTTON-CORPUS LEGENDARY**. Surviving fragments (eight small pieces) of a manuscript possibly copied at Exeter in the early tenth century (Exeter Cathedral FMS/3) are likewise from the Euphemius rendering (Ker and Piper 1969–92 2.845; Dumville 1987 pp 170–71; Conner 1993a pp 28–29).

Unfortunately, this important *vita* has not been published in full in its original form. The only complete printed text, in the early editions of Surius's collection (e.g., the second edition, 1576–81 1.4–19), incorporates much stylistic "improvement" by the humanist scholar (see Zettel 1979 pp 198–201); the more widely available 1875–80 edition of Surius (6.319–38) lacks some chapters of the *vita*. The edition of Maior (1544 fols 206v–226v) is textually better but also lacks important parts of the early medieval original.

According to Zettel (1979 p 45), building on the work of Förster (1892 p 28) and, indirectly, Ott (1892 pp 10–11), the Euphemian version appears to lie behind **ÆLFRIC**'s retelling of the legend of Basil's encounter with Julian the Apostate, and the emperor's assassination by Saint Mercurius (discussed by L. Loomis 1949), in Ælfric's first homily for the Assumption of the Virgin, **CATHOLIC HOMILIES** I, 30, lines 199–257 (*ÆCHom* I, B1.1.32; ed. *EETS* SS 17; now sourced by Godden, *EETS* SS 18.254–56). This episode forms chapters VII and VIII of the *Vita Basilii* in the London manuscript listed here (pt 1 fols 64–65; cf. Surius 1576–81 1.10). Ælfric also used it for his fuller life of Basil in **LIVES OF SAINTS** (*ÆLS*; ed. *EETS* OS 76 and 82). See Ott (1892 pp 10–14) and Zettel (1979 pp 45, 47, 180–81 and notes, and 198–201).

Basil's June 14 ordination feast is noticed in several late Anglo-Saxon calendars (see Conner 1993a pp 28–29 note 36; and Lapidge 1996b p 123), as well as in the martyrologies of **ADO** and **USUARD** (*PL* 123.286–87 and 124.151–52), but the Eastern feast day of January 1 is also found in calendars (F. Wormald 1934 pp 128, 254) as well as in the Cotton-Corpus Legendary, in Ælfric's *Lives of Saints*, and in a proper mass in the *Missal of Robert of Jumièges* (see **LITURGY, MASSBOOKS**). For other liturgical reflections of Basil's cult, see Ortenberg (1992 p 115). Conner (1993a p 28) links the Exeter manuscript fragment of the *Vita Basilii* to the cathedral's tenth-century relics collection (Exeter List of Relics, *Rec* 10.8, B16.10.8; ed. Förster 1943 p 76; Conner 1993a p 182).

In addition to the various unsatisfactory editions of the Latin text, it is worthwhile to consult the Greek text, edited by Combefis (1644 pp 155–225) with his parallel Latin translation. For a lively literary appreciation of the Pseudo-Amphilochian Greek life, see Wortley (1980). On the penitential episodes, see Barringer (1980). For a modern English translation of the Julian episode in Ælfric's *Catholic Homilies* I, 30, see Thorpe's edition (1844–46 1.447–53).

Basilla. See **EUGENIA**.

Bathildis. See **BALTHILDIS**.

Beda.

That **BEDE** (*BLS* 2.402–04; *BSS* 2.1006–72) was venerated as a saint in Anglo-Saxon England and abroad is evident from **ALCUIN**'s York poem (**VERSUS DE SANCTIS EUBORICENSIS ECCLESIAE** 1288–318; ed. Godman 1982) and from the numerous manuscripts containing copies of the best-known account of Bede's last days and death, the **EPISTOLA DE OBITU BEDAE** (ed. Colgrave and Mynors 1969 pp 580–86) by his younger contemporary, **CUTHBERT OF JARROW**. The feast day, May 26, shared with **AUGUSTINUS CANTUARIENSIS**, is in several eleventh-century calendars, but these are localized in Winchester (F. Wormald 1934 pp 34,

118, 132, and 160) and Worcester (p 230, graded in capitals like Augustine's). The **OLD ENGLISH MARTYROLOGY** surprisingly lacks a notice for Bede.

His relics apparently remained at Jarrow until the early eleventh century when they were removed ca. 1020 to Durham by one Alfred Westou (great-grandfather of Ailred of Rievaulx), according to the *Historia* usually attributed to Simeon of Durham (Gransden 1974 p 213; Rollason 1989a p 212). Despite Abbot Cuthbert's promise (Colgrave and Mynors 1969 p 586.7–8) to write a *vita*, he does not seem to have done so. Various *vitae* are extant, however, but in manuscripts only of the twelfth century and later (see *BHL* 1069–76). They contain little historical information beyond what could be gleaned from Bede's own works and from Cuthbert's *Epistola*.

Of these *vitae* the most elaborate and possibly the earliest is *BHL* 1069 (ed. *PL* 90.41–54). It does not mention the removal of Bede's relics from Jarrow to Durham and thus may pre-date this event (Whiting 1936 pp 183–84), but Glastonbury also claimed to have acquired his relics in the tenth century (Rollason 1989a p 152) and the vagueness of *BHL* 1069 about such matters may be a deliberate ploy on the part of a late-eleventh-century author. A copy in London, BL Cotton Nero E. i is among the twelfth-century additions and is not part of the **COTTON-CORPUS LEGENDARY**. Regrettably this *vita*, biographically worthless but culturally interesting, has not been studied, either for its own sake or in relation to the numerous others, although it was translated by Joseph Stevenson (1853 pp xxxix–xlviii) from John Smith's 1722 edition. On some of the extant copies see Hardy (*RS* 26/1.450) and Mynors (1939 p 41). A somewhat erratic but still useful account of Bede's posthumous cult is that of Whiting (1936).

Benedictus Biscopus: *BLS* 1.72–74; *BSS* 2.1212–16; Farmer (1987) pp 39–41.

Benedict Biscop (628–90, feast day January 12) was a Northumbrian nobleman (family name Baducing) and much-traveled monk who founded the famous twin monasteries of Wearmouth (674) and Jarrow (681/82). Here **BEDE** spent most of his life, working in the library that Benedict Biscop put together in the course of "twenty years of continuous pilgrimage" in Gaul and Italy (Campbell et al. 1982 p 78), including six trips to Rome and back. His importance in Anglo-Saxon cultural history merits a separate entry here, although the relevant texts are the subjects of other entries.

Benedict's life, along with those of his immediate successors, Ceolfrith (**CEOLFRIDUS**), Eosterwine, Hwaetbert, and Sigfrid, is narrated in the collective biography dated ca. 715, the so-called anonymous life of Ceolfrith, *BHL* 1726 (recently attributed to Bede himself: see the entry for Ceolfridus). Bede in turn drew on this earlier work for his treatment of much the same subject matter in **HISTORIA ABBATUM**, *BHL* 8968 (ca. 720); Benedict is also mentioned several times in the **HISTORIA ECCLESIASTICA** (e.g., IV.xviii). A summary of his life, based on Bede's *Historia abbatum*, is given in the ninth-century **OLD ENGLISH MARTYROLOGY** (*Mart*, B19.u; ed. Kotzor 1981 2.14–15, 283).

The first part of London, BL Harley 3020 (HG 433), late tenth/early eleventh century, constitutes a *libellus* of early Wearmouth-Jarrow saints, containing the oldest and best copy of the *Historia abbatum* (Plummer 1896 1.cxxxii–cxxxiii), along with Bede's **HOMILIAE** I.xiii for Benedict's feast (*BHL* 1101; ed. *CCSL* 122.88–94) and the life of Ceolfrith.

The Harley manuscript (an important hagiographic collection) is complicated, and its provenance is in dispute. The most recent study, that of James Carley (1994), argues persuasively for Glastonbury, where Ceolfrith's relics were venerated in the tenth century (Rollason 1989a p 152), as the origin of the *libellus* portion, as opposed to Canterbury, which is the home of the second section of the manuscript (Dumville 1992 p 110 note 92; Carley 1994 p 277). Benedict's relics were also brought south, to Thorney Abbey in East Anglia, in the later tenth century (Rollason 1989a p 179). On the historical and Continental context of his life as depicted by Bede, see P. Wormald (1976). A recent English translation of Bede's *Historia abbatum* is that of Farmer in Webb and Farmer (1983 pp 185–208). A new edition of the *Historia abbatum* is being prepared by David Dumville (see Carley 1994 p 276 note 58).

Benedictus Casinensis, miracula [ADREVALD.FLOR.Mir.Benedict.]:
BHL 1123; *BLS* 1.650–55; *BSS* 2.1105–71; *DHGE* 8.225–41; *DTC* 1.446;
Farmer (1987) pp 38–39.
ed.: De Certain 1858 pp 15–89.
MSS Cambridge, St John's College 164: HG 153.
Lists – Refs none.

The cult of **BENEDICT OF NURSIA** (ca. 480–550), first abbot of Monte Cassino and one of the fathers of Western monasticism, was established in England by at least the late seventh century (and almost certainly before). **ALDHELM** eulogizes him in his DE VIRGINITATE (*Carmen* 842–80; *Prosa* 268–69; ed. *MGH* AA 15), and ecclesiasts such as **BONIFACE** (BONIFATIUS) and Willibrord helped establish Benedict's monastic rule as the norm of regular life in the Frankish empire (an eighth-century English manuscript contains the oldest extant copy). For a brief survey of Benedict's liturgical cult and its English repercussions, see Ortenberg (1992 pp 113–14, 123–25); see also Deshusses and Hourlier (1979 pp 157–59, 170). On the varied evidence for English knowledge of the influential Latin life in DIALOGI II, see **GREGORY THE GREAT**. For English manuscripts and knowledge of the other narrative texts associated with Benedict's cult at Fleury-sur-Loire, where his relics were supposedly removed in 673, see further in this and the next entry. For the homily on Benedict's feast day, extant in three pre-1100 English manuscripts, see **ODO OF CLUNY**.

The cult of Benedict, originally centered on Monte Cassino in Italy, acquired a second center in the late seventh century when the monks of Fleury-sur-Loire claimed to have taken his relics to France. The first collection of posthumous Fleury miracles was composed ca. 870 by Adrevald of Fleury (Head 1990 p 39 notes 78 and 82; see also the article in *DTC*, above, and *Lexikon des Mittelalters* 1.165–66) and subsequently continued by several other writers in the eleventh and twelfth centuries (Rollason 1985; Vidier 1965 pp 153–62). While the early Anglo-Saxon hagiographic sources, including the ninth-century **OLD ENGLISH MARTYROLOGY**, do not allude specifically to Benedict's Fleury cult (see, however, the late-ninth-century calendar in F. Wormald 1934 p 8), the numerous contacts between English ecclesiasts and Fleury in the tenth century (Stenton 1971 pp 447–50; Ortenberg 1992 pp 237–38) ensured the widespread appearance of Benedict's translation feast (July 11, sometimes called the "depositio") in English monastic calendars of the reform era and the eleventh century. **BYRHTFERTH**, former pupil of **ABBO OF FLEURY** during the latter's two-year sojourn at Ramsey (985–87), refers to Benedict's relics and miracles at Fleury in his life of **OSWALDUS WIGORNIENSIS** (*RS* 71/1.422) as does **ÆLFRIC** at the close of his homily on Benedict, **CATHOLIC HOMILIES** II, 11, lines 572–76 (*ÆCHom*, B1.2.12; ed. *EETS* SS 5), and in his life of Edmund, lines 1–2, 10–12, in **LIVES OF SAINTS** (*ÆLS*, B1.3.31; ed. *EETS* OS 94 and 114), although neither shows knowledge of the *miracula* (but see next entry).

Only one Anglo-Saxon copy of Adrevald's *Miracula* attests to this intercourse. The St John's College manuscript, apparently from St Augustine's, Canterbury, is an elaborately written *libellus* on Benedict, containing the *translatio* narative, Adrevald's *Miracula* I, and the homily on Benedict by Odo of Cluny (hymns for **AUGUSTINUS CANTUARIENSIS** and Adrian of Canterbury were added in the eleventh century on blank leaves, fols 15–16: see Gneuss 1968 pp 114–15). It is thus similar in contents and arrangement to a handful of other manuscripts listed by Vidier (1965 p 139). James (1913 p 197) dates the *libellus* in the tenth century; since Odo was abbot of Cluny from 927–42, the St John's manuscript is presumably of the second half of the century. The text of the *Miracula* is preceded by a set of prefatory verses (*ICL* 11436) and concludes with an elaborate colophon in black and red capitals (both printed by James 1913 pp 198–99). The *explicit* given by James is not the same as in the printed editions of Adrevald's work. The manuscript does not appear to have been studied, nor is it listed by Vidier (1965 pp 151–52) whose survey of copies of Adrevald's collection concentrates on manuscripts of French origin.

The most recent edition, by Holder-Egger (*MGH* SRM 15.478–500), like most editions except that of De Certain, omits some portions of the text, and De Certain's unsatisfactory text remains standard. For a recent assessment of Adrevald's hagiography, see Head (1990 pp 39–41,

138–52). I have not seen Lysaght's dissertation on the cult of Benedict at Fleury (1984).

Benedictus Casinensis, translatio [ADREVALD.FLOR.Trans.Benedict]:
BHL 1117; *BLS* 1.292–93; *BSS* 11.742–49.
ed.: De Certain 1858 pp 1–14.
MSS 1. Cambridge, St John's College 164: HG 153.
2. Cambridge, Corpus Christi College 9 (HG 36) + London, BL Cotton Nero E. i (HG 344).
Lists – AS Vers none.
Quots/Cits Trans.Benedict. 12.7–8, 14.19–20: BYRHTFERTH.Vit. Oswald. 422.9–12.
Refs see below.

An especially interesting aspect of **GREGORY THE GREAT**'s life of **BENEDICT OF NURSIA** is the saint's close relationship with his sister SCHOLASTICA, a nun at a nearby convent, with whom he would meet every year and whose body eventually shared his coffin at Monte Cassino (DIALOGI II.xxxiii–xxxiv; ed. *SC* 260). According to Fleury legend, Scholastica's relics were brought with her brother's from Italy to France, hers to Le Mans (but see Goffart 1967) while his went to Fleury (commemorated July 11). The account of the double translation is a mid-ninth-century work usually known as the *Historia translationis* and traditionally attributed to Adrevald of Fleury, author of the first book of Benedict's miracles (see previous entry), but it is probably not Adrevald's work (Hourlier 1979 p 226). It is the most widely represented, if not the earliest, of the various versions of the translation (on the other versions, see Hourlier 1979). **BYRHTFERTH** of Ramsey echoes some phrases while summarizing it in his life of Archbishop Oswald (OSWALDUS WIGORNIENSIS: BYRHTFERTH.Vit.Oswald.; ed. *RS* 71/1.422.2–14). Links between Ramsey and Fleury were long-standing. Oswald, founder of Ramsey (ca. 971), had been ordained at Fleury, and the English abbey's most distinguished schoolmaster was **ABBO OF FLEURY**, who taught Byrhtferth, so the latter's familiarity with this text is not surprising.

In addition to the copy in the tenth-century manuscript from St Augustine's, Canterbury (see previous entry), another later copy, made at Worcester in the mid-eleventh century, is now split between the two main eleventh-century components of the **COTTON-CORPUS LEGENDARY**, beginning in the Cambridge manuscript and continuing in the London portion. Neither is among the long list of copies printed by Vidier (1965 pp 141–44), who focuses on manuscripts of French origin, and we have no information as to the English copies' affiliations with one another or with the Continental manuscripts.

There is no critical edition of the text. The unsatisfactory edition of De Certain is still standard (see also *PL* 124.901–10). See Vidier (1965 pp 144–49) and Hourlier (1979). On generic aspects of the *Historia translationis*, see Geary (1990 pp 120–22). The standard modern study of the *translatio* genre as a whole is that of Heinzelmann (1979).

Benignus, passio [ANON.Pas.Benign.]: *BHL* 1153; *BLS* 4.236; *BSS* 2.1231–32; *CPL* 2114; *DACL* 4.835–49; *DHGE* 7.1314–15.
ed.: Van der Straeten 1961 pp 465–68.
MSS – Lists none.
A-S Vers 1. BEDA.Mart. 198.11–30.
2. *Mart* (B19.iq).
Quots/Cits – Refs none.

Benignus of Dijon (November 1) is the central figure in a cycle of texts on Burgundian saints (see **ANDOCHIUS**) purporting to narrate the preaching, miracles, and martyrdoms of missionaries from Asia Minor sent by **POLYCARPUS** to east central Gaul in the second century. The saint's cult was already active in the time of **GREGORY OF TOURS** (Van der Straeten 1961 pp 126–31), and the *passio* is usually dated likewise in the sixth century, although Gregory does not show awareness of its extravagant claims. It was known to **BEDE**, whose notice for Benignus in his **MARTYROLOGIUM** (BEDA.Mart.; ed. Dubois and Renaud 1976) is sourced by Quentin (1908 pp 61–62), and also to the author of the **OLD**

ENGLISH MARTYROLOGY (*Mart*; ed. Kotzor 1981 2.245–46). The specific version of the source has not been ascertained in either case and there are no Anglo-Saxon manuscript copies. However, if Van der Straeten's view concerning a Farfa manuscript and the "cycle benignien" is correct, and if Cross also is correct in seeing the Farfa-type text as the source of the *Old English Martyrology*'s account of Andochius, then the *Martyrology*'s notice for Benignus would presumably depend likewise on the Farfa-type version of the cycle.

It is puzzling that the **COTTON-CORPUS LEGENDARY** includes the older Burgundian texts that were among the original sources of the Benignus legend, namely the martyrdoms of **SPEUSIPPUS** and **SYMPHORIANUS** (Van der Straeten 1961 pp 132–34), but lacks texts for Andochius and Benignus. Ortenberg (1992 pp 248–49) gives the misleading impression that the cult of Benignus was unknown in England before the later Anglo-Saxon period.

For another edition of the legend, see *AS* Nov. 1.155–59.

Bertinus, vita [ANON.Vit.Bertin.]: *BHL* 763; *BLS* 3.493–94; *BSS* 3.101–02; *DHGE* 8.1006–07.

ed.: *MGH* SRM 5.765–69 and 778–80.

MSS 1. London, BL Cotton Nero E. i: HG 344.
  2. Salisbury, Cathedral Library 222 (formerly Oxford, Bodleian Library Fell 1): HG 754.6.

Lists none.

A-S Vers Mart (B19.gt).

Quots/Cits – Refs none.

Bertin (September 5, died 698) was associated with Omer (**AUDOMARUS**) in the conversion of the region known today as the Pas-de-Calais. The abbey at Sithiu, which they founded together and which later adopted Bertin's name, came to have strong links with Anglo-Saxon England. An important figure in King Alfred's ecclesiastical and educational program, Grimbald (died 901 or 903), was a monk of Saint-Bertin (see Ortenberg

1992 p 24 for bibliography). Other monks of Saint-Bertin migrated to Bath in the reign of King Athelstan (ca. 944) in protest against reforms and doubtless brought books with them, including perhaps a copy of their patron's *vita* (Grierson 1940). Later alumni of Saint-Bertin to migrate to England were the hagiographers Goscelin and Folcard, both resident in England in the later eleventh century (see Gransden 1974 pp 107–11).

The oldest version of Bertin's life forms part two of the three-part life (Vita I) of Omer, Bertin, and **WINNOCUS**, written ca. 800. It was known to the author of the ninth-century **OLD ENGLISH MARTYROLOGY** (*Mart*; ed. Kotzor 1981 2.200–01, sourced pp 347–48). Levison, who numbers the Cotton and Salisbury manuscript copies of the *vita* $4a^{1-2}$ (*MGH* SRM 5.742), describes them (p 747) as more faithful to the original Vita I than the Legendary's text of the life of Omer.

For some remarks on Bertin's liturgical cult in England, see Ortenberg (1992 p 37), who mistakenly states, however, that, of the three saints, only Bertin appears in the *Old English Martyrology*.

Bertinus, miraculum [ANON.Mir.Bertin.]: *BHL* 1289b.
  ed.: *MGH* SRM 5.778–80.

MSS 1. London, BL Cotton Nero E. i: HG 344.
  2. Salisbury, Cathedral Library 222 (formerly Oxford, Bodleian Library Fell 1): HG 754.6.
List – Refs none.

An additional Bertin miracle, printed by Levison from the English manuscript copies of the *Vita Bertini* (*MGH* SRM 5.778–80; see also Jackson and Lapidge 1996 p 140), is dated by him no later than the mid-ninth century.

Birinus: *BLS* 4.500–01; *BSS* 3.193–94; *DHGE* 8.1530–31; Farmer (1987) pp 47–48.

Birinus (Birin/Berin; feast days December 3, September 4), an early missionary among the West Saxons (ca. 635), was their first known bishop, consecrated by the Archbishop of Milan in Genoa before leaving for England. He established his see at Dorchester (near Oxford) and built other churches elsewhere, including Winchester. His relics were translated to Winchester by Bishop Hedda (ca. 690) and retranslated by Bishop ÆTHELWOLDUS to a new shrine (980), and the feretory was moved again to the new Anglo-Norman minster (1093). Birinus's December 3 feast day is quite common in later Anglo-Saxon calendars (especially with Winchester associations), and some from the eleventh century also have the September 4 translation (see the references in Townsend 1989 p 129). But he is one of several notable Anglo-Saxon saints for whom we lack convincing evidence of a pre-Conquest *vita*. The only early narrative is **BEDE**'s brief account (mainly **HISTORIA ECCLESIASTICA** III.vii; ed. Colgrave and Mynors 1969 p 232), on which most of the above information is based. The earliest extant *vita* (*BHL* 1361, ed. Love 1996 pp 1–46) is regarded by Townsend (1989 p 130) as a product of the Winchester diocese shortly after the Norman Conquest, but Love (1996 pp liv–lviii), while agreeing as to the place of origin, argues for a date nearer the turn of the eleventh century, suggesting that the work was composed by the anonymous Winchester author of a life and miracles of **SWITHUNUS** (see Lapidge 1989/90 p 260) most probably around the time of the construction of the new cathedral (ca. 1093). Love and Townsend agree that the hagiographer adds little new material to that supplied by Bede, other than two miracles derived from oral tradition or other hagiographies. Love does not completely dismiss the possibility of an earlier *vita*, but considers it unlikely and describes the work as mainly a rhetorical tour de force by an apparently learned author (Love 1996 pp lii–liv). The most important manuscript copy, Oxford, Bodleian Library Digby 39 (*SC* 2672; HG 609), is a composite of originally separate booklets. The portion containing the *Vita Birini* (along with a copy of Osbern's life of ÆLFEGUS) is by two scribes of the turn of the century. On this and other manuscripts, see Townsend (1989 pp 131–34) and Love's introduction to her edition (1996 pp xlix–lxxxviii), which also includes a facing translation of the Latin text (pp 2–47). The text is also edited by Townsend (1989 pp 138–57).

Blandina: *BLS* 2.454–58; *BSS* 3.202–03.

Blandina (feast day June 2) was a slave woman whose faith and courage under torture and in the arena made her one of the most venerated of the "Martyrs of Lyons," A.D. 177 (under Marcus Aurelius). Their story is told in a letter (*BHL* 6839, *Passio Photini*), from the churches of Vienne and Lyons to those of Asia and Phrygia, describing their trials, tortures, and deaths. It is one of the earliest documents in Christian hagiography. The original is lost, but **EUSEBIUS PAMPHILUS**'s account incorporates substantial extracts, which passed to the West in **RUFINUS**'s translation (**HISTORIA ECCLESIASTICA** V.i–iii; ed. *GCS* 9/2.403.9–435.6); thus the story was accessible throughout the Anglo-Saxon period. Only **BEDE**, however, devotes a separate notice to Blandina in his **MARTYROLOGIUM** (ed. Dubois and Renaud 1976 p 100.9–22), quoting several passages from, and citing, the Latin version of the Eusebius/Rufinus account (see Quentin 1908 p 98). On the extant English manuscripts, see the main entry for Rufinus. The Greek text is separately printed, with English translation, by Musurillo (1972 pp 62–85).

Blastus. See **MARIUS ET MARTHA**.

Bonifatius [WILLIBALD.Vit.Bonifat.]: *BHL* 1400; *BLS* 2.477–81; *BSS* 3.308–17; *DHGE* 9.883–95; Farmer (1987) pp 51–53; *LTK* 2.591–93.
ed.: Levison 1905 pp 1–61.

MSS   Salisbury, Cathedral Library 223 (formerly Oxford, Bodleian Library Fell 3): HG 754.7.
Lists – Quots/Cits   none.
Refs   see below.

BONIFACE, originally named Wynfrith, was a West Saxon by birth and upbringing who interrupted a successful career as monk, teacher, and scholar in the monastery at Nursling to begin work in 716 as a missionary under Willibrord among the heathen Frisians and later among other

Germanic peoples beyond the Rhine, where he became Archbishop of Mainz (he was renamed Bonifatius by Pope Gregory II). He was killed while preaching among the Frisians in 755.

Boniface was famous and revered among his English contemporaries (see, e.g., a letter of Sigebald, abbot of Chertsey, *MGH* ES 1.61; Rau 1968 p 116; see also Levison 1946 p 76). After his martyrdom, his feast day (June 5) was publicly instituted in England as of equal solemnity with those of the English "apostles" (**GREGORIUS MAGNUS** and **AUGUSTINUS CANTUARIENSIS**: see *MGH* ES 1.240; Rau 1968 pp 344–46), and Bishop Milret of Worcester wrote to Lullus, Boniface's successor at Mainz, requesting a life and passion of the martyr (*MGH* ES 1.244; Rau 1968 p 352.17–19). He is duly celebrated in verses 32–33 of the York metrical calendar (ed. Wilmart 1934 p 66). It is probable that Milret was indeed sent a copy of the *Vita Bonifatii* (*BHL* 1400) composed shortly afterwards by the priest Willibald, but no pre-Conquest copy of English provenance has turned up. While his cult flourished in Germany, English devotion to Boniface's memory seems to have diminished markedly as time passed (Sisam 1953 pp 205–06; Liebermann 1889 p iii). He is omitted by the compiler of the ninth-century **OLD ENGLISH MARTYROLOGY**; his feast day is not among the more important during the tenth and eleventh centuries; and of the many letters Boniface is known to have sent to England, only a handful were preserved in Anglo-Saxon contexts (see Levison 1946 pp 280–82). Among the earliest extant English copies of the *Vita Bonifatii* is that in the Salisbury manuscript, dated early twelfth century by Ker (1964 p 172) and by Webber (1992 p 169) who places it among her Group II manuscripts, but it is included by Gneuss among the pre-1100 manuscripts (HG 754.7: Gernot Wieland urged upon me the relevance of this copy). According to Webber (1992 p 169 note 77) the Salisbury copy is "damaged at the beginning," lacking chapters I–V and beginning part way through chapter VI at "Hugoberti" (Levison 1905 p 35.20; Rau 1968 498.30) with a further lacuna in chapter VIII (see Levison 1905 p XXVI); the ninth and final chapter, which is probably not by Willibald (Rau 1968 p 453), was omitted by the scribe (as in three other English copies: see Levison 1905 p XXVI). According to Levison (pp XXV–XXVI), the English manuscripts form a distinct family, among which is London, Gray's Inn 3 (provenance Chester), dated early twelfth century by Ker and Piper (1969–92 1.52–53; Levison 1905 p XXVI). Although the Salisbury and Gray's Inn manuscripts are late witnesses, they could be representatives of an earlier English (i.e., pre-Conquest) textual tradition. It is unlikely, however, given their textual differences from Levison's best manuscript, that they derive from the putative early copy that would have been sent from Saxony (Mainz or Fulda) soon after its composition in response to the request of Bishop Milret.

The standard edition of Boniface's correspondence, by M. Tangl (*MGH* ES 1), and of Willibald's *Vita Bonifatii*, by Levison (1905), are now printed in one volume with facing German translations by Rau (1968).

Bonifatius Tarsi, passio [ANON.Pas.Bonifat.Tars.]: *BHL* 1413; *BLS* 2.305–06; *BSS* 3.324–25.
ed.: *AS* Mai. 3.280–83.

MSS 1. London, BL Cotton Nero E. i: HG 344.
2. Salisbury, Cathedral Library 221 (formerly Oxford, Bodleian Library Fell 4): HG 754.5.

Lists – Refs none.

The Boniface whose *passio* is preserved in the **COTTON-CORPUS LEGENDARY** is not the famous English missionary but the martyr of Tarsus (Zettel 1979 p 21). His cult began to flourish in Rome in the seventh century, at which time an early Greek *passio* (now lost) was translated into Latin (Siegmund 1949 p 230) before being revised and expanded in the ninth (*BHG* 276). It represents Boniface as the Roman agent (and lover) of a dissolute patrician woman who, repenting of her ways, sent him to the East to acquire relics of martyrs during the Diocletian persecution. In Tarsus he defied the persecutors and was tortured and executed himself.

Puzzling, however, is the position of this text in the English legendary, in early June, where one would expect to find Boniface of Mainz (feast day June 5) or Pope Boniface (feast day June 6). Boniface of Tarsus's normal feast day is May 14. See Jackson and Lapidge (1996 p 138). There was probably some Anglo-Saxon confusion of the Tarsus martyr with the Mainz martyr or the martyred Pope Boniface, who is commemorated explicitly in the eleventh-century Winchester (Nunnaminster) calendar (F. Wormald 1934 p 35) on June 5.

Botolphus: *BLS* 2.567–68; *BSS* 3.370–71; *DHGE* 9.1433–34.

Botolph (alias Botulf; feast day June 17), who flourished in the late seventh century, is known to have been a widely revered abbot of one of the earliest monasteries in East Anglia, at "Icanho" (more probably Iken, Suffolk, than Boston, Lincolnshire), where he was visited by CEOLFRIDUS (*Vita Ceolfridi*, ed. Plummer 1896 1.389.13–15), but he is otherwise a shadowy figure (see Whitelock 1972 pp 10–12 for a trenchant discussion of the evidence). His absence from the **OLD ENGLISH MARTYROLOGY** is noteworthy.

The monastery was supposedly destroyed in the Danish invasions of the ninth century. Part of the relics of Botolph, and of his even more shadowy "brother" Adwulf (Adulf), were later retrieved (ca. 972) by the agents of Bishop ÆTHELWOLD of Winchester (ÆTHELWOLDUS) for his new foundation at Thorney (along with relics of Thancred, Torthred, and Tova, East Anglian hermits supposedly murdered by the Vikings in 870). On the Thorney foundation charter, see Hart (1966 pp 165–72) and Clark (1979 p 46, with notes 18 and 20). Relics were also claimed by the eleventh-century monks of Bury, Ely, and, later, Westminster (but see Scarfe 1984 pp 298–300). There is no trace of a formal *vita* until one was written by the Flemish hagiographer Folcard and dedicated to Bishop Walkelin of Winchester (*BHL* 1428: *AS* Iun. 3.402–05; the prologue is printed in *RS* 26/1.373–74). Folcard, a former monk of Saint-Bertin, was abbot of Thorney shortly after the Norman Conquest (in addition to Whitelock 1972, see also Clark 1979). An account of Æthelwold's translation of the relics (*BHL* 1431) may also be by Folcard, in Clark's opinion. The Botolph *vita* is thought to be largely fabricated, and

Folcard's vague allusions in his prologue to information in "old books" and oral tradition lack conviction, but it is possible that, at least since the foundation under Æthelwold, the Thorney community had preserved some traditions about Botolph that Folcard adapted. On the archeology of Iken (excavated in 1977) and for a further attempt to place Botolph in his historical context, see the studies of Clark and Hart, and the joint study of West, Cramp, and, especially, Scarfe (1984), who largely ignores, however, Folcard's contribution.

It should be mentioned that one modern scholar (Wilkinson *TU* 79.527–33), whose contribution has not been noted by any of the above, has a quite different hypothesis as to the historical value and composition of the *Vita Botolphi*, arguing that paragraphs 4–11 of the *AS* edition represent an early, possibly eighth-century life of Botolph himself; that paragraphs 2–3, which mainly concern his putative brother Adwulf, were added in the late tenth, around the same time as the translation of the relics; that Folcard was responsible for revising the whole and adding the prologue; and finally that lections for Botolph's feast (*BHL* 1430) preserved in an early printed breviary from Sleswig represent a different pre-Conquest tradition, that of the Danes of East Anglia before the monastic revival, carried to Denmark by English missionaries of Danish descent. Unfortunately these intriguing ideas are presented in summary form without supporting evidence or analysis, either textual or historical.

Briccius, vita [GREG.TUR.Vit.Brit.]: *BHL* 1452; *BSS* 3.542–44; *DHGE* 10.670–71.
ed.: *MGH* SRM 1/1.37–38 [2nd ed.].

MSS 1. Cambridge, Corpus Christi College 9: HG 36.
2. Cambridge, Trinity Hall 21: HG 201.
3. Hereford, Cathedral Library O.VI.11: HG 264.
4. Vatican, Reg. lat. 489: HG 915.

Lists – Refs none.

Closely associated with Martin of Tours (**MARTINUS TURONENSIS**) whom he succeeded as bishop (397), Brice, who died in 444 (feast day

November 13), plays an interesting and cantankerous role in **SULPICIUS SEVERUS**, DIALOGI II.xv (*BHL* 1451; ed. *CSEL* 1.213–14) where it transpires that Brice was no great friend of his more illustrious predecessor. **GREGORY OF TOURS**, in his HISTORIA FRANCORUM II.i, develops this "difficult" persona in his brief life of the saint but suppresses the Sulpician anecdote in favor of others somewhat less offensive. Brice's cult spread with that of Martin, and the *vita* (entitled "Narratio" in *BHL*) is preserved, separately from Gregory's *Historia*, in many if not all collections of "Martiniana." Of this type are the four Anglo-Saxon copies listed above (another, now lost, was formerly in Salisbury, Cathedral Library 222: Webber 1992 p 157). For a later copy linked to the **COTTON-CORPUS LEGENDARY**, see Zettel (1979 p 31). In their edition of Gregory's *Historia*, Krusch and Levison (*MGH* SRM 1/1.XXXII–XXXIV [2nd ed.]) collate the text of *Historia* II.i with extracts in some collections of Martiniana but do not mention any of the English manuscripts listed above, and we have no additional information about their affiliations. Some Martiniana (e.g., the Vatican manuscript) also include the Brice anecdote by Sulpicius himself, which was often omitted from early manuscripts of his *Dialogi* (Delehaye 1920 pp 13–15).

Although Brice's feast was evidently of some liturgical importance in later Anglo-Saxon England (see the graded feast days in F. Wormald 1934 pp 68, 236, 250, 264), **ÆLFRIC** chose not to include any Brice material in either his shorter or longer version of Martin's life, CATHOLIC HOMILIES II, 34 (*ÆCHom*, B1.2.42; ed. *EETS* SS 5) and LIVES OF SAINTS (*ÆLS*, B1.3.30; ed. *EETS* OS 94 and 114). In the year 1002, for whatever reason, King Æthelred chose St Brice's day for the infamous massacre of Danes resident in England, which probably precipitated a renewal of the Viking invasions.

We have not seen the monograph by Schoenen (1981).

Brigida, vita [COGITOS.Vit.Brigid.]: *BHL* 1457; *BSS* 3.430–37; *CPL* 2147–48; *DHGE* 10.716–19; Farmer (1987) pp 62–63; *SEHI* 147.
  ed.: *AS* Feb. 1.135–41.

MSS 1. London, BL Cotton Nero E. i: HG 344.
2. Salisbury, Cathedral Library 221 (formerly Oxford, Bodleian Library Fell 4): HG 754.5.
Lists – Refs none.

Veneration of Saint Brigid (also Brigit, Bride; feast day February 1), an early Irish nun and abbess, originated at the monastery of Kildare, which according to tradition she had founded in the fifth century. The date of her death is estimated at ca. 525. Her cult followed Irish missionaries to the Continent where it was widely represented in the areas of Celtic Christian influence. Despite the supposed existence, by the end of the seventh century, of at least two *Vitae Brigidae* (by Aileran/Ultan, *BHL* 1455–56, and Cogitosus, *BHL* 1457) she is not mentioned in the main early Anglo-Saxon sources, but neither is her putative baptizer, **PATRICIUS** (on the Irish saints' lack of influence on Anglo-Saxon liturgy and hagiography, see Rollason 1989a pp 78–81). The February–March portion of the ninth-century **OLD ENGLISH MARTYROLOGY**, in which she might have been noticed, is lost from all the manuscripts. The *Martyrology* does have a notice for Patrick, however (see below, the entry for Patricius), and since both his and Brigid's feasts are in a late-ninth-century Anglo-Saxon calendar (F. Wormald 1934 pp 3–4), it seems likely that the *Martyrology* would also have had a notice for Brigid. Almost all the surviving Anglo-Saxon calendars have Brigid's feast (unlike Patrick's), and proper masses are provided for her in some eleventh-century sacramentaries (Corrêa 1993 pp 249–52). A piece of her cheek bone appears in the relics collection (Exeter List of Relics, *Rec* 10.8, B16.10.8; ed. Förster 1943 p 80; Conner 1993a p 187) said to have been donated by King Athelstan, and in the Old English list there is an effusive three-line eulogy of "that precious virgin" who worked many miracles and "lightened the hearts of many men by the example of her holy living." Of her several *vitae*, rich in mythic and folkloric elements, and copiously represented in Continental libraries especially, the only one preserved in English manuscripts of our period is the most popular one, "Vita II" by Cogitosus (ca. 620–80), in the Worcester and Salisbury recensions of the **COTTON-CORPUS LEGENDARY** (Jackson and Lapidge 1996 p 136;

Webber 1992 p 155). Facsimiles of the opening and closing leaves of each copy are printed by Esposito (1912/13, Plates XXXII–XXXV), who nonetheless characterizes the Legendary's text as "carelessly written," with one large lacuna (paragraph 34 of the *AS* edition) and numerous minor omissions (Esposito 1912/13 pp 310, 312).

Other evidence for English interest in Brigid's hagiography is from Canterbury in the late eleventh century and later. One of the delightful miracles narrated by Cogitosus (the garment hung on a sunbeam: ed. *AS* Feb. 1.136, paragraph 9) is attributed to **DUNSTANUS** in the life written ca. 1090 by Osbern of Canterbury (ed. *RS* 63.160); a more elaborate rendering is in the life of Dunstan by Eadmer (p 204) some years later. This link between the two saints is made explicit in a sermon on Dunstan preserved in a late-twelfth-century English manuscript (p 456.10–11), cited by Ogilvy (*BKE* p 45). Osbern may be alluding to an established, possibly pre-Conquest tradition, but the miracle does not appear in either of the early-eleventh-century lives of Dunstan.

Despite the flurry of recent scholarly attention to the *Vitae Brigidae* (see bibliography in Lapidge and Sharpe 1985 p 84 and recent articles by S. Connolly and Picard 1988 and by O'Riain 1990), the early printed editions listed in *BHL* have not yet been replaced. Of these, the Bollandists' is regarded as superior. The list of manuscripts of Cogitosus's work drawn up by Esposito (1912/13 pp 309–19, 325–26) has been superseded and considerably augmented by Ludwig Bieler (see Hayes 1965 1.332–34; 1979 1.78–79). On the verse life of Brigid by Laurence of Durham (died 1154), see *SEHI* 151(iv).

Caecilia, passio [ANON.Pas.Caecil.]: *BHL* 1495; *BLS* 4.402–05; *BSS* 3.1064–86; *CPL* 2171; *DACL* 2.2712–38 (especially 2713–21). See also **VALERIANUS ET TIBURTIUS**.
ed.: Delehaye 1936 pp 194–220.
MSS 1. Cambridge, Corpus Christi College 9: HG 36.
2. Paris, Bibliothèque Nationale lat. 10861: HG 898.
Lists none.

A-S Vers 1. ALDH.Carm.uirg. 1710–35.
2. ALDH.Pros.uirg. 292.13–23.
3. BEDA.Mart. 211.16–19.
4. *Mart* (B19.ja).
5. *ÆLS* Cecilia (B1.3.32).
Quots/Cits – Refs none (see below).

According to their colorful legend, the Roman martyrs with the crowns of roses and lilies, Cecilia (feast day November 22) and Valerianus (April 14), were virgin spouses, like **CHRYSANTHUS ET DARIA** and **IULIANUS ET BASILISSA**, but in this case the bride persuaded the groom (and later his brother, Tiburtius) to remain chaste on the wedding night (and ever after) and to convert to Christianity. On the names of the principal characters and their historical connections, see Delehaye (1936 pp 80–88). By the beginning of the Anglo-Saxon period, Cecilia was already established as one of the best known and most widely venerated of the female Roman saints, while Valerianus also became important in his own right (see his entry, below). In England, Caecilia is prominent in calendars from the early and later Anglo-Saxon periods (Wilmart 1934 p 68; F. Wormald 1934 p 54) and in liturgical books (see Ortenberg 1992 p 179). On the cult in general, see the standard modern study of Kirsch (1910) and more recently T. Connolly (1979, 1980). On chaste spouses in hagiography, see De Gaiffier (1947); for a historical study, see D. Elliott (1993).

Modern scholarship regards the legend itself as a literary creation of the late fifth century or early sixth, modeled perhaps on an episode in Victor of Vita's *Historia persecutionis* I.x–xii (ed. *CSEL* 7.13–17), written in Africa in 486 (see *DACL* 2.2718–19, citing earlier studies). For the intriguing hypothesis that the story and characters are an allegory of alchemical synthesis, see Grennen (1966).

The *passio* appears to have been known in England throughout the Anglo-Saxon period. The earliest Anglo-Saxon copy is the Paris manuscript listed here (Canterbury, early ninth century: see M. P. Brown 1986), designated P and collated with a tenth-century Chartres copy (manuscript C) in Delehaye's edition (1936 pp 191–92). Of the **COTTON-CORPUS LEGENDARY** manuscripts, the Cambridge manuscript listed here (from

Worcester, second half of the eleventh century) contains the *passio* (Jackson and Lapidge 1996 p 142), but it has been lost, along with other November and December saints' texts, from Salisbury, Cathedral Library 222. For other important later (twelfth-entury) copies in affiliated manuscripts, especially one in Hereford, see Zettel (1979 pp 12–13, 31, 36–39, 160–73, and below). The copy of the *Passio Caeciliae* in the Cotton-Corpus Legendary is very similar to Delehaye's manuscript C from Chartres and clearly represents a textual tradition different from that of the Paris manuscript.

BEDE certainly knew the *passio*. While his summary of Cecilia's story in his **MARTYROLOGIUM** (BEDA.Mart.; ed. Dubois and Renaud 1976, sourced by Quentin 1908 p 64) lacks verbal echoes, his indebtedness is more specific in the separate notice for her husband (see below, the entry for Valerianus). **ALDHELM**'s tributes to Cecilia, immediately after the Virgin Mary in the series of female virgins in his verse and prose **DE VIRGINITATE** (ALDH.Carm.uirg., Pros.uirg.; ed. *MGH* AA 15), focus primarily on the episode of the wedding night, ignoring Cecilia's martyrdom (see Ehwald's sourcing, *MGH* AA 15.292, 424–25; Lapidge and Herren 1979 pp 177, 195–96, and note 20). Regarding the substantial account of Cecilia in the **OLD ENGLISH MARTYROLOGY** (*Mart*; ed. Kotzor 1981 2.253–55), see Herzfeld's brief notes on sources (*EETS* OS 116.xlii and 239, using the edition of Mombritius). Unlike Aldhelm's, the *Martyrology*'s account of the wedding night follows the wording of the *passio* closely, for the most part, and at the end briefly describes Cecilia's martyrdom and last words, with interesting variations from the *passio*, which may or may not be due to textual variants in the Latin source. For the *Martyrology*'s separate notice for Valerianus, see his entry below.

C. Loomis (1931 p 6) notes that **ÆLFRIC** used a copy of the *Passio Caeciliae* similar to that in Mombritius's edition (1910 1.332–41, 638–39) for the account in **LIVES OF SAINTS** (*ÆLS*; ed. *EETS* OS 94 and 114). Zettel (1979 pp 256–57), who does not mention Delehaye's edition, confirms that Mombritius's text is a good guide to Ælfric's source, but he points to some passages for which Hereford, Cathedral Library P.VII.6, a twelfth-century affiliate of the Cotton-Corpus Legendary, is closer to

Ælfric's presumed exemplar than either Mombritius or the other two representatives of the Legendary. For example, in lines 356–57 of his *Cecilia* Ælfric briefly explains the law that forbids the executioner to strike Cecilia more than three times. Zettel points out that this important detail, lacking in Delehaye's manuscripts and Mombritius's text, is found in the Hereford manuscript but not in the earlier English copies. With slightly different wording, however, it is recorded as a variant in the textual apparatus to the modern edition of Mombritius (1910 1.639), so it is not, apparently, unique to the English tradition in the way Zettel implies. See the interesting analogue in Ælfric's sermon on Ash Wednesday, *In Caput Ieiunii* 180–242 (*ÆLS* Ash Wed, B1.3.13; ed. *EETS* OS 76 and 82), drawing on **JEROME**'s **EPISTOLAE** I (ed. *CSEL* 54.1–9).

On other studies of Ælfric's *Cecilia*, see Moloney (1982), who cites earlier studies, and Reames (1980). In the absence of a critical edition of the *passio*, Delehaye's edition should be used in conjunction with those of Mombritius and others cited in *BHL NS*.

Caesarius, passio [ANON.Pas.Caesar.diac.]: *BHL* 1511; *BSS* 3.1154–55; *CPL* 2172; *DHGE* 12.185.
   ed.: *AS* Nov. 1.106–17.
MSS   Cambridge, Corpus Christi College 9: HG 36.
Lists   none.
A-S Vers   1. BEDA.Mart. 199.2–23, 201.3–18.
   2. ?*Mart* (B19.ip).
Quots/Cits – Refs   none.

The cult of Caesarius (feast day November 1), for which there is fifth-century Roman evidence, was well known throughout the Christian West through its inclusion in the Roman sacramentaries. In the early Latin *passio* (dated fifth or sixth century by Lanzoni 1923 p 148), he is said to have been an African deacon who, together with a companion, the priest Julian, traveled to Terracinum in Campania (Italy) in the reign of Claudius. There they combatted idolatry, endured tortures, and suffered martyrdom by order of the city governor Luxurius. Their bodies were retrieved from the sea by a monk, Eusebius, and a priest, Felix, who were executed shortly afterwards (feast day November 5). Caesarius also has a small role in the *passio* of **NEREUS ET ACHILLEUS**.

BEDE's substantial narrative entries for both pairs of saints in his **MARTYROLOGIUM** (BEDA.Mart.; ed. Dubois and Renaud 1976) are sourced by Quentin (1908 pp 64–65) with reference to the Bollandists' printed edition.

The somewhat garbled rendering in the **OLD ENGLISH MARTYROLOGY** (*Mart*; ed. Kotzor 1981 2.244–45, partially sourced p 366) honors only Caesarius himself and focuses almost exclusively on the vengeance suffered by the pagan persecutor, not on the martyrdom. In the absence of a rigorous sourcing, it is uncertain which version of the *Passio Caesarii* lies behind the *Martryology*'s account. In later Anglo-Saxon England the extant calendars are erratic in their observance of the feasts associated with the legend (e.g., F. Wormald 1934 pp 26, 40, 54, 180).

Among somewhat later English copies of the *passio* is London, BL Arundel 91 (HG 305). The *AS* edition (pp 105–06) lists fifty-five manuscripts collated in the apparatus criticus, none of which are English, and there is no attempt at classification, but the *AS* text is preferable to that of Mombritius (1910 1.346–48).

Calepodius. See **CALLISTUS**.

Callistus, passio [ANON.Pas.Callist.]: *BHL* 1523; *BLS* 4.107–08; *BSS* 3.680–89; *CPL* 2173; *DACL* 2.1657–754; *DHGE* 11.421–24; Farmer (1987) pp 70–71.
  ed.: Mombritius 1910 1.268–71.
MSS 1. Cambridge, Corpus Christi College 9: HG 36.
  2. London, BL Harley 3020: HG 433.
Lists none.
A-S Vers BEDA.Mart. 187.2–15: see below.

Quots/Cits none.
Refs BEDA.Mart. 84.18, 191.10–11.

Numerous details of Callistus's colorful historical life as slave, banker, brawler, miner, cemetary keeper, and controversial pope (217–22) are provided by hostile witnesses such as Hippolytus (his rival for election to the papacy) and **TERTULLIAN**. Callistus (also Callixtus) was killed during a city riot and is venerated as a martyr (feast day October 14), but the *passio*, which preserves little or nothing of the biographical facts, tells how he was thrown from a window then drowned in a "puteus" (cistern) with a stone tied to his neck. The *passio* is believed to be a source of the account in the sixth-century **LIBER PONTIFICALIS** and also the main source of the *passio* of **MARIUS ET MARTHA** (Verrando 1984 p 1050).

BEDE draws extensively on the *Passio Callisti* in his **MARTYROLOGIUM** (BEDA.Mart; ed. Dubois and Renaud 1976), including separate notices not only for Callistus himself, cited above, but also for his aging attendant, Calepodius (p 84.6–18, May 10), and for his priest, Asterius, martyred shortly after Callistus (p 191.6–11, October 21). See Quentin (1908 pp 66–67).

The author of the **OLD ENGLISH MARTYROLOGY** shows his independence of Bede by drawing his entire notice for Callistus (*Mart*, B19.hx; ed. Kotzor 1981 2.229) from the *Liber Pontificalis* XVII, not from the *passio* (see Cross 1979 pp 191 and 202). However, the brief obit for Calepodius (ed. Kotzor 1981 2.100.12–102.2) is most probably from Bede's account.

Although the feast of Callistus is marked as important in two Canterbury calendars of the late tenth century (F. Wormald 1934 pp 53 and 67), the copy in the Harley manuscript, from Canterbury (see **BENEDICTUS BISCOPUS**), roughly contemporary with the two calendars, is not marked for lections like some other texts in the same manuscript. The Harley copy appears, on the basis of a short sample, to be unrelated textually to that in the Cambridge manuscript (from Worcester) of the **COTTON-CORPUS LEGENDARY**.

According to Verrando, the edition of Mombritius is preferable to that of *AS* Oct. 6.401–08.

Cassianus Augustodunensis, vita [ANON.Vit.Cassian.Aug.]: *BHL* 1632; *BSS* 3.908; *DHGE* 11.1317.
ed.: unpublished (see below).

MSS 1. London, BL Cotton Nero E. i: HG 344.
2. Salisbury, Cathedral Library 222 (formerly Oxford, Bodleian Library Fell 1): HG 754.6.

Lists – Refs none.

Cassian of Autun (feast day August 5) was apparently a historical bishop of the fourth century with an early cult (**GREGORY OF TOURS**, DE GLORIA CONFESSORUM LXXIII–LXXIV; ed. *MGH* SRM 1/2.791.16–792.22), but his *passio*, according to which he was an Egyptian bishop before he became a missionary in Gaul, is regarded as a literary fabrication, heavily indebted to the **GALLICANUS** episodes (*BHL* 3236) in the legend of **IOHANNES ET PAULUS** and to earlier lives of Burgundian saints such as **ANDOCHIUS**, **BENIGNUS**, and **SYMPHORIANUS** (De Gaiffier 1948). The earliest form of the *vita* (*BHL* 1630, Vita 1) is of uncertain date but earlier than the 840s, when the saint's relics were transferred from Autun to Saint-Quentin and a revision (*BHL* 1631, Vita 2a) was produced (De Gaiffier 1948 p 50). According to Zettel (1979 p 23) and Jackson and Lapidge (1996 p 139), the copies of the *Vita Cassiani episcopi* preserved in the manuscripts of the **COTTON-CORPUS LEGENDARY,** listed here, represent a variant version, Vita 2b, of the revised life, Vita 2a (*BHL* 1631); which was composed earlier is uncertain. The narrative portion of Vita 2b is unpublished but its more elaborate preface and its variants from Vita 2a are printed (from a manuscript in Brussels) in the notes to the Bollandists' edition of Vita 2a (Bollandists 1885 pp 159–66). The English manuscripts are not noted, although these also have the preface, identical to that in the Brussels manuscript (see, e.g., the Cotton manuscript, pt 1 fol 64r).

Cassianus Augustodunensis, vita metrica [ANON.Carm.Cass.Aug.]: *BHL* 1633.
ed.: *MGH* PLAC 4.181–96.

MSS – A-S Vers none.
Quots/Cits see below.
Refs none.

FRITHEGOD of Canterbury may have known a metrical version (possibly composed in ninth-century Laon: see Manitius 1911–31 1.703–04) of the *Vita Cassiani* (see previous entry). For an apparent verbal echo, see his **BREVILOQUIUM VITAE WILFRIDI** 131 (ed. Campbell 1950), corresponding to the metrical life (*Carmen de Sancto Cassiano*), line 349.

Cassianus Ludimagister, passio [ANON.Pas.Cassian.Lud.]: *BHL* 1626; *BLS* 4.484; *BSS* 3.909–11; *CPL* 2060.
ed.: Mombritius 1910 1.280 and 636.
MSS London, BL Cotton Otho A. xiii: HG 351.
Lists none.
A-S Vers 1. BEDA.Mart. 149.8–18.
2. ?*Mart* (B19.fu).
Quots/Cits none.
Refs BEDA.Vit.Felic. 789.

According to the earliest version of his legend, as recounted by **PRUDENTIUS**, Cassian of Imola, near Ravenna (feast day August 13), was a schoolmaster ("ludimagister") martyred for his Christian faith by his pupils with their "styli," on the order of an unnamed prosecutor. The anonymous *passio* in question here, a prose adaptation of Prudentius's poem, **PERISTEPHANON** IX (ed. *CCSL* 126.326–29), can be dated only after Prudentius (ca. 405) and before **BEDE** (ca. 730). He cites the prose *Passio Cassiani* as a precedent for his own **VITA FELICIS** (ed. *PL* 94; *BHL* 2873), itself a prose rendering of **PAULINUS OF NOLA**'s poems on the life of Felix of Nola (**FELIX NOLANUS PRESBYTER**). Bede also summarizes part of the *Passio Cassiani* in his **MARTYROLOGIUM** (BEDA.Mart.; ed. Dubois and Renaud 1976), in which a note, possibly Bede's own, misattributes the *passio* to Prudentius (Quentin 1908 p 68).

GREGORY OF TOURS's knowledge of Cassian's martyrdom, as evidenced in **DE GLORIA MARTYRUM** XLII (ed. *MGH* SRM 1/2.516–17), appears to derive from Prudentius and oral testimony.

Cross (1985b pp 241–42) points to both the *passio* and Bede's *Martyrologium* as the sources of the notice for Cassian in the **OLD ENGLISH MARTYROLOGY** (*Mart*; ed. Kotzor 1981 2.180).

The copy of the *passio* surviving in fragmentary, badly burnt state in the Cotton manuscript listed here (dated first half of the eleventh century by HG) closely matches the text as printed by Mombritius, but seems to have an expanded ending (only partially legible) not recorded in *BHL*.

William of Malmesbury in his *Gesta Regum* (ed. *RS* 90/1.131.24–26) records a story, of uncertain date, that may have been modeled on that of Cassian: namely, that John the Scot was stabbed to death by his pupils while teaching in England during the reign of King Alfred (perhaps confusing John the Scot with John the Saxon, as Stubbs suggests, *RS* 90/1.131 note 1).

Bless-Grabher (1978 pp 75, 78–79) in her survey of the legend's literary history discusses the Bedan material but not the *Old English Martyrology*.

Cassius Narniensis: *BSS* 3.921–22; *DHGE* 11.1409.

Cassius bishop of Narni (536–58, feast day June 29) does not seem to have had any liturgical cult or commemorations in Anglo-Saxon England. English awareness of him may be attributed solely to the influence of **GREGORY THE GREAT**, who wrote about the bishop in his **HOMILIAE XL IN EVANGELIA** XXXVII.ix (ed. *PL* 76.1279–81) and in his **DIALOGI** III.vi and IV.lviii (ed. *SChr* 260.276–78 and 265.194–96). On **WAERFERTH**'s Old English version of the *Dialogi*, where the episodes concerning Cassius are translated in full (ed. *BaP* 5/1.187.10–188.4 and 346.10–21), see the main entry for Gregory the Great. The single anecdote in the **OLD ENGLISH MARTYROLOGY** (*Mart*, B19.ea; ed. Kotzor 1981 2.135–36), however, is based on Gregory's homily alone, as confirmed by Cross (1985a p 107) and Kotzor (1981 2.324–25, reproducing the source text), following earlier scholars. I have found no evidence of Anglo-Saxon knowledge of *BHL* 1638 (a *vita* combining the homily extract with the second of the relevant chapters from *Dialogi*).

Castus et Aemilius: *BLS* 2.365–66; *CPL* 42.

The only English reference to these two North African martyrs of the third century (to whom **AUGUSTINE** devotes **SERMONES** CCLXXXV; ed. *PL* 38.1293–97) is a brief notice in **BEDE**'s **MARTYROLOGIUM** (ed. Dubois and Renaud 1976 p 91.10) mentioning simply their death by fire. Bede identifies his source as **CYPRIAN, DE LAPSIS** 259–66 (ed. *CCSL* 3.228, sourced by Quentin 1908 pp 97–98). The Castus commemorated on May 22 in the tenth-century English calendar (F. Wormald 1934 p 48) in the *Leofric Missal* (see **LITURGY, MASSBOOKS**) is probably a Capuan saint of the same name.

Ceadda (Chad): *BLS* 1.457–59; *BSS* 3.1058–59; *DHGE* 12.33–34; Farmer (1987) p 83.

The center of the cult of Chad, prominent among the small number of saints from the English Midlands, was Lichfield, where he established a bishopric (669) during the late-seventh-century reorganization of the church under Archbishop **THEODORE OF CANTERBURY**. His earlier career had been spent in Northumberland as a monk of Lindisfarne, then as monk and abbot of Lastingham and bishop of York (see the brief account and further references in Farmer 1987 p 83). Chad died in 672 (feast day March 2).

Something of his life and a detailed account of his death are narrated by **BEDE** in his **HISTORIA ECCLESIASTICA** III.xxviii and IV.iii (ed. Colgrave and Mynors 1969 pp 316 and 336–46), from which in turn derive the three main vernacular accounts, two from the later ninth century and a third of uncertain date. Probably the earliest is that in the **OLD ENGLISH MARTYROLOGY** (*Mart*, B19.as; ed. Kotzor 1981 2.27, sourced

289–90), which concentrates on Chad's death and that of his brother, Cedd, bishop of the East Saxons (see Farmer 1987 pp 80–81), and draws mainly on Bede's *Historia* IV.iii (see also Cross 1982d p 24). Somewhat later is the literal translation of the relevant portions of the *Historia* in the **OLD ENGLISH BEDE** (*Bede*, B9.6; ed. *EETS* OS 96 pt 1/2.246.5–28, 260.3–10, and 260.26–272.11). Finally, the Old English *Chad* homily (*LS* 3 [Chad], B3.3.3; ed. Vleeskruyer 1953), which survives only in an early-twelfth-century manuscript from Worcester (NRK 333), is believed to be an early composition, either mid- to late ninth century (Vleeskruyer 1953 p 70) or tenth century (Bately 1988 p 118). The homily (possibly imitating the life of **GUTHLACUS**) opens and closes with material from **SULPICIUS SEVERUS**, **VITA MARTINI** (Vleeskruyer 1953 pp 163, 185), but otherwise it follows the Bedan narrative for the most part. See, however, the recent study by Roberts (2000 pp 435–41), who suggests the homily as we have it may be a twelfth-century compilation, possibly based on "an older homily" that need not be earlier than the later tenth century and whose archaic linguistic features may be attributed to the influence of the *Old English Bede*. In Vleeskruyer's edition (1953 pp 162–85) the two Old English texts are conveniently juxtaposed with Bede's Latin.

For later lives of Chad, see *BHL* 1716–17.

Ceolfridus, vita [ANON.Vit.Ceolfrid.]: *BHL* 1726; *CPL* 1377; *SEHI* 64. ed.: Plummer 1896 1.388–404.

MSS London, BL Harley 3020: HG 433.
Lists none.
A-S Vers BEDA.Hist.abb. 364–87.
Quots/Cits see below.
Refs none.

Traditionally regarded as the composition of an anonymous monk of Wearmouth-Jarrow, the *Vita Ceolfridi* mainly recounts the life of Ceolfrith (feast day September 25), second abbot of the monastery of

Wearmouth-Jarrow, who succeeded BENEDICTUS BISCOPUS (whose life is also commemorated in the *Vita Ceolfridi*) in 690. Ceolfrith resigned his abbacy in 716 in order to make a final pilgrimage to Rome, taking with him one of the three copies of the Vulgate BIBLE made at Wearmouth-Jarrow from a copy brought from Rome earlier by Benedict Biscop. Ceolfrith died en route at Langres. His remains were eventually returned to Northumberland, but they were removed to Glastonbury after the Danish invasions (Rollason 1989a p 152). His feast day is graded in the *Bosworth Psalter* calendar (ca. 1008; F. Wormald 1934 p 66; see also LITURGY, PSALTERS). The Bible, evidently intended as a gift to the Pope, found its way to Lombardy and is now, as the Codex Amiatinus, in the Bibliotheca Laurentiana in Florence.

The life was used by Milred, bishop of Worcester, in the later eighth century. From it he copied into his collection of verses the dedicatory inscription in the Codex Amiatinus. See Sims-Williams (1990 pp 182 and 348, note 84) and Lapidge (1975b pp 806–07).

J. McClure (1984) has argued, on grounds of style, context, and contents, that the *Vita Ceolfridi* was in fact written by BEDE himself. That it is the chief source for his own account of Ceolfrith and the events of 716 in HISTORIA ABBATUM (BEDA.Hist.abb.; ed. Plummer 1896 vol 1) is widely accepted. Kotzor regards the notice for Ceolfrith in the OLD ENGLISH MARTYROLOGY (*Mart*, B19.hm; ed. Kotzor 1981 2.219–20, sourced 355–56) as dependent on Bede's *Historia abbatum* rather than on the *Vita Ceolfridi*.

On the Harley manuscript, see above, the entry for Benedict Biscop. For an English translation of the life of Ceolfrith, with further references, see *EHD* 155. See also Berschin (1986–91 2.284–89) on the work in the context of Bede's hagiography.

Chad. See CEADDA.

Chione. See AGAPE, CHIONIA, ET IRENE.

Christina, passio [ANON.Pas.Christin.1d]: *BHL* 1751; *BLS* 3.173–74; *BSS* 4.330–32; *DHGE* 12.774.
ed.: *AS* Iul. 5.524–28.
MSS – Lists none.
A-S Vers ALDH.Pros.uirg. 300.15, 300.24–301.20.
Quots/Cits – Refs none.

Christina, whose portrait is among those in the procession of virgins in the sixth-century frescoes of Sant'Apollinare Nuovo, Ravenna, may have been a genuine martyr of Bolsena (Tuscany), but her identity became confused with a more dubious Christina of Tyre (Phoenicia). The elaborate and sensational *passio* (apparently based on a Greek original: Siegmund 1949 p 231) exists in numerous versions, all relating the same basic story and frequently sharing the same language but differing in details of substance and phrasing and in additions and omissions. Some early medieval manuscripts containing variant versions are listed by Siegmund (1949 p 231; see next entry). The climax of Christina's story is the attempt of her father (Urbanus), after various other bizarre tortures, to drown her at sea as a punishment for her militant Christianity and stubborn virginity.

Christina's legend appears to have been known to both the early and later Anglo-Saxons, and the puzzling variety of her feast days in the Anglo-Saxons' calendars testifies perhaps to the variety of the sources of their veneration of her (Ortenberg 1992 pp 120–21 lists July 17, 19, and 24 as Christina's English feast days; see also October 5 in F. Wormald 1934 p 53). The Bollandists in *BHL* originally listed ten variant versions of Passio 1, to which Cross and Tuplin (1980), after surveying early manuscripts, have added another, *BHL* 1748b (see next entry). The Anglo-Saxons appear to have known at least three variant versions, discussed in this and the next two entries in the chronological order suggested by the Anglo-Saxon evidence rather than the order adopted in *BHL*.

Ehwald (*MGH* AA 15.301) identifies the version edited in *AS* as the likely source of **ALDHELM**'s account, which occurs only in his prose DE VIRGINITATE (ALDH.Pros.uirg.; ed. *MGH* AA 15). In addition to

Ehwald's list of echoes, see also Aldhelm's allusion (301.16–17) to the "Marsi" (*Passio Christinae* 527b.40). Aldhelm's apparent dependence on this version attests to its early currency. For the other versions known in England, see the next two entries.

The study of the Christina cult and legend by Zucconi, which was not available to us, is apparently a misguided attempt to find historical substance in the *passio* itself. See Halkin's review (1980b). For other literature, see the reference sources cited above (headnote).

Christina, passio [ANON.Pas.Christin.1b *bis*]: *BHL* 1748b.
ed.: Cross and Tuplin 1980 pp 173–87.

MSS – Lists none.
A-S Vers Mart (B19.es).
Quots/Cits – Refs none.

Less clearly affiliated to the printed editions is the source of the ample notice for Christina (July 19) in the ninth-century **OLD ENGLISH MARTYROLOGY** (*Mart*; ed. Kotzor 1981 2.152–53). Cross and Tuplin (1980), who have surveyed numerous early manuscripts of the *Passio Christinae*, first identified the version listed here (*BHL* 1748b). They regard it as the variant closest to, but not identical with, the Old English martyrologist's source. They publish the first edition of this version from a ninth-century German copy, now in London, that is closely related to Passio 1b, *BHL* 1748, also printed by Cross and Tuplin from early manuscripts in Turin and Zurich. They suggest (p 164) that the Old English martyrologist may have made use of **ALDHELM**'s account in places (see previous entry).

Christina, passio [ANON.Pas.Christin.1i]: *BHL* 1756.
ed.: unpublished.

MSS Cambridge, Corpus Christi College 9: HG 36.
Lists – Refs none.

At the end of the Anglo-Saxon period another variant version of the *Passio Christinae*, *BHL* 1756, was known in England, as represented in the Cambridge portion of the **COTTON-CORPUS LEGENDARY** (Jackson and Lapidge 1996 p 143), where it is one of the group of texts out of normal calendar order among a disorderly group of December saints at the end of the manuscript, but with the usual feast day July 24. Another copy of the same version, similarly oddly positioned, was formerly in Salisbury, Cathedral Library 222 (Webber 1992 p 157). See Zettel (1979 p 33) for an additional later copy.

Christophorus, passio [ANON.Pas.Christoph.1]: *BHL* 1764; *BLS* 3.184–87; *BSS* 4.349–53.
   ed.: Fábrega Grau 1953–55 2.299–309.

MSS – Lists none.
A-S Vers Mart (B19.cf).
Quots/Cits – Refs none.

One of the best known of medieval Christian saints, Christopher (feast days April 28, July 25) probably was a genuine third-century martyr of Asia Minor, but his legend, originally Greek (*BHG* 309), may have been composed as much as three centuries later (Rosenfeld 1937 pp 8–9). Its fantastic story of his conversion, preaching, sufferings, and martyrdom depicts Christopher as one of the fabled *cynocephali* or dog-headed men (see Lecouteux 1981). The famous episode in which the saint carries the heavy Christ-child across a river is a later medieval development, unknown in our period.

The occurrence of several distinctive Latin versions of the *passio* in early medieval legendaries (Siegmund 1949 p 232) indicates the complex textual tradition that the legend had developed in Latin by the eighth or ninth century. Rosenfeld (1937 pp 357–65) has distinguished two main branches: the "eastern" (closest to the Greek, Syriac, and other oriental versions), corresponding to the Bollandists' Passio 1 and Passio 2 (*BHL* 1764, 1765); and the "western," which comprises the numerous variants of Passio 3 (*BHL* 1766 and higher numbers). Besides various differences of content and language, the two main branches also reflect different traditions as to the saint's feast day: the Eastern date is April 28, the Western July 25. For the Anglo-Saxons' knowledge of Rosenfeld's Western tradition, see next entry.

The Bollandists' Passio 1, from Rosenfeld's Eastern branch of the Christopher tradition, was evidently known outside the Christian orient, not only in Spain but also in England and Ireland, and elsewhere in the West (Ortenberg 1992 p 121). Rosenfeld (1937 p 96) and Ortenberg may be mistaken in attributing the Syrian feast day, April 28, to **BEDE**'s MARTYROLOGIUM (the short notice, ed. Dubois and Renaud 1976 p 74.3, is only in the post-Bedan amplified copies; see Quentin 1908 p 50), but the *passio*, *BHL* 1764, with the Syrian feast day, was used by the authors of the Irish *Leabhar Breac* (preserved in Middle Irish but believed to be tenth century or earlier) and the **OLD ENGLISH MARTYROLOGY** (*Mart*; ed. Kotzor 1981 2.68–71), as analyzed by Leinbaugh (1985) incorporating information supplied by J. E. Cross. The only other English notice of the April feast day is in an idiosyncratic eleventh-century Nunnaminster calendar (F. Wormald 1934 p 33).

Besides the most recent edition by Fábrega Grau, based on Spanish manuscripts, see that of the Bollandists (1891).

Christophorus, passio [ANON.Pas.Christoph.3a]: *BHL* 1766.
ed.: Rosenfeld 1937 pp 520–29.

MSS ?Paris, Bibliothèque Nationale lat. 5574: HG 885.5.
Lists none.
A-S Vers ?*LS* 4 (Christopher, B3.3.4).
Quots/Cits – Refs none.

Among the later Anglo-Saxons, Christopher's Western calendar date (July 25) is generally observed and the Western branch of the *Passio Christophori* is represented in the Paris manuscript (Avril and Stirnemann 1987 p 11; Clayton and Magennis 1994 pp 95–96, and the review by Biggs 1996a). This text, which lacks a leaf between folios 1 and 2, is unedited. Although its *incipit* and *explicit* match *BHL* 1770 (Passio 3c), a cursory examination of the opening passages reveals numerous variant readings in common with *BHL* 1766, especially as represented in the *AS* edition and a Turin manuscript (eighth/ninth century) collated by Rosenfeld in his edition. The Old English prose *Christopher* (*LS* 4; ed. *EETS OS* 161.68–76), extant in two incomplete recensions, has not been thoroughly sourced (Orchard 1995 p 14), but Rypins in his edition points implicitly to *BHL* 1766 by partially reprinting the *AS* text (*EETS OS* 161.108–10). Some variants in the Paris manuscript, and in the Turin manuscript collated by Rosenfeld, also seem significant.

Sisam (1953 pp 69–70) speculates that the Old English version was composed in the mid-tenth century to promote the cult of Christopher's relics. For example, Christopher figures in the Exeter List of Relics, supposedly donated by King Athelstan (*Rec* 10.8, B16.10.8; ed. Förster 1943 p 112; Conner 1993a pp 180, 195, and 203).

In the absence of a comprehensive critical edition of Passio 3, the preferred edition here is that of Rosenfeld, especially important for the Turin manuscript's variants, although the Bollandists' edition (*AS* Iul. 6.146–49) is still valuable.

For a stimulating discussion of the Old English Christopher texts, especially in relation to the monsters in the *Beowulf* manuscript, see Orchard (1995 pp 12–18). On the literary artistry of the Old English version, see Frederick (1989). We have not seen the unpublished dissertation by Pickles (1971; see Orchard 1995 p 12 note 73).

Chrysanthus et Daria, passio [ANON.Pas.Chrysanth.Dar.]: *BHL* 1787; *BLS* 4.196–97; *BSS* 4.300–06; *CPL* 1636 (note); *DACL* 3.1560–68.
 ed.: Mombritius 1910 1.271–78, 635.

MSS Cambridge, Corpus Christi College 9: HG 36.
Lists none.
A-S Vers 1. ALDH.Carm.uirg. 1123–250.
 2. ALDH.Pros.uirg. 276.23–280.7.
 3. *Mart* (B19.jf).
 4. *ÆLS* Chrysanthus (B1.3.33).
Quots/Cits – Refs none.

As with many of the Roman saints, there are grounds for accepting Chrysanthus and Daria (feast day varies; see below), and some of the minor figures in their saga, as genuine martyrs who may well have been executed in one of the sand pits known to have existed near the New Salarian Way, ca. 257 during the reign of the emperor Valerian (rather than that of Numerianus almost thirty years later, as their legend asserts: *DACL* 3.1567). The largely fictional *passio* was known to **GREGORY OF TOURS**, DE GLORIA MARTYRUM XXXVII, "ut historia passionis declarat" (*MGH* SRM 1/2.511.32). The Greek text *BHG* 313 (printed in parallel with the Latin in *AS* Oct. 11.469–87) now appears to be a translation of the Latin, not vice-versa (Noret 1972; Siegmund 1949 p 198).

No study of the manuscripts and recensions of the *passio* appears to have been done, and thus the affiliations of the sole pre-1100 English copy, in the Cambridge manuscript of the **COTTON-CORPUS LEGENDARY**, are uncertain (its variant readings show more affinity with the text printed by Mombritius than with that in *AS*). The text has been emended in places, obscuring some of its original readings. A later copy, mentioned by Zettel (1979 p 32), is in Hereford, Cathedral Library P.VII.6 (see below), which is consulted by Noret (1972 p 111) for variants.

For **ALDHELM**'s use of specific passages from the *passio*, in his verse and prose DE VIRGINITATE (ALDH.Carm.uirg., Pros.uirg.; ed. *MGH* AA 15), see Ehwald's source notes in his edition (*MGH* AA 15.276–80). Regarding the account in the **OLD ENGLISH MARTYROLOGY** (*Mart*; ed. Kotzor 1981 2.258–59), Kotzor notes that the martyrologist depends on Aldhelm as well as on the *passio* (2.372; see also Cross 1985b p 231).

Zettel (1979 pp 258–59) confirms and corrects C. Loomis's sourcing (1931 p 6) of **ÆLFRIC**'s version of the legend in LIVES OF SAINTS (*ÆLS*; ed. *EETS* OS 94 and 114) detecting in Hereford, Cathedral Library P.VII.6 a slightly more faithful witness to Ælfric's source than either the printed texts or the copy in the Cambridge manuscript. Zettel (1979 p 258 note 164) also points out that Ælfric appears to have made use of the opening lines of the Latin prologue for his own lines 341–45. His choice of the legend of Chrysanthus and Daria for the *Lives of Saints* may have been influenced by Aldhelm's extravagant tributes to the two virgin spouses, whose feast day is not common in late Anglo-Saxon calendars.

Among the infrequent calendar references, there is some variety as to the date of the saints' feast day. In the Cambridge copy of the *passio*, no feast day is mentioned, as pointed out by Jackson and Lapidge (1996 pp 142–43), who tentatively suggest November 29 is meant, pointing to the calendar in the *Leofric Missal* (see **LITURGY, MASSBOOKS**, and F. Wormald 1934 p 54; the same date is given in Skeat's edition of Ælfric's *Lives of Saints*, ed. *EETS* OS 94 and 114 p 378). December 1 (as in **ADO**'s ninth-century martyrology, ed. *PL* 123.407–08), however, is the date in the Worcester calendar in the Cambridge manuscript (F. Wormald 1934 p 237; see also pp 125 and 167) and is implied by the position of the text in the Hereford manuscript (Bannister 1927 p 174). October 23 appears in an earlier calendar (F. Wormald 1934 p 25).

On the virgin spouse theme, see the references above in the entry for CAECILIA.

Chrysogonus, passio [ANON.Pas.Chrysog.]: *BHL* 1795; *BLS* 4.418–19; *BSS* 4.306–08; *CPL* 2163; *DHGE* 12.786.

Chrysogonus of Rome (feast day November 24) will have been merely the founder of a church, *titulus Chrysogoni*, on the site of the present basilica, probably in the third century, but by the early sixth century he is confused or conflated with a martyr of Aquileia with the same name. Hence the need to provide a legend linking the titular Roman saint to Aquileia, as in the *Passio S. Chrysogoni*, which, while sometimes appearing separately, properly forms chapters 2–9 (*BHL* 1795; ed. Delehaye 1936 pp 222–28) of the *passio* of **ANASTASIA** (another titular founder converted into a saint). Here Chrysogonus is said to have been Anastasia's Roman tutor and confessor. See the Anastasia entry for manuscript information and further references.

Chrysogonus, who is one of the saints of the Canon of the Mass and whose feast day invariably appears in later Anglo-Saxon calendars, has separate notices, dependent on the *Passio*, in both **BEDE**'s

MARTYROLOGIUM (ed. Dubois and Renaud 1976 p 213.2–4) and the OLD ENGLISH MARTYROLOGY (*Mart*, B19.jd; ed. Kotzor 1981 2.257). On the brief notice in Bede, see Quentin (1908 p 58). The cult and literature are studied by Delehaye (1936 pp 151–71) and Kennedy (1938 pp 128–30).

Cirycus et Iulitta, passio [ANON.Pas.Ciryc.Iul.]: *BHL* 1802–08; *BSS* 10.1324–28; *BLS* 2.252–54; *DHGE* 13.1168; Farmer (1987) pp 108–09. ed.: *AS* Iun. 3.28–33.

MSS – Lists none (see below).
A-S Vers ?*Mart* (B19.ep).
Quots/Cits – Refs none.

The original Greek legend of Cirycus (Cyricus, Ciricus), a child martyr of Antioch (more accurately, Tarsus), and his mother, Iulitta, was listed as heretical in the **GELASIAN DECREE**. This was probably, as Siegmund thinks (1949 p 217), in response to the recommendations of a certain Theodore, the author of a new blander version (*BHG* 314). This "colorless" revision lies behind the surviving Latin versions. The evidence for English knowledge of the legend is sparse and uncertain. It is interesting that the long notice in the **OLD ENGLISH MARTYROLOGY** (*Mart*; ed. Kotzor 1981 2.148–51) is for July 15, the feast day commonly observed in the East and reflected in the non-narrative short notice in **BEDE**'s **MARTYROLOGIUM** (Dubois and Renaud 1976 p 128; see Quentin 1908 p 52) and one English calendar of the late tenth century (F. Wormald 1934 p 50). The source of the *Old English Martyrology* account, which consists almost entirely of Cirycus's prayer promoting his cult, is problematic according to Cross (1982d pp 32–33 and private communication) and awaits proper identification (see also Hohler 1995 p 224).

No authentically Anglo-Saxon manuscript copies of the *passio* are extant. That in Cambridge, Corpus Christi College 9 (HG 36) is a later (i.e., twelfth-century) addition to the manuscript, not part of the original **COTTON-CORPUS LEGENDARY** (see Jackson and Lapidge 1996 p 133).

Claudius et soc., passio [ANON.Pas.Claud.1a.]: *BHL* 1836; *BLS* 4.293–95; *BSS* 10.1276–304.
ed.: *AS* Nov. 3.765–79.
MSS Paris, Bibliothèque Nationale lat. 10861: HG 898.
Lists none.
A-S Vers ?*Mart* (B19.it).
Quots/Cits – Refs none.

The "Four Crowned Ones" (feast day November 8), who are actually five in their original legend (Claudius, Nicostratus, Symphorianus, Castorius; the fifth is the convert, Simplicius), were reputedly expert stonemasons martyred for their Christianity under Diocletian in the marble quarries of Pannonia; their names were later bestowed on four Roman soldiers whose names had been forgotten but who were martyred under Diocletian in Rome. The original epithet "coronati" is unexplained in the *passio*, or anywhere else. Modern scholarship on the legend and on the nine martyrs it includes has failed to reached a convincing conclusion as to who the original *Coronati* (four or five) really were, where they were martyred, or how old and reliable their *passio* is. Among the more important discussions are those of Delehaye (1936 pp 64–73; 1966 pp 236–46) and Amore (1965), the former arguing for and the latter against the authenticity of the "Pannonian" *passio*. See the useful surveys and bibliographies of Amore in *BSS* and *LTK*. See also Berschin (1986–91 1.69–70).

Certainly in Rome itself, where a cult of four martyrs seems to have been established by the mid-fourth century, according to an early calendar, there was evidently considerable confusion as to who they were. By the mid-fifth century there was a church in their honor on the Coelian Hill (Delehaye 1936 pp 66–70), but the fifth-century *passio* of **SEBASTIANUS** depicts Claudius and Nicostratus as Roman officials (e.g., *AS* Ian. 2.270, §33). The *passio* in its present form, thought to have been composed in the later sixth century (Amore in *BSS* 10.1286 and 1965 p 223), is apparently an attempt to reconcile the conflicting traditions. On the unity of the *passio* (the last two chapters have been regarded as later additions), see Amore (1965 especially pp 235–43).

Anglo-Saxon knowledge of the saints is plentiful, but somewhat puzzling. **BEDE** in his **HISTORIA ECCLESIASTICA** II.vii (ed. Colgrave and Mynors 1969 p 158.1) mentions a Canterbury church, "martyrium," dedicated to the *Coronati Quattuor* before the death of Archbishop Mellitus (624), but Bede's **MARTYROLOGIUM** does not include a narrative for their feast day. The earliest evidence for English knowledge of the text of the *passio* is the important Canterbury passional, the Paris manuscript listed above, of the early ninth century (M. P. Brown 1986), which has the rare colophon identifying the author of the *passio* as "Porphyrius." Delehaye in his edition (see *AS* Nov. 3.750) labels this manuscript "A1," selecting it as the principal witness to the original form of the *passio*. For English witnesses to the more plentiful "B" group, see next entry.

The ninth-century **OLD ENGLISH MARTYROLOGY** (*Mart*; ed. Kotzor 1981 2.248–49) devotes a substantial notice to Claudius and his companions, which has not been properly sourced, although it clearly depends on a *passio* of this type (*EETS* OS 116.xlii). The only detail not represented in the Latin versions is the martyrologist's closing remark (Kotzor 1981 2.249.15–16) that the relics of the saints have worked many miracles, which may be merely a lame substitute for the bewildering final chapter of the *passio* (cf. *AS* Nov. 3.778–79).

The feast of the *Coronati* appears in all later Anglo-Saxon calendars and is marked as of high grade in two of the late tenth century (F. Wormald 1934 pp 54 and 68). **BYRHTFERTH** (in his *Vita Oswaldi, RS* 71/1.463) mentions the feast as important at Ramsey, during his account of a visit by Bishop Oswald (**OSWALDUS WIGORNENSIS**). He describes some of the liturgical and ceremonial features of the occasion (Millinger 1979 p 241) after quoting the appropriate verse (112) of the metrical calendar of Ramsey (ed. Lapidge 1984). ÆLFRIC, for whatever reason, did not include the feast in his **LIVES OF SAINTS** (Lapidge 1996b p 120).

For earlier editions of this version of the *passio*, see *BHL* and *BHL NS*. For literary discussion, see Berschin (1986–91 1.66–74).

Claudius et soc., passio [ANON.Pas.Claud.1b.]: *BHL* 1837.
ed.: Mombritius 1910 1.288–92, 636–37.

MSS Cambridge, Corpus Christi College 9: HG 36.
Lists – Refs none.

The text of the *passio* of the "Four Crowned Ones" surviving from later Anglo-Saxon England in the Cambridge manuscript (part of the mid-eleventh-century Worcester copy of the **COTTON-CORPUS LEGENDARY**) belongs to the textual tradition that Delehaye (*AS* Nov. 3.750) labels "B," corresponding to the text as printed by Mombritius. For another similar but later copy, see Zettel (1979 p 28).

Clemens, passio [ANON.Pas.Clement.]: *BHL* 1848; *BLS* 4.405–08; *BSS* 4.38–48; *CPL* 2177; *DHGE* 12.1089–93.
  ed.: Funk and Diekamp 1913 2.51–81.
MSS Cambridge, Corpus Christi College 9: HG 36.
Lists none.
A-S Vers 1. BEDA.Mart.212.2–8.
  2. *Mart* (B19.jb).
  3. *ÆCHom* I, 37 (B1.1.39) 1–33, 51–127.
Quots/Cits – Refs none.

Clement (feast day November 23), author of a celebrated pastoral letter to the Corinthians, was fourth bishop of Rome, although upholders of apostolic tradition believed him to have been Peter's direct successor as pope: see, for example, **BEDE**'s **HISTORIA ECCLESIASTICA** II.iv (ed. Colgrave and Mynors 1969 p 144.18–21) and **ÆLFRIC**'s **CATHOLIC HOMILIES** I, 37, lines 10–14 (*ÆCHom*; ed. *EETS* SS 17; see also Godden, *EETS* SS 18.309–10). The legend of Clement's martyrdom by drowning while in exile in the Crimea, as recounted in the Latin *passio* (*BHL* 1848), was known at least as early as the 520s (Funk and Diekamp 1913 2.77, note on Theodosius, *De situ terrae sanctae*), but it was apparently unknown to the earlier Church Fathers. On the legend in its historical context, see Delehaye (1936 pp 96–116). An eleventh-century English copy of the *passio*, with the typical appendage of two posthumous miracles (see next entry), is in the Cambridge (originally Worcester)

ACTA SANCTORUM   146

manuscript of the **COTTON-CORPUS LEGENDARY**. Presumably the text lost from Salisbury, Cathedral Library 222 (Webber 1992 p 157) was of the same type.

ALDHELM, in his eulogies of Clement in DE VIRGINITATE (*Carmen* 524–38, *Prosa* 257.3–15; ed. *MGH* AA 15), draws on the **LIBER PONTIFICALIS** and PSEUDO-CLEMENS, RECOGNITIONES (see **APOCRYPHA**, APOCRYPHAL ACTS), but not on the *passio*. Bede, however, in his MARTYROLOGIUM (BEDA.Mart.; ed. Dubois and Renaud 1976) summarizes the *passio* (sourced by Quentin 1908 pp 68–69).

According to Cross (1979 pp 196–98), who compares the notice in the **OLD ENGLISH MARTYROLOGY** (*Mart*; ed. Kotzor 1981 2.255–56) with the edition by Mombritius and several early manuscripts, the martyrologist made use of a text of *BHL* 1848 similar to, but not identical with, that of Mombritius, sharing some variants with unprinted copies. Cross (1979 p 199) finds the martyrologist may also have used the *Liber Pontificalis* (see also next entry for the *Martyrology*'s posthumous miracle).

The tenth-century Old English verse *Menologium* 210–14 (*Men*, A14; ed. *ASPR* 6) briefly mentions Clement's drowning but the source could easily have been a martyrology or oral report.

Most of the first half of Ælfric's homily on Clement in *Catholic Homilies* I draws on the *passio* (for the posthumous miracle, see next entry). It has been sourced by Zettel (1979 pp 162–63, 242–44, superseding Förster 1892 pp 29–31; see also Zettel 1982 pp 34–35). Zettel finds evidence for the importance of Hereford, Cathedral Library P.VII.6 (mid-twelfth century) as a late witness to the text of the Latin legendary used by Ælfric. The Hereford manuscript shares a series of variants with Ælfric's homily that are found neither in the printed texts that he consulted nor in Cambridge, Corpus Christi College 9. Most of these variants, however, occur in the edition of Funk and Diekamp cited here, which Zettel apparently did not consult. One detail, in line 113 of Ælfric's version, "þurh engla þenunge," is also reflected in a Turin manuscript collated by Funk and Diekamp (1913 2.79.11; see also Mombritius 1910 1.344.34–35, as noted by Cross 1979 p 198). It is also perhaps worth noting that the Hereford copy does not, apparently, have the appended posthumous miracles (as far as one can tell from the new catalogue: Mynors and Thomson 1993 p 110, art. 13) that are in the Cotton-Corpus Legendary and would have been in Ælfric's source (see next entry).

Ælfric's homily on Clement omits the bulk of the *passio*'s account of Clement's career in Rome, except for the introductory generalities in lines 1–33 (cf. Funk and Diekamp 1913 2.51–53), inserting instead (33–50) a brief summary of material from the *passio* of Saint Denis of Paris, which Ælfric treats more fully in LIVES OF SAINTS (see DIONISIUS). The second part of the Clement homily (148–280) replaces hagiography with apologetics in order to answer, from mainly biblical sources, the question posed by "men of slight faith" as to why God allows the heathen to torture and kill the saints.

In addition to Clemoes's *EETS* edition cited here, see that of Thorpe (1844–46 1.556–66), which includes a facing translation. Also see now Godden's detailed sourcing and comments, *EETS* SS 18.308–18. Ælfric's homily is also discussed by Lapidge (1991a pp 257–58).

The standard edition of the Latin *passio*, that of Funk and Diekamp (1913), based on three manuscripts of the tenth and eleventh centuries and an early printed edition, gives prominence to the Greek text; but the Latin text appears to have been the original and has much in common with other classic examples of the Roman *passio*, for example, those of AGNES and SEBASTIANUS: see Delehaye (1936 pp 102–04).

Clemens, miracula [ANON.Mir.Clement.]: *BHL* 1855, 1857.
   ed.: Mombritius 1910 1.344–46, 640.
MSS Cambridge, Corpus Christi College 9: HG 36.
Lists none.
A-S Vers 1. ?*Mart* (B19.jb).
   2. *ÆCHom* I, 37 (B1.1.39) 128–47.
Quots/Cits – Refs none.

GREGORY OF TOURS, DE GLORIA MARTYRUM XXXV–XXXVI (*MGH* SRM 1/2.510–11), refers to the account in the *Passio Clementis* of the saint's drowning at sea and adds posthumous miracles said to have occurred at the saint's undersea island shrine (*BHL* 1854) and at a spring near Limoges (*BHL* 1856). The Bollandists distinguish Gregory's accounts of the miracles from those in question here, which represent the work of an anonymous author who rewrote Gregory's by providing them with homiletic prologues and other flourishes. In this revised form, the miracles are often appended to the *Passio Clementis* in the manuscripts: for example, in the Cambridge manuscript of the **COTTON-CORPUS LEGENDARY** (Zettel 1979 p 31; Jackson and Lapidge 1996 p 142). The earliest Anglo-Saxon evidence of knowledge of the miracles, however, at least of the first of them, is in the **OLD ENGLISH MARTYROLOGY** (*Mart*; ed. Kotzor 1981 2.256.7–12), which briefly summarizes the story of the child who slept unharmed in Clement's undersea shrine for a year. The *Martyrology*'s precise source cannot be determined, but, as Cross explains (1979 p 199), it is more likely to have been the later anonymous version (*BHL* 1855), which is coupled with the *passio* in early manuscripts, than Gregory's version. **ÆLFRIC**'s account of the same miracle in his **CATHOLIC HOMILIES** I, 37 (*ÆCHom*; ed. *EETS* SS 17), as Förster showed (1892 pp 30–31), is sufficiently detailed to indicate clearly his dependence on the anonymous *BHL* 1855.

Columba Hiensis: *BSS* 3.126–28; *CPL* 1133–34; Farmer (1987) pp 95–96; *SEHI* 214.

After founding three monasteries in his native Ireland, Columba (Colum-cille, 521–97) came to Pictish Scotland as a missionary monk in 565 and established the famous community on Iona, from which later Irishmen such as Aidan (**AIDANUS**) evangelized Anglo-Saxon Northumberland. There is no clear evidence, however, that the influential life of Columba written by **ADOMNAN**, 688–92, was known to the Anglo-Saxons (see the edition of Anderson and Anderson 1991). Although **BEDE** knew and wrote a précis of Adomnan's **DE LOCIS SANCTIS**, providing extracts in his **HISTORIA ECCLESIASTICA** V.xv–xviii (ed. Colgrave and Mynors 1969 pp 506–12), in his brief account of Columba in *Historia* III.iv (pp 220–24) Bede shows no knowledge of the *vita*, although he was aware that there were written records concerning the saint: "nonulla . . . feruntur scripta haberi" (p 224.3–4).

Similarly Cross (1981e pp 177–78) finds the **OLD ENGLISH MARTYROLOGY** notice for the saint (*Mart*, B19.dj: ed. Kotzor 1981 2.117–18) independent of Adomnan, drawing instead on Bede's *Historia* and on another otherwise unknown tradition for the miracle of the couple who spoke of Columba all night and whose house was spared in a great fire. Thacker (1989 p 112), in view of an episode in the anonymous Life of Cuthbert (see **CUTHBERTUS**, vita), suggests that "Melrose . . . may have possessed an early life of Columba" but not necessarily Adomnan's.

Columba Senonum, passio [ANON.Pas.Columb.Sen.]: *BHL* 1893; *BLS* 4.645; *BSS* 4.103–06; *DACL* 15.1206–07.
ed.: Chastel 1939 pp 325–28.
MSS London, BL Cotton Nero E. i: HG 344.
Lists none.
A-S Vers 1. ?BEDA.Mart.4.11–12.
2. ?*Mart* (B19.h).
Quots/Cits – Refs none.

Columba (feast day December 31) may have been a genuine martyr of Sens in the late third century, and there is early evidence of a developed cult (*AS* Nov. 2/2.18) not only in Sens (where a basilica was built in her name in 620) and elsewhere in Francia but also in Spain, her reputed birth-place. The *passio*, however, is regarded as a synthesis of topoi familiar in written legends of virgin martyrs, including exposure in a brothel and protection by a wild beast. Such episodes in the *Passio Columbae* are borrowed, partly verbatim, from the *passio* of **CHRYSANTHUS ET DARIA** (Van der Straeten 1962 p 116). The oldest version of the *passio* survives in several variant forms, labeled 1a, 1b, 1c by the Bollandists, and numbered *BHL* 1892–94, respectively, all of which are represented in early manuscripts (Van der Straeten 1962 p 116).

The sole Anglo-Saxon manuscript copy listed here, in the Cotton manuscript of the **COTTON-CORPUS LEGENDARY**, has been identified as 1c (*BHL* 1893) by Zettel (1979 p 34) and Jackson and Lapidge (1996 p 144). It is one of a block of texts (near the end of the manuscript) that are out of expected calendar order and formerly part of Cambridge, Corpus Christi College 9. The *passio* is copied by a different scribe from that of the preceding text (SILVESTER), which is in the main hand of the other legendary texts. For a later affiliated English copy, see Zettel (1979 p 34).

The other Anglo-Saxon witnesses have eluded precise sourcing. The notice in BEDE's MARTYROLOGIUM (BEDA.Mart.; ed. Dubois and Renaud 1976) is too brief to classify his source text precisely (Quentin 1908 p 69), and the acephalous notice in one manuscript of the ninth-century OLD ENGLISH MARTYROLOGY (*Mart*; ed. Kotzor 1981 2.9) could be related to either Passio 1a or 1c or an unrecorded version of 1b, according to Cross (1983d), who mentions early medieval manuscript copies as well as printed editions of each of the variant versions.

Chastel's edition, which does not allude to the English manuscript copies, supersedes that of Mombritius (1910 1.370–71 and 645).

Conon, passio [ANON.Pas.Conon.]: *BHL* 1912; *BSS* 4.152; *DHGE* 13.461.

ed.: *AS* Mai. 7.5–7.

MSS   1. London, BL Cotton Nero E. i: HG 344.
2. Salisbury, Cathedral Library 221 (formerly Oxford, Bodleian Library Fell 4): HG 754.5.

Lists – *Refs*   none.

The Syrian Conon (feast day May 29), honored as a martyr of Iconium with his twelve-year-old son, is said to have left his wife and taken his son to live a chaste life as hermit and miracle-worker until arrested, tortured, and eventually martyred by hammer blows, under the emperor Aurelian (270–75). The Bollandists suggest that the Greek *passio* recounting this story (*BHG* 360) was translated into Latin in the ninth century in connection with the veneration of Conon's relics at Acerra, in Campania, Italy. According to Siegmund (1949 p 232), who lists three tenth-century manuscript copies of the Latin *passio*, the earliest witness to its existence is the summary by the martyrologist **ADO** (ca. 870), but **HRABANUS MAURUS**, writing about fifty years earlier, includes a detailed summary of the *passio* (emphasizing the life rather than the martyrdom) in his *Martyrologium*, MAI. 211–37 (ed. *CCCM* 44.48–49). See also Quentin (1908 p 503 note 7).

Conon does not appear to have had any English cult, early or late. We have not seen the study of Caporale (1885).

Constantia. See **CONSTANTINA**.

Constantina: *DACL* 3.2609–15; *DHGE* 13.587.

Constantina, daughter of Constantine the Great, wife of Gallus, dedicated a basilica (before 354, perhaps 326–35) to the memory of **AGNES** and inscribed the dedication stone with some verses in praise of the saint. This much, and an earlier marriage, seem to be historical. Later legend, as narrated in the *Passio Agnetis* (*BHL* 156), has Constantina (here Constantia the virgin) healed of leprosy by praying to Agnes. In the legend of **IOHANNES ET PAULUS** (her eunuch servants), she is instrumental in the conversion of her betrothed, **GALLICANUS**, and his daughters (*BHL* 3236).

BEDE in his **MARTYROLOGIUM** merely mentions Constantina, in his brief account of Iohannes and Paulus (ed. Dubois and Renaud 1976 p 114.3), but **ALDHELM** devotes separate eulogies to her in his **DE VIRGINITATE** (*Carmen* 2051–120, *Prosa* 302.10–303.6; ed. *MGH* AA 15), telling how she aroused the zeal for Christian chastity in the women of Rome, including the daughters of Gallicanus. The verse account is longer, devoting more attention to Gallicanus's Scythian campaign. Aldhelm's editor Ehwald (*MGH* AA 15.302 notes 2–4) identifies the source for the prose and verse accounts as *BHL* 3236 and 3238, but Lapidge and Herren (1979 p 178) are uncertain.

ÆLFRIC, in addition to relating the account of Constantia's vision of Agnes in **LIVES OF SAINTS**, *Agnes* 261–95 (*ÆLS*, B1.3.8; ed. *EETS* OS

76 and 82), also renders the same story as Aldhelm in somewhat more detail in the appended "Alia Sententia," *Agnes* 296–429. For further details, see below, the entry for Iohannes et Paulus.

For an exhaustive account of Constantina's place in the cult and legend of Agnes, see Jubaru (1907 pp 202–67). Additional bibliography is in *DACL* and *DHGE*.

Cornelius, passio [ANON.Pas.Cornel.]: *BHL* 1958; *BLS* 3.560–61; *BSS* 4.182–89; *CPL* 2180; *DHGE* 13.891–94; Farmer (1987) pp 100–01.
ed.: Mombritius 1910 1.373 and 646.

MSS   1. London, BL Harley 3020: HG 433.
       2. ?London, BL Cotton Otho A. xiii: HG 351.
       3. London, BL Cotton Nero E. i: HG 344.
       4. Salisbury, Cathedral Library 222 (formerly Oxford, Bodleian Library Fell 1): HG 754.6.

Lists   none.
A-S Vers   1. BEDA.Mart. 168.7–11.
           2. *Mart* (B19.gy).
Quots/Cits – Refs   none.

The surviving correspondence of the patrician Pope Cornelius (251–53) and **CYPRIAN**, bishop of Carthage (see also **CYPRIANUS CARTHAGENSIS**), attests to their joint role in combatting the Novatian schism that followed the Decian persecution of the mid-third century (see also **EUSEBIUS PAMPHILUS, HISTORIA ECCLESIASTICA** VI.xliii; ed. *GCS* 9/2.615–25). Cornelius appears to have died in exile when the persecution was revived, but his later legend, composed in the late fifth or early sixth century (Kennedy 1938 p 123), asserts that he was tortured and martyred by decapitation, after converting some of his guards and their families, who were martyred with him. He shares the same feast day (September 14) as Cyprian himself, with whom he also shares the distinction of being among the saints of the Canon of the Mass (Kennedy 1938 pp 119–23).

Of the extant Anglo-Saxon copies of his *passio*, the earliest is that from Canterbury (late tenth or early eleventh century) in the second section of the Harley manuscript listed here (see **BENEDICTUS BISCOPUS**). All four manuscripts have the text entitled "Passio brevior" by the Bollandists, *BHL* 1958 (Passio 1a). To judge from a short sample of text, the Harley copy is very similar to, and possibly affiliated with, that in the **COTTON-CORPUS LEGENDARY**, represented here by Cotton Nero E. i and Salisbury 222, but the version in the badly burnt and fragmentary Cotton Otho copy (fols 30–33, new foliation 23v–26) has a different, expanded preamble, apparently adapted from the first few lines of the notice for Cornelius in **LIBER PONTIFICALIS** (Duchesne 1955 1.150). The legible portions of the remainder correspond, with minor variations, to Mombritius's edition.

This *passio* is also the version used by **BEDE**, in his **MARTYROLOGIUM** (BEDA.Mart.; ed. Dubois and Renaud 1976), according to Quentin (1908 p 69). He cites a seventeenth-century edition (Schelstrate 1692–97); this, according to the Bollandists' classification, uses a text similar to that printed by Mombritius. Cross (1979 p 201), in confirming Herzfeld's sourcing of the brief notice in the **OLD ENGLISH MARTYROLOGY** (*Mart*; ed. Kotzor 1981 2.205–06), likewise points out that Mombritius's edition is just as good as the rarer edition of Schelstrate.

Coronati Quattuor. See CLAUDIUS ET SOC.

Cosmas et Damianus, passio [ANON.Pas.Cosm.Dam.1]: *BHL* 1967; *BLS* 3.659–61; *BSS* 4.223–25; *DHGE* 13.930; Farmer (1987) p 101.
ed.: *AS* Sept. 7.471–72.

MSS – Lists none.
A-S Vers ?BEDA.Mart.178.2–6.
Quots/Cits – Refs none.

The cult of Cosmas and Damian (feast day September 27 in Anglo-Saxon England), twin brothers and physicians, supposedly martyred for their faith under Diocletian, originated in Syria. Modern scholarship has found little or no historical basis for their legend, which survives in several *passiones*, but their cult seems genuine. In the West it began at Rome in the early sixth century, promoted by Popes Symacchus and Felix IV (Delehaye 1933a pp 190–91), when a Greek *passio* was rendered into Latin (Siegmund 1949 p 216). They are among the select group of saints mentioned in the Canon of the Mass (Kennedy 1938 pp 137–40). See also **GREGORY OF TOURS, DE GLORIA MARTYRUM** XCVII (ed. *MGH* SRM 1/2.553.34–554.6).

The simplest form of the Latin *passio*, *BHL* 1967 or Passio 1, based on a Greek original *BHG* 378 (Siegmund 1949 p 216), records only the trial and martyrdom of the two saints, indicating briefly at the outset that they were doctors. A more elaborate Greek expansion of the short legend (*BHG* 372) appears in Latin as *BHL* 1970, Passio 3, complete with a prologue, details of the saints' upbringing by their pious Christian mother, Theodota, and some anecdotes of their life as healers, before a rather abrupt transition to the *passio* account. Later in the same work there are further additional anecdotes, mainly in the form of posthumous miracles (including a talking camel). Passio 3 is sometimes entitled "Acta et passio" to reflect the structure of the story. A third version, *BHL* 1969, Passio 2, derives from Passio 3.

All three versions of the legend appear to have been known in Anglo-Saxon England from at least the early eighth century. According to Quentin (1908 p 70), **BEDE**'s brief notice in his **MARTYROLOGIUM** (BEDA.Mart.; ed. Dubois and Renaud 1976) is based on Passio 1, since he mentions none of the material added to the legend in the expanded versions, for which see the next two entries.

Cosmas et Damianus, passio [ANON.Pas.Cosm.Dam.2]: *BHL* 1969. ed.: *AS* Sept. 7.473–74.

MSS – Lists none.
A-S Vers 1. ?ALDH.Carm.uirg. 1071–122.
2. ?ALDH.Pros.uirg. 275.8–276.22.
Quots/Cits – Refs none.

Unlike **BEDE**, **ALDHELM** reveals in his verse and prose **DE VIRGINITATE** (ALDH.Carm.uirg., Pros.uirg.; ed. *MGH* AA 15) some knowledge of the expanded legendary tradition concerning Cosmas and Damian: for example, that their mother was a pious Christian who saw to the twins' education and that they accepted no fees for their medical work. For Aldhelm's source, however, Ehwald in his edition (*MGH* AA 15.275 note 4; also Lapidge and Herren 1979 p 177) points not to the fullest version of this tradition, *BHL* 1970 (see next entry), but to one that the early Bollandists regarded as an abridgement of the latter (*AS* Sept. 7.474 note a). Confusingly this has been classified as Passio 2 in *BHL*, implying it is earlier than the longer version. Although it has Passio 3's introductory account of the saints before their arrest, it suppresses all the more fanciful episodes, which are also lacking in Aldhelm's account. Ehwald, compounding the confusion, refers to this Passio 2 as "Acta Tertia," following the terminology used in the *AS* edition. In the absence of a critical edition or study of the surviving manuscripts, we cannot be sure if Aldhelm actually used such an abridged version, or if, alternatively, the abridged version was inspired by his example.

Cosmas et Damianus, passio [ANON.Pas.Cosm.Dam.3]: *BHL* 1970. ed.: *AS* Sept. 7.474–78.

MSS 1. London, BL Cotton Nero E. i: HG 344.
2. Paris, Bibliothèque Nationale lat. 10861: HG 898.
3. Salisbury, Cathedral Library 222 (formerly Oxford, Bodleian Library Fell 1): HG 754.6.

Lists none.
A-S Vers Mart (B19.hp).
Quots/Cits – Refs none.

According to Herzfeld (*EETS* OS 116.236) and Cross (1983b), this longer version of the legend of Cosmas and Damian, which alone has the story of the talking camel that insisted the brothers be buried together, was used by the author of the ninth-century **OLD ENGLISH MARTYROLOGY** (*Mart*; ed. Kotzor 1981 2.221–23). The printed edition, however, as so often, is not a reliable guide to the early medieval text used by the martyrologist. In more than one instance Cross, who cites several ninth-century manuscripts, finds the Paris manuscript listed above (from Christ Church, Canterbury, early ninth century: see M. P. Brown 1986) closer to the Old English than the version printed in *AS*. Cross argues that also available to the martyrologist may have been another text, similar to a ninth-century copy in Zurich, from which he took the information that Palladia's gift to Damian was three eggs. The Zurich text is of the Passio 3 type but with numerous omissions and variant readings. Cross also detects the martyrologist's occasional use of **ALDHELM**'s summary of the legend.

The textual relationship between the affiliated copies in the eleventh-century London and Salisbury manuscripts (Zettel 1979 p 26 note 79) and the earlier Paris manuscript has not been studied.

For some information on the liturgical cult of Cosmas and Damian in Anglo-Saxon England, where their feast day was of the second highest rank and celebrated with proper masses, see Ortenberg (1992 p 162). For recent work on the cult and iconography of these saints, see Julien and Ledermann (1985).

Crispinus et Crispinianus, passio [ANON.Pas.Crispin.Crispinian.]: *BHL* 1990; *BLS* 4.197–98; *BSS* 4.313–18; *DHGE* 13.1022.
ed.: *AS* Oct. 11.535–37.
MSS Cambridge, Corpus Christi College 9: HG 36.
Lists – Refs none.

The initially obscure cult of these Roman saints (Delehaye 1936 pp 128–30) developed more vigorously at Soissons, to which their relics were taken in the sixth century (feast day October 25). Their later *passio* (pre-ninth century, since it was known to the early-ninth-century Lyons martyrologist: Quentin 1908 pp 136, 154) claims that they came to Soissons from Rome and lived as shoemakers while preaching the Christian faith until their arrest and martyrdom. Despite their later English fame, there is little evidence among the Anglo-Saxons of active devotion to Crispin and his companion, except for the text in the eleventh-century Cambridge copy of the **COTTON-CORPUS LEGENDARY** (Worcester provenance; a copy was also formerly in Salisbury, Cathedral Library 222: Webber 1992 p 157). Zettel (1979 p 28) confirms that the text in the Cambridge manuscript (and a later copy) is *BHL* 1990, but varies in some details.

Cuthbertus, vita [ANON.Vit.Cuthb.]: *BHL* 2019; *BLS* 1.637–41; *BSS* 4.413; *CPL* 1379; *DHGE* 13.1118–20; Farmer (1987) pp 104–06. ed.: Colgrave 1940 pp 60–138.

MSS Arras, Bibliothèque Municipale 1029 (812): HG 781.
Lists Saewold: ML 8.19 (= Arras 1029).
A-S Vers 1. BEDA.Vit.Cuth.metr.
  2. BEDA.Vit.Cuth.pr. 143–206.
Quots/Cits 1. Vita Cuthberti 60.11–62.13, 62.24–64.1: STEPH.HRYP. Vit.Wilfr. 2.5–20; see below.
  2. ?*ÆCHom* II, 10 (B1.2.11): see below.
  3. Vita Cuthberti 68.17–18, 25: ANON.Hist.Cuth. 196.9–11, 18.
Refs BEDA.Hist.eccles. 6.12–14.

Cuthbert (ca. 634–87, feast day March 20) was a Northumbrian monk and prior, first of Melrose abbey, then of Lindisfarne, also bishop of Lindisfarne and hermit of Farne Island, where he died. He was undoubtedly one of the most important native English saints in the eyes of **BEDE** and later generations of Anglo-Saxons and modern scholars. While his cult was strongest in the north of England, first at Lindisfarne, then Chester-le-Street, and finally Durham, Cuthbert is said to have achieved the status of "national saint" in the tenth century when the West Saxons showed a great deal of interest in his cult and hagiography (Rollason 1989a pp 144–52, 1989b; Dumville 1992 p 109).

Of the four eighth-century accounts of his life, three are the work of Bede. His metrical **VITA CUTHBERTI**, *BHL* 2020 (BEDA.Vit.Cuth.metr.; ed. Jaager 1935), was first composed ca. 705, then revised ca. 720, as

Lapidge has argued (1989a pp 84–85). His prose *vita*, BHL 2021 (BEDA. Vit.Cuth.pr.; ed. Colgrave 1940), was produced ca. 721; an epitome of these is in Bede's HISTORIA ECCLESIASTICA IV.xxvii–xxx (ed. Colgrave and Mynors 1969 pp 430–44), which was completed ca. 731. The main source of Bede's two *Vitae Cuthberti*, however, is the anonymous life, *BHL* 2019, while from the tenth and eleventh centuries another anonymous compilation, the *Historia de sancto Cuthberto*, *BHL* 2024–25, witnesses to the later development of Cuthbert's cult. The eighth-century anonymous *vita* is the subject of the present entry; for the later *Historia*, see the next entry. For further information on Bede's works on Cuthbert, see the main entry on Bede.

The earliest *Vita Cuthberti* was composed by a monk (or monks) of Lindisfarne ca. 699–705. Bede only acknowledges once, in the preface to his *Historia ecclesiastica*, his indebtedness to this earlier work, but while Bede's lives certainly overshadowed it, the anonymous life was not neglected completely. Stephen of Ripon (Eddius Stephanus) in his life of WILFRIDUS (STEPH.HRYP.Vit.Wilfr.; ed. Colgrave 1927), drew on the anonymous life extensively, incorporating lengthy passages without acknowledgement. In addition to a long passage in Stephen's prologue, drawn from the prologue and preface of the anonymous Cuthbert life, as cited above, see *Vita Wilfridi* VI and XI (Colgrave 1927 pp 14.2–4, 24.10–22), which borrow from *Vita Cuthberti* II.ii and IV.i, respectively (Colgrave 1940 pp 76.12–14, 110.27–112.15); see also Thacker (1976 pp 264–65, and 1989 p 117 note 109).

According to Colgrave (1940 p 27) an eleventh-century English scribe added some proper names from the anonymous *vita* as glosses in a tenth-century manuscript of Bede's prose life (London, BL Cotton Vitellius A. xix: HG 401). See also the marginal note "Iuxta flumen Ledir" in Colgrave's manuscripts C3 and O3 (1940 pp 164–65 note 29), both from Durham; this phrase seems to have been copied from a text of the anonymous *Vita Cuthberti* I.v (p 68.16–17).

While no manuscript copies of the work have surfaced in English collections, Colgrave in his edition (pp 17–20) lists seven now in Continental libraries, one of which, the Arras manuscript listed here (late tenth or early eleventh century), is believed to be one of the English books donated to Saint-Vaast, Arras, by Abbot Saewold, formerly of Bath, in the mid-eleventh century. Bullough (1998) describes and collates a ninth-century Salzburg manuscript with insular traits, which was not known to Colgrave. Although Förster (1892 pp 35–37) speaks only of Bede's prose and verse lives as the sources of ÆLFRIC's homily on Cuthbert in CATHOLIC HOMILIES II, 10 (*ÆCHom*, B1.2.11; ed. *EETS* SS 5), there is some textual evidence to suggest that Ælfric had a text of the anonymous *vita* and made occasional use of it. For example, Ælfric's phrase "mid gesibsumum wordum swæslice grette" in lines 33–34 (ed. *EETS* SS 5.82) is closer to "salutansque uerbis pacificis" from the anonymous *Vita Cuthberti* I.iv (ed. Colgrave 1940 p 66.24) than to the equivalent "mansueto illum saluteret alloquio" from Bede's *Vita Cuthberti* II (p 160.2–3). While Ælfric's "swaeslice" seems to depend on Bede's "mansueto," the phrase "gesibsumum wordum" echoes the "uerbis pacificis" in the anonymous life. Similarly, in the same episode of Ælfric's version, line 30, "under sunnanbeame" is closer to "in solis ardore" in the anonymous life (ed. Colgrave 1940 p 66.20) than to Bede's "sub diuo" (p 158.27). Compare also Ælfric's line 49, "heofenas opene" (*EETS* SS 5.82), with the anonymous *vita* I.v, "coelo aperto" (ed. Colgrave 1940 p 68.20–21). A more detailed sourcing of the Old English version in relation to the anonymous *vita* and Bede might yield further examples. For a contrasting view of the sources of Ælfric's homily on Cuthbert, see Blokhuis (1996; I am grateful to Malcolm Godden for this reference; see now his detailed sourcing of the homily, *EETS* SS 18.412–29).

Another reputedly tenth-century work (see next entry), the anonymous *Historia de sancto Cuthberto* (*BHL* 2024–25, ed. *RS* 75/1.196–214) chapter II, appears to echo some phrases from *Vita Cuthberti* I.v (cited above, headnote), although Arnold in his edition (*RS* 75/1.196.17) refers only to Bede's prose life, chapter IV (ed. Colgrave 1940 pp 164–66), as the episode's source. The phrase "in coelum deferri" in the *Historia* (*RS* 75/1.196.18) corresponds to a variant from the Paris manuscript of the anonymous *Vita Cuthberti* (Colgrave 1940 p 69 note 36). It is possible, however, that by this time monastic communities and larger churches had liturgical texts that combined material from both Bede and the anonymous life (see also below). For other Anglo-Saxon evidence of such mixed texts, see **AIDANUS**.

On Bede's adaptations of the anonymous life, see most recently Abraham (1976), Berschin (1986–91 2.266–84, and 1989), and Stancliffe (1989). On the attribution of the anonymous *vita* to other contemporaries of Bede, see *CPL* 1342, 1379. The *Historia*'s use of the anonymous *vita* has been noted independently by Johnson-South (1990). He cautions, however, that the eleventh-century compiler of the extant *Historia* was apparently drawing on older intermediate sources, which may have been responsible for the actual borrowings from the anonymous life and Bede's.

On the cult of Cuthbert in the Anglo-Saxon period, see Rollason (1989a pp 104–09, 144–52, and passim). For an important analysis of Ælfric's handling of the Cuthbert legend, see Godden (1996 pp 276–82).

Cuthbertus, historia [ANON.Hist.Cuthb.]: *BHL* 2024.
ed.: *RS* 75/1.196–214.

MSS Oxford, Bodleian Library Bodley 596 (*SC* 2376): HG 586.
Lists – A-S Vers none.
Quots/Cits see below.
Refs none.

Believed to have been composed at Chester-le-Street, the *Historia de sancto Cuthberto* deals briefly with the life of Cuthbert but is largely concerned with narrating the posthumous fortunes of his relics and their guardians up to ca. 945, including the growth of the saint's landed "patrocinium" and relations with friendly West Saxon kings and hostile Vikings (in the *Historia Regum* generally associated with the name of Simeon of Durham, the work is described, erroneously if understandably, as a cartulary: *RS* 75/1.72). Several posthumous miracles are included, which later formed the nucleus of the large post-Conquest miracle collections compiled at Durham (Colgrave 1950 pp 307–08).

The earliest surviving manuscript, listed here, which also contains a copy of **BEDE**'s prose life of Cuthbert (*BHL* 2021), is a Canterbury,

St Augustine's, manuscript dated by HG around the turn of the eleventh century (see also Colgrave 1940 pp 24–25; 1950 p 307; Simpson 1989 pp 397–98). Neither the date of composition nor the internal makeup of the work is settled, but a recently cogent argument (Simpson 1989, endorsed Rollason 1989a pp 144–46 and Johnson-South 1991 pp 619–21) is that sections 1–28 of Arnold's edition, including an episode involving Cuthbert and King Alfred (*RS* 75/1.204.11–205.24), were probably composed in the mid-tenth century, while the remaining sections were added in the eleventh amid some general revision. Johnson-South and Simpson apparently arrived independently at quite similar views as to the political context of the *Historia*; Johnson-South in particular (1991 pp 619–21) regards the Alfred/Cuthbert episode as a product of the West Saxon royal court in the mid-tenth century. Simpson (1989 pp 409–10) supports her argument for the mid-tenth-century date of the *Historia* with reference to the brief account of the same episode in the *Historia Regum*, in the early portion now attributed to **BYRHTFERTH** of Ramsey, since Byrhtferth's source in this instance seems to be the *Historia*. Johnson-South (1991), who seems to be unaware of the Byrhtferth attribution, posits a more complicated origin for the Alfred/Cuthbert story, which we have no space to discuss here.

Simpson also suggests that the Alfred/Cuthbert episode in the anonymous *Historia* was the model for a comparable incident in the mid-eleventh-century *Vita Prima S. Neoti* chapters XI–XVI (Dumville and Lapidge 1985 pp 124–32: see **NEOTUS**), although Lapidge refers to oral tradition as the source of the Neot/Alfred story (Dumville and Lapidge 1985 p cv).

In addition to the studies, cited above, by Colgrave, Johnson-South, Rollason, and Simpson, see the basic papers of Craster (1925 and 1954), and also that of Gransden on the work in the context of Durham historiography (1974 pp 76–77).

Cyprianus Carthaginensis, acta proconsularia [ANON.Act.Cypr.1.a.I]: *BHL* 2038; *BLS* 3.561–67; *BSS* 3.1260–74; *CPL* 53; *DHGE* 13.1149–60.
   ed.: Reitzenstein 1913 pp 12–18.

MSS 1. London, BL Cotton Nero E. i: HG 344.
2. Salisbury, Cathedral Library 222 (formerly Oxford, Bodleian Library Fell 1): HG 754.6.
Lists none.
A-S Vers 1. ?BEDA.Mart.168.20–23.
2. ?*Mart* (B19.gz).
Quots/Cits – Refs none.

The third-century work known to scholars as the "Acta proconsularia" (*BHL* 2037–38, 2039) purports to record the official court proceedings that led to the exile and subsequent martyrdom of **CYPRIAN**, bishop of Carthage (248–58, feast day September 14), the Christian apologist and theologian executed under the emperor Valerian. Although well known through his letters and theological tracts, and through a late-third-century biography (that of "Pontius," *BHL* 2041: see Cyprianus Carthaginensis, vita), Cyprian's life and death were early subject to legendary embellishment and confusion; for example, in **PRUDENTIUS, PERISTEPHANON** XIII (*CPL* 1443; ed. *CCSL* 126), who attributes to Cyprian of Carthage the necromantic exploits of the fictitious Cyprian of Antioch (**CYPRIANUS ET IUSTINA**). **AUGUSTINE**, on the other hand, in his sermons on Cyprian's feast day (especially **SERMONES** CCCIX, *PL* 38.1410–12) appears to draw only on the trial portions of the *acta* under consideration here.

What follows is merely a sketch, as brief as possible, of the complicated textual tradition of Cyprian's *acta* and the accompanying scholarly debate.

Delehaye (1966 pp 62–69) regards the *acta* as partly authentic, the result of an effort to present the original proconsular documents as a coherent narrative, composed shortly after Cyprian's death in 258 (see also Berschin 1986–91 1.338). Delehaye (1966 p 75) also argues (following Reitzenstein 1913 and Corssen 1914) that the complete *acta* was known, soon after Cyprian's death, to "Pontius," author of the formal *vita* (*BHL* 2041).

Following Reitzenstein (1913 p 4), Delehaye divides the proconsular *acta* into three parts: 1, the first trial, before the proconsul Paternus, resulting in Cyprian's exile; 2, the second trial a while later, before proconsul Galerius Maximus, resulting in the death sentence; 3, the execution itself and burial. Part 1 existed separately during Cyprian's own lifetime (Delehaye 1966 p 62; Berschin 1986–91 1.58); part 2 seems to have been composed independently shortly after his death, with or, more likely, without part 3. Part 1, however, survives in the manuscripts usually in combination with parts 2 and 3, to which it is linked, in different recensions, by more than one kind of transitional passage. This "complete" version (*BHL* 2037, variant 2038), designated "A" by Delehaye, is represented in the early printed editions (frequently in inferior recensions) and is critically edited by Reitzenstein (1913 pp 12–18; manuscripts listed on p 10) and others (see *BHL NS* p 235). It is found in passionals and legendaries from the early Middle Ages on. There are numerous variant versions, particularly of the widespread *BHL* 2038, which initially dates the narrative with reference to the consuls Tuscus and Bassus, rather than the emperor Valerianus as in *BHL* 2037 (Reitzenstein 1913 pp 18–19).

The A version appears to be of somewhat later origin, and its manuscripts of lesser historical authority, however, than the "incomplete" or "B" version (*BHL* 2039), as discussed and edited by Reitzenstein (1913 pp 20–22; manuscripts on pp 6–7); B is usually found among the manuscript copies of Cyprian's letters. It consisted originally, Reitzenstein argues, of part 2 only (the second trial resulting in the sentence of death), and it survives in many manuscripts in this form, but it is occasionally followed by the *passio* portion (part 3) appended from a copy of the A version (Reitzenstein 1913 p 22; 1919 p 179).

The precise chronology of all this is unclear, but it appears that both the A and B versions originated in the late third century and were well known to the fourth-century Fathers. The *Acta Cypriani* is thus among the very oldest hagiographical works known to the Anglo-Saxons. The surviving evidence suggests that, with one exception (see next entry), their knowledge was limited to the A version.

BEDE, in Quentin's opinion (1908 p 70), appears to have known the longer A version, although his brief **MARTYROLOGIUM** notice (BEDA. Mart.; ed. Dubois and Renaud 1976) is not taken into account by Reitzenstein or Delehaye. It is unclear whether Bede's source corresponded to *BHL* 2037 or 2038. Among Quentin's evidence for Bede's knowledge of the *acta* is his statement (Dubois and Renaud 1976 p 168.22) of the long duration of Cyprian's exile (cf. *CSEL* 3/3.CXI.13). Bede thus supplies early witness to a controversial portion of the A text, the "Verbindungsstück" linking part 1 to part 2 in the early printed editions, which Reitzenstein excludes from his edition, dismissing it as a late medieval or "humanist" interpolation (1913 p 11). Against this view, see Delehaye (1966 pp 64–65).

Cross (1985a pp 107–08 note 4) confirms Herzfeld's statement (*EETS* OS 116.xii) that the ninth-century **OLD ENGLISH MARTYROLOGY** (*Mart*; ed. Kotzor 1981 2.206–07) draws on the A version of the *acta* (*BHL* 2037 or 2038). Also confirmed by Cross is the *Martyrology*'s additional dependence, for one portion of the notice (Kotzor 1981 2.207.1–3), on Augustine, Sermones CCCIX (*PL* 38.1411.19–30; see also Cross 1982d p 31). In addition Cross suggests the *Martyrology*'s use of a sermon printed among those of **FULGENTIUS OF RUSPE** in Migne's edition (*PL* 65.741), specifically the words "virginum pudicitiam . . . custodivit," for the phrase "þa bebead he þat mon heolde his mædenu clæne" (ed. Kotzor 1981 2.206.14; Cross 1985a pp 107–08). But a variant reading from the *Acta Cypriani* manuscripts, "castigari puellas praecepit" (ed. Reitzenstein 1913 p 15.3 and note), could as easily be the source here. See *CPL* 836 for doubts about the attribution of the Cyprian sermon to Fulgentius (it is omitted from the modern edition, *CCSL* 91A).

Surviving from the later Anglo-Saxon period, in the two eleventh-century manuscripts of the **COTTON-CORPUS LEGENDARY** listed here, there are four virtually identical copies of a recension of the A version, corresponding to *BHL* 2038, but not identical to any of the various editions cited in *BHL NS*; for example, the English copies omit the final statement, found in many other recensions and clearly echoed in the *Old English Martyrology* (ed. Kotzor 1981 2.207.5–6), about the death of the proconsul shortly after Cyprian's martyrdom. In a curious arrangement, reflecting the confusion over the relationship between Cyprian of Carthage and his namesake of Antioch, the London and Salisbury manuscripts both supply a text of the *acta* for the African Cyprian's feast day (September 14) plus the *same* text again for the feast of Cyprian and Justina of Antioch (in addition to their separate *passio*). See Jackson and Lapidge (1996 pp 140–41) and Webber (1992 pp 156–57). The first of the two Cotton manuscript copies (fols 122v–123v) for Cyprian's feast day has been revised in places by a twelfth-century hand, with some unusual variant readings (some possibly improvized) not reflected in Reitzenstein's collation. The basic text of all four copies, however, is clearly derived from an exemplar closely related to that of Reitzenstein's FIK group of Roman manuscripts (Reitzenstein 1913 p 10), but doubtless there are other examples elsewhere. We have not seen Philippart's 1975 dissertation (cited Philippart 1977 pp 12 and 13 note 3).

Of the numerous modern editions of the *Acta Cypriani* (see *BHL NS* p 235), Reitzenstein's (1913), although not definitive, is the most scholarly, superseding that of Hartel (*CSEL* 3/3). Musurillo's edition (1972) is based on Reitzenstein's and has a facing English translation. On Cyprian as one of the saints of the Canon of the Mass (with CORNELIUS), see Kennedy (1938 pp 119–23). For a recent assessment of the *Acta Cypriani*, see Saxer (1994 pp 35–39).

Cyprianus Carthaginensis, acta [ANON.Act.Cypr.1.at.II]: *BHL* 2038t.
  ed.: unpublished.
MSS Paris, Bibliothèque Nationale lat. 10861: HG 898.
List – Refs none.

This Paris manuscript (from Canterbury, early ninth century) is the earliest English copy of the *Acta Cypriani*. It is not mentioned in previous discussions of the **CYPRIAN** literature, to my knowledge, although it is in Philippart's list of medieval legendaries containing the *Acta* (1977 pp 13–16). According to the Bollandists in their hagiographic catalogue of Paris manuscripts (Bollandists 1889–93 2.605), as confirmed by M. P. Brown (1986 p 122), the text in the Paris manuscript begins as *BHL* 2038, but ends as *BHL* 2039, the shorter (B) version, omitting the *passio* proper. We have not examined the manuscript, but on this evidence the text appears to comprise parts 1 and 2 only. This unique textual situation is recognized in *BHL NS* where it is designated "1 at. II Recensio Brevior" with the number *BHL* 2038t. Corssen (1914 pp 226–27) argues that **AUGUSTINE** himself must have known such a text, but Delehaye (1966 p 63) denies this, for lack of manuscript evidence, although he certainly knew and used this manuscript for work on other saints' legends (e.g., **CAECILIA**). The argument may need to be reopened to take account of this manuscript.

Cyprianus Carthaginensis, vita (PONT.Vit.Cypr.]: *BHL* 2041; *CPL* 52.
ed.: Bastiaensen 1975a pp 4–48.

MSS Dublin, Trinity College 174: HG 215.
Lists – Refs none.

"Pontius," whose name as author of the *Vita Cypriani* is supplied by **JEROME**, claims to have been the confidant of **CYPRIAN**, but his life and passion of the saint tell little or nothing that could not have been gleaned from the proconsular *Acta Cypriani* (see previous entries), Cyprian's letters and other writings, and "enfin son imagination" (Delehaye 1966 pp 69–77). Despite some vigorous arguments to the contrary, most modern scholars accept the *Vita Cypriani* as the genuine, if historically disappointing, work of Cyprian's deacon, ca. 260. Among recent literary assessments, more balanced and appreciative than many is that of Berschin (1986–91 1.57–65, with bibliographical notes). See also Saxer (1995).

The only sign of the Anglo-Saxons' knowledge of Pontius's work is the copy in the Dublin manuscript, by Webber's Group II scribes, and therefore probably ca. 1100 or after (1992 p 159). The textual affiliations of this copy (from Salisbury) are unknown. It omits most of the last five chapters, terminating deliberately with an "explicit" after "placentiam dei" (Colker 1991 1.326), corresponding to "placentem Dei" in *Vita Cypriani* XV.1–2 (ed. Bastiaensen 1975a p 38). The same ending is in manuscripts F and R in Bastiaensen's collation. Evidently in some communities there was a preference for the account of Cyprian's martyrdom in the A version of the *Acta Cypriani* (*BHL* 2037/38). The final chapters of Pontius's *Vita* were therefore expendable and are only preserved in late medieval manuscripts (Bastiaensen 1975a p 2).

Cyprianus et Iustina, passio [ANON.Pas.Cypr.Iustin.]: *BHL* 2047, 2050; *BLS* 3.652–54; *BSS* 3.1281–86.
ed.: Mombritius 1910 2.70–75 and 669–70.
MSS 1. London, BL Cotton Nero E. i: HG 344.
2. Salisbury, Cathedral Library 222 (formerly Oxford, Bodleian Library Fell 1): HG 754.6.
Lists none.
A-S Vers 1. ?ALDH.Carm.uirg. 1842–82.
2. ALDH.Pros.uirg. 295.1–296.14.
3. ?BEDA.Mart.177.15–20.
4. *Mart* (B19.hn).
Quots/Cits see below.
Refs ?ALDH.Pros.uirg. 295.4–5.

One of the earliest precursors of the Faust legend is the Christian romance of the sorcerer Cyprian of Antioch and the virgin Justina (feast day September 26; see the study by Zahn 1882). After his familiar demons have failed to coerce Justina into accepting the marital advances of his client, Aglaidas, Cyprian abandons his sorcery and is converted to Christianity, eventually becoming bishop of Antioch. Later, after being arrested and tortured, he and Justina are martyred by decapitation, on the order of Diocletian. The legend survives in various versions (summarized by Delehaye 1921b) in Greek, Syriac, and Latin and was known, for example, to **GREGORY NAZIANZUS** and **PRUDENTIUS** (Delehaye 1921b pp 323–32). In the early medieval West (after relics supposedly were brought to Rome) the legend became widely known in three basic forms, classified as three parts of a single set of "Acta" by the Bollandists: part one, the "Conversio," *BHL* 2047–48, comprising the conversion of Justina, her resistance to her attackers, and the subsequent conversion of Cyprian; part two, the "Confessio," *BHL* 2049, which records a somewhat different version of the events of the "conversio" narrative; and part three, the *passio* proper, *BHL* 2050, narrating the martyrdoms of Cyprian and Justina, apparently intended as a sequel to the "Conversio" but by a different author (Delehaye 1921b pp 321–22). Siegmund (1949 p 233) lists one late-eighth-century manuscript now in Munich that contains all three texts, whereas others have only the "Conversio" and *passio*. Delehaye and other scholars postulate, on the basis of internal and external evidence, that these several parts and forms of the legend, and the earlier epitomes by Gregory and Prudentius, derive from one or more earlier texts that are now lost. Since the "Conversio" and *passio* regularly form one continuous text in the manuscripts, they are treated here together.

BEDE and ALDHELM were both familiar with the legend, and Aldhelm vaguely refers to written versions in his verse and prose DE VIRGINITATE (ALDH.Carm.uirg., Pros.uirg.; ed. *MGH* AA 15), but Quentin (1908 p 71) says Bede's MARTYROLOGIUM notice (BEDA.Mart.; ed. Dubois and Renaud 1976) is too general to be linked specifically to any of the extant published texts, but that he probably knew the whole story, as undoubtedly did Aldhelm (see Ehwald, *MGH* AA 15.295 note 1). As different as are Bede's and Aldhelm's accounts in their style and emphases (Aldhelm's on Justina's virginity, Bede's on her Christianity), each mentions that Cyprian and Justina suffered under both Diocletian and Claudius and each stresses the efforts of Justina's attackers to overcome her by means of magical delusions.

The immediate source of the brief notice for Cyprian and Justina in the ninth-century OLD ENGLISH MARTYROLOGY (*Mart*; ed. Kotzor 1981 2.220–21) is uncertain. The simile "swa swa . . . weax þonne hit for fyre gemelteð" (pp 220.14–221.1) is apparently based on "liquefactus est sicut cera a facie ignis" from the "Conversio" (Mombritius 1910 2.72.23), as pointed out by J. E. Cross in an unpublished analysis. Cross adds, however, that Aldhelm has the same image in his *De uirginitate*, prose version (*MGH* AA 15.295.7–9), somewhat abbreviated, and the Old English martyrologist could have adapted it from Aldhelm alone or from the "Conversio" under Aldhelm's influence, since in both Aldhelm and the *Old English Martyrology* it is coupled with a similar image of vanishing smoke (see also *EETS* OS 116.236). Other details of the *Martyrology* notice are equally ambiguous.

The copies of the "Conversio" and *passio* texts in the mid- to late-eleventh-century Cotton and Salisbury manuscripts of the **COTTON-CORPUS LEGENDARY** correspond to the printed edition of Mombritius (Jackson and Lapidge 1996 p 141), although the *passio* text is not identical (Zettel 1979 p 26; Webber 1992 p 157 misidentifies Salisbury's copy of the *passio* portion as *BHL* 2047, instead of 2050). That the Anglo-Saxons, like others before them, were prone to confuse Cyprian of Antioch with his more historical namesake of Carthage is evident in that the calendars containing the rare September 26 feast do not have the African bishop's much more common feast of September 14 (see F. Wormald 1934 pp 10, 38). See the above entry, **CYPRIANUS CARTHAGINENSIS**, acta proconsularia, for the duplication of texts in the Cotton-Corpus Legendary.

In addition to Mombritius's edition of the "Conversio," see also *AS* Sept. 7.217–19.

Cyrilla.

Cyrilla (feast day October 28), identified as a daughter of the emperor Decius in the legend of Saint Laurence, is the subject of separate brief narrative notices in **BEDE**'s **MARTYROLOGIUM** (ed. Dubois and Renaud 1976 p 196.12–15) and the **OLD ENGLISH MARTYROLOGY** (*Mart*, B19.ij; ed. Kotzor 1981 2.241), taken independently from *Passio Laurentii* XXXV (sourced by Cross 1983a p 212). See **LAURENTIUS**. There are no indications of a separate cult in England.

Demetrias, epistola [PELAG.Ep.Dem./PS.HIER., PS.IVL.ECL.]: *BCLL* 7; *CPL* 737; *DHGE* 14.194; *NCE* 4.744.

Demetrias (ca. 398–460, feast day February 24) was one of several Roman patrician women of the fourth and fifth centuries whose adoption of an ascetic way of life is celebrated in contemporary documents. The best known of these, a lengthy *Epistola ad Demetriadem* (*PL* 30.15–45), full of praise and advice on the celibate life, with some information about the saint herself, is now firmly attributed to the controversial British priest **PELAGIUS** although it was formerly attributed to **AUGUSTINE** and **JEROME**, among others. It was known to **ALDHELM**, who includes Demetrias and EUSTOCHIUM as exemplary virgins in his DE VIRGINI-TATE. The eulogy of Demetrias in the prose version (ed. *MGH* AA 15.304.4–23; see also *Carmen* 2162–93) departs from Aldhelm's usual practice of adapting his sources, being largely composed of substantial verbatim quotations from chapters I and XXX of the *Epistola* (*PL* 30.15–16 and 44; see *MGH* AA 15.304, notes 1–3). Aldhelm does not name his source's author, and Lapidge and Herren (1979 p 196 note 25) assert that he would have been "horrified" to realize that the letter was actually written by the infamous heretic. **BEDE**, on the other hand, to whom the *Epistola* was also familiar, mentions the attribution to Jerome and rejects it, in the prologue to his COMMENTARIUS IN CANTICA CANTICORUM (*Prologus* 332–36; ed. *CCSL* 119B), in favor of **JULIAN OF ECLANUM**, the supporter of Pelagius. Shortly after this (*Prologus* 344–83), as indicated in the *CCSL* edition, Bede also goes on to quote several passages verbatim from the early pages of the *Epistola* (ed. *PL* 30.16–23). Ogilvy (*BKE* pp 187 and 218) mentions another passage, in Bede's COMMENTARIUS IN PROVERBIA SALOMONIS (III.179–80; ed. *CCSL* 119B), where he borrows a maxim from the *Epistola*, chapter XIX (*PL* 30.34), on avoiding idle gossip, attributing the maxim cryptically to "a certain man of God." This is not noticed in the *CCSL* edition.

On Demetrias and her circle, see Gonsette (1933) and P. Brown (1972). The letter by Pelagius is translated in a recent collection by Rees (1991 pp 29–70).

The Bollandists assign the number *BHL* 2121c to Aldhelm's eulogy of Demetrias, apparently confusing her with a more historically dubious "Demetria" (feast day June 21: see *DHGE* 14.194) who figures in the legend of Bibiana (Viviana).

Dionisius, passio [ANON.Pas.Dion./PS.VEN.FORT.]: *BHL* 2171; *BLS* 4.66–67; *BSS* 4.650–61; *CPL* 1051; *DHGE* 14.263–65; Farmer (1987) pp 116–17.
ed.: *PL* 88.577–84.
MSS – Lists none.
A-S Vers ?*Mart* (B19.hv).
Quots/Cits – Refs none.

The cult of Denis (Denys; feast day October 9) was already important in the sixth and seventh centuries, when the church dedicated to him in Paris (ca. 475) became a frequent burial place for Merovingian royalty (Wallace-Hadrill 1983 pp 126–31; on the history of the abbey in general, see Crosby 1987 and, on Hilduin's chapel, Formige 1960 pp 169–72). **GREGORY OF TOURS**, HISTORIA FRANCORUM I.xxx (ed. *MGH* SRM 1/1.22.15–23.8 [2nd ed.]), describes him as one of seven Roman missionaries (including **SATURNINUS TOLOSANUS**), sent to evangelize Gaul in the third century, who were martyred after establishing Christian centers in their several provinces.

By the mid-ninth century, three successive *passiones*—two anonymous, the third by Hilduin of Saint-Denis, who also produced a version in verse —had progressively elaborated the basic story told by Gregory, eventually identifying the martyr of Paris with the first-century Dionysius the Areopagite (Acts 17.13–34) and the fifth-century Neoplatonist **PSEUDO-DIONYSIUS AREOPAGUS**. On the chronological order of the three works, which is misrepresented in the first edition of *BHL*, see Loenertz (1951) and Moretus Plantin (1948). See also Luscombe (1988 pp 135–40) on the two later texts in the context of literary forgery. Bibliographies for Hilduin are in *DHGE* 24.515–22 and *RFHMA* 5.495–96. The first anonymous *passio*, with which this entry is concerned, and those by Hilduin were known in Anglo-Saxon England. On English witnesses to Hilduin's prose and verse versions, see the next two entries. See Lapidge (1987 pp 77–79) on English relations with the abbey of Saint-Denis in Paris, and for other tenth- and eleventh-century evidence of the importance of the cult of Denis in England: for example, at Wilton (where **EDITHA** was especially devoted to him) and at Winchester, New Minster. See also

Ortenberg (1992 pp 246–47, drawing on D. Hoare's unpublished 1978 thesis) for liturgical evidence of the cult in later Anglo-Saxon England. On the importance of Denis to the Capetian dynasty, see Spiegel (1983).

The earliest *passio*, once attributed to **VENANTIUS FORTUNATUS** and dated variously sixth (Loenertz 1951 pp 217–21) or eighth century (*BSS* 4.650–53), is simply a more detailed version of the story told by Gregory of Tours, with the addition of two missionary companions, Rusticus a priest and Eleutherius a deacon, martyred with Denis. Most of the contents of the notice in the **OLD ENGLISH MARTYROLOGY** (*Mart*; ed. Kotzor 1981 2.227–28) could be explained with reference to this *passio*, with which it shares details of phrasing. Similarities occur between the *Martyrology* and the Latin of Hilduin's version only in contexts where Hilduin's phrasing is borrowed verbatim from the earlier work (see Kotzor 1981 2.227.7–9 and compare the anonymous *Passio Dionisii*, ed. *PL* 88.582.18–20, with Hilduin's *Passio Dionisii*, ed. *PL* 106.48.14–16). Details in the *Martyrology* that are not found in any of the printed Latin texts may indicate, however, the martyrologist's knowledge of a recension of the oldest *passio* not represented in the printed editions. For example, the *Martyrology* (Kotzor 1981 2.227.10–12) is unique in saying that the executioners "handed over" the bodies of the martyrs to the matron Catulla and that she had her servants steal them away "by night."

The first *passio* has also been edited by Bruno Krusch (*MGH AA* 4/1.101–05).

Dionisius, passio [HILDVIN.Pas.Dion.]: *BHL* 2175.
ed.: *PL* 106.23–50.

MSS 1. Cambridge, Corpus Christi College 9: HG 36.
2. Salisbury, Cathedral Library 222 (formerly Oxford, Bodleian Library Fell 1): HG 754.6.

Lists none.

AS Vers 1. *ÆLS* Denis (B1.3.29).
2. *ÆCHom* I, 37 (B1.1.39) lines 39–50.

Quots/Cits – Refs none.

The most elaborate prose *passio* of Denis, composed by Hilduin of Paris in the 830s, draws on the language of both the earlier versions (Loenertz 1951 pp 228–31) while providing a great deal of new material, especially on the supposed Athenian phase of the saint's life and his supposed authorship of the Pseudo-Dionysian writings. This is the version preserved in the surviving **COTTON-CORPUS LEGENDARY** manuscripts listed here (Zettel 1979 p 27; Jackson and Lapidge 1996 p 141) in each of which it is entitled "Passio S. Dionisii Martyris Ariopagitae." A somewhat later copy is in London, BL Arundel 91 (HG 305; from St Augustine's, Canterbury, early twelfth century).

ÆLFRIC's life of Denis in his **LIVES OF SAINTS** (*ÆLS*; ed. *EETS* OS 94 and 114) is based on this version (C. Loomis 1931) but, as Zettel points out (1979 p 236), the Old English account is more an epitome than a close rendering, omitting a great deal of the contents of Hilduin's expansive work. Zettel finds no significant differences between the Cotton-Corpus texts and the printed editions as a guide to Ælfric's source. See Zettel (1982 p 34 note 3) on Ælfric's even more rapid summary of the *Passio Dionisii* in his First Series homily on Clement (**CLEMENS**, passio). Thorpe provides a facing translation of the passage in the homily (1844–46 1.558.31–560.15). See also Godden's sourcing (*EETS* SS 18.310–11).

For another edition of Hilduin's *Passio Dionisii*, see Mombritius (1910 1.394–409 and 651–52).

Dionisius, passio metrica [HILDVIN.Pas.Dion.metr.].
ed.: unpublished.

MSS ?Oxford, Bodleian Library Bodley 535 (*SC* 2254): HG 582.
Lists – Refs none.

Scholars have long known that Hilduin produced a verse version of his prose *Passio Dionisii*, thus completing a typically Carolingian *opus gemminatum*. This metrical version was believed lost until Lapidge (1987) determined that it survives in a late-eleventh-century copy in the Oxford manuscript cited here (fols 1–37), from Winchester, a center of English devotion to Denis. Hilduin's authorship cannot be proved beyond a doubt, as Lapidge admits (p 74), but he builds an impressive case for the poem's Carolingian origins and incidentally demonstrates (p 75) that it was the major source of Hrotswitha of Gandersheim's own verses on the saint of Paris. Unfortunately, there is no way of knowing if Hilduin's poem came to England during the Anglo-Saxon period or as a post-Conquest import. For notice of an edition in progress, see Lapidge (1987 p 69 note 85).

Domitilla et soc. See NEREUS ET ACHILLEUS.

Donatus Aretii, passio [ANON.Pas.Donat.]: *BHL* 2289; *BSS* 4.773–82; *CPL* 2183.
  ed.: Lazzeri 1938 pp 117–21.
MSS   1. London, BL Cotton Nero E. i: HG 344.
  2. Salisbury, Cathedral Library 222 (formerly Oxford, Bodleian Library Fell 1): HG 754.6.
Lists none.
A-S Vers ?*Mart* (B19.fm).
Quots/Cits see below.
Refs none.

Donatus had an authentic early cult as second bishop of Arezzo (died ca. 362, feast day August 7), but according to his legend, which borrows material from that of GALLICANUS, Donatus was a pupil, in company with the future emperor Julian, of Saint Pimenius. Later, when Julian as emperor executed not only his former master but also Donatus's parents, the young man fled to Arezzo, taking sanctuary with the hermit HILARINUS. Later still, as bishop of Arezzo, he was martyred on Julian's orders. The *passio* that relates this legend appears to have been known to GREGORY THE GREAT, who may be borrowing from one of its episodes, the broken chalice, in DIALOGI I.vii.31–42 (ed. De Vogüé, *SChr* 260; see his note, pp 268–69). For analysis of the legend's sources, and for further references, see De Gaiffier (1956 pp 28–29, 36–37).

While **BEDE** in his **MARTYROLOGIUM** (ed. Dubois and Renaud 1976 p 145.2–4) only records the chalice miracle, citing Gregory's account, he regards the saint as a martyr and includes a detail from the *passio* lacking in Gregory (Quentin 1908 p 102).

No sourcing of the notice in the **OLD ENGLISH MARTYROLOGY** (*Mart*; ed. Kotzor 1981 2.173) has been published, but J. E. Cross (personal communication) believes the *Martyrology* draws on Bede's *Martyrologium*, Gregory's *Dialogi*, and probably the *passio*. The copies of the *passio* in the **COTTON-CORPUS LEGENDARY** are said to correspond to *BHL* 2289 (Zettel 1979 p 23), but Jackson and Lapidge (1996 p 139) also cite the closely related unpublished variant *BHL* 2291. For two other variant versions of the same text, see the two editions of Mombritius (1480 1.234–35, *BHL* 2292, and 1910 1.416–18, *BHL* 2292a).

Dormientes (Septem), passio [ANON.Pas.Dorm.sept.]: *BHL* 2316; *BLS* 3.193–96; *BSS* 11.900–07.
ed.: Magennis 1994 pp 74–90.

MSS 1. London, BL Cotton Nero E. i: HG 344.
    2. Salisbury, Cathedral Library 222 (formerly Oxford, Bodleian Library Fell 1): HG 754.6.
Lists none.
A-S Vers 1. *ÆCHom* II, 27 (B1.2.34) 182–231.
    2. *LS* 34 (SevenSleepers, B3.3.34).
Quots/Cits 1. *ÆCHom* I, 16 (B1.1.18): see below.
    2. ?ANON.Vit.Edward.Conf.: see below.
Refs none.

BEDE and his contemporaries do not mention the legend of the Seven Sleepers (feast day July 27), and evidence for Anglo-Saxon knowledge of specific versions comes from only late in the period. The legend was known, however, to some of the English community in late-eighth-century Germany. According to Huneberc's *Vita Willibaldi* (*MGH* SRM 15/1.93.16), Saint Willibald and his brother visited the spot (near Ephesus) where the remains of the Seven Sleepers lay.

Two main versions of the story were known in the early medieval West, one by **GREGORY OF TOURS** (*BHL* 2313: see next entry), and the anonymous *passio* of this entry; see Huber (1910 pp 59–62). The two are apparently independent of one another. The earliest manuscripts of this version (*BHL* 2316), a Frankish translation from Greek (Siegmund 1949 p 218), are ninth-century (see also Huber 1910 p 61 and Magennis 1991 p 43); it is also represented in the eleventh-century London and Salisbury manuscripts of the **COTTON-CORPUS LEGENDARY**.

The anonymous *passio* has been shown (initially by Ott 1892 pp 56–58) to be the source of the much expanded Old English *Seven Sleepers* (*LS* 34; ed. Magennis 1994 pp 33–57), surviving in two eleventh-century copies, one complete (London, BL Cotton Julius E. vii) and the other fragmentary (Otho B. x). Although not written by ÆLFRIC, this version is generally regarded as roughly contemporary with his work. Among extant texts of the *passio*, the closest to the source of the anonymous Old English version is not the Cotton-Corpus Legendary recension, but an eleventh-century manuscript (London, BL Egerton 2797) of Continental provenance and closely related to a later text in BL Harley 3037. See Huber (1910 p 161), Whitelock (1961), and Magennis (1985a; see also 1985b on the style of the Old English version). For other manuscripts of importance for determining the source text of the anonymous Old English *Seven Sleepers*, see Magennis (1991 and 1994 pp 11–13). His edition of the Latin *passio* is based on the Egerton manuscript and includes a facing translation (pp 75–91) and bibliography (pp 29–30). Skeat's edition of the Old English *Seven Sleepers* (in *EETS* OS 76 and 82) may still be consulted for its facing translation (pp 489–541).

Despite the brevity of Ælfric's account of the Seven Sleepers in his **CATHOLIC HOMILIES** (*ÆCHom* II; ed. *EETS* SS 5; see also SS 18.576, 580–82), it can be seen to depend on the anonymous *passio,* as Huber (1910 p 157) first showed. Although the *passio* was unknown to Förster (1892), it corresponds closely to the hypothetical source (containing elements of *BHL* 2313 and the Greek of Simeon Metaphrastes) that he posited (p 40). Zettel (1979 pp 192–94) suggests that the version of the *passio* Ælfric used is that in the Cotton-Corpus Legendary, but various discrepancies suggest that his source was not identical with the Legendary's text, and further that he also drew on the *passio* written by Gregory of Tours (see next entry).

Ælfric also briefly mentions the Seven Sleepers, as an exemplum of the resurrection of the body, in a passage that he added (in the period 1002–05) to his First Series homily for the first Sunday after Easter, *Catholic Homilies* I, 16, between lines 125 and 126 (B1.1.18; ed. *EETS* SS 17, Appendix B.2.34–41; also SS 18.135). Omitted from Thorpe's edition, it appears in six of the eleven extant manuscripts of the homily (see Gatch 1977 pp 86–87 and Magennis 1991 p 45; the passage is translated by Magennis 1996a p 322). Here, as in the Second Series homily cited above, Ælfric says the length of the sleep is 372 years, which suggests his dependence on a text of the *passio* different from that in the Cotton-Corpus Legendary.

The *Vita Edwardi regis* (*BHL* 2421: see **EDWARDUS CONFESSOR**), dated ca. 1067 and attributed by Barlow to Goscelin of Canterbury, contains (II.vii) Edward the Confessor's vision of the Sleepers turning over onto their left sides (Barlow 1992 pp 102–10). The sole authoritative manuscript copy (London, BL Harley 526; HG 420), however, is deficient at this point and the vision has to be supplied from later revised versions, the most reliable of which now appears to be in the Bury St Edmunds copy (1130s) of "Florence" of Worcester, from which the episode is printed in Barlow's 1992 edition (cf. the first edition, 1962 pp 66–71, from Osbert of Clare's redaction). Barlow, while convinced (1992 p xli) that Harley 526 contained such an episode, does not think it was in the original *Vita Edwardi* (p xliii). Heningham (1975 p 32 note 39) disagrees. As it stands, however, this episode and other materials in Book II of the *vita* appear to be no earlier than ca. 1081, when a (probably) Canterbury reviser expanded the miraculous content of the original work (Barlow 1992 pp xliii–xliv). The details of the Sleepers' legend as presented in the *Vita Edwardi* are not specific enough to indicate any particular source. Barlow (p 104 note 259) sees the figure of 272 years as a harmonization of more than one tradition.

Hugh Magennis

Dormientes (Septem), passio [GREG.TVRON.Pas.Dorm.Sept.]: *BHL* 2313; *CPL* 1029.
 ed.: *MGH* SRM 7.761–69.
MSS – A-S Vers none.
Quots/Cits see below.
Refs none.

Some features in ÆLFRIC's rendering of the Seven Sleepers' legend, in the second part of his CATHOLIC HOMILIES II, 27 (*ÆCHom* II, B1.2.34; ed. *EETS* SS 5), suggest that he was familiar with the *passio* by GREGORY OF TOURS, as well as with the independent anonymous version (see previous entry). For details, see Magennis (1996a). Additional evidence that Gregory's version might have been known in Anglo-Saxon England is provided by the Old English prose "Fever Charm" (*Charm* 17, B23.1.17; ed. Stokes 1891 p 144; see also Bonser 1945), where the list of the Sleepers' names corresponds, although with some corruption, to the first of the two lists as given by Gregory (*MGH* SRM 7.761.17–18). The anonymous *passio*, on the other hand, has only the second list. A metrical charm, "Against a Dwarf" (*MCharm* 3, A43.3; ed. *ASPR* 6.121–22), contains, in its prose preface, the second list of Sleepers' names as given by Gregory in his *passio* (*MGH* SRM 7.762.2–3) and also in DE GLORIA MARTYRUM XCIV (*BHL* 2314; ed. *MGH* SRM 1/2.551.28–552.1). While this second set also appears in the anonymous *passio*, it is possible that the Old English metrical charm is indebted, like the prose charm, to Gregory's version.

Hugh Magennis

Dorothea, passio [ANON.Pas.Doroth.]: *BHL* 2323; *BLS* 1.261–62; *BSS* 4.820–24; *DHGE* 14.684.
 ed.: *AS* Feb. 1.773–76.
MSS – Lists none.
A-S Vers ALDH.Pros.uirg. 300.15–16, 301.21–302.9.
Quots/Cits – Refs none.

The Western cult of Dorothea, who was martyred apparently at Caesaria in Cappadocia, under Diocletian, was early centered in Rome where her relics were believed to be. Although she was one of the more popular female saints in the later Middle Ages, Dorothea's legendary *passio*, which includes the bitter-sweet story of the sarcastic Theophilus and the apples and roses of paradise, was apparently little known in Anglo-Saxon England. Her cult is not reflected in English pre-Conquest calendars, where February 6, her usual feast day, is invariably given over to **VEDASTUS** and **AMANDUS**. The only Anglo-Saxon witness we have encountered is **ALDHELM**'s summary in his prose **DE VIRGINITATE** (ALDH.Pros.uirg.; ed. *MGH* AA 15). Dorothea, moreover, is one of the few saints who do not appear in both the prose and verse versions. For Aldhelm's source, Ehwald in the *MGH* edition (p 300) points to the text printed by the Bollandists in *AS*. For early medieval manuscripts of this and other versions, see Siegmund (1949 p 234). Another edition of this version is by Fábrega Grau (1953–55 2.226–32).

Dunstanus, vita [B.Vit.Dunst.]: *BHL* 2342; *BLS* 2.349–51; *BSS* 4.869–71; *DHGE* 14.1063–68; Farmer (1987) pp 122–24.
ed.: *RS* 63.3–52.
MSS 1. Arras, Bibliothèque Municipale 1029 (812): HG 781.
2. London, BL Cotton Cleopatra B. xiii: HG 323.
3. St Gallen, Stadtbibliothek 337: HG 928.
Lists Saewold: ML 8.19.
A-S Vers ADELARD.Vit.Dunst.
Quots/Cits none.
Refs BYRHTFERTH.Vit.Oswald. 457.11–12; see below.

Thanks to the idiosyncracies and limitations of Dunstan's first hagiographers, much more is known about his early life and his career as abbot at Glastonbury (939–55) than about his later career as Archbishop of Canterbury (960–88, feast day May 19), which spanned the first period of the ecclesiastical reform and the anti-monastic reaction. Many of the problematic aspects of Dunstan's life, character, and cult are explored in a valuable commemorative collection of essays (Ramsay and Sparks 1992a), among which is Lapidge's authoritative discussion (1992b) of the identity and motives of Dunstan's former secretary "B," the author of the earliest *Vita Dunstani*. Lapidge regards B as a native Englishman (resident for many years as a cathedral canon in Liège) and not a German as has always been assumed. Composed not long after Dunstan's death in 988 (probably soon after the accession of the dedicatee, Archbishop Ælfric, in 995: Lapidge 1992b p 247), B's work has survived in the three pre-Conquest manuscripts listed above, discussed by Stubbs in his edition (*RS* 63.xxvi–xxx, xxxviii–xli). Stubbs was not aware, however, that Arras 1029, which in his opinion best preserves the original form of B's text and was used by the Bollandists for their edition (*AS* Mai. 4.346–58), is one of the Bath Abbey books given to the monks of Saint-Vaast, Arras, by the exiled English abbot Saewold shortly after the Conquest (see Lapidge's note on the booklist, ML 8.19). The St Gall and London manuscripts both originated at St Augustine's, Canterbury.

B's composition, valued by modern scholars for its contents but not for its style, was also apparently unsatisfying in its own day, and his effort failed to secure the appointment he desired in England. The work was also subject to considerable correction and revision. Two of the manuscripts listed above represent a revised, corrected version of the original. But whereas Stubbs treated the copies from St Gall (ca. 1000) and London (early twelfth century) as revisions, more recent work offers an alternative view, pointing to the St Gall text as closest to the original version and positing a revised version as the common exemplar of the Arras and Cotton texts (Winterbottom 2000). The St Gall manuscript was sent by Abbot Wulfric (989–1006) to **ABBO OF FLEURY** in the hope (unfulfilled) that he would compose a metrical version of the *Vita Dunstani*. See Stubbs's edition (*RS* 63.xxviii and 409) and Lapidge (1992c p 247 note 2; I am grateful to Christine Rauer for drawing my attention to Michael Winterbottom's important new study and for sending me an offprint).

BYRHTFERTH of Ramsey in his life of Oswald (997–1002; see OSWALDUS WIGORNIENSIS) indicates that he knew a life of Dunstan, apparently B's, summarizing it in a few lines (BYRHTFERTH.Vit. Oswald.; ed. *RS* 71/1.457.6–12) and adapting two episodes from it (*Vita Dunstani* XVII and XXXVI; ed. *RS* 63.27–28 and 48–49), although with considerable freedom and without verbal echoes (*Vita Oswaldi*; ed. *RS* 71/1.457.13–23 and 457.32–459.13). In the contemporary lives of **ÆTHELWOLD** (see also **ÆTHELWOLDUS**), however, neither **WULFSTAN OF WINCHESTER** nor **ÆLFRIC** seems to refer to or echo B's *vita*, although they recount a story about Dunstan that, while complimentary to Æthelwold, accords with B's depiction of Dunstan as a dreamer and visionary (see, e.g., Wulfstan's **VITA ÆTHELWOLDI** XXXVIII, ed. Lapidge and Winterbottom 1991 p 56). There is also some similarity between B's chapter XV and Wulfstan's chapter XXXI, on the successful ecclesiastical careers of the pupils of each saint.

On Adelard's *Vita Dunstani*, which draws on but also differs considerably from B's, see next entry.

It is possible that during the first half of the eleventh century a vernacular life of Dunstan was composed, combining material from B and Adelard, and incorporating additional material from oral tradition. Osbern of Canterbury, writing during the time of Archbishop Lanfranc, claims to have based his life of Dunstan on such a text (*RS* 63.70.11–13; see Wilson 1970 p 89), but Stubbs assumes that Osbern drew directly on the Latin texts by B and Adelard, and on other Canterbury and Glastonbury traditions.

A new edition of B's life of Dunstan is forthcoming from Lapidge and Winterbottom (Oxford Medieval Texts). Important aspects of Dunstan's cult and hagiography are explored in recent essays by Ramsay and Sparks, Rollason, and Thacker (in Ramsay and Sparks 1992a). Townsend (1991 pp 393–403) briefly explores some aspects of B's and Osbern's lives of Dunstan in the light of reader-response theory.

Dunstanus, vita [ADELARD.Vit.Dunst.]: *BHL* 2343.
ed.: *RS* 63.53–68.

MSS New York, Pierpont Morgan Library 926: HG 865.
Lists none.

A-S Vers see below.
Quots/Cits – Refs none.

Adelard, a monk of "Blandinium" (St Peter's, Ghent), composed the second life of Dunstan apparently at the request of Archbishop Ælfheah (ÆLFEGUS) to whom the preface is addressed and whose death in 1012 provides its terminus ante. Although based in part on B's *Vita Dunstani* (see previous entry), it represents a drastic reworking of the material, omitting a great deal, adding new miracles, and presenting the whole as a set of lections and responsories for liturgical use (the latter omitted in some later copies). Adelard's *vita* was rewritten during the time of Archbishop Lanfranc (1070–89) by Osbern of Canterbury (OSBERN.Vit. Dunst.; ed. *RS* 63.69–128), who also provided a collection of recent miracles (pp 128–61).

The earliest surviving copies of Adelard's *vita* are from around the turn of the eleventh century or early twelfth. The one in the Chester legendary, London, Gray's Inn 3 (Ker and Piper 1969–92 1.53), is collated by Stubbs in his *RS* edition, but that in the New York manuscript listed here (originally from St Albans) was unknown to him (see Hartzell 1975 pp 21 and 42–43).

For a possible Old English version based on this and B's version, and for Osbern's use of them in his late-eleventh-century life of Dunstan, see previous entry. Stubbs discusses his manuscripts, and the author's identity, in his edition (*RS* 63.xxx–xxxi, xli–xlii); he analyzes the contents of the work with little enthusiasm (pp lx–lxii). A new edition is forthcoming from Lapidge and Winterbottom (Oxford Medieval Texts).

Eadberht Lindisfarnensis: *BSS* 4.900; *DHGE* 14.1252; Farmer (1987) pp 127–28.

There is no known separate life of Eadberht, who succeeded CUTH-BERTUS as bishop of Lindisfarne (688–98), promoted his predecessor's cult, and was buried in the same tomb. Although his feast day (May 6) is the subject of a substantial notice in the **OLD ENGLISH MARTYR-OLOGY** (*Mart*, B19.cp; ed. Kotzor 1981 2.90–95), he seems not to have had any cult in Anglo-Saxon England. He figures in several passages of BEDE's historical and hagiographical works, for example, in HISTORIA ECCLESIASTICA IV.xxix–xxx (ed. Colgrave and Mynors 1969 pp 442–44) and the VITA CUTHBERTI XLII–XLIII (ed. Colgrave 1940 pp 292–96). For a detailed sourcing of the *Martyrology* account in relation to Bede's prose life, see Kotzor (1981 2.310–11). Van Doren, in the *DHGE* article on Eadberht, makes the interesting but unsupported statement that Eadberht's name passed into the later versions of USUARD's MARTYROLOGIUM via the *Old English Martyrology*.

Eadmundus. See ABBO OF FLEURY, PASSIO EADMUNDI.

Edburga: *BLS* 2.548–49; Farmer (1987) pp 128–29.

Edburg (Eadburh) of Winchester (feast day June 15), not to be confused with various earlier namesakes distinguished by Ridyard (1988 pp 16–17 note 16), was a daughter of King Edward the Elder and sister of King Athelstan. Her dates are uncertain but she was born before 924 (death of King Edward) and died before the mid-century, having spent her life as a nun at Nunnaminster (St Mary's), Winchester. Her relics were elevated twice, the second time by Bishop ÆTHELWOLD (ÆTHELWOLDUS) between 963 and 984 (translation feast July 18). A portion of them was acquired by Pershore abbey (near Worcester) late in the tenth century, as related by Ridyard (1988 pp 16–19). In a contemporary calendar, now linked with Christ Church, Canterbury, Edburg's June 15 feast is graded (F. Wormald 1934 p 63).

There is no extant *vita* from the Anglo-Saxon period, but Ridyard (1988 p 29) posits the existence of a lost mid-eleventh-century (or later) life, probably from Winchester, which was then revised (ca. 1120–30) by Osbert of Clare for the use of the monks of Pershore. His life survives as *BHL* 2385. The lost life was drawn on independently by William of Malmesbury (1120s) and is also reflected in a variety of later narrative texts (for details, see Ridyard 1988 pp 25–29).

Ridyard's work on Edburg's literature and cult, with its ecclesiastical and political context (1988 pp 16–37, 96–139), complements and corrects that of Braswell (1971), who prints some of the later Latin texts. The life by Osbert is edited by Ridyard (1988 pp 259–309) from two manuscripts in Oxford. Rollason (1989a pp 138–39) also discusses the political context of the early cult.

Editha: *BSS* 4.915; *DHGE* 14.1438–39; Farmer (1987) pp 130–31.

Eadgyth (Edith) of Wilton (961–84, feast day September 16) was the daughter of King Edgar and his wife (or concubine) Wulfthryth. Eadgyth's short life was spent almost entirely in the royal convent of Wilton where her mother was first a novice and later abbess. Besides other works of piety and charity, Eadgyth promoted the cult of Saint Denis (**DIONISIUS**), in whose honor a shrine was constructed in the convent. Eadgyth's devotion to Denis was perhaps due to the influence of her French tutors, one of whom, Benno of Trèves, decorated the shrine with scenes from the passions of Christ and Denis. On the cult of Denis in England, see the entry for Dionisius.

Although Eadgyth's relics were translated in 997, the earliest extant *Vita Edithae* is that of Goscelin of Canterbury (*BHL* 2388, written ca. 1078–87; ed. Wilmart 1938b). Although he does not specify a full earlier life, Goscelin does mention, as Wilmart (1938b pp 39, 292) and Ridyard (1988 p 40) point out, that there was an Old English account ("patriis litteris") of Eadgyth's posthumous cure of one of the famous dancers of Colbeck during the time of Abbess Brihtgifu (reign of Edward the Confessor).

The fullest modern treatment is that of Ridyard (1988 pp 37–44, 140–54). See also Rollason (1989a pp 139–40); for bibliography on the dancers of Colbeck, see *DHGE* 14.1439.

Edwardus confessor, vita [ANON.Vit.Edward.Conf.]: *BHL* 2421; *BLS* 4.100–03; *BSS* 4.921–25; *DHGE* 14.1448–51; Farmer (1987) pp 133–35. ed.: Barlow 1992 pp 2–127.

MSS London, BL Harley 526: HG 420.
Lists – A-S Vers none.
Quots/Cits – Refs see below.

The anonymous life of King Edward the Confessor (1002–66, feast days January 5, October 13), usually, though not firmly, attributed to Goscelin the hagiographer, of St Bertin, later of Canterbury, was composed in two books in mixed prose and verse ca. 1067, then revised and amplified ca. 1080. It has some attributes of a saint's life, but its main purpose apparently was more to honor Queen Edith and her brothers than to foster a cult of the thaumaturgic and reputedly celibate king himself. It survives in one sadly imperfect manuscript of the turn of the century, possibly from Christ Church, Canterbury. Edward's cult, centered on his relics at Westminster Abbey, did not develop in earnest, however, until after the end of the century. The *vita* was used by a Westminster monk and historian, Sulcard, ca. 1080 (Heningham 1946 pp 450–54), but he does not appear to have regarded Edward as a saint. The cult's first energetic promoter was Osbert of Clare, prior of Westminster, who in the 1130s revised and recast the life to create a new version (*BHL* 2422), which remains an important witness (along with William of Malmesbury and "Florence" of Worcester) to the missing portions of the text of Book Two. The standard edition of the first *vita*, with full and complex introduction to the textual problems arising from the imperfect state of the manuscript, is that of Barlow (2nd edition, 1992) who has also written an authoritative biography of Edward (1970). Also important is the work of Heningham (1946 and 1975). For a detailed but mainly discredited discussion of the relation between the first life and Osbert's, see Bloch (1923). On Edward's vision of the Seven Sleepers, see **DORMIENTES (SEPTEM)**.

Edwardus martyr: *BLS* 1.627–28; *BSS* 4.926–27; *DHGE* 14.1452–53; Farmer (1987) pp 135–36.

King Edward (Eadward) when still a teenager succeeded to the English throne vacated by his father Edgar in 975, but he was murdered by supporters of his half-brother Æthelred's rival claim to the throne, on March 18, 978 (or 979). In a short time, miracles were reported at Edward's grave at the convent of Wareham and his body was elevated, proclaimed incorrupt, and translated with all due ceremony to Shaftesbury. The annal for 978 in the E version of the **ANGLO-SAXON CHRONICLE** (*ChronE*, B17.9; ed. Plummer 1892–99; see **CHRONICLES**) extolls him, in rough verses, as a martyr; in 1008 his feast day was officially declared a national holy day (C. Fell 1971 p xxi).

Before 1005, **BYRHTFERTH** of Ramsey included in his life of Bishop Oswald (**OSWALDUS WIGORNIENSIS**) a brief account of the martyrdom, also alluding to miracles at Shaftesbury (*BHL* 6374; ed. *RS* 71/1.448–52). On the literary character of Byrhtferth's account, see Lapidge's brief discussion (1996a pp 79–80). Liturgical evidence of the development of his cult is surveyed by C. Fell (1971 pp xxi–xxiv).

The earliest extant *passio* (ed. C. Fell 1971 pp 1–16) was not composed until almost a century after Edward's death, probably by Goscelin the hagiographer (although its style is not typical of his known work). Fell (pp xix–xx, xxv) argues, however, that the *passio* is based closely on an earlier, lost work most likely composed at or before the end of the tenth century, since the existing account by Goscelin contains no information that postdates 1001, except for three miracles from Edward the Confessor's reign, which follow the conclusion of the *passio* proper and for which the author acknowledges oral testimony. Ridyard (1988 pp 48–50) endorses Fell's argument while echoing (p 50 note 167) her supposition that Byrhtferth's account probably was not derived from the lost work.

It should be pointed out that two mass prefaces with narrative details, composed specifically for Edward's feast day in the first half of the eleventh century, make no mention of the crucial role ascribed in the *passio* to Edward's stepmother Ælfthryth. See the *Missal of New Minster, Winchester* (ed. *HBS* 93.80–84) and the *Missal of Robert of Jumièges* (ed. *HBS* 11.3–4; see **LITURGY, MASSBOOKS**).

On Edward's cult in the context of late-tenth-century English history and politics, see Keynes (1980 pp 169–71), Folz (1980, 1984 pp 49–52), Rollason (1983 pp 2, 14, 17–19; 1989a pp 142–44), Ridyard (1988 pp

154–71), and Thacker (1996a pp 248–50). On the literary, hagiographic character of the *passio*, see C. Fell (1978).

See also C. Fell (1971 p 17) for a transcription of some Latin verses (beginning "Omnibus est recollenda dies," not listed in *ICL*) lamenting Edward's death and celebrating, as an eyewitness, the translation in 980. It is copied on to a blank leaf of a Canterbury Cathedral manuscript from ca. 1000, which also contains **BEDE**'s two lives of **CUTHBERTUS** and anthems for Cuthbert, **BENEDICTUS CASINENSIS**, and **GUTHLACUS**. See also Colgrave (1940 p 28). For other editions of Goscelin's *Passio Edwardi*, see the entry for *BHL* 2418 in *BHL NS*.

Egwinus, vita [BYRHTFERTH.Vit.Egwin.]: *BHL* 2432; *BLS* 4.643; *BSS* 4.972–73; *DHGE* 15.32–33.
ed.: Giles 1854 pp 349–96.
MSS London, BL Cotton Nero E. i: HG 344.
Lists – *Refs* none.

Ecgwine was bishop of Worcester (ca. 692) and founder and first abbot of nearby Evesham. He is presumed to have died in 717 (feast day December 30). He was unknown to, or ignored by, **BEDE** and did not become the subject of hagiography or other writing until Evesham began to prosper as a reformed monastery in the late tenth and eleventh centuries. The oldest life, written in the early eleventh century in the hermeneutic style, is now believed to be the work of **BYRHTFERTH**. The latter was linked to Evesham through the two houses' mutual dependency on the see of Worcester through the powerful Bishop **OSWALDUS WIGORNIENSIS** and through Evesham's abbot Ælfweard (ca. 1014–44), formerly a monk of Ramsey.

To suit the different stylistic tastes of the Anglo-Norman era, Byrhtferth's life was rewritten, and a book of miracles added, by Prior Dominic of Evesham (*BHL* 2433) shortly before the turn of the eleventh century (Lapidge 1978 pp 71–73).

The unique manuscript copy of the *Vita Egwini* in the London manuscript is accompanied by the only surviving copy of Byrhtferth's life of

Oswald (*BHL* 6374). These texts, along with a copy of **LANTFRED**'s translation and miracles of SWITHUNUS (*BHL* 7944–45), are of approximately the same date (third quarter of the eleventh century) as the **COTTON-CORPUS LEGENDARY**, which makes up the bulk of the manuscript, but the English lives were not part of the original Legendary and were added as a supplement to the beginning of Worcester's copy of the Legendary. All three texts have been the object of close attention by Michael Lapidge in recent years, and he has separate editions of each in progress. For discussion of Ecgwine's cult and hagiography, including Dominic of Evesham's late-eleventh-century reworking of Byrhtferth's *Vita Egwini*, see Lapidge's published papers of 1977, 1978, and 1979. See also Thacker (1996a pp 261–64).

Eleutherius et Antia, passio [ANON.Pas.Eleuth.Ant.]: *BHL* 2451; *BLS* 2.120–21; *BSS* 4.1012–16; *DHGE* 15.146.
    ed.: Mombritius 1910 1.443–46 and 658.
MSS 1. London, BL Cotton Nero E. i: HG 344.
    2. Salisbury, Cathedral Library 221 (formerly Oxford, Bodleian Library Fell 4): HG 754.5.
Lists none.
A-S Vers Mart (B19.bx).
Quots/Cits – Refs none.

The origins and development of the legend of the martyred bishop Eleutherius and his mother, Antia, are unclear. Some relationship exists between the Greek versions represented in *BHG* 568–71b and the Latin texts *BHL* 2450 and 2451, but priorities and dates are in dispute (Siegmund 1949 p 234). The earlier of the Latin versions, however, certainly seems to be the text in Mombritius, the Bollandists' Passio 2, of which there are copies in Continental legendaries of the late eighth and ninth centuries (Siegmund 1949 p 234). According to this version, Eleutherius is elevated to the episcopacy of Aeca (Troja) in Apulia at the age of twenty, during the reign of the emperor Hadrian (early second century), but is arrested and taken to Rome for trial where a series of sensational torments, emphasizing the use of fire, culminate in his martyrdom. His widowed mother and several companions are also executed.

This older Latin version was known to the Anglo-Saxons in one form or another. J. E. Cross (personal communication) confirms Herzfeld's opinion that the April 18 notice for the two saints in the **OLD ENGLISH MARTYROLOGY** (*Mart*; ed. Kotzor 1981 2.54–57) is based on this text, rather than on *BHL* 2450. Closely related to the version in Mombritius is the copy of the *passio* in the **COTTON-CORPUS LEGENDARY** manuscripts listed above (Jackson and Lapidge 1996 p 137).

The feast of Eleutherius and Antia (April 18) is only rarely recorded in Anglo-Saxon calendars (see F. Wormald 1934 p 19).

Eligius, vita [ANON.Vit.Elig.]: *BHL* 2477; *BSS* 4.1064–69; *CPL* 2094; *DHGE* 15.260–63; *DTC* 4.340–49; Farmer (1987) pp 156–57.
ed.: unpublished.
MSS Cambridge, Corpus Christi College 9: HG 36.
Lists – Refs none.

Before becoming bishop of Noyon in 641, Eligius (Eloi, Loy; feast day December 1) had been an important and productive goldsmith and moneyer in the service of the Merovingian kings Lothar II (died 629) and Dagobert I (died 639). During his busy ecclesiastical career as preacher and founder of monasteries, besides being a close friend of Saint Ouen (**AUDOENUS**), he was also associated with Queen Bathilde (**BALTHILDIS**) in anti-slavery legislation. Shortly after Eligius died in 660 a life, no longer extant, was written by Ouen himself. This lost life was the basis of the elaborately expanded *Vita Eligii* (*BHL* 2474–76) by an anonymous monk of Noyon in the eighth century, edited by Krusch (*MGH* SRM 4.663–742) with numerous omissions. The text listed here in a manuscript of the **COTTON-CORPUS LEGENDARY** is an epitome (pre-eleventh century) of this longer life. See Levison (*MGH* SRM 7.573) and Zettel (1979 p 32 note 106) regarding a copy formerly in Salisbury Cathedral Library 222 and now lost but listed in the table of contents. Other copies are mentioned by Krusch (*MGH* SRM 4.657), one of which, originally from St Gall, he assigns to the late tenth century. The epitome has apparently not been printed or studied. For further bibliography on the longer life (*BHL* 2474–76), see *CPL* and Berschin (1986–91 2.58–63).

Elphegus. See ÆLFEGUS.

Emerentiana: *BLS* 1.152–53; *BSS* 4.1161–66.

The legendary martyrdom of Emerentiana is narrated briefly as part of the legend of **AGNES**, *Passio Agnetis* XV (ed. *PL* 17.741), on which the brief notices in **BEDE**'s **MARTYROLOGIUM** (ed. Dubois and Renaud 1976 p 20.17–20) and the **OLD ENGLISH MARTYROLOGY** (*Mart*, B19.am; ed. Kotzor 1981 2.24–25) are based, but the story is believed to be a fifth-century interpolation rather than an integral part of the legend. Emerentiana was probably an authentic Roman martyr (with a feast day originally on September 16), but her incorporation into the legend of Agnes, as the latter's "collactanea" (foster sister) is probably due to the physical proximity of their early shrines on the Via Nomentana. In the ninth century, Emerentiana's relics were removed to the basilica of St Agnes. Emerentiana's feast day, commemorated in some Anglo-Saxon calendars, is January 23, Agnes's January 21. See Ortenberg (1992 pp 179–80) for a brief account of late Anglo-Saxon liturgical devotion to Emerentiana.

ÆLFRIC omits the Emerentiana episode from his account of Agnes in **LIVES OF SAINTS** (*ÆLS*; ed. *EETS* OS 76 and 82), although it is virtually certain that his source contained it. For further information, see above, the entry for Agnes.

Eosterwinus: Farmer (1987) pp 142–43.

The life of Eosterwine (650–86, feast day March 7), a cousin of **BENEDICTUS BISCOPUS**, is narrated in the collective biographies of the abbots of Wearmouth and Jarrow, BEDE's HISTORIA ABBATUM (ed. Plummer 1896 1.364–87) and the life of CEOLFRIDUS (1.388–404). The ninth-century OLD ENGLISH MARTYROLOGY also allots him a quite detailed separate notice (*Mart*, B19.av; ed. Kotzor 1981 2.30; sourced p 291). Eosterwine appears to have had no calendar cult in England.

Erasmus, passio [ANON.Pas.Erasm.]: *BHL* 2578–82; *BLS* 2.453–54; *BSS* 4.1289–90; *DHGE* 15.666–67.
ed.: Mombritius 1910 1.485–88 and 665.
MSS 1. London, BL Cotton Nero E. i: HG 344.
2. Paris, Bibliothèque Nationale lat. 10861: HG 898.
3. Salisbury, Cathedral Library 221 (formerly Oxford, Bodleian Library Fell 4): HG 754.5.
Lists none.
A-S Vers *Mart* (B19.dg).
Quots/Cits – Refs none.

Erasmus (Elmo; feast day June 2) is known to have had a cult at Formiae in Campagna (of which probably he was once bishop) during the time of **GREGORY THE GREAT**. His relics were later translated to Gaeta, perhaps in 842 owing to Saracen invasions, but his origins and true identity remain obscure (see *AS* Nov. 2/2.296–97). In the Latin *passio*, a ninth-century composition derived from a Greek original (*BHG* 602) and described by Tillemont as "excellement mauvais" (Halkin 1983 p 5), he is conflated with another Bishop Erasmus, of Antioch in Syria, where he is said to have suffered numerous spectacular tortures, including the famous disemboweling, before being rescued and brought by **MICHAEL ARCHANGELUS** to Formiae, where he died peacefully a week later.

The Anglo-Saxons were familiar with one or more recensions of the widely diversified Passio 1. Cross (1984a pp 28–29, 34–36) closely sources the notice in the **OLD ENGLISH MARTYROLOGY** (*Mart*; ed. Kotzor 1981 2.112–14) in relation to printed sources and several manuscripts of the eighth–ninth century, finding the Old English account dependent on a Latin source similar to, but not identical with, the text of the *passio* in the Paris manuscript listed here (Canterbury, ninth century) and a closely related manuscript now in Vienna. M. P. Brown (1986) identifies the Paris text as *BHL* 2578, but with the *explicit* of the variant version *BHL* 2582, as printed in the edition of Mombritius (1910). Cross's analysis, however, makes clear that there are numerous textual variants distinguishing the copy in the Paris manuscript from the printed editions. The copies of the *passio* in the eleventh-century manuscripts of the **COTTON-CORPUS LEGENDARY** combine features of *BHL* 2578 and 2580, according to Jackson and Lapidge (1996 p 138). As in so many other cases, a comprehensive critical edition of the *passio* would facilitate more rigorous classification of the Anglo-Saxon witnesses to the manuscript tradition.

Erkenwaldus.

The earliest extant Latin vita (*BHL* 2600) of the monk Erkenwald (Eorconwold, Earcenwald), founder of Barking and Chertsey abbeys, bishop of London 675–93 (feast day April 30), is a late-eleventh- or early-twelfth-century composition, probably from St Paul's, London (*BHL* 2600; ed. Whatley 1989 pp 86–96). The only substantial Anglo-Saxon memorial is **BEDE**'s brief account in **HISTORIA ECCLESIASTICA** IV.vi (Colgrave and Mynors 1969 p 354). The evidence of some passages in Goscelin's late-eleventh-century life of Erkenwald's sister, Æthelburh (**ÆTHELBURGA**), suggests there was an earlier, short life of the saint, which probably predated the destruction of the Anglo-Saxon minster of St Paul's (1087) and which was based on Bede but reshaped and slightly expanded with additional material. This short life was later incorporated into the longer life, *BHL* 2600 (see Whatley 1989 pp 19–23).

Accounts of Erkenwald in all the standard reference sources are unreliable. More accurate accounts are noted in Whatley (1989 p 201 note 1); in addition, see P. Wormald (1985 pp 9–11), Blair (1989 pp 97–98, 103), and Yorke (1990 pp 45–57, especially p 56).

Ermino, vita [ANSO.LAUB.Vit.Erm.]: *BHL* 2614.
ed.: *MGH* SRM 6.461–70.
MSS ?Bloomington, Indiana University, Lilly Library, Poole 43: HG 796.6.
Lists – Refs none.

The Poole manuscript, as noted by Bond and Faye (1962 p 181), is a fragment, comprising one folio of a copy of the mid-eighth-century *Vita sancti Erminonis*. Ermino was an eighth-century abbot of Lobbes (feast day April 25), a monastery founded in 654 by Landelin. The work was written about a generation after his death in 737 by one of his successors, Anso, who also composed a life of an earlier abbot, Ursmarus. The manuscript fragment is dated by HG between the late eleventh century and the beginning of the twelfth. The fragment, not surprisingly, went unnoticed by Levison in his *MGH* edition, which is based on several Continental manuscripts dating from the tenth century and later (*MGH* SRM 6.448).

Ethelbertus. See ÆTHELBERHTUS.

Ethelburga. See ÆTHELBURGA.

Etheldreda. See ÆTHELDRYTHA.

Ethelredus et Ethelbertus. See ÆTHELREDUS ET ÆTHELBERHTUS.

Eugenia, passio [ANON.Pas.Eugen.1a/PS.RUFIN.]: *BHL* 2666; *BSS* 5.181–83; *CPL* 2184; *DHGE* 15.1374–76.
ed.: *PL* 21.1105–22.
MSS – Lists none.
A-S Vers 1. ALDH.Carm.uirg. 1883–1924.

2. ALDH.Pros.uirg. 296.15–298.11.
3. *Mart* (B19.c and cz).
Quots/Cits none.
Refs ALDH.Pros.uirg. 298.2.

Eugenia (feast day December 25) is among several early female saints (see also **EUPHROSYNA**) whose legends include "transvestite" episodes. In the first part of her elaborate *passio*, she lives as a monk in an Egyptian monastery until she becomes involved in an episode of attempted seduction, culminating in a trial before her own father. Her martyrdom, in the company of a friend Basilla, takes place after a later, unconnected series of episodes in Rome. On the transvestite theme, see the references supplied by Szarmach (1990 p 156 note 4; see also Patlagean 1976).

Delehaye (1936 pp 171–86) came to the conclusion that the Eugenia legend, which is cited by the poet **AVITUS OF VIENNE** (died 518), originated in Latin, not in Greek as formerly believed, and that she is a composite of two originally separate figures, the one Egyptian, the other Roman. Delehaye distinguished two main recensions of the *passio*, represented respectively by Mombritius's edition (1910 2.391–97 and 715; *BHL* 2667), considered the older and shorter version, and that printed in *PL* among the works of **RUFINUS** and in the **VITAE PATRUM** (*BHL* 2666). Cross (1982b p 392), working with several early medieval manuscript copies, concludes that Delehaye has oversimplified the textual situation, since various kinds of mixed texts, combining elements of *BHL* 2666 and 2667, were common during our period, although copies in two of the early legendaries, now in Würzburg and Turin, preserve a text more nearly resembling the *PL* text.

A version similar to the *PL* text seems to have been current among the early Anglo-Saxons, although **BEDE**'s **MARTYROLOGIUM** notice for September 11 (ed. Dubois and Renaud 1976 p 167.2–3), mentioning Eugenia with her eunuch companions (**PROTUS ET HYACINTHUS**), is too brief to link to the *passio* (Quentin 1908 p 111). **ALDHELM**, on the other hand, in the verse and prose versions of his **DE VIRGINITATE** (ALDH.Carm.uirg., Pros.uirg.; ed. *MGH* AA 15), refers to a "book of Eugenia's life" that Ehwald (*MGH* AA 15.296 note 4) identifies as *BHL*

2666. Aldhelm's usual tendency to rewrite borrowed material makes it difficult to determine the character or affiliations of his source, but Ehwald's notes point out some close verbal parallels between the prose version and the *PL* text; Aldhelm's schooling at Canterbury under **THEODORE OF CANTERBURY** and Hadrian is a probable context for his knowledge of the *passio*. The work is among the texts lemmatized in the Leiden Glossary (preserved in an eighth-century St Gall manuscript: **GLOSSARIES**), which derives from Theodore's Canterbury school. Aldhelm's account contains the rare word *basterna*, one of the Leiden lemmas from the *passio*. See Lapidge (1986a especially pp 54, 58).

Cross (1982b) demonstrates in detail that the separate notices in the **OLD ENGLISH MARTYROLOGY** for Eugenia (*Mart*; ed. Kotzor 1981 2.3–5, December 26), and her Roman friend Basilla, martyred for refusing a pagan suitor (pp 107–08, May 20), depend closely on *BHL* 2666 (with some variant readings reflected in the Würzburg and Turin manuscripts), rather than on *BHL* 2667 or a mixed text. See also below, the entry for Protus et Hyacinthus. Basilla's story is retold in Old English by **ÆLFRIC** as part of his *Eugenia*, lines 326–68, in LIVES OF SAINTS (ed. *EETS* OS 76 and 82) but using a somewhat different recension of the *passio*. See next entry.

Eugenia's feast is listed in a few Anglo-Saxon calendars on March 16 (see F. Wormald 1934 pp 18, 32, 46, 60).

Eugenia, passio [ANON.Pas.Eugen.1ab]: *BHL* 2666m.
  ed.: Fábrega Grau 1953–55 2.83–98.
MSS Cambridge, Corpus Christi College 9: HG 36.
Lists none.
A-S Vers *ÆLS* Eugenia (B1.3.3).
Quots/Cits – Refs none.

In later Anglo-Saxon England the available evidence indicates the currency of a *Passio Eugeniae* of the mixed type (see previous entry for older version). While Ott (1892 pp 8–10) in his sourcing of **ÆLFRIC**'s *Eugenia* in LIVES OF SAINTS (*ÆLS*; ed. *EETS* OS 76 and 82) specifies

BHL 2666, Zettel (1979 pp 62–64 and 110–21) shows that Ælfric used a text combining features of *BHL* 2666 and 2667, as in the version preserved in the eleventh-century Worcester copy of the **COTTON-CORPUS LEGENDARY** (the Cambridge manuscript above) and its later affiliates. According to Zettel, this mixed text is also represented in a Brussels manuscript (1979 pp 33, 37), but he does not refer to any of the earlier mixed texts cited by Cross (1982b). Both Cross and Zettel refer to the edition of Fábrega Grau, based on a tenth-century Spanish manuscript, as representative of the mixed type of text that the Bollandists distinguish as *BHL* 2666m. It is also cited by Roy (1992 p 21 note 3) as identical to the Cotton-Corpus Legendary text. On Mombritius's edition, see previous entry.

Magennis (1986 pp 322–24) has a brief but valuable analysis of Ælfric's adaptation of his Latin sources but does not focus on the precise version. For critical analysis of Ælfric's *Eugenia*, see Szarmach (1990) and Roy (1992); the latter closely compares Ælfric's Old English text with the *passio* in question here and with the English manuscripts of the Cotton-Corpus Legendary.

Eulalia Barcinone, passio [ANON.Pas.Eul.Barc.]: *BHL* 2696; *BLS* 4.530; *CPL* 2069a; *DHGE* 15.1380–84.
  ed.: Narbey 1899–1912 2.62–64.
MSS Paris, Bibliothèque Nationale lat. 10861: HG 898.
Lists none.
A-S Vers 1. BEDA.Mart. 221.1–5.
  2. *Mart* (B19.hi).
Quots/Cits – Refs none.

Eulalia of Barcelona (feast day February 12), supposedly martyred as a young girl under the prefect Dacian during the Diocletian persecution, is regarded by many as a doublet of **EULALIA EMERITAE** (feast day December 10), but the question is by no means settled, especially in Spain where Fábrega Grau has argued that this Eulalia's Passio 1 (*BHL* 2693) is a mid-seventh-century composition by Bishop Quirinus of Barcelona, based on oral tradition surrounding the saint's authentic cult in Barcelona, and that it is entirely independent of the cult of Eulalia of Merida (see Fábrega Grau's bibliography and summary of his position, *DHGE* 15.1380–84). The Bollandist De Gaiffier (1959), along with other scholars outside Spain, does not accept Fábrega Grau's arguments. The assessment of García Rodríguez (1966 pp 289–90) is also unfavorable.

The earliest *Passio Eulaliae* known to the English is the one used by **BEDE** in his **MARTYROLOGIUM** (BEDA.Mart.; ed. Dubois and Renaud 1976; sourced by Quentin 1908 p 71) and also represented in the Paris manuscript (from ninth-century Canterbury). It relates the martyrdom of Eulalia of Barcelona, but associates her with December 10 (on Anglo-Saxon calendar entries for both Eulalias, see the next entry). According to Fábrega Grau, this version was composed in the early eighth century, outside Spain. The same *passio* also lies behind the notice in the **OLD ENGLISH MARTYROLOGY** (*Mart*; ed. Kotzor 1981 2.261–62; sourced by Cross 1981c), likewise for December 10. **ALDHELM**'s brief but vague effusion, in his **DE VIRGINITATE** (*Carmen* 2009–23, *Prosa* 300.10–12; ed. *MGH* AA 15), indicates only his awareness that Eulalia was a virgin martyr, but his precise source is undetermined. He may well have had in mind Eulalia of Merida, since he appears to have known **PRUDENTIUS**'s **PERISTEPHANON** (see next entry).

Eulalia Emeritae, passio [ANON.Pas.Eul.Emer.]: *BHL* 2700; *CPL* 2069b; *DHGE* 15.1384–85.
 ed.: Fábrega Grau 1953–55 2.68–78.
MSS Cambridge, Corpus Christi College 9: HG 36.
Lists – Refs none.

The cult of Eulalia, virgin, martyred at Merida, Spain, for her defiant Christianity under Maximian in the early fourth century, is attested in the early fifth century by the poet **PRUDENTIUS** in **PERISTEPHANON** III (ed. *CCSL* 126), his hymn on her shrine and martyrdom (see also IV.38 and XI.238), and by other early Christian writers. According to the most recent editor, Fábrega Grau (*DHGE* 15.1384), the *passio* in question here was composed in the late seventh century, drawing not only on Prudentius but also on a lost "texte primitif" that was itself Prudentius's source. This argument is not completely convincing, since there is no tangible evidence for the existence of the lost "acta." The *passio*'s non-Prudentian features need not necessarily derive from a pre-Prudentian source. Fábrega Grau admits in the end (1385) that all we know for sure about Eulalia is in Prudentius.

Given the currency of Prudentius's poems in later Anglo-Saxon England, it is not surprising that the *passio* current among the later Anglo-Saxons is the one that most clearly matches Prudentius's treatment of Eulalia, for example in the eleventh-century **COTTON-CORPUS LEGENDARY** and its twelfth-century affiliates (Zettel 1979 p 32; Jackson and Lapidge 1996 p 143). The influence of the Barcelona tradition (see previous entry), however, is evident in the late-tenth- and eleventh-century English calendars, several of which have both December 10 and February 12 feasts (F. Wormald 1934 pp 31 and 41, 45 and 55, 227 and 237), while one (p 27) has December 10 and 12.

For further information on Eulalia, see Roger Collins (1980) and García Rodríguez (1966 pp 284–89).

Euphemia, passio [ANON.Pas.Euphem.]: *BHL* 2708; *BLS* 3.567–68; *BSS* 5.154–60; *DACL* 5.745–46.

ed.: Mombritius 1910 1.454–59 and 660–61.

MSS 1. Dublin, Trinity College 174: HG 215.
   2. London, BL Cotton Nero E. i: HG 344.
   3. Paris, Bibliothèque Nationale lat. 10861: HG 898.
   4. Salisbury, Cathedral Library 222 (formerly Oxford, Bodleian Library Fell 1): HG 754.6.

Lists none.

A-S Vers 1. BEDA.Mart. 171.2–9.
   2. *Mart* (B19.hc).

Quots/Cits – Refs none.

Nothing certain is known about Euphemia (feast day September 16) except that she was martyred under Diocletian in 303 at Chalcedon, future site of the fourth council of the church (451). By the late fourth century, her cult and a varied legendary tradition are attested not only at Chalcedon by Asterius of Amasea, but also in the West in Aquileia, Milan, and Rouen (*BSS* 5.154–58; Schrier 1984). The earliest surviving *passio*, featured here, was originally composed in Greek in the fifth century (*BHG* 619d), probably on the occasion of, or soon after, the Chalcedon council of 451, and was rendered into Latin in the sixth/seventh century; it is now an important witness to the state of the poorly preserved Greek text (Halkin 1965 pp 10–12; Siegmund 1949 pp 234–35). The *passio*, filled with typically sensational tortures, has not been much valued by most modern scholars for its contents (*AS* Nov. 2/2.511), but see Schneider (1951).

Attesting to the importance of Euphemia's cult in Anglo-Saxon England are four manuscript copies of her *passio*, spanning the early and later Anglo-Saxon periods, all more or less conforming to the version printed by Mombritius. As might be expected, however, given the apparent complexity of the *passio*'s textual transmission (see *BHL NS* p 309), the English manuscripts exhibit numerous minor textual variants from the printed edition. In the eleventh-century Cotton manuscript, for example, some of the variants in the closing prayer are shared with a Paris manuscript collated in Mombritius (1910 1.661).

The text in the Dublin manuscript (Colker 1991 1.321–22) is among those copied by the Group I scribes at Salisbury Cathedral in the late eleventh century (Webber 1992 p 142). It appears to be somewhat abridged and reworded, by comparison with Mombritius's text (according to J. D. Pheifer, personal communication, to whom I am also grateful for a copy of his transcription of the text). For the Paris manuscript (from ninth-century Canterbury), see M. P. Brown (1986).

BEDE draws on a text of the *passio* in his **MARTYROLOGIUM** (BEDA. Mart.; ed. Dubois and Renaud 1976; sourced by Quentin 1908 pp 71–72), as well as in the brief allusion to Euphemia in his hymn to **ÆTHELDRYTHA**, line 20 (**HISTORIA ECCLESIASTICA** IV.xx; ed. Colgrave and Mynors 1969 p 398). Surprisingly, she is not mentioned by **ALDHELM**.

In discussing the account in the ninth-century **OLD ENGLISH MARTYROLOGY** (*Mart*; ed. Kotzor 1981 2.210–11), Cross (1983c) confirms that the source is this *passio*. He lists the Paris manuscript among several early copies but does not suggest that it has any special relation to the *Martyrology*. He points out (p 21) that in the phrase "sigefæst fæmnan" (Kotzor 1981 2.211.11) the *Martyrology* echoes the epithet "virgo . . . triumphatrix" in a preface for Euphemia's feast day in the Ambrosian liturgy, which has no equivalent in the *passio*. The Ambrosian preface is among those reckoned to be of fifth- or sixth-century composition (Paredi 1937 pp 191 and 218; Schrier 1984 pp 330, 336) and could therefore have been among the older liturgical materials brought to England in the seventh century or even earlier. The author appears to be referring to ancient tradition, written or remembered, rather than a recent import when he says of Euphemia "ure fædras hi nemdon þa sigefæstan fæmnan" ("our fathers named her the victorious maid"). Euphemia's September 16 feast (not discussed by Ortenberg 1992) is widely commemorated in calendars and service books of the later Anglo-Saxon period. There is no critical edition of the *passio*, those of Mombritius and Fábrega Grau (1953–55 2.338–45) being based on one or two manuscripts with minimal apparatus.

For further bibliography on the historical context of Euphemia's legend and cult, see Delehaye (1966) and Schrier (1984).

Eupraxia (Euphrasia), vita [ANON.Vit.Euphrax.]: *BHL* 2718; *BLS* 1.581–83; *BSS* 5.233–35; *DHGE* 15.1411–12.
ed.: *AS* Mart. 2.265–74.
MSS 1. Dublin, Trinity College 174: HG 215.
2. London, Lambeth Palace 173: HG 508.
Lists – Refs none.

The Greek life (*BHG* 631) of Eupraxia (ca. 380–410, feast day March 13) is believed to be a faithful record, composed soon after her death in an Egyptian monastery, of the saint's early vocation for the religious life and her subsequent fulfilment of the monastic ideals of asceticism, humility, and charity. The dates and affiliations of the various Latin translations are not known, but an important early legendary now in Turin, of the eighth/ninth century, contains a copy of the version discussed here (Siegmund 1949 p 235, who also remarks that copies of the legend are comparatively few in the early medieval period). We have found no evidence for Anglo-Saxon knowledge of the *vita* before the two late-eleventh-century copies listed above, although the saint's name is substituted for that of EUPHROSYNA of Alexandria (a common confusion: see *BSS* 5.233) in the rubrics of the main copy of the anonymous Old English *Euphrosyne* (NRK 162, art. 44); see next entry. The text of the *passio* in the Lambeth Palace manuscript breaks off early, fol 221v, after "Et dum aliqua earum aliquando contingeret infirmari, nullum ei" (James and Jenkins 1930–32 p 274; cf. "et cum aliquam earum aliquando contigerat infirmari, nullum ei," *AS* Mart. 2.267a.49). The Dublin text, however, copied by the Group I Salisbury Cathedral scribes (Webber 1992 p 142) in the late eleventh century, appears to be complete (Colker 1991 1.322–23).

For another edition, see *PL* 73.623–44.

Euphrosyna, vita [ANON.Vit.Euphros.]: *BHL* 2723; *BLS* 1.4–5; *BSS* 5.175–76.
ed.: *AS* Feb. 2.537–41.

MSS – Lists none.
A-S Vers *LS* 7 (Euphr, B3.3.7).
Quots/Cits – Refs none.

According to her legend, Euphrosyne of Alexandria (feast day February 11) was a female ascetic who disguised herself as a man and changed her name to Smaragdus in order to become a monk. Evidence so far adduced for Anglo-Saxon knowledge of the originally Greek *vita* of Euphrosyne (*BHG* 625, translated into Latin in the eighth century; see Siegmund 1949 p 235) is confined to the anonymous Old English prose

Euphrosyne listed here, which occurs in two eleventh-century manuscripts in the British Library (*LS* 7; ed. *EETS* OS 94 and 114). The source was identified first by C. Loomis (1931 pp 5–6); see also Magennis (1985a p 299). Loomis, following the work's editor, Skeat, had assumed that the Old English *Euphrosyne* was ÆLFRIC's work. Although this is not the case (Magennis 1986 pp 342–47), the similarity of approach to the Latin source supports the generally accepted view that *Euphrosyne* is contemporary with Ælfric. Wenisch (1979 pp 57, 291) finds in its vocabulary occasional traces of Anglian influence. For a recent critical assessment, see Szarmach (1996a).

Further work remains to be done on the Latin *vita*, Rosweyde's edition of which is reprinted in *PL* 73.643–52. The *AS* edition cited above is based on several manuscripts and collated with Rosweyde's. Neither is satisfactory as a guide to the early medieval state of the text.

Hugh Magennis

Euplus, passio [ANON.Pas.Eupl.]: *BHL* 2729; *BLS* 3.313–14; *BSS* 5.231–33; *DHGE* 15.1417.
   ed.: Mombritius 1910 1.448–49 and 659.
MSS 1. London, BL Cotton Nero E. i: HG 344.
      2. Salisbury, Cathedral Library 222 (formerly Oxford, Bodleian Library Fell 1): HG 754.6.
Lists none.
A-S Vers 1. BEDA.Mart. 148.15–17.
      2. *Mart* (B19.fs).
Quots/Cits – Refs none.

The *Passio Eupli*, long regarded as one of the select corpus of historically authentic accounts of an early Christian martyr's trial and execution, tells how Euplus (or Euplius; feast day August 12) provoked his own arrest and subsequent martyrdom (303/04) by loudly proclaiming his Christian faith outside the courtroom in Catania, Sicily, while flaunting a personal copy of the gospels. A Latin translation of the original Greek *passio* (*BHG* 629–30) has assumed several variant forms, one of which, classified by the Bollandists as Passio 1a (*BHL* 2728), has appeared in numerous modern editions, including most recently that of Musurillo (1972 pp 314–18). Siegmund (1949 pp 235–36), however, citing the findings of Franchi de' Cavalieri (1928), pronounces *BHL* 2728 a post-medieval translation of a later Greek recension! Undoubtedly of the early medieval period, however, is Passio 1b, printed by Mombritius, which is extant in several early legendaries (see Siegmund 1949 p 236; Cross 1981e p 191) and has been identified as the text used by **BEDE** in his **MARTYROLOGIUM** (BEDA.Mart.; ed. Dubois and Renaud 1976; sourced by Quentin 1908 p 72) and by the ninth-century author of the **OLD ENGLISH MARTYROLOGY** (*Mart*; ed. Kotzor 1981 2.178–79), partially sourced by Cross (1981e pp 191–92), who notes the apparently Irish manner in which the *Martyrology*, expanding on the *passio*, depicts Euplus carrying his book of gospels (Kotzor 1981 2.178.6–7). The same version is also represented in the two eleventh-century manuscripts of the **COTTON-CORPUS LEGENDARY** (Zettel 1979 p 23; cf. Jackson and Lapidge 1996 p 139 who refer to both *BHL* 2728 and 2729).

Euplus was not important liturgically among the Anglo-Saxons, to judge from surviving calendars and service books. His August 12 feast day, in the crowded octave of Saint **LAURENTIUS**, is commemorated in the highly eclectic Nunnaminster calendar of the eleventh century (F. Wormald 1934 p 37).

Eusebius Romae, passio [ANON.Pas.Euseb.Rom.]: *BHL* 2740; *BLS* 3.328; *BSS* 5.260–61; *DHGE* 15.1472–73.
 ed.: Mombritius 1910 1.459 and 661.
MSS 1. London, BL Cotton Nero E. i: HG 344.
 2. Salisbury, Cathedral Library 222 (formerly Oxford, Bodleian Library Fell 1): HG 754.6.
Lists – Refs none.

Originally the founder of a Roman church that bore his "titulus," Eusebius "presbyter" became the subject of a martyrdom legend probably fabricated in the sixth or seventh century, after the church became known as "ecclesia sancti Eusebii" following a common pattern (see, e.g., ANASTASIA). His feast day (August 14) is provided with a mass in some of the sacramentaries of Roman origin and hence among the Anglo-Saxons (e.g., in the so-called *Missal of Robert of Jumièges*, early eleventh century; see **LITURGY, MASSBOOKS**), but usually with the title of confessor, as is true of most of the entries for his feast day in Anglo-Saxon calendars. In two calendars of the late tenth or early eleventh century, associated with Canterbury, his feast is graded and he is entitled "presbyter," as in the rubric to the English copies of the *passio* in manuscripts, listed above, of the **COTTON-CORPUS LEGENDARY** (F. Wormald 1934 pp 51, 65; also p 233).

Eusebius Vercellensis, vita [ANON.Vit.Euseb.Verc.]: *BHL* 2748–49; *BLS* 4.569–71; *BSS* 5.263–70; *DHGE* 15.1477–83.
ed.: Ughelli 1644–62 4.1030–48.

MSS – Lists none.
A-S Vers Mart (B19.ff).
Quots/Cits – Refs none.

Eusebius of Vercelli (Anglo-Saxon feast day August 1; see *DHGE* 15.1481) was born in Sardinia early in the fifth century, was educated in Rome, and became bishop of Vercelli in N. Italy ca. 344. He rose to become one of the leaders of the Western church and a champion of Athanasian orthodoxy during the reign of the Arian sympathizer Constantius, who exiled Eusebius for his role in the council of Milan (355). For his sufferings in exile Eusebius was later credited with martyrdom although he apparently died peacefully in his diocese (371). The life printed by Ughelli (*BHL* 2748–49), in which he is said to have been martyred by the Arians, is a legendary composition of the eighth or ninth century.

Quentin (1908 p 100) suggests that **BEDE**'s **MARTYROLOGIUM** notice (BEDA.Mart.; ed. Dubois and Renaud 1976 p 140.7–9) depends on the *passio*, but Cross (1977a pp 102–03) points out problems in Quentin's argument and identifies **PSEUDO-MAXIMUS OF TURIN**,

SERMONES VII (*BHL* 2752b; ed. *CCSL* 23.24–26), as Bede's source for Eusebius's martyrdom. Cross (1977a pp 101–02) argues, however, that the **OLD ENGLISH MARTYROLOGY** (*Mart*; ed. Kotzor 1981 2.167–68) draws on the *passio* cited here as well as on Pseudo-Maximus, *Sermones* VIII (*BHL* 2752d; ed. *CCSL* 23.28–29).

Besides Ughelli's first edition, the *passio* is reprinted in the second edition (1717–22 4.749–61). I have not seen the modern edition of the *passio* by China or that in the *Miscellanea Augustana* (see bibliography in *BHL NS* p 313).

Eusebius et Felix. See CAESARIUS.

Eustachius, passio [ANON.Pas.Eust.]: *BHL* 2760; *BLS* 3.606–07; *BSS* 5.281–89.
  ed.: Mombritius 1910 1.466–73 and 663.
MSS 1. London, BL Cotton Otho A. xiii: HG 351.
  2. Cambridge, Corpus Christi College 9: HG 36.
Lists none.
A-S Vers 1. *LS* 8 (Eust, B3.3.8).
  2. ?ANON.Pas.Eust.metr.
Quots/Cits – Refs none.

The first mention of Eustace (Eustachius, Eustathius) in the West (Anglo-Saxon feast day November 2) is considered to be that of John of Damascus, *De imaginibus* (*PG* 94.1382), a work translated into Latin immediately after its composition in 726 (Heffernan 1973 p 65). A considerable number of Latin versions of the legend of Eustace was produced from the ninth century on, of which at least two were known in Anglo-Saxon England: one the prose *passio* (*BHL* 2760), the other (*BHL* 2767) a hexameter rendering of the prose text (see the next entry for the possibility that England was the original home of the hexameter version). The prose *passio* is itself a reworking of an older text, *BHL* 2761, believed by Siegmund (1949 p 236) to have been translated from the

Greek of *BHG* 641, possibly in connection with the introduction of the cult of Eustace into Rome under Pope Gregory II (715–33).

The date of the composition of *BHL* 2760 is unknown, but the earliest extant manuscripts are tenth century (Monteverdi 1908–11 p 397), and the original may have been composed in the ninth (see the reference in Lapidge 1988b p 257 note 10). This *passio* was included in the **COTTON-CORPUS LEGENDARY**, as represented by the mid-eleventh-century Cambridge manuscript above (provenance Worcester). From somewhat earlier, in the first half of the eleventh century, fifteen burnt fragments survive of the copy originally on fols 1–20 of the Cotton manuscript (new foliation 1–15). See also Zettel (1979 p 28) for a twelfth-century manuscript affiliated with the Cotton-Corpus Legendary.

Other evidence indicates that copies of the *passio* were known in England at least as early as the later tenth century. As first pointed out by C. Loomis (1931 pp 4–5), it is the source of the Old English prose *Eustace*, surviving in two manuscripts from which it was edited by Skeat (*LS* 8; ed. *EETS* OS 94 and 114) as a work of **ÆLFRIC**. Magennis (1985) shows that the Cotton-Corpus texts of the *passio* represent the Old English writer's source more closely than the printed editions used by C. Loomis. Although the Old English version is not Ælfric's work (Magennis 1986 pp 336–42), as C. Loomis also assumed, it is reasonable to date it in Ælfric's time, around the turn of the tenth century. Examination of the vocabulary has led Wenisch (1979 pp 57, 258, 291, and passim) to suggest Anglian influence on its composition, although Lapidge (1988b p 263) has suggested the possibility that the translator worked in collaboration with Ælfric.

In addition to the edition in Mombritius, see also *AS* Sept. 6.123–35. On the cult of Eustace in Anglo-Saxon England, see Lapidge (1988b pp 259–60).

Hugh Magennis

Eustachius, passio metrica [Anon.Pas.Eust.metr.]: *BHL* 2767; *ICL* 14237; *ICVL* 16700.

ed.: Varnhagen 1881 pp 4–25.

MSS none.
Lists 1. ?Æthelwold: ML 4.9.
2. Peterborough: ML 13.60.
A-S Vers – Refs none.

The "Passio Eustachii Placide uersifice" mentioned in a booklist thought to come from Peterborough ca. 1100 (ML 13.60), and probably identical to the "Vita Eustachii" donated to Peterborough in the late tenth century (ML 4.9) by Bishop **ÆTHELWOLD** (see also **ÆTHELWOLDUS**) is probably, if not definitely, the hexameter poem preserved in a late-tenth-century manuscript of South German provenance, now in Oxford and printed by Varnhagen (1881). The poem is discussed by Lapidge (1988b), who adduces evidence, which he admits is "not decisive" (p 265), for the possibility that the poem was composed in England (perhaps at Abingdon, where Æthelwold's foundation possessed a relic of Eustace), in time for Æthelwold to send a copy to Peterborough ca. 970. The German copy would presumably be based on a tenth-century English exemplar (Lapidge 1988b pp 264–65).

See also Monteverdi (1908–11 p 407).

Hugh Magennis

Eustochium: *BLS* 5.302–04; *DHGE* 16.43–45.

Eustochium (died 420, feast day September 28) and her mother Paula were two important members of **JEROME**'s circle of female disciples and patrons. Under his influence Eustochium took vows of perpetual virginity. **ALDHELM** in D**E** **VIRGINITATE** (*Carmen* 2121–61, *Prosa* 303.7–304.3; ed. *MGH* AA 15) praises Eustochium's learning, along with that of her mother, and credits them with prompting Jerome to write many of his biblical commentaries for their edification, as well as the treatise on virginity (**EPISTULAE** XXII; ed. *CSEL* 54.143–211), addressed to Eustochium, which is Aldhelm's principal source for his eulogy and to which he refers explicitly (*Carmen* 2153–57, *Prosa* 304.2–3).

See the main entry for Jerome for information about manuscripts and other witnesses to this text's circulation in Anglo-Saxon England.

The spurious letter of Jerome to Eustochium and Paula, "Cogitis me," composed in the ninth century by **PASCHASIUS RADBERTUS**, contains a discussion of the assumption of the Virgin Mary, used by **ÆLFRIC** in CATHOLIC HOMILIES I, 30, lines 1–184 (*ÆCHom*, B1.1.32; ed. *EETS* SS 17; see Clayton 1990 pp 235–40).

Eutyches et Victorinus et Maro. See NEREUS ET ACHILLEUS.

Evurtius, vita [LUCIFER.Vit.Evurt.]: *BHL* 2799; *BSS* 5.401; *DHGE* 16.97–98.
ed.: *AS* Sept. 3.52–58.

MSS – A-S Vers none.
Quots/Cits see below.
Refs none.

Evurtius (Euverte; feast day September 7), about whom very little is known, is believed to have been the fourth bishop of Orléans, immediately preceding **ANIANUS** (Aignan), and probably identical to the "Eortius" present at the council of Valence in 374 (*DHGE* 16.97–98). The Exeter List of Relics (*Rec* 10.8, B16.10.8; ed. Förster 1943 p 76; Conner 1993a pp 182–83) briefly describes one of the more celebrated episodes in his legend: the hand of God appears above his head during Mass, blessing the host just as Evurtius himself is elevating it. The wording of the Old English passage ("Of sanctus Euurties lichaman þæs biscopes þam atiwde dextera Dei, þæt is Godes swiðre þa þa he mæssode, 7 þa offrunge mid heofenlicre bletsunge gebletsode") may be an echo of a passage in the ninth-century *Vita Evurtii* XIV (56.17–22). There is an account of the same episode, however, with similar wording, in the martyrology of Saint-Quentin (*PL* 94.1036; see Dubois and Lemaitre 1993 p 118), although it is unlikely this was known in England. The relics list alone refers to the hand with the Latin phrase "dextera Dei." Admittedly a commonplace, this may be the Exeter author's own embellishment, or it may reflect the wording of a lost source or unpublished manuscript variant of the *vita*. Other Anglo-Saxon references to Evurtius are rare. For a solitary occurrence in a litany along with Anianus, see Lapidge (1992a p 103).

The earliest extant English manuscript copy of the *vita* is Lincoln Cathedral B. 1. 16 (mid-twelfth century).

Exaltatio Sanctae Crucis. See IESUS CHRISTUS, EXALTATIO SANCTAE CRUCIS.

Fausta et Evilasius, passio [ANON.Pas.Faust.Evil.]: *BHL* 2833; *BSS* 5.478–79.
ed.: *AS* Sept. 6.144–47.
MSS see below.
Lists none.
A-S Vers BEDA.Mart. 174.2–19.
Quots/Cits – Refs none.

Although the legend of Fausta (feast day September 20) was known to **BEDE** in the form of this *Passio Faustae et Evilasii* (BEDA.Mart.; ed. Dubois and Renaud 1976; sourced by Quentin 1908 pp 72–73), **ALDHELM** either did not know the story or passed over it, despite the heroic conduct of the thirteen-year-old virgin, which so impressed her prosecutors, Evilasius and Eusebius, that they happily joined her in a cauldron of boiling pitch. The notice in the **OLD ENGLISH MARTYROLOGY** (*Mart*, B19.he; ed. Kotzor 1981 2.212), in the opinion of Kotzor (p 213 and 1986 p 314 note 70) and Cross (1985b p 241 note 71), is probably based on Bede rather than on any of the *passiones*.

The badly burnt, fragmentary manuscript, London, BL Cotton Otho A. xiii (HG 351), dated first half of the eleventh century by HG (but see

Dumville 1992 p 140), contains the remnants of a version of the *passio* that is textually related to the present version, but with a substantially different preamble and much verbal variation elsewhere (see fols 57–66v, new foliation 41–50v).

Felicitas cum septem filiis, passio [ANON.Pas.Felic.Sept.Fil.]: *BHL* 2853; *BLS* 3.62–64; *BSS* 5.605–08; *CPL* 2187; *DACL* 5.1259–98.
    ed.: K. Künstle 1894 pp 60–63.
MSS   1. London, BL Cotton Nero E. i: HG 344.
    2. London, BL Harley 3020: HG 433.
    3. Salisbury, Cathedral Library 222 (formerly Oxford, Bodleian Library Fell 1): HG 754.6.
Lists   none.
A-S Vers   1. BEDA.Mart. 124.2–9 (Septem filii).
    2. BEDA.Mart. 212.27–28 (Felicitas).
    3. *Mart* (B19.ej, jc).
Quots/Cits – Refs   none.

The Roman matron Felicity (feast day November 23), and the seven young men (Januarius, Felix, Philip, Alexander, Vitalis, Martial, Silvanus: feast day July 10) who in her sixth century *passio* are said to be her sons, were most probably historical martyrs, but the family relationship appears to be a pious fiction influenced by a similar story in 2 Maccabees 7.1–42 (Delehaye 1936 pp 116–23; the recent objections of Vogt 1984 are reviewed by Halkin 1985). The *passio* was paraphrased by **GREGORY THE GREAT, HOMILIAE XL IN EVANGELIA** III (ed. *PL* 76.1086–89), but it also traveled separately to England. The brief notice for Felicity and the more detailed one for the seven brothers in **BEDE**'s **MARTYROLOGIUM** (BEDA.Mart.; ed. Dubois and Renaud 1976) are drawn from the *passio* (sourced by Quentin 1908 pp 73–74).

    Cross (1985a p 107 note 3) corrects Herzfeld (*EETS* OS 116.xli and xlii) as to the sources of the **OLD ENGLISH MARTYROLOGY** entries for these saints. He finds that while the *Martyrology*'s notice for Felicitas herself, on November 23 (*Mart*; ed. Kotzor 1981 2.256), draws mainly on

Gregory's third homily on the gospels, one detail (that Felicity is a "holy widow") echoes the *passio* directly. On the other hand, the *passio* (as printed in Künstle and *AS* Iul. 3.12–13, not Mombritius 1910 1.549, used by Herzfeld) is the main source for the *Martyrology*'s notice for the seven sons on July 10 (ed. Kotzor 1981 2.145), and Cross doubts if the martyrologist drew at all on Bede's *Martyrologium* in this case.

The copy of the *passio* in Harley 3020 (late tenth or early eleventh century, Canterbury), while related to Künstle's manuscript D, displays numerous variants and errors, especially near the beginning, which a somewhat later scribe has tried to correct, apparently without the help of another copy. The eleventh-century Cotton and Salisbury manuscripts of the **COTTON-CORPUS LEGENDARY** preserve a less corrupt text, but that in the Cotton manuscript is vitiated by the typical minor errors of the Worcester scribe. The *AS* edition is preferable to that of Mombritius, an interpolated text, but both are superseded by the critical edition of Künstle, although this is not definitive.

The more recent edition by Ruiz Bueno (1968 pp 293–98), with a Spanish translation of the *passio* and of Gregory the Great's homily, is not a critical edition.

Felix episcopus Anglorum Orientalium: Farmer (1987) p 157.

This Felix was, according to **BEDE, HISTORIA ECCLESIASTICA** II.xv (ed. Colgrave and Mynors 1969 p 190), a Burgundian who became the first bishop of the East Angles (630–647/48). No other account besides Bede's is known from the Anglo-Saxon period, but in the late-twelfth-century *Liber Eliensis* I.vi the author refers to an English account ("In Anglico quippe legitur") of Felix's supposed foundation of a monastery at "Seham," usually identified with Soham, Cambridgeshire (ed. Blake 1962 p 17 and note 3). If there was an English life of Felix, it could have been written at Ramsey after Felix's relics were taken there, as indicated in the same chapter of *Liber Eliensis*, in the reign of Canute (see Thacker 1996a pp 259–60, 264 note 129). It is also possible, however, that the Old English text referred to was a charter.

The "vita inedita" listed in *BHL NS* (p 326) is a set of liturgical lections in a manuscript later than the Anglo-Saxon period.

Felix II papa, passio [ANON.Pas.Fel.II.Pap.]: *BHL* 2857; *BLS* 3.206–07; *BSS* 5.576–79.
ed.: Mombritius 1910 1.550–51 and 671–72.
MSS 1. London, BL Cotton Nero E. i: HG 344.
2. London, BL Harley 3020: HG 433.
3. Salisbury, Cathedral Library 222 (formerly Oxford, Bodleian Library Fell 1): HG 754.6.
Lists – Refs none.

Pope Felix "II," actually an Arian anti-pope under the emperor Constantius, was confused in the **LIBER PONTIFICALIS** with Pope Liberius and thereafter honored as a martyr for the cause of orthodox Christianity. See Duchesne (1955 1.CCXXIV–CCXXV and 211), De Gaiffier (1963). Felix's feast day (July 29) is widely commemorated (and sometimes graded) in Anglo-Saxon calendars. Its relative importance is indicated by the provision of a text of the *passio* in the Harley manuscript (Canterbury, late tenth or early eleventh century) as well as in the much larger and less selective **COTTON-CORPUS LEGENDARY** (Zettel 1979 p 23; Jackson and Lapidge 1996 p 139), represented here by the Cotton and Salisbury manuscripts from the later eleventh century.

Felix Nolanus presbyter.

The prose and verse lives of Felix of Nola are treated under the author entries for **BEDE** and **PAULINUS OF NOLA**, but this Felix's confusing relationship with **FELIX ROMANUS PRESBYTER** requires some comment here.

The earliest literary records concerning this saint of Campania are several poems (*BHL* 2870) by Paulinus of Nola who adopted Felix as his patron on retiring from public life to Nola in 394 (P. Brown 1981 pp

53–60). Among the score of Felixes in the Roman calendar, two share the feast day January 14: Felix "priest of Nola," and Felix "priest of Rome" ("in Pincis"). It is generally accepted that Felix of Nola is the authentic original of the two January 14 saints and that the church "in Pincis" was originally a locus of Roman devotion to the Campanian saint (for this later, spurious Felix of Rome, see next entry).

Paulinus's poems on Felix of Nola were well known in early Anglo-Saxon England and are quoted and echoed many times by **ALDHELM**, Bede, and **ALCUIN**. In addition, Bede wrote a prose epitome (**VITA FELICIS**, *BHL* 2873; ed. *PL* 94.789–98) of the poems, which he knew to be Paulinus's work (see the main entry for Paulinus). According to Cross (1985b p 241 note 73), the author of the ninth-century **OLD ENGLISH MARTYROLOGY**, in his January 14 notice for Felix (ed. Kotzor 1981 2.15.19–16.7), drew on both Bede's **MARTYROLOGIUM** (ed. Dubois and Renaud 1976 p 13.2–6) and life of Felix, but the vernacular martyrologist already shows the influence of the confusing development of Felix's cult in Rome, since he identifies Felix as a priest of Rome "in the place called Pincis" (Kotzor 1981 2.16.1) bypassing Bede's "in Campania" (ed. Dubois and Renaud 1976 p 13.2).This suggests that the *Martyrology* may depend, in this instance, on a calendar or liturgical book, as well as on Bede.

In the later Anglo-Saxon period, the Paulinus-Bede tradition concerning Felix seems to have been displaced by the Roman tradition represented in *BHL* 2885, since there is no trace of the prose and verse lives of Felix of Nola in the **COTTON-CORPUS LEGENDARY** or other later manuscripts, except for ÆTHELWOLD's booklist (ML 4.7; see also 13.38).

Felix Romanus presbyter, vita [ANON.Vit.Fel.Rom.]: *BHL* 2885; *BSS* 5.535, 552; *CPL* 2189; *DHGE* 6.909.
 ed.: Mombritius 1910 1.543–44 and 670.
MSS 1. London, BL Cotton Nero E. i: HG 344.
 2. Salisbury, Cathedral Library 221 (formerly Oxford, Bodleian Library Fell 4): HG 754.5.
Lists – Refs none.

Reputed brother of another Felix of Rome (feast day August 30: Felix and Adauctus, *BHL* 2878–84), Felix "in Pincis" (January 14) is believed to be a doublet of FELIX NOLANUS PRESBYTER, in whose honor the church on the Pincio was originally built (Delehaye 1897a p 23). The *vita* in question here was probably composed in the seventh century (or sixth: see *CPL* 2189) by the same author as the *passio* of Felix and Adauctus (*BHL* 2878). The work was known to **HRABANUS MAURUS** (*Martyrologium*, IAN. 172–79; ed. *CCCM* 44.11) but not, apparently, to **BEDE**. The notice for January 14 in the ninth-century **OLD ENGLISH MARTYROLOGY** (*Mart*; B19.y; ed. Kotzor 1981 2.16) speaks of a Felix "priest of Rome, in the place called Pincis," but the remainder of the brief narrative is drawn word for word from Bede's writings on Felix of Nola (Cross 1985b p 241 note 73). This *Vita Felicis*, therefore, does not appear to have been known to the early Anglo-Saxons.

The only Anglo-Saxon witnesses are the copies of the *vita* in the mid-eleventh-century English manuscripts listed above, representing the **COTTON-CORPUS LEGENDARY** (see Zettel 1979 p 16; Jackson and Lapidge 1996 p 135), which are not collated in the Mombritius edition. *BHL* identifies Felix's *vita* as a *passio*.

Felix Tubzacensis, passio [ANON.Pas.Fel.Tub.1a]: *BHL* 2894; *BLS* 4.188; *BSS* 5.585–87; *CPL* 2054; *DHGE* 16.884.
  ed.: *AS* Oct. 10.625–28.

MSS 1. London, BL Cotton Nero E. i: HG 344.
  2. Salisbury, Cathedral Library 221 (formerly Oxford, Bodleian Library Fell 4): HG 754.5.
Lists – *Refs* none.

Bishop Felix of Thibiuca, near Carthage, apparently suffered martyrdom in the N. African city early in the Diocletian persecution (303) for refusing to hand over the Christians' sacred books to the local magistrate. The ancient *passio* is lost but its substance is believed to survive in several later recensions (see Delehaye 1921a pp 268–70 for an attempt to reconstruct the original, designated *BHL* 2893s). The two versions known in Anglo-Saxon England, in both of which the saint's death is said to take place in Italy, probably originated among different groups of refugees from the Vandal invasions of N. Africa in the fifth century (Saxer 1994 p 54). The more widely represented of the two, designated the N recension by modern editors (Delehaye 1921a pp 245–46), in which the martyrdom takes place in Nola, appears in the London and Salisbury manuscripts of the **COTTON-CORPUS LEGENDARY** (Jackson and Lapidge 1996 p 135, misidentifying the saint as Felix of Trier).

Although Felix's original feast day was probably July 15 or 16, it was early transferred to August 30, probably owing to confusion with the feast of the martyrs Felix and Adauctus (*BHL* 2878), and later to October 24, its present position in the Roman calendar. The Cotton-Corpus Legendary assigns the text to a January date, immediately after **FELIX ROMANUS PRESBYTER**, in apparent confusion with **FELIX NOLANUS PRESBYTER**.

The London manuscript contains a second copy of the N type, although in the later (twelfth-century) portion of the manuscript, not in the Legendary proper. Bishop Fell, as an appendix to his edition of **LACTANTIUS**'s DE MORTIBUS PERSECUTORUM (J. Fell 1680 pp 47–56), prints an edition of the N recension based on that of Baluzius (1678–1715 1.77–81) but provides variant readings from the Salisbury manuscript. Delehaye mistakenly states (1921a p 245) that the edition by Fell is based on the Salisbury manuscript.

It is necessary to note that Delehaye's edition of the N recension (1921a pp 252–59) is based on the text in a ninth-century manuscript now in London, formerly from St Emmeram, Regensburg, which differs sufficiently from that in the other printed editions for him designate it N1, distinguishing it from the other family, N2, to which the English copies belong (pp 245–46). Accordingly in this entry we cite the most accessible edition of the N2 recension here, but readers are advised to consult Delehaye's edition and apparatus of variants.

For the V recension, which was known in early Anglo-Saxon England, see next entry. For a more recent edition of Delehaye's reconstructed text, see Musurillo (1972 pp 266–70).

Felix Tubzacensis, passio [ANON.Pas.Fel.Tub.1b]: *BHL* 2895b.
ed.: Quentin 1908 pp 526–27.
MSS Paris, Bibliothèque Nationale lat. 10861: HG 898.
A-S Vers 1. ALDH.Pros.uirg. 264.13–14.
2. BEDA.Mart. 160.9–17.
3. *Mart* (B19.gj).
Quots/Cits – Refs none.

The second of the two main branches of the *Passio Felicis Tubzacensis* places the martyrdom in Venosa in Apulia and is thus designated V by modern scholars (see Delehaye 1921a pp 243–45). This version occurs in the ninth-century Canterbury manuscript now in Paris (see M. P. Brown 1986 p 122) and is edited from that manuscript by Quentin (cited above). Delehaye, who collates the manuscript in his more recent edition (1921a pp 247–52), designates it a member of the second recension (V2); his edition is based on what he considers the older manuscript tradition, V1, represented by an early printed edition and two eleventh-century manuscripts. The V2 recension, however, seems to underlie the account by **ALDHELM** (ALDH.Pros.uirg.; ed. *MGH* AA 15) and almost certainly those of **BEDE** in his **MARTYROLOGIUM** (BEDA.Mart.; ed. Dubois and Renaud 1976; see Quentin 1908 p 74) and the ninth-century **OLD ENGLISH MARTYROLOGY** (*Mart*; ed. Kotzor 1981 2.194–95, sourced p 343).

Ferreolus et Ferrucio, passio [ANON.Pas.Ferreol.Ferruc.]: *BHL* 2903; *BLS* 2.552; *BSS* 5.652–54; *CPL* 2116; *DHGE* 16.1244–47.
ed.: *AS* Iun. 3.7–8.
MSS – Lists none.
A-S Vers 1. ?BEDA.Mart. 109.14–19.
2. *Mart* (B19.dn).
Quots/Cits – Refs none.

The legend of the deacons Ferreolus and Ferrucio (feast day June 16) tells how they were sent by Bishop Irenaeus of Lyon as missionaries to

Besançon where their success in converting souls was eventually crowned with martyrdom under "Aurelian." Their *passio* is closely linked to that of the martyrs of Valence (Felix and companions, *BHL* 2896). On these two texts depend the other members of the so-called Burgundian cycle of legends discussed by Van der Straeten (1961; see also BENIGNUS; SPEUSIPPUS). The *passio* in question here, apparently known to GREGORY OF TOURS (see DE GLORIA MARTYRUM LXX; ed. *MGH* SRM 1/2.535.8) and dated in the early sixth century by Van der Straeten (1961 p 143), is said to be the source of the accounts of the two saints in BEDE's MARTYROLOGIUM (BEDA.Mart.; ed. Dubois and Renaud 1976; sourced by Quentin 1908 pp 74–75) and in the OLD ENGLISH MARTYROLOGY (*Mart*; ed. Kotzor 1981 2.121–22; sourced by J. E. Cross, personal communication). Quentin implies, however (1908 p 74 note 5), that Bede's actual source may have been somewhat narrower in scope than the *passio*. A fresh sourcing might take account of the primitive *passio, BHL* 2903b, thought to be of the late fifth century, of which the better known version, at issue here, is a stylistic revision (see *DHGE* 16.1245).

I have found no evidence that the later Anglo-Saxons were aware of the legend or cult.

Ferreolus Viennae, passio [ANON.Pas.Ferreol.Vienn.]: *BHL* 2912; *BLS* 3.591–92; *BSS* 5.651–52; *DHGE* 16.1243–44. See also *CPL* 2100.
ed.: *AS* Sept. 5.766–67.
MSS London, BL Cotton Otho A. xiii: HG 351.
Lists – Refs none.

The late-fifth-century account of the martyrdom of this Ferreolus (feast day September 18) describes him as a military tribune of Vienne and associates him with Saint Julian of Brioude. While the cult of this Ferreolus appears to be of genuine antiquity (*AS* Nov. 2/2.517–18), the *passio* is not apparently historical, despite its early date, and is much indebted to the legend of GENESIUS ARELATENSIS. The fragmentary copy in the badly burnt Cotton manuscript (fols 33–37v, new foliation 26–30v) corresponds closely to the slightly later of the two variant versions (for the earlier, see *BHL* 2911). I have found no other evidence of Anglo-Saxon knowledge of this saint or his legend.

Filibertus. See **PHILIBERTUS**.

Firminus Ambianensis, passio [ANON.Pas.Firmin.]: *BHL* 3002; *BLS* 3.632–33; *BSS* 5.866–69; *DHGE* 17.252–57.
ed.: Bosquet 1636 2.146–56.
MSS 1. London, BL Cotton Nero E. i: HG 344.
2. Salisbury, Cathedral Library 222 (formerly Oxford, Bodleian Library Fell 1): HG 754.6.
Lists – Refs none.

The earliest textual evidence for the Anglo-Saxons' knowledge of the legend of the Spaniard Firminus (feast day September 25), venerated as an early bishop of Amiens martyred in the second half of the third century, is the copies of this version of the *passio* in the London and Salisbury manuscripts of the **COTTON-CORPUS LEGENDARY** (Zettel 1979 p 26; Jackson and Lapidge 1996 p 140). Firmin's cult, however, was known in England in previous centuries, to judge from the occurrence of his feast day in some early calendars (F. Wormald 1934 pp 10, 24, and 38). The surviving *passio* was composed probably no earlier than the later ninth century, since, according to Dubois in his *DHGE* article on Firmin, **USUARD** the martyrologist (865) does not seem to have known it, and the oldest manuscript of a variant version of the *passio*, *BHL* 3003 (ed. *AS* Sept. 7.46–50), is of the late tenth or early eleventh century (*DHGE* 17.253–54). Dubois does not mention the version in question here, but the Bollandists (*AS* Sept. 7.24–25) regard it as a less complete and less reliable text than *BHL* 3003, which they edit from their own manuscripts. As Dubois points out, the history of the text and manuscripts of the *passio* have not been properly studied.

Fructuosus Tarroconensis, passio [ANON.Pas.Fruct.Tarr.]: *BHL* 3200; *BLS* 1.137–38; *BSS* 5.1296–97; *CPL* 1293; *DHGE* 19.231–36.
   ed.: unpublished (see below).
MSS 1. London, BL Cotton Nero E. i: HG 344.
   2. Salisbury, Cathedral Library 221 (formerly Oxford, Bodleian Library Fell 4): HG 754.5.
Lists – Refs none.

Fructuosus (feast day January 21), bishop of Tarragona in Spain, was martyred with two of his clerics, Augurius and Elogius, in 259 by being burned alive. His *passio*, most of which is believed to have been composed in the early fourth century (Musurillo 1972 p xxxii), is regarded as an authentic record of the event. Anglo-Saxons would know the story through **PRUDENTIUS**, PERISTEPHANON VI (ed. *CCSL* 126), and **AUGUSTINE**, SERMONES CCLXXIII (ed. *PL* 38.1248–50, especially 1249), but there is no evidence of a liturgical cult in England. The place of the eleventh-century English copies in the complex textual history of the *passio* is unknown, and the particular variant version they contain is not printed or collated in any of the numerous modern editions listed by the Bollandists in *BHL NS* (p 365). The English text corresponds in some instances with the text preserved in the great early-thirteenth-century legendary of St Maximinus of Trier, occasionally cited in the notes to the Bollandists' edition (*AS* Ian. 2.341).

The most useful modern edition, with variants from numerous manuscripts, is that of *BHL* 3196 by Franchi de' Cavalieri (1935 pp 182–94), on which Musurillo's text, with facing English translation, is based (1972 pp 176–84).

Furseus, vita [ANON.Vit.Furs.1β]: *BHL* 3210; *BSS* 5.1321–22; *CPL* 2101; *DHGE* 19.476–83; *SEHI* 296.
   ed.: *MGH* SRM 4.423–49 and 7.837–42 (*vita* only); Ciccarese 1984–85 pp 279–303 (*visiones*).
MSS 1. London, BL Cotton Otho A. xiii: HG 351.
   2. London, BL Cotton Nero E. i: HG 344.

3. Salisbury, Cathedral Library 221 (formerly Oxford, Bodleian Library Fell 4): HG 754.5.
Lists Peterborough: ML 13.51.
A-S Vers 1. BEDA.Hist.eccles. 268-76.
 2. *Mart* (B19.aa).
 3. *ÆCHom* II, 20 (B1.2.25) 19-268.
Quots/Cits Vita Fursei 435.1-10: FELIX.Vit.Guth. 84.13-21 and 26-28.
Refs BEDA.Hist.eccles. 270.19-20 and 34.

Fursey was a wandering Irish monk (from Ulster: see Ó Riain 1986 p 407) and eventually a bishop. As a missionary he founded monasteries in East Anglia (630s) and in northern France (640s), where he died (648/49, feast day January 16). He was venerated at Lagny (his foundation) and at Péronne (his shrine), where his body was found to be incorrupt four years after his death. Fursey's chief fame, however, was due to the richly detailed stories of his visions that are included in the so-called "Vita Prima" composed probably at Péronne not long after his death. Of the several extant Latin lives of Fursey, the Anglo-Saxons appear to have known only this one.

The standard critical edition of the *Vita Fursei*, that of Krusch, unfortunately omits most of the text of the visions on which the saint's reputation rests, but the visions have been edited afresh by Ciccarese (1984-85). Krusch's edition includes variants from the Cotton Nero manuscript above, but not from the Salisbury manuscript (he confirms later, *MGH* SRM 7.632, that the Salisbury copy is identical to the Cotton text). Ciccarese's edition of the *visio* portion is based mainly on two manuscripts of Krusch's class A and one of class C, but she argues that the latter represents the subarchetype of the large and complex B class.

While Krusch in his *MGH* edition does not adhere to the Bollandists' distinction between two main variant versions of the *Vita Prima*, *BHL* 3209 and 3210, it happens that three of the extant Anglo-Saxon manuscript copies match the *explicit* of *BHL* 3210 while the fourth matches that of *BHL* 3209. Although Krusch groups all four Anglo-Saxon copies in his large B family (*MGH* SRM 4.429-30), his subgroupings imply that the three manuscripts listed in the present entry are textually closely related, forming subgroup B2a (all matching *BHL* 3210), and distinct from the fourth Anglo-Saxon copy (see next entry, on *BHL* 3209). The Cotton Nero and Salisbury copies, each numbered B2a1 by Krusch, are eleventh-century representatives of the **COTTON-CORPUS LEGENDARY** (see Zettel 1979 p 16; Jackson and Lapidge 1996 p 135); Cotton Otho, a badly burnt, fragmentary copy, where legible shares most of its variants with Cotton Nero, so that Krusch classifies it as B2af (*MGH* SRM 7.838). It should be noted that Hardy's reference (*RS* 26/1.239) to another copy of the *vita* in Oxford, Bodleian Library Fell 3 is an error, presumably for Fell 4, now Salisbury Cathedral Library 221.

Fursey's *vita* was known early in England. **BEDE** incorporated a lengthy extract, mainly from the visionary portion, in his **HISTORIA ECCLESIASTICA** III.xix (BEDA.Hist.eccles.; ed. Colgrave and Mynors 1969), which did much to spread Fursey's fame beyond his cult sites. Bede evidently used a manuscript close to the subarchetype of Krusch's B class, as represented in his manuscript C2a (Ciccarese 1984–85 pp 248–77, especially 253, 273).

Sims-Williams (1990 pp 243–72) has recently argued that **BONIFACE** was influenced by the Fursey vision, and not just the **VISIO SANCTI PAULI (APOCRYPHA)**, in composing his account, in a letter to Eadburga, of a vision of a monk of Wenlock (*MGH* ES 1.7–15), which in turn was translated into Old English in the tenth or eleventh century (*Lett* 1, B6.1; ed. Sisam 1953 pp 199–224).

Felix, the East Anglian author (ca. 740) of the life of **GUTHLACUS** (FELIX.Vit.Guth.; ed. Colgrave 1956) adapts a substantial passage from the *vita* to describe Guthlac's virtues; he may also have been influenced by Fursey's visions in composing Guthlac's vision of hell (Colgrave 1956 pp 104–06; on the same subject see Ciccarese 1982).

Cross (1981e pp 178–80) shows that the ninth-century **OLD ENGLISH MARTYROLOGY** (*Mart*; ed. Kotzor 1981 2.16–17) draws on a version of the life as well as on Bede's extract. **ÆLFRIC** in his homily on the Greater Litany (Feria III), in the Second Series of **CATHOLIC HOMILIES** (*ÆCHom*; ed. EETS SS 5), draws extensively on the vision portions of a B text of the life, not on Bede, translating some passages closely but greatly abridging the whole (Förster 1892 p 39; Godden *EETS*

SS 18.529–38). The effect, and presumably the intention, is quite different from Bede's. Zettel argues for Ælfric's dependence on a text very similar to that in the Cotton-Corpus Legendary (1979 pp 152–54, 189–91). Szarmach (1987) briefly discusses Ælfric's treatment of Fursey's visions in relation to the Old English *Dream of the Rood*.

Krusch (*MGH* SRM 4.429–33) discusses earlier editions of the *Vita Fursei* by Mabillon and the Bollandists, pointing out that neither is based on reliable manuscripts. However, the Bollandists' text (*AS* Ian. 2.36–41), particularly in tandem with the extant English manuscripts, seems to be a useful guide to the sort of text used by the Anglo-Saxons. A thorough study of the English "reception" of the *Vita Fursei*, in relation to the English manuscript tradition, would be desirable, if only to modify the impression given recently (Ó Riain 1986 p 405) that there is no English textual history of the *vita* apart from Bede's extracts.

Furseus, vita [ANON.Vit.Furs.1α]: *BHL* 3209.
   ed.: see previous entry.

MSS London, Lambeth Palace 173: HG 508.
Lists – Refs none.

The text of the *Vita Fursei* preserved in this slightly imperfect late-eleventh-century manuscript is of the type *BHL* 3209 (*explicit* α) and is numbered B2d in Krusch's classification of manuscripts, distinguishing it from B2a, the other, more closely interrelated subgroup of Anglo-Saxon copies (see previous entry). Its readings are not included in Krusch's apparatus. For a description of the manuscript and its missing leaves see the catalogue of James and Jenkins (1930–32 p 273).

Fuscianus et soc., passio [ANON.Pas.Fuscian.]: *BHL* 3226; *BLS* 4.538–39.
   ed.: Jonsson 1968 pp 210–13.

MSS Cambridge, Corpus Christi College 9: HG 36.
Lists – Refs none.

The December 11 feast day of Fuscianus, Victoricus, and Gentianus (Victoricus often appearing first) commemorates what appears to have been a genuine martyrdom (see *AS* Nov. 2/2.643), but their narrative legend, in which the first two are said to have been Roman missionaries, active in the Boulogne-Amiens region during the time of **QUINTINUS**, is an inventive derivative of the equally fabulous *Passio S. Quintini* (*BHL* 6999–7000: see Quintinus). The version preserved in the eleventh-century Cambridge manuscript of the **COTTON-CORPUS LEGENDARY**, originally designated Passio 2 in the first edition of *BHL*, is now regarded as the oldest version, composed no later than the eighth century. See *BHL NS* (p 367) and especially Jonsson (1968 pp 82–93), whose useful edition is based on an early manuscript now in Paris (see *CLA* 5.644a and 644b). The rubric in the Corpus manuscript has "Faustinus" in error for Fuscianus.

Gallicanus: *BLS* 2.638–39; *BSS* 6.12–13; *CPL* 2193; *DHGE* 19.843–45.

Gallicanus (feast day June 25) was Roman consul with Symmachus in 330 and a known benefactor of the church built by the emperor Constantine at Ostia. There is no historical evidence for the legend that he was a Roman general, betrothed to **CONSTANTINA**, converted by the eunuch brothers John and Paul (**IOHANNES ET PAULUS**), then later, after a period as a hermit at Ostia with Saint **HILARINUS**, exiled in Egypt and ultimately martyred under Julian. His story, which seems to have arisen partly out of a misinterpretation of portions of the *Gesta Silvestri* (**SILVESTER**) regarding donations to churches at Ostia and elsewhere, is an integral part of the legend of the brothers John and Paul, whose cult was more ancient and more important liturgically than that of Gallicanus. The Bollandists treat the three saints under the heading "Gallicanus, John and Paul," and classify the two parts of the *passio* separately as *BHL* 3236 (Gallicanus) and 3238 (John and Paul), but these appear as one continuous text in most of the Anglo-Saxon witnesses and elsewhere (ed. Mombritius 1910 1.569–72, 677). Gallicanus figures only in the first part, which ends in his martyrdom, but John and Paul play prominent roles in both parts. For

Anglo-Saxon manuscripts and versions of the *Passio Gallicani, Iohannis et Pauli*, see the entry for Iohannes et Paulus.

Gallicanus is not mentioned separately in the **OLD ENGLISH MARTYROLOGY** or in **BEDE**'s **MARTYROLOGIUM**, but the story of his short-lived betrothal to Constantina, and his military victory, appealed to **ALDHELM**, who draws on it in his **DE VIRGINITATE** (*Carmen* 2051–120, *Prosa* 302.20–303.6; ed. *MGH* AA 15). His summary account of the virtues of Constantina, and Gallicanus's conversion, in the prose version seems based on the first part of the *passio* (*BHL* 3236), but does not include Gallicanus's martyrdom or mention John and Paul. The longer verse account includes the Scythian war (*Carmen* 2075–94), briefly mentioning John and Paul. **ÆLFRIC**, perhaps influenced by Aldhelm, summarizes the whole story, with emphasis on Gallicanus, in the second part ("Item alia") of his legend of **AGNES**, lines 296–403, in **LIVES OF SAINTS** (*ÆLS* Agnes, B1.3.8; ed. *EETS* OS 76 and 82).

Gallicanus seems to have had no separate liturgical cultus in Anglo-Saxon England. On the historical background of his hagiographical legend, see most recently the studies of Grégoire and Orgels (1954, 1957) and De Gaiffier (1948, 1956).

Gaugericus, vita [ANON.Vit.Gaug.]: *BHL* 3287; *BLS* 3.305–06; *CPL* 2013; *DHGE* 20.1102–03.

ed.: *AS* Aug. 2.672–75.

MSS 1. London, BL Cotton Nero E. i.: HG 344.
2. Salisbury, Cathedral Library 222 (formerly Oxford, Bodleian Library Fell 1): HG 754.6.

Lists – Refs none.

Gaugericus or Géry (feast day August 11) was bishop of Cambrai from ca. 585 to 625 but his long episcopacy was unremarkable (Krusch *MGH* SRM 3.649). He is valued today chiefly for the antiquity of his *Vita prima* (*BHL* 3286), believed to be a late-seventh-century composition. The *Vita secunda*, however, which apparently is no later than the ninth century (Krusch *MGH* SRM 3.651), is the version preserved in the **COTTON-CORPUS LEGENDARY** (Zettel 1979 p 23; Jackson and Lapidge 1996 p 139).

Bolton (1959 p 37) mistakenly adduces the *Vita secunda* as source of a commonplace phrase in Felix's *Vita Guthlaci* (**GUTHLACUS**), and likewise errs in positing the *Vita Gaugerici prima* as a source of Felix.

On the historical context of Géry's mission and episcopacy, see the collection of papers edited by Rouche (in Heuclin 1986), which includes his French translation of the *Vita prima* (pp 281–88).

Genesius Arelatensis, passio [ANON.Pas.Genes.Arl./PS.PAULIN.]: *BHL* 3304; *BSS* 6.115–17; *CPL* 509; *DHGE* 20.408–10.
ed.: Cavallin 1945 pp 160–64.

MSS 1. London, BL Cotton Nero E. i: HG 344.
2. Salisbury, Cathedral Library 222 (formerly Oxford, Bodleian Library Fell 1): HG 754.6.
Lists none.
A-S Vers Mart (B19.ie).
Quots/Cits – Refs none.

Genesius of Arles, the notary, unlike his namesake the actor (**GENESIUS MIMUS ROMAE**) with whom he shares the feast day of August 25, is accepted as an authentic martyr of the early fourth century (*AS* Nov. 2/2.463–65), although the earliest form of his legend, the *passio* formerly ascribed to **PAULINUS OF NOLA**, appears to be of the sixth century (Cavallin 1945 p 173).

The ninth-century **OLD ENGLISH MARTYROLOGY** (*Mart*; ed. Kotzor 1981 2.238) commemorates Genesius the notary on October 24, but Cross (1984c pp 151–52) finds no evidence of cult or commemoration of Genesius of Arles in English calendars. He confirms and refines Herzfeld's sourcing of the *Old English Martyrology* in relation to the *passio*.

The copies of the *Passio Genesii* in the eleventh-century London and Salisbury manuscripts of the **COTTON-CORPUS LEGENDARY** have the more usual date (August 25), ascribe the work to Paulinus's authorship, and, as Jackson and Lapidge indicate (1996 pp 139–40), include an appended collection of miracles (see next entry).

The *passio* is also printed in *AS* Aug. 5.135. Hartel's edition (*CSEL* 29.425–28) is not recommended by modern scholars. The more valuable critical edition of Cavallin (1945) analyzes and collates numerous manuscripts, but ignores the English copies. He includes an edition (pp 165–68) of the source of the *passio* (*BHL* 3306), a fifth-century sermon from among the spuria of EUSEBIUS GALLICANUS.

Genesius Arelatensis, miracula [ANON.Mir.Genes.Arl./PS.HILAR.]: *BHL* 3307; *CPL* 504.
ed.: *AS* Aug. 5.133–34.

MSS 1. London, BL Cotton Nero E. i: HG 344.
2. Salisbury, Cathedral Library 222 (formerly Oxford, Bodleian Library Fell 1): HG 754.6.
Lists – Refs none.

Frequently following the *Passio Genesii* in manuscripts is this elaborately narrated account of a posthumous miracle, according to which crowds marooned on a pontoon bridge adrift in the Rhone are saved by praying to the saint for help. The episode is said to take place during the time of Bishop Honoratus (427–30), and this account has often been attributed to his successor, Hilary of Arles, "with some probability" (Van Dam 1988 p 92 note 82). A shorter version of the same story (*BHL* 3309) is the first of several miracle episodes recorded by **GREGORY OF TOURS**; see DE GLORIA MARTYRUM LXVIII (ed. *MGH* SRM 1/2.533.27–534.6).

Genesius mimus Romae, passio [ANON.Pas.Genes.mim.Rom.]: *BHL* 3320; *BLS* 3.398–400; *BSS* 6.121–24; *DACL* 6.903–09; *DHGE* 20.414–16.
ed.: Weismann 1977 pp 38–43.

MSS – Lists none.
A-S Vers Mart (B19.gc).
Quots/Cits – Refs none.

The legend of Genesius, Roman mime and martyr (who shares his feast day, August 25, with **GENESIUS ARELATENSIS**, the notary), has provoked much interest in its theatrical content but little confidence in its authenticity (the analogous account of the actor Gelasinos of Heliopolis, whose story may have been the model for that of Genesius of Rome, has inspired more credence: see Weismann 1977 pp 23–25, and 1975). The Bollandists' original classification of the variant forms of the *passio* (*BHL* 3315–25) has been modified through the work of Mostert and Stengel (1895 pp 41–50), Quentin (1908 pp 533–41), and, more recently, Weismann (1977). Instead of a single *passio* in numerous recensions, they distinguish two significantly different texts, Quentin's A and B versions, each surviving in several recensions and epitomes, but represented respectively by *BHL* 3320 and 3318. Surprisingly, in view of its evident popularity in medieval Europe, the legend is not preserved in either form in Anglo-Saxon manuscripts. The sole evidence of its currency among the early English is in the **OLD ENGLISH MARTYROLOGY** (*Mart*; ed. Kotzor 1981 2.188–89), where it is interesting to note that the martyrologist, in abbreviating his source, has suppressed any suggestion that Genesius's vision and conversion occur during his theatrical performance spoofing Christian rituals and belief. Cross (1984c p 151 note 23) argues that the *Martyrology*'s source text must have been an A text, on the grounds that in A and in the Old English only one angel (not several as in the B tradition) appears to Genesius during his vision and baptism. The textual importance of the single angel is confirmed independently by Weismann's 1977 study (apparently unknown to Cross) of the manuscript traditions, in which the angel is the distinctive "Leitfehler" of a large family of A manuscripts. Among these is a ninth-century manuscript in the Bollandists' library, referred to by Cross as a check on Mombritius's printed edition (1910 1.597–98), which is based on a contaminated manuscript (Weismann 1977 p 36). The Weismann edition, which clearly supersedes that of Mombritius, is based on a collation of fifty-eight manuscripts.

Genovefa, vita [ANON.Vit.Genov.]: *BHL* 3336; *BLS* 1.28–30; *BSS* 6.157–64; *CPL* 2104; *DHGE* 20.455–64.
    ed.: C. Künstle 1910 pp 1–20.
MSS 1. London, BL Cotton Nero E. i: HG 344.
      2. Salisbury, Cathedral Library 221 (formerly Oxford, Bodleian Library Fell 4): HG 754.5.
Lists – Refs none.

According to the ancient *Vita Genovefae* (generally accepted as sixth century: see below), Genevieve (feast day January 3) as a young girl in her birthplace of Nanterre was blessed by Saint **GERMANUS AUTISIODORENSIS** while he was on his way to preach against the Pelagians in Britain (ca. 430), and henceforth she dedicated herself to religion. Taking the veil at age fifteen, she led a busy and controversial life as a consecrated virgin and died in Paris ca. 500. The conflicts in which she herself was involved have been surpassed in vehemence, however, by the modern scholarly dispute over the authenticity of the ancient *vita*, generally accepted as having been composed not long after her death, but regarded by some scholars (including Bruno Krusch) as an eighth-century forgery. For bibliography, see the recent work of Poulin (1983) and Poulin and Heinzelmann (1986), which incorporates and supersedes all previous studies. Of the several variant versions of the first life, the oldest is believed to be *BHL* 3335 (ed. *MGH* SRM 3.215–38). Despite the local importance of her cult (see **GREGORY OF TOURS**, DE GLORIA CONFESSORUM LXXXIX; ed. *MGH* SRM 1/2.805.5–8), and the apparently international scope of her fame during her lifetime, Genevieve is not mentioned by any of the chief early Anglo-Saxon sources, although her feast day is noted in the Epternach recension of the Hieronymian Martyrology (*AS* Nov. 2/2.23) and is variously commemorated in later Anglo-Saxon calendars, notably that in the *Leofric Missal* (see **LITURGY, MASSBOOKS**), where her feast is graded (F. Wormald 1934 p 44). Copies of the C version of the *vita*, *BHL* 3336, printed by Künstle, are in the eleventh-century **COTTON-CORPUS LEGENDARY** (Zettel 1979 p 15; see also Levison *MGH* SRM 7.602, 632). According to Poulin

(1983 pp 121–30) the C text is a mid-eighth-century abridgement and stylistic revision of A, the sixth-century *vita*. C appears to have circulated widely, especially in Germany.

In addition to the edition by Künstle, see also *AS* Ian. 1.143–47. For a recent English translation of version A (as edited by Krusch), see McNamara and Halborg (1992 pp 17–37).

Georgius, passio [ANON.Pas.Georg.1a]: *BHL* 3363; *BSS* 6.512–25; *DHGE* 20.633–41.
  ed.: Arndt 1874 pp 49–70.
MSS – Lists none.
A-S Vers ?*Mart* (B19.bz and cd).
Quots/Cits – Refs none.

The early legends of Saint George (feast day April 23), the supposed martyr of Cappadocia (more properly Lydda), originated in Greek (*BHG* 670–80) in the early fifth century and rapidly thereafter proliferated in most of the literary languages of East and West. The Latin versions fall into two main groups: the so-called "first" and "second" legends, which are sometimes, but erroneously, referred to as "apocryphal" and "canonical" respectively. The Anglo-Saxons knew versions of the "first" legend only, in which the saint's enemy is the Persian emperor Datian; they seem not to have known the "second" (*BHL* 3386–92) in which George's opponent is Diocletian. The earliest Latin versions of the "first" legend, which itself is extant in numerous variant forms (see most recently Haubrichs 1979), are believed to date from the fifth century. The sixth-century **GELASIAN DECREE** (Siegmund 1949 p 219) proscribes as heretical a *Passio Sancti Georgii*, version unknown.

ALDHELM either did not know or ignored George's legend and **BEDE** omits the saint from his **MARTYROLOGIUM**, evidently because he had no traditions available to him that he regarded as sufficiently reliable and orthodox to form the basis of a brief narrative (J. Hill 1985–86 pp 207–08). In the ninth century, however, the author of the **OLD ENGLISH MARTYROLOGY** (*Mart*; ed. Kotzor 1981 2.58–62 and

66–67) provides detailed notices on George himself (April 23) and on the emperor Datian's wife Alexandria, converted by George's preaching and later tortured by her husband's order (April 27). The martyrologist seems to have known two versions (or an undiscovered conflation of two versions) of the "first" legend, corresponding to *BHL* 3363 (Passio 1a) and 3379 (Passio 1n), which represent respectively the "X" and "Y" branches identified by Matzke (1902) and further explored and reconstructed in Haubrichs's comprehensive study (1979). For a detailed sourcing of the *Old English Martyrology* entries, see Cross (1982c pp 45–51) who finds the main source to be the "X" version, with one substantial passage (George's final prayer on behalf of his future devotees) from the "Y" version. Haubrichs (1979 pp 329–30), while noting the *Martyrology*'s "undoubted" dependence on a text of the "X" type, surprisingly does not remark on the *Martyrology*'s verbatim quotations from the "Y" version.

In addition to Arndt's edition of the "X" version, see also that of Haubrichs (1979 pp 407–73). For the "Z" branch, see below, the third Georgius entry.

Joyce Hill

Georgius, passio [ANON.Pas.Georg.1n]: *BHL* 3379.
   ed.: Matzke 1902 pp 525–29.

MSS – A-S Vers   none.
Quots/Cits   see below.
Refs   none.

On the apparent use, in the **OLD ENGLISH MARTYROLOGY**, of the "Y" as well as the "X" version of the "first" legend of Saint George, see the previous entry. This version of the *passio* represents the "Y" version. For another edition of the "Y" version, see Haubrichs (1979 pp 474–99).

Georgius, passio [ANON.Pas.Georg.1i.β/γ]: *BHL* 3373/74.
   ed.: Huber 1906 pp 194–203.

MSS 1. London, BL Cotton Nero E. i: HG 344.
2. Salisbury, Cathedral Library 221 (formerly Oxford, Bodleian Library Fell 4): HG 754.5.
Lists none.
A-S Vers *ÆLS* George (B1.3.15).
Quots/Cits – Refs none.

While Ott (1892 p 39) fails to find a source for the version of the George legend related by ÆLFRIC in his LIVES OF SAINTS (*ÆLS*; ed. *EETS* OS 76 and 82), Cross (1977b) concludes that Ælfric's source was from the group *BHL* 3372–75; this corresponds to the "Z" branch in the classifications of Matzke (1902) and Haubrichs (1979). Zettel (1979 pp 19, 146, and 223–24), following Matzke (1902), narrows Ælfric's source to *BHL* 3373–74, as preserved in the London and Salisbury manuscripts of the COTTON-CORPUS LEGENDARY, which postdates Ælfric's composition, but which Zettel argues is a good witness to the legendary used by Ælfric as his principal source for *Lives*. The Legendary's text of the *Passio Georgii* combines features of both *BHL* 3373 and 3374, and, in common with other examples of the "Z" type, represents a toned-down version of the "X" type of the "first" legend. Ælfric in turn has modified the narrative further (J. Hill 1989). He refers obliquely at the outset (lines 1–4) to the GELASIAN DECREE, but evidently assumes, not necessarily on the basis of direct knowledge, that the heretical legends differ from the version circulating in Benedictine reform circles (J. Hill 1989).

On George's cult and growing popularity in tenth- and eleventh-century England, see J. Hill (1985–86 pp 289–92).

Joyce Hill

Germanus Autisiodorensis, vita [CONSTANT.Vit.German.Autiss.]: *BHL* 3453; *BSS* 6.232–36; *CPL* 2105; *DHGE* 20.901–04; *SEHI* 27. ed.: *MGH* SRM 7.247–83.

MSS – Lists none.
A-S Vers 1. BEDA.Hist.eccles. 54–67.

2. BEDA.Mart. 139.15–17; Dubois and Renaud 1976.
3. BEDA.Chron.mai. 1630–42; *CCSL* 123B.
Quots/Cits   *Vita Germani* 259.15–260.5: ADOMN.Vit.Columb. 144.20–25.
Refs none.

Germanus (born ca. 380), bishop of Auxerre (418–48, feast day July 31), is believed to have visited Britain, with **LUPUS TRECENSIS**, on two occasions to combat outbreaks of Pelagian heresy, as **BEDE** relates in detail in his **HISTORIA ECCLESIASTICA** I.xvii–xxi (BEDA.Hist.eccles.; ed. Colgrave and Mynors 1969). Bede's source was this life of Germanus by Constantius of Lyons (a correspondent of **SIDONIUS**), who wrote it ca. 475–80, when he was an old man, and dedicated it to Bishop Patiens of Lyons and Censurius of Auxerre. See Bardy and De Gaiffier (1950) and *SChr* 112.13–17. Over one hundred manuscripts of the *vita* are extant, none earlier than the eighth century. A much expanded and interpolated version (*BHL* 3454) was composed in the ninth century, incorporating some of Bede's account of **ALBANUS** (see Levison's edition, *MGH* SRM 7.245). Plummer in his edition of Bede's *Historia* (1896) depended on this interpolated version and thus his source attributions are inaccurate in places.

In addition to Bede, the learned **ADOMNAN**, Abbot of Iona, borrows from the *Vita Germani* an episode in his life of **COLUMBA HIENSIS**, *BHL* 1886 (ADOMN.Vit.Columb.; ed. Anderson and Anderson 1991; see p xlii), composed ca. 696 (his contemporary Muirchu claims that Saint Patrick was a novice of Germanus: see *SEHI* 27). Levison (*MGH* SRM 7.233 and 237–39) regards Adomnan's text of the *Vita Germani* as belonging to the same group as Bede's (viz., group B, admittedly a large and varied one). Bede's text may have derived from Iona, like his copy of Adomnan's **DE LOCIS SANCTIS** (*Historia* V.xv–xvii; ed. Colgrave and Mynors 1969 pp 504–12), but, as Borius points out (*SChr* 112.61–62), Anglo-Saxon pilgrims had ample opportunity to secure copies of the *Vita Germani* in Auxerre, since they evidently passed through there in sufficient numbers to have their own "xenodochium" (hostel).

After Bede, there is no specific evidence of Anglo-Saxon knowledge of Constantius's life of Germanus independent of Bede's account, although there was evidently a rich oral tradition among the Welsh (see next entry). The saint continued to be remembered, though without special veneration, in later Anglo-Saxon calendars. After the Norman Conquest, in 1069, a monk of Auxerre, Benedict, brought a finger of Germanus with him to Selby (Yorkshire), where he was granted a charter (1070) by William I to found a monastery (Knowles and Hadcock 1972 p 76). An account of Benedict's experiences, and of various miracles and events of the twelfth-century history of the foundation, was composed in 1184 (*Historia Selebiensis Monasterii, BHL* 3464; ed. *AS* Iul. 7.290–304), possibly from earlier written and/or oral traditions. In addition to the bibliography in *BHL*, see Fowler (1891, 1893 1.1–54), as cited by Gransden (1974 p 295).

Cross (1982d p 24) agrees with Herzfeld (*EETS* OS 116.xl) that the notice for this Germanus in the ninth-century **OLD ENGLISH MARTYROLOGY** (*Mart*; ed. Kotzor 1981 2.167 and 334) is based on Bede's extracts in his *Historia*. The **OLD ENGLISH BEDE**, however, omits altogether the chapters dealing with the missions of Germanus and Lupus (*Bede*, B9.6; ed. *EETS* OS 95.54).

The text in the later (twelfth-century) portion of London, BL Cotton Nero E. i (HG 344), pt 2, fols 205–08, is, according to Levison (*MGH SRM* 7.602), "a fragment of the interpolated life" of Germanus, that is, *BHL* 3454. Later English copies of the interpolated life are listed in Levison's edition (*MGH SRM* 7.244–45 note 1).

The brief notice of Germanus in the Exeter List of Relics (*Rec* 10.8. B16.10.8; ed. Förster 1943 p 76; Conner 1993a p 182) is insufficient to indicate knowledge of the *vita*.

For recent studies of Germanus and Britain, see E. Thompson (1984) and Wood (1984). Among other work on the literary and cultural backgrounds of Germanus and his biographer, see N. Chadwick (1955) and Griffe (1965). In addition to Levison's edition, see that of Borius (*SChr* 112), with French translation and extensive introduction. An English translation of Levison's text is in F. Hoare (1954 pp 284–320). For additional bibliography, see *RFHMA* 3.316–18. For detailed analysis of Bede's use of the *Vita Germani* in his narratives of AUGUSTINUS CANTUARIENSIS and Mellitus, as well as of Germanus himself, see Elfassi (1998).

Gavin Richardson and E. Gordon Whatley

Germanus Autisiodorensis, miracula.

By the ninth century in England the Romano-Gallic literary tradition concerning Germanus had been reduced to the abbreviated form represented in **BEDE** (see previous entry); similarly a richly legendary native British tradition was also being reduced to a few extracts incorporated in another larger work of historical narrative associated with the name of **NENNIUS** (*CPL* 1325), hardly an "Anglo-Saxon author," but someone in contact with Anglo-Saxon traditions. Included in his **HISTORIA BRITTONUM** are hagiographic episodes (*BHL* 3461; ed. J. Morris 1980 pp 67–68, 70, and 73–74) drawn from a now lost "Liber Sancti Germani" (p 73.33). The earliest full text of the *Historia Brittonum*, London, BL Harley 3859 (HG 439), was copied in Wales in the late eleventh century, but probably derived from a tenth-century exemplar (Chadwick and Chadwick 1954 p 24); a fragmented copy in Chartres is dated ca. 900. On Nennius, see N. Chadwick (1958 pp 37–46).

In some form or other, the material on which "Nennius" draws in the *Historia Brittonum* was brought to Burgundy in the later part of the ninth century by, among others, Marcus, a Welsh bishop educated in Ireland but living in Soissons ca. 873. He was in contact with various Carolingian scholars, including Heiric of Auxerre, who used the Germanus materials from Britain in his prose *Miracula S. Germani* (*BHL* 3462). On Marcus, Heiric, and the early medieval cult of Saint Germanus in Wales and Burgundy, see N. Chadwick (1958 pp 106–15). On Vortigern and Germanus, see Chadwick and Chadwick (1954). For the Germanus episodes in the most recent edition of Nennius, see Dumville (1985 pp 83–95, 99–103, 106).

Germanus Parisiensis, vita [VEN.FORT.Vit.German.Par.]: *BHL* 3468; *BLS* 2.410–11; *BSS* 6.257–59; *CPL* 1039; *DHGE* 20.927–29. See **VENANTIUS FORTUNATUS**.
ed.: *MGH* SRM 7.372–418.

MSS 1. London, BL Cotton Nero E. i: HG 344.
2. Salisbury, Cathedral Library 221 (formerly Oxford, Bodleian Library Fell 4): HG 754.5.

Lists – Refs none.

Germanus was bishop of Paris under King Childebert I and Chilperic. He died in 576, aged 80 (feast day May 28). The *vita* composed by Venantius Fortunatus shortly after Germanus's death is described by Berschin as a "Sensationsgeschichte," startlingly lacking in the sort of biographical information one might have expected from a writer who had known his subject personally for a long time (1986–91 1.282–84).

Evidence of Anglo-Saxon knowledge of Germanus is confined to the copies of the *vita* extant in the London and Salisbury manuscripts of the **COTTON-CORPUS LEGENDARY**. They correspond to group 2c in the classification of manuscripts in the newer edition of Krusch and Levison (*MGH* SRM 7.350), who remark on the frequent carelessness of the Cotton Nero E. i scribe. They list several other later English copies of the same closely related group (*MGH* SRM 7.349–50).

The edition by Krusch and Levison replaces Krusch's earlier edition (*MGH* AA 4/2.11–27).

Gervasius et Protasius, passio [ANON.Pas.Gerv.Prot./PS.AMBROSIUS]: *BHL* 3514; *BSS* 6.298–304; *CPL* 2195; *CPPM* IIA.28a; *DHGE* 20.1073–76.
ed.: *PL* 17.742–47.

MSS 1. London, BL Cotton Nero E. i: HG 344.
2. Paris, Bibliothèque Nationale lat. 10861: HG 898.
3. Salisbury, Cathedral Library 221 (formerly Oxford, Bodleian Library Fell 4): HG 754.5.

Lists none.
A-S Vers 1. ALDH.Carm.uirg. 881–94.
2. *Mart* (B19.dr).
Quots/Cits – Refs none.

Even when their cult first arose in Milan (386), during the episcopacy of **AMBROSE**, nothing much was known about how or when these two saints (feast day June 19) were martyred, or who they were, except their names and those of their parents. The story of the discovery of their bodies is told by Ambrose ca. 386 in a well-known letter to his sister Marcellina (*BHL* 3513), number XXII in the older editions (*PL* 16.1019–26), now LXXVII (ed. *CSEL* 82/3.126–40), an early example of the hagiographic subgenre of the *inventio*. The Pseudo-Ambrosian *Passio Gervasii et Protasii* at issue here, variously dated in the mid-fifth or early sixth century, purports to reproduce the contents of a small book, "libellus," written by one "Philippus" and left in the saints' tomb (*PL* 744.17–20). The aim was clearly to provide the cult with a conventional legend involving the two saints and various other characters, including their parents, **VITALIS ET VALERIA** (feast day April 28), whose story sometimes appears separately (*BHL* 8699) and whose cult was important in its own right. The *passio*'s story of Ursicinus the physician (see below) also sometimes appears separately in the manuscripts (*BHL* 8410), but not in England. Zanetti (1979) argues, on the basis of his studies of the Latin and Greek recensions, that in its earliest form the *passio* also included the legend of **NAZARIUS ET CELSUS** (in a form similar to *BHL* 6042), whose relics were unearthed along with those of Gervasius and Protasius. In this connection, in one Anglo-Saxon calendar of the late tenth century the feast of June 19 is that of "Sanctorum Geruasii. Protasii. et Nazari" (F. Wormald 1934 p 49).

The text in the Paris manuscript listed here (early ninth century, Canterbury) is imperfect, breaking off early at "Et exclamavit vitalis dicens" (*PL* 17.744.41–42), according to M. P. Brown (1986 p 125) who remarks, without explanation, that this text is "conflated" with the *Passio Gallicani, Iohannis et Pauli* (*BHL* 3236–38). This seems to mean that where the former text breaks off, the latter, which is acephalous, begins. See **IOHANNES ET PAULUS**.

The text in the **COTTON-CORPUS LEGENDARY**, as noted by Zettel (1979 p 19), conforms closely but not exactly to that printed in *PL*, somewhat abridged (crudely at times). Entitled *Passio Sancti Vitalis Martyris et Sanctorum Protasii et Geruasii*, this copy is entered among the April saints, with the feast day (April 28) of Vitalis. See Jackson and Lapidge (1996 p 137). There is no separate provision for Gervasius and Protasius. For a later manuscript in which the two feast days have separate texts, see below, the entry for Vitalis et Valeria.

While **ALDHELM** in his verse **DE VIRGINITATE** (ALDH.Carm.uirg.; ed. *MGH* AA 15) draws on a text similar to the *passio* for his brief eulogy of the twin saints (sourced by Ehwald, *MGH* AA 15.391), **BEDE** does not use the *passio* for Gervasius and Protasius in his **MARTYROLOGIUM** (ed. Dubois and Renaud 1976 p 110.13–17); instead, according to Quentin (1908 p 101), he combines material from **AUGUSTINE**'s **CONFESSIONES** and Paulinus of Milan's *Vita Ambrosii* (see **AMBROSIUS**).

Herzfeld (*EETS* OS 116.xxxix) points to the Pseudo-Ambrosian *passio* as the source of the notice for the two saints in the **OLD ENGLISH MARTYROLOGY** (*Mart*; ed. Kotzor 1981 2.124–25); J. E. Cross (private communication) confirms this but adds that the martyrologist also appears to have made some use of the genuine Ambrosian letter (*BHL* 3513).

The *Old English Martyrology* draws on the *passio* for two other notices: the doctor Ursicinus (December 13, *Mart*, B19.jk; ed. Kotzor 1981 2.264) and the twins' parents, Vitalis and Valeria (see their entry below, for further details). In the brief account of Ursicinus's martyrdom in the *passio* (*PL* 17.744.25–50), Vitalis plays a prominent role, but the Old English martyrologist keeps him anonymous, referring to him merely as "a certain Christian" ("sum christen man": Kotzor 1981 2.264.7). Conversely in the *Martyrology* notice for Vitalis, Ursicinus is reduced to the "other men" whom Vitalis "exhorted to have faith in Christ" (p 67.13; see also p 374). To describe Ursicinus's martyrdom, however, the martyrologist borrows a sentence from the part of the Latin *passio* that recounts Vitalis's own martyrdom: "he gave up to God the precious gem that the devil wished to seize, that is the holy soul" (p 264.11–13, echoing the *passio, PL* 17.745.12–14).

On Ursicinus, see *BSS* 12.1229–31. For recent discussions of Ambrose's role in promoting the cults of the brothers Gervasius and Protasius, and Nazarius and Celsus, see Dassman (1975) and P. Brown (1981 pp 36–37).

Getulius, passio [ANON.Pas.Getul.]: *BHL* 3524; *BLS* 2.517–18; *DHGE* 20.1123–24.
ed.: Mara 1964 pp 134–46.
MSS London, BL Cotton Nero E. i: HG 344.
Lists – Refs none.

Getulius (feast day June 10), according to his legend, was a retired army veteran and husband of **SYMPHOROSA**, martyred like her under the emperor Hadrian. Although conventional in many respects, the *Passio Getulii* (dated sixth–eighth century) is unusual for its emphasis on biblical knowledge and doctrine (Mara 1964 pp 127–30). Anglo-Saxon interest in Getulius and the related legend of his wife's martyrdom with her seven sons is indicated only by the evidence of the **COTTON-CORPUS LEGENDARY**. As Zettel points out (1979 p 21), in Anglo-Saxon England the *passio* is preserved only in the Cotton manuscript (in a form not quite identical to *BHL* 3524) and was lost from the Salisbury Cathedral manuscript at the division between Salisbury 221 and 222 (Webber 1992 p 156 note 65). The Cotton text, not mentioned in Mara's edition, is very like the text edited by her from a ninth- or tenth-century manuscript in the Vatican.

Gislenus: *BSS* 6.1149–50; *DHGE* 20.1180–82.

The earliest life of Gislenus (Ghislain), *BHL* 3552, composed ca. 900, describes him as a Basilian monk of seventh-century Athens who came first to Rome and thence to northern France where he founded a monastery now identified with Celle (Hainault) and was associated with various contemporary saints, including **AMANDUS** and Aldegonde. Modern scholars, however, are less confident than their predecessors that the tenth-century *vita* is based on an authentic earlier text, and the story may well have been created in support of a cult for which there is no evidence before the date of the *vita*. A life of the saint is mentioned in the Peterborough Abbey booklist from around the turn of the eleventh century (ML 13.42), but as Lapidge points out in his note on this item, there is no way of establishing which of the several prose and verse *vitae* is indicated. For a somewhat parallel story, see **IVO**.

Gordianus et Epimachus, passio: *BHL* 3612; *BLS* 2.265; *BSS* 7.117–18.
ed.: Mombritius 1910 1.603–04 and 682–83.
MSS 1. London, BL Cotton Nero E. i: HG 344.
2. Salisbury, Cathedral Library 221 (formerly Oxford, Bodleian Library Fell 4): HG 754.5.
Lists – Refs none.

There is archeological evidence for early cults of these two saints in Rome (feast day May 10), but the late *passio*, according to which Gordianus was a high Roman official martyred under the emperor Julian and buried in the tomb of an earlier martyr, Epimachus, is generally regarded as spurious by modern scholars. Although Gordianus is mentioned as a Roman martyr in the **OLD ENGLISH MARTYROLOGY** (*Mart*, B19.cu; Kotzor 1981 2.100.9–12), there is no narrative, and the martyrologist's source is probably a mass set in a sacramentary (see Amore's article in *BSS*; cf. Kotzor 1981 1.211 and 225). However, in one of the late-tenth-century Canterbury calendars, the joint feast appears and is graded (F. Wormald 1934 p 48), implying possibly the use of the *passio* for lections. I have no information about the textual traditions of the *passio* or the affiliations of the two English copies in the **COTTON-CORPUS LEGENDARY**. Zettel (1979 p 20) identifies these as corresponding to the text edited by Mombritius. Most of the text in the London manuscript has been lost (Jackson and Lapidge 1996 p 137).

Gregorius Magnus, vita [ANON.Vit.Greg.Mag.2]: *BHL* 3637; *BLS* 1.566–71; *BSS* 7.222–78; *CPL* 1722; *DHGE* 21.1387–407; Farmer (1987) pp 189–90.
   ed.: Colgrave 1968 pp 72–138.
MSS – Lists none.
A-S Vers see below.
Quots/Cits – Refs none.

   Although the monks of St Augustine's, Canterbury honored their patron (**AUGUSTINUS CANTUARIENSIS**) with the title "apostle of the English," **BEDE** and most other English writers gave this honor to Pope **GREGORY THE GREAT** (ca. 540–604), who sent others to preach the gospel to the angelic Angles only because he could not go himself. For a recent reassessment and reinterpretation of the historical context and sources, and for bibliography, see Wood (1994). In addition to being familiar with most of his literary output, the Anglo-Saxons knew several early and later lives of Gregory, including that in the **LIBER PONTIFICALIS** LXVI (*BHL* 3636). English authors themselves produced two Latin lives and two Old English lives. One of the Latin lives is the subject of this entry. See the following entries for the others. On English liturgical devotion to Gregory, and for further references, see Ortenberg (1992 pp 180–84). See also Thacker (1998).

   Although the earliest full Latin life of Gregory is known to have been written at Whitby in Northumberland early in the eighth century, and although it proved influential in the development of Gregory's legend on the Continent (as an important source for two of the lives discussed below), it has left no apparent trace in English manuscripts and texts, not even in those of the earliest period. Until recently, it was even customary to argue that Bede in **HISTORIA ECCLESIASTICA** II.i (ed. Colgrave and Mynors 1969 pp 122–34) drew on a common tradition, and not the Whitby life, for his report of Gregory's famous puns on "Angli" and "angeli," "Deira" and "de ira," and "Aelle" and "Alleluia" (pp 132–34 and 133 note 2; compare the Whitby *Vita Gregorii* IX–X, ed. Colgrave 1968 pp 90–92). Goffart, however (1988 pp 264–67), following Richter

(1984 pp 101–02), has insisted afresh that Bede *did* know the Whitby life but used it selectively, drawing more on the *Liber Pontificalis* and Gregory's own writings and letters for his more sophisticated account. It has been suggested that early in the eighth century a copy of the *vita*, "perhaps the only copy" (Colgrave 1968 p 49), traveled to the Continent where it was known in Rome in the ninth and tenth centuries. The sole extant manuscript is from St Gall. For notes on minor deficiencies of Colgrave's edition, see Löfstedt (1990). For a recent literary appreciation, see Berschin (1986–91 2.261–66). We have not seen the unpublished edition of Mosford (1988).

Gregorius Magnus, vita [PAVL.DIAC.Vit.Greg.Mag.]: *BHL* 3639; *CPL* 1723.

ed.: Grisar 1887 pp 162–73.

MSS 1. London, BL Cotton Nero E. i: HG 344.
2. Salisbury, Cathedral Library 221 (formerly Oxford, Bodleian Library Fell 4): HG 754.5.

Lists none.

A-S Vers *ÆCHom* II, 9 (B1.2.10).

Quots/Cits – Refs none.

As established by Godden (1968), **ÆLFRIC** in composing his life of Pope **GREGORY THE GREAT** for the Second Series of **CATHOLIC HOMILIES** (*ÆCHom*; ed. *EETS* SS 5) drew not only on the Latin and Old English versions of **BEDE**'s **HISTORIA ECCLESIASTICA** but also on the original, uninterpolated version of the *Vita Gregorii* composed by the Lombard **PAUL THE DEACON** (alias Warnefried) in the later eighth century (probably in the 780s; see Limone 1988 p 898). The uninterpolated version is also preserved in the eleventh-century London and Salisbury copies of the **COTTON-CORPUS LEGENDARY**, as indicated by Levison somewhat vaguely (*MGH* SRM 7.602 and 632) and confirmed by Zettel (1979 p 18) and Jackson and Lapidge (1996 p 136). Zettel (1979 pp 144 and 184–46) finds close textual links between the Legendary text and Ælfric's homily. It is not impossible that the life of Gregory listed in the late-eleventh-century Peterborough booklist (ML 13.57) was also this version, but more probably it was that of John the Deacon (*BHL* 3641). Limone (1988 pp 910–11 and 915–53) provides a list and descriptions of the manuscripts of Paul's original *Vita Gregorii*. He mistakenly identifies (p 893) the version in the Cotton manuscript, however, as the "Vita Interpolata" (see next entry) and misses the Salisbury copy of Paul's life, as well as the evidence provided by Ælfric's rendering. For a literary analysis, characterizing Paul's work as "eine studierte Variante von Bedas Porträt," see Berschin (1986–91 2.150–53). For a recent discussion of Ælfric's treatment of the *vita*, see Godden (1996 pp 275–76 and *EETS* SS 18.403–12 and 522).

Gregorius Magnus, vita [PAVL.DIAC.Vit.Interp.Greg.Magn.]: *BHL* 3640.
ed.: *PL* 75.41–60.

MSS – Lists none.
A-S Vers ?*Mart* (B19.ax).
Quots/Cits – Refs none.

The interpolated version of **PAUL THE DEACON**'s life of **GREGORY THE GREAT** was composed in Rome, apparently shortly after the life by John the Deacon (see next entry) in the late ninth or early tenth century (Colgrave 1968 p 60). It is thus unlikely that it was known to the author of the brief but distinctive tribute to Gregory in the **OLD ENGLISH MARTYROLOGY** (*Mart*; ed. Kotzor 1981 2.32), which is believed to have been written in the late ninth century or earlier, far from Rome. Yet of the several early medieval versions of the life of Gregory, the "Interpolata" provides the closest parallels to the second part of the *Martyrology* notice that briefly summarizes episodes concerning Gregory's salvation of Trajan (p 32.6–9) and the inspirational white dove (p 32.9–12). It is true that both episodes occur in the Whitby *Vita Gregorii* XXVI and XXIX (*BHL* 3637; ed. Colgrave 1968 pp 120–22 and 126–28; see above, the entry for *BHL* 3637), but only in the *Martyrology* and the present *vita* (XXVII–XXVIII; *PL* 75.56–58) do they form consecutive episodes. Moreover, only in this *vita* (*PL* 75.58.2–5 and 9–10) and the *Martyrology* is the dove said to have been sitting on the saint's head and also close to his mouth.

One might tentatively suggest that these parallels imply the existence of an intermediate form of the life of Gregory, or an earlier recension of the "Interpolated" version, to which the *Martyrology* and the "Interpolata," as printed, are both independently indebted. Further study seems necessary. For a handlist of "Interpolata" manuscripts, see Limone (1988 pp 892–95).

Gregorius Magnus, vita [IOH.DIAC.Vit.Greg.Magn.]: *BHL* 3641.
ed.: *PL* 75.59–242.
MSS 1. London, BL Royal 6. A. vii: HG 465.
2. Oxford, Bodleian Library Bodley 381 (*SC* 2202): HG 570.
3. Oxford, Jesus College 37: HG 674.
Lists ?Peterborough: ML 13.57.
A-S Vers none.
Quots/Cits see below.
Refs none.

The longest and, ultimately, most widely known of the early medieval lives of **GREGORY THE GREAT** is that of John the Deacon, surnamed Hymmonides, written in Rome (ca. 873–76) for Pope John VIII. Among John's sources was the Whitby life (see the entry above for *BHL* 3637), which he knew to be of English origin: see John's *Vita Gregorii* I.xliv (*PL* 75.104–05) and Limone (1978 pp 42–43, 50–51). There is no modern critical edition and the affiliations of the three extant Anglo-Saxon manuscripts, all *libelli* containing only this text, are unknown. The Royal manuscript, written in the early eleventh century, is from Worcester (Ker 1964 p 208); the Bodley manuscript (eleventh century) was at St Augustine's, Canterbury in the later Middle Ages (p 46); the Jesus College manuscript was later at Hereford, St Guthlac's (p 99).

The "Vita Gregorii" in the eleventh-century Peterborough booklist (ML 13.57) may well have been this *vita*.

According to Thomas N. Hall (private communication), an anecdote adapted from John's *Vita Gregorii* I.x (*PL* 75.66), about an angel disguised as a shipwrecked sailor who tests Gregory's charity, occurs in an unpublished Latin sermon for Palm Sunday, extant in two late-eleventh-century manuscripts from Salisbury: London, BL Cotton Tiberius C. i (HG 376), fols 172r–173r, and Royal 5. E. xix (HG 461), fols 19r–20r. Hall has in progress an edition of this sermon.

On the Roman historical context of John's *Vita Gregorii*, see Leonardi (1977); for further bibliography, see his brief article in *Lexikon des Mittelalters* 5.569. See also the valuable literary analysis (and bibliographical notes) of Berschin (1986–91 3.372–87).

Gregorius Naziazenus.

While **ALDHELM** in his DE VIRGINITATE appears to use several sources for his eulogy of **BASIL**, his account of Basil's life-long friend, Gregory of Nazianzen (*Carmen* 710–29, *Prosa* 262.8–263.10; ed. *MGH AA* 15), draws only on **RUFINUS**'s continuation of **EUSEBIUS PAMPHILUS**, HISTORIA ECCLESIASTICA XI.ix (ed. *GCS* 9/2.1014–17). See Lapidge and Herren (1979 p 176), who follow Ehwald (*MGH* AA 15.262). Cross (1985b pp 231–32) shows that the **OLD ENGLISH MARTYROLOGY** notice for this Gregory (*Mart*, B19.bc; ed. Kotzor 1981 2.35) is probably based on Aldhelm's account rather than directly on the "Vita Contractior" attributed to Rufinus as suggested by Kotzor (p 293).

Guthlacus, vita [FELIX.Vit.Guth.]: *BHL* 3723; *BLS* 2.72–73; *BSS* 7.546–47; *CPL* 2150; *DHGE* 22.1214–18; Farmer (1987) pp 198–99. ed.: Colgrave 1956 pp 60–170.

MSS 1. Arras, Bibliothèque Municipale 1029 (812): HG 781.
2. Boulogne, Bibliothèque Municipale 106: HG 804.
3. Cambridge, Corpus Christi College 307: HG 88.
4. Cambridge, Corpus Christi College 389: HG 103.

5. Dublin, Trinity College 174: HG 215.
6. London, BL Cotton Nero E. i: HG 344.
7. London, BL Royal 4. A. xiv: HG 456.
8. London, BL Royal 13. A. xv: HG 484.
Lists 1. Saewold: ML 8.19.
2. Peterborough: ML 13.16.
A-S Vers 1. ?*GuthA* (A3.2).
2. *GuthB* (A3.2).
3. *Mart* (B19.s, B19.bv).
4. *LS* 10 (Guthlac, B3.3.10).
Quots/Cits – Refs none.

Although his death seems to have occurred in 714, Guthlac, the hermit of the Fens (feast day April 11), is not mentioned by **BEDE**, and the Latin life by the monk Felix is dated 730–49 by Colgrave (1956 p 19), that is, after the completion of Bede's **HISTORIA ECCLESIASTICA**. Felix's *Vita Guthlaci*, while written in the ornate Insular style, is heavily indebted in its content and structure to Bede's **VITA CUTHBERTI** and to early classics of monastic hagiography such as Evagrius's life of **ANTONIUS** and **SULPICIUS SEVERUS**'s **VITA MARTINI**; see Kurtz (1926) and Colgrave (1958).

Guthlac was widely venerated in Anglo-Saxon England and his popularity is reflected in the number of extant pre-Conquest copies of the life and related vernacular texts. Among the manuscripts listed above, a late-eighth- or early-ninth-century fragment of the life survives as the fly leaves of the tenth-century manuscript Royal 4. A. xiv, and the complete copy in Corpus Christi College 307, of unknown provenance, is dated in the ninth century. The other Latin manuscripts listed here range from the tenth to the late eleventh centuries. Colgrave remarks (1956 p 31) that the copy in the Cotton manuscript of the **COTTON-CORPUS LEGENDARY** seems to have been "added as an afterthought," between the lives of **MARIA AEGYPTIACA** and **AMBROSIUS**, since it is neither in the Salisbury manuscript of the Legendary nor in the Cotton table of contents. The text hand of the Cotton copy, however, is that of the main scribe, and other signs indicate that the decision to add the *Vita Guthlaci* was made while the main legendary was being copied. Colgrave also notes (p 32) that the Cotton text is the only one in the manuscript to be supplied with Old English glosses and that the glosses seem related to those in Corpus Christi College 389 (see below). For descriptions of all the manuscripts and their affiliations, see Colgrave (1956 pp 26–51; stemma p 51).

Lapidge identifies the manuscript itemized in the Saewold booklist as the Arras manuscript, which is textually very close to the Boulogne manuscript. Lapidge also suggests the manuscript in the Peterborough list may be London, BL Harley 3097, omitted by HG, as a twelfth-century manuscript, but dated mid-eleventh century by Colgrave (1956 p 85).

Guthlac's importance to the Anglo-Saxons is reflected also in vernacular versions in both prose and verse. According to Kotzor, the substantial account of Guthlac in the ninth-century **OLD ENGLISH MARTYROLOGY** (*Mart*; ed. Kotzor 1981 2.52–53, sourced p 301) appears to draw mainly on Felix's life, as does the *Martyrology*'s shorter notice for Guthlac's sister, **PEGA** (p 13), although Roberts (1970 pp 203–04) thinks it more likely that the martyrologist's immediate source was liturgical. The anonymous Old English prose *Guthlac (LS* 10; ed. Gonser 1909), a translation of Felix's life surviving in a late West Saxon recension (London, BL Cotton Vespasian D. xxi, formerly part of a manuscript now in Oxford; NRK 344), was probably composed in the ninth or early tenth century in Mercia (Roberts 1986). A portion of the translation (corresponding to *Vita Guthlaci* XXVIII–XXXII, concerning Guthlac and the demons), independent of the Vespasian copy or its immediate exemplar, appears among the homilies in the Vercelli Book (*VercHom* 23; ed. *EETS OS* 300; also ed. Szarmach 1981 pp 97–101; see **HOMILIARIES, ANONYMOUS OLD ENGLISH HOMILIES**). Bolton (1961) points to Corpus Christi College 389 or Cotton Nero E. i (or a similar text of Colgrave's group IV type) as the Latin source text of the prose *Guthlac*; Roberts in her 1967 Oxford thesis specifies Corpus Christi College 389 (a Canterbury manuscript). The Old English glosses in these manuscripts are apparently not related to the Old English prose life.

Two vernacular poems, *Guthlac A* (*GuthA*; ed. *ASPR* 3), which recounts the saint's encounters with demons in his fenland retreat, and

Guthlac B (*GuthB*; ed. *ASPR* 3), which describes his death, survive in one manuscript, the so-called *Exeter Book* in Exeter Cathedral Library. In addition to the edition of the poems in *ASPR*, it is important to consult the fuller edition by Roberts (1979). *Guthlac B* is widely accepted as a rendering of chapter L of Felix's life (Roberts 1979 pp 36–43), but while *Guthlac A* corresponds in some respects to the subject matter of *Vita Guthlaci* XXVIII–XXXII (see the remarks of T. Hill 1979 pp 186–87), the few verbal correspondences formally adduced to indicate the poet's knowledge of the Latin are not decisive. The ending of *Vercelli Homily* 23 (which departs from the *vita*), later iconographic evidence, and the contents of *Guthlac A* suggest the existence of some lost literary sources regarding Guthlac's visionary experiences, or a flourishing oral tradition, or both (Roberts 1979 pp 19–29; also 1988).

The dating and provenance of both poems are uncertain; they have usually been regarded as no later than the late ninth century, *Guthlac A* possibly being older than *Guthlac B*; see Roberts (1979 pp 70–71). For a recent argument in favor of a later tenth-century date for *Guthlac A*, see Conner (1993b). See also Roberts's dissertation (1967 pp 241–524) for further discussion of the prose *Guthlac,* and editions of the Old English text and of the Latin text from Cambridge, Corpus Christi College 389. Olsen (1981 and 1983) interprets the relation of the Old English Guthlac writings to their putative sources.

Hadrianus et Natalia, passio [ANON.Pas.Hadrian.Nat.]: *BHL* 3744; *BSS* 1.269–70; *DHGE* 1.608–11.
   ed.: Mombritius 1910 1.22–30.
MSS 1. London, BL Cotton Nero E. i: HG 344.
      2. Salisbury, Cathedral Library 222 (formerly Oxford, Bodleian Library Fell 1): HG 754.6.
Lists none.
A-S Vers Mart (B19.at).
Quots/Cits – Refs none.

According to this *passio*, Hadrianus was an officer of the imperial court at Nicomedia, husband of Natalia, who witnessed his martyrdom and encouraged him therein. Her role in the story is colorful and assertive. Although she died a natural death, she is also reckoned among the martyrs. Scholars appear still undecided as to whether the legend of Hadrianus and Natalia was composed first in Greek or Latin. As so often, the oldest Latin copies predate the oldest Greek manuscripts, but Siegmund (1949 pp 236–37), who mistakenly says **BEDE**'s **MARTYROLOGIUM** has a notice for the two, suggests the Latin version was translated from the Greek in Rome, where already by the early seventh century a church was dedicated to them. Initially their feast day was March 4 and this was still the case in England in the ninth century to judge from the **OLD ENGLISH MARTYROLOGY** (see below), but September 8 became the normal feast day in Rome in the eighth or ninth century and this is reflected in the later English manuscript copies listed above. March 4 is retained, however, in a late-eleventh-century calendar from Exeter; see F. Wormald 1934 p 88; also pp 46 and 52, where the calendar in the *Leofric Missal* (see **LITURGY, MASSBOOKS**) has both March 4 and September 8.

In the absence of a critical edition, any picture of the textual tradition of the *passio* in England must remain vague. Cross (1986b p 281 note 37) confirms that the source of the substantial notice for these married saints in the *Old English Martyrology* (*Mart*; ed. Kotzor 1981 2.28–29) is similar to the version printed by Mombritius. According to Zettel (1979 p 25), the text preserved in the Cotton and Salisbury manuscripts is also of the same type, but in its present state it seems to share features with *BHL* 3744b (see Jackson and Lapidge 1996 p 140) and/or *BHL* 3745e. Many of the original readings in the Cotton copy have been corrected or rewritten in a twelfth-century hand.

Besides the edition by Mombritius, see also that of Fábrega Grau (1953–55 2.266–79).

Helena. See **IESUS CHRISTUS, INVENTIO SANCTAE CRUCIS**.

249   ACTA SANCTORUM

Hermes. See ALEXANDER PAPA.

Hewaldi Duo: cf. *BHL* 2803; *BLS* 4.17; *BSS* 5.401–02; Farmer (1987) p 205.

The chief source for the Anglo-Saxons' knowledge of the brothers Hewald (Ewaldi), martyred members of Willibrord's mission to the Frisians and Saxons (who died ca. 695, feast day October 3), is **BEDE**'s HISTORIA ECCLESIASTICA V.x (Colgrave and Mynors 1969 pp 480–84) from which are drawn the notices in his MARTYROLOGIUM (see Quentin 1908 pp 105–06) and in the **OLD ENGLISH MARTYROLOGY** (B19.ht; ed. Kotzor 1981 2.225–26; detailed sourcing, p 359). See also the eighth-century York metrical calendar (verse 63; ed. Wilmart 1934 p 68). In later Anglo-Saxon England their feast was apparently forgotten. There are several anonymous reworkings of the Bedan narrative (*BHL* 2804–2807d).

Hieronymus, vita [ANON.Vit.Hieron./PS.GENNADIUS]: *BHL* 3869; *BHM* 903; *BLS* 3.686–93; *BSS* 6.1108–32; *CPL* 623; *DACL* 7.2235–304. ed.: *PL* 22.175–84.

MSS 1. London, BL Cotton Nero E. i: HG 344.
       2. Salisbury, Cathedral Library 222 (formerly Oxford, Bodleian Library Fell 1): HG 754.6.
Lists – Refs none.

JEROME (341–420, feast day September 30) was not only one of the four Doctors of the Western Church, author of numerous works of biblical scholarship, exegesis, polemic, Christian instruction, and hagiography, which were well known to the Anglo-Saxons; he was also one of the early Western champions of asceticism and the spiritual culture of the desert. Despite the importance of his life's story, however, he was apparently the last of the four Doctors to be commemorated with a formal *vita*. During the four or five hundred years after his death, his biography was known only through his own works and the notice (largely a bibliography) in his own DE VIRIS INLUSTRIBUS CXXXV (ed. *TU* 14/1a.55.17–56.11), which was one of the sources of **ALDHELM**'s eulogy in the DE VIRGINITATE (*Carmen* 1619–52; ed. *MGH* AA 15). The notice for Jerome in the **OLD ENGLISH MARTYROLOGY** (*Mart*, B19.hr; ed. Kotzor 1981 2.224–25 and 358) is based ultimately on **ADOMNAN**'s DE LOCIS SANCTIS (Cross 1981e p 180).

As is evident from the copies in the **COTTON-CORPUS LEGENDARY**, however, the later Anglo-Saxons had access to the ninth-century life of Jerome by an unknown writer, "Pseudo-Gennadius." This, and the other ninth-century fabrication, "Pseudo-Sebastian" (*BHL* 3870), formed the basis of the later medieval lives, although these would be greatly expanded from other sources. Since it was used by **ADO** in his martyrology, ca. 850 (*PL* 123.370–72), the Pseudo-Gennadius life must be somewhat earlier than this date.

Another copy is in the early-twelfth-century Canterbury legendary, London, BL Arundel 91 (HG 305), along with the famous "miraculum de leone," *BHL* 3872, presumably excerpted from the Pseudo-Sebastian life where it first appears. Ogilvy (*BKE* p 47) refers to a copy of the Pseudo-Sebastian life in Siwold's booklist, but I could not confirm this in ML. Also from the turn of the century, what appears to be an abridged version of the Pseudo-Gennadian life, divided into eight lections, is the last item in Cambridge, University Library Kk.4.13 (HG 24), a Norwich cathedral manuscript otherwise comprising a copy of the expanded version of **PAUL THE DEACON**'s HOMILIARIUM (see also **HOMILIARIES**). Thomas N. Hall kindly drew my attention to this manuscript.

On the development of the hagiography concerning Jerome, see most recently Rice (1985 pp 23–45 especially p 23 notes 1 and 2), who draws on the fundamental study of Vaccari (1958, especially pp 35–41). To Lambert's list of extant manuscripts of Pseudo-Gennadius (*BHM* 903), Rice (1985 p 23 note 1) adds three more from the ninth century.

ACTA SANCTORUM

Hilarinus.

Hilarinus (feast day July 16) is a minor figure in the legend of GALLICANUS, which in turn is part of the *passio* of IOHANNES ET PAULUS. He is said to have been martyred at Ostia, the port of Rome, where the Roman general, Gallicanus, had been his guest after converting to Christianity. For **BEDE**'s dependence on this *passio* for his separate but brief notice in **MARTYROLOGIUM** (ed. Dubois and Renaud 1976 p 129.2–4), see Quentin (1908 p 75).

Hilarion, vita [HIERON.Vit.Hilar.]: *BHL* 3879; *BHM* 262; *BLS* 4.163–65; *BSS* 7.731–33; *CPL* 618; *DHGE* 24.471–72.
ed.: *PL* 23.29–54.
MSS ?Worcester, Cathedral Library F.48: HG 761.
Lists none.
A-S Vers 1. ALDH.Carm.uirg. 797–826; *MGH* AA 15.
2. ALDH.Pros.uirg. 266.1–267.12.
3. *Mart* (B19.id).
Quots/Cits Vit.Hilar. 50.39–42: BEDA.Nom.reg.loc. 225–27; *CCSL* 121.
Refs 1. ALDH.Pros.uirg. 266.4.
2. BEDA.Mart. 191.4–5; Dubois and Renaud 1976.

A native of Gaza, Hilarion (ca. 291–371, feast day October 21) was educated in Egypt, where he converted to Christianity. After a sojourn with Saint Antony (**ANTONIUS**) in the desert, and after adopting the eremitic life in Palestine at Maiuma (where he was later buried), he traveled widely in quest of solitude, eventually settling near Paphos on Cyprus. Here he was visited by Bishop **EPIPHANIUS** of Salamis, who later wrote a eulogy of his life, now lost, but reputedly used by **JEROME** (HIERONYMUS, died 421) in composing his *Vita Hilarionis*.

As is evident from the sources listed in the headnotes here, the *vita* was well known in early Anglo-Saxon England. Prago (1938) points to one detail in the account of Hilarion in **ALDHELM**'s prose DE VIRGINITATE (ALDH.Pros.uirg.; ed. *MGH* AA 15.266.13–14) not reflected in the *vita*: the designation of Epidaurus as a "municipium" rather than an "oppidum" as in Jerome. He attributes the choice of word to Aldhelm's knowledge (gleaned on his visit to Rome) of Epidaurus/ Ragusa as an episcopal city.

The use of the *vita* by the author of the **OLD ENGLISH MARTYROLOGY** in his ample notice for Hilarion (*Mart*; ed. Kotzor 1981 2.236–38) was noted by Cockayne (*RS* 35/1.141) and Herzfeld (*EETS* OS 116.xli), though without close analysis. Particularly detailed are the *Martyrology*'s renderings of episodes and dialogue from *Vita Hilarionis* XXI and XLV (*PL* 23.38–39, 52; cf. Kotzor 1981 2.236.12–237.14 and 237.16–238.5). For Cross's discussion (1984b p 21) of another connection, see our entry for **ANTONINUS APAMEAE**.

On the uncertainties surrounding the Worcester manuscript, see above, the entry for Antonius. The Worcester text of the *Vita Hilarionis* belongs in the same group (L) as an eighth- or ninth-century Chartres manuscript, but it is most closely related to a twelfth-century English manuscript, now in Cambridge (see McNeil in Oldfather 1943 pp 285–86; see also p 106). McNeil remarks that the printed editions appear to have been based on manuscripts of the L type.

In addition to the *PL* text, which reprints a commendable eighteenth-century edition by D. Vallarsi, see also *AS* Oct. 9.43–58 and Bastiaensen (1975b) pp 69–143, neither of which is a critical edition. Paul B. Harvey Jr., of Pennsylvania State University, has announced a new edition in progress. McNeil's list of known manuscripts of the *vita* (in Oldfather 1943 pp 251–305) is enlarged by Lambert (*BHM* 262). For a brief but enlightening appreciation of the *Vita Hilarionis* in comparison with Jerome's other hagiographies, see Berschin (1986–91 1.138–40 and 143–44). For a more detailed study, see De Vogüé (1991–93 2.163–236). For a recent survey and further bibliography, see Bastiaensen (1994). The latest English translation is that of White (1998) pp 89–115.

Hilarius Pictavensis, vita [VEN.FORT.Vit.Hilar.Pict.]: *BHL* 3885; *BLS* 1.77–80; *BSS* 7.719–25; *CPL* 1038; *DHGE* 24.459–61; *DTC* 6.2388–96. ed.: *MGH* AA 4/2.1–7.

MSS 1. London, BL Cotton Nero E. i: HG 344.
2. Salisbury, Cathedral Library 221 (formerly Oxford, Bodleian Library Fell 4): HG 754.5.
Lists none.
A-S Vers ?BEDA.Mart. 12.9–11.
Quots/Cits – Refs none.

Hilary, bishop of Poitiers ca. 350–67 (feast day January 13), was well known, during and after his time, as a champion of catholic orthodoxy against Arianism. According to **SULPICIUS SEVERUS, VITA MARTINI** V.i (ed. *SChr* 133.262), Hilary was also an early mentor and teacher of Saint Martin of Tours (**MARTINUS TURONENSIS**). The earliest full life of Hilary, however, was written 200 years after his death by **VENANTIUS FORTUNATUS** (probably between 565 and 573: see Krusch's *MGH* edition p VII). Quentin (1908 p 108) suggests that Fortunatus's *Vita Hilarii* (*MGH* AA 4/2.4.2–5.6) may be the source of **BEDE**'s brief notice for Hilary in the **MARTYROLOGIUM** (BEDA.Mart.; ed. Dubois and Renaud 1976), where he alludes to his resuscitation of a corpse by prayer. Quentin cautions (1908 p 107) that the notice is too brief to admit of a conclusive sourcing.

The same is true of the four-line notice for Hilary in the **OLD ENGLISH MARTYROLOGY** (*Mart*, B19.w; ed. Kotzor 1981 2.15), which Herzfeld (*EETS* OS 116.xxxvii) regarded as dependent on Bede's *Martyrologium* alone, but Kotzor includes this one among other *Martyrology* entries that contain more material than Bede provides (Kotzor 1981 1.208–16; see also Cross 1985b p 241 and note 70). It is by no means certain, however, that the *Martyrology* author knew the *Vita Hilarii*.

The later Anglo-Saxons, on the other hand, did have copies of the *vita*, as evidenced in the London and Salisbury manuscripts of the **COTTON-CORPUS LEGENDARY** (see the next entry for the forged letter of Hilary to his daughter Abra). Neither of the English copies is collated by Krusch, and their affiliations with the Continental tradition have not been studied (the Cotton manuscript shares numerous variants with Krusch's V and A manuscripts, but does not seem to be directly related to either).

On relations between Anglo-Saxon England and Poitiers in the later Anglo-Saxon period, see Beech (1990 pp 87–88, 92–93), who points to the role of Queen Emma, wife of Cnut, in the rebuilding of the church of Saint-Hilaire-le-Grand in Poitiers (dedicated 1049). This is probably not the reason, however, for the presence of the *Vita Hilarii* in the two English manuscripts. As Krusch remarks (*MGH* AA 4/2.VII) the work is included in virtually every important medieval legendary.

Hilarius Pictavensis, epistola [ANON.Ep.Hilar.Abra./PS.HILAR.]: *BHL* 3887a.
ed.: *CSEL* 65.237–44.
MSS 1. London, BL Cotton Nero E. i: HG 344.
2. Salisbury, Cathedral Library 221 (formerly Oxford, Bodleian Library Fell 4): HG 754.5.
Lists – Refs none.

In common with many other medieval manuscripts containing copies of the *Vita Hilarii* by **VENANTIUS FORTUNATUS** (see previous entry), the London and Salisbury manuscripts of the **COTTON-CORPUS LEGENDARY** append to the *vita* a letter purporting to be from Saint Hilary to his daughter Abra, but now known to be spurious. See the Bollandists' remarks (*BHL NS* p 426) on *BHL* 3887a. The text in the Cotton manuscript is not collated by Feder in his *CSEL* edition, but it appears to differ only in minor ways from his printed text. An earlier edition is in *PL* 10.549–52.

Hilda: *BLS* 4.369–70; *BSS* 7.754–56; *DHGE* 24.480–82; Farmer (1987) pp 206–07.

Hild (feast day November 17) was born in 614, of royal Northumbrian and East Anglian stock, converted to Christianity in the time of King Edwin, and later planned to become a nun at **BALTHILDIS**'s foundation at Chelles in Francia. **AIDANUS** persuaded her, however, to settle in Northumbria where she eventually founded, and was abbess of, the double monastery of Whitby (657). The monastery became a veritable nursery of bishops and, according to **BEDE**, the well-spring of Old

English Christian poetry (see **CAEDMON**). Hilda died in 680, arguably among the most important figures in early Anglo-Saxon religious and cultural history. Bede is the main source of modern knowledge about her (chiefly **HISTORIA ECCLESIASTICA** IV.xxiii; ed. Colgrave and Mynors 1969 pp 404–14) but according to Cross (1982d pp 21–24 and passim), significant details and a distinct episode in the **OLD ENGLISH MARTYROLOGY** (*Mart*, B19.iz; ed. Kotzor 1981 2.252–53) strongly presuppose another account besides that of Bede. Cross posits a Whitby life of Hild, lost like that of **ÆTHELBURGA** of Barking (see also that of **GREGORIUS MAGNUS** from Whitby, lost until rediscovered in the nineteenth century in a Continental library). Cross reckons the author of the *Old English Martyrology* drew on both Bede and the lost life, but it is possible that the lost life was a reworking of Bede's account with added material. The martyrologist does not mention Bede as his source, as he does often elsewhere.

For a recent critical study of Hild and Bede's depiction of her, see Hollis (1992 pp 248–50, 253–58, 261–70). For a late medieval poem on the life of Hilda, which incorporates various non-Bedan traditions, see Rigg (1996).

Hippolytus: *BLS* 3.315–16; *BSS* 7.868–79; *CPL* 2219; *DHGE* 24.626, 627–35; Farmer (1987) pp 208–09.

The Hippolytus known to the Anglo-Saxons, and venerated on August 13 in all their later calendars, bears little resemblance to the priest and controversial theologian, celebrated by modern church historians, who died on this day in exile on Sardinia in 235 and was buried on the Via Tiburtina in Rome. The hagiographical Hippolytus, on the other hand, is said to have been a Roman deputy, "vicarius" (Old English *tungerefa*, "town-reeve"), under the prefect Valerian and emperor Decius, charged with collecting the church's treasures from **LAURENTIUS**. His story forms part five (*BHL* 3961) of the epic cycle of the *Passio Laurentii* (ed. Delehaye 1933b pp 93–98). In the legend, Hippolytus, who is charged with custody of Laurence during the saint's persecution and martyrdom, is inspired by his conduct and teaching to become a Christian; then, with his whole household, including his old nurse Concordia, he is martyred some days after Laurence. Hippolytus himself is killed by being dragged behind a team of wild horses, like his namesake in the myth of Theseus and the play *Hippolytus* by Euripedes. The early-fifth-century poem by **PRUDENTIUS** (**PERISTEPHANON** XI, *BHL* 3960; ed. *CCSL* 126), which was certainly known to the Anglo-Saxons (see Gernot Wieland's entry for Prudentius in Biggs, Hill, and Szarmach 1990 p 155), is among the first to attribute this mode of death to Hippolytus the theologian. Time and the legend-making process further contrived to obscure the original clerical identity of the Hippolytus buried on the Via Tiburtina, providing him with a secular identity in the legend of Laurence, whose basilica was close by.

For discussion of the longer and shorter versions of the *Passio Laurentii*, and surviving Anglo-Saxon manuscript copies, see below, the entry for Laurentius. The longer version was the source of the brief accounts of Hippolytus's conversion and martyrdom in **BEDE**'s **MARTYROLOGIUM** (ed. Dubois and Renaud 1976 p 149.2–7, sourced by Quentin 1908 p 80) and the **OLD ENGLISH MARTYROLOGY** (*Mart*, B19.ft; ed. Kotzor 1981 2.179–80, sourced by Cross 1983a pp 208–10). It also lies behind **ÆLFRIC**'s more extended account of Laurence and Hippolytus in his **CATHOLIC HOMILIES** I, 29, lines 75–265 (*ÆCHom*, B1.1.31; ed. *EETS* SS 17), sourced by Zettel (1979 pp 178–79 and 300). See now Godden (*EETS* SS 18.241–46).

Hucbertus Leodiensis, vita [IONAS.AUREL.Vit.Hucb.]: *BHL* 3994; *BLS* 4.247–48; *BSS* 12.736–43; *Lexikon des Mittelalters* (1977–) 5.149–50.

ed.: *AS* Nov. 1.806–16.

MSS Cambridge, Corpus Christi College 9: HG 36.
Lists – Refs none.

Hubert (also Hugbertus, Hugberhtus) of Liège, famous in the later Middle Ages for the story (borrowed from the legend of **EUSTACHIUS**) of his conversion by a stag while hunting on Good Friday, was a missionary in the Ardennes region and succeeded LAMBERTUS as bishop of Maastricht ca. 705, later transferring his see, and Lambert's relics, to Liège. He died in 727 (feast days May 30, November 3). He appears to have had no liturgical cult in England before the Conquest. The only extant English text of his *vita*, in the Cambridge manuscript (eleventh century, from Worcester) of the **COTTON-CORPUS LEGENDARY**, is the second life of the saint. It was composed in 825 (when Hubert's relics were translated to the monastery later known as Saint-Hubert) by **JONAS OF ORLÉANS**, who succeeded **THEODULPH** as bishop of Orléans. The Worcester copy lacks Jonas's epistle and prologue and the appended *Translatio* (*BHL* 3995). Another copy was formerly in Salisbury, Cathedral Library 222, where it is listed in the table of contents (Webber 1992 p 157; Zettel 1979 p 28). The critical edition by De Smedt does not collate or list the English copy (*AS* Nov. 1.763–64). For a recent bibliography on Jonas, see *RFHMA* 6.431–33.

Hyacinthus, passio [ANON.Pas.Hyacinth.]: *BHL* 4053; *BSS* 1.161–62.
  ed.: Mara 1964 pp 104–08.
MSS 1. London, BL Cotton Nero E. i: HG 344.
  2. Salisbury, Cathedral Library 222 (formerly Oxford, Bodleian Library Fell 1): HG 754.6.
Lists – Refs none.

This saint, said to have been martyred "in portu Romano," has no relation with **PROTUS ET HYACINTHUS**, the eunuch slaves of **EUGENIA**, although the text of his *passio* refers to the same feast day (September 11) as that of the more famous pair. In other manuscripts the legend is associated with September 9 (Mara 1964 p 104) or July 26, as in *BHL*. Various possibilities regarding the saint and his origins are explored in the introduction to Mara's edition (pp 87–96), which contains ample bibliographical references. The *Passio Sancti Iacincti* in the London and Salisbury manuscripts of the **COTTON-CORPUS LEGENDARY**

(Zettel 1979 p 25; Jackson and Lapidge 1996 p 140) seems to be virtually identical to that printed by Mara from a Vatican manuscript of the ninth–tenth century, except that the London text has been emended idiosyncratically by a later hand. Mara's edition supersedes that of Mombritius (1910 2.28–29 and 668).

Hyacinthus et Protus. See PROTUS ET HYACINTHUS.

Iacobus Maior, passio. See APOCRYPHA: PSEUDO-ABDIAS, HISTORIAE APOSTOLICAE; PASSIO IACOBI MAIORIS.

Iacobus Minor, passio. See APOCRYPHA: PSEUDO-ABDIAS, HISTORIAE APOSTOLICAE; PASSIO IACOBI MINORIS.

Ianuarius et Sosius, passio [ANON.Pas.Ian.Sos.]: *BHL* 4132; *BLS* 3.594–96; *BSS* 6.135–51.
ed.: Mallardo 1940 pp 253–59 and *AS* Sept. 6.869.
MSS – Lists none.
A-S Vers 1. BEDA Mart. 173.2–16.
2. BEDA.Mart. 176.2–15.
3. ?*Mart* B19.hd.
Quots/Cits – Refs none.

Ianuarius (Gennaro; feast day September 19), bishop of Benevento during the period of the Diocletian persecution, and Sosius, deacon of Miseno (feast day September 23), were martyred with other clerics and lay supporters near Pozzuoli; Ianuarius's cult was later centered on Naples. Although there is ample early evidence of the antiquity of the cults (Mallardo 1940), the earliest witness to the hagiographic legend is BEDE's two notices in his MARTYROLOGIUM (BEDA Mart.; ed. Dubois and Renaud 1976, sourced by Quentin 1908 pp 75–77). Of the various extant forms of the legend, the earliest, used by Bede, is taken to be the so-called "Bolognesa" version, Passio 5 in the Bollandists' classification, extant only in a twelfth-century manuscript but frequently printed. This version includes, at the end, an account of the *translatio* of Ianuarius's relics to Naples (*BHL* 4116). It seems likely, however, that Bede's source was not identical to Malardo's text, in that it also must have included the other two *translatio* accounts (*BHL* 4117-18), regarding the relics of Sosius and other martyred companions; Bede summarizes all of these together (Dubois and Renaud 1976 p 173.12-16) at the end of his notice for Ianuarius. The *passio* thus constituted might have been taken to England by Hadrian, Neapolitan first abbot of St Augustine's, Canterbury, but other English travelers, such as **BENEDICTUS BISCOPUS**, could as easily have brought the text to Northumbria.

The source of the much briefer notices in the ninth-century **OLD ENGLISH MARTYROLOGY** (*Mart*; ed. Kotzor 1981 2.211-12 and 215) is less clear. The notice for Ianuarius himself and his companions is bare of narrative detail, assigns the martyrdom to Benevento (unlike the *passio*), and calls both his companions deacons (in the *passio* one is a lector). In the longer notice, for Sosius (p 215), Ianuarius is said to have been his teacher (which is not in the known forms of the *passio*), and the episode of Sosius's flaming head, as he reads the gospel, differs significantly in the *Martyrology* from the wording of the Bologna *passio*, as Cross demonstrates (1986a pp 236-37). Either the martyrologist is handling Passio 5 (or Bede's summaries) very freely here, or he had access to a different recension. These South Italian saints and their legend seem to have been unknown to, or disregarded by, the later Anglo-Saxons.

Iesus Christus, Exaltatio Sanctae Crucis, historia [ANON.Exalt.cruc]: *BHL* 4178; *DACL* 3.3131-39. See also **IESUS CHRISTUS, INVENTIO SANCTAE CRUCIS**.

ed.: Mombritius 1910 1.379-81, 648.

MSS 1. Paris, Bibliothèque Nationale lat. 5574: HG 885.5.
2. London, BL Cotton Nero E. i: HG 344.

Lists none.
A-S Vers *ÆLS* Exalt of Cross (B1.3.27) 6–142.
Quots/Cits – Refs none.

As early as the middle of the ninth century, in the Latin West, the feast of the Exaltation of the Holy Cross (September 14) commemorated the recovery, in 628, of the Jerusalem cross relic by the Byzantine emperor Heraclius from its Persian captors and its restoration to Jerusalem in 630. It is uncertain how long the Heraclian legend and the Exaltation feast had been associated in this way. The feast is first mentioned in the West in the **LIBER PONTIFICALIS** under Pope Sergius (687–701; Duchesne 1955 1.374–78). In the Eastern church, however, September 14 was a multiple commemoration, celebrating the feast of the dedication of the two principal churches in Jerusalem on the putative sites of Golgotha and the Holy Sepulchre, as well as the feast of the finding of the cross (see below, the entry for Iesus Christus, *Inventio Sanctae Crucis*). This also apparently was a day in Jerusalem for the "ostension" or public display of the wood of the cross to the faithful, as indicated in the legend of Mary of Egypt (**MARIA AEGYPTIACA**), *Vita Mariae Ægyptiacae* XV (*PL* 73.671–90). In Constantinople, by the early seventh century, the September 14 feast was also being observed, along with the "hypsosis" (lifting up, hence Latin "exaltatio"), a ceremonial exhibiting of the portion of the cross relic said to have been brought to the imperial capital. It is likely that the late-seventh-century feast in Rome was an imitation of this Eastern tradition and need not have been linked as yet to the military legend in question here. This would explain why the feast's most ancient mass texts focus solely on the theology of the cross as the instrument of Christ's passion and of the protection and redemption of the faithful.

The history of the relationship between the Western feasts of the Exaltation and the Invention (May 3) is too complicated and problematic for even summary treatment here (see Chavasse 1958 pp 350–59; Hesbert 1935 pp lxxii–lxxxiii; Jonsson 1968 pp 44–54; Leclercq *DACL* 3.3131–39; for a useful digest and further bibliography, see that of Hansjörg auf der Maur in H. Meyer et al. 1983– 5.186–88). Suffice it to say that the clear distinction, found in eleventh- and twelfth-century service books and legendaries, between the two feasts and their respective legends is not evident in the extant liturgical books of the earlier medieval period. For example, the Compiègne *Liber Responsalis* (860–80) has anthems derived from the *Inventio Sanctae Crucis* legend (*BHL* 4169) for use at Matins of the Exaltation feast (Hesbert 1963–79 1.302–05; *PL* 78.704–05).

In Anglo-Saxon England, there is no evidence for the observance of the September 14 feast of the Exaltation before the tenth century, considerably later than the May 3 Invention, for which ninth-century evidence is substantial. The Exaltation feast, although important liturgically, especially in monasteries, was of lesser rank than the Invention, to judge from its treatment in calendars and by ÆLFRIC (see below and compare the entries for the two feasts in F. Wormald 1934 pp 6 and 10, 20 and 24, 48 and 52, 62 and 66).

The composition date and origins of the *Exaltatio Sanctae Crucis* legend (also known as *Reversio Sanctae Crucis*) are unknown. It is not the work of **HRABANUS MAURUS**, as often assumed, although it appears at the end of a collection of his sermons (*PL* 110.131–34), dedicated to Archbishop Haistulf of Cologne (814–26). Faral (1920 p 520) thinks that the *Exaltatio* sermon is a later addition to Hrabanus's original collection. The legend, in a recension independent of the Hrabanus text (in which one scribal misreading, for example, substitutes "Gracchus" for Heraclius), was certainly known to various other mid-ninth-century authors (cited in Fourrier 1960 pp 211–12) including **ADO**, whose martyrology (853–60) incorporates a substantial portion of the *Exaltatio* narrative in the notice for the September 14 feast (Dubois and Renaud 1984 pp 313–15, also *PL* 123.356–57; cf. Quentin 1908 p 506). Another witness is Wandelbert of Prüm, somewhat earlier, who briefly but clearly alludes to the *Exaltatio* in his metrical martyrology (ca. 848), verses 558–59 (ed. *MGH* PLAC 2.594). On the other hand, Wandelbert's older contemporary, **FLORUS OF LYONS**, whose martyrology, completed ca. 825–40, is regarded as the main source of Wandelbert's and Ado's (Dubois 1961 p 261), seems not to have known the story, although he took pains to provide an elaborate notice for the Exaltation feast (sourced by Quentin 1908 p 324). Information provided by Stephan Borgehammar suggests, however, that the *Exaltatio* in its present form is at least as old as the early ninth/late eighth century (date of the copy in Vienna: see *CLA* 10.1479) and possibly older. Borgehammar also suggests that the text designated *BHL* 4181a is an independent version of the same legend and may be pre-Carolingian, to judge from its latinity.

It is not surprising, therefore, that **BEDE** does not seem to have known the *Exaltatio* proper, although he knew something of the history behind the legend. In his **CHRONICA MAIORA** 1785–809 (ed. *CCSL* 123B), drawing on the seventh-century Latin *Passio Sancti Anastasii* (see **ANASTASIUS**), he mentions the conquest of Jerusalem and abduction of the Cross by the Persians, and also Heraclius's later reconquest of the city and the return of Persian Christians from captivity; but he says nothing of the return of the cross to Jerusalem, with the attendant miracles, as described in the *Exaltatio*. Whereas the second edition of the Greek life of Anastasius has a brief account of Heraclius restoring the cross to Jerusalem (*BHG* 88, ed. Flusin 1992 2.98–99), this was not included in the first edition (*BHG* 84) from which the first Latin translation (*BHL* 410b), known to Bede, was made (see the entry on Anastasius for references to the work of Carmela Franklin and Paul Meyvaert).

The ninth-century **OLD ENGLISH MARTYROLOGY** has no provision for the Exaltation, which strongly suggests that neither the text nor the feast had reached England by the late ninth century.

The earliest evidence for the Anglo-Saxons' knowledge of the text is the copy in the early-tenth-century Paris manuscript listed here, believed to be of Mercian provenance. Its copy of the *Exaltatio* is not mentioned in the recent catalogue description by Avril and Stirnemann (1987 p 11), perhaps because the preceding text, the *Inventio Sanctae Crucis*, breaks off at fol 12v, and the *Exaltatio* narrative ends on fol 18r with, misleadingly, "explicit inventio sancte crucis"; see the Bollandists' catalogue of hagiographical manuscripts in Paris (Bollandists 1889–93 2.482–83).

According to Zettel (1979 p 231), enlarging on the work of C. Loomis (1931 pp 3–4), Ælfric's interesting sermon-like rendering of the Heraclius legend, to which he appends that of **LONGINUS** in his late-tenth-century **LIVES OF SAINTS** (*ÆLS*; *EETS* OS 94 and 114), is based on a Latin text similar to that in the **COTTON-CORPUS LEGENDARY**, as represented in the eleventh-century Cotton manuscript and a twelfth-century affiliate, Oxford, Bodleian Library Bodley 354 (*SC* 2432, twelfth century). This text is closer to Ælfric's source than either of the printed editions (Mombritius or *PL*). The Cotton copy (fols 167–68) is incomplete, but in Zettel's view it can be reliably supplemented with Bodley 354. However, the dislocation of the text from its expected place in the Cotton manuscript (Jackson and Lapidge 1996 p 143), and its absence from Salisbury Cathedral Library 221–22 and the table of contents, have yet to be explained. Nor does Zettel's sourcing take account of the much older copy in the Paris manuscript. It is possible that, if the Cotton-Corpus Legendary were not Ælfric's source for the legend, he could have found it in a homiliary or in a more specialized collection.

Borgehammar informs me that *BHL* 4181f–g are short adaptations of the *Exaltatio* for homiletic purposes. He also says that the "Sermo in exaltatione S. Crucis" beginning "Quia favente" in the tenth-century manuscript Orléans, Bibliothèque Municipale 342 (290), HG 869 (see Van der Straeten 1982 p 72), does not refer to the legend in question here.

In addition to Mombritius's edition, see also *PL* 110.131–34. There is no critical edition or modern study of the text of the *Exaltatio Sanctae Crucis* legend, to my knowledge, and little of substance is known about its origins, Greek or otherwise, although historians have given a good deal of attention to contemporary accounts, in a variety of Eastern languages, of Heraclius's reign (see Frolow 1953 and more recently Flusin 1992 2.293–309). I am grateful to Stephan Borgehammar, who is working on a critical edition, for generously supplying me with various kinds of information from his unpublished notes on the Latin Exaltation legend.

Iesus Christus, Imago Berytensis, miracula [ANON.serm.Beryt.cruc./ PS.ATHANASIUS]: *BHL* 4230; *CPG* 2262.
   ed.: *PG* 28.819–24.

MSS Dublin, Trinity College 174: HG 215.
Lists – Refs none.

This "sermon" recounts how a crucifix, left in the house of a Jew of Beirut by a Christian visitor, was subjected to the physical torments of Christ's passion by other Jews but later became the agent of various miracles that resulted in the conversion and baptism of its erstwhile violators. Extant in a variety of Greek versions (*BHG* 780–88) and Latin translations (*BHL* 4227–30), the text was introduced at the second council of Nicea (787) as a work of **ATHANASIUS** of Alexandria to support the case against iconoclasm. In the chronicle of Sigebert of Gembloux (late eleventh century) the episode is said to have occurred in the year 766 (*MGH* Scriptores 6.333.23–33).

For other information about the legend surrounding the crucifix (translated to Constantinople in 975), see Von Dobschütz (*TU* 18/2 Beilagen pp 280–83).

The copy of *BHL* 4230 in the Dublin manuscript above was copied by one of Webber's Group II scribes at Salisbury, probably in the early twelfth century (Webber 1992 p 158). It is imperfect, breaking off at "acoetum et fel dederunt ei porrecta" (Colker 1991 2.325); compare *PG* 28.821. Von Dobschütz (*TU* 18/2 Beilagen p 281 note 2) lists six manuscripts of this version, which he labels "c," but not the Dublin manuscript.

Iesus Christus, Inventio Sanctae Crucis, inventio [ANON.Invent.cruc]: *BHL* 4169; *BLS* 2.220–23; *DACL* 3.3131–39. See also **IESUS CHRISTUS, EXALTATIO SANCTAE CRUCIS**.

ed.: Borgehammar 1991 pp 254–71.

MSS 1. Cambridge, Pembroke College 24: HG 131.
2. Cambridge, Trinity College O.10.31 (1483): HG 200.
3. Salisbury, Cathedral Library 221 (formerly Oxford, Bodleian Library Fell 4): HG 754.5.
4. Paris, Bibliothèque Nationale lat. 5574: HG 885.5.

Lists none.

A-S Vers 1. *El* (Elene, A2.6).
2. *LS* 6 (InventCrossMor, B3.3.6).
3. *Mart* (B19.ck).

Quots/Cits – Refs see below.

The *Inventio Sanctae Crucis* (also *Acta Cyriaci*; feast day May 3) recounts the discovery of the holy cross and nails in Jerusalem by the empress Helena with the help of a converted Jew, Judas, later Bishop Cyriacus (**QUIRIACUS**), whose *passio* sometimes accompanies the *Inventio* in the manuscripts (as in the Trinity College manuscript). According to the most recent scholarly study, the *Inventio* was composed in Greek in fifth-century Palestine and quickly translated into Latin and other languages (Borgehammar 1991 pp 146–54). The earliest surviving Latin copy, a sixth-century Italian manuscript (which may have passed through a Continental Anglo-Saxon center in the eighth century: *CLA* 5.550), is transcribed in Holder's edition (1889 pp 1–13). Various other kinds of evidence suggest that by the sixth century the legend and May 3 feast —the date that is firmly embedded in the text of *BHL* 4169—were established in Rome (Chavasse 1958 pp 350–57; Borgehammar 1991 pp 202–03). Either from there, or by other routes, the legend spread into Gaul (for some early Frankish witnesses, see Whatley 1993), although there is no evidence for the celebration of the May 3 feast day in the Frankish liturgy until the eighth century. Nor is the feast or legend mentioned by **BEDE** or **ALDHELM**, while the early-eighth-century calendar of the Anglo-Saxon Willibrord (*HBS* 55) assigns the feast to May 7 (for an explanation, see Chavasse 1958 p 351 and note 2). By the later ninth century, however, the feast is marked as of high rank in a monastic calendar (F. Wormald 1934 p 6), and there is abundant tenth-century evidence that it had become one of the most important feast days. See, for example, the Old English verse *Menologium* 83–86 (*Men*, A14; ed. *ASPR* 6).

The Anglo-Saxon manuscript copies of the *Inventio* legend listed here are all of the late eleventh century, except for the Paris manuscript (early tenth century; see Avril and Stirnemann 1987 p 11); this copy, which is followed in the manuscript by the *Exaltatio Sanctae Crucis*, is imperfect owing to missing leaves, breaking off (fol 12v) after "cum in ilio et troade factum est bellum et omnes nunc" (*Inventio S. Crucis* 130). The text is also included in the **COTTON-CORPUS LEGENDARY**, represented here by the late-eleventh-century copy from Salisbury. Another copy, closely affiliated with the Salisbury copy, was formerly in London, BL Cotton Nero E. i (HG 344).

The earliest literary evidence for Anglo-Saxon knowledge of the legend and feast is the Old English *Elene* by Cynewulf (*El*; ed. *ASPR* 2; usually dated early ninth century, but extant in a manuscript of the late tenth), based closely on a text that, in Gradon's view (1958 p 19), must have been similar to that preserved in a ninth-century St Gall manuscript. Details in the brief entry for the May 3 feast in the ninth-century **OLD ENGLISH MARTYROLOGY** (*Mart*; ed. Kotzor 1981 2.78–81) seem to be drawn from the *Inventio* (see *EETS* OS 116.xxxviii). It is also the main source of an eleventh-century anonymous homily for the feast of the Invention (*LS* 6; ed. *EETS* OS 46), although the most recent editor argues that the homily's ultimate source was an abbreviated version of the *Inventio* and more immediately a lost Old English version, influenced by *Elene* (Bodden 1987 pp 36–56).

ÆLFRIC is probably looking askance at the *Inventio* legend in a remark near the close of his brief homily for the May 3 feast, in **CATHOLIC HOMILIES** II, 18, lines 52–53 (*ÆCHom*, B1.2.22; ed. *EETS* SS 5); the homily is drawn mainly from an alternative account by **RUFINUS**, **HISTORIA ECCLESIASTICA** IX.ix and X.vii–viii (ed. *GCS* 9/2.827–33 and 969–71; see also Godden's sourcing, *EETS* SS 18.513–16). The *Inventio* has also been cited as a possible source for two passages in the *Dream of the Rood* (*Dream*, A2.5; ed. *ASPR* 3): the vision of the cross in the sky (4–7) and the discovery of the cross (76–78). See Patch (1919), who admits, however, the uncertainty of the first parallel. It should be pointed out also that the *Dream*'s brief reference to the cross's burial and invention could equally be dependent on other accounts, such as that of Rufinus. Similarly indefinite are the intriguing allusions to Helena, the finding of the cross, and the Jews in the Old English charms "For Loss of Cattle" and "For Theft of Cattle" (*MCharm* 5, 9, and 10, A43.5, A43.9, and A43.10; ed. *ASPR* 6).

For a detailed study of the legend's origins and a list of early manuscripts, see Borgehammar's edition (1991 passim, especially pp 146–50, 209–12). Although his edition of the Latin text is an eclectic reconstruction of the archetype, he provides a more readable text and a fuller critical apparatus than the older, scarcer edition of Holder (1889 pp 1–13), which is, however, still useful as a transcript of an early manuscript. See also the text edited from a tenth-century Spanish manuscript by Fábrega Grau (1953–55 2.260–66; for translation of this text, and of the account by Rufinus, see Whatley 2000).

In addition to Gradon's introduction (1958 pp 15–22), see the source studies on *Elene* listed in Greenfield and Robinson (1980 pp 220–22). On possible sources of the anonymous prose homily (*LS* 6), see Bodden (1987 pp 127–32), whose edition prints the *AS* text below the Old English (pp 60–103); for bibliography on the *Dream of the Rood*, see Greenfield and Robinson (1980 pp 215–17). For a recent discussion of *Elene* and the *Dream* in relation to one another and the source tradition, see M. Irvine (1986). For a general discussion of cross lore in Anglo-Saxon England, see Stevens (1904), and for information on Irish materials, see McNamara (1975 pp 78–79).

Frederick M. Biggs and E. Gordon Whatley

Indractus: *BLS* 1.258; *BSS* 7.794–96; *SEHI* 228.

Indract (feast day May 8), venerated at Glastonbury as a martyr from the late tenth or early eleventh century, was supposedly an Irish prince returning from a pilgrimage to Rome with his companions, via Glastonbury (where he wished to venerate the relics of Saint Patrick [**PATRICIUS**]), when he was murdered there by a thane of King Ine of Wessex (late seventh century). It is possible this story is a reworking of one concerning another Irish Indract, an abbot of Iona, killed in the west of England in 854 according to the Annals of Ulster.

Various pieces of literary evidence from the twelfth and later centuries, including the writings of William of Malmesbury, are adduced by Lapidge (1982b) to lend credence to the statement by the anonymous author of a Latin *passio* (*BHL* 4272) that he is translating from an Old English account. Since the sole copy of the *passio* is of the twelfth century (Oxford, Bodleian Library Digby 112 [*SC* 1713], from Winchester or Glastonbury: Carley 1994), and since William of Malmesbury, early in the twelfth century, also seems to have used the Old English work independently, it is likely that the lost text existed in the eleventh century. But in Lapidge's view there is no way of dating it more precisely than between the mid-tenth and early twelfth centuries.

It seems likely that the Latin *passio* itself, since it was evidently unknown to William of Malmesbury, was probably not composed long before the date of the Digby copy, that is, second quarter of the twelfth century. Although it was traditional to attribute the Digby *passio* to William of Malmesbury, Lapidge rejects this on grounds of style and content. He provides the first edition of the Latin text (1982b pp 199–212); for English translations of the *passio*, see Doble (1942) and Platts (1921–23).

Iohannes Baptista, inventio [DION.EXIG.Inv.Cap.Iohan.]: *BHL* 4290–91; *BSS* 6.599–616.
ed.: *PL* 67.423–32.

MSS – Lists none.
A-S Vers ?*Mart* (B19.gh).
Quots/Cits – Refs see below.

John the Baptist is a frequent subject of Anglo-Saxon writers and was honored with no less than four feast days in the ninth-century **OLD ENGLISH MARTYROLOGY** (*Mart*; ed. Kotzor 1981 2.26.13–18, February 27; 130–31, June 24; 192, August 29; 217, September 24) and in some later English calendars (February 27 was set aside for the *Inventio capitis*). Nevertheless, specifically hagiographical, as opposed to homiletic, material on John is rare in the West. An exception to this is the posthumous adventures of the head. The account cited here is a Greek narrative translated by **DIONYSIUS EXIGUUS**, to which Quentin refers (1908 p 108) as the source of **BEDE**'s brief **MARTYROLOGIUM** notice for August 29 (ed. Dubois and Renaud 1976 p 160.5–7); see also his **CHRONICA MAIORA** 1446–55 (ed. *CCSL* 123B) for the history of John's bones (derived from **RUFINUS, HISTORIA ECCLESIASTICA** XI.xxviii; ed. *GCS* 9/2.1033–34) and *Chronica maiora* 1626–29 on the *Inventio capitis*. According to Cross (1975 pp 158–60), Bede's knowledge of John's head derived mainly from the chronicle of **MARCELLINUS COMES** (ed. *MGH* AA 11/2.84–85), but Cross presents evidence to suggest that the notice for the February 27 feast in the *Old English Martyrology* may depend on the fuller *Inventio* account. Unfortunately only the last few lines of the original *Martyrology* notice survive.

In **ÆLFRIC**'s homily on the August 29 feast of John's decollation in CATHOLIC HOMILIES I, 32, lines 153–62 (*ÆCHom*, B1.1.34; ed. *EETS* SS 17), he mentions the translation of John's bones from Sebaste to Alexandria, after alluding disapprovingly to a story (told by "gedwolmen," "fools" or "heretics") about the head's causing Herodias to be blown around the world by the winds; to this he adds a greatly compressed account of the *Inventio capitis* by the two Eastern monks from "Emesa." His source for all except the winds story could have been Bede's *Chronica*, but J. E. Cross (private communication) suggests a homiliary (see now Godden's sourcing, *EETS* SS 18.266–75). A variant version of the Herodias story rejected by Ælfric appears later in the thirteenth-century *Legenda aurea*, chapter CXXV (ed. Graesse 1890 p 573) where it is characterized as a folk or vernacular tradition.

Iohannes Eleemosynarius, vita [ANASTAS.BIB.Vit.Ioh.Elemos.]: *BHL* 4388; *BLS* 1.153–55; *BSS* 6.750–56; *CPG* 7882.
  ed.: *PL* 73.337–84.
MSS 1. Hereford, Cathedral Library P.II.5: HG 267.
  2. New York, Pierpont Morgan Library 926: HG 865.
Lists – Refs none.

Saint John the Almsgiver (feast day January 23), a wealthy member of the Alexandrian patrician class, became patriarch of Alexandria in 610, in the wake of the violent succession of Heraclius I (see **IESUS CHRISTUS, EXALTATIO SANCTAE CRUCIS**). Until his death in 619 or 620 John devoted himself, and vast sums of his money, to the relief of poverty and famine in Egypt and to the care of refugees in Palestine during the Persian invasions. The text of the Greek life, by the Cypriot Leontios (*BHG* 886–886c), was translated into Latin by Anastasius the Librarian ("Bibliothecarius") in Rome in the third quarter of the ninth century. John's cult came late to the West and his story is absent from all the major martyrologies of our period. There is no trace of his cult among the pre-Conquest Anglo-Saxons, and the Hereford copy of the *vita* dates from the end of the Anglo-Saxon period (Mynors and Thomson 1993 p 76). The New York copy, from around the same time or somewhat later, is from St Albans: see Hartzell (1975 p 21 and note 6).

Gelzer, in his critical edition of the Greek text, discusses the quality of the Latin translation (1893 pp XXXV–XL) but not its textual history. There is no modern critical edition of the hagiographic works of Anastasius. For a brief assessment of the latter, and further bibliography, see Berschin (1980 pp 199–204, especially p 199 and note 19). In addition to Rosweyde's edition, reprinted in *PL* 73, see also that in *AS* Ian. 2.498–517, based on Rosweyde's with variants from other manuscripts.

Iohannes Eremita, vita: *BHL* 4329; *BLS* 1.691–92; *BSS* 6.818–22.

The life of John, the hermit of Lycopolis in Egypt (feast day March 27), forms the lengthy first chapter of **RUFINUS**'s HISTORIA MONACHORUM (ed. Schulz-Flügel 1990 pp 241–75; also *PL* 21.391–405) in the **VITAE PATRUM**. **ALDHELM** in his DE VIRGINITATE (*Carmen* 827–41, *Prosa* 267.13–268.6; ed. *MGH* AA 15) glorifies John's 90-year preservation of his virginity and retells one anecdote from the life, regarding the saint's refusal to receive a visit from the wife of a military tribune, and his supernatural remedy for her persistence (*Historia monachorum* I.41–73). At one point in his prose version (*MGH* AA 15.268.2–3), Aldhelm quotes a sentence of his source verbatim and shares the variant *conclusisset* with the *PL* edition (*PL* 21.392.25–26) against Schulz-Flügel's *contulisset* (*Historia monachorum* I.45–46).

John's political prophesying may have influenced the portrayal of similar qualities in the lives of English hermit saints such as CUTHBERTUS and GUTHLACUS. His chaste living is mentioned by ÆLFRIC in his LETTER TO SIGEFYRTH 217 (*ÆLet* 5, B1.8.5; ed. *BaP* 3.23).

On the *Historia monachorum*, see above, the entry on AMOS NITRIAE.

Iohannes Evangelista, passio. See APOCRYPHA: PSEUDO-ABDIAS, HISTORIAE APOSTOLICAE; PSEUDO-MELLITUS, PASSIO IOHANNIS.

Iohannes et Paulus, passio [ANON.Pas.Ioh.Paul.]: *BHL* 3236 and 3238; *BLS* 2.645–46; *BSS* 6.1046–49; *CPL* 2193.

ed.: Mombritius 1910 1.569–72 and 677.

MSS 1. London, BL Cotton Nero E. i: HG 344.
2. Paris, Bibliothèque Nationale lat. 10861: HG 898.
3. Salisbury, Cathedral Library 222 (formerly Oxford, Bodleian Library Fell 1): HG 754.6.

Lists none.

A-S Vers 1. ?ALDH.Pros.uirg. 302.20–303.6.
2. ?ALDH.Carm.uirg. 2051–120.
3. BEDA.Mart. 114.2–6, 129.2–4.
4. *Mart* (B19.dy).
5. *ÆLS* Agnes (B1.3.8) 296–429.

Quots/Cits – Refs none.

In the course of the fifth century, the reputed relics of the Roman brothers John and Paul (feast day June 26) became the object of a cult at the church on the Coelian Hill (mentioned in a tenth-century itinerary from Salisbury: see *BLS* 2.645), which came to be associated with their names but which may originally have been dedicated to the apostles by the same names. The brothers' names appear in the canon of the Roman Mass, and they have offices in the Gelasian and Gregorian sacramentaries (see **LITURGY, MASSBOOKS**). They are believed to have been genuine martyrs of the Diocletian persecution (Franchi de' Cavalieri 1902 p 55), but in the present *passio* their deaths occur under Julian the Apostate. The *passio* seems to be entirely borrowed or invented, and late. Dated in the sixth century by Franchi de' Cavalieri (see also Duchesne 1955 1.199 note 99 for the suggestion that it borrows from the second edition of the **LIBER PONTIFICALIS**, which is dated ca. 540), the *passio* records John and Paul's transfer to military service under **GALLICANUS** from their original positions as officers in the household of the virgin daughter of Constantine, **CONSTANTINA**, the conversion of Gallicanus in Scythia under their influence, his later experiences and martyrdom in Egypt, and their martyrdom for refusing to serve under Julian. Gallicanus's portion of the *passio* has the separate number *BHL* 3236. The work purports to have been written by one Terentianus, the imperial prosecutor, who is finally converted by the brothers' miracles and conduct. The listing of John and Paul in *BHL* as companions of Gallicanus suggests their subordination to him, but their feast and cult were in fact much more important and widespread than Gallicanus's in Anglo-Saxon England and elsewhere.

The *passio* was apparently known to **BEDE**, whose **MARTYROLOGIUM** (BEDA.Mart.; ed. Dubois and Renaud 1976; sourced by Quentin 1908 p 75) has brief notices for the brothers and the hermit **HILARINUS**, but not for Gallicanus or Constantina. The latter, however, are the main focus of **ALDHELM**'s adaptations of the legend in his **DE VIRGINITATE** (ALDH.Carm.uirg, Pros.uirg; ed. *MGH* AA 15; sourced by Ehwald, *MGH* AA 15.302 notes 2–4; see also Lapidge and Herren 1979 p 178, who express uncertainty regarding Aldhelm's precise source).

According to M. P. Brown (1986), the copy of the *passio* preserved in the ninth-century Paris manuscript from Canterbury begins imperfectly at "misericordia gloriantes nihil terrenum desiderunt" (Mombritius 1910 1.570.28) in the story of Gallicanus but contains in full this version of the *passio* of John and Paul (see also **GERVASIUS ET PROTASIUS**). The other English manuscripts contain complete copies. The **OLD ENGLISH MARTYROLOGY** (*Mart*; ed. Kotzor 1981 2.133–34) has a notice for John and Paul, but not for Gallicanus or Hilarinus. Herzfeld (*EETS* OS 116.231) comments that the martyrologist mistakenly describes the brothers as members of Constantine's family. See Kotzor's note (1981 2.324) and Cross (1986b p 288).

Ott (1892 pp 24–26) demonstrates ÆLFRIC's dependence on the *Passio Iohannis et Pauli* in his LIVES OF SAINTS (*ÆLS*; *EETS* OS 76 and 82), the second part of the legend of AGNES (numbered 7B by Skeat in his *EETS* edition), with the subtitle "Alia sententia quam scripsit Terentianus" in the principal manuscript. Zettel (1979 pp 213–15) argues that the text of the *passio* in the eleventh-century COTTON-CORPUS LEGENDARY seems closer to Ælfric's source than either of the texts printed in Mombritius and *AS*.

On the probable source of the legend's account of the brothers' martyrdom, see Franchi de' Cavalieri (1902). In addition to the edition of Mombritius, see also *AS* Iun. 5.37–39, 159–60. As in so many other cases, a critical edition of this legend is a *desideratum*.

Irenaeus et Abundius: *BHL* 4464; *BSS* 7.900–01.

Although assigned a separate number in *BHL*, and copied separately in some medieval manuscripts, the story of the martyrs Irenaeus and Abundius (variant spellings include Hereneus, Habundius) is part of the *passio* of HIPPOLYTUS, which in turn forms Part V of the "epic" *passio* of LAURENTIUS (*Passio Laurentii* XXXII; ed. Delehaye 1933b pp 95–96). Irenaeus is there said to be a sewer worker ("cloacarius") and secret Christian who, with another Christian, Abundius, retrieves the body of Concordia, martyred nurse of Hippolytus, from the Roman sewers. The brief narrative notices for Irenaeus and Abundius in BEDE's MARTYROLOGIUM (ed. Dubois and Renaud 1976 p 157.11–15) and the OLD ENGLISH MARTYROLOGY (*Mart*, B19.gd; ed. Kotzor 1981 2.189) are sourced by, respectively, Quentin (1908 p 80) and Cross (1983a p 210). ÆLFRIC omits the story of these saints from his homily on Laurence in CATHOLIC HOMILIES I, 29 (*ÆCHom*, B1.1.31; ed. *EETS* OS 17), but Abundius's feast day, August 27, is listed ("Sancti Habundi") in a late-tenth-century West Saxon calendar (F. Wormald 1934 p 51).

Iudocus, vita [ANON.Vit.Iudoc.]: *BHL* 4504; *BLS* 4.550; *BSS* 6.1159–63; *BCLL* 1315.
   ed.: Le Bourdellès 1993 pp 916–28.
MSS 1. Cambridge, Corpus Christi College 9: HG 36.
   2. Rouen, Bibliothèque Municipale 1384 (U. 26): HG 925.5.
Lists none.
A-S Vers ANON.Vit.Iudoc.metr.
Quots/Cits – Refs none.

Relics of Judoc (Josse), a seventh-century Breton warrior turned hermit who died ca. 668 in Picardy at Saint-Josse (feast day December 13; English translation feast January 9), were brought to the New Minster, Winchester, early in the tenth century by refugees from Viking incursions, and the cult flourished there throughout the remainder of the Anglo-Saxon period. The earliest life, *Vita Prima*, has been dated ca. 800 (Trier 1924 p 15) and has been associated with **ALCUIN** (see *BCLL* p 352: "arguably by Alcuin"; Lapidge 1989/90 p 255: "doubtfully attributed to Alcuin"). Le Bourdellès (1993 pp 902–04), however, has rejected this attribution, arguing that the work, which merely borrows from Alcuin and other Carolingian hagiographers, was composed (913–31) by exiled Breton monks at Montreuil, near Saint-Josse.

Whether the copy of the *vita* in the **COTTON-CORPUS LEGENDARY** (represented here by the Cambridge manuscript) is due to the Winchester cult or to the saint's importance in North France (the putative home of the Legendary) is uncertain. Other copies are in important twelfth-century manuscripts now in Oxford (Zettel 1979 p 33) and Hereford (Mynors and Thomson 1993 p 111). For a survey of manuscripts, showing the affiliations of the English copies, see Le Bourdellès (1993 pp 910–15). His edition (which is followed by a translation, pp 928–34) is based on the Cambridge and Rouen manuscripts, the oldest and best from Le Bourdellès's first recension group. Le Bourdellès is aware of the Worcester provenance of the Cambridge manuscript, but he ascribes the Rouen manuscript to Jumièges and dates it in the eleventh century. The first four folios of the *Vita Primi Iudoci*, however, are listed by HG (revised version) as comprising an Anglo-Saxon manuscript from the last quarter of the tenth century. According to Le Bourdellès (1993 p 911), the *vita* occupies fols 1–6.

Le Bourdellès's edition supersedes that of Trier (1924 pp 19–33). On the Winchester metrical life of Judoc listed here as a version of the *Vita Prima*, see below.

Iudocus, vita [ISEMB.FLOR.Vit.Inv.Mir.Iudoc.]: *BHL* 4505–10; *RFHMA* 6:454.

ed.: none (see below).

MSS London, BL Royal 8. B. xiv: HG 474.5.

Lists – Refs none.

The collection of liturgical and hagiographical texts for the feast of Iudocus (Josse) that forms part D (fols 118–44) of the composite manuscript listed here includes the *Vita Secunda*, an early-eleventh-century work by Isembard, monk of Fleury (De Gaiffier 1979). It comprises a *vita* proper (*BHL* 4505), followed by the *Inventio*, *Translatio* (*BHL* 4506, 4508), and an accompanying *sermo* (*BHL* 4509), all relating to events purporting to have occurred in 977, with a set of *Miracula* from the intervening period (*BHL* 4510). Despite the different *BHL* numbers, both the Bollandists and Le Bourdellès (1996 p 880) imply that Isembard's work is a single assemblage, which invariably survives as a whole in the manuscripts. An edition of this hitherto unprinted work is in preparation by Le Bourdellès. The Royal manuscript copy of the *Vita Secunda*, which is described as "incomplete" in the catalogue (Warner and Gilson 1921 1.225), was written in France in the first half of the eleventh century but was in Winchester by the late eleventh century.

Iudocus, vita [ANON.Vit.metr.Iudoc.]: *BHL* 4512; *ICL* 16714.

ed.: unpublished.

MSS London, BL Royal 8. B. xiv: HG 474.5.

Lists – Refs none.

Lapidge has argued (1989/90 pp 255–56, 260) that a metrical reworking of the *Vita Iudoci Prima* (*BHL* 4504: see first **IUDOCUS** entry above), surviving in a collection of liturgical and hagiographical materials for Judoc in the Royal manuscript, was composed at the Winchester school during the late Anglo-Saxon period, possibly as a metrical exercise. The portion of the manuscript containing the poem (fols 118–44) appears to have been copied at Winchester in the late eleventh century, unlike the manuscript's other Judoc texts, which were copied in France but brought to Winchester before the poem was added to the saint's dossier.

Iuliana, passio [ANON.Pas.Iulianae]: *BHL* 4522–23; *BLS* 1.349–50; *BSS* 6.1176–77; *CPL* 2201.
   ed.: Mombritius 1910 2.77–80 and 671.
MSS   1. London, BL Cotton Nero E. i: HG 344.
   2. London, BL Harley 3020: HG 433.
   3. Paris, Bibliothèque Nationale lat. 5574: HG 885.5.
   4. Paris, Bibliothèque Nationale lat. 10861: HG 898.
   5. Salisbury, Cathedral Library 221 (formerly Oxford, Bodleian Library Fell 4): HG 754.5.
Lists   none.
A-S Vers   1. BEDA.Mart.35.7–17.
   2. *Jul* (Juliana, A3.5).
Quots/Cits   see below.
Refs   none.

The earliest Latin *passio* of the virgin martyr Juliana of Nicomedia (feast day February 16) is now believed to be the original form of the legend, not a translation from the Greek, despite the saint's purported Eastern origin and the Greek form of her name in an early Neapolitan calendar (Siegmund 1949 p 197; Geith 1965 pp 12 and 27). The latest opinion of the Bollandists, on the evidence of the early martyrologies, is that Juliana was originally a local Cumae martyr whose cult became general in the Naples area before spreading elsewhere and whose martyrdom in Nicomedia (along with the whole legend) is a fabrication (see *AS* Nov. 2/2.301–02).

Geith (1965) regards England in the late seventh to early eighth century as an early locus of devotion to Juliana. As evidence he points to **BEDE**'s use of the *passio* in his **MARTYROLOGIUM** (BEDA.Mart.; ed. Dubois and Renaud 1976; sourced by Quentin 1908 p 77); Juliana's feast day in the eighth-century English recension of the *Martyrologium Hieronymianum* (Paris, Bibliothèque Nationale lat. 10837—the Epternach manuscript); and Neapolitan influence through Abbot Hadrian of Canterbury. He argues that two of the three main families of extant manuscripts of the *passio* originated in England (note that Geith's classification of manuscripts does not retain the Bollandists' distinctions btween *BHL* 4522 and 4523).

Five manuscripts now known to be of English provenance contain copies of the *passio*. The oldest, Bibliothèque Nationale lat. 10861, was almost certainly written at Christ Church, Canterbury, in the early ninth century (M. P. Brown 1986) and belongs to Geith's Würzburg family of manuscripts, which he links to the Anglo-Saxon missions to Germany. The Harley text, on the other hand, is a member of Geith's Corbie family (1965 pp 58–59). The manuscript has now been shown to be a composite of the late tenth century, part of which is also from Canterbury, but the originally separate Juliana portion, with the story of **THEOPHILUS**, may be from Winchester (see Carley 1994 pp 277–79 and notes 66–67). Geith associates most of the other members of his Corbie family with Anglo-Saxon influence on the monastery at Corbie founded by the former English slave Queen Bathild (**BALTHILDIS**). Geith was unaware that the Paris and Harley manuscripts are actually of English provenance, as pointed out by Price (1986) in her study of the Middle English *Liflade*, and none of these scholars mentions the copies in the **COTTON-CORPUS LEGENDARY** (the Cotton and Salisbury manuscripts listed here). These have not been classified (Zettel 1979 p 18 lists them as examples of *BHL* 4522), but they appear to be textually close to Harley. Among the Corbie manuscripts, although in a different group from Harley, is Bibliothèque Nationale lat. 5574, which Geith describes (1965 p 57) as considerably abridged in places, especially in Juliana's prayers and farewell speech. Avril and Stirnemann (1987 p 11) regard this manuscript as of early tenth-century English, possibly Mercian, provenance. The *passio* is the source of the Old English poem *Juliana* (*Jul*; ed. *ASPR* 3) by the poet Cynewulf, usually dated ninth century (see Woolf 1966a pp 5–7). Geith points to Bibliothèque Nationale lat. 10861 as the Latin text closest to the Old English poem. The absence of Juliana from the ninth-century **OLD ENGLISH MARTYROLOGY** is doubtless due to the loss of most of the February notices.

The brief Old English description of Juliana in the Exeter List of Relics (*Rec* 10.8, B16.10.8; ed. Förster 1943 p 79; Conner 1993a p 184) probably derives from a martyrology rather than from the *passio*, although it appears to echo faintly *Juliana* 614–17.

Despite the increasing amount of interpretive analysis of *Juliana*, there is as yet no modern critical edition of the Latin *passio*: those of Brunöhler (1912), d'Ardenne (*EETS* OS 248), and Mombritius (1910), which reproduce specific manuscripts, are to be preferred to the contaminated text in *AS* Feb. 2.873–77 (see Geith 1965 pp 24–25). Studies of the surviving medieval manuscripts (e.g., Brunöhler 1912, Geith 1965) have been done mainly with the German tradition in mind. Geith's is the most thorough and useful but is not definitive. English studies of Cynewulf's *Juliana* have tended to rely on the *AS* text, and it is used by Calder and Allen (1976 pp 121–32) for their translation. Despite Geith's opinion as to the importance of Bibliothèque Nationale lat. 10861 for sourcing *Juliana*, a detailed study of the Old English poem in relation to this and other English copies of the *passio* remains to be undertaken.

For other, earlier studies dealing with the *passio* and the Old English and other vernacular versions, see Strunk (1904), Glöde (1889), Backhaus (1899), and Garnett (1899). For a review of Geith's dissertation, see Berschin (1973).

Iulianus Cenomanensis, lectiones [ANON.Vit.Iul.Cenoman.]: *BHL* 4546d; *BLS* 1.183; *BSS* 6.1199–201.
  ed.: unpublished.

MSS Dublin, Trinity College 174: HG 215.
Lists – Refs none.

In his ninth-century acts, this Saint Julian is identified as one of the first-century missionaries sent to Gaul by Pope Clement I (**CLEMENS**), but historically he seems to have been an early (possibly the first) bishop of Le Mans in the fourth century. His cult in England seems to have been mainly late medieval, promoted perhaps by King Henry II who was born at Le Mans (Farmer 1987 p 243). One pre-Conquest Wessex calendar has a garbled notice ("Sancte Juliani virginis") for what appears to be his January 27 feast day (F. Wormald 1934 p 16). The three lections for the feast in the Dublin manuscript cited above are not identified by Colker (1991 1.352), but Webber (1992 p 158) points to *BHL* 4546d. This number refers only to the Dublin manuscript text, which is labeled by the Bollandists "Vita 4 bis," no other examples having yet been located. The Dublin text is among those copied by Webber's Group II scribes at Salisbury Cathedral, around, and probably after, 1100.

Iulianus et Basilissa, passio [ANON.Pas.Iul.Bas.1]: *BHL* 4529; *BLS* 1.56–57; *BSS* 6.1120–23; *DHGE* 6.1240–41.
 ed.: Salmon 1944–53 pp 27–56.

MSS none.
Lists ?Saewold: ML 8.19.
A-S Vers 1. ALDH.Carm.uirg. 1251–449.
 2. ALDH.Pros.uirg. 280.8–284.17.
 3. ?*Mart* (B19.q).
Quots/Cits none.
Refs ALDH.Pros.uirg. 281.6.

Julian and Basilissa, martyrs of Antinoe in Egypt (not Antioch) during the Diocletian persecution (feast day January 9), belong to the subcategory of saints who were virgin spouses, discussed by De Gaiffier (1947). According to their legendary *passio*, they devoted their lives after their chaste wedding night to founding and presiding over communities of celibates.

Basilissa and her sister nuns were granted a peaceful death but Julian and his male companions endured persecution and eventual martyrdom. Early witnesses to the currency of the cult are **VENANTIUS FORTUNATUS** (CARMINA VIII.iii.35; ed. *MGH* AA 4/1) and notices for the feast day in a fifth-century martyrology (January 6: *AS* Nov. 2/2.27–28). The original Greek *passio*, *BHG* 970–71, edited by Halkin (1980a), was translated into Latin in the seventh century or earlier (Siegmund 1949 p 238). A recension of this Latin *passio* was known to **ALDHELM**, whose verse and prose DE VIRGINITATE (ALDH.Carm.uirg., Pros.uirg.; ed. *MGH* AA 15) contain quite lengthy summaries of the legend. To judge from his verbatim renderings of some passages of direct speech, he seems to have used a text more like Salmon's, from the seventh-century Luxueil lectionary, than that in the *AS* edition (Ian. 1.575–87), which is based on a thirteenth-century legendary.

The ninth-century **OLD ENGLISH MARTYROLOGY** (*Mart*; ed. Kotzor 1981 2.12–13) also draws on some version of the *passio* for a brief account of Julian and Basilissa (for January 6), as Cross (1986a pp 232–34) points out; but although he notes the existence of several early manuscript copies of the *passio*, he finds nothing in the *Martyrology* notice that might permit a precise sourcing.

The feast day of Julian and Basilissa is not widely recorded in Anglo-Saxon calendars. See F. Wormald (1934 pp 58 and 254) and Lapidge (1996b p 123).

Another edition of the *passio* is that of Fábrega Grau (1953–55 2.118–44), based on a tenth-century manuscript from Spain, where the cult seems to have flourished.

Iulianus et Basilissa, passio [ANON.Pas.Iul.Bas.2]: *BHL* 4532.
ed.: unpublished.

MSS 1. ?Dublin, Trinity College 174: HG 215.
2. ?London, BL Cotton Nero E. i: HG 344.
3. ?Salisbury, Cathedral Library 221 (formerly Oxford, Bodleian Library Fell 4): HG 754.5.

Lists none.

A-S Vers ?*ÆLS* Julian & Basilissa (B1.3.5).
Quots/Cits – *Refs* none.

In the absence of a critical edition of the *Passio Iuliani et Basilissae*, identification of the texts in these manuscripts, which have been variously described as hybrids and abridgements of *BHL* 4529, must remain uncertain, but they seem sufficiently different from the printed editions of the *passio* to merit this separate entry. The Bollandists recognize that the *passio* was liable to abridgement, identifying one such recension as *BHL* 4532, which omits most of the last chapter of *BHL* 4529. According to Zettel, however (1979 pp 15, 47, 143, and 201–08), the text found in both the London and Salisbury manuscripts of the **COTTON-CORPUS LEGENDARY** is a previously unidentified text, considerably shorter than *BHL* 4532. On the other hand, Jackson and Lapidge (1996 p 135) refer to it merely as a hybrid of *BHL* 4529 and 4532. Zettel does not indicate whether there are other copies of this particular abridged version or if it is unique to the Legendary.

The text in the Dublin manuscript was copied by Webber's Group II scribes at Salisbury Cathedral, probably shortly after 1100. Webber (1992 p 158) identifies the text as *BHL* 4529, as does Colker (1991 1.324), but Colker adds that it "differs greatly" from the *AS* edition. The *incipit* and *explicit*, however, point towards *BHL* 4532, and it may thus be the sort of hybrid suggested by Jackson and Lapidge.

Zettel (1979 pp 201–08), developing the earlier source work of Ott (1892 pp 14–17) on ÆLFRIC's characteristically abbreviated account of Julian and Basilissa in LIVES OF SAINTS (*ÆLS*; ed. *EETS* OS 76 and 82), argues that the Latin *passio* used by Ælfric was the abridged text in the Cotton-Corpus Legendary. Zettel's sourcing should not be considered conclusive. In *BHL NS*, which appeared after his work was complete, the Bollandists list several other variant versions of *BHL* 4532, any one of which might be relevant here. The textual transmission of the legend and its relation to the Anglo-Saxon texts clearly require further study in the light of a more thorough survey of manuscript evidence.

Iustus Bellovacensis, passio [ANON.Pas.Iust.]: *BHL* 4590; *BLS* 4.143–44; *BSS* 7.24–25; *CPL* 2119a.
ed.: Coens 1956 pp 94–96 (partial).
MSS Düsseldorf, Universitätsbibliothek K1:B.215, K2:C.118, and K15:00: HG 819.
Lists none.
A-S Vers Mart (B19.ib).
Quots/Cits see below.
Refs none.

The legend of the boy martyr Justus of Beauvais (feast day October 18), one of the "céphalophores" (Moretus Plantin 1953; Coens 1956), is believed to be based in part on that of Justinus of Paris (*BHL* 4579). Interesting indirect evidence for early Anglo-Saxon knowledge of the legend is provided in Coens's discussion of the early manuscripts of the *passio*, which contain some rare words that are omitted from the later recensions and from the *AS* edition (*AS* Oct. 8.338–39). Coens (1956 pp 104–05) points out that three of these words also occur together (and nowhere else) in the eighth-century *Corpus Glossary* (see **GLOSSARIES**) from Canterbury, implying the existence of a copy of the *passio* in England during the eighth century. Coens also links the oldest manuscript fragment of the *passio* (mid-eighth century, now in Düsseldorf) to Anglo-Saxon England, since the script (according to Bischoff, quoted by Coens) is either Northumbrian, Kentish, or Continental Anglo-Saxon. The immediate Continental provenance of the fragments is Beyenberg, near the early-ninth-century monastery of Werden, founded by the Frisian Liudger who is known to have been a student of **ALCUIN**'s at York (up to 772) and whom Coens regards as a supplier of Anglo-Saxon manuscripts to Werden. More recently the fragment has been firmly described by Lowe (*CLA* 8.1187) as "written in England, and apparently in the North, to judge from the script," a judgement echoed by Gneuss (see HG 819).

The probability of an English origin for the Düsseldorf fragment is reinforced by Cross's sourcing (1977a pp 103–07) of the long notice for Justus in the ninth-century **OLD ENGLISH MARTYROLOGY** (*Mart*;

Kotzor 1981 2.231–33), which he finds most closely related, among all the extant versions, to the Düsseldorf text itself. Kotzor (1981 2.362–63) notes that one of the glosses mentioned above turns up in the C manuscript of the *Martyrology*. See also Cross (1986b pp 282–83, notes 44 and 49).

The early currency of the Justus legend in England is further indicated in a calendar of the ninth century, of Northern English origin (F. Wormald 1934 p 11), where Justus's name is coupled with that of Justinian, his uncle in the legend (as in a late-tenth-century calendar, p 25). The later cult of Justus's relics at Winchester, New Minster, in the eleventh century is reflected in several calendars (pp 123, 137, 165, 235, 263) and the so-called *Missal of Robert of Jumièges* (*HBS* 11.219–20; see **LITURGY, MASSBOOKS**). Unspecified relics of Justus were also said to be at Exeter: see the Exeter List of Relics (*Rec* 10.8, B16.10.8; ed. Förster 1943 p 74; Conner 1993a pp 180–81). A twelfth-century Winchester account claims the head was given to the community by King Athelstan in 924. See Coens (1956 p 109 note 3).

The edition of Coens, cited above, is limited to the text preserved in the Düsseldorf fragment; this may be supplemented, for the earlier portions of the *passio*, by the edition of Narbey (1899–1912 2.111–13), which is based on a ninth-century manuscript in Paris.

Ivo: *BSS* 7.997.

Various kinds of post-Conquest evidence, especially a *Vita Ivonis* by Goscelin of Canterbury (ed. *PL* 155.81–90), written 1087–91 for Herbert Losinga and the monks of Ramsey, suggest the existence of pre-Conquest literary memorials of this saint, whose name survives in the East Anglian town of St Ives (see Gransden 1974 p 108). According to the *vita*, Yvo was a Persian bishop of the sixth century who left his homeland with a few companions to become a missionary "peregrinus" in Europe, preaching the word and performing miracles, before finally settling in East Anglia where, after many years, "Yvo Domini ivit ad Dominum" (*PL* 155.84.1). Goscelin, who deals only briefly and very vaguely with Ivo's actual life and wanderings, focuses mainly on the events and miracles surrounding the *inventio* of the mysterious corpse (unearthed by a ploughman) at Slepe (St Ives), one of the greatest of the Ramsey Abbey properties, in 1002 during Ædnoth's abbacy. At first, all that was known of the discovered saint was his rank and name (which he revealed in a dream) but according to Goscelin in his prologue (*PL* 155.81–82), a later abbot, whom Goscelin calls Andrew (alias Witman or Withman, a German, 1016–20), had gone on pilgrimage to Jerusalem, learned of Ivo's fame among the Greeks, and, on his return, wrote up the life along with an account of the *inventio* and *miracula*. Goscelin does not reveal that Abbot Andrew/Witman had left Ramsey because he had quarreled with his monks (*Chronicon Rameseiensis*, ed. *RS* 83.121–25; for other relevant passages in the chronicle, see pp 64 and 114–15). Goscelin claims in his prologue to be providing a somewhat briefer version of Andrew's narrative and to have corroborated the local events from living witnesses.

The "discovery" of a body at Slepe may well have occurred in the early eleventh century as part of an effort by Ramsey monks to consolidate their hold on the substantial manor of Slepe itself, which was in dispute (Thacker 1996a pp 257–59). But the life of the foreigner Ivo, particularly his journey from the East and retirement in the fens, is dubious and unsupported by any external evidence; it may have been fabricated by Andrew himself or whoever wrote the version Goscelin revised.

Goscelin's *vita*, *inventio*, and succeeding miracles at Slepe and elsewhere (*BHL* 4622) are printed, partially, in *PL* 155.81–89 from the Bollandists' edition (*AS* Ian. 2.288–91) of an unknown English manuscript that lacked most of the miracles; these are printed by Macray (*RS* 83.lix–lxxiv) from Oxford, Bodleian Library Bodley 285 (*SC* 2430). He also prints (*RS* 83.lxxv–lxxxiv) a version of the early-twelfth-century *translatio* (*BHL* 4623) of Yvo's companions that is much fuller than the other printed version (*PL* 155.89–90). See also Hardy (*RS* 26/1.184–86). Colker (1991 1.309) itemizes another text, in Dublin, that likewise appears to differ from the printed editions. Another manuscript copy, apparently similar to the Bodley recension, is in Douai (see the *Bulletin* section of *Analecta Bollandiana* 54 [1936]: 204).

Kenelmus, passio [ANON.Vit.Mir.Kenelm.]: *BHL* 4641n, 4641p, 4641r; *BLS* 3.127–28; *BSS* 3.1182–83.
ed.: Love 1996 pp 50–88.

MSS – Refs none.

The historical Kenelm (Cynehelm; feast day July 17) was a Mercian prince who appears to have died while still a young man soon after 811, when Cenwulf (probably his father) was still king of Mercia (Levison 1946 p 249; Love 1996 pp lxxxix–xc). According to the hagiographical legend, however, Kenelm succeeded as a child of seven to the throne vacated by his father in 819 (821) and was murdered in the same year at the instigation of his sister, Cwenthryth. She ruled the kingdom for a time after the murder, attempting to keep it quiet, but a dove dropped a letter on the altar of St Peter's in Rome revealing the body's location, and Cwenthryth suffered a suitably gruesome end while attempting to recite a psalm backwards. Various kinds of evidence suggest that a martyr cult and (probably) the core of the surviving legend were in place by the late tenth century. Bassett (1985) has advanced the interesting hypothesis that Kenelm and his father were originally buried in a royal mausoleum (similar to others at Repton and Worcester) in a chapel of St Pancras (**PANCRATIUS**) at Winchcombe. By the time Bishop Oswald of Worcester (**OSWALDUS WIGORNIENSIS**) refounded Winchcombe Abbey (ca. 969) and a new church (St Mary's) was built, oral tradition or clerical ingenuity had transformed Kenelm into a child martyr under the influence of the Saint Pancras story; the royal bodies would have been translated to the new church at this time and not, as the legend has it, soon after Kenelm's death. Not quite congruent with this scenario is the suggestion of Thacker (1996a pp 252–53), building on earlier studies (Rollason 1983 pp 9–10; Thacker 1985 pp 8–12), that the formation of Kenelm's legend was influenced by the murder of Edward the Martyr (978) and that Kenelm's cult may have been fostered originally at Ramsey by the refugees from Winchcombe, which was a casualty of the "anti-monastic reaction" following King Edgar's death in 975. This view is favored by the legend's most recent editor, Love (1996 pp cxi–cxiii).

The hagiographic legend of Kenelm, as it survives, is difficult to date and the earliest manuscript evidence is from the very end of the Anglo-Saxon period, but there is sufficient likelihood of pre-Conquest traditions for it to merit specific treatment here. The manuscripts with one exception are later than the eleventh century, all representing, although in various forms, what Love regards as a self-contained whole, the *Vita et miracula*, although in *BHL* a more differentiated impression is given by the three numbers, *BHL* 4641n, p, and r. To be distinguished from the *Vita et miracula* is the *Vita brevior*, designated *BHL* 4641m, which comprises a set of lections for the feast day, preserved in an eleventh-century manuscript (see next entry).

There is general agreement among modern scholars such as Love, Antropoff, and others that the *Vita et miracula* was composed (apparently as a single work) in the third quarter of the eleventh century, probably at Winchcombe, the center of Kenelm's cult, and probably 1066–75 (Love 1996 p xci; Antropoff 1965 p 60; see also Thacker 1985 pp 8, 23 note 59, and Hayward 1993 p 82 note 5), and that the copy of the set of lections was made around the same time. Most other basic questions about the legend's origins and transmission are still unresolved, including the relationship of the *Vita brevior* and *Vita et miracula*. While some have assumed (e.g., Antropoff 1965 pp 50 and 59–60 and Rollason 1983 p 10) that both derive from a lost, early-eleventh-century original, to which the relevant portions of the *Vita et miracula* provide a more faithful witness, and while the Bollandists' title for the lection set, *Vita antiquior*, implies it was composed earlier than the other version, Love concludes that neither explanation is valid. Both versions, she suggests, are the work of one author soon after the Conquest (1996 pp cix–cx).

According to a preface that occurs in several of the later manuscripts, the author of the *Vita et miracula* drew on oral traditions associated with a Worcester monk Wulfwine (died 1017), on a song, on "writings in English," and on the testimony of Queen Edith as to the contents of other earlier writings (pp 50–52). Another such intermediary mentioned in one manuscript may have been the mid-eleventh-century Abbot Ælfwine of Ramsey (p xcvi). Love thinks it likely, if not provable, that the author of the *Vita et miracula* was Goscelin the hagiographer at an early stage of his career (pp lxxxix–cx).

The surviving Latin texts, along with Latin chronicles that draw on it, and also the Middle English *South English Legendary* (late thirteenth century), all preserve more or less identically some verses of late Old English type, in the "letter" dropped by the dove on the Roman altar, announcing the location of Kenelm's body after his murder. It is uncertain whether the verses are from a lost vernacular narrative, written or oral, or are merely "a commemorative snatch" (Bennett and Smithers 1966 pp 96–97; also Wilson 1970 p 99), but there is some evidence that the verses were known in the early eleventh century (Love 1996 pp cxvii–cxix).

For another edition of the *Vita et miracula*, see Antropoff (1965 pp IV–XXIV). Love's edition has a facing English translation. For earlier discussions and bibliography on Kenelm, see Levison (1946 pp 249–51) and Bennett and Smithers (1966 p 312). All previous work on the Kenelm legend and texts, however, is superseded by Love's edition (which, unfortunately, has no separate bibliography). On the general theme of "innocent martyrdom" among Anglo-Saxon saints, including Kenelm, see Hayward (1993 p 83 note 7).

Kenelmus, passio [ANON.Vit.Kenelm.brev.]: *BHL* 4641m.
ed.: Love 1996 pp 126–29.

MSS Cambridge, Corpus Christi College 367: HG 100.
Lists – Refs none.

Once considered (e.g., by Antropoff 1965) the older of the two main versions of the legend of Kenelm, this set of originally eight lections for the saint's feast, called *Vita brevior* in the most recent edition, is preserved uniquely and imperfectly (lection I and part of II are lost, owing to a missing folio) in an interesting manuscript written probably at Worcester Cathedral Priory in the third quarter of the eleventh century (see the description in Love 1996 pp cxxi–cxxii; see also ML 11). Unlike the much longer *Vita et miracula*, the lections describe only the saint's murder and the events preceding it, but not the miraculous aftermath or the later cult history. Love argues persuasively against the view that the

Vita brevior is the source of the longer life or that it represents a lost source from the early eleventh century. The text has also been edited by Antropoff (1965 pp XXIII–XXVI).

Kiaranus (Clonmacnois or Sagiriensis): *SEHI* 166 or *SEHI* 124.

A *Vita Kyerrani* is among the texts listed in a booklist (ML 11.24) of the late eleventh century, written on some blank folios at the end of an early-eleventh-century copy, now in Oxford, of the **DIALOGI** of **GREGORY THE GREAT**. Although the later (twelfth-century) provenance of the manuscript is Worcester, its original home is unknown. Nor is it possible to determine if the booklist notice refers to Kieran (Ciaran) of Clonmacnoise (feast day September 9, *BHL* 4654–55) or his more shadowy namesake of Saighir (feast day March 5, *BHL* 4657–58). We have found no other evidence of Anglo-Saxon interest in either saint.

Lambertus, vita [ANON.Vit.Lambert.]: *BHL* 4677; *BLS* 3.579–80; *BSS* 7.1079–80; *CPL* 2121.
ed.: *MGH* SRM 6.353–84.

MSS 1. London, BL Cotton Nero E. i: HG 344.
2. Salisbury, Cathedral Library 222 (formerly Oxford, Bodleian Library Fell 1): HG 754.6.
Lists – Refs none.

Lambert (feast day September 17), bishop of Tongres-Maastricht (Belgium) in the late seventh century, was murdered (ca. 705) in the course of a feud between rival aristocratic clans. A cult developed in the years following his death, his relics were translated by his successor Bishop Hubert (**HUCBERTUS LEODIENSIS**) from Maastricht to the village of Liège (the place of his death), which now became the episcopal center, and this *vita* celebrating Lambert as a martyr was composed there ca. 727–43 (see Krusch, *MGH* SRM 6.308–10, and Kupper 1984 pp 6–22). It is heavily dependent on the life of Saint Eloi (**ELIGIUS**), *BHL* 2477.

Copies of this earliest *Vita Lamberti* survive in the eleventh-century recensions of the **COTTON-CORPUS LEGENDARY**, classified 2A.2 (the Cotton manuscript) and 2A.6 (the Salisbury manuscript) by Krusch in his edition (*MGH* SRM 6.312–13; see also Levison, *MGH* SRM 7.602 and 632). Lambert's feast is regularly recorded in later Anglo-Saxon calendars. For further bibliography, see Kupper (1984 p 6 note 1).

Laurentius, passio [ANON.Pas.Laurent.]: *BHL* 4753; *BLS* 3.297–99; *BSS* 8.108–21; *CPL* 2219. See also **ABDON ET SENNEN, CYRILLA, HIPPOLYTUS, IRENAEUS ET ABUNDIUS, POLYCHRONIUS, QUADRAGINTA SEX MILITES, ROMANUS MILES, SIXTUS II**, and **TRYPHONIA**.
ed.: Delehaye 1933b pp 72–98.

MSS 1. Edinburgh, National Library of Scotland, Advocates 18.7.8: HG 255.
2. London, BL Cotton Nero E. i: HG 344.
3. Salisbury, Cathedral Library 222 (formerly Oxford, Bodleian Library Fell 1): HG 754.6.
Lists none.
A-S Vers 1. BEDA.Mart. 147.8–11.
2. *Mart* (B19.fq).
3. *ÆCHom* I, 29 (B1.1.31).
Quots/Cits Passio Laurentii 83.1: WVLF.WINT.Vit.Æthelwold. 46.8–9; see below.
Refs BEDA.Mart. 36.5 and 68.26–27.

Laurence the deacon, whose name was invoked in the Canon of the Mass along with that of his bishop, Pope Sixtus II, was one of the seven deacons of Rome at the time of the persecution under the emperor Valerian; his execution (feast day August 10) followed that of his fellow deacons and the pope (August 6) in 258. During the fourth century and later, Laurence became one of the most widely venerated saints in Christian Europe, including England. As **BEDE** reports in **HISTORIA ECCLESIASTICA** III.xx (ed. Colgrave and Mynors 1969 p 320.29), Pope

Vitalian sent relics of Laurence and other principal Roman saints to King Oswiu of Northumbria in response to the adoption of Roman Christianity at the Council of Whitby (664), and his feast is prominent (frequently of the first rank) in all extant English calendars.

The legend of his distribution of church wealth to the poor and his martyrdom by roasting on a grill developed early, as in **PRUDENTIUS**'s verse narrative, **PERISTEPHANON** II, written ca. 400 (*BHL* 4752; ed. *CCSL* 126). On **AMBROSE**'s knowledge of another episode in the story, see Berschin (1986–91 1.84). The prose *passio*, variously dated fifth or sixth century, is an epic "Passionszyklus" combining several previously distinct martyrs' stories into a single, somewhat unwieldy narrative of the persecution, which is anachronistically conducted by the emperor Decius and his "prefect" Valerian. There appear to be two main versions, a longer and a shorter version, the latter omitting some of the numerous other martyrs (see below) distributed throughout the longer version (Cross 1983a p 203). *BHL* divides and distributes the longer version among several numbers with cross-references (in narrative order: *BHL* 6884, 6, 7801, 4754, 3961), reflecting the practice of some medieval legendaries, which divided up the narrative into separate *passiones*. The complete longer version is that edited from three manuscripts by Delehaye, superseding earlier editions, and cited here. Cross (1983a p 201) lists additional early manuscripts from Continental libraries. For the portion in which Laurence himself is the main protagonist (*BHL* 4753), see pp 80–93 of the edition; the shorter version (*BHL* 7812) is edited by Narbey (1899–1912 2.234–43) who, along with Cross (1983a p 202), considers it the "primitive" version. But this shorter version is not, apparently, widely preserved. The longer version is the text in the **COTTON-CORPUS LEGENDARY**. Of the eleventh-century copies listed here, the Salisbury manuscript preserves the more original readings, the London copy having been frequently altered and "corrected" by a later scribe. According to Ker (NRK p 174), text fragments surviving in the eighth- or ninth-century palimpsest in the Edinburgh manuscript (fols 19, 22) represent the "earliest extant manuscript" of the text edited by Delehaye.

The longer *passio* was drawn on by Bede for his notices for Laurentius in **MARTYROLOGIUM** (BEDA.Mart.; ed. Dubois and Renaud 1976) and similarly by the author of the **OLD ENGLISH MARTYROLOGY** (*Mart*; ed. Kotzor 1981 2.176–77). For specific details on those other saints of the cycle (cross-referenced above, headnote) who had seperate feast days and/or notices in more than one of our sources, see their separate entries. For Bede's notice for Olympias and Maximus, see the entry for Abdon et Sennen. Bede's notices for Laurence and Sixtus are among the shortest in the group, but this may be because he assumed that his readers would be well acquainted with the legends of the two principal saints of the cycle. Cross, however (1983a p 204 note 23), questions Quentin's attribution to Bede himself of the *Martyrologium* notices for the feast days after July 25, where the only authoritative early manuscript breaks off. Cross (1983a) has sourced the entries in the *Old English Martyrology* in detail. He finds Delehaye's text generally a reliable guide to the form of the *Martyrology*'s source, but cites several variants from early manuscripts, not collated by Delehaye, that agree more closely with the Old English (pp 204–05).

ÆLFRIC drew on the *Passio Laurentii* proper in a homily for the saint's feast, in the First Series of his **CATHOLIC HOMILIES** (*ÆCHom* I; ed. *EETS* SS 17); for his use elsewhere of earlier portions of the *passio*, see above, the entry for Abdon et Sennen. In the homily Ælfric abridges his source considerably and covers only those stories in the cycle that are set in Rome and clearly linked together: the martyrdoms of Sixtus, Laurence, Romanus, and Hippolytus, and the conversions (but not the deaths) of Decius's wife and daughter, Tryphonia and Cyrilla, and the Forty-Six soldiers (Quadraginta Sex Milites). See the separate entries on these saints for further details. For a translation, see Thorpe's edition (1844–46 1.416–36).

Zettel's sourcing (1979 pp 178–79) of Ælfric's homily on Laurence, superseding that of Förster (1892 pp 27–28), shows that Ælfric's source text must have been similar to Delehaye's text of the longer cycle, but closer in places to the copy in the Cotton-Corpus Legendary. The latter, however, is not identical with Ælfric's immediate source, as is shown in several instances where his text agrees with Delehaye's edition against the Legendary (Zettel 1979 pp 179 and 300), and in one instance, pointed out by Cross (1983a p 208), in which Delehaye's edition (1933b p 83.5) and the Legendary (fol 69ra.12) have the reading "per regiones," where Ælfric's source must have had the variant "peregrinos," found by Cross in two early manuscripts (see *EETS* SS 17.419.43, "ælþeodigum"). See now Godden's sourcing of the whole homily (*EETS* SS 18.238–47).

Magennis (1986 pp 320–22) offers a brief but valuable analysis of Ælfric's adaptation of the *passio*.

The eleventh-century *Caligula Troper* (see **LITURGY, TROPERS**) contains, in the form of an inscription or *titulus* bordering a picture of Saint Laurence (fol 25r), six verses in leonine hexameters briefly narrating the saint's arraignment before Decius and his subsequent roasting, "piscis ut assatur" ("as a fish is roasted"), on the celebrated iron grill. Teviotdale (1991 pp 306–07) argues that although convincing verbal echoes are lacking, the wording and narrative details of the verses suggest that the poet probably knew the *passio*.

The author of the tenth/eleventh-century Exeter List of Relics (*Rec* 10.8, B16.10.8, ed. Förster 1943 p 73; Conner 1993a p 180) mentions that among Laurence's relics at Exeter were some of the coals with which he was roasted. This may indicate knowledge of the *passio*. More definite is the case of **WULFSTAN OF WINCHESTER** in VITA ÆTHELWOLDI (WVLF.WINT.Vit.Æthelwold.; ed. Lapidge and Winterbottom 1991) where he compares Bishop **ÆTHELWOLD** with Laurence for his philanthropic use of church wealth. In a similar context, and imitating Wulfstan, the Anglo-Norman Osbern of Canterbury alludes to Laurence in his life of **ÆLFEGUS**, composed ca. 1080 (ed. *AS* April. 2.637 col. ii.28; cf. *Passio Laurentii* 83.1–3).

In addition to Delehaye's edition of the *passio*, see also that of Mombritius (1910 2.92–95).

Leo IX, miracula [LIBUIN.Mir.Leon.]: *BHL* 4821a–c; *BLS* 2.126–28; *BSS* 7.1293–301; Kelly (1986) pp 147–48.

ed.: *PL* 143.534–39.

MSS London, BL Cotton Nero E. i: HG 344.

Lists – Refs none.

The first of the energetic reformist popes of the eleventh century, Leo IX (formerly Bruno, bishop of Toul in Alsace, born 1002, a close kinsman of the emperor Henry III) died April 19, 1054, worn out by the travels and exertions of his six years in office. Even before he died, his evident virtues had elicited a biography of the first part of his life, by Wibert of Toul, who wrote a continuation later in the century (*BHL* 4818). Miracles associated with Leo's relics immediately began to be reported, in Rome and elsewhere, in the weeks and months following his death. A collection of the Roman miracles, labeled "Tertia die" (from the *incipit*) by Tritz (1952 pp 321–41), and attributed in *BHL NS* to one of Leo's clerks, the subdeacon Libuinus, was composed presumably not long after the miracles are said to have occurred in 1054, although Tritz is non-committal on the composition date; the author of this original collection, according to Tritz (1952 p 338), was not necessarily Libuinus himself, who was apparently responsible for a somewhat later expanded edition of the same set. The copy of the collection in the eleventh-century Cotton manuscript, from Worcester, of the **COTTON-CORPUS LEGENDARY** represents what Tritz terms the earlier "Northern" recension and is most closely affiliated textually with the lost "Hubertinus" manuscript, on which the *PL* edition (reprinted from *AS* April. 2.669–71) is based, and with another manuscript now in Paris (see Tritz 1952 pp 329–33; stemma on p 337). The English copy (Cotton Nero E. i, pt 2, fols 151–153v) is not a complete copy of the Libuinus collection. The series of short miracle episodes in the Cotton manuscript, numbered separately I–LVII, comprises only parts I–V of the whole work as it is divided (I–VIII) in *BHL NS*, or numbers 1–22 of the *PL* edition's 34 chapters. The Cotton text ends abruptly after its episode LVII (concerning the crippled boy Leo of Monte Cassino) with the words "membrorum secum reportauit" (*PL* 143.538.50).

The *Miracula Leonis* in the Cotton manuscript is preceded by an abridged version of a sermon for All Saints, "Legimus in ecclesiasticis historiis" (ed. Cross 1977c pp 105–22; see **PSEUDO-BEDE, HOMILIAE**), and followed by neumed lections for Saint Nicholas (see **NICOLAUS**, lectiones). These three texts are added, out of calendar order, at what was once the end of this portion of the Worcester legendary. The Leo text, noticed by Levison in his "Conspectus" (*MGH* SRM 7.602), is not mentioned by Zettel (1979) or Jackson and Lapidge (1996) in their lists of the contents of the Legendary.

None of the three additional texts (including the *Miracula Leonis*) in the Cotton manuscript is or was in the Salisbury legendary (Webber 1992 pp 154–57) that derives from the same exemplar as Worcester's. The three additional texts must be local Worcester supplements to the legendary. Since the scribal hands of the additions are similar to those of the main text of the legendary, it seems unlikely they were added much later than the date normally attributed to the main text (third quarter of the eleventh century). Doubtless, like the Nicholas lections, the Leo collection represents some special devotional interest of the Worcester community during or just before the episcopacy of Bishop Wulfstan II (1062–95; **WULFSTANUS II**).

Leo IX's cult was not widely celebrated in later eleventh-century England, but he is mentioned as "the holy pope" and "Pope St Leo" in the annal for 1054 in the so-called D and E copies of the **ANGLO-SAXON CHRONICLE** (*ChronD*, B17.8, ed. Classen and Harmer 1926; *ChronE*, B17.9, ed. Plummer 1892–99; see **CHRONICLES**); D was at Worcester during the mid- to late eleventh century, while E is a Peterborough copy of a Canterbury original. Notice of the April 19 feast of Leo IX was added, presumably at Exeter, to the calendar in the so-called *Leofric Missal* (F. Wormald 1934 p 47; see **LITURGY, MASSBOOKS**). Barlow (1979 p 84 note 4) draws attention to Leo's name in a litany likewise from Exeter in Leofric's time. The pope's important relations with the Anglo-Saxon church are touched on by Stenton (1971 pp 465 and 467); see also Barlow (1979 pp 48, 301–02, 307) who mentions Leofric of Exeter as a solitary supporter of Leo IX's cult (he does not mention the Worcester office).

Without a more precise dating of the compilation of the miracle collection itself, one can only speculate as to when and how it reached Worcester, but opportunities were not lacking. Archbishop Ealdred of Worcester and York visited Rome in 1061 to receive the pallium from Alexander II, and papal legates came back with Ealdred to arrange for his replacement as bishop of Worcester, 1062, when prior Wulfstan was elected. The papal legates spent about six weeks (Lent) in Worcester as

Wulfstan's guests. For a detailed account, see Mason (1990 p 78), who does not, however, mention this text.

Another possibility, which would require the *Miracula Leonis* to have been composed and circulated immediately after the events it describes, has been suggested to me by Richard Pfaff, namely that Archbishop Ealdred might have brought a copy of the *Miracula* to Worcester from Cologne, where he spent most of the year of Leo's death, 1054, being entertained by the archbishop and by the emperor Henry III, Leo's kinsman. On Ealdred's liturgical interests, see Lapidge (1983), a reference that I also owe to Professor Pfaff.

Leodegarius, vita [ANON.Vit.Leodeg.]: *BHL* 4853; *BSS* 7.1180–93; *RFHMA* 2.1421; *DACL* 8.2460–93.
  ed.: *AS* Oct. 1.463–81.
MSS 1. Cambridge, Corpus Christi College 9: HG 36.
  2. Salisbury, Cathedral Library 222 (formerly Oxford, Bodleian Library Fell 1): HG 754.6.
List – Refs none.

Although the two earliest lives of Léger were both in circulation before the end of the eighth century, the cult of the bishop of Autun, murdered in 679, former abbot of Saint-Maxence, Poitou (where his relics were kept and his cult first fostered), is not clearly reflected in England before the later Anglo-Saxon period, when we find a proper mass assigned to him in the early-eleventh-century Winchester *Missal of Robert of Jumièges* (ed. *HBS* 11.216–17; see **LITURGY, MASSBOOKS**). His feast day occurs regularly (on October 2 or 3) in English monastic calendars of the late tenth and eleventh centuries.

The two eleventh-century English manuscript copies of Léger's *vita* listed here represent a third recension, compiled by an anonymous monk of Saint-Maxence, around the turn of the eighth century. He spliced together portions of the two earlier versions to form the new work, which has been studied and discussed in modern scholarship mainly as a means of reconstructing the original Vita 1, as in Krusch's edition, *MGH* SRM 5.283-22 (see also Krusch 1891). The Salisbury copy is collated in Krusch's edition; Levison (*MGH* SRM 7.573) pronounces the Cambridge text to be of the same recension (Krusch's C3 family of manuscripts). The composite text known to the later Anglo-Saxons, and similar to that printed in *AS* and *PL*, is not, however, reedited by Krusch. For a full critical appraisal of the textual history of the various recensions of the *vita*, see now Poulin (1977-78). On the historicity of the earliest life, and its methodological similarities to Stephen of Ripon's life of **WILFRIDUS**, see Fouracre (1990 pp 11-21).

RFHMA (2.1421) misidentifies the text in the former Fell manuscript (Salisbury 222) as a copy of Vita 1. *CCSL* 117 (1957) contains reprints of Krusch's editions of the two earlier *vitae*.

Leodegarius, vita metrica [ANON.Vit.Leodeg.metr.]: *BHL* 4854.
   ed.: *MGH* PLAC 3.5-37.

MSS – A-S Vers none.
Quots/Cits see below.
Refs none.

Possible echoes of phrases in this Carolingian verse life of Léger have been noted by Campbell in his edition of two tenth-century Anglo-Latin hagiographic poems. See **FRITHEGOD**'s **BREVILOQUIUM VITAE WILFRIDI** 20 (ed. Campbell 1950) and *Vita Leodegarii metrica* II.245; see also **WULFSTAN OF WINCHESTER**'s **NARRATIO METRICA DE SANCTO SWITHUNO** I.1188, 1552 (Campbell 1950) and *Vita Leodegarii metrica* I.153, 338.

Leonardus Nobiliacensis, vita [ANON.Vit.Leonard.]: *BHL* 4862; *BLS* 4.273-74; *BSS* 7.1198-204.
   ed.: *AS* Nov. 3.150-55.

MSS Dublin, Trinity College 174: HG 215.
List – Refs none.

The only witness to possible Anglo-Saxon knowlege of the literature commemorating Leonard (feast day November 6), the putative sixth-century hermit saint of "Noblac" (Saint-Léonard-de-Noblat, near Limoges), is the copy of the *Vita Leonardi* (composed ca. 1025) in the Dublin manuscript, originally from Salisbury Cathedral (Colker 1991 1.324) and written ca. 1100 or somewhat later by one of Webber's Group II scribes (Webber 1992 p 158). According to Colker the text is divided into five lections (for a sixth, see next notice). The complete absence, however, of any earlier English liturgical devotion to Leonard, whose feast day is invariably dedicated to Winnoc (**WINNOCUS**) in Anglo-Saxon calendars, suggests that the Salisbury copy probably derives from a Norman import, intended to supplement rather than continue existing English traditions. Another, slightly later copy of the *vita* is in the Canterbury legendary, now London, BL Arundel 91 (Levison, *MGH* SRM 7.603), which is the only manuscript of English provenance collated in the Bollandists' edition (*AS* Nov. 3.148).

Leonardus Nobiliacensis, miracula [ANON.Mir.Leonard.]: *BHL* 4863.
   ed.: *AS* Nov. 3.155–56.

MSS Dublin, Trinity College 174: HG 215.
List – Refs none.

The late-eleventh-/early-twelfth-century Dublin manuscript listed in the previous entry also has the *Miracula Leonardi* I.i–ii, forming a sixth lection along with the *vita*'s five (Colker 1991 1.324). The Arundel manuscript referred to in the body of the previous entry has the full set of miracles, I–IX (*BHL* 4863–71).

Longinus, passio [ANON.Pas.Longin.]: *BHL* 4965; *BLS* 1.594–95; *BSS* 8.89–95.
   ed.: *AS* Mart. 2.384–86.

MSS Cambridge, Corpus Christi College 9: HG 36.
Lists none.

A-S Vers ÆLS Exalt of Cross (B1.3.27) 184–217.
Quots/Cits – Refs none.

The figure of Longinus (feast day usually March 15) is a conflation of the Roman centurion who uttered the words "Vere hic filius dei erat" (Mark 15.29) and the soldier who lanced Christ's side (John 19.34). On the origins and development of the legend, according to which Longinus eventually became a Cappadocian monk and then a martyr, see Peebles (1911) and Dölger (1933 pp 81–94).

The Latin *passio* of Longinus, apparently a rendering of an earlier Greek text (*BHG* 988), appears in several early medieval legendaries (Siegmund 1949 p 238) and was known to the major martyrologists of the ninth century, but not to those of the eighth. The earliest English memorial is a brief, free rendering of the *passio* that concludes ÆLFRIC's compilation of narrative and polemic texts for the feast of the Exaltation in LIVES OF SAINTS (*ÆLS*; ed. *EETS* OS 94 and 114; see IESUS CHRISTUS, EXALTATIO SANCTAE CRUCIS), sourced by C. Loomis (1931 p 4 notes 1 and 2) and Zettel (1979 p 234). Liturgical evidence for an Anglo-Saxon cult of Longinus is scarce, but, as pointed out by Jackson and Lapidge (1996 p 142), the soldier's feast is given the unusual date of November 22 not only in the COTTON-CORPUS LEGENDARY manuscript listed above, but also in the late-tenth-century calendar in the *Leofric Missal* (F. Wormald 1934 p 54; see LITURGY, MASSBOOKS) where after the notice for CAECILIA we read "et Longini qui latus domini aperuit," an echo of John 19.34 (see also the martyrologies of ADO and USUARD, *PL* 123.343 and 843–44). The lost copy of the *passio* that was formerly in Salisbury, Cathedral Library 222 also would have had the November 22 date (see Webber 1992 p 157). However, the copy extant in the early-twelfth-century legendary from Chester (London, Gray's Inn 3) has the more usual feast day of March 15 (Ker and Piper 1969–92 1.52).

Lucas Evangelista, laudatio [ANON.Laud.Luc.Evang./PS.PAUL.DIAC.]: *BHL* 4973.
ed.: *PL* 95.1530–35.

MSS Dublin, Trinity College 174: HG 215.
List – Refs none.

There is no developed Western tradition of apocryphal *acta* concerning the evangelist Luke (feast day October 18). All the hagiographic texts associated with him are labeled *laudationes*, eulogies, in *BHL*. The earliest of these occur as prologues to his gospel and thence in major non-hagiographic works described elsewhere in *SASLC*, including the brief but influntial account by **JEROME** in **DE VIRIS INLUSTRIBUS** VII (ed. *TU* 14/1a.11–12). This in turn influenced **ISIDORE, DE ORTU ET OBITU PATRUM** LXXXI (ed. Chaparro Gomez 1985 p 217), and **PSEUDO-ISIDORE, DE ORTU ET OBITU PATRUM** LV (*PL* 83.1292–93), on which depend the early Anglo-Saxon eulogies of Luke in **ALDHELM**'s **DE VIRGINITATE** (*Carmen* 503–23, *Prosa* 256.15–257.2; ed. *MGH* AA 15) and in the **OLD ENGLISH MARTYROLOGY** (*Mart*, B19.hz; ed. Kotzor 1981 2.230). On Aldhelm, see Ehwald's edition (*MGH* AA 15.256); on the *Old English Martyrology*'s notice and for further references on Isidore and Pseudo-Isidore, see Cross (1981e pp 189–91 and 1986b p 285). According to Quentin (1908 p 97), **BEDE**'s eulogy of Luke in his **MARTYROLOGIUM** (ed. Dubois and Renaud 1976 p 189.1–6) is adapted directly from a gospel prologue, the so-called *Vetus argumentum* (*BHL* 4970; I would have overlooked this but for Rosalind Love's sourcing of the *Martyrologium* in the Fontes Anglo-Saxonici on-line database).

The anonymous eulogy in question here is the second of two such pieces in the late-eleventh-century Dublin manuscript, originally from Salisbury (for the other work, see next entry). The second text appeared in late medieval editions of the **HOMILIARUM** of **PAUL THE DEACON** and hence is attributed erroneously to him in *PL* and later authors. In the Dublin manuscript this work is headed "Expositio Decorosi presbiteri in laude Luce euangeliste" and is divided into six lessons (Colker 1991 1.320).

Lucas Evangelista, laudatio [ANON.Laud.Luc.Evang.]: *BHL* 4976d.
 ed.: unpublished.

MSS Dublin, Trinity College 174: HG 215.
List – Refs none.

The first of the two *laudationes* of Luke the evangelist in the Dublin manuscript (Colker 1991 1.320) is an anonymous gospel prologue. I have found no printed edition or study of this version.

Luceia Romae, passio [ANON.Pas.Lucei.Rom.]: *BHL* 4980; *BSS* 8.236–38.
ed.: *AS* Iun. 5.13–14.
MSS 1. Cambridge, Corpus Christi College 9: HG 36.
2. Dublin, Trinity College 174: HG 215.
Lists none.
A-S Vers Mart (B19.dx).
Quots/Cits – Refs none.

The most usual feast day for the virgin Luceia (Lucia), along with the pagan convert Auceia and numerous companions, reputedly martyrs of Rome under Diocletian, is June 25, half a year away from that of her more famous Sicilian namesake (**LUCIA SYRACUSIS**; feast day December 13). The two Lucys are properly distinguished in the ninth-century **OLD ENGLISH MARTYROLOGY** (see below) and, somewhat garbled, in at least one later Anglo-Saxon calendar ("Sanctae Lucianae," June 25, in F. Wormald 1934 p 49, presumably a mistake for "Sanctae Luceiae"). Their *passiones* are found in close and apparently confused proximity, however, with the same December 13 feast day, in the eleventh-century Cambridge manuscript (from the **COTTON-CORPUS LEGENDARY**) and formerly in Salisbury, Cathedral Library 222 (see Webber 1992 p 157 and Jackson and Lapidge 1996 p 143; for later, affiliated manuscripts, see Zettel 1979 p 33 note 108). Colker (1991 1.322) identifies the text in the Dublin manuscript (from Salisbury Cathedral) as *BHL* 4980 and 4980b but comments that it "differs greatly" from the *AS* edition.

The substantial notice for Luceia in the *Old English Martyrology* (*Mart*; ed. Kotzor 1981 2.132–33) is briefly sourced by Cross

(1986a p 238) in relation to the *AS* edition and some early manuscripts of the *passio*.

Lucia Syracusis, passio [ANON.Pas.Luci.Syrac.]: *BHL* 4992; *BLS* 4.548–49; *BSS* 8.241–52; *CPL* 2204.
ed.: Surius 1570–75 6.892–94.
MSS Cambridge, Corpus Christi College 9: HG 36.
Lists none.
A-S Vers 1. ALDH.Carm.uirg. 1779–841.
2. ALDH.Pros.uirg. 293.15–294.24.
3. BEDA.Mart. 223.6–14.
4. *Mart* (B19.jj).
5. *ÆLS* Lucy (B1.3.10).
Quots/Cits – Refs none.

Lucy, virgin martyr of Syracuse, Sicily (December 13), is one of a select number of saints whose legends were current in both the earlier and later Anglo-Saxon periods and in several slightly different recensions. There is no critical edition of the *passio* and the source studies by the scholars listed below avail themselves of a variety of printed editions and manuscripts.

Lucy is a devotee of **AGATHA**, according to her legend, and **ALDHELM** juxtaposes his eulogies of the two saints in his **DE VIRGINI-TATE** (ALDH.Carm.uirg., Pros.uirg.; ed. *MGH* AA 15) on the grounds that they are linked together in the Canon of the Mass and by virtue of their shared Sicilian homeland (see *Prosa* 293.15–20). For Aldhelm's source, Ehwald (*MGH* AA 15.293–94), followed by Lapidge and Herren (1979 p 177), cites Surius's edition, apparently in preference to that of Mombritius (1910 2.107–09), as the text closest to Aldhelm's source for his prose eulogy of Lucy. Quentin (1908 p 81) on the other hand chooses that of Beaugrand (1892, "annexes" pp XLI–LXIV) for the source of **BEDE**'s **MARTYROLOGIUM** (BEDA.Mart.; ed. Dubois and Renaud 1976). Cross (1986b pp 277–80) uses Mombritius for his sourcing of the

OLD ENGLISH MARTYROLOGY notice (*Mart*; ed. Kotzor 1981 2.262–63) but finds various early manuscripts nearer to the *Martyrology*'s evident source. See also Cross (1981d p 486).

ÆLFRIC, in **LIVES OF SAINTS** (*ÆLS*; ed. *EETS* OS 76 and 84), may have taken his cue from Aldhelm in deviating from normal calendar order (his *Agatha* and *Lucy* form chapters 8 and 9 of *Lives of Saints*). Following Ott (1892 pp 31–34), Zettel (1979 pp 251–53) in sourcing Ælfric's version rejects Mombritius's edition in favor of Surius and cites a late recension of the **COTTON-CORPUS LEGENDARY**, Hereford, Cathedral Library P.VII.6 (late twelfth century), as most closely corresponding to Ælfric's source, rather than the earlier copy in the Cambridge manuscript listed here. Morini (1990 pp 315–17) confirms that the Surius edition, not that of Mombritius, represents the type of text used by Ælfric, but adds (pp 317–19) that Ælfric's puzzling identification of Lucy's suitor with her persecutor Paschasius (*Lucy* 57–58), while it could also be construed from Aldhelm's account (see also Lapidge and Herren 1979 p 196 note 22), must derive from a corrupt exemplar, such as she points to in early manuscripts now in Munich and Verona. See her quotations of variant readings from these manuscripts (p 319). It should be noted that the identification of Paschasius and the suitor is not, according to Zettel, reflected in any of the manuscripts of the Cotton-Corpus Legendary that contain the Lucy *passio*, including the Hereford copy. He suggests that Ælfric himself was responsible for conflating Paschasius with the suitor (1979 p 253 note 153).

Lucia et Geminianus, passio [ANON.Pas.Luci.Gemin.]: *BHL* 4985; *BSS* 8.260–62; *CPL* 2203.
  ed.: Mombritius 1910 2.109–14.
MSS 1. London, BL Cotton Nero E. i: HG 344.
  2. Salisbury, Cathedral Library 222 (formerly Oxford, Bodleian Library Fell 1): HG 754.6.
List – Refs none.

The September 16 feast day and seventh-century legend of the widowed Roman matron, Lucia, and her companion martyr, the patrician convert Geminianus, were not apparently known in earlier Anglo-Saxon England, but the feast is widely represented, and occasionally graded, in Anglo-Saxon calendars of the tenth and eleventh centuries, while copies of the *passio* are included in the London and Salisbury manuscripts of the **COTTON-CORPUS LEGENDARY** (Zettel 1979 p 25). For further bibliography, see the article in *BSS*.

Lucianus Bellovacensis, passio [ANON.Pas.Lucian.]: *BHL* 5010; *BLS* 1.51–52; *BSS* 8.268–69.
  ed.: Moretus Plantin 1953 pp 74–82.
MSS 1. London, BL Cotton Nero E. i: HG 344.
  2. Salisbury, Cathedral Library 221 (formerly Oxford, Bodleian Library Fell 4): HG 754.5.
Lists ?Saewold: ML 8.23.
A-S Vers – Refs none.

A late and dubious legendary tradition describes Lucianus (hereafter Lucian) with his companions Maximianus and Julianus as early missionaries to Gaul in the third (or first) century, supposedly martyred at Beauvais, of which in later accounts Lucian is also said to have been bishop. Modern scholars have tended to regard the entire story as a literary invention. There are three basic versions of the legend: anonymous *passiones* of the eighth century (*BHL* 5008) and ninth (*BHL* 5010), and a later ninth-century life (*BHL* 5009) composed ca. 860–69 by Odo of Beauvais (Moretus Plantin 1953 p 30). The ninth-century texts derive from but also embellish and rework the eighth-century "passion primitive" in various ways: *BHL* 5010, for example, associates Lucian closely with **QUINTINUS**, whereas Odo's version underlines the saint's connections with **DIONISIUS** of Paris.

The text devoted to Lucian's feast in the eleventh-century London and Salisbury manuscripts of the **COTTON-CORPUS LEGENDARY** is identified by Zettel (1979 p 15) as *BHL* 5010, numbered Passio 3 by the

Bollandists but the second in order of composition, according to Moretus Plantin in his collective edition of all three texts, in which he does not use or refer to the English manuscripts. He briefly suggests some affiliations among the twenty-four manuscripts that he lists, all from French libraries (1953 pp 71–73). It has not yet been determined which version of the *passio* corresponds to that mentioned in the list of books donated in the mid-eleventh century by Bishop Saewold of Bath to Saint-Vaast, Arras (the *passio* mentioned in the booklist is misidentified in ML as *BHL* 5015: see ML p 62, note on item 23).

Lucian's January 8 feast does not seem to have been widely observed in Anglo-Saxon England (see the January 8 notice in the late-tenth-century calendar from Canterbury, F. Wormald 1934 p 58). For some Lucian relics at Exeter, see the Exeter List of Relics (*Rec* 10.8, B16.10.8; ed. Förster 1943 p 73; Conner 1993a p 180).

Lupus Trecensis, vita [ANON.Vit.Lup.]: *BHL* 5087; *BLS* 3.207–08; *BSS* 8.390–91; *CPL* 989.
    ed.: *MGH* SRM 7.295–302.

MSS – Lists none.
A-S Vers 1. BEDA.Mart. 138.6–11.
    2. *Mart* (B19.fa).
Quots/Cits Vita Lupi 302.2–3: BEDA.Hist.eccles. 64.20–21.
Refs none.

Lupus (Loup), bishop of Troyes (427–79, feast day July 29), was best known to the Anglo-Saxons through **BEDE**'s stories (adapted from the life of Germanus of Auxerre, **GERMANUS AUTISIODORENSIS**) in **HISTORIA ECCLESIASTICA** I.xvii–xx (BEDA.Hist.eccles.; ed. Colgrave and Mynors 1969 pp 54–64), where he describes the mission Germanus undertook against the Pelagian heresy in Britain, with Lupus as his companion. The question of Bede's knowledge of the *Vita Lupi* itself is part of the controversy over the work's date and authenticity. French scholars (and the Bollandists) believe it to be of the late fifth century (e.g., Griffe 1964–66 2.301–04), but Krusch, the work's modern editor, insisted at first (e.g., in his earlier edition, *MGH* SRM 3.119) that it was an early Carolingian forgery, postdating Bede. Later, after an eighth-century manuscript had come to light, Krusch was prepared to allow that Bede was indebted to the *Vita Lupi*, not vice versa, as demonstrated, among others, by Quentin (1908 p 81) with regard to Bede's **MARTYROLOGIUM** (BEDA.Mart.; ed. Dubois and Renaud 1976). Krusch still maintained, however, that "this noble piece of fiction" was "concocted" in the eighth century (*MGH* SRM 7.285, 289). Wallace-Hadrill, in his recent commentary on Bede's *Historia* (1988 p 29), apparently relies on Krusch's older opinions (*MGH* SRM 3.124 note 1) when he contradicts Colgrave and Mynors (1969 p 64 note 1) regarding Bede's dependence on the *Vita Lupi* for his information about Lupus's disciple, Severus (*MGH* SRM 7.302 note 1). Another study, in favor of the historical reliability of the *vita*, is that of Ewig (1978). For additional bibliography, see Wood (1984).

Among other Anglo-Saxons, only the author of the **OLD ENGLISH MARTYROLOGY** (*Mart*; Kotzor 1981 2.162–63) shows knowledge of the *vita*. The **OLD ENGLISH BEDE** (*Bede*, B9.6; ed. *EETS* OS 95.54) completely omits the chapters dealing with Lupus and Germanus. Cross (1982d pp 25–26) corrects Herzfeld's erroneous sourcing (*EETS* OS 116.xl) of the curiously selective *Martyrology* notice to show that it draws independently on the *vita* (not on Bede's *Historia*) and may borrow a detail from Bede's *Martyrologium*.

Krusch's edition of the *Vita Lupi*, cited above, supersedes his earlier one in *MGH* SRM 3.120–24.

Macarius Aegyptius: *BHL* 5093; *BSS* 8.425–29.

Macarius of Egypt (feast day January 15), also known as Macarius the Elder or the Great, was one of the pioneers of the eremitic life in the Egyptian desert, where he lived (at Skete) for sixty years, dying at the age of ninety. His life and miracles were known in the West in several of the works that make up the **VITAE PATRUM**, including **RUFINUS**'s **HISTORIA MONACHORUM** XXVIII (for further references, see the entry on **AMOS NITRIAE**).

ÆLFRIC twice uses, as an exemplum, one of Macarius's miracles from Rufinus's *Historia* (XXVIII.30–57; ed. Schulz-Flügel 1990) in which the saint detects a devilish delusion whereby a young woman was perceived, erroneously, to have been changed into a mare: see Ælfric's *Swithun* 471–93, in LIVES OF SAINTS (*ÆLS*, B1.3.22; ed. *EETS* OS 76 and 82); see also the revised ending found in two manuscripts of his treatise *On Auguries*, lines 10–34 of Pope's edition, *Homilies of Ælfric* 29 (see OTHER HOMILIES), where the Latin is reprinted (*ÆHom*, B1.4.30; ed. *EETS* OS 260.790–92; see also Pope's discussion, pp 786–88; for the original text of *Auguries*, see *Lives of Saints*, ed. *EETS* OS 76 and 82; see also Meany 1985). Ælfric also alludes to Macarius as one of the desert fathers in his treatise on virginity, the LETTER TO SIGEFYRTH 216 (*ÆLet* 5, B1.8.5; ed. *BaP* 3.23). The saint is also included in numerous Anglo-Saxon litanies (see Lapidge's index, *HBS* 106.313).

Machabei: *BSS* 8.434–37. See also **BIBLE**.

In the later Anglo-Saxon church, there is ample calendar evidence for English veneration of the seven Hebrew brothers and their mother who were martyred by the Greek tyrant Antiochus (probably at Antioch) in 168 B.C. (2 Macc. 7) and whose cult as saints was the only one celebrated by both Jews and Christians (Schatkin 1974; *DACL* 1.2375–79 and 10.724–27). In one graded calendar of the late tenth century, associated with Canterbury, the August 1 feast day is of the second rank (F. Wormald 1934 p 51) and is widely represented in others, although the feast of Saint Peter "in Chains," on the same day, tends to assume greater importance later in the eleventh century. Nevertheless, there do not seem to be any surviving Anglo-Saxon copies of any of the various *passiones* (*BHL* 5106–11) that were based on the scriptural account. A fragmentary portion of the scriptural text of Maccabees (1 Macc. 6.59–7.2), written in Italy in the sixth century, and doubtless brought to England with the Italian missionaries, survives in Durham B. IV (HG 245). See Lowe (*CLA* 2.153, also 1960 p 7 and plate IIb).

The notice in the **OLD ENGLISH MARTYROLOGY** (*Mart*, B19.fd; ed. Kotzor 1981 2.165–66), recounting the martyrdoms, with the resulting punishment of Antiochus, is based on 2 Macc. 7.1–41 and 9.5–12 (Cook 1903 p 17). **ÆLFRIC**, to provide a lengthy reading for the August 1 feast, paraphrases 1–2 Macc. in his *Maccabees* in **LIVES OF SAINTS** (*ÆLS*, B1.3.25; ed. *EETS* OS 94 and 114). He mainly focuses on the military adventures of Judas Machabeus and his brothers, but includes also (as the first of the eleven sections of the reading, lines 1–204) the separate story of the martyrdom of the anonymous seven and their mother, preceded by that of the scribe Eleazar. Ælfric's scriptural sources, which he appears to have adapted independently, are listed by Skeat in the *EETS* edition at the head of each section; see also Cook (1903 pp 202–03). See also Ælfric's brief characterization of the book of Maccabees, at the end of his **LETTER TO SIGEWEARD** 781–838 (*ÆLet* 4, B1.8.4; ed. *EETS* OS 160). Among recent work on Ælfric's version, see Wilcox (1994) and Lee (1995).

Machutus, vita [BILI.Vit.Machut.1a]: *BHL* 5116a; *BLS* 4.49–50; *BSS* 8.461–64; *DACL* 10.1293–318; Lapidge and Sharpe (1985) p 825.
  ed.: Lot 1907 pp 331–430 (variants only).
MSS London, BL Royal 13. A. x: HG 482.
Lists – Refs none.

Machutus (Machutis, Machu, Malo, Maclou; feast day November 15) was a Breton saint of uncertain, and possibly mixed, origins, but according to his legend he was born in Gwent in South Wales, educated as a monk under Saint Brendan at Llancarfan, and after accompanying his master on his famous voyages, migrated to the north Breton coast to live as a hermit, preacher, founder of monasteries, and also bishop of Alet (now Saint-Malo) in the late sixth or early seventh century. His cult is also associated with Saintes (Saintonges) in Aquitaine, where he is supposed to have retreated after a rupture with his flock in Brittany. Of the various extant *vitae*, the two oldest, which apparently drew on a lost common source, are believed to be the anonymous ninth-century *vita*, *BHL* 5117 (not 5118 as has been widely asserted: see Poulin 1990 pp 164–68), and *BHL* 5116a–b, versions of a life written by Bili, a deacon of Alet, for Bishop Ratuili between 866 and 872 (Yerkes 1984 p xxvi). There is no evidence that the anonymous lives of Malo were known in England, but the two best surviving manuscript copies of Bili's work are of English provenance. During the reign of King Athelstan (924–39), Breton immigrants fleeing Viking inroads brought Malo's cult to southern England, where it flourished especially, it seems, in Winchester (for discussion and bibliography, see Yerkes 1984 pp xxxix–xli and most recently C. Brett 1991 pp 45–48; see also **IUDOCUS**). The tenth-century copy of the *Vita Machuti* listed here (provenance unknown, but probably Winchester, according to Dumville 1992 p 110) is a greatly abridged version of Bili's work, of which the full list of the chapter headings of Book I (the *vita* proper) is preserved in the same manuscript (Yerkes 1984 pp xlv–xlvi). In addition to some elaborate prefatory material by Bili and a sermon, the manuscript also includes a hymn containing some narrative material from the saint's legend. The Latin sermon for Malo's feast day, also in BL Royal 13. A. x, is drawn from **ALCUIN**'s sermon on **VEDASTUS**, *BHL* 8509 (R. Brown and Yerkes 1981), and various other Carolingian texts: see Dolbeau (1983b). For a longer recension of the *Vita Machuti*, see the next entry.

Machutus, vita [BILI.Vit.Machut.1b]: *BHL* 5116b.
    ed.: Lot 1907 pp 331–430.
MSS   Oxford, Bodleian Library Bodley 535 (*SC* 2254): HG 582.
Lists   none.
A-S Vers   LS 13 (Machutus, B3.3.13).
Quots/Cits – Refs   see below.

Another recension of Bili's *Vita Machuti* survives in a twelfth-century copy bound up with late-eleventh-century material in the Bodley manuscript listed here (see **DIONISIUS**, and Lapidge 1987; also Yerkes 1984 pp xxxiii–xxxvi). This copy is considerably longer than the Royal manuscript (see previous entry) and appears to represent something closer to the complete work: hence the Bollandists' separate number (*BHL* 5116b).

This version was in existence at least as early as the tenth century, since something like it appears to have been the source of the Old English prose *Machutus* (*LS* 13; ed. Yerkes 1984), preserved only in a badly burned early-eleventh-century manuscript (London, BL Cotton Otho A. viii: HG 348). The Bodley manuscript version, while it is not exactly what Bili wrote, or what the Old English writer had in front of him, nonetheless "corresponds closely" to the vernacular text. Yerkes in his edition of the Old English text, of which approximately two-thirds survive in the Cotton manuscript, prints on facing pages that portion of the Bodley Latin text that corresponds to the surviving Old English life, with variants from the Royal manuscript (which is occasionally closer than Bodley to the Old English: Yerkes 1984 p xxxv). Yerkes posits Winchester as the place of composition of the Old English life (1984 p xlii), during the tenth or earlier eleventh century, but points finally to Worcester as the provenance of the Cotton manuscript itself (1986 p 111).

Hereford, Cathedral Library P.VII.6, a twelfth-century manuscript that may have textual links to pre-Conquest English traditions (see Zettel 1979 pp 38–39; 1982 p 20), contains a *Vita Machuti* that, as Poulin (1990 pp 171–72) guessed, seems to be an abridgement of Bili's work, although it is mistakenly identified as *BHL* 5118 in the recent Hereford library catalogue (Mynors and Thomson 1993 p 110). It corresponds closely to much of *BHL* 5116b, especially the earlier chapters (I am grateful to Michael Lapidge for access to a microfilm of the manuscript), and represents the sort of text on which John of Tynemouth (early fourteenth century) may have based his more drastic abridgement (*BHL* 5122).

Yerkes's pioneer edition of the Old English *Machutus* is a formidable achievement and his facing transcription of the Bodley Latin text (1984 pp 2–100) is convenient for comparison with the Old English, but it lacks several chapters of Bili's Book I and all of Book II, making it necessary to consult the more complete editions of the Latin text by Lot (cited above) and Le Duc (1979 pp 2–256), which is useful for its French translation. Le Duc's parallel edition of the Old English text, however, is not reliable. For critiques, see Dolbeau (1983a) on the Latin and Rowland Collins (1981) on the Old English.

For bibliography, besides Yerkes's edition, see Lapidge and Sharpe (1985 pp 226, 254–55), and for the most recent summary discussion of Machutus's cult and hagiographic dossier, see Julia Smith (1990 pp 331–34), and especially Poulin (1990), although the fullest discussion, that of Lot (1907 pp 97–206), if no longer authoritative, is still valuable. On the numerous literary sources of Bili's Book I, which prompted Dolbeau (1983a p 196) to characterize the author as "un vulgaire centonisateur," see the references assembled by Julia Smith (1990 p 333 note 103) and Poulin (1990 pp 174–75). For some analysis of the Old English translator's treatment of the source, see Whatley (1997 pp 198–207). I am grateful to Christine Rauer for her advice on this entry.

Malchus, vita [HIERON.Vit.Malch.]: *BHL* 5190; *BHM* 263; *BSS* 8.585–87; *CPL* 619.

    ed.: Mierow 1946.

MSS – Lists none.

A-S Vers 1. ALDH.Pros.uirg. 270.4–18.

    2. *LS* 35 (VitPatr, B3.3.35) 124–424.

    3. *ÆHomM* 15 (Ass 9 [Judith], B1.5.15) 445–51.

Quots/Cits none.

Refs ALCVIN.Epist. 341.37.

Malchus (feast day October 21) was a fourth-century Syrian monk who yearned for the world, deserted his cloister, was captured by slave-merchants and forcibly married to a beautiful fellow slave, but managed to preserve his own virginity and the chastity of his "wife," who had been married before. His diverting adventures would doubtless have been widely read in medieval monasteries even if described by someone less illustrious and authoritative than **JEROME**. The latter's prestige guaranteed the legend's prominence in early medieval collections, although modern scholars are less impressed. Over 350 manuscripts are listed by Lambert in *BHM*. On their classification, see Jameson (in Oldfather 1943 pp 449–511) and Mierow (1945, 1946). No Anglo-Saxon copies have survived, but there is varied evidence that the work was known in

England from the earliest times. Summaries were written by **ALDHELM** in his DE VIRGINITATE (ALDH.Pros.uirg.; ed. *MGH* AA 15) and by **ÆLFRIC**, who ended his homiletic paraphrase of the book of Judith (see Clayton 1994) with the story of Malchus, as a further example of chastity. Unfortunately this final part of the homily, after line 445, is mutilated and the Malchus story lost (*ÆHomM* 15; ed. *BaP* 3.115–16), only the last six lines being extant in a seventeenth-century transcription of the *explicit* of the only other copy, burnt in the Cotton fire (see Assmann, *BaP* 3.258–59; and NRK 178, item 1).

ALCUIN in one of his letters (cited in the headnote) refers to the *vita* and echoes a phrase, "raro diabolus aperta fronte" (ALCVIN.Epist.; ed. *MGH* ECA 2.341.40–41; cf. *Vita Malchi* 64: "Numquam diabolum aperta fronte"), using Malchus's experience as a warning to monks to resist wandering away from the cloister, even for apparently virtuous motives.

An Old English translation, the anonymous prose *Malchus* (*LS* 15; ed. *BaP* 3.199–207), preserved in an eleventh-century Worcester manuscript, was unskillfully composed in the tenth century (dated by Sisam 1953 pp 209–11; see Jackson 1992). There is no separate listing for the Old English *Malchus* in AC, where the text's separate identity is obscured under the collective rubric of *Vitas Patrum* (B3.3.35), comprising *Malchus* and an Old English translation of two anecdotes from the **VERBA SENIORUM** (**VITAE PATRUM**), copied in the same manuscript as *Malchus* but in a different hand. The manuscript, texts, and their sources are discussed by Jackson (1992). Despite the familiarity of his legend, the saint's feast day is not remembered in Anglo-Saxon calendars, although that of **HILARION**, on the same day, whose life was also composed by Jerome, is widely recorded. The **OLD ENGLISH MARTYROLOGY**, suprisingly, has no notice for Malchus.

We have no information concerning textual affiliations between the Old English texts based on the *Vita Malchi* and the manuscript traditions analyzed by Jameson (in Oldfather 1943) and Mierow (1945). The most recent scholarly edition is that of Mierow, cited above, but more accessible is *PL* 23.53–60. Paul B. Harvey Jr., of Pennsylvania State University, has announced a new edition in progress. Among modern studies of the *Vita Malchi* as hagiographical literature, see Berschin

(1986–91 1.140–43) and Coleiro (1957). See also De Vogüé (1991–93 1.78–101) and Bastiaensen (1994–), the latter with extensive bibliography on Jerome's hagiographies in general.

Mamas, passio [ANON.Pas.Mamm.]: *BHL* 5194; *BLS* 3.339–40; *BSS* 8.592–612.
ed.: Mombritius 1910 2.126–29 and 681–82.
MSS – Lists none.
A-S Vers Mart (B19.fw).
Quots/Cits – Refs none.

Mamas (Mammes; feast day August 17) was apparently a shepherd of Cappadocia, martyred for his faith under Aurelian. He is eulogized in a homily by **BASIL** (Delehaye 1966 pp 140 and 144–45). His legend, marked by its interest in friendly animals, was popular in the West, to judge from the number of variant early Latin versions of the originally Greek legend (*BHG* 1018: Siegmund 1949 pp 238–39), which are extant in manuscripts of the eighth century and later. Queen Radegund, founder of Holy Cross, Poitiers, is said to have acquired a finger of Mamas in the late sixth century. See Baudonivia's *Vita Sanctae Radegundis* (ed. *MGH SRM* 2.386–87).

Cross (1986a pp 238–40) discusses the only substantial English record of Mamas (Old English *Mommos*), the notice in the **OLD ENGLISH MARTYROLOGY** (*Mart*; ed.Kotzor 1981 2.182–83), the Latin source of which appears to have been a text similar to that printed by Mombritius, the Bollandists' Passio 1b. As so often, Cross is able to show that an early manuscript is evidently much closer to the *Martyrology's* source than Mombritius's exemplar. Other early manuscripts are cited by Siegmund (1949 p 239), and by Bernt (1971 pp 144–45) in his study of the sources of **WALAHFRID**'s metrical version (*BHL* 5197) of the *passio*.

The text classified as Passio 1a by the Bollandists (ed. Delehaye 1940) is extant in the tenth-century Bobbio manuscript Turin, Biblioteca Nazionale F.III.16, which Carmela Franklin believes to have strong connections with early Anglo-Saxon England (see ANASTASIUS). It apparently represents a different recension (*BHL* 5191d) from that known to the Old English martyrologist.

Mamilianus.

The hermit monk Mamilianus, one of whose adventures is told at some length in the ninth-century **OLD ENGLISH MARTYROLOGY** for the feast day September 15 (*Mart*, B19.hb; ed. Kotzor 1981 2.208–10), is otherwise unknown. Kotzor (p 352) remarks that Mamilianus of Palermo also has the feast day September 15 but that there is no other link between the *Martyrology* notice and the fifth-century Sicilian bishop (*BHL* 5204d). Herzfeld (*EETS* OS 116.236) points out that stories containing the motif of the talking infant, such as that in the *Martyrology* (p 209.4–14), are told in the acts of Simon and Jude (**APOCRYPHA, PASSIO SIMONIS ET JUDAE**) and also in the eleventh-century life of **ALDHELM**. But Kotzor (1981 2.352), citing Canart (1966), finds the closest analogue to the *Martyrology* anecdote in the life of the hermit Goar (*BHL* 3565–68: ed. *MGH* SRM 4.417–19). Cross (1985b p 248), however, posits a lost life of a Mamilianus as yet unidentified. Whatever its source, the story as told in *Martyrology* appears to celebrate hospitable monks at the expense of hypocritical bishops.

Marcellinus et Petrus, passio [ANON.Pas.Marcellin.Petr.]: *BHL* 5231; *BLS* 2.452–53; *BSS* 8.757–58; *CPL* 2206.
 ed.: *AS* Iun. 1.171–73.
MSS 1. London, BL Cotton Nero E. i: HG 344.
 2. Salisbury, Cathedral Library 221 (formerly Oxford, Bodleian Library Fell 4): HG 754.5.
Lists none.
A-S Vers 1. BEDA.Mart. 100.2–8.
 2. *Mart* (B19.dh and di).
Quots/Cits – Refs none.

The cult of the Roman martyrs Marcellinus the priest and Peter the exorcist (feast day June 2) was known in England throughout the Anglo-Saxon period. On the Continent, it is attested as early as a fourth-century epitaph by Pope **DAMASUS**, the emperor Constantine having built a church over the saints' tomb, in which he buried his mother **HELENA**. The anonymous *passio* of this entry is dated late fifth to early sixth century by Lanzoni (1923 p 83). The saints' reputation is indicated by the inclusion of their names in the Canon of the Mass (Kennedy 1938 pp 158–61); in northern Europe their cult was further enhanced when their relics were translated to Germany in 827, as related by **EINHARD** (*BHL* 5233, translated Wendell 1926). The verse *passio* (*BHL* 5232) attributed to Einhard is an important witness to the textual tradition of the earlier prose *passio*, as demonstrated by Cross (1982a p 103) in his discussion of the inferior readings of the printed editions.

Quentin (1908 p 82) links the notice in **BEDE**'s **MARTYROLOGIUM** (BEDA.Mart.; ed. Dubois and Renaud 1976) to this *passio,* but what recension Bede had is uncertain. He does not mention Artemius, the converted jailor, by name, but he devotes half his notice to the converted executioner, Dorotheus, who is also prominent in the Damasus epitaph (Ferrua 1942 pp 160–63).

The ninth-century **OLD ENGLISH MARTYROLOGY** (*Mart*; ed. Kotzor 1981 2.114–16) has notices (both June 2) for Marcellinus and Petrus, and for Artemius and his family (see *BSS* 2.490), whose story is told early in the *passio*. Both the *Martyrology* notices are independent of Bede and the wording of the notice for Artemius in particular suggests that it is based on a text of the *passio* somewhat different from and "more sensible" than that printed by Mombritius and *AS*. It must have been also closer to, if not identical with, a text represented in some of the earlier manuscripts (Cross 1982a p 104). The name of Artemius's daughter should apparently be "Virgo" as in the early manuscripts and the *Martyrology*, not "Paulina" as in the printed texts and *BHL* (see also Cross 1986b pp 287–88). Cross also points out (1982a pp 105–06) that among martyrologies only the *Old English Martyrology* and **ADO** (*PL* 123.281–82) provide a separate feast day for Artemius, although in Ado it is June 6, not June 2 as in the English work.

The text preserved in the eleventh-century London and Salisbury manuscripts of the **COTTON-CORPUS LEGENDARY** appears to represent an inferior textual tradition. The London manuscript (pt 2, fol 17r–v), for example, follows the printed editions in omitting or corrupting passages analyzed by Cross.

In addition to the *AS* edition, cited above, see also that of Mombritius (1910 2.179–81 and 689–90).

Marcellus Cabillonensis, passio [ANON.Pas.Marcel.Cab.]: *BHL* 5245; *BLS* 3.483–84; *BSS* 8.663.
ed.: *AS* Sept. 2.196–97.

MSS – Lists none.
A-S Vers Mart (B19.gr).
Quots/Cits – Refs none.

According to his legend, which historians consider to be largely fiction, Marcellus of Chalons (feast day September 4) suffered under the same persecutor as **VALERIANUS TRENORCHII**, his relative and companion, in the reign of the emperor Antoninus. Of the two surviving versions of his legend listed by the Bollandists, Passio 1, at issue here, seems to be the earlier, since it echoes **GREGORY OF TOURS, DE GLORIA MARTYRUM** LII–LIII (*MGH* SRM 1/2.525), in regarding Marcellus simply as a martyr, whereas the second *passio* (*BHL* 5246) entitles him "bishop" and was apparently composed after the promotion of the idea that Memmius, putative first bishop of Chalons, was a first-century "apostle" rather than a third-century missionary. On the origins of Christianity in Chalons, see *DHGE* 12.313–14.

Marcellus is notable for the unusual manner of his martyrdom, being buried alive up to his waist (like **VITALIS**), and this story was known to the ninth-century author of the **OLD ENGLISH MARTYROLOGY** (*Mart*; ed. Kotzor 1981 2.198–99). Kotzor (p 346) does not specify which of the two versions of Marcellus's *passio* was the *Martyrology*'s source (*BHL* 5245 or 5246). Herzfeld (*EETS* OS 116.xli) points to *BHL* 5245.

The brief Old English account, for example, styles the saint as martyr only, not as bishop. On the historicity or otherwise of Marcellus, see Griffe (1964–66 1.143, 160).

Marcellus papa, passio [ANON.Pas.Marcel.pap.]: *BHL* 5235; *BLS* 1.100; *BSS* 8.671–76. See also **SATURNINUS ET SISINNIUS**.
   ed.: Mombritius 1910 2.169–73.
MSS 1. London, BL Cotton Nero E. i: HG 344.
   2. Salisbury, Cathedral Library 221 (formerly Oxford, Bodleian Library Fell 4): HG 754.5.
Lists none.
A-S Vers BEDA.Mart. 14.2–14; see below.
Quots/Cits none.
Refs BEDA.Mart. 26.13; see below.

According to his fourth-century epitaph, attributed to Pope **DAMASUS**, Marcellus was not martyred. His brief pontificate in 308 ended when he was banished by the emperor Maxentius, and he died in exile in 309. By the mid-sixth century, however, in the second edition of the **LIBER PONTIFICALIS** (ca. 540), Marcellus's death is said to be brought about by a period of forced labor as a groom, his church having been converted into a stable by Maxentius (Duchesne 1955 1.164). In Duchesne's opinion, the papal biographer adapted this account from the elaborate *passio*, comprising a lengthy narrative cycle recounting the imprisonments, trials, and martyrdoms of several pairs and groups of characters, who had their own cults and feast days. These include two Roman soldiers, Papias and Maurus (January 29), and several deacons, including Cyriacus, Largus, and Smaragdus (March 16), Crescentianus (November 24), and Saturninus et Sisinnius (November 29). The whole cycle was known to **BEDE**, who refers to it by name as the *Gesta Marcelli papae* several times in his **MARTYROLOGIUM** (BEDA.Mart.; ed. Dubois and Renaud 1976, sourced by Quentin 1908 pp 82–85), where the account of Marcellus and his companions is divided up among several notices, of which the Marcellus notice is cited here in the headnote (*A-S Vers*). The reference to the *Gesta* (see above, *Refs*) is from the notice for the Roman soldiers Papias and Maurus, January 29 (*Martyrologium* 26.2–13). Similar reference is also made in the notices for the deacons Cyriacus, Largus, and Smaragdus, March 16 (50.2–22 at 21), and Crescentianus, November 24 (213.10–19 at 18–19), as well as in the notice for the remaining deacons Saturninus et Sisinnius, November 29 (216.18), whose story, which was sometimes extracted from the *Gesta* to form a separate *passio* (*BHL* 7493), is the subject of a separate entry below. Cyriacus, Largus, and Smaragdus (see *BLS* 3.280) also have a separate *passio* (see *BHL* 2056), but not in surviving Anglo-Saxon manuscripts.

The whole *Gesta Marcelli* is represented in the London and Salisbury manuscripts of the **COTTON-CORPUS LEGENDARY**. While Zettel (1979 p 16) identifies these copies as Mombritius's version, Jackson and Lapidge (1996 p 135) imply it is a hybrid of *BHL* 5234 and 5235.

According to Cross (1979 p 191) the notice for Marcellus in the **OLD ENGLISH MARTYROLOGY** (*Mart*, B19.z; ed. Kotzor 1981 2.16), which ignores the cast of characters above, is based on the *Liber Pontificalis*, not on Bede's *Martyrologium* or the *passio*.

In addition to Mombritius's edition of the *Passio Marcelli*, see also *AS* Ian. 2.5–9. For a summary of scholarly views on the historical Marcellus, see Kelly (1986 pp 25–26).

Marcellus Tingi, passio [ANON.Pas.Marcel.Ting.]: *BHL* 5253; *BLS* 4.220–21; *BSS* 8.665–68; *CPL* 2053; *DACL* 11.1138–39.
ed.: Delehaye 1923a pp 260–63.

MSS 1. London, BL Cotton Nero E. i: HG 344.
2. Salisbury, Cathedral Library 221 (formerly Oxford, Bodleian Library Fell 4): HG 754.5.
Lists – Refs none.

According to his legend, Marcellus the Centurion (feast day October 30) was condemned to death (at Tangiers, N. Africa, ca. 298) for openly repudiating the gods of Rome and his military service in the imperial army. Later medieval elaborations of his story in Spain transformed him into a married citizen of Leon with twelve children (De Gaiffier 1943), but some modern scholars regard the core of the older legend historically valuable (Saxer 1979 pp 127–30).

Delehaye (1923a), who considers the surviving texts of the *passio* to be based on a lost contemporary account of the martyrdom, distinguishes two recensions of the *passio*. The N recension (*BHL* 5254y–5255a) is mainly that of the texts from Spain, which he considers further removed from the lost original than the larger M group (*BHL* 5253–54). Of the M group of manuscripts, a small subgroup (M1, *BHL* 5254) seems to represent fairly closely the lost original, while the majority (M2, *BHL* 5253) have an interpolated introductory chapter. The two English manuscripts are among the oldest copies of M2 listed and collated by Delehaye (1923a) for his edition. He does not indicate at what time the M2 recension was composed. No other evidence of Anglo-Saxon knowledge of Marcellus of Tangiers has been found.

Delehaye's edition combines readings from his M1 and M2 groups. De Gaiffier (1943 pp 118–20) prints the oldest copy of Delehaye's M1 recension, from a tenth-century Paris manuscript. Musurillo's edition (1972 pp 250–54) is a corrected version of Delehaye's (see also pp xxxviii–xxxix). For the numerous other modern editions, see *BHL NS* (pp 568–69).

Marcus et Marcellinus. See SEBASTIANUS.

Marcus evangelista, passio. See **APOCRYPHA, PASSIO MARCI.**

Margareta, passio [ANON.Pas.Marg./PS.THEOTIMUS]: *BHL* 5303; *BLS* 3.152–53; *BSS* 8.1150–60.
 ed.: Clayton and Magennis 1994 pp 194–218.
MSS 1. Paris, Bibliothèque Nationale lat. 5574: HG 885.5.
 2. ?Saint-Omer, Bibliothèque Municipale 202.
Lists none.

A-S Vers 1. ?*Mart* (B19.ei).
2. *LS* 14 (Margaret I, B3.3.14).
3. ?*LS* 15 (MargaretKer, B3.3.15: *incipit* and *explicit* only).
4. ?*LS* 16 (Margaret II, B3.3.16).
Quots/Cits – Refs none.

The virgin martyr known as Margareta to the later Anglo-Saxons (frequently but not always with the feast day July 20) was known in England earlier by her Greek name of Marina, which also appears (June 18) in the martyrology of **HRABANUS MAURUS** (ed. *CCCM* 44.59, IVN. 202–08; see also IVL. 120–27, his similar entry for "Margareta," pp 67–68). On the occurrence of these and other feast days, and apparent confusion regarding the identity of Margaret/Marina, in Anglo-Saxon England, see the survey of her cult by Clayton and Magennis (1994 pp 72–83). The transmission and interrelationship of early medieval versions of the *Passio Margaretae* still remain to be studied in detail. Examination of Latin versions has so far revealed the existence of several independent translations from closely interrelated Greek versions. See Francis (1927 pp 94–95), and Siegmund (1949 p 240) who regards all the Latin versions as ultimately dependent on a common source, to which *BHG* 1165 (ed. Usener 1886), while not itself the source, is an important witness. The most widely found Latin version is Passio 1, by Pseudo-Theotimus, *BHL* 5303, the earliest texts of which date from the ninth century (Siegmund 1949 p 240). See Clayton and Magennis for the most recent survey of the various Latin versions (1994 pp 7–23).

Among early copies of *BHL* 5303, of English provenance, is the Paris manuscript, BN lat. 5574 (early tenth century), possibly of Mercian origin (Avril and Stirnemann 1987 p 11; Clayton and Magennis 1994 pp 95–96), printed with facing translation by Clayton and Magennis (1994 pp 194–219; commentary pp 220–23). The copy of *BHL* 5303 in London, BL Cotton Nero E. i (HG 344) is a later addition and was not part of the **COTTON-CORPUS LEGENDARY** believed to be in use in England during the tenth and eleventh centuries. Saint-Omer 202, written at Saint-Bertin in the ninth century, which also includes a copy of *BHL* 5303 (Lechat 1929 p 244), was in England at some point during the second half of the eleventh century, before 1072, the end of the episcopacy of Bishop Leofric of Exeter (see Cross 1996 p 19; see also Clayton and Magennis 1994 pp 41 and 192).

Four Old English versions of Margaret's story are known to have been composed. One of these, *LS* 15, is no longer extant (see below). The remaining versions are of considerable interest, not only for their own sakes, but also for the information they give concerning the transmission of *BHL* 5303. Despite their general similarity to *BHL* 5303, no known Latin manuscript represents the exact source of any of them. The earliest, a vigorous summary notice in the ninth-century **OLD ENGLISH MARTYROLOGY** (*Mart*; ed. Kotzor 1981 2.141–44), is notable for the use of the old Greek name Marina (as also in the Monte Cassino manuscript, *BHL* 5304, ed. Clayton and Magennis 1994 pp 224–34), the omission of the dragon-devil episode during the saint's imprisonment, and a number of other significant disagreements with the "standard" texts of *BHL* 5303, as represented in, for example, BN lat. 5574 and the editions by Mombritius (1910 2.190–96), Assmann (*BaP* 3.208–20), and others. Research by Magennis and Cross indicates that the martyrologist used a highly distinctive form of the Latin, apparently no longer extant, whose distinguishing features are not represented elsewhere in the *BHL* 5303 tradition but are shared in several instances with the Old English prose life in *LS* 16 (Margaret II, preserved in the mid-eleventh-century manuscript, Cotton Tiberius A. iii, NRK 186). The presence of some of these features in the Greek tradition also (and occasionally in *BHL* 5304) attests to the antiquity of the lost version. See Cross's sourcing of the *Old English Martyrology* in relation to the Latin texts and *LS* 16 (Cross 2000); Clayton and Magennis (1994 pp 53–56) summarize and corroborate Cross's findings, supplying additional evidence, from the Greek tradition and *BHL* 5304. For further discussion of *LS* 16, see Clayton and Magennis (1994 pp 56–61), who provide a "composite" edition of the Old English text, incorporating later scribal corrections (with facing translation, pp 112–39, and detailed commentary, pp 140–48), and a semi-diplomatic edition of the original text (pp 181–90). For earlier editions, see Cockayne (1861 pp 39–49) and Herbst (1976).

A second Old English prose version, *LS* 15 (MargaretKer), formerly in BL Cotton Otho B. x (NRK 177), from the first half of the eleventh century, was destroyed in the Cotton fire of 1731 and is known only from the *incipit* and *explicit* transcribed by Wanley (see NRK p 228). The *incipit* is a literal translation of the beginning of *BHL* 5303, but the *explicit* does not correspond to the Latin.

LS 14 (Margaret I), the late Old English prose life of Margaret preserved in Cambridge, Corpus Christi College 303 (NRK 57), from the first half of the twelfth century, is adapted from a source that did not share the distinctive features reflected in the *Old English Martyrology* and *LS* 16 and was apparently closer to the "standard" Latin texts. Nonetheless, *LS* 14 also shows significant disagreements with the latter. See Clayton and Magennis for discussion (1994 pp 61–71), edition with translation (pp 152–71), and commentary (172–80). The text was previously edited by Assmann (*BaP* 3.170–80).

A critical edition of the *passio* is lacking. For the numerous texts printed from individual manuscripts or small groups, see *BHL* 5303 in *BHL NS*. The text printed by Clayton and Magennis is based on two Anglo-Saxon manuscripts: Paris BN lat. 5574, collated with the editions of Assmann (*BaP* 3, from BL Harley 5327) and Mombritius (1910 2.190–96), and supplemented where imperfect with Saint-Omer 202. For recent studies of different aspects of the legend in early England, see Price (1985).

Hugh Magennis

Maria Aegyptiaca, vita [PAUL.DIAC.NEAP.Vit.Maria.Aeg.]: *BHL* 5415; *BLS* 2.14–16; *BSS* 8.981–91.

ed.: Jane Stevenson 1996b pp 51–79.

MSS 1. London, BL Cotton Claudius A. i: HG 312.
2. London, BL Cotton Nero E. i: HG 344.
3. Salisbury, Cathedral Library 221 (formerly Oxford, Bodleian Library Fell 4): HG 754.5.

Lists none.
A-S Vers LS 23 (MaryofEgypt, B3.3.23).
Quots/Cits – Refs none.

This text, which was translated from the Greek (attributed to Sophronius of Jerusalem, *BHG* 1042) by Paulus Diaconus "Neapolitanus" in the ninth century (Siegmund 1949 p 269; Kunze 1969 pp 26–28), was known in England in the late Anglo-Saxon period, although it is uncertain when it was first introduced (Mary of Egypt's April 10 feast day appears in some Anglo-Saxon calendars of the late ninth and tenth centuries; e.g., F. Wormald 1934 pp 5, 19, 47). Of the manuscripts listed above, Cotton Claudius A. i has been dated mid-tenth century, but was written on the Continent. The other two manuscripts (from Worcester and Salisbury) are copies of the **COTTON-CORPUS LEGENDARY**, a version of which is thought to have been in England by the late tenth century, if not earlier, although the earliest extant copies are of the mid-eleventh.

The Old English prose life of Mary of Egypt (*LS* 23; ed. *EETS* OS 94 and 114) is a fairly literal translation of Paul's Latin life (*BHL* 4515). Comparative study of the Old English and Latin versions reveals that the Old English translator must have worked from a text very like that in the Cotton-Corpus Legendary, which is also close to Cotton Claudius A. i. *LS* 23 shares with these Latin manuscripts many features that contrast with what we find in the printed editions (see Magennis 1985a pp 294–97). Chase (1986) argues that despite its close dependence on a Latin source *LS* 23 is nonetheless a distinctive literary document, controlled, like other versions of the life, by the presuppositions of the age in which it was written.

The Old English translation is preserved complete in London, BL Cotton Julius E. vii (NRK 162), containing **ÆLFRIC**'s **LIVES OF SAINTS**, and there are also fragments in two other manuscripts of the first half of the eleventh century (NRK 117A and 177). Although not written by Ælfric himself (see Magennis 1986 pp 332–36), *LS* 23 has generally been regarded as coming from the same period. Elements of its vocabulary, however, have been seen as suggesting an Anglian original (Wenisch 1979 pp 56, 257–58, 291, and passim).

For further bibliography on the Neapolitan context, see Mary Clayton's entry on THEOPHILUS.

Hugh Magennis

[*Addendum*: Jane Stevenson's new edition, which includes a translation of the Latin text (1996b pp 80–98), is based on the three English manuscripts listed here, with selected variants from the standard edition of Rosweyde (1615 pp 381–92, reprinted PL 73.671–90). Stevenson (1996a p 45) generally confirms Magennis's view of the textual similarities between the Cotton-Corpus Legendary copies and Cotton Claudius A. i. She provides a gendered analysis of the original Greek legend's literary sources and cultural context, and the pre- and post-Conquest English reception of the Latin version. For a literary study of the Old English version in its Ælfrician manuscript context, see Magennis (1996b). —E. Gordon Whatley]

Maria Magdalena, vita [ANON.Vit.Maria.Magd.]: *BHL* 5453; *BLS* 3.161–63; *BSS* 8.1078–104; *DACL* 8.2038–96.
ed.: Cross 1978 pp 21–22.

MSS – Lists none.
A-S Vers Mart (B19.ev).
Quots/Cits – Refs none.

The Mary Magdalen of medieval hagiography (feast day July 22) is a conflation of several women named Mary (and one unnamed) whom Jesus encounters in the gospels, only two of whom are said to have been sinners (Luke 7.37–50 and 8.2), and only one is "Maria quae vocatur Magdalene." The growth of her legend is one of the more complicated stories in medieval hagiography as her cult shifted from Ephesus, where she was supposed to have traveled with John the Evangelist and the Virgin Mary, to Provence, where she was later believed to have gone as a missionary with her brother and sister, Lazarus and Martha. See Saxer's studies of the legend and cult (1959, 1986, 1989a, plus his entry in *BSS*).

Evidence for Anglo-Saxon interest in Mary Magdalen is widespread. Her shrine at Ephesus was visited by an Anglo-Saxon pilgrim, Willibald, later bishop of Eichstatt, in the eighth century, and her figure is carved in relief on the eighth-century Northumbrian Ruthwell Cross. **BEDE**'s brief notice for her in his **MARTYROLOGIUM** (ed. Dubois and Renaud 1976 p 133.2) is the earliest Western record of the Eastern feast of July 22 that later became standard in the West, replacing that of January 19, a Gallic feast of Mary and Martha that apparently resulted from a misreading of the notice for the Roman martyrs **MARIUS ET MARTHA** on the same day (Saxer 1959 p 45) and that recurs in some Anglo-Saxon calendars and a service book (F. Wormald 1934 pp 16, 30, 44, and 226; *HBS* 11.153). The July 22 feast is recorded in a ninth-century northern English calendar adapted for Canterbury use and is graded in a Crowland calendar of the mid-eleventh century (F. Wormald 1934 pp 8 and 261; see also p 22). Mary's finger bone leads the roster of female saints' relics at Exeter, believed to be of tenth-century date (Exeter List of Relics, *Rec* 10.8, B16.10.8; ed. Förster 1943 p 79; Conner 1993a pp 184–85), thus constituting the earliest Western record of a Magdalen relic, in Saxer's view, who also believes (1959 p 54) that the Latin and Old English texts associated with this relic may be based on **ADO**'s notice for Mary in his mid-ninth-century martyrology (*PL* 123.195). Many Anglo-Saxon calendars, however, have neither feast, or that of July 22 had to be added to them in Norman times or later.

It used to be believed that the hagiographic legend of Mary Magdalen as a desert hermit did not develop until the eleventh century, in conjunction with her cult in Provence, but the **OLD ENGLISH MARTYROLOGY** has a substantial notice (*Mart*; ed. Kotzor 1981 2.156–57) combining material from the gospels with an account of Mary's thirty-year sojourn in the desert as a hermit and ascetic (apparently imitating **MARIA AEGYPTIACA**) miraculously fed by angels. Cross has shown (1978) that the *Martyrology*'s main narrative source is a version of the Magdalen legend known from its *incipit* as "Narrat Josephus" (*BHL* 5453–56). Cross narrows the source down to the *vita* numbered 6a (*BHL* 5453) by the Bollandists. Cross edits this version, previously unpublished, from tenth- and eleventh-century manuscripts now in Rome and Florence respectively. The evidence of the *Old English Martyrology* proves that the legend known as the "Narrat Josephus" (Cross's title) or *Vita eremitica* (Saxer's title) existed at least as early as the later ninth century. It was composed, Saxer now thinks (1986 p 24), in Italy under the influence of the Latin version of the life of Mary of Egypt (*BHL* 5415), which he dates 875, but this hardly allows time for the life of Mary Magdalen to reach the Old English martryologist, unless the *Martyrology*'s composition date were not until the very end of the ninth century. A more thorough study of the relationship between the Latin lives of the two penitent sinners seems necessary before firmer conclusions can be reached.

FRITHEGOD, the Frankish poet active in England during the time of Archbishop Oda (942–58), apparently wrote a metrical version, now lost, of Mary's life (Lapidge 1988a pp 48–49). The omission of any version of her life from the **COTTON-CORPUS LEGENDARY** is surprising, unless one accepts Zettel's view (1982 p 18) that the Legendary's contents were already fixed by the later ninth century.

The intriguing remark by Thurston and Attwater in their 1932 edition of *BLS* (7.310) that a life of Mary Magdalen supposedly by **HRABANUS MAURUS** is contained in a ninth-century manuscript at Magdalen College, Oxford, is erroneous. The manuscript is of the fifteenth century (Oxford, Magdalen College 89).

Cross (1978) prints other variant versions of the "Narrat Josephus" version of Mary's life. See his article and the various studies by Saxer for further bibliographical information. See also Hohler (1995 pp 224–25). On Mary's liturgical cult in later Anglo-Saxon England, see Ortenberg (1992 pp 250–55). Among numerous other recent studies of the Magdalen phenomenon, mainly interpretive, see that of Ward (1987 pp 10–25).

Maria Meretrix. See ABRAHAM ET MARIA.

Mariae Beatae Virginis Assumptio. See **APOCRYPHA, DE TRANSITU MARIAE; PASCHASIUS RADBERTUS.**

Mariae Beatae Virginis Nativitas. See **APOCRYPHA, DE NATIVITATE MARIAE, GOSPEL OF PSEUDO-MATTHEW, PROTO-EVANGELIUM OF JAMES.**

Marina. See **MARGARETA.**

Marinus, passio [ANON.Pas.Marin.]: *BHL* 5538; *BSS* 8.1171–72.
   ed.: Bollandists 1889–93 2.184–91.
MSS Cambridge, Corpus Christi College 9: HG 36.
Lists – Refs none.

The *passio* of Marinus (feast day December 26), reputedly a youth from a high senatorial family under the emperor "Martian," is a catalogue of tortures and repetitive dialogues between martyr and emperor. The saint had no cult in Anglo-Saxon England, but copies of this *passio* are preserved in the **COTTON-CORPUS LEGENDARY**, here represented only by the Cambridge manuscript, the copy formerly in the Salisbury collection having been lost. Later affiliated copies are now in Oxford and Hereford (Zettel 1979 p 33; Webber 1992 p 157). The Bollandists print the *passio* from a Brussels manuscript.

Marius et Martha, passio [ANON.Pas.Marii.Marth.]: *BHL* 5543; *BLS* 1.117; *BSS* 8.1186–88; *CPL* 2208.
   ed.: *AS* Ian. 2.216–19.

MSS – Lists none.
A-S Vers 1. BEDA.Mart. 16.9–14; see below.
   2. *Mart* (B19.ah, dp).
Quots/Cits none.
Refs BEDA.Mart. 54.9–10.

BEDE has a short notice (January 19) for these saints and for others associated with them in his **MARTYROLOGIUM** (BEDA.Mart.; ed. Dubois and Renaud 1976). The legend describes Marius and Martha as Persian nobles on pilgrimage to Rome with their two children, Audifax and Abachum. Bede also has a notice (34.2–4) for Valentinus, priest of Rome (feast day February 14; see *BSS* 12.896–97), who assists the Persians in burying the remains of numerous Christians martyred by the emperor Claudius the Goth (260). Eventually they all suffer the same fate. Among the martyrs buried by Marius and Martha is Quirinus (Cyrinus), another Roman priest (March 25), whom also Bede treats separately (ed. Dubois and Renaud 1976 p 54.7–10), referring to his source as *Passio Sancti Valentini*. The relics of Quirinus migrated in the early medieval period to Tegernsee, Bavaria (*BSS* 3.1339), and as a result he is the subject of a separate hagiographic tradition (*BHL* 7029; ed. *MGH* SRM 3.11–20), derived from this *passio* but not relevant here. For Bede's dependence on the *passio*, see Quentin (1908 pp 86–87).

Marius and Martha, with their two sons, are commemorated in the **OLD ENGLISH MARTYROLOGY** on January 20 (*Mart*; ed. Kotzor 1981 2.22), in a brief and bland notice. It would be hard to prove that the ninth-century martyrologist had any source besides Bede (see Herzfeld, *EETS* OS 116.xxxvii), but the *Martyrology*'s short notice on June 17 for the military tribune Blastus (ed. Kotzor 1981 2.122.8–12), another martyr buried by Marius and Martha, and not mentioned by Bede, confirms the martyrologist's indebtedness to the *passio* (see *AS* Iun. 3.216, paragraphs 2 and 3), although in a form not necessarily identical to the printed edition. Blastus (see *DHGE* 9.161–62) was probably an authentic Roman martyr originally honored on the Via Salaria near the "clivus cucumeris" (see *AS* Iun. 3.285–86). The *Martyrology* probably also had a notice for Valentinus in the lost February portion.

Texts associated with this group of saints appear to be lacking in Anglo-Saxon England after the ninth century, and their January feast day is attributed in some later calendars to "Maria et Martha" (see **MARIA MAGDALENA**). For a recent study of this problem, see Pfaff (1998).

Martialis, vita [ANON.Vit.Martial.]: *BHL* 5551; *BLS* 2.675–76; *BSS* 8.1310–13; *DACL* 9.1094–155.

ed.: Arbellot 1892 pp 238–43.

MSS – Lists none.
A-S Vers ?*Mart* (B19.eb).
Quots/Cits – Refs none.

The earliest traditions about Martial of Limoges (feast day June 30) regard him as one of several missionaries who preached in Gaul during the third century: see, for example, **GREGORY OF TOURS**, DE GLORIA CONFESSORUM XXVII–XXVIII (ed. *MGH* SRM 1/2.764–65), and HISTORIA FRANCORUM I.xxx (*MGH* SRM 1/1.23.6–7 and 17–20 [2nd ed.]). As early as the ninth century, however, if not earlier, it came to be widely believed, though not without some opposition, that Martial was one of the original seventy-two disciples of Christ and was later sent from Rome by Saint Peter to be apostle to the Gauls. This legend is related in this, the earliest extant *vita* of the saint, one manuscript of which, originally from Reichenau, is of the ninth century, pre-dating the 848 foundation of the new abbey of Saint-Martial, Limoges (*DACL* 9.1094, 1113–14). Martial's apostolicity was eventually confirmed, at a council in Poitiers, 1031, after considerable debate and promotional activities. The most vigorous proponent of Martial's cause, Ademar of Chabannes, claimed in Limoges, 1031, that according to a recent report from the monks of St Augustine's, Canterbury, the English church had venerated Martial as apostle since the time of **GREGORY THE GREAT**. Ademar's informants also reported, however, that while the English preserved Martial's name in their litanies and martyrologies, "non habent librum de actibus beati Martialis" (Beech 1990 p 85). The lack of a text of Martial's *vita* at Canterbury at this time is paralleled by its rather surprising absence from the **COTTON-CORPUS LEGENDARY**, extant manuscripts of which derive from eleventh-century Worcester and Salisbury.

A version of this *vita* of the apostolic Martial does seem to have been known in England in the ninth century, however, since the author of the **OLD ENGLISH MARTYROLOGY** (*Mart*; ed. Kotzor 1981 2.136) summarizes some episodes. There are minor discrepancies between the *Martyrology*'s account of Martial's mission and that in *BHL* 5551 (for a more striking discrepancy in an appended miracle story, see next entry). Thus the Old English work may be a unique witness to narrative traditions about Martial that predate, or at least were in competition with, the earliest extant *vita*.

On relations between England and Aquitaine in the eleventh century, affecting English veneration of saints such as Martial, see Beech (1990), who, however, omits mention of the notice for Martial in the ninth-century *Martyrology* but is probably correct in stating (p 93) that English liturgical veneration of Martial did not begin until the eleventh century. For the numerous modern editions of ninth- and eleventh-century texts concerning Martial, see *BHL* and *DACL* 9.1094–95.

Martialis, miracula [ANON.Mir.Martial.]: *BHL* 5561.
  ed.: Arbellot 1892 pp 243–48.

MSS – Lists none.
A-S Vers ?*Mart* (B19.eb).
Quots/Cits – Refs none.

The **OLD ENGLISH MARTYROLOGY** (*Mart*; ed. Kotzor 1981 2.137) recounts a posthumous miracle of Martial (see previous entry) that corresponds in some particulars and phrasing to chapter IV of this first set of miracles, usually appended to manuscript copies of the *Vita Martialis* (see Arbellot's edition, p 245). It is noteworthy that in the printed editions of the Latin text of this miracle, the fornicating couple miraculously ejected from the vicinity of Martial's tomb comprises a female prostitute and her male client; in the *Martyrology*, however, the fornicators are apparently both male (see also *EETS* OS 116.231). Either the Old English author retold the miracle with some freedom, for personal or local reasons, or his source differed in this respect from the extant Latin versions. For another edition of the Latin version, see also *AS* Iun. 5.553.

Martina, passio [ANON.Pas.Martinae]: *BHL* 5588; *BLS* 1.203; *BSS* 8.1220-21.
 ed.: unpublished.
MSS 1. London, BL Cotton Nero E. i: HG 344.
 2. Salisbury, Cathedral Library 221 (formerly Oxford, Bodleian Library Fell 4): HG 754.5.
Lists – Refs none.

According to Franchi de' Cavalieri (1903), the *passio* of the Roman martyr Martina (feast day January 1) is a work of fiction based on the equally fictitious Greek *passio* of Tatiana (*BHL* 7989). Both were probably composed in Rome in the seventh century. There is no proof Martina ever existed.

There does not seem to have been any particular devotion to this saint in Anglo-Saxon England, but the copy of the *Passio Martinae* in the Cotton manuscript, with its splendid decorated initial "R" (fol 55v: Martina's *passio* is the first text in the Legendary proper), shows signs of having been read attentively. The text exhibits numerous small variants from those printed in Mombritius (1910 2.246–56 and 695–97) and *AS* Ian. 1.11–17; its *incipit* and *explicit* agree with those of the manuscripts listed by Bandini (1791–93 1.300, number VI; 2.286, number IX), classified separately by the Bollandists as *BHL* 5588 (Zettel 1979 p 15), rather than with those of Mombritius (*BHL* 5587).

Martinus Turonensis. See **SULPICIUS SEVERUS, DIALOGI, EPISTOLAE, VITA MARTINI**; see also **ALCUIN, VITA MARTINI**.

Martinus Turonensis, narrationes [GREG.TUR.Narr.Mart.]: *BHL* 5619–23.
 ed.: *MGH* SRM 1/1.32–34 (2nd ed.) and *MGH* SRM 1/2.589–91.
MSS 1. Cambridge, Corpus Christi College 9: HG 36.
 2. Cambridge, Trinity Hall 21: HG 201.
 3. Hereford, Cathedral Library O.VI.11: HG 264.

4. Salisbury, Cathedral Library 222 (formerly Oxford, Bodleian Library Fell 1): HG 754.6.
5. Vatican, Reg. lat. 489: HG 915.
Lists – A-S Vers   see below.
Quots/Cits – Refs   none.

In addition to the writings of **SULPICIUS SEVERUS** on Martin of Tours (feast day November 12), medieval collections of "Martiniana" frequently included several extracts from the works of **GREGORY OF TOURS**, entitled by the Bollandists in *BHL* "Narrationes de miraculis in obitu et de prima translatione." Since it is unlikely, however, that they were known in England as works of Gregory of Tours *per se*, it seems appropriate to list them here rather than in the main *SASLC* entry on Gregory. Further, it would be misleading and tedious to devote separate entries here to the different extracts. Of the manuscripts listed, the two in Cambridge and those in Hereford and Rome contain these stories as a standard cluster among their Martinian texts. The Salisbury manuscript now preserves only *BHL* 5623 (Webber 1992 p 156), on Martin's translation, among the July feasts (presumably for the July 4 feast of Martin's translation), but it is likely that the lost portion of the manuscript contained the other *narrationes* along with the other *Martiniana* (see Webber 1992 p 157 note 68).

BHL 5619–20 are entitled "epistola" in the two Cambridge manuscripts above, but this brief two-part *narratio* concerning the rivalry of Tours and Poitiers for possession of Martin's body after his death is based closely on Gregory of Tours, **HISTORIA FRANCORUM** I.xlviii (ed. *MGH* SRM 1/1.32–34 [2nd ed.]).

BHL 5621–23 are variously titled in the manuscripts listed above. In the Corpus manuscript, *BHL* 5621 is termed "Versiculus de transitu S. Martini" while 5622 is "Epistola S. Ambrosi Ep. de transitu." In Trinity Hall 21, *BHL* 5622 is entitled "Sermo S. Ambrosii de transitu S. Martini." The three items comprise, in fact, Gregory of Tours's **DE VIRTUTIBUS SANCTI MARTINI** I.iv–vi (ed. *MGH* SRM 1/2.589–91).

For ÆLFRIC's apparent use of such a collection of *Martiniana* as the source of some episodes of his two lives of Martin, see Zettel (1979 pp

121–26 superseding and correcting Gerould 1925). He points to *BHL* 5619–20 as the source of CATHOLIC HOMILIES II, 34, lines 314–27 (*ÆCHom* II; ed. *EETS* SS 5), and of LIVES OF SAINTS, *Martin* 1441–95 (*ÆLS*; ed. *EETS* OS 94 and 114), and *BHL* 5621–22 as the source of *Martin* 1385–441. On Ælfric's use of his various Martin sources, see now Biggs (1996b) and Godden (*EETS* SS 18.622–33).

Martinus Turonensis, vita metrica [PAVL.PETR.Vit.Mart.]: *BHL* 5617; *CPL* 1474.

ed.: *CSEL* 16/1.17–159.

MSS – A-S Vers none.
Quots/Cits see below.
Refs none.

The life of Martin of Tours by **SULPICIUS SEVERUS** was rendered into hexameters by two poets of late classical Gaul, the better known of whom is the late-sixth-century bishop of Poitiers, **VENANTIUS FORTUNATUS**, *BHL* 5624 (see next entry). His predecessor was the more obscure fifth-century Gallic poet, Paulinus of Périgueux, who produced six books of hexameters based on Sulpicius's writings about Martin. Although Ogilvy (*BKE* 217–18), relying on Manitius, is dubious about the early Anglo-Saxons' knowledge of Paulinus's poem, the research of Jaager, on **BEDE**'s metrical **VITA CUTHBERTI** *(BHL* 2020), and of Orchard on **ALDHELM**'s verse **DE VIRGINITATE**, has detected a substantial number of convincing verbal parallels, confirming the use of the Gallic poet by both English writers. For citations, see Jaager (1935 pp 63, 91, 98, 103, 110, and 126) and Orchard (1994 pp 181–82 and 232).

Martinus Turonensis, vita metrica [VEN.FORT.Vit.Mart.]: *BHL* 5624; *CPL* 1037.

ed.: *MGH* AA 4/1.293–370.

See the main entry on **VENANTIUS FORTUNATUS** (530–609) for Anglo-Saxon knowledge of the writings of the late-sixth-century poet, hagiographer, bishop of Poitiers, and confidant of Queen Radigund. His longest poem (over two thousand hexameter verses in four books) is a life of Martin of Tours, to whose cult Fortunatus was drawn when he left his native Italy for Gaul in 565. The poem, like that of Paulinus of Périgueux (see previous entry), is based closely on the *Martiniana* by **SULPICIUS SEVERUS**. Its early circulation among the Anglo-Saxons is evident from the number of verbal echoes detected in the hagiographic poetry of **BEDE, ALDHELM**, and, most of all, **ALCUIN**. For citations, see Jaager (1935 pp 66 and 82), Orchard (1994 pp 235–36), and Godman (1982 pp lxx–lxxi, lxxiv, 148). For late Anglo-Saxon knowledge of Fortunatus's prose hagiographies, see the entries for **ALBINUS ANDEGAVENSIS, GERMANUS PARISIENSIS, HILARIUS PICTAVENSIS**, and **MEDARDUS**.

Mattheus apostolus. See **APOCRYPHA, PASSIO MATTHAEI**.

Mauritius, passio [EVCHER.Pas.Maurit.1]: *BHL* 5737; *BLS* 3.619–21; *BSS* 9.193–205; *CPL* 490; *DACL* 10.2699–729; *RFHMA* 2.1472–74.
  ed.: *MGH* SRM 3.32–41.

MSS – Lists none.
A-S Vers ?*Mart* (B19.hg).
Quots/Cits see below.
Refs none.

As many as three different versions of the legend of Maurice and the Theban legion ("Thebaei"; also known as "Agaunenses": see below) may have been known to the Anglo-Saxons, but since this view is speculative rather than confident, and given the lack of detailed studies of the Maurice legend in English sources, I have organized the relevant materials into two entries.

Mauritius, Exsuperius, and Candidus (feast day September 22), principal officers of the Theban legion, along with the veteran Victor, are the earliest recorded names associated with the famous martyrdom of an entire legion of the Roman army under the co-emperor Maximian at

Agaunum, now Saint-Maurice-en-Valais, Switzerland, 285/86. According to Dupraz (1961) there are two early versions of their story, and one of later but indeterminate date (given below in their *BHL* order):

Passio 1, *BHL* 5737–40, by Bishop **EUCHERIUS** of Lyons (428–50), variously interpolated in the later fifth and sixth centuries; for manuscripts, see Krusch (*MGH* SRM 3.22–26). According to this version, the soldiers, who were Christians from Egypt, were executed for refusing to carry out Maximian's orders to persecute and kill Christians in the Alpine region. Although Eucherius's version survives in the oldest manuscript of the *passio* (of the sixth or seventh century, now in Paris), and was formally considered the "original," equal importance is now attached to the oldest anonymous version (see below). A recent edition of this oldest manuscript copy of Eucherius is that of Dupraz (1961 pp 1*–5*). Most manuscripts of this version exhibit the additions of one or more interpolators (B–D: Krusch, *MGH* SRM 3.23), printed by Dupraz (1961 pp 5*–8*).

Passio 2a, *BHL* 5741–45, anonymous, composed 475–500 at Agaunum and usually referred to as version X2. This version, long considered a mere reworking of Eucherius, is now believed (e.g., by Dupraz 1961 and Zufferey 1983) to draw on a more authentic tradition than that used by Eucherius. It relates that when Maximian ordered his army to sacrifice to the gods to ensure victory against a rebellious tribe of Gauls (Bagaudae), the Christian legion refused.

Passio 2b, *BHL* 5746, a third version, X1, apparently dependent on X2 and of indeterminate date, but pre-tenth century, omits details specific to the cult center of Agaunum and seems to have been composed in Cologne.

The number of men in the legion varies between the three versions: Eucherius, 6,600; X2, 6,660; X1, 6,666 (see Dupraz 1961 p 55).

The most recent detailed discussion is that of Dupraz (1961, generally endorsed by Zufferey 1983), on which the above summary is based. See especially Dupraz pp 41–68 (on relationship and dates of the three *passiones*), pp 289–98 (conclusions), and pp 1*–18* (three "Appendices" containing editions of the oldest manuscripts of each version). On the historical context of the original composition and subsequent revisions of the *passio*, see Berchem (1956 pp 45–54) and most recently Zufferey

(1983). For a brief but valuable literary appreciation, see Berschin (1986–91 1.261–65). There is copious earlier bibliography in *RFHMA* 2.1472–74 and *DACL* (see headnote).

Neither **BEDE** nor **ALDHELM** shows awareness of Maurice and his companions, but a ninth-century northern English calendar (F. Wormald 1934 p 10), later at Canterbury, has their feast day, and the ninth-century **OLD ENGLISH MARTYROLOGY** (*Mart*; ed. Kotzor 1981 2.214–15) has a brief, fairly free summary account of the martyrdom. Some features of the *Martyrology* account point to the version of Eucherius: for example, the legion has 6,600 men (Kotzor 1981 2.214.10–11), not 6,660 as in X2; it is sent to Maximian's aid, "to fultume Maximiane" (p 214.12–13), as in Eucherius: "in auxilium Maximiano ... acciti" (*MGH* SRM 3.33.18; cf. X1 and X2, "Cui ad supplementum . . . dedit," ed. Dupraz 1961 p 8*.28–29, p 13*.12–13). The *Martyrology* says that "their blood flowed across the earth like a flood" (Kotzor 1981 2.215.1–2), as in Eucherius, "fluxerunt pretiosi sanguinis rivi," an image absent from X in its basic form, though incorporated in some mixed texts (see *AS* Sept. 6.349, note b). The Old English account mentions fewer martyrs' names—only Mauritius, Exsuperius, Candidus—than even the earliest texts of Eucherius, which always add that of Victor. The *Martyrology* strangely never refers to the Theban origin of the martyrs, but says they were from Cappadocia (Kotzor 1981 2.214.12).

For **ÆLFRIC**'s possible use of a Eucherian text, or of a mixed recension, see next entry.

Mauritius, passio [ANON.Pas.Maurit.2b]: *BHL* 5746.
   ed.: Surius 1576–81 5.356–60.

MSS 1. Cambridge, Corpus Christi College 361: HG 99.
    2. London, BL Cotton Nero E. i: HG 344.
    3. Salisbury, Cathedral Library 222 (formerly Oxford, Bodleian Library Fell 1): HG 754.6.
Lists none.
A-S Vers ?*ÆLS* Maurice (B1.3.28) 1–118.
Quots/Cits – Refs none.

The textual history of the legend of Maurice and the Theban Legion is even more complex than is indicated in the previous entry. Very few of the extant manuscripts used by Krusch and other scholars actually conform to the three basic versions (**EUCHERIUS**, X1, X2) that modern scholarship has isolated. Most of the manuscripts of the X versions contain interpolations and additions from the Eucherius version and display so many variants one from another that even Krusch declined to try to sort them out (*MGH* SRM 3.27). The text in the surviving eleventh-century copies of the **COTTON-CORPUS LEGENDARY** (represented in the Cotton and Salisbury manuscripts cited here) is of this mixed type. After following X2 mainly (with some passages from Eucherius interspersed!) up to the death of Victor (*promeruit*: Dupraz 1961 p 17*.9), the Cotton manuscript, for example, switches to a D recension of Eucherius for the closing paragraphs (as in Dupraz pp 7*–8*).

The text of the Cotton manuscript, in other words, appears to be substantially that of Passio 2b, or "X1" (*BHL* 5746), as printed by Surius, but without the prologue and epistle that Surius takes from Eucherius. Zettel (1979 pp 234–35) follows C. Loomis (1931 p 4) in linking the Cotton-Corpus Legendary text to that of Surius, but then identifies it as *BHL* 5743 ("X2"); in my opinion, however, it is textually closer to *BHL* 5746, that is, the mixed text ("X1") used by Surius. To complicate matters further, the Cotton *incipit* conforms to that of *BHL* 5747d (although lacking the prologue attached to the latter), of which Zettel was apparently unaware. Another problem in Zettel's discussion is his statement (1979 p 235) that the martyrdom of Victor is an eighth-century interpolation: it is in fact in the earliest recensions of Eucherius and, more elaborately, X1. The first part of the Cotton text is marked in short lections I–VII and has various marginal annotations and excisions of the text.

Another manuscript of Anglo-Saxon provenance, the Cambridge manuscript (eleventh century, Malmesbury), has the beginning of a *Passio Mauritii* on its last folio: "Temporibus diocliani [*sic*] imperatoris cum ipse ad consortium." It breaks off as follows: "Tunc hi preerant legioni mites affatu. dixerunt ad." James (1911–12 2.194) notes that the *incipit* does not correspond to those listed in *BHL*. It is in fact an abbreviated form of the *incipit* in the Cotton manuscript, and the wording of the last sentence, though corrupt, points likewise to a text like Cotton, of the "X1/X2" type (see Dupraz 1961 p 14*.10; *AS* Sept. 6.345b.33–34).

In the tenth and eleventh centuries, the Theban legion's feast day was among the more important in the Anglo-Saxon calendars (e.g., F. Wormald 1934 pp 52, 66). **ÆLFRIC**'s *Maurice* in **LIVES OF SAINTS** (*ÆLS*; ed. *EETS* OS 94 and 114) is sourced by C. Loomis (1931 p 4), who relates it to the Latin text printed in Surius. Zettel (1979 pp 234–35) argues that Ælfric's version is somewhat closer to the recension preserved in the Cotton and Salisbury manuscripts (see above) than to Surius. Zettel's proofs, however, are not conclusive. For example, he compares Ælfric's "æfter þysre cyþnysse" (*Maurice* 111) with the Cotton manuscript's "post professionem" against Surius's "ob professionem," but in fact the Surius reading is an unusual variant, and "post professionem," far from being unique to Cotton, is apparently the more common reading among X manuscripts (*AS* Sept. 6.348b.10; Dupraz 1961 p 17*.7). Another problem is the fact that Ælfric (*Maurice* 19) adds a fourth name, Vitalis, to the list of the legion's officers, but the Cotton manuscript preserves just the traditional names. Nor does the Cotton manuscript have the passage, common to Ælfric (*Maurice* 71–73) and Eucherius (Dupraz 1961 p 3*.32 and *MGH* SRM 3.37.12), about the martyrs offering their necks willingly to their executioners: in Cotton and the printed versions of the X recension, this detail is part of the exhortation of Exsuperius, whereas in Eucherius and Ælfric it is simply narrated in the third-person description of the soldiers' unresisting deaths. Other, similar considerations make it possible that Ælfric (or his source) is combining more than one version.

The closing section of Ælfric's version (*Maurice* 119–78), which departs from the Maurice story altogether, is sourced by Cross (1965b pp 327–30 and 1977c pp 130–31).

The eleventh-century Exeter List of Relics records in Old English the church's possession of Maurice's tooth (*Rec* 10.8, B16.10.8; ed. Förster 1943 p 75; Conner 1993a p 182) and gives the number of legionaries as 6,066, probably a garbled version of 6,666. Apart from the unusual number, the Exeter passage is very like the notice for Maurice and his companions in the martyrology of **FLORUS OF LYONS** (Quentin 1908 p 280).

The verse *passio* of the Theban legion mentioned but not identified by Ogilvy (*BKE* p 49) in Oxford, Trinity College 4, a manuscript from St Augustine's, Canterbury, is in fact outside our period. It is *BHL* 5752 (*PL* 171.1625–30) by Marbod of Rennes (died 1123). See Coxe (1852 vol 2 *Catalogus codicum MSS. collegii S. Trinitatis* p 2).

Maurus, vita [ODO.GLAN.Vit.Maur./PS.FAUST.]: *BHL* 5773; *BSS* 9.210–19; *BLS* 1.97; *DACL* 6.1285–319.

ed.: *AS* Ian. 1.1039–50.

MSS   Hereford, Cathedral Library O.VI.11: HG 264.
Lists   Saewold: ML 8.23.
A-S Vers   *ÆLS* Maur (B1.3.7).
Quots/Cits – Refs   none.

Maur (feast day January 15) figures in several episodes of the life of **BENEDICT OF NURSIA (BENEDICTUS CASINENSIS)** by **GREGORY THE GREAT (DIALOGI** II.vii.1–28, II.viii.58–67; ed. *SChr* 260), but by the later ninth century he was given a life and career of his own and identified with the putative founder of the abbey of Glanfeuil, later Saint-Maur-sur-Loire. The *vita* purports to be written by a companion of Maurus named "Faustus," but it is now generally accepted as the work of Odo, abbot of Glanfeuil, after his community evacuated the monastery to escape the Northmen in 862. He claimed to have found the earlier *vita* just as he was leaving Glanfeuil with Maur's relics, which had been discovered during the abbacy of Gauslin in 845.

Not surprisingly, given the lack of either cult or separate *vita* before the later ninth century, there is no separate mention of Maur in early Anglo-Saxon memorials, but the saint's reputation grew in the later period, as evidenced by **ÆLFRIC**'s *Maur* in **LIVES OF SAINTS** (*ÆLS*; ed. *EETS* OS 76 and 82). Moreover, although Maur is not prominent in pre-Conquest calendars, according to Alicia Corrêa (private communication) there are proper masses for Maur in some Anglo-Saxon service books. John (1983 p 306) suggests that Ælfric and the Benedictine reform party would naturally be interested in a saint whose story associated him with both Benedict and the early monasticism of the Fleury region, and H. Bloch (1950 pp 185–86) points out that the *vita* presents Maur's foundation at Glanfeuil as the oldest Benedictine monastery in France. His importance in Ælfric's time is indicated by the fact that when Saint Adalbert of Prague (956–97) made a pilgrimage to France, Maur's shrine at Glanfeuil was one of the four pilgrimage sites he chose to visit (the others being those of **Dionisius, Martinus Turonensis**, and Benedict himself).

Ott (1892 pp 21–24) suggests that Ælfric's source for his *Maur* was closer to those printed by Mabillon and *AS* than to Surius's edition (see *BHL*). The *Vita Mauri* is not included in the surviving eleventh-century copies of the **COTTON-CORPUS LEGENDARY**, but it appears (though not in calendar order) in the table of contents in Salisbury Cathedral Library 222, and there is a copy in the later but affiliated manuscript, Oxford, Bodleian Library Bodley 354 (*SC* 2432). Zettel (1979 p 34) argues, therefore, that it was in the original legendary and uses this (p 9) as the earliest year in which the legendary could have been compiled. He presents some evidence (pp 211–13) for Ælfric's dependence on a version of the *vita* similar to that in Bodley 354. He does not mention the text in the Hereford manuscript listed here, which has not been studied in relation to the printed editions or other later English copies.

In Lapidge's note in ML (p 62) the *Vita Mauri* in the Saewold booklist is identified as *BHL* 5783, that is, the *passio* of Maurus priest of Rheims, but since the booklist itself identifies the work as a "vita," it may have been a copy of *BHL* 5773.

For the controversy over the identity of Maur of Glanfeuil, see Leclercq's article in *DACL*. See also H. Bloch (1950, especially pp 182–88).

Maximus, Severa, et Flavianus, passio [ANON.Pas.Max.Sev.]: *BHL* 5857d–e; *BSS* 11.957.

ed.: Poncelet 1909 pp 473–78.

MSS Cambridge, Corpus Christi College 9: HG 36.
Lists – Refs none.

Maximus and his fellow martyrs (feast day October 24 in the above manuscript) are among the more obscure saints known to the Anglo-Saxons. Since the usual reference sources say little about their legend, a brief summary is in order here. According to the unsophisticated, poorly written *passio* (*BHL* 5857d–e), remarkable for its chronological mistakes and lack of miracles, Maximus was a Christian and an officer, "comes milinarius," in the Roman army, who preached to and converted one hundred and twenty four of the soldiers under his command, thereby arousing the anger of the emperor Constantius (*sic!*). After being subjected to various punitive hardships (e.g., digging and transporting sand) and a trial before a tribune Marcus, Maximus and his converts were eventually executed. They are said to have been buried at the site of their forced labor, in the Via Salaria "in clivo Cucumeris." As Poncelet (1909 pp 471–72) demonstrates, the details of the martyrs' burial and cult site are apparently adapted from the *passio* of the Forty-Six Martyrs (QUADRAGINTA SEX MILITES), which forms the conclusion of the epic cycle of LAURENTIUS. The remainder of the *passio* (*BHL* 5857e) relates the martyrdom, under Constantius's successor Claudius (*sic*), of Maximus's wife, Secunda, and their children, Severa, Calendinus, and Marcus, and the conversion and martyrdom of the emperor's "vicarius," Flavianus (feast day January 28).

The Anglo-Saxons' knowledge of these dubious martyrs is evidenced only by the copy of the *passio* in the **COTTON-CORPUS LEGENDARY**. Zettel (1979 p 33) identifies the *passio* in the Cambridge manuscript, along with another affiliated copy of the later twelfth century, as similar but not identical to *BHL* 5857d–e (see also Jackson and Lapidge 1996 p 143). More precisely, the text in the Cambridge manuscript contains a somewhat abridged version of the *passio*, very similar to two manuscripts of the eleventh and twelfth centuries now in Rome, collated by Poncelet (1909 p 470) with his base text, a ninth-century manuscript from the Farfa collection. The English text is independent of any of these, however, and appears to preserve some of the place-names of the *passio* more accurately. The heading in the manuscript (p 434) states that the martyrs' relics are in the chapel of Saint John "in cliuium Cucumeris." Amore's entry in *BSS* surprisingly ignores Poncelet's edition.

Medardus, vita [VEN.FORT.Vit.Med.]: *BHL* 5864; *BLS* 2.502–03; *BSS* 9.262–64; *CPL* 1049; *DACL* 11.102–08.
  ed.: *MGH* AA 4/2.67–73.
MSS 1. London, BL Cotton Nero E. i: HG 344.
  2. Salisbury, Cathedral Library 221 (formerly Oxford, Bodleian Library Fell 4): HG 754.5.
Lists – Refs none.

Born ca. 470, Médard became bishop of Vermandois, probably with his seat at Saint-Quentin, and died ca. 560 (feast day June 8). His cult, widespread in France, especially northern France, during the Middle Ages, was initially promoted by Clothar I, who had the body transferred to his capital, Soissons. King Sigibert (died 575) founded the monastery church of Saint-Médard over the tomb. The *vita*, long attributed to **VENANTIUS FORTUNATUS** and of early date (shortly after 602), is no longer definitely accepted as Fortunatus's work, although probably based on his metrical life of Médard (*BHL* 5863). For Krusch's doubts, see *MGH* AA 4/2.XXVI.

The presence of a text of the *Vita Medardi* in the London and Salisbury manuscripts of the **COTTON-CORPUS LEGENDARY** is doubtless due to the north French milieu in which the Legendary appears to have been compiled prior to its importation into England (see Zettel 1979 p 9; see also Jackson and Lapidge 1996 p 133). Krusch in his edition does not list the English copies of *BHL* 5864, but they seem to be descended from his Q manuscript (eighth century, from Corbie, now in Paris: see *MGH* AA 4/2.XXIII–XXIV and XXVII).

Mennas, passio [ANON.Pas.Menn.]: *BHL* 5921; *BLS* 4.314–16; *BSS* 9.324–42; *DACL* 11.324–97.
  ed.: Miedema 1913 pp 105–21.

MSS Cambridge, Corpus Christi College 9: HG 36.
Lists none.
A-S Vers ?*Mart* (B19.iw).
Quots/Cits – Refs none.

Mennas (feast day November 11), patron saint of desert merchants and camel caravans (Farmer 1987 p 299), was the object of an early Christian cult in Egypt, which spread throughout the Christian world (in **GREGORY THE GREAT**'s time there was a basilica of St Mennas not far from Rome where Gregory preached on the saint in his **HOMILIAE XL IN EVANGELIA XXXV**; ed. *PL* 76.1259). Twentieth-century archaeology has revealed extensive remains of a pilgrimage center at Bumma, near Alexandria, which flourished at least until the seventh century (Meinardus 1965 pp 141–45), but the history of Mennas himself remains obscure. His legend, which presents him as a Roman soldier of Egyptian birth martyred in Phrygia during Diocletian's persecution, and brought back to Egypt for burial, is a literary fiction, borrowed from the story of Saint Gordius as related by **BASIL** (*CPG* 2862, *BHG* 703). It survives in several Greek recensions (*BHG* 1250–54) of a lost Greek original (see Delehaye's survey, 1966 pp 273–76). The anonymous Latin *passio* has been thought to derive from this lost Greek *passio* (Siegmund 1949 p 242; see also Miedema 1913).

It is by no means certain that this version of Mennas's *passio* was known in Anglo-Saxon England before the tenth century. **BEDE** has no narrative notice for the saint in his **MARTYROLOGIUM**, and the post-Bedan second recension merely records the feast day (Quentin 1908 p 55). The brief notice in the **OLD ENGLISH MARTYROLOGY** (*Mart*; ed. Kotzor 1981 2.251) is puzzling, in that it pairs Mennas with a companion, Heliodorus, as well as naming the persecuting judge, Pyrrhus. The latter is prominent in the *passio* but Heliodorus appears only briefly as an unsympathetic pagan courtier who urges the saint's execution, not as a fellow soldier and martyr, as in the *Martyrology*. Herzfeld's listing (*EETS* OS 116.xlii) of this *passio* as the source of the *Martyrology* notice seems therefore debatable.

Evidence for the later Anglo-Saxons' awareness of the *passio* is a text in the **COTTON-CORPUS LEGENDARY**, represented by the mid-eleventh-century copy (from Worcester) in the Cambridge manuscript listed above (Jackson and Lapidge 1996 p 142). For a later affiliated copy, see Zettel (1979 p 30). None of the English manuscripts is mentioned in the published studies and editions of the *passio*. A preliminary comparison of the Corpus text with the manuscripts collated by Miedema for his edition (1913) suggests that it is a good text, closer in most of its readings to Miedema's base text than to Mombritius's printed edition (1910 2.286–89 and 702–03), but difficult to affiliate with the other manuscripts.

Michael archangelus, apparitio [ANON.Appar.Michael.]: *BHL* 5948; *BLS* 3.677–80; *BSS* 9.410–46.
ed.: Waitz 1878 pp 541–43.
MSS 1. Canterbury, Cathedral Library Add. 127/1: HG 209.
2. London, BL Cotton Nero E. i: HG 344.
3. Salisbury, Cathedral Library 179: HG 753.
4. Salisbury, Cathedral Library 222 (formerly Oxford, Bodleian Library Fell 1): HG 754.6.
Lists none.
A-S Vers 1. *Mart* (B19.cr).
2. *BlHom* 25 (MichaelMor, B3.3.25).
3. *ÆCHom* I, 34 (B1.1.36) 1–132.
Quots/Cits – Refs none.

September 29, the feast day associated with the archangel Michael in the West, is believed to have originated as the commemoration of the dedication of the basilica on the Via Salaria, six miles north of Rome, in the fifth century; May 8 appears to have been the feast day introduced by the Lombards of central Italy in the late eighth and early ninth centuries (e.g., in the Naples calendar), commemorating the archangel's famous appearance on Monte Gargano in Apulia, as described in the work in question here, the "Liber de apparitione" (Otranto 1981 p 440). In most ninth-century and later martyrologies, however, the Gargano feast and legend are associated with September 29, and it invariably appears in the manuscripts in connection with this day. Since the work already appears in **HOMILIARIES** and legendaries of the early and mid-ninth century (Cross 1981b p 12 note 4), it seems likely that its composition preceded the ninth-century date assigned to it by Waitz in his edition (1878 p 540). Otranto (1988 p 383) regards the *Apparitio* as a composition of the second half of the eighth century or early ninth century. However, his earlier insistence (1981 p 435) that the legend was circulating only in Italy in the mid-ninth century, is contradicted by manuscript evidence, by the occurrence of the text in the homiliary of **HRABANUS MAURUS** (*PL* 110.60–63) dedicated to Archbishop Haistulf of Mainz (813–26), and by its currency in England early enough to be used in the May 8 notice for Michael in the ninth-century **OLD ENGLISH MARTYROLOGY** (*Mart*; ed. Kotzor 1981 2.96 and 97).

This work, unnoticed by Otranto, is unusual among martyrologies in having narrative notices for both the May 8 feast and September 29 (Kotzor 1981 2.96–97 and 223–24). The source of the story told for September 29 is unknown, but according to Cross must have been similar to one of the sources of the anonymous Old English homily preserved in Cambridge, Corpus Christi College 41 (MichaelTristr, *LS* 24, B3.3.24; ed. Tristram 1970 pp 152–61). On the *Martyrology* notice, see Cross (1981b pp 11–13), who disagrees with Herzfeld's note (*EETS* OS 116.236) as to the sourcing of the September 29 notice. For a different discussion of the sources of the homily, see R. Grant (1982) who adduces several biblical and apocryphal texts and commonplaces of angel lore for the homily's sources. He does not note the parallels between the homily and the *Martyrology*. Johnson (1998a) examines the Corpus homily in light of Coptic and Irish traditions of devotion to the Archangel, arguing that the Corpus text could reflect a degree of Coptic influence mediated by a Hiberno-Latin source.

The earliest extant English manuscript containing a text of the *Apparitio* is the fragmentary copy of **PAUL THE DEACON**'s augmented **HOMILIARUM**, preserved at Canterbury Cathedral and dated in the first half of the eleventh century by Ker and Piper (1969–92 2.315–16). See Cross and Hall (1993 p 189) for this text and for another Canterbury fragment, **HAYMO OF HALBERSTADT**'s exegetical homily for Michael's feast (for ÆLFRIC's use of both, see below). Complete copies of the *Apparitio* are preserved in the eleventh-century manuscripts of the **COTTON-CORPUS LEGENDARY** (Cotton Nero E. i and Salisbury 222; see Jackson and Lapidge 1996 p 141). Unfortunately in several places the text in both these copies has been erased and revised, making it impossible to determine their affiliations (Zettel 1979 p 183). From the end of the eleventh century, also from Salisbury, a copy of the *Apparitio* is included in another augmented recension of the homiliary of Paul the Deacon (Salisbury 179). None of the English copies is collated in the published editions. I am grateful to Thomas N. Hall for drawing my attention to the Canterbury fragments and to Salisbury 179.

In the anonymous tenth-century **BLICKLING HOMILIES** (*BlHom*; ed. *EETS* OS 58, 63, and 73), the *Apparitio* is the source for the Michaelmas homily, which translates the Latin narrative very closely (see Förster 1893 pp 193–200). Ælfric's homily on the Dedication of St Michael's Church, in the First Series of the **CATHOLIC HOMILIES** (*ÆCHom* I; ed. *EETS* SS 17), is likewise based on the *Apparitio* (Förster 1892 pp 28–29). Zettel (1979 pp 182–83) points out that Ælfric's source did not correspond exactly to any of the printed editions, or, in this case, to the recension preserved in the Cotton-Corpus Legendary, although the latter provides some readings closer to Ælfric's than those of the three printed editions that Zettel consulted (viz., Mombritius 1910 1.389–91 and 649–50; *AS* Sept. 7.61–62; and Waitz 1878). It will now be necessary to take account of the Salisbury homiliary copy and the Canterbury fragments mentioned above, of which Zettel was apparently unaware. Particularly interesting is the conjunction in the Canterbury manuscript (and other augmented copies of Paul the Deacon's homiliary to judge from the edition in *PL* 95.1522–30) of the *Apparitio* narrative and Haymo of Halberstadt's exegetical homily for the feast, which was Ælfric's source for the second part of his Michael homily. Godden (*EETS* SS 18.281–89) sources the homily in relation to the *PL* edition of Paul's homiliary.

Given the amount of verbal agreement between Ælfric's version and that in *Blickling* (briefly noted by Förster 1892 p 195), the two texts deserve to be more closely studied in relation to one another.

We have not seen the dissertation of Rushing (1949). The most important recent study is that of Richard Johnson (1998b), to whom I am grateful for various kinds of help with this entry. His dissertation traces the establishment and diffusion of Michael's cult in Anglo-Saxon England, and includes a thorough review of the scholarship on the Old English texts concerned with the archangel, and an edition of the *Apparitio* in Salisbury 222, which he regards as the best of the English copies, collated with the others listed here.

For a review of recent scholarship on the *Apparitio* and the Gargano cult site, see Arnold (2000) pp 567–73.

Milburga: *BLS* 1.405–06; *BSS* 9.479–82; Farmer (1987) p 302.

This entry has been written more in the hope of provoking further work on the hagiography of Milburga (Mildburg; feast day February 23) than in the conviction that the Anglo-Saxons possessed a written life (Latin or Old English) of the saint. She was one of the three saintly daughters of Princess Ermenburg (alias "Domneva") of Kent and the Mercian Merewald, king of the Magonsaetan (see also **ÆTHELREDUS ET ÆTHELBERHTUS** and **MILDREDA**). Mildburg spent most of her life as the second abbess of Much Wenlock, a double monastery in Shropshire (founded by her father, Merewald, ca. 670 under the direction of **BOTOLPHUS**), and died ca. 715. **BONIFACE** in a famous letter (**EPISTOLAE** X, to Eadburh; ed. *MGH* ES 1.7–15) gives an account of a Wenlock monk's otherworld vision, later rendered into Old English (*Lett* 1, B6.1; ed. Sisam 1953 pp 199–224). It now appears that the Wenlock foundation endured throughout the Anglo-Saxon period, although after the ninth century as a secular minster of clerics, not a monastery (Finberg 1972 pp 197–98).

As is often the case with Anglo-Saxon saints, no Anglo-Saxon life of Mildburg has survived and the post-Conquest texts, a *vita* and *translatio*, appear to have been composed in association with the Anglo-Norman *inventio* of the saint's body in an abandoned church in 1101. See Finberg (1972 pp 198–201) and Sims-Williams (1990 pp 55–56), who give conflicting dates for the unique manuscript copy of the *vita* (London,

BL Additional 34633). Neither text is listed in *BHL* or *BHL NS* (*BHL* 5959 is a fourteenth-century abbreviated version by John of Tynemouth). An account of the 1101 discovery and *translatio* is attributed to Cardinal Odo of Ostia, while the author of the *Vita Milburgae* is thought by modern scholars, on grounds of style, to be the hagiographer Goscelin of Canterbury (Finberg 1972 p 200; see also his references to the relevant work of C. H. Talbot).

The author claims to have based his account of Mildburg and her family on a variety of sources, both oral (a "venerable old priest") and written, Latin and Old English, concerning events of ca. 660, but the nature of the "vetus historia" he mentions is unknown. It seems unlikely, although not impossible, that there was an actual *vita*. He includes what he claims to be a verbatim transcription of the saint's will, but this is probably a later composition based on earlier charters, not an authentic will. See Sims-Williams (1990 pp 55–56) and Rollason (1989a pp 212–13); Finberg (1972 pp 201–06) prints only the will and argues closely for its authenticity (pp 206–15).

Various abbreviated copies of the *vita* are preserved in later manuscripts, including in the several recensions of John of Tynemouth's *Sanctilogium* (see Horstmann's edition, 1901 2.188–92). A fifteenth- or sixteenth-century account of the saint's miracles is listed by Hardy (*RS* 26/1.275). The recent book on Mildburg by Mary Brown (1990) contains a few extracts (and reproductions of two folios) from the *vita*, translated by Keith Workman of Repton School, but Brown gives no bibliographical information about this translation, which seems to be unpublished. She also states (pp 12–13) that the M.A. thesis of Edwards (1960), a study of the 1101 *translatio*, contains a transcription of the *vita*.

Mildreda: *BLS* 3.91; *BSS* 9.479–82.

Mildred (Mildrith) was the daughter of Ermenburg (i.e., Domneva, sister of King Egbert of Kent) and King Merewald of the Magonsaetan of Mercia. She was educated at Chelles, France, before becoming abbess of her mother's foundation, Minster-in-Thanet, where she died ca. 700 (feast day July 13). Little is heard of her cult or relics, however, before the eleventh century (**BEDE** does not mention her) when her relics were "translated" to St Augustine's, Canterbury. With the exception of the late Old English fragments cited below, the surviving information on the Anglo-Saxon textual tradition of her cult is later than the Anglo-Saxon period, and the picture that has emerged from it is complicated and speculative.

What has been identified as the Old English life of Mildred (*LS* 26, B3.3.26; ed. Swanton 1975 pp 24–26) in a mid-eleventh-century manuscript, London, BL Cotton Caligula A. xiv (HG 310), comprises a three-folio fragment of a text composed apparently before 1030. Ostensibly intended to serve as a homily on Mildred's feast day, this life became, in Rollason's view, the basis of a later Latin hagiographic tradition.

For example, Rollason (1982 pp 29–31) notes close similarities between the Old English account of the events leading up to the founding of Minster-in-Thanet and that in a Latin *passio* of the martyred princes ÆTHELREDUS ET ÆTHELBERHTUS preserved in an early-thirteenth-century manuscript in the Bodleian Library, Oxford. This is not the *passio* composed by **BYRHTFERTH** (*BHL* 2643: see our notice for Æthelredus et Æthelberhtus), but was probably a Ramsey composition (it relates the translation of the princes' relics from Wakering, Essex, to Ramsey, 978 x 992). Rollason argues (1982 pp 18–19) that the Oxford *passio* is based on a lost Latin *vita* of Mildred, written at St Augustine's, Canterbury, between 1035 and 1047–59. In his opinion, the Old English life of Mildred may have been a source for such a lost Latin life from St Augustine's, but the Old English version probably originated at Minster-in-Thanet before 1030, when Mildred's relics were brought to Canterbury (Rollason 1982 p 31; the traditional date of the translation, 1035, has been revised to 1030 by Sharpe 1990b).

Goscelin of Canterbury seems to have known and used such a Latin text in composing (1087–91) his *Vita Mildredae* (*BHL* 5960): see Rollason's discussion (1982 pp 18–20, 58–68) and edition (pp 89–104); see Whitney (1984) for historical analysis and Yerkes (1982) for the fragmentary remains of the earliest known manuscript copy of this work and the accompanying *Translatio* (*BHL* 5961).

The 1030 translation also gave rise to a hagiographic tradition that is first reflected in Goscelin's elaborate account, *BHL* 5961 (ed. Rollason 1986), from several manuscripts of the twelfth (and one of the late eleventh) century. The relevance of the lections for Mildred's translation, in London, BL Harley 652 (HG 424), pointed out to me by J. E. Cross, is uncertain. See also the references in *BHL NS* (p 647) to *BHL* 5961a and 5962.

A summary list of the Kentish royal saints and their affiliations and foundations, contained in Cambridge, Corpus Christi College 201 (*KSB* 8, B18.8; ed. Liebermann 1889), includes an outline of Mildred's legend. Rollason refers to this text as *Þa halgan* and provides a summary of its contents (1982 pp 83–84) but does not discuss its origins or form. Later knowlege of the Mildred legend may be reflected in two other items mentioned by Swanton (1975 p 16): that is, a marginal note in the Parker Chronicle concerning the martyrdom of the two princes, and a forged St Augustine's charter.

AC (p 104) offers somewhat problematic information on Mildred. Among the anonymous saints' lives or *Sanctorale* (*LS*) listed in AC there are two consecutive entries for lives of Mildred (B3.3.26, B3.3.27), edited by Cockayne and Förster respectively. Only the first of these, however, the fragment in BL Cotton Caligula A. xiv (HG 310), is identified in the manuscript as a homily for the feast of Mildred, as confirmed by Swanton (1975 p 16) in an edition published after AC. This text is identified in the *Dictionary of Old English*, in its Microfiche "List of Texts and Index of Editions" (*MCOE* 1980 p 136), as "MildredCockayne" (B3.3.26) after its first editor (see *RS* 35/3.422–28). The second text, identified in AC as a second life of Mildred, in London, Lambeth Palace 427 (HG 518), is, in Rollason's view, a fragment of an Old English life of **SEXBURGA**, and the emphasis on Sexburga/Sexburh in the Lambeth fragment is acknowledged in *MCOE* where the first part of the Lambeth fragment, fol 210r–v, is designated B3.3.27.1, "MildredFörst," with reference to the first part of the edition by Förster (1914), but the second part, fol 211r–v, is designated B3.3.27.2 and entitled "SeaxburghFörst." This division reflects the apparently differing content of the two parts and the fact that the adjacent folios 210 and 211 were originally unadjacent. Swanton, however, whose 1975 edition is not cited in *MCOE*, regards all the fragments as portions of what he calls *Lives of the Kentish Royal Saints*, implying this is a single work "compiled some time between 974 . . . and 1030" (1975 p 17). His edition of the fragments from the two manuscripts includes a translation (pp 17–24), Old English texts (pp 24–27), and genealogical charts of the Kentish and East Anglian royal houses.

To complicate matters further, AC cross-references one Mildred fragment, B3.3.27, with B17.10, where the same text fragment is listed as "Kentish Royal Saints" as if it were merely a list. Conversely the other Mildred fragment, B3.3.26, is cross-referenced with B18.8, the notice for both *Þa halgan* and the "List of Saints' Resting Places" (ed. Liebermann 1889 pp 1–19 and discussed by Rollason 1978). In the light of Rollason's researches and arguments regarding the growth and development of the Mildred legend, there is now a need for a new edition and reassessment of *Þa halgan*, as well as of the Old English life of Mildred and other associated vernacular texts. For notice of a recent unpublished paper on the historical context of the Mildred/Sexburga fragments, see the conference abstract by Hollis (1993). The recent study of the Lambeth manuscript by O'Neill (1991) focuses on the original contents of the volume, an eleventh-century Winchester psalter (see **LITURGY, PSALTERS**), and merely comments (p 145 note 11) that the Mildred/Sexburga fragments, originally from another manuscript, were probably added at Lanthony, that is, after 1136.

Milus et Senneus.

MSS – Lists none.
A-S Vers Mart B19.iy.
Quots/Cits – Refs none.

The notice for November 15 in the ninth-century **OLD ENGLISH MARTYROLOGY** (*Mart*; ed. Kotzor 1981 2.251–52) presupposes knowledge of an account of the life and martyrdom of Bishop Milus (or

Mynus) of "Drasythio" and "Leila" (with his deacon Senneus), corresponding to the Eastern text preserved, for example, as *BHG* 2276 (see Herzfeld, *EETS* OS 116.239, who quotes from a modern Latin translation). The *Martyrology* provides a summary sketch of Milus's life and a more detailed account of his passion with special attention to the prediction and performance of retribution on his persecutors. No Latin source text has so far been identified. The *Martyrology*'s account testifies once again to the survival in ninth-century England of Eastern traditions doubtless imported with Archbishop **THEODORE OF CANTERBURY** and Hadrian in the later seventh century. See Kotzor (1981 2.370–71) and Hohler (1995 pp 225–26) for further references.

Nazarius et Celsus, passio [ANON.Pas.Naz.Cel.]: *BHL* 6039; *BLS* 3.200–01; *BSS* 9.780–84; *CPL* 2213.
   ed.: Mombritius 1910 2.326–34.

MSS – Lists none.
A-S Vers *Mart* (B19.ez).
Quots/Cits – Refs none.

Nazarius (July 28) according to his legendary *passio* (fifth century) was converted to the faith by Saint Peter (**PETRUS APOSTOLUS**) in Rome, after which he left the city with Celsus, his young assistant, to preach the gospel far and wide. They were martyred in Milan during Nero's persecution and buried in unmarked graves outside the city. In the late fourth century (386–95) their bodies were among those discovered and translated, with miracles, by **AMBROSE** (see **GERVASIUS ET PROTASIUS**). Their relics were distributed throughout Gaul (see, e.g., **GREGORY OF TOURS**, DE GLORIA MARTYRUM XLVI, LX; ed. *MGH* SRM 1/2.519–20 and 529–30). The textual history of the legend is complicated by its being frequently combined with that of Gervasius and Protasius, but Zanetti (1979) argues for their original independence.

    BEDE would know of their cult through Paulinus of Milan's *Vita Ambrosii* XXXII–XXXIII (ed. Pellegrino 1961 pp 98–100: see **AMBROSIUS**), but he includes only Gervasius and Protasius in his **MARTYROLOGIUM**. The author of the **OLD ENGLISH MARTYROLOGY** notice cited here (*Mart*; ed. Kotzor 1981 2.161–62), however, seems to have known the *passio* itself. Cross (1982d p 32) finds the text printed by Mombritius the closest to the *Martyrology* account, though admittedly on the basis of only one phrase. **PSEUDO-AMBROSE**, *Sermones* LV (*PL* 17.715–19; attributed to **FAUSTUS OF RIEZ**, *CPPM* 1A.65, 1B.5946), may also be a factor, as may be the poem by **ENNODIUS, CARMINA** I.18 (*MGH* AA 7.254).

The Mombritius text, designated Passio 1a in *BHL*, was formerly considered the best representative of the presumed original *passio* composed ca. 450 (see, e.g., Pellegrino 1961 p 97 note 6; Delehaye 1933a pp 79–80). Zanetti (1979), however, on the basis of his study of the Greek versions of the legend (*BHG* 1323–24), and of the language and style of Mombritius's text, argues persuasively that the latter is a sophisticated stylistic revision of the lost work. In his view the best guide to the original *passio* is the Greek texts; further, that among the extant Latin texts, the most primitive version is an unpublished recension of *BHL* 6042 (Passio 2a), found in some of the early legendaries now in Munich and Turin. It remains to be seen if Zanetti's findings will necessitate a revision of Cross's sourcing of the *Martyrology* notice.

Neotus, vita [ANON.Vit.Neot.]: *BHL* 6054–55; *BSS* 9.810–11; *BLS* 3.227–28.
  ed.: Dumville and Lapidge 1985 pp 111–42.

MSS – Lists none.
A-S Vers ?*LS* 28 (Neot, B3.3.28).
Quots/Cits – Refs none.

According to his legend, Neot (feast day July 31) was first a monk of Glastonbury and then later a hermit and founder of a monastery in Cornwall. He is said to have counseled, and interceded for, King Alfred during the Danish wars, died ca. 877, and posthumously ordered his relics translated from St Neot in Cornwall to what was later St Neots, Huntingdonshire. While some hold the view that there were really two saints of this name, one Cornish and one English (Gransden 1974 p 49 note 52), it seems more likely that the "three extant versions of St Neot's life reflect the mixed geographical claims on the saint and his relics evident in the two foundations dedicated to his memory" (Richards 1981 p 262). At issue here are two of these versions: the anonymous Old English prose *Neot* (*LS* 28; ed. *EETS* OS 152.129–34), and the Latin "Vita Prima" (*BHL* 6054, number 3 in the *BHL* Neot listings), which is accompanied by the *translatio* narrative (*BHL* 6055). Extant manuscripts are from the twelfth century. See Lapidge in Dumville and Lapidge (1985 pp lxxviii–lxxxii). Another life, *BHL* 6052, is definitely later than our period and is not dealt with here.

Recent studies of the memorials of Neot disagree about the dates and mutual relationships of the texts. Richards (1981 pp 262–69) has argued that the anonymous Old English *Neot* is of pre-Conquest composition (probably from Crowland) and independent of *BHL* 6054. The latter she dates after 1082 (the refoundation of the St Neots priory from Bec, Normandy). She posits a lost Latin life, composed in the west country, as the common source of all the others. Lapidge (in Dumville and Lapidge 1985 pp xcvi, ci, and cix–cxi) insists, however, on a pre-Conquest date for the "Vita Prima" (possibly by a Cornishman schooled in England) and considers this to be the source of the Old English *Neot*. Lapidge (pp cxvi–cxvii) reckons also that *Neot*, on the basis of its language, is very late, possibly contemporary with its early-twelfth-century manuscript. To judge from the other texts in the manuscript (NRK 209, and see Handley 1974), the unique copy of *Neot* is probably not a reliable witness to the original Old English life of the saint. See Wilcox (1991 p 213) for a passage from **WULFSTAN OF YORK**'s *Sermo lupi* interpolated into the life. On the saint and his cult, see Doble (1929). We have not seen Wright's essay (1995).

Nereus et Achilleus, passio [ANON.Pas.Ner.Achill.]: *BHL* 6058–66; *BLS* 2.284–85; *BSS* 9.813–20; *CPL* 2214. See also **PETRONILLA ET FELICULA**.

ed.: *AS* Mai. 3.6–13.

MSS 1. London, BL Cotton Nero E. i: HG 344.
2. Salisbury, Cathedral Library 221 (formerly Oxford, Bodleian Library Fell 4): HG 754.5.
Lists – A-S Vers none.
Quots/Cits Pas.Ner.Achill. 9.62–10.64: *ÆCHom* I, 26 (B1.1.28) lines 107–56.
Refs none.

Historically, Nereus and Achilleus (feast day May 12) seem to have been pretorian guards in Rome, martyred in the first century, and their early cult is attested in the fourth-century remains discovered by modern archeologists (see Fasola's article in *BSS*, based on his 1967 monograph). They came to be incorporated, however, into an "epic legend" or "Gesta" in seven parts revolving around the exile of Flavia Domitilla during the reign of Domitian. There is sound historical evidence that this Roman noblewoman of the first century was exiled by the emperor for professing Christianity, but in the "Gesta" of Nereus and Achilleus her exile is rewritten as physical martyrdom and the two soldiers are transformed into Domitilla's eunuch attendants (see Quentin 1908 pp 364–65). Although the *BHL* assigns separate numbers to the seven parts (see below) and they do not always appear together in the manuscripts, they nonetheless form one continuous narrative, which is thought by Achelis (*TU* 11/2.23–24) to have been composed first in Greek in the sixth century, but modern opinion considers the Latin text the original. Much of the story is narrated in the form of letters passing among Marcellus (former follower of Simon Magus), Nereus and Achilleus, and other members of the cast of characters. This entry considers the whole work, although two of the protagonists, Petronilla and Felicula, merit a separate entry.

The whole "Gesta" is represented in both the eleventh-century copies of the **COTTON-CORPUS LEGENDARY** (the London and Salisbury manuscripts cited above), comprising I, the prologue and preliminary acts of Nereus and Achilleus (*BHL* 6058); II, ending β, a variant version of the so-called "Rescriptum" of Marcellus, concerning some supernatural encounters between the apostle Peter and Simon Magus (*BHL* 6060), after which follows a succession of accounts of martyrdoms suffered under the prefect Aurelianus; III, Marcellus's account of Peter's daughter, Petronilla, and her companion, Felicula (*BHL* 6061β); IV, the priest Nicomedes (*BHL* 6062); V, Nereus and Achilleus (*BHL* 6063); VI, ending α, Eutyches, Victorinus, and Maro (*BHL* 6064); VII, Domitilla (*BHL* 6066).

Early Anglo-Saxon knowledge of the various components of the cycle is uncertain. **BEDE** does not include any of them in his **MARTYROLOGIUM**. The **OLD ENGLISH MARTYROLOGY** (*Mart*, B19.bf; ed. Kotzor 1981 2.112; see also p 316) mentions Nicomedes (and Priscus) but purely as a liturgical commemoration, lifted from an "older" sacramentary, with no hint of knowledge of the "Gesta." For evidence that the martyrologist knew at least a portion of it, however, see the entry for Petronilla et Felicula.

Ogilvy (*BKE* p 70) incorrectly states that the "Rescriptum Marcelli" portion of the "Gesta" is used by **WULFSTAN OF YORK** in a passage in a homily on the Anti-Christ (*WHom* 1.4, B2.1.4; ed. Napier 1883 pp 94–102) and that it is fully translated in the **BLICKLING HOMILIES** account of Peter and Paul (*BlHom* 15, B3.3.32; ed. *EETS* OS 58, 63, and 73). The source in both cases is the quite different **PASSIO PETRI ET PAULI** (see **APOCRYPHA**, **PSEUDO-MARCELLUS**). The Wulfstan passage in question (Napier 1883 pp 98.5–101.5) is omitted by Bethurum in her edition of Wulfstan's homilies (1957 p 132.70 note) as a spurious addition, although it occurs in two eleventh-century manuscripts.

In **CATHOLIC HOMILIES** (*ÆCHom* I; ed. *EETS* SS 17; translation in Thorpe 1844–46 1.373–75), in the first part of his homily on Peter and Paul, **ÆLFRIC** supplements his main source (Pseudo-Marcellus, *Passio Petri et Pauli*) by drawing on the "Rescriptum Marcelli" from the "Gesta" for further episodes involving Peter and Simon Magus (Förster 1892 pp 18–21; Zettel 1979 pp 177–78; for discussion, see Godden 1996 p 270 and Whatley 1996a pp 477–78). See now Godden's sourcing (*EETS* SS 18.215–16).

For Ælfric's use of the "Gesta," part III, in his **LIVES OF SAINTS**, see the entry for Petronilla et Felicula.

Nicolaus, vita [IOH.DIAC.NEAP.Vit.Nic.]: *BHL* 6104–06, 6108; *BLS* 4.503–06; *BSS* 9.923–39.
   ed.: Treharne 1997 pp 178–97.
MSS 1. Cambridge, Corpus Christi College 9: HG 36.
     2. Cambridge, Trinity Hall 21: HG 201.
     3. Hereford, Cathedral Library P.II.5: HG 267.
     4. Orléans, Bibliothèque Municipale 342 (290): HG 869.
Lists none.
A-S Vers 1. *LS* 29 (Nicholas, B3.3.29).
          2. ?ANON.Vit.Nicol.metr.
Quots/Cits – Refs none.

The Latin life of Nicholas (feast day December 6), fourth-century bishop of Myra in Asia Minor, was composed ca. 880 by the Neapolitan John the Deacon, using as his main sources an otherwise unimportant Greek account (*BHG* 1352y) by one Methodios (patriarch of Constantinople 843–47?) and a Latin version (*BHL* 6119) of a separate episode (*BHG* 1350) from the saint's life, the so-called *Stratilates* composed in the time of Justinian (C. Jones 1963 pp 42–46, 1978 pp 45, 47). The early Latin version of *Stratilates* is believed to date from the seventh century (C. Jones 1978 p 29) or eighth (Siegmund 1949 p 243) and is extant in several early manuscripts (ed. Meisen 1931 pp 527–30; translated C. Jones 1978 pp 29–36). **HRABANUS MAURUS** in the second quarter of the ninth century uses this text for a lengthy notice in his *Martyrologium*, DEC. 35–104 (ed. *CCCM* 44.124–26; see Siegmund 1949 p 243), which in turn is drastically abridged by **USUARD** in his **MARTYROLOGIUM** (ed. *PL* 124.771-72; C. Jones 1978 p 389 note 13). A copy of Usuard's work (ca. 860), made at Abingdon in the late tenth or early eleventh century, is extant in Cambridge, Corpus Christi College 57 (HG 61). *Stratilates* seems to have formed the original conclusion of John the Deacon's *Vita Nicolai* (Treharne 1997 p 39), which thus comprised only the first three parts (*BHL* 6104–06) of the five attributed to it by the Bollandists in the version they designate Vita 1a (ed. Falconi 1751 pp 112–22), although, significantly, they assign to the closely related Vita 1b (ed. Mombritius 1910 2.296–306) only three *BHL* numbers (6111–13), parts I–III together constituting *BHL* 6111.

Nicholas's December 6 feast day, while enabling him to assume in modern times the role of the secular spirit of Christmas, also ensured that his life would remain unedited by the Bollandists (*AS* having ceased publication before the December saints' lives could be attempted); at the same time, the complexity of his hagiographic tradition and the great number of surviving manuscripts of the *vita* have so far deterred other scholars from attempting to rescue Nicholas from his textual limbo. A study of the manuscript tradition has been promised: see Corsi (1979 p 359).

A good deal of evidence has been adduced to argue that the cult of Nicholas did not spread to England until after the Norman Conquest (Schipper 1986; Treharne 1997 pp 36–45). Certainly the surviving manuscripts suggest that John the Deacon's *Vita Nicolai* was not available to the Anglo-Saxons until near the end of the eleventh century, to which period the four manuscripts listed here are assigned. The text in the Orléans manuscript is a palimpsest, written in an apparently English Caroline hand over an unidentified text in an Anglo-Saxon minuscule script of the eighth century (*CLA* 6.820). Van der Straeten (1982 p 72) dates the upper hand in the tenth century, but in HG and *CLA* it is assigned to the eleventh. The manuscript was at Saint-Benoît-sur-Loire by the end of the eighteenth century. I have found no information on its original provenance. It contains parts I–III and V (*BHL* 6104–06, 6108). Only two folios survive of the copy in Cambridge, Trinity Hall 21, which James (1907 pp 38–39) suspects was written at Canterbury. Likewise imperfect is the copy in the Hereford manuscript (Mynors and Thomson 1993 p 76). A later, twelfth-century Hereford manuscript (P.VII.6), however, contains a complete copy of parts I–V accompanied by a substantial collection of miracles (see next entry).

Corroborating the view that Nicholas's cult was a post-Anglo-Saxon phenomenon is the absence of the *Vita Nicolai* from the core collection of the eleventh-century **COTTON-CORPUS LEGENDARY**. The somewhat disorderly text of the *vita* (comprising *BHL* 6104–06, plus supplementary miracles) in volume two of the Worcester copy of the Legendary (the first Cambridge manuscript listed here) is not part of the original Legendary (Jackson and Lapidge 1996 p 133). It is near the beginning of the manuscript (pp 26–53; fols 13v–26v) among the texts added in the late eleventh or early twelfth century. It was then supplemented with two blocks of text, the first in a smaller contemporary hand (possibly the same hand as the original?), the second in a later twelfth-century hand. The original copy of the *vita* occupies pp 26–40 and 53, the two supplements having been inserted abruptly into it part way through the *Stratilates* episode, and occupying pp 41–52. The completion of the *Stratilates* episode occupies most of the two columns of p 53, except for the first three lines of the life of **RUMWALDUS INFANS**. The first supplement (pp 41–46) begins on p 41 with the words *intueri aerumpnas*, which complete the sentence interrupted in the original copy at the end of p 40, at the words *dignatus es* (*Vita Nicolai* 634; in Corsi's edition p 378.39). The rest of the *Stratilates* episode occupies most of p 41, after which the supplement continues with several of the other Nicholas miracles (see below, the entry for Nicolaus, miracula) and a prayer. Thus the ending of *Stratilates* is given twice, on pp 41 and 53. Further codicological study is needed here, but it appears that, although the hand of the first supplement may be the same as that of the original copy, both supplements, which are portions of other legendaries, appear to have been added at the same time.

Also of late-eleventh- or early-twelfth-century origin is the Old English prose *Nicholas* (*LS* 29; ed. Treharne 1997), surviving uniquely in the twelfth-century Rochester homiliary, Corpus Christi College 303 (NRK 57). According to Cross (1971b p 369) it renders the narrative content of the *Vita Nicolai* quite closely but abbreviates its stylistic and biblical flourishes. Treharne (whose valuable edition and study came to hand too late for more than a perfunctory account here) confirms and refines this estimate in detail (1997 pp 46–61) and argues persuasively that the work was most probably composed by the author of the Old English prose life of Saint Giles (see **AEGIDIUS**). She also locates the Old English *Nicholas* in the early textual tradition of John the Deacon's life, in that *Nicholas* contains only the equivalent of parts I–III, ending somewhat abruptly with the *Stratilates*, and omitting any account of the saint's death. "The life in CCC 303 is a translation of an early exemplar of the *vita* of John the Deacon which had not yet reached the expanded stage where later episodes were added to the original" (1997 p 49). Treharne points to the Latin text preserved in the Cambridge portion of the Cotton-Corpus Legendary (discussed above), as well as that in London, BL Cotton Tiberius D. iv (HG 378.5), as the kind of text that formed the source of the Old English prose life. In addition to an edition and translation of the Old English *Nicholas* (pp 131–62), she prints an eclectic edition of the *Vita Nicolai* (cited above, headnote), based mainly on the Cotton Tiberius manuscript, which also contains the *Vita Aegidii*. We have not seen the edition and translation of the Old English *Nicholas* by Lazzari (1997).

In contrast to Schipper and Treharne, C. Jones believes the cult of Nicholas was introduced into England not by the Normans but by Lotharingian clerics before the Conquest, and that under their influence Bishop Wulfstan II (**WULFSTANUS II**) promoted the liturgical veneration of the saint at Worcester, first as prior and then as bishop (1062–92). For a neumed set of lections for Nicholas from mid-eleventh-century Worcester, see the entry for Nicolaus, lectiones. Jones also asserts that the lost late-eleventh-century life of Saint Wulfstan by Prior Coleman, extant only in William of Malmesbury's Latin translation, is partly modeled on the *Vita Nicolai* (C. Jones 1963 pp 9–13, 1978 pp 142–44). Other evidence supporting Jones's position is the grading of Nicholas's feast in a Crowland calendar dated mid-eleventh century by F. Wormald (1934 p 265) and a rather elaborate Old English prose description of a relic of Nicholas in the Exeter List of Relics (*Rec* 10.8, B16.10.8; ed. Förster 1943 p 77; Conner 1993a p 182). See further Ortenberg (1992 pp 71–73), and also Pfaff (**LITURGY, MASSBOOKS**) for remarks on the proper mass for Nicholas in a liturgical book, the so-called "Red Book of Darley" (Cambridge, Corpus Christi College 422: HG 111), written at Winchester ca. 1060 but "used in mid-Derbyshire . . . in a parochial rather than monastic context." See also Lapidge's collections of litanies (*HBS* 106: IV,1,59) for Nicholas's name in a mid-eleventh-century litany originating probably in Cologne. Doubtless closer scrutiny of surviving liturgical manuscripts would yield further instances of Nicholas's cult in England before the Conquest.

It should be pointed out, however, that the liturgical lections for Nicholas in the Cotton-Corpus Legendary do not necessarily imply the existence of the full *Vita Nicolai* in Wulfstan's pre-Norman Worcester. The neumed lections may have been sufficient for the time; hence the later need for a full text of the *vita* as witnessed by the copy added to the Legendary nearer the end of the century.

While the 1751 edition of Falconi appears to be the fullest record of the expanded textual tradition of the *Vita Nicolai*, those of Mombritius, Corsi (1979 pp 361–80, a transcription of a twelfth-century manuscript in Berlin, partially collated with Falconi's text), and Treharne (1997, cited in the headnote) are more generally accessible and appropriate for use in this context; the two last more nearly represent the text known to the English in the late eleventh century.

On the late-eleventh- or early-twelfth-century Latin verse life of Nicholas, based mainly on John the Deacon's *Vita Nicolai*, see the entry for Nicolaus, vita metrica.

Nicolaus, miracula [ANON.Mir.Nicol.]: *BHL* 6150–56, 6160–65 (see below).

ed.: Falconi 1751 pp 122–26.

MSS 1. Cambridge, Corpus Christi College 9: HG 36.

2. Orléans, Bibliothèque Municipale 342 (290): HG 869 (see below).

Quots/Cits – Refs none.

Copies of the first Latin life of Nicholas of Myra, by John the Deacon (see previous entry) are frequently accompanied by various additional chapters recounting miracles from the saint's own lifetime, as well as surrounding his death and afterwards, that are not included in the *vita* proper and were presumably composed later. In *BHL* these form sections 8 (subdivided I–XXVIII) and 9 (I–VII) of Nicholas's *dossier* (the *vitae* are 1–7), comprising *BHL* 6130–76 of the cumulative catalogue. The Orléans manuscript contains a modest selection of these texts appended to the *vita* proper: *BHL* 6154–55 (8.XXV–XXVI: on his sickness and death), 6160–64 (9.I–II, posthumous miracles "ante translationem").

The Nicholas texts added in the late eleventh or early twelfth century to the Cambridge portion of the **COTTON-CORPUS LEGENDARY** include a broader selection of miracula: added as a supplement to the manuscript's original copy of the *Vita Nicolai* are *BHL* 6150–56, 6160–61, 6163–65 (pp 41–46); next were added (in the following order) *BHL* 6172, 6168–69, and 6174 (pp 46–52). Although these two blocks of texts are in different hands and have been culled from other legendaries or booklets (the first contemporary with the original copy of the *vita*, the second later in the twelfth century), they seem to have been added to the manuscript at the same time.

A comparably extensive collection of Nicholas miracles is preserved in the twelfth-century legendary from Hereford, now Hereford, Cathedral P.VII.6 (Mynors and Thomson 1993 p 111).

Nicolaus, translatio [IOH.ARCHIDIAC.BAR.Trans.Nicol.]: *BHL* 6190.
   ed.: Nitti di Vito 1937 pp 357–66.

MSS Dublin, Trinity College 174: HG 215.
Lists – Refs none.

The original and contemporary account of the 1087 translation of the relics of Nicholas from Myra to Bari in Apulia is that of Nicephorus (*BHL* 6179: see C. Jones 1978 pp 175–94 for translation and commentary), who wrote on behalf of the Greek merchants and nobles of Bari. A somewhat later account, however, by Archdeacon John (before February 1089), partly dependent on but opposing that of Nicephorus, became the more widely known. It was composed for the benefit of the Archbishop of Bari, Ursus, who was sympathetic to the Norman party in Apulia. See C. Jones (1978 pp 194–97). The Dublin copy was made at Salisbury by one of Webber's Group I scribes (Webber 1992 p 142) before the end of the eleventh century and thus within a decade or so of its composition.

Nicolaus, lectiones [REG.EICHST.Hist.Nicol.].
   ed.: C. Jones 1963 pp 17–45.

MSS London, BL Cotton Nero E. i: HG 344.
Lists – Refs none.

This set of lessons recounting episodes from the life of Nicholas of Myra is part of a self-contained liturgical office for the saint's December 6 feast day. The office or "historia," as it was called, comprising lections, prayers, anthems, responses, and musical settings, is generally attributed to Reginold of Eichstätt, who became bishop of that city (966–91) apparently as a reward for his composition of this work, which proved popular and influential largely on account of its music (C. Jones 1978 pp 113–14). According to its modern editor, the earliest manuscript copy of the office, complete with neums, is that in the London (originally Worcester) manuscript of the **COTTON-CORPUS LEGENDARY** (eleventh century) where it was added in an eleventh-century hand similar to the main hand, and out of calendar order, along with another supplementary text (see **LEO IX**), after the last item in this portion of the main legendary (see **HIERONYMUS**). This copy of Reginold's *historia* is the basis of C. Jones's edition (1963). Another copy, perhaps "equally early," is in a Vatican manuscript (C. Jones 1978 p 398 note 22). The somewhat later Salisbury Cathedral recension of the Cotton-Corpus Legendary does not preserve, or provide for, the Nicholas *historiae*. The copy in Cotton Nero E. i thus appears to have been a special supplement for the use of the Worcester monks and choir. Jones credits Bishop Wulfstan II (**WULFSTANUS II**) with introducing the cult of Nicholas during his time as prior, even before he became bishop in 1062, under the influence of other English bishops of Lotharingian origin or education (C. Jones 1978 pp 142–43).

As noted by Treharne (1997 p 37), Jones's edition has been criticized by Hohler (1967) because Jones did not recognize that the text in the Cotton-Corpus Legendary is a complex hybrid, containing elements from what Hohler asserts are the two main recensions of Reginold's original work: one German, the other "Anglo-French." While the German recension, the original, is generally accepted as the work of Reginold, the Anglo-French recension (a reworking of Reginold's composition) is attributed to Isembert, monk of Saint-Ouen, Rouen (later abbot of Saint-Cathérine-au-Mont, 1033–54). Copies of the German recension in its original form are scarce (Hohler, p 45, identifes only two, both of Italian provenance), but the Anglo-French is more widely represented, and in various forms: a Benedictine form is extant, for example, in a thirteenth-century Worcester version, and a secular form is extant in a Sarum antiphonal from Barnwell Priory (Hohler 1967 p 41). Hohler (p 44) regards the recension in the Cotton manuscript as "thoroughly anomalous." He describes it as "fundamentally the German secular text adapted to Benedictine use by embodying at mattins 'extra chants' characteristic of the French Benedictine version." Complicating matters, the German secular form incorporated in the Cotton hybrid is "itself anomalous," displaying various "pecularities" that Hohler has found replicated in two later manuscripts associated with the church of "the Madeleine" (*sic*) in Verdun. Since Verdun was at times within the province of Trier, with which Leo IX was "closely associated," Hohler reckons Verdun may be the source of both the Leo lections and the German component of the Nicholas office in the Cotton manuscript. Complicating matters even further, after the hybrid text was copied into the manuscript another scribe, responsible for inserting musical notation, also inserted numerous texts from the French Benedictine recension (and one from the purely German tradition) in apparently random order "by erasure, overwriting, interlining" and in the margins, to produce a textual mess that Jones's edition fails to interpret, with a result that it is "totally unusable" (Hohler 1967 p 45, although he praises Jones's work as containing a "priceless body of references to scattered texts," p 40). Unfortunately, Jones in his later comments on this text (1978 pp 112–23 and 143) does not respond to Hohler's strictures or modify any of his original positions.

According to Jones (p 115) the narrative lections are abbreviated extracts from the *Vita Nicolai* by John the Deacon (see above, Nicolaus, vita), which is also the source of some of the language of the antiphons and other liturgical verses. See Jones's edition of the lections (1963 pp 21–30) for references to the corresponding passages in the *Vita Nicolai*, which he cites from the text printed by Mombritius (1910), not that of Falconi. At least Hohler does not dispute any of this.

Nicolaus, vita metrica [ANON.Vit.Nicol.metr.]: *BHL* 6212–16.
  ed.: Wright and Halliwell 1841–43 2.199–208.
  MSS London, BL Cotton Tiberius B. v: HG 373.
  Lists – Refs none.

The London manuscript listed here, a composite collection, includes a set of miscellaneous texts of Winchester or Battle Abbey provenance (fols 2–73, 77–78 only) dated in the first half of the eleventh century in HG (earlier in *BKE* p 49 and Ker 1964 p 8). Added to blank spaces in this manuscript (fols 55r–56r, 73r–v, 77r), apparently in a contemporary hand, is a metrical life of Nicholas (*BHL* 6212–16), which versifies several episodes from John the Deacon's *Vita Nicolai* (see above, Nicolaus, vita) and two additional episodes of later vintage (*BHL* 6172–73). In the edition cited here, Wright prints the text from this manuscript. Along with HG's attribution to Winchester, other authorities, including Ker (1964), associate the manuscript also with Battle Abbey (founded by William the Conqueror in 1067 and staffed by monks from Marmoutiers-les-Tours). C. Jones (1978 pp 227–28) suggests that the verse life was composed by the monks of William's foundation at Battle or its dependency, the priory of St Nicholas at Exeter (founded 1087), since the Conqueror is believed to have been personally devoted to Nicholas (C. Jones 1978 p 24). We include this text among those known to the Anglo-Saxons only because the dating and provenance of the manuscript are still in doubt and a pre-Norman origin of the poem is not impossible, although unlikely. Jones does not explain how the metrical life, which ends with an account of the 1087 translation to Bari (*BHL* 6216), could be considered "contemporary" with the early-eleventh-century contents of the manuscript.

Nicomedes. See **NEREUS ET ACHILLEUS**.

Ninianus, miracula metrica [ANON.Mir.Nin.]: *BHL* 6240b; *BLS* 3.568–70; *BSS* 9.1012–14; *CPL* 2152.
  ed.: *MGH* PLAC 4.943–62.

MSS – A-S Vers none.
Quots/Cits see below.
Refs ALCVIN.Epist. 431.

Ninian (feast day September 16) was known to BEDE (HISTORIA ECCLESIASTICA III.iv; ed. Colgrave and Mynors 1969 p 222) as the fifth-century missionary of the South Picts and the saint whose relics were venerated at Whithorn (Candida Casa) in modern Galloway. Bede appears not to have seen a *vita* of Ninian, however, but an eighth-century poem on Ninian's miracles survives (*BHL* 6240b) and was probably based on an earlier *vita*, according to Colgrave and Mynors (1969 p 222 note 2). MacQueen (1980 p 2) suggests that the posited lost work depended in turn on an earlier Cumbric life.

Of unknown authorship but probably composed at Whithorn by a pupil of **ALCUIN** in the later eighth century, after Alcuin had departed to pursue his career on the Continent (Godman 1982 p xliv), the surviving Latin poem was sent to Alcuin at his request from England (see Campbell 1967 p xlvii) and is preserved uniquely along with an anthology of texts, compiled by Alcuin, in a manuscript now in Bamberg (see Levison 1940, MacQueen 1980, and most recently Lapidge 1989b pp 166–67).

Apparent echoes of the poem are detected by Alistair Campbell (and confirmed by Lapidge 1989b p 168) in the ninth-century CARMEN DE ABBATIBUS (see ÆTHILWULF) and in the tenth-century hagiographic works by **FRITHEGOD** (BREVILOQUIUM VITAE WILFRIDI 21; ed. Campbell 1950) and **WULFSTAN OF WINCHESTER** (NARRATIO METRICA DE SANCTO SWITHUNO 306; ed. Campbell 1950), implying a continuing textual tradition through the later Anglo-Saxon period, but no English copies have survived. The twelfth-century life and miracles of Ninian written by Ailred of Rievaulx (*BHL* 6239) are independent of the metrical *miracula* but the two evidently share a common source, namely, the lost Latin *vita*, the style of which Ailred describes as "barbarous" (Levison 1940). This may have led a thirteenth-century scribe or rubricator to state that Ailred's life was translated "de Anglico" (see Hardy, *RS* 26/1.45), which in turn misled Wilson (1970 pp 91–92) into positing a lost Old English life of Ninian.

The pioneer study of the poem is that of Strecker (1922), who later produced the standard edition cited here. Other more recent studies of Ninian's hagiography, besides that of Levison (1940), include two earlier articles by MacQueen (1961, 1962). See also the bibliography in Farmer (1987 p 319).

Oethelwaldus: *BLS* 1.664–65.

Æthelwald (also Oidiluald; feast day March 23), formerly a monk at Ripon, succeeded CUTHBERTUS as hermit on Farne Island, where he lived for twelve years, as related by BEDE in HISTORIA ECCLESIASTICA V.i (ed. Colgrave and Mynors 1969 pp 454–56). Originally buried at Lindisfarne, his relics came to Durham after the Viking invasions (he heads the list of anchorites in the Durham *Liber Vitae*). There is no separate *vita* extant and he does not appear in the surviving late Anglo-Saxon calendars. This notice is due solely to his appearance in the OLD ENGLISH MARTYROLOGY (B19.by; ed. Kotzor 1981 2.58–59).

Kotzor (p 302) cites Bede's *Historia* as a source for the *Martyrology* notice for April 21, but, as pointed out by Cross (1985b p 238), the *Martyrology* (Kotzor 1981 2.58.4–6) echoes Bede's prose VITA CUTHBERTI XLVI (ed. Colgrave 1940 p 302.28–29) to describe Æthelwald's death, not the blander phrasing of the *Historia* (ed. Colgrave and Mynors 1969 p 456.7–8). However, the *Martyrology*'s anecdote about the hermit's ability to hear sounds from heaven appears to be condensed from Bede's metrical *Vita Cuthberti* 918–28 (ed. Jaager 1935). See *AS* Mar. 3.463–65.

Olympias et Maximus. See ABDON ET SENNEN.

Oswaldus Rex: *BLS* 3.293–94; *BSS* 9.1250–95; Farmer (1987) pp 328–30.

There does not appear to be any Anglo-Saxon hagiographical tradition beyond that of BEDE concerning Oswald of Northumbria (died 642, feast day August 4), first of the Anglo-Saxon royal martyrs. His cult spread first with the distribution of his relics, both in England and on the Continent (Clemoes 1984), and his story was known through several enthusiastic passages, recounting the king's deeds of war and peace and his posthumous miracles, in Bede's HISTORIA ECCLESIASTICA III.i–vi, ix–xiii, and IV.xiv (ed. Colgrave and Mynors 1969 pp 214–28, 240–54, and 376–80), also III.vii (p 232; still valuable for the cult and literature of Oswald are Plummer's notes to his edition [1896 2.157–58]). ALCUIN devotes a considerable portion of his York poem, VERSUS DE SANCTIS EUBORICENSIS ECCLESIAE 236–506 and 1600–48 (Godman 1982), to a reworking of the Bedan narrative, at times surprisingly bloodthirsty (253–64), but he appears to have known little, if anything, from other traditions. Similarly dependent on Bede is the notice for Oswald in the OLD ENGLISH MARTYROLOGY (B19.fj; Kotzor 1981 2.171–72; detailed sourcing pp 336–37).

The chapters from Bede must have been used as lections on the saint's feast day, which is widely recorded in the surviving Anglo-Saxon calendars and service books as liturgically important (e.g., the graded entries in F. Wormald 1934 pp 9, 51, 65, and 261). The Bedan chapters are found separately extracted in numerous Continental manuscripts and in one of English provenance, in Oxford, Bodleian Library Digby 175 (*SC* 1776; HG 614) of the late eleventh century, suggesting the possibility that such sets of extracts were available during the Anglo-Saxon era. One such set of extracts may have been available to ÆLFRIC, whose vernacular life of Oswald in his LIVES OF SAINTS (*ÆLS*, B1.3.26; *EETS* OS 94 and 114) is a careful reworking of the Bedan narratives (C. Loomis 1931; Needham 1966 pp 18 and 27–42; see also Cross 1965a and McCrea 1976 pp 81–86). A twelfth-century Paris manuscript of English origin, regarded by Lapidge and Winterbottom (1991 pp cxlviii–cxlix) as representing Ælfric's hagiographic commonplace book, does have extracts from Bede relating some posthumous miracles of Oswald (*Historia* III.x–xi), but not his life, at least according to the information in the Bollandists' catalogue (Bollandists 1889–93 2.354–55). Ælfric's Old English life of Oswald, with that of EADMUNDUS, is among the most frequently printed of

Ælfric's hagiographic works: see, for example, the editions of Whitelock (1967 pp 77–85, 252–54), Needham (1966 pp 18–42), and Cassidy and Ringler (1971 pp 239–49).

The *vita* of Oswald generally attributed to Reginald of Durham (*BHL* 6325), partially printed by T. Arnold (*RS* 75/1.326–85), while much indebted to Bede, is also a repository of legends about Oswald and his relics that Bede neglected or that arose later; it is said to be of the later twelfth century (e.g., Rollason 1989a p 127) but this seems inconsistent with the author's statement that he was present at the retranslation of the Bardney/Gloucester relics between 1108 and 1114 (Plummer 1896 2.158). Among scholarly work on Oswald that came to hand too late to take account of here are Thacker's analysis (1996b) of the cult of Oswald's relics cult; see also Jansen (1996).

Oswaldus Wigorniensis, vita [BYRHTFERTH.Vit.Oswald.]: *BHL* 6374; *BLS* 1.439–40; *BSS* 9.1296–97; Farmer (1987) pp 330–31.
  ed.: *RS* 71/1.399–475.

MSS London, BL Cotton Nero E. i: HG 344.
Lists – Refs none.

Oswald of Worcester (feast day February 28) is generally regarded as one of the three chief architects of the English ecclesiastical revival in later tenth-century England. From an aristocratic Danelaw family, which included Archbishop Oda of Canterbury, Oswald, after spending time at Fleury imbibing the spirit of reformed monasticism, became bishop of Worcester (961) and then Archbishop of York (972) while retaining his see at Worcester. He is credited with the foundation or refoundation of several important abbeys, including Ramsey, Evesham, and Pershore, along with Westbury and Winchcombe, and the gradual reform of the Worcester chapter, although he was less successful in reviving monasticism in his northern archdiocese. His literary impact was indirect but important, since as patron of Ramsey he facilitated **ABBO OF FLEURY**'s **PASSIO EADMUNDI** and fostered the school that produced **BYRHTFERTH**, who wrote this life of Oswald, the life of **EGWINUS** of

Evesham, and the martyrdom of the princes ÆTHELREDUS ET ÆTHELBERHTUS, among other literary achievements.

The Ramsey *Vita Oswaldi*, which has been regarded as an important historical source (Gransden 1974 pp 80–87; but see Lapidge 1996a), best known to Anglo-Saxonists for its description of Ealdorman Byrhtnoth at the Battle of Maldon (991), was composed by Byrhtferth within a decade or so of Oswald's death in 992, but the only manuscript copy is that cited above, which was added to the Cotton manuscript somewhat later than the main text of the **COTTON-CORPUS LEGENDARY**, but certainly during the episcopacy of **WULFSTANUS II** (1062–95) who translated Oswald's relics to a new shrine in the late 1080s (see Mason 1990 pp 119–20) and instituted the feast of the translation (October 8). Among the most recent discussions of the manuscript is that of Lapidge (1991b) who provides a text (with manuscript facsimiles) and translation of the Maldon portion, and whose previous discussion (1975a pp 91–95) established Byrhtferth's authorship of the life on a firmer footing. For the *vita*'s liturgical interest, see Millinger (1979). For the liturgy of Oswald's own cult, see Corrêa (1996).

The *vita* was reworked by Eadmer of Canterbury early in the twelfth century (*BHL* 6375), and also appears to be the basis of a lengthy account, *BHL* 6378, in the Ramsey chronicle (which the Bollandists, in *BHL NS* p 676, mistakenly assert concerns not Oswald the archbishop but his namesake, **OSWALDUS REX**, the martyred king of Northumbria).

Raine's *RS* edition of the *Vita Oswaldi* will be replaced by that of Lapidge (forthcoming b) in the series *Oxford Medieval Texts*. For further information on Oswald's career and family connections, and the cultural legacy of his foundations, see the richly informative volume of essays (Brooks and Cubbitt 1996) commemorating the millennium of Oswald's death, which includes the studies by Lapidge (1996a) and Corrêa (1996) cited here.

Pancratius, passio [ANON.Pas.Pancrat.]: *BHL* 6421; *BLS* 2.285; *BSS* 10.82–86; *CPL* 2215.
ed.: Huisman 1939 pp 16–18.

MSS 1. London, BL Cotton Nero E. i: HG 344.
2. Salisbury, Cathedral Library 221 (formerly Oxford, Bodleian Library Fell 4): HG 754.5.
Lists none.
A-S Vers 1. ?BEDA.Mart. 86.2–4.
2. ?*Mart* (B19.cv).
Quots/Cits – Refs none.

Pancras (feast day May 12), by an irreverent accident of history, is known to the modern British as a great Victorian railway station (compare Saint-Nazaire in Paris), but his medieval legend describes him as a Phrygian boy, an orphan, brought to Rome by his uncle, with whom he is said to have been martyred under Diocletian, after earlier having been baptized by Pope **CORNELIUS**. His cult was honored by Pope Symmachus (498–514) who built (or rebuilt) a basilica over his supposed tomb in the former cemetary of **CALEPODIUS** (*BLS* 2.285; however, see Pietri 1976 p 613 note 4). Pancras's cult had spread from Rome to Merovingian Gaul by the late sixth century, as evidenced by **GREGORY OF TOURS, DE GLORIA MARTYRUM** XXXVIII and LXXXII (*MGH* SRM 1/2.512–13 and 544.18). Relics of the saint were in England by the mid-seventh century, a gift of Pope Vitalian to King Oswy of Northumberland (**BEDE, HISTORIA ECCLESIASTICA** III.xxix; ed. Colgrave and Mynors 1969 p 320), and he is one of the select group of saints commemorated in the eighth-century metrical calendar of York, verse 28 (ed. Wilmart 1934). Later medieval tradition and some modern historians claim that Archbishop Augustine (**AUGUSTINUS CANTUARIENSIS**) had dedicated a former heathen temple to Pancras in Canterbury as early as 598, to serve as a house of worship until the church of St Peter and St Paul (now Christ Church Cathedral) was completed (Huisman 1939 pp 39–40). For the possible existence of a chapel dedicated to Pancras at Winchcombe in the early ninth century, see **KENELMUS**.

The *passio* exists in numerous variant versions of the same basic story, the Bollandists' Passio 1. Verrando (1982 p 116; see also Huisman 1939 p 9) has recently argued for the early seventh century as the composition date of the original *passio* (now lost), to which in his view the text in

Mombritius (Passio 1g, *BHL* 6426) most closely corresponds (Verrando 1982 p 118). For other speculation as to which extant recension best preserves the old form, see Leclercq (*DACL* 13.1005), who favors *BHL* 6420 (Passio 1a), and Huisman who insists on the version at issue here, *BHL* 6421, which is preserved in the eleventh-century London and Salisbury manuscripts of the **COTTON-CORPUS LEGENDARY**. Verrando classifies this version, however, along with *BHL* 6424, as representing the "second archetype."

The *passio* seems to have been known in England throughout the Anglo Saxon period. Of the several recensions, Quentin (1908 p 87) cites *BHL* 6420 as a possible source for Bede's brief notice in his **MARTYROLOGIUM** (BEDA.Mart.; ed. Dubois and Renaud 1976), but other recensions would have served equally well. Verrando (1982 pp 123–24) points to either *BHL* 6424 or 6421.

Cross (1986a pp 231–32) analyzes the notice in the **OLD ENGLISH MARTYROLOGY** (*Mart*; ed. Kotzor 1981 2.102) narrowing the source to *BHL* 6421 as printed in *AS* (*AS* Mai. 3.21), but with variant details reflected in earlier manuscripts, and suggests that the martyrologist may have added information from the **LIBER PONTIFICALIS**. The *AS* edition, however, as Huisman points out (1939 p 14; Verrando 1982 p 124), contains late medieval (and modern) editorial changes; as Cross implies, a better guide to the kind of text used by the Old English martyrologist would be the ninth-century Graz manuscript he cites (1986a p 231), or the Salisbury manuscript, listed here and printed by Huisman (1939 pp 16–19). It is uncertain, however, if this variant of the text is descended directly from the *Martyrology*'s immediate source, for the latter clearly had "Cledonius" as the name of Pancras's father, which is cited by the Bollandists from one or more of their manuscripts (*AS* Mai. 3.21 note c) whereas the Cotton and Salisbury manuscripts have "Cleonius."

On the Latin versions of the *passio*, see Franchi de' Cavalieri (1908 pp 77–120) and Verrando (1982). See also Ruggini (1992) on the relationship of the hagiography and cults of Pancratius of Rome and his namesake of Sicily. On the Greek translations, see Declerck (1987). See also Grosjean (1942) for a severely critical review of Huisman's edition.

Pantaleon, passio [ANON.Pas.Pant.1hα]: *BHL* 6437; *BLS* 3.192–93; *BSS* 10.107–16.
   ed.: Pulsiano (forthcoming).
MSS 1. London, BL Cotton Nero E. i: HG 344.
      2. Salisbury, Cathedral Library 222 (formerly Oxford, Bodleian Library Fell 1): HG 754.6.
Lists – Refs none.

According to his spurious legend, Pantaleon (feast day July 28; Greek "Pantaleimon") as a young man was training for a promising career as a physician at the Nicomedian court of the pagan emperor Maximianus when, under the influence of a Christian priest, Hermolaus, he was converted to the faith, gave away his wealth, and as a result of his efforts on behalf of persecuted Christians, suffered torture and finally execution. Numerous variant versions of the *passio* derive from an earlier Greek *passio* (*BHG* 1413). Their wide distribution in the West, and the popularity of the saint's cult, may have begun with the translation of the relics of Pantaleon to Lyons in the ninth century (Siegmund 1949 p 245).

In her unpublished M.A. thesis, Matthews (1966 p 128) classifies the extant manuscripts into three main recensions, A, B, and C, which do not correspond in any orderly way with the classification in *BHL*. Two of these groups are particularly important here. Matthews's A group, "descended from an archetypal translation of the Greek life," includes the text edited by Mombritius (*BHL* 6429) along with *BHL* 6430, 6432, and 6437, represented in the **COTTON-CORPUS LEGENDARY** (as in Cotton Nero E. i and Salisbury 222), which Matthews identifies as *BHL* 6438, apparently a typographical error. Zettel (1979 p 23), Jackson and Lapidge (1996 p 139), and now Pulsiano (forthcoming) number the English recension copies correctly as *BHL* 6437. Matthews's B group includes Florence, Biblioteca Laurenziana Medicea Plut. xx. 3 (twelfth century), which she labels, again mistakenly, *BHL* 6437 for *BHL* 6438 (the Bollandists specifically identify the Florence text as *BHL* 6438).

The impression given by the *BHL* classification here is of only minute variations in *explicits* between *BHL* 6437, Passio 1hα, and *BHL* 6438,

Passio 1hβ, but according to Matthews's grouping they represent significantly different recensions of the legend, although probably ultimately related. Matthews places the Florence manuscript, and several others, including *BHL* 6435, in her group B; these in turn share a common original with the manuscripts of her group C, corresponding to *BHL* 6431, 6436, and 6440. Unfortunately, and surprisingly, she does not explain the textual basis of her classification nor the precise relation of BC to A. Nor does she take account of the potentially important ninth-century Chartres manuscript mentioned by Siegmund (1949 p 245).

There is no evidence for Anglo-Saxon knowledge of the saint before the eleventh century, when his name begins to occur regularly in calendars, for example, that of Winchester, New Minster, dated 1023–35 (F. Wormald 1934 p 120), although his feast is commemorated with narrative histories in the major Carolingian martyrologies, as pointed out by Pulsiano. Matthews draws attention to later, post-Conquest English links with the monastery of St Pantaleon in Cologne, of which Gyda (Gytha), exiled daughter of King Harold II, was a benefactress, according to a twelfth-century sermon by Rupert of Deutz (Coens 1885), but this evidence seems rather late. Earlier links between England and Cologne (see LEO IX, URSULA) could also have helped promote Pantaleon's cult in England. By the mid-eleventh century, the cult is well established in the liturgical devotions of Wells and New Minster, Winchester (proper masses and calendars), and Exeter (calendar). See Ortenberg (1992 pp 75–76). Pulsiano (forthcoming) also refers to relics in Canterbury inventories.

I am grateful to Phillip Pulsiano for arranging for me to see a prepublication copy of his edition. He describes his Latin text as a "composite" edition, selecting readings from both the Salisbury and Cotton manuscripts, of which the former seems to be the superior text, although the two "vary in only a few substantive instances." See also next entry.

For another recension (in Matthews's view affiliated with *BHL* 6427), see Mombritius (1910) 2.347–53 and 769 (*BHL* 6429).

Pantaleon, passio [ANON.Pas.Pant.1hβ]: *BHL* 6438.
ed.: Matthews 1966 pp 132–52.

MSS – Lists none.
A-S Vers LS 30 (Pantaleon, B3.3.30).
Quots/Cits – Refs none.

In addition to the two eleventh-century English copies of the Latin *Passio Pantaleonis* (see previous entry) there also survives a mid-eleventh-century copy (lacking one leaf) of an Old English prose *Pantaleon* in the badly damaged London, BL Cotton Vitellius D. xvii (HG 406; NRK 222, item 14), where it is accompanied by mainly hagiographic texts from ÆLFRIC's CATHOLIC HOMILIES and LIVES OF SAINTS. Matthews's unpublished dissertation (1966) includes a diplomatic edition (pp 38–72), a reconstructed text (pp 92–126), and copious notes. Despite Ker's statement (NRK p 294) that the Latin source of the Old English text is *BHL* 6437 (the recension represented in the COTTON-CORPUS LEGENDARY), Matthews's detailed comparative analysis points to a B-text, closely related to *BHL* 6438, but with some features of the C group. The provenance of the Old English work is uncertain, but in her view the language has some southeastern features, although predominantly West Saxon (Matthews 1966 p 26). That this Old English prose *Pantaleon* was probably composed no earlier than the first half of the eleventh century is corroborated by the liturgical data for Pantaleon's cult in England (see previous entry).

A new edition of the Old English *Pantaleon* is forthcoming by Phillip Pulsiano, which, although presented as a "preliminary edition, the sole purpose of which is to make the texts available in print," is based on a fresh examination of the damaged Vitellius manuscript, incorporating some of Matthews's efforts at reconstruction, but with several new readings of the manuscript and some new reconstructions inspired by the Latin text in the Cotton-Corpus Legendary and the BIBLE. Pulsiano regards *BHL* 6437 (see previous entry) as closest to the source text of the Old English but concedes that "the text as transmitted by the Salisbury and Nero manuscripts does not reflect the ultimate source of the Old English version." We have not seen the recent study by Proud (1997).

Patricius, epistolae [PATRIC.Epist.1and2]: *BHL* 6492–93; *BCLL* 25–26; *BLS* 1.612–17; *BSS* 10.396–407; *CPL* 1100; Farmer (1987) pp 337–38; *SEHI* 29.
   ed.: Bieler 1952 1.56–102.
MSS 1. London, BL Cotton Nero E. i: HG 344.
      2. Salisbury, Cathedral Library 221 (formerly Oxford, Bodleian Library Fell 4): HG 754.5.
Lists – Refs none.

The chief saint of Ireland (feast day March 17), a Roman Briton who labored as a missionary among the *Scotti* during the second half of the fifth century, was certainly venerated among the early English, but the Anglo-Saxon evidence is chiefly late and liturgical rather than hagiographic. For a unique proper mass for Patrick, in a mid-eleventh-century mass book of uncertain provenance (the "Giso" or "Vitellius" sacramentary), see the edition by Alicia Corrêa (1993), to whom I am grateful for this reference. See also **LITURGY, MASSBOOKS**. Patrick's feast day is graded in one Canterbury calendar that includes saints specially culted at Glastonbury, where his feast day was August 24, which also occurs in a Worcester calendar (F. Wormald 1934 pp 65, 233). It is generally accepted that there was an Irish contingent among the clerics at tenth-century Glastonbury, where the body of a Patrick was said to rest during Dunstan's time (see Stubbs, *RS* 63.10–11). The reference to Patrick's relics in the life of the martyred seventh-century Irish pilgrim, **INDRACTUS**, may date from the same period (*Passio Indracti* 14–15, ed. Lapidge 1982b p 199). How old this cult was, and which of the possible Patricks, if any, lay buried there, is unknown (Rollason 1978 pp 66, 92). For the Glastonbury cult, the evidence for which is nearly all post-Conquest, and for further references, see Finberg (1967), Lapidge (1982b pp 182–83), Scott (1981 p 7), and Adams (1993). For a succinct statement of the problem of the two Patricks, see Carley (1985 pp xxxvii–xxxviii).

The monks of Glastonbury had two of the *vitae* of Patrick by the time William of Malmesbury visited them in the 1120s and wrote his lost life of the saint, but there is no evidence that the standard lives were known to the Anglo-Saxons. BEDE surprisingly does not mention Patrick in his HISTORIA ECCLESIASTICA, and although Willibrord's eighth-century calendar has the March 17 feast day, there is no notice in Bede's MARTYROLOGIUM (one was added in a ninth-century Continental recension: ed. Dubois and Renaud 1976 p 50.24). The brief notice for Patrick in the OLD ENGLISH MARTYROLOGY (*Mart*, B19.az; ed. Kotzor 1981 2.33) has not been definitely linked with any known hagiographic source and appears to reflect "access to rare information" (Cross 1981e pp 173–76; also 1985b p 247).

In the eleventh-century London and Salisbury manuscripts of the COTTON-CORPUS LEGENDARY, the copies of Patrick's epistolary "Confessio" (*BHL* 6492) and his letter to Coroticus's Christian soldiers (*BHL* 6493) derive, according to Bieler in his edition (1952 1.7–18, 52), from a Continental textual family rather than from the insular tradition preserved in the Book of Armagh. The Cotton manuscript from Worcester (Bieler's manuscript C) and the Salisbury copy (manuscript G) share a common exemplar, forming the subfamily "Δ^2." Bieler speculates that the ancestor of all such extant Continental copies was carried from Ireland, along with relics of Patrick, by FURSEUS to northern France ca. 630. He doubts that the Patrician letters, however, were included in the French original of the Cotton-Corpus Legendary itself. For recent discussions and translations of the two letters, see Dumville (1993 pp 107–27, 191–202).

Patroclus Trecensis, passio [ANON.Pas.Patroc.]: *BHL* 6520; *BLS* 1.138–39; *BSS* 10.417–18; *CPL* 2130a.

MSS 1. London, BL Cotton Nero E. i: HG 344.
2. Salisbury, Cathedral Library 221 (formerly Oxford, Bodleian Library Fell 4): HG 754.5.

Lists – Refs none.

More interesting than the conventional contents of Patroclus's sixth-century *passio* are the circumstances surrounding the revival, in the time of **GREGORY OF TOURS**, of devotion to this third-century martyr of

Troyes (feast day January 21). As Gregory relates (DE GLORIA MARTYRUM LXIII; ed. *MGH* SRM 1/2.531), Patroclus's cult had been neglected owing to lack of a written *passio*, but the solitary clerk in charge of the delapidated shrine one day claimed to have seen and copied such a *passio* that was in the possession of a passing stranger. The initial angry scepticism of the local bishop was later refuted by another copy of the same work, discovered in Rome and therefore accepted as authoritative by contemporaries.

Copies of Passio 1 are preserved in the London and Salisbury versions of the **COTTON-CORPUS LEGENDARY** (Zettel 1979 p 16; Jackson and Lapidge 1996 p 135), but other evidence of Anglo-Saxon interest in this saint of north-central France is lacking.

On the sources and date of the *passio*, see Van der Straeten (1960).

Paulinus Eboracensis: *BLS* 4.80–81; *BSS* 10.163–64; Farmer (1987) pp 342–43.

The English ministry of Paulinus (feast day October 10) extended from 601, when **GREGORY THE GREAT** sent him with Mellitus and Justus to provide helpers for Augustine of Canterbury (**AUGUSTINUS CANTUARIENSIS**), to his death in 644, serving first as Bishop of York from 625 (or earlier) until the death of his Northumbrian protector, King Edwin, in 633, then as Bishop of Rochester. The main narrative for his life and career, focusing especially on the Northumbrian portion, is **BEDE**'s HISTORIA ECCLESIASTICA II.ix–xx (ed. Colgrave and Mynors 1969 pp 162–206). See also chapter XVI of the anonymous Whitby life of Gregory the Great (*BHL* 3637, ed. Colgrave 1968 p 100; see **GREGORIUS MAGNUS**), and **ALCUIN**'s selective verse epitome of Bede's account (**VERSUS DE SANCTIS EUBORICENSIS ECCLESIAE** 135–215; ed. Godman 1982).

Bede's account of Paulinus's career and death does not include any conventional miracles, but his miraculous involvement in consoling Edwin during his exile is strongly hinted in Bede and affirmed in the Whitby life in the chapter cited above. Later Northumbrians regarded

Paulinus as a saint (see the eighth-century York metrical calendar, verse 64, ed. Wilmart 1934 p 68; also the ninth-century calendar in F. Wormald 1934 p 11), and he is widely commemorated in later Anglo-Saxon calendars, though with various titles. No separate *vita* is known, however, apart from two late medieval versions based on Bede's account (*BHL* 6553 and 6554). Of interest here is the anonymous Old English prose *Paulinus* (*LS* 31, Paulinus, B3.3.31), a one-page digest of the Bedan material, apparently intended as a homily for the saint's feast. It was added in the late eleventh century to the end of an early-eleventh-century Old English homiliary, presumably at Rochester. See the edition and discussion by Sisam (1953 pp 151–52) and the interesting brief analysis by Roberts (2000 pp 434–35). For another possible Old English text, now lost, on this (or another) Paulinus, see Wilson (1970 pp 75–76).

Paulus Apostolus. See **APOCRYPHA: PSEUDO-LINUS, PASSIO PAULI; PSEUDO-MARCELLUS, PASSIO PETRI ET PAULI.**

Paulus Thebaeus, vita [HIERON.Vit.Paul.]: *BHL* 6596; *BLS* 1.91–93; *BHM* 261; *BSS* 10.269–80; *CPL* 617.
    ed.: *PL* 23.17–28.
MSS 1. Cambridge, Corpus Christi College 389: HG 103.
    2. London, BL Cotton Caligula A. xv: HG 311.
    3. ?Worcester, Cathedral Library F.48: HG 761.
Lists none.
A-S Vers 1. ALDH.Carm.uirg. 774–96.
    2. ALDH.Pros.uirg. 265.6–17.
    3. ?BEDA.Mart. 11.5–8.
    4. *Mart* (B19.t).
Quots/Cits Vit.Paul. 22.3–4: FELIX.Vit.Guth. 94.12; see below.
Refs none.

Paul the hermit (Paul of Thebes; feast day January 10 in early Western, including Anglo-Saxon, calendars), whose life in the Egyptian desert near Thebes in the late third and early fourth centuries is the subject of **JEROME**'s *Vita Pauli*, was venerated as one of the founders of monasticism, along with John the Baptist and Antony. According to one influential modern authority, Jerome probably knew virtually nothing about Paul and could therefore draw on his own experience and indulge his imagination and literary gifts to the full (Berschin 1986–91 1.135–36). The result was a work of enduring popularity in the Latin West, to judge from the multitude of extant manuscripts (see the tables in Oldfather 1943 pp 18–35 and in *BHM*). For the manuscripts of the Greek translations, see the chapter in Oldfather (1943 pp 143–250) by Katharine Corey, who reviews (pp 144–45) the earlier controversy surrounding the priority of the Latin or Greek versions.

Anglo-Saxon familiarity with Jerome's *Vita Pauli* was early and continuous. **ALDHELM** in his verse and prose **DE VIRGINITATE** (ALDH. Carm.uirg [*BHL* 6596m], Pros.uirg.; ed. *MGH* AA 15) celebrates Paul's longevity, chastity, heroic asceticism, and the miracle of the crow. One of the *vita*'s episodes (chapter XI, Paul and Antony breaking bread) is depicted on the early-eighth-century Ruthwell Cross (see Meyvaert 1992 pp 131–35 and plate 24). However, although Quentin (1908 p 99) sources the notice for Paul in **BEDE**'s **MARTYROLOGIUM** (BEDA.Mart.; ed. Dubois and Renaud 1976) as if it were Bede's work, according to the modern editors the notice is not of the authentic Bedan "layer."

In addition to the phrases from the *vita* that are echoed in Felix's mid-eighth-century life of **GUTHLACUS**, cited above (FELIX.Vit.Guth.; ed. Colgrave 1956), Colgrave notes several others: *Vita Pauli* 20.7–8, 23.22–23, 26.21–22 with 26.29–31, and 28.25–26, echoed in *Vita Guthlaci* 96, 90, 154, and 116, respectively.

Anglo-Saxon copies of the *Vita Pauli* survive in several interesting contexts. The first part of the Cotton manuscript, the earliest listed here (containing this text and Jerome's **DE VIRIS INLUSTRIBUS**), was written in northeast France in the later eighth century (*CLA* 2.183) but reached St Augustine's, Canterbury, by the tenth. It is one of the two or three most important manuscripts (group K) of the *Vita Pauli*, according to Oldfather's team (1943 p 142; see also pp 102–05). Likewise from St Augustine's is the Cambridge manuscript (second half of the tenth century), which also contains the life of Guthlac. Oldfather (pp 74–75, 77–78) argues that the group of manuscripts to which this belongs derives from a Canterbury exemplar, "D," characterized by the "intelligence" of the scribal additions that, however, detract from its value for reconstructing the archetype. John Cherf (in Oldfather 1943 pp 77–78) reveals that the copy in the Corpus manuscript is preceded by a discussion of the eremitic life that "presupposes wide reading and no mean ability." See also Colgrave's edition of the life of Guthlac (1956). The two St Augustine's manuscripts are from widely different manuscript groups. See Cherf's stemma in Oldfather (1943 p 124).

Unrelated to either of the former manuscripts is the Worcester manuscript (late eleventh century), belonging to the L group of manuscripts (among which it is most closely related to a twelfth-century manuscript now in Cambridge University Library). It also contains Jerome's life of **HILARION**, Evagrius's Athanasian life of **ANTONIUS**, and a selection from portions of the **VITAE PATRUM** (Oldfather 1943 pp 106–07, 113). Cherf speculates (p 113) that the exemplar of the Worcester manuscript came to England "at about the time of the Conquest." On the uncertainties surrounding the manuscript in its Worcester context, see the references above, in the Antonius entry.

An early illuminated manuscript, known to Bede but now lost, that was brought back from Italy to England by the early East Anglian Bishop Cuthwin (716–31) is mentioned by Ogilvy (*BKE* p 50) as containing either a life of Paul the Hermit or Paul the Apostle (**PAULUS APOSTOLUS**), but it clearly concerned the apocryphal acts of the latter, not Jerome's life of Paul the Hermit (Whitelock 1972 p 9).

The ninth-century **OLD ENGLISH MARTYROLOGY** in its substantial notice for Paul the Hermit (*Mart*; ed. Kotzor 1981 2.14) appears to have drawn on both Jerome's life and the eulogy by Aldhelm, cited above (Cross 1985b pp 227–28).

ÆLFRIC includes Paul in a list of chaste desert fathers but does not tell his story. See his **LETTER TO SIGEFYRTH** 216 (*ÆLet* 5, B1.8.5; ed. *BaP* 3.23).

Despite the elaborate study, in Oldfather, of manuscript families and affiliations, there is no modern critical edition of the *Vita Pauli*. That of

Kozik (1968) is a students' edition omitting some chapters. For a useful literary-historical introduction, see Berschin (1986–91 1.134–44, especially 134–37) and more recently Lecler (1988) and De Vogüé (1991, 1991–93 1.150–84). Among modern English translations of the *Vita Pauli* are those of Waddell (1936 pp 29–39) and White (1998 pp 73–84). Paul B. Harvey Jr., of Pennsylvania State University, has announced a new edition in progress.

Pega: *BSS* 10.429.

Pega (feast day January 9) is reputed to have been the sister of the East Anglian hermit **GUTHLACUS**. Apparently a nun or anchoress herself, she buried her brother at his request and a year later translated his incorrupt body, as related in Felix's *Vita Guthlaci* (ed. Colgrave 1956 pp 154–62), which is the source of the brief notice in the **OLD ENGLISH MARTYROLOGY** (B19.s: ed. Kotzor 1981 2.13). The fact that the rarely noticed saint Pega is given a separate obit in the *Martyrology* is regarded by Kotzor (following Sisam) as evidence for a Mercian/East Anglian provenance of the Old English work or its possible Latin source text. See Kotzor (1981 2.282), who cites calendar entries and sources the six-line passage in relation to Felix's text. The unique manuscript copy of the Old English verse account of Guthlac's death, known as *Guthlac B* (A3.2; ed. *ASPR* 3) and based closely on Felix's work, breaks off just before Pega's portion of the story, although her brother's feelings for her are somewhat elaborately developed earlier (lines 1178–96). See also the edition of Roberts (1979 p 118).

Pelagia, vita [EUSTOCH.Vit.Pelag.A]: *BHL* 6605; *BLS* 4.59–61; *BSS* 10.432–37.

ed.: Dolbeau 1981 pp 199–216.

MSS – Lists none.
A-S Vers ?*Mart* (B19.ic).
Quots/Cits – Refs none.

The Pelagia of legend (feast day October 8) was a beautiful, scandalous, gem-loving actress of Antioch converted by Bishop Nonnus of Edessa to a life of ascetic, "transvestite" penitence in a Jerusalem cell. The historical Pelagia was apparently an innocent fifteen-year-old (*BLS* 4.61; see also Delehaye 1955 p 190). The original version of the legend of Pelagia was written in Greek by the pseudonymous "James the Deacon" (*BHG* 1478), probably in the fifth century. Siegmund (1949 p 245) cites a Chartres manuscript, variously dated late seventh to ninth century (see Cross 1984d p 286 and Dolbeau 1981 p 188), as the earliest witness to the Latin translation by a certain Eustochius: *BHL* 6605. Recent studies have distinguished several varieties of this version (entitled "Sacratissimus" from its *incipit*), but chiefly A1 (*BHL* 6605) and B (*BHL* 6607–09), a Carolingian "refection" of the A1 text. Mixed texts combining portions of A and B are also common. For discussion of the manuscript families of the A versions, see Dolbeau (1981 pp 161–98), who lists some uncontaminated English copies of A1 (p 187) and reports (pp 190–91) that the important early-twelfth-century Canterbury legendary, London, BL Arundel 91 (HG 305), has a mixed A/B text. No Anglo-Saxon copies of the A1 version, however, appear to be extant.

Some form or forms of the legend, however, were undoubtedly known in England in the ninth century. There is a lengthy notice for Pelagia's feast day (at October 19) in the **OLD ENGLISH MARTYROLOGY** (*Mart*; ed. Kotzor 1981 2.233–35). In his note on the text, Kotzor (1981 2.363), following Herzfeld, points to the A1 recension (as printed in *AS* and *PL*) as source, but a more recent study concludes that the author of the *Martyrology* drew on both the A1 and B versions (see next entry).

In addition to the edition of A1 by Dolbeau, see also *PL* 73.663–72 and *AS* Oct. 4.261–66. For a recent modern English translation and discussion of the Latin text, as printed in *PL*, see Ward (1987 pp 57–75). On various other aspects of the textual history of the legend of Pelagia, see the valuable collection of essays edited by Petitmengin (1981–84), which includes Dolbeau's edition.

Pelagia, vita [EUSTOCH.Vit.Pelag.B]: *BHL* 6609.
  ed.: Levy et al. 1981 pp 231–49.

MSS London, Lambeth Palace 173: HG 508.
Lists none.
A-S Vers ?*Mart* (B19.ic).
Quots/Cits – Refs none.

As mentioned in the previous entry, it has been argued that the notice for Pelagia the Penitent in the ninth-century **OLD ENGLISH MARTYROLOGY** (*Mart*; ed. Kotzor 1981 2.233–35) makes use of both the A1 and B versions of the *Vita Pelagiae* (Cross 1984d pp 281–86). Another more definite Anglo-Saxon witness to the B recension is the imperfect copy in the eleventh-century Lambeth Palace manuscript listed here (possibly owned later by the monastery of Lanthony, Gloucestershire: Ker 1964 p 112), beginning at ". . . tis. et animabus uestris maximum consolationis" in the Pseudo-James prologue, which is identified by James and Jenkins (1930–32 p 273) as *BHL* 6609 and is affiliated with a ninth- or tenth-century copy at St Gall as well as with the B portions of BL Arundel 91 (Petitmengin et al. 1980 pp 291–92). B constitutes the largest family of the surviving texts of the *vita*. On the B manuscripts as a whole, see Levy et al. (1981 pp 217–30).

Perpetua et Felicitas, passio [ANON.Pas.Perpet.Felic.]: *BHL* 6633; *BSS* 10.493–501; *CPL* 32.
    ed.: Van Beek 1936 pp 4–52.
MSS 1. London, BL Cotton Nero E. i: HG 344.
     2. Salisbury, Cathedral Library 221 (formerly Oxford, Bodleian Library Fell 4): HG 754.5.
Lists none.
A-S Vers 1. BEDA.Mart. 46.2–9.
     2. ?*Mart* (B19.au).
Quots/Cits – Refs none.

The *passio* of Perpetua and Felicitas, martyred in the arena at Carthage in 203 (feast day March 7), is one of the most frequently edited and pondered works in the tradition of Western hagiography (see, e.g., the recent lengthy discussion by Heffernan 1988 pp 185–230 and the edition by Musurillo 1972 pp 106–31; the Bollandists in *BHL* and *BHL NS* list over thirty printed editions). Yet this work is not at all typical of the genre of the female martyr's *passio*, in that its two heroines are a young nursing mother (Perpetua) and a pregnant slave (Felicity), and the former is represented as the author of a substantial portion of her own narrative concerning her dreams and visions during her imprisonment.

As might be expected of saints mentioned in the Canon of the mass (Kennedy 1938 p 61) and honored with proper prayers in the major early medieval sacramentaries, Perpetua and Felicity are widely commemorated in Anglo-Saxon calendars and liturgical books, although their story was evidently not well known to everyone (in a mid-eleventh century Crowland calendar, ed. F. Wormald 1934 p 256, they are identified as virgins!). **BEDE** in his **MARTYROLOGIUM** (BEDA.Mart.; ed. Dubois and Renaud 1976, as sourced by Quentin 1908 p 88) summarizes two episodes of the *passio* but draws the obit from Prosper Tiron (see also Van Beek's edition, 1936 pp 162*–63*). Quentin cites Passio 1 (*BHL* 6633) as Bede's main source, and although two other recensions (*BHL* 6634, 6636) are extant in manuscripts of the eighth and early ninth centuries (Cross 1986b p 284), these differ sufficiently in content and language from Passio 1 for Quentin's sourcing to be exact. All this is now called into question by Dolbeau (1995 pp 94–95).

The notice for the saints in the ninth-century **OLD ENGLISH MARTYROLOGY** (*Mart*; ed. Kotzor 1981 2.29–30) does not correspond fully to any of the extant versions, although clearly based on some form of the *passio* and perhaps, according to Cross (1986b p 284), outside sources. See also Cross (1985b p 237 note 53 and p 240; information from Christine Rauer).

Zettel points out (1979 p 81) that Perpetua and Felicity's feast day was not among those of even secondary rank in the graded calendars of Anglo-Saxon England, and to this he attributes the omission of their story, along with several other important saints, from **ÆLFRIC**'s **LIVES OF SAINTS**. Liturgical importance was doubtless a factor, but the content of the work may also have been problematic for Ælfric.

The copies of the *passio* preserved in the eleventh-century Cotton and Salisbury manuscripts of the **COTTON-CORPUS LEGENDARY** are among a small group of nine important manuscripts on which the authoritative critical edition by Van Beek (1936) is based; the English manuscripts lack the prologue (Zettel 1979 p 18; Van Beek 1936 pp 4–6). Variants from the Salisbury manuscript were published in some early printed editions: see Van Beek (pp 69*–77*), who prints variants not only from the manuscripts cited above, but also from two later English manuscripts, now in London and Canterbury. These four, in his view, together constitute a closely related manuscript family (5a, 5b, 5c, 5d respectively in his apparatus), which shares a common ancestor with Van Beek's manuscript 4, a tenth-century Paris manuscript. On the manuscripts and earlier editions, see the introduction to his edition (pp 17*–83*). For facsimiles of single folios from the Cotton and Salisbury manuscripts, see the plates at the end of his edition.

For another recent critical discussion of the *passio* as hagiographic literature, see Berschin (1986–91 1.46–56).

Petronilla et Felicula: *BLS* 2.434; *BSS* 10.514–17.

Petronilla (feast day May 30) appears to have been an authentic Roman martyr (Delehaye 1927 pp 118–20), but in the account of her in the *Passio Nerei et Achillei* (*BHL* 6058–66: see **NEREUS ET ACHILLEUS**), she has been transformed into the daughter of Saint Peter (**PETRUS APOSTOLUS**), who avoids nuptials with a pagan Roman prefect (Flaccus) by expiring in bed before he arrives to claim her ("une fin banale," remarks Delehaye 1927 p 120). According to the same legend, Felicula, martyred by the same Flaccus, is Petronilla's "foster-sister." In the Anglo-Saxon manuscript copies, the story of the two women is simply part III of the larger *passio* or "Gesta" of Nereus and Achilleus (*AS* Mai. 3.10–11), but the Bollandists give it a separate *BHL* number (6061) because in some legendaries and early printed editions it appears as a separate *passio*.

Petronilla is the only figure in the larger *passio* to have a narrative notice in the **OLD ENGLISH MARTYROLOGY** (B19.dd; ed. Kotzor

1981 2.110–11), but the *Martyrology*'s summary ignores Felicula and differs somewhat from *BHL* 6061. It is possible therefore that the martyrologist drew on another source.

ÆLFRIC was mainly interested in the *passio* for its information about Petronilla's father (see above, the entry for Nereus et Achilleus). He retells her story, from the *passio*, in greater detail than the *Martyrology*, in the course of an interesting reading for the feast of St Peter's Chair, to which he adds his own apology for the fact of Peter's marriage. See LIVES OF SAINTS, *Peter's Chair* 195–201 and 232–93 (*ÆLS*, Peter's Chair, B1.3.11; ed. *EETS* OS 76 and 82). According to Zettel (1979 pp 217–18), Ælfric appears to have followed a text similar to that in the *AS* edition, with no significant variants that might link his rendering more closely to the copy in the **COTTON-CORPUS LEGENDARY**.

Petrus Apostolus. See **APOCRYPHA**: PSEUDO-MARCELLUS, PASSIO PETRI ET PAULI; ACTUS PETRI CUM SIMONE; PASSIO PETRI. See also NEREUS ET ACHILLEUS.

Philibertus, vita [ANON.Vit.Phil.]: *BHL* 6806; *BSS* 5.702–04; *CPL* 2132.
  ed.: *MGH* SRM 5.583–604.
MSS 1. Arras, Bibliothèque Municipale 1029 (829): HG 781.
  2. Boulogne, Bibliothèque Municipale 106: HG 804.
Lists Saewold: ML 8.19.
A-S Vers – Refs none.

Filibert of Jumièges (ca. 608–85, feast day August 24) was a Gascon disciple of Saint Ouen (AUDOENUS) and founder of monasteries at Jumièges in Normandy and Noirmoutier in Poitou. His life was written by an anonymous Jumièges monk in the late eighth or early ninth century. His cult among the Anglo-Saxons appears to have been limited to the Flemish community at Bath in the tenth century, with which all the evidence listed above is linked. The Arras and Boulogne copies (classified as "B1b" and "B1a" in Levison's edition, *MGH* SRM 5.575–76) were written at Bath in the tenth or early eleventh century; they probably derive, at one or two removes, from a common Flemish exemplar. For the other hagiographic contents of the two manuscripts, see Van der Straeten (1971 pp 62–63, 137). Some of the Bath manuscripts were brought to the Continent by the Anglo-Saxon abbot of Bath, Saewold, shortly after the Norman Conquest, according to the list of books he bequeathed to Saint-Vaast, Arras (1068/69), among which Arras 1029 has been identified. How the Boulogne manuscript came from England is unknown. Levison includes its variants in the apparatus of his *MGH* edition. For further information and bibliography regarding the Bath/Flanders connection, see **AICHARDUS** and **GUTHLACUS**. There is a recent geographical analysis of the manuscripts of Filibert by Guy Philippart (1992 pp 37–41), to whom I am grateful for this reference.

Philippus Apostolus. See **APOCRYPHA, PASSIO PHILIPPI**.

Phocas, passio [ANON.Pas.Phoc.]: *BHL* 6838; *BLS* 3.617–19; *BSS* 5.948–50; Farmer (1987) p 355.
　　ed.: Mombritius 1910 2.417–22 and 718–19.

MSS – Lists none.
A-S Vers 1. ?BEDA.Mart. 127.2–6; Dubois and Renaud 1976.
　　2. *Mart* (B19.en).
Quots/Cits – Refs none.

The cult of Phocas the gardener, of Sinope on the Black Sea, was already active in the East in the early fifth century and quickly spread to Byzantium, Sicily, and Rome (Western feast day July 14). In the Greek text (*BHG* 1536), however, from which the present Latin *passio* derives (Siegmund 1949 p 247 note 1), Phocas is a bishop, not a gardener as in the earliest Eastern accounts (e.g., the panegyric of Saint Asterius of

Amasea, *PG* 40.300–13). Alban Butler's account in *BLS* 3.617–18 is a paean to cultivated nature; see also the English verse rendering by L. Morris (1892 pp 71–80). **GREGORY OF TOURS** in the late sixth century, who remarks on Phocas's fame at Antioch for protection against snake bites (**DE GLORIA MARTYRUM** XCVIII; ed. *MGH* SRM 1/2.554.7–15), also reveals the existence of some relics at Vienne, the city where the Northumbrian abbot Benedict (**BENEDICTUS BISCOPUS**) is said to have put together the collection of books that he brought home to Wearmouth in the 670s (**BEDE, HISTORIA ABBATUM** IV; ed. Plummer 1896 1.367). Bede, to judge from his **MARTYROLOGIUM** (BEDA.Mart.; ed. Dubois and Renaud 1976), certainly seems to have known a version of the legend, but not necessarily one that was identical to the extant *BHL* 6838 (Quentin 1908 pp 88–89). The author of the ninth-century **OLD ENGLISH MARTYROLOGY** in his notice for Phocas (*Mart*; ed. Kotzor 1981 2.147–48) used Bede as well as a recension of the *passio* (private communication from J. E. Cross). There is no evidence of knowledge of the text among the later Anglo-Saxons.

Piato, passio [ANON.Pas.Piaton.]: *BHL* 6845; *BSS* 10.544–49.
    ed.: Moretus Plantin 1953 pp 123–31.

MSS 1. Cambridge, Corpus Christi College 9: HG 36.
    2. Salisbury, Cathedral Library 222 (formerly Oxford, Bodleian Library Fell 1): HG 754.6.

Lists – Refs none.

    Piato (also Piatus) the priest (feast day October 1) is reputed to have been among the missionary companions of Saint Denis (**DIONISIUS**), each of whom came to be associated with specific areas of northern Gaul. Piato is linked with the region of Tournai. The earliest evidence for the cult is the seventh-century life of Saint Eloi (**ELIGIUS**) who is said to have located and translated Piato's body. On the other hand, the earliest *vita* (largely dependent on the *passio* of another saint of the same group, **LUCIANUS BELLOVACENSIS**) is dated only in the tenth century.

According to Zettel (1979 p 27) the text of the *passio* in the **COTTON-CORPUS LEGENDARY**, represented here by the eleventh-century Cambridge and Salisbury manuscripts, is not identical to that printed in *AS* Oct. 1.22–24. The edition of Moretus Plantin, cited above, does not take account of the English copies listed here or of that in the early-twelfth-century legendary (from St Augustine's, Canterbury), London, BL Arundel 91 (HG 305). Piato's cult is not reflected in Anglo-Saxon calendars of our period.

Polycarpus, passio [MARCIAN.Pas.Polycarp.]: *BHL* 6870; *BLS* 1.167–71; *BSS* 10.986–88.
    ed.: Ussher 1647 pp 13–30.
MSS 1. London, BL Cotton Nero E. i: HG 344.
      2. Salisbury, Cathedral Library 221 (formerly Oxford, Bodleian Library Fell 4): HG 754.5.
Lists – Refs none.

One of the "Apostolic Fathers," Bishop Polycarp of Smyrna was burned alive in the arena at Smyrna ca. 155 (feast day January 26). His martyrdom forms the subject of what is generally agreed to be one of the earliest surviving hagiographic narratives, the celebrated and much discussed Greek epistle written by a certain Marcianus on behalf of the members of Polycarp's church of Smyrna shortly after Polycarp's death. The epistle survives separately and is also incorporated in the form of long extracts in the church history of **EUSEBIUS PAMPHILUS** (*BHG* 1556–60). It and would be familiar in the West in the Latin version by **RUFINUS** (HISTORIA ECCLESIASTICA IV.xv; ed. *GCS* 9/2.337.4–353.12), but an important Latin version of the original Greek letter circulated in the West in the early Middle Ages. An abridged copy of this is in a late-eighth-century Munich manuscript (Siegmund 1949 p 248).

Surprisingly, **BEDE**'s brief notice for Polycarp (for January 26) in his MARTYROLOGIUM (ed. Dubois and Renaud 1976 p 23.2–5) does not draw on either the *passio* or the Eusebian extracts but depends on **JEROME**'s DE VIRIS INLUSTRIBUS XVII (ed. *TU* 14/1a.18–19, as sourced by Quentin 1908 p 100). There would almost certainly have been a notice for Polycarp in the ninth-century **OLD ENGLISH MARTYROLOGY**, but the notices for January 26–February 27 are lost. Polycarp's feast day is celebrated in the eighth-century York metrical calendar on February 1 (Wilmart 1934 pp 57 and 66), likewise in two other Anglo-Saxon calendars from the ninth and tenth centuries (F. Wormald 1934 pp 3 and 17), but among the eleventh-century calendars, surprisingly, the feast is only occasionally noted (e.g., F. Wormald 1934 pp 30, 226, and 240, all January 26).

The two surviving Anglo-Saxon copies of the Latin text of the *passio* have been important in its modern publication history, since they were used by Archbishop James Ussher of Dublin for his 1647 edition, which formed the basis of most subsequent and more accessible printed editions (e.g., Ruinart 1859 pp 77–82) until the first critical edition, that of Zahn (1876 pp 133–67), which privileges the variant readings of the manuscripts used by the Bollandists for their *AS* edition (*AS* Ian. 2.705–07, unknown to Ussher). See Zahn's introduction (1876 pp XLVIII–LV) and Harnack (1878 p 80). Siegmund (1949 p 248) draws attention to an older manuscript, now in Karlsruhe, apparently unknown to Zahn and the other editors. A recent English translation of the Greek narrative is in Musurillo (1972 pp 2–21).

Polychronius: *BSS* 10.339–40, 990–91; *CPL* 2219.

Polychronius (feast day February 17) according to his legend was a bishop of Babylon who was martyred along with several of his priests and deacons during persecution of Eastern Christians by the emperor Decius (mid-third century). Parmenius (feast day April 22), one of the priests, is distinguished in the legend by having his tongue torn out for mocking the persecutor (while Polychronius remains silent), but the disembodied tongue continues speaking. Their story, which forms Part I (*BHL* 6884) of the epic cycle associated with **LAURENTIUS**, is summarized in **BEDE**'s separate MARTYROLOGIUM notices for Polychronius and Parmenius (ed. Dubois and Renaud 1976 pp 36.2–5 and 68.20–27; sourced by Quentin 1908 p 78). For full texts of the *Passio Laurentii* in English manuscripts of the **COTTON-CORPUS LEGENDARY**, see above, the entry for Laurentius. For another copy, containing only Parts I and II, see **ABDON ET SENNEN**.

It is possible that there was originally a separate notice for Polychronius in the **OLD ENGLISH MARTYROLOGY**, but it was lost along with the other entries for January 26–February 27. The feast day of Polychronius, ungraded, is occasionally recorded in Wessex calendars of the tenth and eleventh centuries. See F. Wormald (1934 pp 31, 45).

Potitus, passio [ANON.Pas.Potit.]: *BHL* 6908; *BSS* 10.1072–74.
    ed.: *AS* Ian. 1.754–57.

MSS 1. London, BL Cotton Nero E. i: HG 344.
      2. Salisbury, Cathedral Library 221 (formerly Oxford, Bodleian Library Fell 4): HG 754.5.
Lists – Refs none.

Although he is said to have been a native of Sardica in lower Dacia, Potitus's cult is associated chiefly with the site of his martyrdom at age thirteen, Apulia, from where it must have spread to Naples and Rome. Siegmund (1949 p 248 note 1) suggests that the Latin *passio*, the earliest extant copies of which occur in eighth-century manuscripts, is a translation of a Greek original that, however, he does not identify. There is no evidence for Anglo-Saxon interest in or knowledge of this south Italian saint other than the texts of his *passio* in the manuscripts of the **COTTON-CORPUS LEGENDARY** listed here.

Praxedis, vita [ANON.Vit.Prax.]: *BHL* 6920; *BLS* 3.157; *BSS* 10.1062–72; *CPL* 2224.
    ed.: *AS* Mai. 4.300.

MSS 1. London, BL Cotton Nero E. i: HG 344.
   2. Salisbury, Cathedral Library 222 (formerly Oxford, Bodleian Library Fell 1): HG 754.6.
List – Refs none.

The *vita* of the virgin Praxedis (July 21) was not originally a separate work but rather formed the second part (*BHL* 6989) of the joint life, by Pseudo-Pastor, of Praxedis and her supposed sister **PUDENTIANA** (Potentiana). Praxedis's cult is undoubtedly that of a genuine Roman martyr buried in the catacomb of Priscilla, but she became associated with the nearby church of Pudentiana as sister of its supposed saint: hence the joint *vita* (see below, the entry for Pudentiana). The two lives frequently appear separately in the legendaries, with numerous minor variants, as in this case where the compilers of the eleventh-century London and Salisbury manuscripts of the **COTTON-CORPUS LEGENDARY** have included a version of the life of Praxedis corresponding most nearly to *BHL* 6920 (identified by Zettel 1979 p 23 and Jackson and Lapidge 1996 p 138).

A similar text, now lost, was formerly in the badly burnt manuscript London, BL Cotton Otho A. viii (HG 348; early eleventh century). Yerkes (1986 p 109) notes that Archbishop Ussher of Dublin appears to have collated the Salisbury text with both the manuscripts in the Cotton collection. In addition to the *AS* edition, see also Mombritius (1910) 2.353–54.

Primus et Felicianus, passio [ANON.Pas.Prim.Felic.]: *BHL* 6922; *BLS* 2.509–10; *BSS* 10.1104–05; *CPL* 2222.
   ed.: Mombritius 1910 2.411–14 and 717–18.

MSS 1. London, BL Cotton Nero E. i: HG 344.
   2. Salisbury, Cathedral Library 221 (formerly Oxford, Bodleian Library Fell 4): HG 754.5.
Lists – Refs none.

The fifth- or sixth-century legend of these Roman saints (feast day June 9) depicts them as patrician brothers, one of whom (Felicianus) was of advanced age, martyred under Diocletian near the site of their future tomb (and later their church) on the Via Nomentana, twelve miles from Rome. Although the legend is not thought to be of historical value, the early date of their cult is evidence for their authenticity. In 640 their relics were translated by Pope Theodore to a church in Rome itself (San Stefano in Rotondo). Their importance in Rome and in sacramentaries of Roman origin secured them a place in all later Anglo-Saxon calendars, where their feast is sometimes graded. It is not surprising therefore that a copy of the *passio* is preserved in the eleventh-century London and Salisbury manuscripts of the **COTTON-CORPUS LEGENDARY**. The text differs in only minor details from the version printed by Mombritius. The copy in the late-eleventh-century Salisbury manuscript lacks a few lines, ending on fol 277v at "corpora eorum proiecerunt" (*Passio Primi* 414.33), as noted by Zettel (1979 p 21 note 59) and Webber (1992 p 156 note 65).

Processus et Martinianus, passio [ANON.Pas.Proc.Mart.]: *BHL* 6947; *BLS* 3.7–8; *BSS* 10.1138–40; *CPL* 2223.
   ed.: Franchi de' Cavalieri 1953 pp 47–52.

MSS   1. London, BL Cotton Nero E. i: HG 344.
       2. Salisbury, Cathedral Library 222 (formerly Oxford, Bodleian Library Fell 1): HG 754.6.

List – Refs   none.

Processus and Martinianus (feast day July 2) appear for the first time in one of the later recensions of the apocryphal acts of the apostles as prison guards of Peter and Paul (**PAULUS APOSTOLUS, PETRUS APOSTOLUS**). According to their sixth-century *passio*, they were converted and baptized by the apostles before being tortured and martyred for their new faith (Verrando 1987 pp 356–60 and 366), but historically little is known about these two martyrs whose cult already had its own church on the Via Aurelia in the fourth century. The saints' relics were transferred to the basilica of St Peter in the ninth century.

Their feast day is common in Anglo-Saxon calendars and graded in some. They also have proper masses in some service books, but the only direct textual evidence for Anglo-Saxon knowledge of the *passio* is the rather careless copy found in both the London and Salisbury manuscripts listed here (**COTTON-CORPUS LEGENDARY**), which shares many textual variants with Franchi de' Cavalieri's manuscript P (a Vatican manuscript of the tenth century). His edition is to be preferred to the older printed texts (e.g., that in *AS* Iul. 1.303–04), although the differences between these and other versions are minor.

The short notice in the ninth-century **OLD ENGLISH MARTYROLOGY** (*Mart*; B19.ed; ed. Kotzor 1981 2.138) does not use the *passio*, recounting instead an anecdote taken from **GREGORY THE GREAT**, HOMILIAE XL IN EVANGELIA XXXII (ed. *PL* 76.1237). See also Kotzor (1981 1.255–56), Herzfeld (*EETS* OS 116.xxxix and 231–32), and Cross (1985a p 107).

Procopius Caesareae, passio [ANON.Pas.Procop.]: *BHL* 6949; *BLS* 3.39–40; *BSS* 10.1159–66.
ed.: Cureton 1861 pp 50–51.

MSS – Lists none.
A-S Vers 1. BEDA.Mart. 121.14–16.
2. *Mart* (B19.eh).
Quots/Cits – Refs none.

Procopius (feast day July 7 or 8) was one of the late-third-century martyrs of Palestine whose collective story was told by **EUSEBIUS PAMPHILUS** in a lost work, *On The Martyrs of Palestine*, of which only a Syriac translation, some Greek fragments, and Eusebius's own Greek abridgement survive. This abridgement was included in a revised version of his HISTORIA ECCLESIASTICA but was not part of the text translated by **RUFINUS** and was therefore unknown in medieval Latin Christendom, except for some individual sections. One of these is the *Passio Procopii*, which corresponds closely to the Syriac version and appears to be an important witness to the contents of Eusebius's original Greek account. The Latin *passio* was known to **BEDE** who summarizes it briefly in his MARTYROLOGIUM (BEDA.Mart.; ed. Dubois and Renaud 1976; sourced by Quentin 1908 p 89), as does the OLD ENGLISH MARTYROLOGY (*Mart*; ed. Kotzor 1981 2.140–41) but with more details than Bede and apparently independently of him. Herzfeld (*EETS* OS 116.232), in his note on the source of the *Martyrology* notice, misleadingly cites an eighteenth-century Latin translation of a Syriac text, not the Latin *passio* proper. Bede's *Martyrologium* account was the source of those in all the later Continental martyrologies. We have found no further attention to Procopius in Anglo-Saxon England.

On the development of the legend, see Delehaye (1955 pp 119–39). The Latin text of the *passio* printed by Cureton (like that of Violet 1896 pp 6–7) is simply reproduced from the earliest printed text, by H. Valesius (as cited in *BHL*). See also Siegmund (1949 p 207 and note 1, and pp 248–49).

Protus et Hyacinthus: *BSS* 10.1221–23; *DACL* 6.2328–31, 14.1929.

There is early evidence for a genuine Roman cult of the martyred brothers Protus and Hyacinthus (feast day September 11; see *AS* Nov. 2/2.501–02), including verses in their honor by Pope **DAMASUS** (mid-fourth century; Ferrua 1942 pp 190–94), but there is no separate legend. Their story is incorporated in the diverting but unreliable romance of **EUGENIA**, whose eunuch slaves and later companions they are supposed to have been. **BEDE**'s very brief notice in his **MARTYROLOGIUM** (ed. Dubois and Renaud 1976 p 167.2–3) may, as Quentin says (1908 p 111), be based only on the fifth-century *Martyrologium Hieronymianum*, but Bede's "qui erant eunuchi sanctae Eugeniae," a detail absent from early manuscripts of the older martyrology, suggests he may have known the *passio*. The **OLD ENGLISH MARTYROLOGY** also has a brief notice for their September 11 feast day (B19.gx; ed. Kotzor 1981 2.204–05) based on the *Passio Eugeniae* and sourced by Cross (1982b p 397). Protus and Hyacinthus also figure in **ÆLFRIC**'s version of the Eugenia legend in his **LIVES OF SAINTS** (see above, the entry for Eugenia). The eunuchs' feast is graded in the early-eleventh-century Canterbury calendar preserved in the *Bosworth Psalter* (F. Wormald 1934 p 52; see **LITURGY, PSALTERS**).

The Hyacinthus whose *passio* is listed separately in BL Cotton Nero E. i is unrelated to the two eunuchs of Eugenia. See **HYACINTHUS**.

Pudentiana, vita [ANON.Vit.Pudent./PS.PASTOR]: *BHL* 6991; *BLS* 2.347–48; *BSS* 10.1062–72; *CPL* 2224. See also **PRAXEDIS**.
 ed.: Mombritius 1910 2.390–91.

MSS 1. London, BL Cotton Nero E. i: HG 344.
 2. Salisbury, Cathedral Library 221 (formerly Oxford, Bodleian Library Fell 4): HG 754.5.

Lists – Refs none.

There was an early Christian church in Rome on land given by a certain Pudens, hence it was known as "ecclesia Pudentiana." Later this was misinterpreted as the name of a woman saint who in her spurious *vita* is said to have been the daughter of Pudens and sister of Praxedis. On the cult of Pudentiana or Potentiana (feast day May 19) and her sister, in Rome and England, see Ortenberg (1992 pp 179–80). On the legend, see Vanmaele (1965 pp 79–96). The *vita* is dated after the eighth century by Thurston and Attwater in *BLS*, but much earlier (fifth or sixth century) by Dekkers in *CPL*. This latter view is endorsed by Vanmaele (1965 p 80) who cites the opinion of Dufourcq that the passionary preserved in a tenth-century Vienna manuscript represents a sixth-century Roman passionary. The separate life of Pudentiana incorporated in the **COTTON-CORPUS LEGENDARY**, represented by the eleventh-century London and Salisbury manuscripts listed here, is a variant version of part I of the *vita* by Pseudo-Pastor (identified by Zettel 1979 p 21 and Jackson and Lapidge 1996 p 137), corresponding more closely to the text in Mombritius than to that in *AS* Mai. 4.299. A supplementary thirteenth-century portion of the London manuscript has another copy of the same text (pt 2 fol 195r–v).

Quadraginta Martyres (Milites). See SEBASTENI.

Quadraginta Sex Milites.

The story of the "46 soldiers" (feast day October 25) is the final episode in Part V (or *Passio Hippolyti*, BHL 3961) of the epic *Passio Laurentii*. The soldiers are said to have been in the service of the emperor Decius, but converted to Christianity after his death, like his wife and daughter (see TRYPHONIA, CYRILLA), and were martyred in turn by Claudius. For the text, see Delehaye's edition of the *Passio Laurentii* (1933b pp 97–98). On English manuscript copies of the *passio*, see above, the entries for LAURENTIUS.

BEDE, in his MARTYROLOGIUM (ed. Dubois and Renaud 1976 p 194.17–22), and the OLD ENGLISH MARTYROLOGY (*Mart*, B19.if, October 24; ed. Kotzor 1981 2.239) devote separate narrative notices to the episode, sourced respectively by Quentin (1908 pp 80–81) and Cross (1983a pp 211–12). ÆLFRIC, in his homily for Laurence's feast day in CATHOLIC HOMILIES, I, 29, lines 283–87 (*ÆCHom* I; ed. *EETS* SS 17), drastically abridges the legend's account of the soldiers, mentioning only their conversion with their wives, so that, misleadingly, they appear to become part of the Christian congregation that lives on after the persecution. Their feast does not appear to have been recognized anywhere in later Anglo-Saxon England.

Quattuor Coronati. See CLAUDIUS ET SOC.

Quintinus, passio [ANON.Pas.Inv.Quint.1.a]: *BHL* 6999, 7000; *BLS* 4.229–30; *BSS* 10.1313–15.
  ed.: *AS* Oct 13.781–87.
MSS Cambridge, Corpus Christi College 9: HG 36.
Lists none.

A-S Vers 1. BEDA.Mart. 197.19–22.
2. *Mart* (B19.ik).
Quots/Cits – Refs none.

The early cult of this saint (feast day October 31), who is reputed to have been a missionary companion of Lucian of Beauvais (**LUCIANUS BELLOVACENSIS**) in the time of the emperors Maximian and Diocletian, is attested by **GREGORY OF TOURS, DE GLORIA MARTYRUM LXXII** (ed. *MGH* SRM 1/2.536–37), who tells how Quintin's relics were venerated at the place now called after him in the Vermandoix region of northern France. Gregory's account says nothing about Quintin's life and martyrdom, but he repeats several details from the legend of the "Inventio Prior," by the blind nun Eusebia, of the saint's body, which had lain for 55 years on the bed of the River Somme. Since most versions of the saint's legend contain the *passio* and *inventio* together, they are dealt with together here also. There is a good deal of evidence for Anglo-Saxon knowledge of Quintin's legend in various versions throughout our period.

BEDE's brief notice in his **MARTYROLOGIUM** (BEDA.Mart.; ed. Dubois and Renaud 1976) is sourced by Quentin (1908 p 89) as deriving from what seems to be the oldest version of the *Passio et Inventio Prior* (in *BHL* designated Passio 1.a, parts I and II). Herzfeld (*EETS* OS 116.xii) identifies the same text as the source of the notice for Quintinus in the **OLD ENGLISH MARTYROLOGY** (*Mart*; ed. Kotzor 1981 2.241–42). Although the *Martyrology*'s account repeats incidents that are common to all basic versions of the *passio*, it compares the smell of Quintin's body, after it emerged from the Somme, to "roses and lilies" (*AS* Oct. 13.786a.50), a detail that is unique to Passio 1 among the Latin versions. See also Förster (1901 pp 260–61).

Passio 1 is also preserved in the Cambridge portion of one of the eleventh-century copies of the **COTTON-CORPUS LEGENDARY** (it was also formerly in Salisbury Cathedral Library 222: see Webber 1992 p 157 note 68). This text has the prologue (beginning "Sanctum atque perfectum") that is omitted in the *AS* edition but supplied in the editors' notes (*AS* Oct. 13.783 note b).

It is likely that this text or a similar one was current also in tenth-century England, since it would be needed for lections on the feast day, which was apparently of high rank at this time, for example, at Canterbury (F. Wormald 1934 pp 53 and 67).

For the source of the fragmentary Old English prose *Quintin*, see below, the entry for *Passio et Inventio Quintini* 3.

Quintinus, passio [ANON.Pas.Inv.Quint.2]: *BHL* 7005–07.
ed.: *AS* 13.787–92.

MSS Paris, Bibliothèque Nationale lat. 5575: HG 885.6.
Lists – Refs none.

According to HG (revised version), fols 1–41 of the Paris manuscript, a composite collection, are of English provenance of the second half of the tenth century. These folios contain a recension of the *Passio et Inventio Prior Quintini* that is Passio 2 and listed third in *BHL* (after 1.a and 1.b). The Bollandists identify a prologue (*BHL* 7005), *passio* (*BHL* 7006), and *inventio* (*BHL* 7007). We have no information as to the date or origins of this recension, but in this manuscript it was copied along with the *Inventio altera* and a ninth-century collection of miracles. See the relevant entries below.

Quintinus, passio [ANON.Pas.Inv.Quint.3]: *BHL* 7008–09.
ed.: *AS* Oct. 13.794–800.

MSS – Lists none.
A-S Vers *LS* 33 (Quintin, B3.3.33).
Quots/Cits – Refs none.

An elaborate revision of the first *Passio et Inventio Quintini* survives in an illuminated twelfth-century manuscript from Saint-Quentin itself, and is classified as Passio III in *BHL*. This version appears to be the source of the Old English prose *Quintin* (*LS* 33, B3.3.33; ed. Förster 1901 pp 258–59). Sadly, only the brief prologue of the Old English text survives (corresponding to the Latin prologue, *AS* Oct. 13.794a.1–10). It occupies the last page of a miscellany of Old English prose texts (see NRK 215) copied in the twelfth century and owned later (thirteenth–fourteenth century) by the Augustinian priory of St Mary, Southwick, in Hampshire (see also Carnicelli 1969 p 3). Despite the lateness of the manuscript, Scragg considers it possible (1979 p 264) that, in view of the fact that the other Old English texts in the manuscript are known to have originated in the late ninth or tenth century, the Old English *Quintin* itself may be of a similar age. See also Kiernan's codicological analysis (1981 pp 110–19), which challenges earlier work but not so as to invalidate Scragg's hypothesis. The late date (twelfth and thirteenth centuries) of the extant manuscripts of the putative Latin source, however, is problematic, and the Bollandist editor, Benjamin Bossue, despite a lengthy discussion (*AS* Oct. 13.727–30), throws no light on the matter. A later Bollandist, Poncelet (1901 p 7), remarks in passing, however, that a *Passio metrica Quintini* or *Carmen de Sancto Quintino* (*BHL* 7010, *ICL* 5685), which is at least as early as the late ninth century, is based on, and therefore later than, *BHL* 7008, the prose *passio* that is at issue here. Thus the Latin source of the Old English *Quintin* may be ninth century or earlier, despite its late manuscripts. Further research on the Latin hagiography of Quintin is needed to clarify all this, but if Poncelet's unsubstantiated statement is correct, it supports Scragg's suggestion of an early date for the Old English *Quintin*.

Quintinus, passio metrica [ANON.Pas.Inv.Metr.Quint.]: *BHL* 7011–12; *ICL* 8766, 4238.
 ed.: *MGH* PLAC 4.979–96.

MSS – A-S Vers none.
Quots/Cits see below.
Refs none.

It is possible that **WULFSTAN OF WINCHESTER** knew this work, a Carolingian verse rendering of the second of the prose *passiones* of Quintinus (*Passio et Inventio Prior* 2; *BHL* 7006–07). Campbell (1950 p 101) notes that Wulfstan's **NARRATIO METRICA DE SANCTO**

SWITHUNO I.473, "uirtutibus . . . coruscis," echoes the *Passio et Inventio Prior Metrica Quintini* 33: "virtutes . . . choruscae."

Quintinus, inventio [ANON.Inv.Quint.]: *BHL* 7014.
    ed.: *AS* 13.740–41 (paragraphs 51–55).

MSS   Paris, Bibliothèque Nationale lat. 5575: HG 885.6.
Lists – Refs   none.

The second *inventio* of the relics of Quintinus, said to have been carried out by the seventh-century Bishop ELIGIUS of Noyon, is described in the *Vita Eligii* book II, chapter 6, and often found as a separate extract, as here in the Paris manuscript (see previous entry). See also Krusch's edition of the *Vita Eligii* in *MGH* SRM 4.697.13–699.32.

Quintinus, miracula [ANON.Mir.Quint.]: *BHL* 7017–18.
    ed.: *AS* 13.801–11.

MSS   Paris, Bibliothèque Nationale lat. 5575: HG 885.6.
Lists – Refs   none.

This Carolingian collection of the miracles of Quintinus (*BHL* 7017), compiled after 827, is supplemented with an account of the translation of the relics in 835 (*BHL* 7018). On the Paris manuscript, see the above entry for *Passio et Inventio Quintini* 2 (*BHL* 7005–07).

Quiriacus (Judas), passio [ANON.Pas.Quiriac.]: *BHL* 7024; *BLS* 2.220–23, 229; *BSS* 3.1296–97.
    ed.: unpublished.

MSS   1. Cambridge, Trinity College O.10.31 (1483): HG 200.
        2. Salisbury, Cathedral Library 221 (formerly Oxford, Bodleian Library Fell 4): HG 754.5.
Lists – Refs   none.

The best known account of Judas Quiriacus (or Cyriacus; feast day May 4) is in the fifth-century legend of the finding of the Holy Cross,

Inventio S. Crucis (*BHL* 4069), which the Bollandists call "Acta Quiriaci" in their edition (*AS* Mai. 1.445-48) and in which Judas first defies and then cooperates with the empress Helena in her search for the buried cross, before he himself is converted to Christianity and becomes bishop of Jerusalem. The invention legend, associated in the West with the feast day of May 3, was well known to the Anglo-Saxons (see above, IESUS CHRISTUS, INVENTIO SANCTAE CRUCIS). The text in question here, however, the *Passio Quiriaci*, which takes the form of a conventional martyr's passion, continues Judas's story after Helena's departure and describes chiefly his confrontation with and torture by Julian the Apostate (De Gaiffier 1956 p 39), who finally orders his execution (as predicted by the devil in *Inventio S. Crucis* 190–92, ed. Borgehammar 1991). While introducing a new character into the legend, Judas's mother, Anna, the *passio* contrives to echo or imitate many features of the *Inventio* narrative, including Helena's interrogation of Judas. It has been plausibly suggested that the original Greek *passio* (not represented fully by extant versions, e.g., *BHG* 465, 465b) is by the same author as the Greek version of the *Inventio*, that the ancient Syriac version is based on the Greek, and that the Latin draws on both the Greek and Syriac versions of the story (Pigoulewsky 1927–28, with an edition and French translation of the Syriac version).

As Zettel (1979 p 20) and Webber (1992 p 155) point out, in the Salisbury copy of the **COTTON-CORPUS LEGENDARY** the *passio* seems to correspond best to the unpublished Passio 1b (*BHL* 7024). The Bollandists' printed text, *BHL* 7022–23 (*AS* Mai. 1.449–51), inserts the text of the *Inventio* (*BHL* 4169) between the prologue (*BHL* 7022) and the *Passio Quiriaci* narrative, an arrangement not normally found in manuscript copies (Pigoulewsky 1927–28 p 312); the *AS* text is also somewhat abridged by comparison with the Salisbury copy, although in only minor ways. Formerly there was another, slightly earlier copy of the same text in manuscript Cotton Nero E. i, since it is present in the table of contents (see Jackson and Lapidge 1996 p 137). I have not seen the Cambridge manuscript, which is probably from Christ Church, Canterbury, and formerly part of a larger manuscript (see Ker 1964 p 34 note 9). Ker and

Piper (1969–92 1.53) identify a *passio* of Quiriacus and Anna in the early-twelfth-century Chester legendary (London, Gray's Inn 3) as *BHL* 7022, but, more accurately, this must also be *BHL* 7024.

It should be noted that an important tenth-century Bobbio manuscript that, in Franklin's opinion (1995), represents an insular passional from the time of **ALDHELM**, contains a text of the *passio* of Judas Quiriacus. On the relics cult of the saint and his mother at Ancona, Italy, in the Middle Ages, see *BSS*, as cited above.

Quirinus. See **MARIUS ET MARTHA**.

Remigius, vita, translatio, miracula [HINCMAR.Vit.Remig.]: *BHL* 7152–59; *BLS* 4.1–3; *BSS* 11.104–12.
   ed.: *MGH* SRM 3.250–336.
MSS 1. Cambridge, Corpus Christi College 9: HG 36.
     2. Salisbury, Cathedral Library 222 (formerly Oxford, Bodleian Library Fell 1): HG 754.6.
Lists – Refs none.

Remigius (Rémy), "Apostle of the Franks" (feast day October 1), was born at Laon in 437, became Archbishop of Rheims when only 22 (459), and held the see until his death ca. 530 (for his own extant writings, see *CPL* 1070–72). Probably his most famous act was his baptism of Clovis, king of the Franks, in 496. A late-eighth-century *vita* survives (*BHL* 7150), formerly attributed to **VENANTIUS FORTUNATUS** (ed. *MGH* AA 4/2.64–67), and a much earlier one, now lost, was apparently known to **GREGORY OF TOURS**, **HISTORIA FRANCORUM** II.xxxi (ed. *MGH* SRM 1/1.76–78 [2nd ed.]). But the Anglo-Saxons appear to have known only the massively elaborate mid-ninth-century life (comprising two prologues, *Vita, Translatio, Miracula, Testamentum,* and *Carmina*) by **HINCMAR** (Archbishop of Rheims 845–82). Copies of this, lacking only the *Testamentum* and *Carmina* (*BHL* 7160–62), are in the eleventh-century Cambridge and Salisbury manuscripts of the **COTTON-CORPUS LEGENDARY**. They are not collated or listed by Krusch in his *MGH* edition, nor are they mentioned by Devisse (see below).

The feast of Remigius's translation, October 1, the major liturgical celebration after Hincmar's time, is represented in all the calendars of later Anglo-Saxon England and, with proper masses, in the service books. There is a rather detailed Old English notice of several relics of Remigius in the tenth-/eleventh-century Exeter List of Relics (B16.10.8, *Rec* 10.8; ed. Förster 1943 p 77; Conner 1993a pp 182–83). The fullest treatment of Hincmar's life and works is that of Devisse (1975–76; see especially pp 1008–37 on the *Vita Remigii)*, who is critical of Krusch's edition. See also Berschin (1986–91 3.365–72).

Richarius, vita [ALCVIN.Vit.Richar.]: *BHL* 7224; *BLS* 2.164; *BSS* 11.155–57.
   ed.: *MGH* SRM 4.389–401.

MSS 1. Cambridge, Corpus Christi College 9: HG 36.
   2. Salisbury, Cathedral Library 222 (formerly Oxford, Bodleian Library Fell 1): HG 754.6.
Lists ?Saewold: ML 8.18.
A-S Vers – Refs none.

Richarius (Riquier; feast day April 26, translation October 9), founder and abbot of Celles, near Amiens, hermit of Forêt-Montiers in his old age (died ca. 645), is the subject of a life by **ALCUIN**, written at the request of Angilbert, abbot of Saint-Riquier, near modern Abbeville, after Easter 800, and dedicated to the emperor Charles (see also Alcuin, **EPISTOLAE** CCCCLXV; ed. *MGH* ECA 2). Alcuin's life of Richarius is a rewriting of a seventh-century "libellus" identified by Krusch (1904) as *BHL* 7245 (*MGH* SRM 7.438–53; *CPL* 2134; see also Poncelet 1903). A *librum uite sancti Richarii* is included in the list of former Bath Abbey books given to the abbey of Saint-Vaast by the exiled Abbot Saewold, shortly after the Conquest. In ML (p 61), Lapidge follows Grierson (1940 p 109) in identifying the text mentioned in the Saewold booklist as "probably" the Alcuinian life. The eleventh-century Cambridge and Salisbury manuscripts of the **COTTON-CORPUS LEGENDARY** also include the Alcuinian life (but without the prologue, *BHL* 7223) in association with October 8, the saint's translation day. Among later (twelfth-century) English copies is that in London, BL Arundel 91 (HG 305), a legendary from St Augustine's, Canterbury.

Richarius's name is not common in Anglo-Saxon calendars. A mid-eleventh-century Bury calendar (F. Wormald 1934 p 243) records his April 26 feast, but earlier calendars note his day as October 8 (pp 25 and 39) or October 9 (p 11). For a recent literary study of Alcuin's *Vita Richarii* in relation to the older *libellus*, see I Deug-Su (1983 pp 115–65).

Romanus Miles: *BSS* 11.326–28.

Romanus (feast day August 9) is a minor figure in the epic *passio* of Saint Laurence of Rome (**LAURENTIUS**), a soldier converted by Laurence's words and miracles during his tortures under Decius and Valerian and quickly martyred for his new faith (see *Passio Laurentii*, ed. Delehaye 1933b pp 90–91). The brief notices for Romanus's feast day in **BEDE**'s **MARTYROLOGIUM** (ed. Dubois and Renaud p 147.3–6) and the **OLD ENGLISH MARTYROLOGY** (*Mart*, B19.fp: ed. Kotzor 1981 2.175) are sourced by Quentin (1908 p 79) and Cross (1983a p 206) respectively. Romanus also appears in **ÆLFRIC**'s homily on Laurence in **CATHOLIC HOMILIES** I, 29, lines 169–82 (*ÆCHom* I, B1.1.31; ed. *EETS* SS 17; see also Thorpe 1844–46 1.427–29). For information on manuscripts of the *passio*, and for other references, see above, the entry for Laurentius.

Rufina et Secunda, passio [ANON.Pas.Rufin.Secund.]: *BHL* 7359; *BLS* 3.64; *BSS* 11.460–64; *CPL* 2227.
  ed.: *AS* Iul. 3.30–31.

MSS 1. London, BL Cotton Nero E. i: HG 344.
2. Salisbury, Cathedral Library 222 (formerly Oxford, Bodleian Library Fell 1): HG 754.6.
Lists none.
A-S Vers 1. ALDH.Carm.uirg. 2279–349.
2. ALDH.Pros.uirg. 307.5–308.5.
3. *Mart* (B19.em).
Quots/Cits – Refs none.

Rufina and Secunda (July 10) are described in their unhistorical *passio* as Christian Roman sisters who abandoned their fiancés and fled from Rome when the men foreswore their Christianity during Valerian's persecution. After arrest, tortures (including an attempted drowning in the Tiber), and execution they were buried on the Aurelian Way by a patrician lady converted by their example. The spot, Silva Candida, became an episcopal see. The sisters' cult is early, but nothing is known about them for sure. In Anglo-Saxon England, their feast day is invariably occupied by the more important feast of **FELICITAS CUM SEPTEM FILIIS**. **ALDHELM** provides detailed energetic accounts of Rufina and Secunda in his verse and prose **DE VIRGINITATE** (ALDH.Carm.uirg., Pros.uirg.; ed. *MGH* AA 15), which are based on, and in places quote, the *passio* represented here; see the source notes in Ehwald's edition (*MGH* AA 15.307–08). The **OLD ENGLISH MARTYROLOGY** (*Mart*; ed. Kotzor 1981 2.147) on the other hand recalls only the episode of the failed drowning attempt and borrows a simile from Aldhelm (Cross 1982d p 31).

For another edition of the *passio*, see Mombritius (1910 2.444–45 and 725–26).

Rufinus et Valerius, passio [PASCH.RAD.Pas.Rufin.Val.]: *BHL* 7374; *BLS* 2.542; *BSS* 11.483–84.
ed.: *PL* 120.1489–508.

MSS Dublin, Trinity College 174: HG 215.
Lists – Refs none.

There is little evidence before the end of the eleventh century that the hagiography of these two martyrs of the Soissons region (feast day June 14) was known to the Anglo-Saxons. The Dublin manuscript (Colker 1991 1.326) contains a copy, in the hand of one of Webber's Group II Salisbury scribes (1992 p 158), of the *passio* composed by **PASCHASIUS RADBERTUS**, a native of the Soissons area (died ca. 860), who claims to be revising an earlier *libellus* (presumably *BHL* 7373, which is no earlier than the eighth century and much indebted to the legend of **QUINTINUS**). Unlike most of Paschasius's other works, his *Vita Rufini et Valerii* has not been critically edited.

One Wessex calendar, possibly from Shaftsbury and dated ca. 969–78, records the June 14 feast day (F. Wormald 1934 p 21).

Rumwaldus infans, vita [ANON.Vit.Rumwald.]: *BHL* 7385; *BSS* 11.384.
 ed.: Love 1996 pp 92–114.
MSS Cambridge, Corpus Christi College 9: HG 36.
Lists – Refs none.

Rumwold (Rumbald; feast day November 2 or 3) is said to have been the son of a seventh-century Northumbrian king, Alhfrith, and Cyneburh, daughter of king Penda of Mercia; Rumwold died when he was only three days old but not before he had miraculously proclaimed his Christianity and preached on the Holy Trinity. The cult existed in Buckingham by the tenth century, if not earlier, to judge from the notice in the first and older layer of the so-called *Secgan* or "List of Saints Resting Places" (see Rollason 1978 pp 63, 64, 70). There are also entries (for November 2 or 3) in some calendars of the late tenth or early eleventh century (F. Wormald 1934 pp 26, 40, 69). The November 3 feast was added in the later eleventh century at Worcester (F. Wormald 1934 p 236), and the earliest surviving copy of the saint's Latin *vita* also comes from Worcester, where it was part of a fragmentary late-eleventh-century legendary added to the beginning of the eleventh-century Cambridge manuscript of the **COTTON-CORPUS LEGENDARY**. Other copies are all of the twelfth century or later, despite calendar evidence that the cult waned after the end of the eleventh century (Love 1996 pp cxli and clix). Later medieval evidence of other kinds suggests that the cult was widespread in Buckinghamshire, Northamptonshire, and Kent, but the provenance, authorship, and date of the *vita* remain obscure. As the most recent editor points out (Love 1996 p clxi), the author does not mention written sources of any kind, and the work appears to have been composed to provide documentary support for a cult based purely on oral tradition. Certainly the story, whatever its origins, was too good to lose.

The new edition by Love, with English translation, commentary on the text, and full discussion of cult evidence and manuscript traditions, supersedes that of the Bollandists (*AS* Nov. 1.682–90), with its incomplete collation and survey of manuscripts.

Sabina Romae, passio [ANON.Pas.Sabin.Rom.]: *BHL* 7407; *BLS* 3.442–43; *BSS* 11.540–42; *CPL* 2234.
   ed.: *AS* Aug. 6.503–04.

MSS 1. London, BL Cotton Nero E. i: HG 344.
     2. Salisbury, Cathedral Library 222 (formerly Oxford, Bodleian Library Fell 1): HG 754.6.

Lists – Refs none.

There is a certain amount of confusion surrounding the two female saints known to the Anglo-Saxons as Sabina (Savina), one a martyr of Rome and another whose relics are associated with the city of Troyes (see **SABINA TRECENSIS**). The fifth- or sixth-century *passio* in question here concerns a Roman martyr (feast day August 29), a patrician widow converted to Christianity by her Syrian slave girl, the virgin **SERAPIA**, whose trial she witnessed and on whose account she was herself executed. The alleged time period is the reign of Hadrian (second century). There was an early Christian church, "titulus Sabinae" in Rome, but historians are doubtful that there was ever a martyr of that name. Although the *Passio Sabinae* is listed separately from that of Serapia in *BHL*, reflecting the separate treatment of the two in the Carolingian martyrologies (e.g., **ADO**, *PL* 123.341–42 and 345–46), it is merely the last portion of, or sequel to, the *Passio Serapiae*. The two are printed as one work, the *Passio Serapiae et Sabinae*, in the *AS* edition, where the brief account of Sabina occupies chapter 3.

In the *Gregorian Sacramentary* (see **LITURGY, MASSBOOKS**), however, Sabina (but not Serapia) has a proper mass on August 29, along with John the Baptist (**IOHANNES BAPTISTA**). Many of the Anglo-Saxon calendars and service books commemorate her on this day, including the ninth-century **OLD ENGLISH MARTYROLOGY** (*Mart*, B19.gi; ed. Kotzor 1981 2.193), but the *Martyrology*'s notice is merely an obit, not a narrative notice. Her name is in capitals in a late-eleventh-century Winchester calendar (F. Wormald 1934 p 163; see also Pfaff in Gibson et al. 1992 p 75), possibly implying the need for lections and therefore, perhaps, a local copy of the *passio*. In the eleventh-century versions of the **COTTON-CORPUS LEGENDARY** (Zettel 1979 p 25; Jackson and Lapidge 1996 p 140), Sabina's brief *passio* is presented separately from but immediately after that of Serapia.

Sabina Trecensis, vita [ANON.Vit.Sabina.Trec.]: *BHL* 7408; *BSS* 11.538–40.
    ed.: *AS* Ian. 2.944–46.
MSS 1. London, BL Cotton Nero E. i: HG 344.
    2. Salisbury, Cathedral Library 222 (formerly Oxford, Bodleian Library Fell 1): HG 754.6.
Lists – Refs none.

The text listed here concerns the virgin Sabina (Savina), reputedly of the island of Samos and sister of the martyr Sabinianus. While her brother is reported to have migrated secretly to Gaul to preach the gospel and to have died a martyr under the emperor Aurelian (*BHL* 7438–41), Sabina is said to have gone in search of him and, after various adventures in Rome and Ravenna, expired on her brother's new grave in Troyes, in 288.

Her feast day is properly, like her brother's, January 29, and in three of the earlier (i.e., ninth-/tenth-century) English calendars it is variously January 29, 24, and 28 (F. Wormald 1934 pp 2, 16, and 30; see also p 50 for the puzzling notice "Sanctae Sabinae uirginis" on July 19). In the eleventh-century London and Salisbury manuscripts of the **COTTON-CORPUS LEGENDARY**, however, the text (extensively revised by a twelfth-century hand in the Cotton manuscript) is located immediately before the legends of the Roman martyrs SERAPIA and SABINA ROMAE, and all three are given the date August 29 (Zettel 1979 p 24; also Jackson and Lapidge 1996 p 140). A similar juxtaposition is found earlier in the influential ninth-century MARTYROLOGIUM of USUARD (*PL* 124.411–12) and is reflected later in the thirteenth-century *Legenda aurea* CXXVII (*BHL* 7442, ed. Graesse 1890 pp 576–78).

Sabinus Spoleti, passio [ANON.Pas.Sabini.Spol.]: *BHL* 7451; *BLS* 4.641–42; *BSS* 11.705–16; *CPL* 2228.
ed.: Azevedo 1752 pp 467–77.
MSS Cambridge, Corpus Christi College 9: HG 36.
Lists – Refs none.

On the basis of the ancient cult of Sabinus (Savino) of Spoleto (feast day December 7), Delehaye (1933a p 317) believes Sabinus to have been a genuine martyr, but the sixth-century *passio*, probably composed in Rome, has no credibility (Lanzoni 1903). The only evidence of the Anglo-Saxons' awareness of this important Italian saint is the copy of the *passio* in the eleventh-century Cambridge manuscript of the **COTTON-CORPUS LEGENDARY**, the beginning and ending of which correspond most closely to the version printed by Azevedo (Passio 1a.α, *BHL* 7451). Zettel remarks (1979 p 32 note 106) on the omission of this text from one of the later, twelfth-century recensions of the Legendary. Another copy, however, is in Hereford, Cathedral Library P.VII.6, which is numbered *BHL* 7453k in *BHL NS*.

Salvius Valencenarum: *BHL* 7472; *BLS* 2.648; *BSS* 11.610–11.

There is no evidence of a pre-Conquest Anglo-Saxon cult or knowledge of any of the several saints with the name Salvius. Some relics of a saint Salvius were brought to the newly rebuilt Canterbury cathedral by archbishop Lanfranc (1070–89), and it is possible, according to Farmer (1987 p 379), that the monks associated them with the missionary bishop Salvius of Valenciennes who was murdered (ca. 768) for his costly cloak and girdle (feast day June 26). A copy of his ninth-century *passio* (*BHL* 7472) is preserved among the supplementary texts added in the later eleventh century to the second part (Cambridge, Corpus Christi College 9) of the **COTTON-CORPUS LEGENDARY**, from Worcester. See also the early-twelfth-century Chester legendary (Ker and Piper 1969–92 1.54). One portion of a Christ Church, Canterbury legendary, London, BL Arundel 91 (HG 305, early twelfth century), contains the life of another Salvius, bishop of Amiens (feast day October 28): *BHL* 7460. See *BSS* 11.688–95.

Saturninus et Sisinnius, passio [ANON.Pas.Saturn.Siss.]: *BHL* 7493; *BLS* 4.445; *BSS* 11.688–95.
   ed.: Mombritius 1910 2.169–170.27.

MSS   Cambridge, Corpus Christi College 9: HG 36.
Lists   none.
A-S Vers   BEDA.Mart. 216.3–18.
Quots/Cits – Refs   none.

An authentic Roman martyr named Saturninus (November 29), apparently a priest from Carthage, was buried on the Via Salaria. In the sixth or seventh century, however, Saturninus and his fellow clerics were incorporated into the large cast of characters that make up the "Gesta Marcelli" (*BHL* 5234–35: **MARCELLUS PAPA**). **BEDE** devotes a separate notice in his **MARTYROLOGIUM** (BEDA.Mart.; ed. Dubois and Renaud 1976) to the aged Saturninus and his companions and refers to the source as the "Gesta Marcelli papae" (sourced by Quentin 1908 pp 82–83). The separate importance of Saturninus's feast is also reflected in the eleventh-century Cambridge manuscript of the **COTTON-CORPUS LEGENDARY**, in which the first part of the "Gesta Marcelli" is extracted and adapted to form a *Passio Saturnini* (Zettel 1979 p 31), despite appearing earlier in the Legendary as part of the full "Gesta" (see above, the entry for Marcellus papa); thus the story of Saturninus and his companions appears twice in almost identical form in the Legendary. The separate *passio* is apparently widely represented in this way in medieval manuscripts. Another copy was formerly in Salisbury, Cathedral Library 222 (Webber 1992 p 157) and recurs in affiliated twelfth-century manuscripts now in Oxford (see Zettel 1979 p 31) and Hereford (Bannister 1927 p 174).

The Saturninus in the **OLD ENGLISH MARTYROLOGY**, although he has the same feast day as Saturninus of Rome, is the martyr of Toulouse, Saint Sernin (**SATURNINUS TOLOSANUS**).

Saturninus Tolosanus, passio [ANON.Pas.Saturn.Tol.]: *BHL* 7495–96; *BLS* 4.445–46; *BSS* 11.673–80; *CPL* 2137.
 ed.: Devic and Vaissete 1872–1905 2 Preuves cols 29–34.

MSS   ?London, BL Cotton Otho A. xiii: HG 351.
Lists   none.
A-S Vers   ?*Mart* (B19.je).
Quots/Cits – Refs   none.

Saturninus (Sernin; feast day November 29) is venerated as a missionary and first bishop of Toulouse, active in the third century. According to the earliest extant *passio* (dated ca. 420–30 in *CPL*, but see below), his presence in the city silenced the local oracles. The enraged pagan priests had him tied by the feet to a bull and then goaded the animal into dragging him down the temple steps until he was battered to death. A version of this *passio* was known to writers such as **GREGORY OF TOURS**, HISTORIA FRANCORUM I.xxx (ed. *MGH* SRM 1/1.22.15–23.16 [2nd ed.]), and **VENANTIUS FORTUNATUS**, CARMINA II.vii (ed.

MGH AA 4/1.35–36), but the printed editions differ in some important particulars from that evidently used by Gregory, and one suspects that the extant texts are revised versions of the original fifth-century *passio*. The oldest extant copy is in an eighth-century manuscript now in Turin (*CLA* 4.466).

The feast of Saturninus is widely represented in English calendars and has a mass in the *Missal of Robert of Jumièges* (early eleventh century; see **LITURGY, MASSBOOKS**). Knowledge of the *passio* in Anglo-Saxon England, however, is indicated only by the summary in the **OLD ENGLISH MARTYROLOGY** (*Mart*; ed. Kotzor 1981 2.257–58) and the fragmentary text in the badly burnt eleventh-century Cotton manuscript (fols 38–41, new foliation 31–34), which has not been studied. A cursory check revealed that, although lacking the usual prologue, it includes part two (*BHL* 7496, on the translation of the relics) and its text of the *passio* proper (*BHL* 7495) is somewhat fuller than that printed by Devic and Vaissete.

As the *Martyrology*'s source, Herzfeld (*EETS* OS 116.xlii) cites the text printed by Ruinart (substantially the same as that of Devic and Vaissette), but a thorough sourcing has not been published. One or two details in the *Martyrology* notice (e.g., that the obit is November 28, not 29, and the fact that the bull drags the saint along "unsmeðe eorðan," "rough ground," instead of down the capitol steps) may permit of a more precise sourcing among manuscript variants.

Other editions of potential relevance for further study are those of Arbellot (see *BHL* 7498) and Fábrega Grau 1953–55 2.57–59. On the development of the hagiography of Saturninus, see Gilles (1982).

Scholastica: *BLS* 1.292–93; *BSS* 11.742–49.

The sister of **BENEDICT OF NURSIA** (**BENEDICTUS CASINENSIS**), abbess of a nunnery close to Monte Cassino, Scholastica is the subject of two chapters (*BHL* 7514) in **GREGORY THE GREAT**'s life of Benedict: **DIALOGI** II.xxxiii–xxxiv (ed. *SChr* 260.230–34), which mainly relate the episode of their last meeting. She also figures in the *translatio* narratives (*BHL* 1116–17), relating the arrival of their relics in France (see above, the entry on Benedictus Casinensis, translatio). Anglo-Saxon calendars invariably have the February 10 feast day of Scholastica (the same day as Sotheris, **AMBROSIUS**'s sister, whom Scholastica displaces in all but the earliest calendars). **ALDHELM** draws on the episode in Gregory's *Dialogi* II.xxxiii twice in **DE VIRGINITATE** (ed. *MGH* AA 15): the brief eulogy in the *Prosa* (300.17–24) and the more elaborate account in *Carmen* 2024–50 (*BHL* 7518). See also the Old English prose versions edited by Hecht (*BaP* 5/1.166–69) and **ÆLFRIC**'S homily on Benedict, in **CATHOLIC HOMILIES** II, 11, lines 486–521 (*ÆCHom* II, B1.2.12; *EETS* SS 5; see also SS 18.445–46). She is not mentioned in **BEDE**'s **MARTYROLOGIUM** or in the **OLD ENGLISH MARTYROLOGY**, but the relationship between **GUTHLACUS** and his sister **PEGA** in Felix's life of Guthlac must surely owe something to Gregory's account of Benedict and Scholastica (for this and other Anglo-Saxon analogues to their relationship, see Hollis 1992 pp 284, 289, 292).

For English manuscripts of the various Latin sources, see the appropriate entries cross-referenced above. On Scholastica's Le Mans cult, see Beau (1980), Goffart (1967), and Hourlier (1971 and 1979b). For some preliminary information on Scholastica's cult in Anglo-Saxon England, see Ortenberg (1992 pp 180–81 note 184). On Benedict and Scholastica, see De Vogüé (1981, 1983) and, for a gendered reading, Morissey (1990). On Aldhelm's eulogy, see most recently Forman (1990).

Scillitani, passio [ANON.Pas.Scill.]: *BHL* 7531; *BLS* 3.124–26; *BSS* 11.733–41; cf. *CPL* 2049.
    ed.: *AS* Iul. 4.214.

MSS – Lists none.
A-S Vers 1. BEDA.Mart. 129.10–15.
    2. ?*Mart* (B19.eq).
Quots/Cits – Refs none.

The primitive *passio* or "Acta proconsularia" (*BHL* 7527) of Speratus and his eleven male and female companions (feast day July 17), martyrs of Scillium in North Africa under the emperor Commodus (ca. 180), is among those usually regarded by modern hagiographers (e.g., Delehaye 1966 pp 47–49 and 278–83) as historically authentic and virtually contemporary with the events described (for recent arguments against the authenticity of the Scillitani *Acta*, see Gärtner 1989). The version that was known to the early Anglo-Saxons, however, differed somewhat from the primitive *passio*. **BEDE** in his **MARTYROLOGIUM** (BEDA.Mart.; ed. Dubois and Renaud 1976, sourced by Quentin 1908 pp 89–90) used a somewhat expanded, interpolated, version, designated Passio 2 in *BHL*.

Neither Herzfeld (*EETS* OS 116.232) nor Kotzor (1981 2.329) indicates which specific version of the *passio* was used for the brief notice in the **OLD ENGLISH MARTYROLOGY** (*Mart*; ed. Kotzor 1981 2.151), but it appears to be based on one that differed in some details from the *passio* cited here, since the martyrologist designates Speratus as bishop (151.11).

For a modern edition of the primitive *Acta* (*BHL* 7527), see Musurillo (1972 pp 86–88); see also *BHL NS* and *CPL* 2049 for further bibliographical details. The most recent study of the legend is that of Ruggiero (1991).

Sebasteni, passio [ANON.Pas.Sebast.1]: *BHL* 7537; *BLS* 1.541–44; *BSS* 11.768–71; *DACL* 14.2003–06, 15.1107–11.

   ed.: *Bibliotheca Casinensis* 1873–94 3 *Florilegium* pp 58–61.

MSS   1. ?London, BL Cotton Nero E. i: HG 344.
   2. ?Salisbury, Cathedral Library 221 (formerly Oxford, Bodleian Library Fell 4): HG 754.5.

Lists – Refs   none.

The Forty Martyrs (feast day March 10) were soldiers in the Roman garrison of Sebastea (Sivas, Turkey) who refused to sacrifice to idols as ordered by the emperor Licinius (ca. 320). According to their legend they died by being exposed naked on a frozen lake outside the city walls. The cult in the Christian East is very early and well attested. Panegyrics for these martyrs were composed by several of the fourth-century Greek Fathers. An early Greek *passio* (*BHG* 1201) is the source of most later versions (for discussion and bibliography, see Karlin-Hayter 1991). **GREGORY OF TOURS** wrote a summary of their story in his **DE GLORIA MARTYRUM** XCV (ed. *MGH* SRM 1/2.552–53), probably based on an oral report (Van Dam 1988 p 119 note 108). Their feast day, usually March 9 in England, is widely commemorated in Anglo-Saxon calendars of the later period (graded in one: F. Wormald 1934 p 46). At least two different versions of the legend, labeled Passio 1 and Passio 2 in *BHL*, appear to have traveled to Anglo-Saxon England. Passio 2 seems to have been known in the early and later Anglo-Saxon periods, Passio 1 only in the later period. For Passio 2, which was known to **BEDE** and **ÆLFRIC**, see next entry.

Siegmund (1949 p 250) suggests that the text designated Passio 1, and printed from a Monte Cassino manuscript, is a later translation from the Greek than Passio 2. Zettel (1979 p 18) identifies the version in the eleventh-century London and Salisbury manuscripts of the **COTTON-CORPUS LEGENDARY** as a variant of the recension that the Bollandists number 1b, as yet unprinted, but Jackson and Lapidge (1996 p 136) identify the copy in the Legendary as a hybrid of 1a and 1b. Zettel notes (1979 p 219) that a small number of the readings in Ælfric's rendering of Passio 2 (see below) are paralleled in the Cotton-Corpus text of Passio 1. Clearly the early medieval textual history of the *passio* is more complicated than the original *BHL* classification implies (as evidenced in the proliferation of variant versions of Passio 1 in *BHL NS*), and further work on the extant manuscripts is necessary before the affiliations of the Cotton-Corpus version and Ælfric's rendering can be properly determined.

Sebasteni, passio [ANON.Pas.Sebast.2]: *BHL* 7539.
   ed.: *AS* Mart. 2.19–21.

MSS Paris, Bibliothèque Nationale lat. 10861: HG 898.
Lists none.
A-S Vers 1. BEDA.Mart.47.2–11.
   2. *Mart* (B19.aw).

3. ?*ÆLS* Forty Soldiers (B1.3.12) 1–277.
Quots/Cits – Refs none.

BEDE's source for his notice on the Forty Soldiers (or Forty Martyrs) in his MARTYROLOGIUM (BEDA.Mart.; ed. Dubois and Renaud 1976) is the text classified in *BHL* as Passio 2 (sourced by Quentin 1908 p 90), which is the version printed in *AS* and also represented in an early-ninth-century Paris manuscript, of Canterbury provenance (M. P. Brown 1986 p 122; see also Siegmund 1949 p 249). Cross (1986a pp 234–36, 243–44) shows in detail that the notice in the OLD ENGLISH MARTYROLOGY (*Mart*; ed. Kotzor 1981 2.31) also derives from a text similar to that in the Paris manuscript.

Zettel (1979 pp 18, 218–23), following Ott (1892 pp 36–39), finds that ÆLFRIC's rhythmic prose version, *Forty Soldiers* in his LIVES OF SAINTS (*ÆLS*; ed. *EETS* OS 76 and 82), is mainly dependent on a version of Passio 2 as printed in *AS*, rather than on the variant version of Passio 1 preserved in the COTTON-CORPUS LEGENDARY, which Zettel frequently cites elsewhere as a source of Ælfric's work as a hagiographer. Zettel finds some variants in Ælfric's version of the legend, however, that have parallels in the Legendary's text (see the previous notice, on Passio 1). Following Algeo (1960 p 49), Zettel also posits (1979 pp 220–23) Ælfric's dependence, in *Forty Soldiers* 278–364, on an as yet unidentified Latin homily based probably on sermons by BASIL and GREGORY OF NYSSA. Algeo (1960 pp 90–91) suggests also that Ælfric's emphasis on temperance at the end of the piece (*Forty Soldiers* 356–61) is explicable as his own response to the Lenten season in which the feast of the Forty Martyrs occurs.

Sebastianus, passio [ANON.Pas.Sebastian./PS.AMBROSIUS]: *BHL* 7543; *BLS* 1.128–30; *BSS* 11.7773–89; *CPL* 2229.
ed.: *AS* Ian. 2.265–78.

MSS 1. London, BL Cotton Nero E. i: HG 344.
2. Paris, Bibliothèque Nationale lat. 10861: HG 898.

3. Salisbury, Cathedral Library 221 (formerly Oxford, Bodleian Library Fell 4): HG 754.5.
Lists none.
A-S Vers 1. BEDA.Mart. 17.4–23.
2. *Mart* (B19.af); see below.
3. *ÆLS* Sebastian (B1.3.6).
Quots/Cits ABBO.Flor.Pas.Eadmund.: see below.
Refs ABBO.Flor.Pas.Eadmund. 78.21.

Sebastian (feast day January 20), a soldier saint reputedly martyred at Rome under Diocletian ca. 288, appears to have had an early cult at Milan as well as at Rome where his tomb was on the Appian Way. The epic *passio* (*BHL* 7543), which interweaves the story of Sebastian with those of numerous other martyrs whom he supposedly converted or encouraged, was traditionally though falsely attributed to **AMBROSE**; it is now reckoned to have been composed later, in the fifth or early sixth century (Berschin 1986–91 1.75); Pesci (1945 pp 180–84) points to the pontificate of Sixtus III (432–40), as the most probable date of composition; the earliest surviving copy is a seventh-century palimpsest fragment (*CLA* 7.866). Narbey (1899–1912 2.257) has argued that the surviving form of the *passio* not only has been much interpolated but also differs considerably in length and structure from the original: see Cross (1988 p 40), who is skeptical of Narbey's theory. At any rate, it is clear that in this case the printed editions reflect the form of most of the early medieval texts that would have been known to the Anglo-Saxons. For a list of early manuscript copies, see Cross (1988 pp 39–40).

This *passio* was apparently well known throughout the Anglo-Saxon period. Quentin (1908 p 91) identifies it as **BEDE**'s source for his **MARTYROLOGIUM** notice (BEDA.Mart.; ed. Dubois and Renaud 1976), and it figures in a tradition of glosses linked with the school of Archbishop **THEODORE OF CANTERBURY** (Pheifer 1987). There is a copy of the same text in the early-ninth-century Paris manuscript (from St Augustine's, Canterbury: see M. P. Brown 1986 p 122). And while Herzfeld (*EETS* OS 116.xxxvii) considers the brief account of Sebastian in the **OLD ENGLISH MARTYROLOGY** (*Mart*; ed. Kotzor 1981 2.21) to be based on Bede's *Martyrologium*, Cross (1988 p 41) objects that since the *Martyrology* author, as Herzfeld acknowledges, elsewhere shows detailed knowledge of stories of some of the other saints in the Sebastian cycle not mentioned in Bede, it is likely that his Sebastian notice also uses the *passio*. See the *Martyrology* notices for Marcus and Marcellianus, June 18 (ed. Kotzor 1981 2.123–24); Tiburtius, August 11 (pp 177–78); Tranquillinus, July 6 (p 140); and Zoe, July 5 (p 139), briefly sourced by Cross (1988 pp 42–45) with respect to the *passio*. Moreover, one passage that he notes (p 41) in the *Martyrology* notice for Sebastian agrees with the *passio* as printed in the *AS* and not with Bede. Finally he suggests (p 45) that the *Martyrology*'s failure to mention the translation of the saint's relics to Soissons in 826 is additional evidence for dating the *Martyrology* earlier rather than later in the ninth century.

ABBO OF FLEURY, in PASSIO EADMUNDI (ABBO.Flor.Pas.Eadmund.; ed. Winterbottom 1972), probably written in England ca. 885–87, explicitly compares the martyrdom of King Edmund to that of Sebastian, echoing isolated phrases from the *Passio Sebastiani*'s description of the famous arrows episode and the comparison of the saint's body to a hedgehog, as noted by Winterbottom in his edition (1972 p 78.12–20 and note on line 21). He cites as Abbo's source *PL* 17.1021–58, at 1056, which corresponds to 278a.29–34 in the *AS* edition. *Passio Eadmundi* 78.12, "fustigatus," probably echoes *Passio Sebastiani* 278a.58, "fustigari."

ÆLFRIC's dependence, in his *Sebastian* legend in LIVES OF SAINTS (*ÆLS*; ed. *EETS* OS 76 and 82), on a text of the *passio* similar to the *AS* edition was established by Ott (1892 pp 17–20). Zettel (1979 pp 16 and 208–10) confirms Ott's findings in general but notes readings that Ælfric's source must have had in common with the text used by Mombritius and that in the London and Salisbury manuscripts of the **COTTON-CORPUS LEGENDARY** listed here (Zettel does not collate the Paris manuscript).

In addition to the three manuscripts listed above, which definitely fall within our period, it is worth noting that a somewhat later manuscript, Salisbury, Cathedral Library 223 (HG 754.7, formerly Oxford, Bodleian Library Fell 3), copied by the Salisbury Group II scribes in the late eleventh or (more likely) early twelfth century, contains an excerpt from the *passio*, corresponding roughly to paragraphs 22–23 in the *AS* edition (pp 276–78), entitled "Passio Sce Zoe," and recounting the deaths not only of Zoe, but also of Tranquillinus, Tiburtius, Marcus and Marcellianus, and Sebastian himself (Webber 1992 p 170).

There is no modern critical edition of the *Passio Sebastiani*. In addition to the *AS* and *PL* editions, see also Mombritius (1910 2.459–76 and 728–30). The edition of Fábrega Grau (1953–55 2.148–76), based on a tenth-century Spanish manuscript, purports to represent an early (i.e., pre-ninth-century) version of the text. For a literary appreciation of the *passio*, see Berschin (1986–91 1.74–82).

Serapia, passio [ANON.Pas.Serap.]: *BHL* 7586; *BSS* 11.540–42; *CPL* 2233.

ed.: *AS* Aug. 6.500–03.

MSS 1. London, BL Cotton Nero E. i: HG 344.
2. Salisbury, Cathedral Library 222 (formerly Oxford, Bodleian Library Fell 1): HG 754.6.

Lists – Refs none.

As is indicated in *BHL*, the *passio* of the virgin martyr Serapia (Seraphia; Roman feast day September 3), a Syrian slave, normally forms the first part (chapters 1 and 2) of the joint *passio* of Serapia and her Roman mistress, Sabina or Savina (**SABINA ROMAE**). In the manuscripts, the two parts of the *passio* usually have separate rubrics, as in the eleventh-century London and Salisbury manuscripts of the **COTTON-CORPUS LEGENDARY** listed here, but the Bollandists in their edition print the text as one *passio*. While Sabina is commemorated in some Anglo-Saxon calendars, Serapia, whose portion of the *passio* is longer than that of Sabina, seems to have had no separate cult among the English, which may explain why her legend shares Sabina's August 29 feast day in the Legendary (see Jackson and Lapidge 1996 p 140).

Sergius et Bacchus, passio [ANON.Pas.Serg.Bacc.]: *BHL* 7599; *BLS* 4.50–51; *BSS* 11.876–79.
   ed.: *AS* Oct. 3.863–69.
MSS Cambridge, Corpus Christi College 9: HG 36.
Lists – Refs none.

According to their legend, the Syrians Sergius and Bacchus (feast day October 1) were Roman officers, and secretly Christians, serving under the emperor Maximian (early fourth century) on the Syrian frontier. When they eventually made their Christian faith public, the emperor had them paraded through the streets in women's clothes before sending them to Mesopotamia for gruseome tortures and martyrdom. Their cult is early and widespread in the East especially, but also in the West, both in Gaul and Rome (Siegmund 1949 p 250; see also **GREGORY OF TOURS, DE GLORIA MARTYRUM** XCVI, ed. *MGH* SRM 1/2.552–53). Their legend is extant in Syriac, Greek (*BHG* 1624), and various Latin versions of the Greek version. Despite their fame, however, their liturgical cult does not seem to have spread to Anglo-Saxon England early or late, although the legend is represented in the eleventh-century Cambridge manuscript (from Worcester) of the **COTTON-CORPUS LEGENDARY** in a form, Passio 1a, that Siegmund (1949 p 250) finds elsewhere in legendaries of the early "Roman" as opposed to the Spanish or "Gallic" type (Passio 1c, *BHL* 7601). Zettel (1979 p 27) mentions another copy of *BHL* 7599 in a later (twelfth-century) recension of the Legendary. See also the early-twelfth-century Canterbury legendary, London BL Arundel 91 (HG 305).

In addition to the *AS* edition, see that of Mombritius (1910) 2.482–89 and 731.

Servatius, sermo [RADBOD.Serm.Fest.Servat.]: *BHL* 7614; *BLS* 2.297–98; *BSS* 11.889–92.
   ed.: Bollandists 1882a pp 104–11.
MSS Dublin, Trinity College 174: HG 215.
Lists – Refs none.

Servatius (Servais) of Tongres, whose relics cult was important in the Netherlands and Belgium during the Middle Ages (feast day October 13), is believed to have been an Armenian who served as bishop of Tongres and Maastricht in the mid-fourth century and was active at church councils during the Arian controversy. His hagiographic dossier is extensive and complex, and the oldest extant life (*BHL* 7611) has been dated in the eighth century (see *CPL* 2139), but the Anglo-Saxons seem to have been unaware of Servatius and his hagiographies until the very end of our period. At the end of the eleventh century or in the early twelfth, the sermon on Servatius's feast day by Radbod, bishop of Utrecht (ca. 900–17), was copied by a Salisbury Group II scribe (Webber 1992 p 158) into a miscellaneous collection of hagiographic texts, now in Dublin (Colker 1991 1.324), that was apparently intended as a supplement, of previously unavailable texts, to the cathedral chapter's existing legendaries. The sermon, which is based on the old *vita*, was edited by the Bollandists from eleventh- and twelfth-century manuscripts in Belgium, but they do not mention the Dublin manuscript copy.

Sexburga: *BLS* 3.25–26; *BSS* 11.1007–08; Farmer (1987) pp 384–85.

Sexburga (Seaxburgh; feast day July 6) was the sister of **ÆTHELDRYTHA**, whom she succeeded as abbess of Ely. Earlier she had been married to King Eorcenberht of Kent (640–64), by whom she had a son, Egbert (king of Kent 664–73), and two daughters, Saint Eormenhild of Ely (mother of **WERBURGA**) and Saint Eorcengota of Faremoutier. The compiler of the late-twelfth-century *Liber Eliensis* (Blake 1962 p 51) in summarizing and giving extracts from a Latin *Vita Sexburgae* (= *BHL* 7693, early twelfth century, unprinted) refers also to an Old English source for this life. Rollason (1982 p 30) adds that, in the unpublished Latin *vita*, the Old English life is said to be "ancient." He believes that this Old English life is represented by the fragmentary Old English text, associated by AC with the name of Saint Mildred (**MILDREDA**; *LS* 27, B3.3.27), in London, Lambeth Palace 427 (HG 518), most recently edited by Swanton (1975 pp 22–24 and 26–27). Like Wilson (1970 p 89),

Rollason is convinced that this represents the Old English life of Sexburga (the Lambeth fragment is not necessarily, however, a unity, since its adjacent leaves were originally non-adjacent: see above, the entry for Mildred, and the divison of the text in *MCOE*). This copy was made in the late eleventh century, probably in Exeter (NRK 281). Rollason suggests the original was composed at Minster-in-Sheppey, after the Viking invasions. See also Ridyard (1988 pp 57–58). The unpublished Latin life (*BHL* 7693) believed to derive from it is presumably an Ely composition, made from the Old English life for liturgical purposes and for the benefit of monks who could not read the vernacular (for a comparable case, see WULFSTANUS II). For manuscripts of the Latin life, see Blake (1962 p xxxiv and note 1); for further references, see our entry for Mildred.

Sigfridus abbas. See BENEDICTUS BISCOPUS, CEOLFRIDUS.

Silvester, vita [ANON.Gest.Silvest.1D]: *BHL* 7742b–f; *BLS* 4.644–45; *BSS* 11.1077–79; *CPL* 2235.
    ed.: Narbey 1899–1912 2.166–68, 171, 172–74, and 175–76 (partial).

MSS – Lists none.
A-S Vers 1. ?ALDH.Carm.uirg. 539–650.
    2. ?ALDH.Pros.uirg. 257.16–260.4.
Quots/Cits – Refs none.

Not a great deal is known about the historical Pope Silvester, who held office early in the church's new era of freedom from persecution (314–35, feast day December 31). The so-called *Actus* or *Gesta Silvestri* (as his *vita* is usually called), believed by modern scholars to have been composed in the fifth century, and certainly known by the early sixth (Loenertz 1975 p 427), is a sprawling amalgam of intriguing and influential legends, probably of mixed Roman and Eastern origins, which include the earliest form of the notorious "Donation of Constantine" (Levison 1924) along with an account of the emperor's conversion and baptism that contradicts in various ways earlier historians as well as the INVENTIO SANCTAE CRUCIS (see IESUS CHRISTUS), one of its sources (Loenertz 1975 pp 428–30, 438). It is not possible to give anything other than a tentative account of the influence of the *Gesta Silvestri* in Anglo-Saxon England, because, despite a great deal of preliminary textual work, especially by Levison, there is no comprehensive modern edition. Levison has distinguished three main and several mixed versions of the legend, of which the history and variant forms are formidably complex. The standard edition by Mombritius (1910 2.508–31, *BHL* 7725–32) is based on the third and least ancient version (designated "C" by Levison and dated ninth century), which is in fact a synthesis and continuation of the two earlier versions (Levison 1924 pp 170 and 215; Loenertz 1975 pp 435–38). Mombritius is thus not a reliable guide to the *Gesta Silvestri* known to the Anglo-Saxons, although he remains the only way in print of gaining an impression of the character of the legend in its entirety. The edition promised by S. De Vaere (see *CPL* 2235) has not appeared; another is said to be in preparation by Pohlkamp (1983 p 61 note 1). See also his 1983 and 1984 studies of certain aspects of the Silvester legend.

In the opinion of Levison (1924 p 170) and Narbey (1899–1912 2.166–76), the earliest extant version of the *Gesta*, Levison's A1, composed probably in the late fifth century, corresponds to that now classified as version D by the Bollandists in *BHL NS* (*BHL* 7742b–f). Another early version, possibly by the same author in Levison's opinion (1924 p 201), which is somewhat shorter than A1, with some reordering of episodes, is version B1 in Levison's scheme and corresponds to *BHL* 7739. Narbey's edition from fragments of a Paris manuscript is only partly the genuine A1 version (for the influence of version B1 and its variant, B2, in Anglo-Saxon England, see the next notice).

In his source notes on **ALDHELM**'s verse and prose tributes to Silvester in DE VIRGINITATE (ALDH.Carm.uirg., Pros.uirg; ed. *MGH AA* 15), Ehwald (pp 257–58) points to a source other than Mombritius's text, but was apparently unaware of Narbey's edition. Levison (1924 pp 211–12) concludes that Aldhelm drew on a text of the A1 version for his account of the episode of the founding of Constantinople. As Levison allows, however, other aspects of Aldhelm's account (e.g., the placement of the dragon episode, Pros.uirg. 258.3–10) seem to reflect the influence of a B version. Since, as Levison makes clear throughout his study of the *Gesta*, mixed and contaminated versions proliferated in the early Middle Ages, it seems equally possible that Aldhelm knew one of these.

Although A is generally believed to be the original version, there are no copies older than the tenth century (Loenertz 1975 p 435).

Silvester, vita [ANON.Gest.Silvest.1B]: *BHL* 7739.
   ed.: unpublished.

MSS London, BL Cotton Nero E. i: HG 344.
Lists none.
A-S Vers ?*Mart* (B19.g and ga).
Quots/Cits 1. ANON.Vit.Cuth. 64.1–3 and 76.3–6: see below.
   2. ADOMN.Vit.Columb. 6.18–21: see below.
   3. BEDA.Mart. 154.2–11.
Refs BEDA.Mart. 154.11.

Other early Anglo-Saxon writers besides **ALDHELM** (see previous entry) show familiarity with the *Gesta Silvestri*, but apparently in the form of the late-fifth-century B version, according to Levison (1924 p 214). Among such witnesses is the anonymous Lindisfarne *Vita Cuthberti* (ANON.Vit.Cuth., *BHL* 2019; ed. Colgrave 1940; see **CUTHBERTUS**) in which Colgrave, relying on Levison, notes verbal echoes from the *Gesta*'s prologue and the catalogue of virtues in Book I (see also Colgrave 1940 p 316). **ADOMNAN** in his life of **COLUMBA HIENSIS** (ADOMN.Vit.Columb.; ed. Anderson and Anderson 1991; see Levison 1924 p 213) adapts the same catalogue of virtues, independently, it seems, and more selectively, with greater emphasis on chastity. In neither case here does Mombritius's edition match the B text.

BEDE does not provide a narrative account of Silvester himself in his **MARTYROLOGIUM** (BEDA.Mart.; ed. Dubois and Renaud 1976), in which he devotes little space to confessors, but he does refer to and quote from what he calls the "historia sancti Silvestri" for his notice regarding the martyred Syrian preacher Timotheus (feast day August 22) whose story, including his relationship with the future pope Silvester, forms the first distinct episode in *Gesta Silvestri* I (cf. Mombritius 1910 2.508.27–59). The passage in Bede is sourced by Quentin (1908 p 92) with reference to Mombritius's edition, but Levison (1924 p 214) confirms Bede's use of a B text here and in his **DE TEMPORIBUS** IV.7–9 (ed. *CCSL* 123C).

Somewhat later than Bede, correspondents of **BONIFACE** (**BONIFATIUS**) frequently echo the closing formulas found in the exchange of letters between **HELENA** and her son Constantine in *Gesta Silvestri* II (cf. Mombritius 1910 2.515.20–21 and 37–38), as noted by Levison, although these may be indirect echoes, since the phrases in question found their way into formula books and one of them was a "favorite phrase" of Aldhelm's. See Levison's numerous references (1946 p 285).

In the ninth century, the **OLD ENGLISH MARTYROLOGY** (*Mart*; ed. Kotzor 1981) provides brief narrative notices for both Silvester (2.8) and Timotheus (2.185–86). Cross (1979 pp 201–02 and 1986b p 281 and note 35) endorses Herzfeld's view (*EETS* OS 116.xxxvi) that the brief Silvester notice in the *Martyrology* depends on a text of the *Gesta*. Although Cross and Herzfeld rely on Mombritius's edition (the C text), it is likely that a B text would be the martyrologist's source.

According to Zettel (1979 p 34) and Jackson and Lapidge (1996 pp 143–44), the version of the *Gesta Silvestri* preserved in the eleventh-century **COTTON-CORPUS LEGENDARY** is that designated by the Bollandists 1B, that is, *BHL* 7739, as pointed out by Levison (1924 p 193) who lists the Cotton manuscript along with several others of the ninth–twelfth centuries as examples of what he calls "B2," a variant form of his B version, incorporating some elements of the A version (as Jackson and Lapidge imply, by identifying the English copy as *BHL* 7725–26 as well as 7739). The same text was also formerly in (but now lost from) Salisbury, Cathedral Library 222 (Webber 1992 p 157), of the late eleventh century, and is found in a twelfth-century recension of the Legendary (Zettel 1979 p 34). The copy in the Cotton manuscript (pt 2, fols 168r–180r) is among a group of texts formerly located at the end of Cambridge, Corpus Christi College 9. It has been extensively corrected and rewritten in places, by a hand that has been identified as belonging to the twelfth-century chronicler John of Worcester (Jackson and Lapidge 1996 p 144; Levison 1924 p 223). Two of the original folios (175–76) have been removed and replaced by two that are wholly in John's hand. The text from which he drew his corrections and substitutions was the C version.

The oldest extant manuscript of the unprinted B version of the *Gesta Silvestri* is an eighth-century legendary now in Munich (Levison 1924 p 192).

Simon et Iudas (Thaddeus). See APOCRYPHA, PASSIO SIMONIS ET JUDAE.

Simplicius, Faustinus, et Beatrix, passio [ANON.Pas.Simp.Faust.Beat.]: *BHL* 7790; *BLS* 3.206; *BSS* 11.1204–05; *DACL* 6.866–900.
    ed.: *AS* Iul. 7.36.
MSS 1. London, BL Cotton Nero E. i: HG 344.
    2. London, BL Harley 3020: HG 433.
    3. Salisbury, Cathedral Library 222 (formerly Oxford, Bodleian Library Fell 1): HG 754.6.
Lists – Refs none.

The late, brief legend of these genuine Roman martyrs (feast days July 29, May 11) is remarkable chiefly for its account of the miraculous manner in which a certain Lucretius, the covetous neighbor and denouncer of Beatrice (Viatrix), sister of the martyred brothers Simplicius and Faustinus, was himself denounced by a new-born infant at a dinner party and died soon afterwards. The translation of the brothers' and sister's relics to two Roman churches and the consequent provision of masses in their honor in the Roman sacramentaries were doubtless among the reasons for the relative importance of their cult among the later Anglo-Saxons, as attested in calendars and service books and as evidenced in the provision of copies of the *passio* in the early-eleventh-century Canterbury passional that forms part two of Harley 3020 (Carley 1994) and the eleventh-century recensions of the **COTTON-CORPUS LEGENDARY** from Worcester and Salisbury. In addition to the *AS* edition, see also that of Mombritius (1910 2.531–32).

Sixtus II: *BLS* 3.269–70; *BSS* 11.1256–61.

The martyrdom of Pope Sixtus (Xystus) II, with some of his deacons, under the emperor Valerian in 258 (feast day August 6) is well documented in quasi-historical sources such as the **LIBER PONTIFICALIS**, but the story told in his *passio* (in which Decius is the emperor in charge) is a literary invention. Although sometimes edited as a separate work (*BHL* 7801) in medieval legendaries, his legend properly forms the middle section of the "epic" *Passio* (or *Gesta*) *Laurentii*, also known as *Passio Polychronii* (see **LAURENTIUS** and **POLYCHRONIUS**). See Delehaye's edition (1933b pp 80–85). **BEDE** refers to the whole work as "Passio sancti Xysti" once, in his **MARTYROLOGIUM** (ed. Dubois and Renaud 1976 p 194.22), the notice for **QUADRAGINTA SEX MILITES**, but elsewhere he calls it *Passio Laurentii*. See the Laurentius entry, above, for information on the legend and manuscripts.

Sixtus was one of the saints of the Canon of the Mass and devotion to him among the Anglo-Saxons seems to have been very early (see Brooks 1984 p 20) and continuous. Bede's separate *Martyrologium* notice (ed. Dubois and Renaud 1976 p 144.2–6), like that for Laurentius, is very brief and draws on the *Liber Pontificalis,* as well as on the *passio*. See Quentin (1908 p 79). According to Cross (1983a p 205), the notice in the ninth-century **OLD ENGLISH MARTYROLOGY** (*Mart*, B19.fk; ed. Kotzor 1981 2.172) mingles some details from the *Liber Pontificalis* or Bede's *Martyrologium* with material, some of it verbatim, from the *passio*.

ÆLFRIC does not provide a separate legend, but he gives prominence to Sixtus at the beginning of his homily for Laurence: see **CATHOLIC HOMILIES** I, 29, lines 1–74 (*ÆCHom* I, B1.1.31; ed. *EETS* SS 17; translation in Thorpe 1844–46 1.417–21).

Sosius. See IANUARIUS ET SOSIUS.

Speratus. See SCILLITANI.

Speusippus, passio [ANON.Pas.Speus.1]: *BHL* 7828; *BLS* 1.109–10; *BSS* 11.1349–50.
    ed.: *AS* Ian. 2.74–76.
MSS – Lists none.
A-S Vers *Mart* (B19.ac).
Quots/Cits – Refs none.

    Speusippus and his companions, Eleusippus and Meleusippus, are usually referred to as "Tergemini," the triplets (feast day January 17). Although they were originally connected only with Cappadocia, as in a Greek legend (*BHG* 1646) and in the Latin *passio* under consideration here, the legend was interpolated in the sixth century, probably by the anonymous Dijon priest who wrote the cycle of **BENIGNUS** and **ANDOCHIUS**, to assert that the three boy martyrs, baptized by Benignus, died under the emperor "Aurelian" at Langres. On the sources and relations of the two versions, Passio 1 and Passio 2, see Van der Straeten (1961 pp 132–34) and Siegmund (1949 pp 224–25). Although the Tergemini do not appear to have been culted as calendar saints by the Anglo-Saxons, the legend nonetheless found its way to Anglo-Saxon England in both forms. For evidence of English knowledge of the interpolated version, Passio 2 (*BHL* 7829), see the next entry.
    Cross (1986b pp 285–86) follows Herzfeld (*EETS* OS 116.226) in positing the older *passio* as the source of the substantial notice in the **OLD ENGLISH MARTYROLOGY** (*Mart*; ed. Kotzor 1981 2.18–19), where it is implied that the triplets are baptized in the blood of their martyrdom (whereas *BHL* 7829 states that they were baptized by Benignus). Cross also shows how the *Martyrology* shares a correct variant reading with an eighth-century copy (now in Munich) of the *passio*,

which was used by the Bollandists for their *AS* edition, but which in this instance they copied wrongly. Cross (1986b p 287) reproduces a page from the Munich text.

Speusippus, passio [ANON.Pas.Speus.2/WARNAHARIUS]: *BHL* 7829; *CPL* 1309.
ed.: *AS* Ian. 2.76–80.
MSS 1. London, BL Cotton Nero E. i: HG 344.
2. Salisbury, Cathedral Library 221 (formerly Oxford, Bodleian Library Fell 4): HG 754.5.
Lists none.
A-S Vers BEDA.Mart.15.6–24.
Quots/Cits – Refs none.

This interpolated version, Passio 2, of the *Passio Speusippi* was apparently better known in the medieval period than *BHL* 7828 (see previous entry). It is traditionally attributed to Warnaharius, priest of Langres in the early seventh century (see *BHL* and Siegmund 1949 p 224), but he is now agreed to have written merely the dedicatory epistle (ca. 610–14) in the extant manuscripts, the *passio* itself having originated in the previous century.

BEDE's notice for these saints in his **MARTYROLOGIUM** (BEDA. Mart.; ed. Dubois and Renaud 1976) depends on Passio 2 according to Quentin (1908 pp 60–63) who, following earlier scholarship, also links it (p 60 note 5) with the *passiones* of **ANDOCHIUS** and **BENIGNUS**.

Copies of Passio 2 are also preserved in the eleventh-century London and Salisbury manuscripts of the **COTTON-CORPUS LEGENDARY** (Zettel 1979 p 16), where Speusippus's name is rendered "Pseusippus." Both Zettel and Jackson and Lapidge (1996 p 135) indicate that the Legendary's text of the *Passio Speusippi* is preceded by Warnaharius's *passio* of Saint Desiderius of Langres and the "Gemini," but the manuscript rubrics are misleading. What seems to be two separate texts is actually Warnaharius's prologue to the *Passio Speusippi*, merely mentioning the *Passio Desiderii* (*BHL* 2145, *CPL* 1310), followed immediately by the *passio* of Speusippus and his brothers, that is, the "Tergemini." The *Passio Desiderii* proper is not included in the English legendary at all and does not appear to have been known in Anglo-Saxon England.

In addition to the edition in *AS*, see *PL* 80.185–96.

Stephanus diaconus protomartyr, inventio [LUCIAN./AVIT.Rev. Steph.A]: *BHL* 7851; *BLS* 3.250–51; *BSS* 11.1376–87; *CPL* 575; *DACL* 5.624–71.
  ed.: Vanderlinden 1946 pp 190–216 (left-hand pages only).

MSS – Lists none.
A-S Vers Mart (B19.d and fi).
Quots/Cits Revelatio Stephani 194.12–196.13: BEDA.Retract.Act. VIII.40–58.
Refs 1. BEDA Comm.epist.cath. II.305–07.
  2. BEDA.Retract.Act. V.44–46 and VIII.37–40.
  3. BEDA.Chron.mai.1545–49.

The story of Stephen's "protomartyrdom" (ca. 35 A.D., feast day December 26) is told in Acts 6–7, but his cult began to flourish after the supposed discovery of his relics not far from Jerusalem in 415 (feast day August 3) by the priest Lucian, whose written account survives in various forms and languages. Additional impetus to the cult was given by **AUGUSTINE, DE CIVITATE DEI** XXII.viii (ed. *CCSL* 48), in his detailed accounts of Stephen's posthumous miracles in North Africa (*BHL* 7863–72).

Lucian's Greek account is represented in the Latin West by the *Revelatio*, surviving in two main versions, formerly designated by the Bollandists "a" (comprising *BHL* 7850, translator's prologue; *BHL* 7851–52, narrative) and "b" (*BHL* 7853–56), usually referred to as the A and B versions by twentieth-century scholars. Both versions claim to be the work of Lucian, but the first is associated, by an epistolary prologue (*BHL* 7850) and other evidence, with Avitus, a Spanish priest resident in Palestine, who purportedly commissioned Lucian's Greek account, translated it into Latin, and then entrusted his translation, with some relics of Stephen's body, to **OROSIUS** who was to take them with him to Spain. The A version is generally accepted by modern scholars as the genuine work of this Avitus and the best witness to Lucian's Greek text, the original version of which has not so far been found. Version B is regarded as an inferior witness reflecting a revised "official" account of Lucian's experiences (as in *BHG* 1649) emanating from the party of Bishop John of Jerusalem whom Avitus and Orosius had failed to convert from his Pelagian sympathies. See Vanderlinden (1946 p 186) and Lagrange in *DACL* 5 (especially cols 631–47).

Vanderlinden, the modern editor (1946 especially pp 185–87), has seriously modified the analysis of the textual tradition first offered in *BHL*, as reflected in the revised classification in the *BHL NS* (pp 798–99). He determined that version A has survived in relatively pure form, which he labels A", in only a few manuscripts, since most of the extant copies of the straight A version are contaminated to a greater or lesser degree with readings from the B tradition. The widely used text printed by the Maurists, reprinted in *PL* 41.805–16 (left-hand cols), is just such a contaminated text, which Vanderlinden calls A'. He finds that Mombritius's edition (1910 2.492–93), on the other hand, reproduces the genuine A" version but without the Avitus prologue (Vanderlinden 1946 p 181). In *BHL NS* this preferred A" version is now redesignated a.I, "Recensio genuina" (*BHL* 7851), while the A' version is now a.II and "mixta" (*BHL* 7851b). Vanderlinden's A" recension (the Bollandists' a.I version) is the focus of the remainder of this entry (see next entry for recension B). On early manuscripts not included in Vanderlinden's collation, which was limited to the collections of Brussels and Paris (Vanderlinden 1946 p 180 note 23), see Siegmund (1949 pp 223–24) and Cross (1982c pp 40–41).

Earlier Anglo-Saxon knowledge of the Latin *Revelatio* is represented first by **BEDE**, who, to judge from the lengthy extract in his **RETRACTIO IN ACTUS APOSTOLORUM** (BEDA.Retract.Act.; ed. *CCSL* 121), appears to have had a fairly good A text, although Laistner's note (*CCSL* 121.185) refers the reader to the B version. The first of Bede's two references in the *Retractio* also contains details drawn from the work (Vanderlinden 1946 p 190); Laistner's note (*CCSL* 121.129) refers the reader to the *Epistula*

Aviti, but Bede's specific reference to Avitus in CHRONICA MAIORA 1550–52 (BEDA.Chron.Mai.; ed. *CCSL* 123B) echoes GENNADIUS's DE VIRIS INLUSTRIBUS XLVII–XLVIII (*TU* 14/1a.78), as noted by C. Jones (*CCSL* 123B.514), and need not show knowledge of the *Epistula Aviti* even though the *Revelatio* is a source for the preceding lines (*Chronica* 1545–49). Similarly, the remark in his COMMENTARIUS IN EPISTOLAS SEPTEM CATHOLICAS (BEDA Comm.epist.cath.; ed. *CCSL* 121) is too general to prove his knowledge of other versions or texts. While all modern scholars, including Vanderlinden, appear to accept the genuineness of Avitus's authorship of both epistle and narrative, it is puzzling that none of Vanderlinden's authoritative A manuscripts of the *Revelatio* have the epistle. (I am indebted to Fred Biggs for most of the points in this paragraph.)

Herzfeld (*EETS* OS 116.233) refers to the *Revelatio* as a source for the substantial notice for August 3 in the OLD ENGLISH MARTYROLOGY (*Mart*; ed. Kotzor 1981 2.5–6 and 169–71). Cross (1982c pp 40–45) has shown that the *Revelatio* also acounts for several details in the notice on Stephen on December 26. Indeed, Cross argues from the two entries that the martyrologist could have used both the A and B versions or, as he seems to favor, a mixed text. He offers readings from a Vienna manuscript, not collated by Vanderlinden, as particularly close to the Old English. Cross (1982c p 44; 1985a p 125) also finds the martyrologist, for his December notice, dependent on the miracle narratives in Augustine's *City of God*, but possibly by way of a homiliary.

After the ninth century the *Revelatio* seems to drop from view in England until the end of the eleventh century (see next entry) despite the evident importance of Stephen's feast days in Anglo-Saxon calendars. The COTTON-CORPUS LEGENDARY contains nothing on Stephen, nor do ÆLFRIC's two homilies on the protomartyr mention the *Revelatio*. Fred Biggs has privately informed me that Ælfric's CATHOLIC HOMILIES I, 3 (*ÆCHom* I, B1.1.4; ed. *EETS* SS 17) relies on the biblical Acts, CAESARIUS OF ARLES, SERMONES CCXIX, and FULGENTIUS OF RUSPE's SERMONES III (Förster 1894 p 34 and Smetana 1959 pp 183–84), and that Ælfric's *Catholic Homilies* II, 2 (*ÆCHom* II, B1.2.3; ed. *EETS* SS 5) relies primarily on Augustine's *De civitate Dei* XXII.viii, most likely as an extract in sermon form (Förster 1892 pp 31–34 and Cross 1971a pp 450–53). Biggs also points to Augustine's **SERMONES** CCCXIX and CCCXXII (*PL* 38.1440–42, 1443–45) and **PSEUDO-AUGUSTINE**, **SERMONES** CCCLXXXII (*CPPM* 748; ed. *PL* 39.1684–86), and, from the "Appendix" of the Benedictines' edition, **SERMONES** CCXV (*CPPM* 1000; ed. *PL* 39.2145–46).

But see now Godden's sourcing of both the Ælfric homilies (*EETS* SS 18.21–28 and 355–62).

Stephanus diaconus protomartyr, inventio [LUCIAN./AVIT.Rev. Steph.B]: *BHL* 7854.
    ed.: Vanderlinden 1946 pp 191–217 (right-hand pages only).

MSS Dublin, Trinity College 174: HG 215.
Lists – Refs none.

The late-eleventh-century hagiographic miscellany listed here, originally from Salisbury Cathedral, has several texts relating to the cult of Stephen protomartyr, copied towards the end of the eleventh century by Webber's Group I scribes (Webber 1992 p 142), including the *Revelatio* itself, and sermons by **AUGUSTINE, PSEUDO-AUGUSTINE,** and **CAESARIUS OF ARLES**. According to Colker (1991 1.321), the copy of the *Revelatio* represents one of the variant forms of version B. Besides Vanderlinden's edition of recension B, see also the somewhat contaminated text edited by the Maurists, reprinted in *PL* 41.808–18 (right-hand columns only, in italics: *BHL* 7853).

Stephanus papa, passio [ANON.Pas.Steph.pap.]: *BHL* 7845; *BLS* 3.249; *BSS* 12.22–24; *CPL* 2236.
    ed.: *AS* Aug. 1.139–44.

MSS 1. London, BL Harley 3020: HG 433.
    2. London, BL Cotton Nero E. i: HG 344.
    3. Salisbury, Cathedral Library 222 (formerly Oxford, Bodleian Library Fell 1): HG 754.6.
Lists – Refs none.

Pope Stephen I (254–57, feast day August 2) is of interest to modern historians as one of the more disputatious protagonists in the ecclesiastical controversies of the mid-third century (including, e.g., the validity of baptism by heretics). Early sources say nothing of a martyrdom, but the persecution under emperor Valerian began in the year of Stephen's death and the probably sixth-century *passio* depicts him as one of its victims, borrowing a good deal from the earlier *passio* of LAURENTIUS and SIXTUS II (Farmer 1987 p 392).

BEDE's MARTYROLOGIUM (ed. Dubois and Renaud 1976 p 142.2–3) and the **OLD ENGLISH MARTYROLOGY** (*Mart* B19.fg; ed. Kotzor 1981 2.168) do not draw on the *passio* for their brief notices for Pope Stephen but use the sixth-century **LIBER PONTIFICALIS**, which also reflects the tradition that Stephen was a martyr (see Quentin 1908 p 103; Kotzor 1981 2.334; Cross 1979 pp 191 and 202). In later Anglo-Saxon England, Pope Stephen's feast day, which figures prominently in the *Gregorian Sacramentary* (see **LITURGY, MASSBOOKS**), was apparently of some importance, and this is reflected in the existence of copies of the *passio* in the early-eleventh-century Canterbury passional, Harley 3020, and in the eleventh-century London and Salisbury manuscripts of the **COTTON-CORPUS LEGENDARY** (Zettel 1979 p 23; Jackson and Lapidge 1996 p 139). The textual relationship of these copies has not been studied. In addition to the *AS* edition, see also Mombritius (1910 2.495–500 and 733–34).

Sulpitius Bituricensis, vita [ANON.Vit.Sulpit.]: *BHL* 7928; *BLS* 1.111–12; *BSS* 12.62–63; cf. *CPL* 2142.
ed.: *AS* Ian. 2.174–76.

MSS 1. London, BL Cotton Nero E. i: HG 344.
2. Salisbury, Cathedral Library 221 (formerly Oxford, Bodleian Library Fell 4): HG 754.5.
Lists – Refs none.

Usually called Sulpitius Pius (feast day January 17) to distinguish him from an earlier bishop of Bourges, and from Sulpitius of Maastricht, this

Sulpitius was bishop from the 620s to 646/647, renowned for his concern for the poor and for defending the people from their Frankish overlords, as well as for his miracles. According to Krusch (*MGH* SRM 4.368), the original *vita*, now lost, was composed ca. 647–71 and is most closely represented in Krusch's recension A (Vita 1a, *BHL* 7927), which survives in only one ninth-century manuscript; but since the more popular and more recent B recension, Vita 1b (*BHL* 7928), although much revised, occasionally preserves readings from the original *vita*, Krusch prints the two side by side (*MGH* SRM 4.372–80), interwoven in a tortuous format, so as to reconstitute the original lost text.

Despite the early textual tradition of the *vita*, there is no trace of Anglo-Saxon interest in the saint except for copies of Vita 1b that are preserved in eleventh-century representatives, listed here, of the **COTTON-CORPUS LEGENDARY** (specifically manuscript B1c: see Krusch in *MGH* SRM 4.369 and Levison in *MGH* SRM 7.602 and 632). The much more readable *AS* edition, cited here, has a B-type text apparently very similar to that of the English copies.

Swithunus, miracula et translatio [LANTFRED.Trans.mir.Swith.]: *BHL* 7944–45; *BLS* 3.108–09; *BSS* 12.91–92; Farmer (1987) pp 395–96.
    ed.: *AS* Iul. 1.324–25, 331–37 and Sauvage 1885 pp 372–410.
    MSS 1. London, BL Cotton Nero E. i: HG 344.
        2. London, BL Royal 15. C. vii: HG 496.
        3. Rouen, Bibliothèque Municipale 1385: HG 927.
        4. ?Vatican, Reg. lat. 566.
Lists none.
A-S Vers 1. WVLF.WINT.Narr.metr.Swith.
        2. ÆLFR.Epitom.trans.mir.Swith.
Quots/Cits none.
Refs *ÆLS* Swithun (B1.3.22) 334.

Swithun (deposition, July 2; translation, July 15) was bishop of Winchester (852–62) under King Ethelwulf of Wessex, but little is known about his life and career. His cult does not seem to have developed until during the period of the monastic revival a century later, when the relics were translated in 971 by ÆTHELWOLD (ÆTHELWOLDUS, bishop of Winchester 963–84) into the new cathedral. Early in the next century, another bishop of Winchester, Ælfheah (ÆLFEGUS), on becoming Archbishop (1005), took Swithun's head to Canterbury. The cult was widely celebrated throughout the country. The earliest hagiography is the Latin account of the translation and miracles (*BHL* 7944–45) composed ca. 975 by a Frankish cleric, **LANTFRED** (Old English "Landferth"), who later retired to Fleury (Lapidge 1989/90 pp 249 note 3, and 251–52). Four of the five extant manuscripts of Lantfred's *Miracula* are of the eleventh century (the most important, in Lapidge's view, BL Royal 15. C. vii, is dated late tenth century). The text in the Cotton manuscript listed here is not part of the **COTTON-CORPUS LEGENDARY** proper, however, having been added some time after the copying of the main collection. A full description of the manuscripts and textual affiliations will be provided in Lapidge's edition (forthcoming a).

On Lantfred's work, with some additional material, **WULFSTAN OF WINCHESTER** based his **NARRATIO METRICA DE SANCTO SWITHUNO**, *BHL* 7947 (WVLF.WINT.Narr.metr.Swith.; ed. Campbell 1950 pp 65–177), which he composed in 996 to form an *opus geminatum* (Lapidge 1986b p 28; 1989/90 p 252). **ÆLFRIC** refers to Lantfred in his Old English prose *Swithun*, in **LIVES OF SAINTS** (*ÆLS*; ed. *EETS* OS 76 and 82, composed 995–1002), but *Swithun* is based on a Latin prose epitome (ÆLFRIC.Epitom.trans.mir.Swith.; unpublished: see next entry) rather than directly on Lantfred's work.

At the end of the eleventh century, at Sherborne, Lapidge argues, Wulfstan's poem in turn was rendered back into prose by an anonymous writer, and more miracles were added. This version, not fully recognized in *BHL* or *BHL NS*, survives, in expanded or abbreviated form and preceded by the life attributed to Goscelin, in several manuscripts of the twelfth century and later. See Lapidge (1989/90 p 260 and forthcoming a). See also Grosjean (1940 pp 187–96) for an edition of portions of a fourteenth-century redaction (*BHL* 7948z) of the Sherborne anonymous; for other manuscripts, see Hardy (*RS* 26/1.513–14, nos. 1078–79).

Neither of the editions of Lantfred's *Translatio et Miracula Swithuni* cited here is complete. That by Sauvage is a supplement (based on the Rouen manuscript) to the earlier incomplete edition in *AS*, which in turn is based on the fragmentary manuscript in Rome, Vat. Reg. lat. 566 (Poncelet 1910 p 375; note that *AS* and Sauvage cite this manuscript by its old catalogue number, Vat. Reg. lat. 769). Lapidge's forthcoming edition will thus provide the first complete text of Lantfred's work, along with new editions of Wulfstan's metrical version, Ælfric's Old English prose version and his Latin prose epitome, and the late-eleventh-century *Vita Swithuni* commonly attributed to Goscelin of Canterbury (*BHL* 7943), and the first edition of the anonymous Sherborne *Translatio et Miracula Swithuni*. Lapidge's edition will also include an account of the influence of Lantfred's *Translatio et miracula* on other writings (including liturgies) in the late tenth and eleventh centuries, which we have not considered here.

Swithunus, miracula [ÆLFRIC.Epitom.trans.mir.Swith.]: *BHL* 7948.
ed.: *AS* Iul. 1.328–30.

MSS   none (see below).
Lists   none.
A-S Vers   *ÆLS* Swithun (B1.3.22).
Quots/Cits – Refs   none.

An epitome of **LANTFRED**'s life and miracles of Swithun (see previous entry) is preserved in a twelfth-century manuscript, Paris BN Lat. 5362, along with other texts relating to English saints (see **ÆLFRIC**, and Lapidge and Winterbottom 1991 pp cxlviii–cxlix). Lapidge regards this epitome as Ælfric's own composition and the immediate source for his Old English *Swithun* in **LIVES OF SAINTS** (*ÆLS*; ed. *EETS* OS 76 and 82). Both these texts share details not in Lantfred's version (see also Needham 1966 pp 20–21). A new edition of the epitome will be included in Lapidge's edition of the Swithun materials (forthcoming a).

Symeon Stylites, vita [ANON.Vit.Symeon.]: *BHL* 7956–57; *BLS* 1.34–37; *BSS* 11.1116–38; Farmer (1987) pp 436–37.
   ed.: *PL* 73.325–34.
MSS – Lists none.
A-S Vers ?*Mart* (B19.ey).
Quots/Cits – Refs none.

   Symeon (Simeon) the Stylite or pillar saint (feast days January 5, July 27) died on top of his pillar in Syria in 459, after a long career as one of the most famous and audacious ascetic heroes of the early church. In his own lifetime, his fame spread to Gaul, where he is mentioned in the sixth-century life of GENOVEFA and by **GREGORY OF TOURS, DE GLORIA CONFESSORUM** XXVI (*MGH* SRM 1/2.314), who draws on an early Latin version, *Vita Symeonis* 1 (*BHL* 7956, ed. Leitzmann *TU* 32/4.21–78), of the widely known Greek life by Symeon's disciple "Antonius" (*BHG* 1682–83: see Siegmund 1949 p 224); "cet impossible Antoine" is not highly regarded by modern scholars (e.g., Peeters 1943 p 43).

   It is uncertain if Symeon was known to the earliest Anglo-Saxons. His January 5 feast day, the usual one in the West, is regularly noted in later Anglo-Saxon calendars; two pre-eleventh-century calendars (F. Wormald 1934 pp 8, 22) have July 27, an Eastern date, as does the narrative notice in the ninth-century **OLD ENGLISH MARTYROLOGY** (*Mart*; ed. Kotzor 1981 2.159–61), the earliest Anglo-Saxon allusion to Symeon. The *Martyrology* notice has not been properly sourced but, as suggested by Herzfeld (*EETS* OS 116.xl), it appears to be based on a Latin life similar to that in question here, *Vita Symeonis* 2, longer and later than *BHL* 7956, translated from *BHG* 1685 (Siegmund 1949 p 224). While the *Martyrology*'s version of the opening exchange between the young Symeon and the old monk (Kotzor 1981 2.160.5–8) is verbally closer to that in the shorter Vita 1 (*TU* 32/4.21 and 23), most of the other details of the narrative are found only in Vita 2. So a mixed text may have been the *Martyrology*'s source. Surprisingly, the Old English author avoids mentioning Symeon's famous column and represents him instead as simply standing in the desert "on a dry stone": perhaps he misunderstood his source text or the latter was corrupt (see Kotzor 1981 2.161.3–4 and *PL* 73.328.2–9). See also Quentin (1908 p 188), who remarks on a similar lack of interest in the column on the part of the anonymous martyrologist of Lyons (late eighth century).

Leitzmann's modern edition of the Latin *Vita Symeonis* has only the shorter, much rarer text (*BHL* 7956), from two late manuscripts, beneath the Greek text, which was Leitzmann's main concern. The *PL* edition of the longer, more successful Latin text, cited here, and that in *AS* Ian. 1.269–74, are reprinted from Rosweyde (1615 pp 170–75). A critical edition is a desideratum. Some early manuscripts are listed by Siegmund (1949 p 224). On the column saints in general, see Delehaye (1923b pp I–XXXIV). On the early hagiography of Symeon (especially in Greek and Syriac), see Peeters (1943).

Symphorianus, passio [ANON.Pas.Symphorian.]: *BHL* 7967–68, 7969; *BLS* 3.380–81; *BSS* 11.1216–17; *CPL* 2143; Farmer (1987) p 467.

    ed.: *AS* Aug. 4.496–97.

MSS 1. London, BL Cotton Nero E. i: HG 344.
      2. Salisbury, Cathedral Library 222 (formerly Oxford, Bodleian Library Fell 1): HG 754.6.

Lists none.

A-S Vers ?*Mart* (B19.fz).

Quots/Cits – Refs none.

Believed to have been a martyr at Autun in the late second century, Symphorianus (feast day August 22) may have become the object of a developing cult at Autun in the fifth century, with the building of a church and possibly the composition of the earliest version (Passio 1a, *BHL* 7967–68) of the *passio* (Delehaye 1933a p 353; Vieillard-Troiekouroff 1976 pp 44–45). The *passio* was certainly known to **GREGORY OF TOURS** in the late sixth century (**DE GLORIA CONFESSORUM LXXVI**; ed. *MGH* SRM 1/2.343.25–26; see also **DE GLORIA MARTYRUM LI**, *MGH* SRM 1/2.74). Symphorianus was venerated early at Tours as well as Autun, and there is place-name evidence of veneration in the southwest of Britain (Doble 1931). The early *passio* exists in two recensions, 1a (*BHL* 7967–68) and 1b (*BHL* 7969), which differ from one another in only minor ways. Later legends incorporated Symphorianus into the "cycle Bourguignon" revolving around the figure of **BENIGNUS**; the *passio* of **PATROCLUS TRECENSIS** (*BHL* 6520) borrows passages from the *Passio Symphoriani* (Van der Straeten 1960 pp 148–50).

The substantial notice in the **OLD ENGLISH MARTYROLOGY** (*Mart*; ed. Kotzor 1981 2.184–85), which highlights short speeches of the young saint and his mother, is discussed by Cross (1981a) in relation to the printed editions of the *passio* and several early medieval manuscripts. Cross concludes (pp 274–75) that the martyrologist may have used a variant of *BHL* 7967–68 (Passio 1a) supplemented with *BHL* 424 (the *passio* of **ANDOCHIUS**), or a variant of *BHL* 7969 (Passio 1b) alone. In the later Anglo-Saxon period, the **COTTON-CORPUS LEGENDARY** displays a text of the *Passio Symphoriani* that corresponds closely to Passio 1a (Zettel 1979 p 24). On the occurrence of the name of Symphorianus with that of **TIMOTHEUS ROMAE** in the calendars and mass prayers for August 22, see the useful note in *BLS* 3.381, based on Delehaye and Quentin (*AS* Nov. 2/2.456–58). I have not seen the edition and studies of Grelier (1952, 1953). *BHL* 7967–68 has been printed several times, including in *AS*, but *BHL* 7969 is unprinted.

Symphorosa, passio [ANON.Pas.Symphoros./PS.JULIUS AFRICANUS]: *BHL* 7971; *BLS* 3.136–37; *BSS* 11.1217–29; *CPL* 2238.
 ed.: *AS* Iul. 4.355 paragraph 22 (prologus), 358–59 (passio).

MSS 1. London, BL Cotton Nero E. i: HG 344.
 2. Salisbury, Cathedral Library 222 (formerly Oxford, Bodleian Library Fell 1): HG 754.6.
Lists none.
A-S Vers 1. BEDA.Mart. 130.2–18.
 2. ?*Mart* (B19.er).
Quots/Cits – Refs none.

The cult of Symphorosa and her seven sons (feast day July 18), who are said to have been martyred under the emperor Hadrian at Tivoli near Rome, is ancient, but it is now thought likely that the *passio*, along with the relationship of the female and seven male martyrs, is a pious invention (similar to the case of **FELICITAS CUM SEPTEM FILIIS**), rather than historically reliable as was formerly believed (e.g., by Ruinart 1859 p 70). See Delehaye (1933a pp 278–79; 1936 pp 121–23). The traditional attribution to **JULIUS AFRICANUS** has also been rejected. To judge from *BHL*, there is remarkably little variation in surviving copies of the text.

The liturgical cult of Symphorosa does not appear to have been commemorated in Anglo-Saxon England, but the *passio* was evidently known throughout our period. **BEDE** certainly draws on it for his detailed **MARTYROLOGIUM** notice (BEDA.Mart.; ed. Dubois and Renaud 1976, sourced by Quentin 1908 pp 92–93), but the much shorter **OLD ENGLISH MARTYROLOGY** notice (*Mart*; Kotzor 1981 2.152) gives little more than the names of the seven sons in the same order as in Bede's account, also mentioning the fact that their relics have occasioned "many heavenly miracles." But the *Martyrology* calls Symphorosa a widow, which Bede does not, and J. E. Cross (private communication) was confident that the *Martyrology* author knew the *passio*. In the eleventh-century **COTTON-CORPUS LEGENDARY**, the text of the *passio* is placed among the June saints, not in July, because of Getulius (June 10), Symphorosa's husband. See *AS* Iul. 4.353 (cited by Jackson and Lapidge 1996 p 138). The Legendary's copy includes the brief prologue of Pseudo-Julius Africanus. Another English copy, of the early twelfth century, is in a Chester legendary, now in London (see Ker and Piper 1969–92 1.54).

Tergemini. See **SPEUSIPPUS**.

Thaïs, vita [ANON.Vit.Thaid.]: *BHL* 8012–13; *BLS* 4.61–62; *BSS* 12.97–99.
    ed.: *CCSL* 85.75 (preface only) and *PL* 73.661–62.

MSS ?Worcester, Cathedral Library F.48: HG 761.
Lists – Refs none.

Modern scholars are agreed that the story of Thaïs (feast day October 8), a beautiful fourth-century Egyptian courtesan who was converted to a life of extreme asceticism by the monk Paphnutius (or Serapion), is a pious fiction, despite the sensational discovery of what was believed to be her grave earlier this century (see the references in *BLS*). The legend is one of several concerning early Christian female saints said to have been reformed prostitutes (see also **AFRA, MARIA AEGYPTIACA, MARIA MAGDALENA, ABRAHAM ET MARIA, PELAGIA**: see Ward 1987, Karras 1990). The model for the Thaïs/Paphnutius story seems to have been a simpler narrative, concerning another desert father, Serapion, and an unnamed prostitute, from the fourth–sixth century Greek collection, *Apophthegmata Patrum*, translated into Latin in the sixth century by Paschasius (*BHL* 6531): see the edition of the Latin text by Freire (1971 1.276–79; also *PG* 65.412–13). See Nau (1903 pp 53–55) and Freire (1971 1.18–24) for contrasting views of the early development of the Thaïs legend.

The Latin life in question here, designated Vita 1a in *BHL*, first printed by Rosweyde (reprinted in *PL* and by Nau 1903 pp 86–113, left-hand pages), was adapted from a (sixth-century?) Greek life (*BHG* 1695–97: Siegmund 1949 p 225). The Latin translation has been firmly attributed to **DIONYSIUS EXIGUUS** (Denis the Little, early sixth century: see *CCSL* 85.75 for the preface lacking in *PL* and most manuscript versions), but Freire considers the work later than the sixth century. As Siegmund implies, we still lack a thorough study of the textual tradition and manuscripts of the Latin lives of Thaïs, only superficially explored by Nau (1903 pp 63–64).

Thaïs seems to have been less familiar to the Anglo-Saxons than some of the other prostitute saints (her feast is not mentioned in the calendars). A fragmentary copy of Vita 1a is preserved in the late-eleventh-century Worcester manuscript listed here, which is inadequately described in the catalogue (Floyer and Hamilton 1906 p 23). The manuscript, the makeup of which is problematic, is discussed by Jackson (1992) chiefly with reference to **RUFINUS**'s **HISTORIA MONACHORUM**, but also in the general context of interest in ascetic texts at Worcester (see ANTONIUS) in the time of Prior Coleman and Bishop Wulfstan II (WULFSTANUS II). According to HG (revised version), the fragmentary copy of the *vita* in the Worcester manuscript was written at "Worcester or York" around the turn of the tenth century. For another late-eleventh-century manuscript, displaying similar interests and containing the lives of two other prostitute saints, see above, the entries for Abraham et Maria and Pelagia.

Thebaei. See MAURITIUS.

Thecla, passio [ANON.Pas.Thecl.1]: *BHL* 8020; *BLS* 3.623–25; *BSS* 12.176–77.
    ed.: *TU* 22/2.2–127.
MSS – Lists none.
A-S Vers 1. ?ALDH.Carm.uirg. 1975–2008.
    2. ?ALDH.Pros.uirg. 299.18–300.10.
    3. ?BEDA.Mart. 124.16–20.
Quots/Cits – Refs none.

According to her well-known legend, Thecla (feast day September 23), a young woman of Iconium, Asia Minor, rejected her fiancé and family after hearing the apostle Paul preach (PAULUS APOSTOLUS). She then survived a series of spectacular ordeals in the arenas at Iconium and Antioch while accompanying Paul on parts of his journeys. She is frequently referred to as a martyr, although she died an old woman at Seleucia after living many years in a cave. The Greek "Acts of Paul and Thecla" was early attached to, if not originally part of, the second-century "Acts of Paul" (see James 1953 pp 270–96), portions of which survive in Greek, Syriac, and Coptic, as well as Latin. The Thecla portion is probably the best known and is among the earliest works of Christian hagiography (see *NTA* 1.323–26; also see Rordorf 1984 p 76 on the possible existence of a Latin version of the late second century). Popular with heretical sects, the work was proscribed in some circles (which may explain ÆLFRIC's silence concerning Thecla), but the text nonetheless circulated freely as the "Passio S. Theclae virginis."

Several Latin versions of the original Greek (*BHG* 1710) survive in numerous recensions, revisions, and epitomes, of which the original *BHL* classification and numbering have been substantially revised in *BHL NS* (see pp 812–16) in the light of the authoritative edition of von Gebhardt in *TU*, who provides descriptions of the versions and manuscript groups. He distinguishes three main redactions, A, B, and C, each subdivided into different families, all of which he prints in parallel columns and blocks, with copious variants. Despite the numerous variants distinguishing these different texts from one another, and despite von Gebhardt's use of the term "Übersetzungen" for the three main redactions, implying independent translations, they are all patently representatives of one original work, which the Bollandists still broadly designate Passio 1.

In early Anglo-Saxon England, both **BEDE** and **ALDHELM** summarize the legend, but not in sufficient detail for their specific sources to be identified, although according to Quentin (1908 p 93) Bede's notice in his **MARTYROLOGIUM** (BEDA.Mart.; ed. Dubois and Renaud 1976) is probably indebted to either von Gebhardt's version A (*BHL* 8020a), Ba (*BHL* 8020b), or Bc (*BHL* 8020f). Thecla's feast day is honored with a verse in the eighth-century York metrical calendar (Wilmart 1934 p 68) and her name was important enough in monastic circles at this time to be adopted by one of the nuns of Barking to whom Aldhelm addressed his **DE VIRGINITATE** (ALDH.Carm.uirg., Pros.uirg.; ed. *MGH* AA 15; for the name, see p 229.4). See also Levison (1946 p 77) on another English Thecla, who followed **BONIFACE** (**BONIFATIUS**) to Germany and became the sainted Abbess of Kitzingen. For evidence of a Thecla cult, possibly very ancient, in the Welsh border area, see Baring-Gould and Fisher (1907–13 4.22–23) and now Sharpe (1990a) who thinks this Thecla may have been merely a local saint with a famous name.

Thecla's feast day is not common in the extant calendars of the tenth and eleventh centuries (see, however, F. Wormald 1934 pp 24, 38, 248, and 262). The remaining Anglo-Saxon evidence, treated separately in the following entries, allows for more precise identification of the recensions available in England after the age of Bede and Aldhelm.

For further bibliography, and a translation of the Greek text edited by Dagron (1978), see *NTA* 2.322, 353–64; see also J. Elliott (1993 pp 350–74).

Thecla, passio [ANON.Pas.Thecl.1a]: *BHL* 8020a; *BLS* 3.623–25; *BSS* 12.176–77.
   ed.: *TU* 22/2.2–127.
MSS ?Dublin, Trinity College 174: HG 215.
Lists – Refs none.

The *Passio S. Theclae* in the Dublin manuscript listed here was copied by one of Webber's Group I Salisbury scribes in the late eleventh century (Webber 1992 p 142). Not noticed by von Gebhardt, it is identified by Colker (1991 1.322), following Grosjean (1928 p 89), as Passio 1a, although it differs slightly from the text as printed by von Gebhardt.

Thecla, passio [ANON.Pas.Thecl.1ba]: *BHL* 8020d; *BLS* 3.623–25; *BSS* 12.176–77.
   ed.: *TU* 22/2.2–127.
MSS London, BL Cotton Otho A. xiii: HG 351.
Lists – Refs none.

Of the *Passio Theclae* in the burnt eleventh-century Cotton manuscript, seven fragments (new foliation 34–40) remain from the original seventeen folios (old foliation 41–57). Not listed by von Gebhardt, this copy has not been properly studied, but on the basis of a cursory examination it appears to correspond closely to his Ba group (Passio 1ba in *BHL*), another representative of which is in a later English manuscript, Lambeth Palace 94 (thirteenth/fourteenth century, possibly West Midlands or Welsh border; see James and Jenkins 1930–32 p 156, and Sharpe 1990a).

Thecla, passio [ANON.Pas.Thecl.1cd]: *BHL* 8020n; *BLS* 3.623–25; *BSS* 12.176–77.
   ed.: *TU* 22/2.2–127.

MSS ?Oxford, Bodleian Library Digby 39 (*SC* 1640): HG 609.
Lists none.
A-S Vers Mart (B19.hi).
Quots/Cits – Refs none.

The brief but interesting notice for Thecla in the **OLD ENGLISH MARTYROLOGY** (*Mart*; ed. Kotzor 1981 2.216–17) has not been formally sourced but the statement (216.12) that Thecla "scear hyre feax" ("cut her hair") as part of her male disguise is echoed in a variant, "incisis crinibus," found only in manuscripts of von Gebhardt's Cd group (*TU* 22/2.115.21–22). Among the Cd manuscripts is the Digby manuscript listed here (from Abingdon), parts of which are late eleventh century, but the Thecla folios are somewhat later, acccording to Macray (1883 col 35). Nonetheless, the Cd version is certainly much older than this (another Cd manuscript is tenth century: *TU* 22/2.XXXII), and in view of the connection with the *Martyrology*, the Digby text may well witness to an earlier Anglo-Saxon tradition. On the maverick character of the Cd group, see von Gebhardt (*TU* 22/2.LXXIV–LXXX).

Thecla, passio altera [ANON.Pas.Thecl.5]: *BHL* 8024g.
   ed.: *TU* 22/2.150–56.

MSS ?Orléans, Bibliothèque Muncipale 342 (290): HG 869.
Lists – Refs none.

The *Passio Theclae* in the Orléans manuscript (Van der Straeten 1982 p 73) is a popular epitome of von Gebhardt's version Bb (*BHL* 8020e) and is now designated Passio 5bb in *BHL NS*. From Van der Straeten's catalogue description, however, it is unclear whether or not the portion of the manuscript containing this text is in the same eleventh-century English hand as the previous portions, or whether the text is of non-English provenance.

Theodora et Didymus, passio [ANON.Pas.Theodor.Didym.]: *BHL* 8072; *BLS* 2.181; *BSS* 12.227–28.
   ed.: *AS* April. 2.573–74.
MSS Dublin, Trinity College 174: HG 215.
Lists – Refs none.

The story of Theodora of Alexandria, a beautiful Christian maiden condemned to prostitution for her faith and rescued by a generous soldier, is closely parallel to the elaborate narrative (*BHL* 9030) by **AMBROSE** in **DE VIRGINIBUS** II.iv (ed. Cazzaniga 1948 pp 98–107). The Alexandrian legend, at least, is no longer regarded as historically authentic. It is a translation of a Greek original (*BHG* 1742), according to Siegmund (1949 p 251, citing Franchi de' Cavalieri 1935), and not commonly found in early medieval manuscripts: Siegmund mentions only one pre-twelfth-century manuscript copy and evidence of a second. The important copy in the Dublin manuscript listed here (see Colker 1991 1.322) is the work of Webber's Group I Salisbury Cathedral scribes (1992 p 142) in the late eleventh century. In the mid-seventeenth century Archbishop Ussher, who had acquired this manuscript with other Fell manuscripts from the Bodleian Library, Oxford, sent a transcription of the text to the Bollandist Daniel Papebroch to be used as the basis of the *AS* edition. On the historical context and sources of the original *passio*, and for further references, see the study by Franchi de' Cavalieri (1935).

Theodoretus, passio [ANON.Pas.Theodoret.]: *BHL* 8074; *BLS* 4.179–80; *BSS* 12.228.
   ed.: *AS* Oct. 10.40–45.
MSS Salisbury, Cathedral Library 221 (formerly Oxford, Bodleian Library Fell 4): HG 754.5.
Lists none.
A-S Vers Mart (B19.bj).
Quots/Cits – Refs none.

In the *Passio Theodoreti* in question here, Theodoret (feast day October 23, but see below) is a Christian priest of Antioch who is tortured and then executed on the orders of the Roman prefect Julian, uncle of Julian the Apostate. The prefect suffers a sordid death shortly afterwards, much chagrined at the cool reception his actions have elicited from his imperial nephew. Various Latin versions of this legend, all deriving from a lost Greek *passio* of undetermined date, are extant (Franchi de' Cavalieri 1920; Siegmund 1949 pp 251–52). The version known to the Anglo-Saxons both early and late is the one designated by the Bollandists as Passio 2a, *BHL* 8074. Apparently it represents a different translation of the lost Greek source than the others studied by Franchi de' Cavalieri, which are interrelated and probably later. Siegmund (1949 p 252) identifies one ninth-century manuscript of *BHL* 8074, now in Karlsruhe.

Although the notice for Theodoret in the **OLD ENGLISH MARTYROLOGY** (*Mart*; ed. Kotzor 1981 2.42–43) is quite brief, Herzfeld's opinion (*EETS* OS 116.xxxviii) that the source is this *passio* (although as printed by Ruinart) was confirmed by J. E. Cross (private communication). In the *Martyrology* Theodoret is honored on March 23, as in other early martyrologies (although often named "Theodore"), not October 23, the more usual date in the Roman calendar. Neither date is celebrated for Theodoret in the extant Anglo-Saxon calendars.

In the eleventh-century **COTTON-CORPUS LEGENDARY**, the *passio* (entitled "Passio Theodori") carries the date March 23, but it is extant only in the Salisbury manuscript, not in Cotton Nero E. i (or Corpus Christi College 9). In the opinion of Zettel (1979 p 18 note 45) the text most probably had a place in what he believes to have been earlier recensions of the Cotton-Corpus Legendary, but he does not suggest why the Worcester scribe omitted the text from the Cotton manuscript: a gap is left at no. xxxiii in the Cotton table of contents (pt 1, fol 53r) where this text would have been listed. There is also a copy in Salisbury, Cathedral Library 223 (HG 754.7), copied by Webber's Group II scribes around or after the turn of the century (Webber 1992 p 170).

Theodorus, passio [ANON.Pas.Theodori]: *BHL* 8077; *BLS* 4.301–03; *BSS* 12.238–41.
  ed.: *AS* Nov. 4.29–39.
MSS Cambridge, Corpus Christi College 9: HG 36.
Lists – Refs none.

Theodore *tiro* ("the recruit"), a young soldier believed to have been martyred in the early fourth century at Amasea in the Helenopontus region of Asia Minor (feast day November 9) while in winter quarters with his legion, is one of the earliest and most celebrated of the military saints (see Delehaye 1909 pp 11–43, 121–202). The Western cult is already evident in Rome in the sixth century, where the dedication of his church at the foot of the Palatine Hill gave rise to the November feast day.

The earliest Latin version of his *passio* appears to be that under consideration here, translated from *BHG* 1761 (Siegmund 1949 p 252). It is not deemed "historical" (Franchi de' Cavalieri, 1912 p 170, calls it a "misero centone"; see also *AS* Nov. 4.13). The edition in *AS* (by Delehaye) is not a critical one, being based on only four manuscripts whose relationship to one another or to earlier editions is not explained.

As befits a saint with a proper mass in the Gregorian service books, Theodore regularly appears in Anglo-Saxon calendars of the tenth–eleventh centuries, in some of which the feast is graded (F. Wormald 1934 pp 54 and 68), but he was not among the Eastern saints celebrated early in Gaul or Spain, and there is no evidence for knowledge of him among the earlier Anglo-Saxons. The sole hagiographic witness in our period is the copy of the *passio* in the Cambridge volume of the **COTTON-CORPUS LEGENDARY**, according to Zettel (1979 p 28, confirmed by Jackson and Lapidge 1996 p 142) who lists a later related copy (neither is mentioned by Delehaye, *AS* Nov. 4.13). A copy of another version of the Theodore *passio*, *BHL* 8079, is the work of Webber's Group II scribes in Salisbury, Cathedral Library 223 (HG 754.7), around or after the end of the eleventh century (Webber 1992 p 170).

Theodosia, passio [ANON.Pas.Theodos.]: *BHL* 8090; *BLS* 2.13–14; *BSS* 12.286–88.
ed.: Bollandists 1886–89 1.164–78.
MSS 1. London, BL Cotton Nero E. i: HG 344.
2. Salisbury, Cathedral Library 221 (formerly Oxford, Bodleian Library Fell 4): HG 754.5.
Lists – Refs none.

Theodosia (feast day April 2) was eighteen years old when she suffered martyrdom at Caesarea under the emperor Maximian in the early fourth century. Her story is told in the *Martyrs of Palestine* by **EUSEBIUS PAMPHILUS**. Much of the original Greek version of this work is lost, but it survives in Eusebius's own abridgement in a late redaction (not translated by **RUFINUS**) of his **HISTORIA ECCLESIASTICA**, as well as in a Syriac version, and piecemeal in some separate Greek narratives. Among the latter is the martyrdom of Theodosia (see *SChr* 55.140–42 for both the longer and shorter Greek versions, with French translations; see also Delehaye 1897b pp 127–28). Siegmund (1949 p 207 note 1, p 252) has suggested that the first version of the saint's Latin *passio* (*BHL* 8090) is a rendering of Eusebius's longer account. He mentions several copies of the Latin *passio* in important early medieval Gallic passionaries, including a seventh- or eighth-century fragment in Berlin and more complete early medieval copies in Vienna, Turin, and Rome. See also the text printed from a Spanish manuscript by Fábrega Grau (1953–55 2.244–54).

Theodosia, however, unlike another Palestinian martyr, **PROCOPIUS CAESAREAE**, appears to have been all but unknown to the early Anglo-Saxons. English evidence in her case is limited to the eleventh-century London and Salisbury copies of the *passio* preserved in the **COTTON-CORPUS LEGENDARY** (Zettel 1979 p 18; Jackson and Lapidge 1996 p 137). Her feast day is rare in Anglo-Saxon calendars (see, e.g., F. Wormald 1934 pp 33 and 229).

Theodota, passio [ANON.Pas.Theodot.1]: *BHL* 8093; *BLS* 3.249–50; *BSS* 12.303–05; *CPL* 2163.

Although in some legendaries the story of Theodota and her three sons (feast day August 2) forms a separate *passio*, in the **COTTON-CORPUS LEGENDARY** and earlier Anglo-Saxon tradition it is included in the third part (chapters XIX–XXXI, especially XIX, XXIX–XXXI) of the four-part epic *passio* of **ANASTASIA** (ed. Delehaye 1936 pp 235–45), which **BEDE** names as the source of his notice for Theodota in his **MARTYROLOGIUM** (ed. Dubois and Renaud 1976 p 142.6–12, sourced by Quentin 1908 p 59). Siegmund (1949 p 252) repeats Delehaye's opinion that a Greek original, more developed than *BHG* 1781, must lie behind the Theodota portion of the *passio*. The same Latin account as Bede's source seems to lie behind the notice in the ninth-century **OLD ENGLISH MARTYROLOGY** (*Mart*, B19.fh; ed. Kotzor 1981 2.168–69; see Herzfeld, *EETS* 116.226 and 239), but a thorough sourcing remains to be done. For the manuscripts of the *passio*, see above, the entry for Anastasia. For another version of the Theodota legend, see the next entry.

Theodota, passio [ANON.Pas.Theodot.2]: *BHL* 8096.
  ed.: Delehaye 1937 pp 220–24.
  MSS Dublin, Trinity College 174: HG 215.
  Lists – Refs none.

The Dublin manuscript listed here contains a *Passio Theodotae* as a separate work (Colker 1991 1.323) in the form of a homily. It is designated Passio 2 by the Bollandists to distinguish it from the better known version that forms part of the legend of **ANASTASIA**. It was copied by Webber's Group I Salisbury scribes in the late eleventh century (Webber 1992 p 142). The homily is described by Delehaye, who edits the text from a tenth-century manuscript in Paris, as a piece of wretchedly literal translating by some "unknown barbarian" in the tenth century or earlier from a Greek original (*BHG* 1781). The existence of this version of the legend in the Dublin manuscript is further grounds for supposing that the texts it contains were collected to form a supplement to the main

Salisbury legendary (**COTTON-CORPUS LEGENDARY**) and probably do not represent pre-Conquest English textual traditions.

Theogenes, passio [ANON.Pas.Theog.]: *BHL* 8107; *BSS* 3.1340.
  ed.: *AS* Ian. 1.134–45.
MSS 1. London, BL Cotton Nero E. i: HG 344.
  2. Salisbury, Cathedral Library 221 (formerly Oxford, Bodleian Library Fell 4): HG 754.5.
Lists – Refs none.

The legend of Theogenes (Theagenes; feast day January 3) recounts how, after being impressed into the Roman army in Phrygia, he was martyred in the Hellespont for refusing to fight for any king but Christ. His feast day was known early in the Christian West (*AS* Nov. 2/2.23–24), but the earliest clear evidence for Anglo-Saxon knowledge of the Latin *passio* is in the eleventh-century London and Salisbury **COTTON-CORPUS LEGENDARY**, containing copies of the work designated Passio 2 in *BHL* (Zettel 1979 p 15; Jackson and Lapidge 1996 p 135). As Siegmund points out (1949 pp 250–51), the study by Franchi de' Cavalieri (1912) is vague as to which of the two main versions is the older, but the one more closely corresponding to the Greek text that he edits (pp 177–85) is that designated Passio 1 by the Bollandists (*BHL* 8106). Delehaye (1909 p 23) has assumed an eighth-century date, or earlier, for the composition of the latter. The English copies of Passio 2 show only minor differences in wording from the edition printed in *AS*.

Theophilus, historia [PAVL.DIAC.NEAP.Hist.Theoph.]: *BHL* 8121; *BLS* 1.247–48; *BSS* 12.340–43.
  ed.: Meersseman 1963 pp 17–40.
MSS 1. London, BL Harley 3020: HG 433.
  2. London, BL Cotton Nero E. i: HG 344.
  3. London, BL Cotton Vespasian D. ii: HG 388.

4. Salisbury, Cathedral Library 221 (formerly Oxford, Bodleian Library Fell 4): HG 754.5.

Lists none.

A-S Vers *ÆCHom* I, 30 (B1.1.32) 190–98.

Quots/Cits 1. Prayer to the Virgin, London, BL Arundel 60 (HG 304): see below.

2. Horae de Beata Maria Virgine in London, BL Cotton Tiberius A. iii (HG 363): see below.

Refs none.

The *Actus* or *Historia Theophili* (also called *Poenitentia Theophili*), an early prototype of the Faust legend, recounts the story of Theophilus (feast day February 23), archdeacon of Adana in Cilicia, who humbly declines a bishopric but is then consumed by envy of the new bishop. He signs away his soul to the devil, but later repents and prays to the Virgin Mary, who regains from the devil the charter that Theophilus has signed in his own blood. The work was composed in Greek in the seventh century (*BHG* 1319–22) and was translated into Latin in the late ninth by Paul, a deacon of Naples, also the presumed author of the life of Mary of Egypt (**MARIA AEGYPTIACA**), in the preface of which (*PL* 73.671–72) the translator refers to the history of Theophilus ("tomulo de cujusdam vicedomini poenitentia"). These two texts (which appear together in several early manuscripts: Siegmund 1949 pp 269–70) are acknowledged as among the earliest to show the Virgin Mary in her role as intercessor for sinners (Fuiano 1961 p 131; cf. Clayton 1990 pp 257–58; see also Chiesa 1989/90 pp 71–72 note 10).

The *Historia Theophili* seems to have been well-known in England in the Benedictine reform era and later. Copies are extant in four manuscripts of our period, including the eleventh-century London and Salisbury manuscripts of the **COTTON-CORPUS LEGENDARY**, which is widely believed to represent **ÆLFRIC**'s main hagiographic source. According to Zettel (1979 p 180), however, Ælfric's Old English version of the story, in his homily for Mary's Assumption in **CATHOLIC HOMILIES** I, 30 (*ÆCHom* I; ed. *EETS* SS 17, translated Thorpe 1844–46 1.449), is too drastically abbreviated to permit any textual comparison with Latin variants. See also Godden (*EETS* SS 18.254).

Several eleventh-century liturgical texts also draw on the *Historia*, especially on the prayers included in the narrative. A substantial such passage (Meersseman's edition p 31) is borrowed and reworked as the second lesson in the Office of the Virgin in London, BL Cotton Tiberius A. iii (ed. *HBS* 21 fols 20–21), from Christ Church, Canterbury (mid-eleventh century; see also Clayton 1990 pp 71–72), and a short echo has been detected by Barré in one of the prayers to Mary in a mid-eleventh-century psalter, probably from Winchcombe (Cambridge, University Library Ff. 1. 23, fol 278r–v: see Barré 1963 p 131 and note 24). The long prayer to Mary in London, BL Arundel 60 (Winchester, Newminster, ca. 1060), printed and translated in Clayton (1990 pp 114–18), is based freely and creatively on the prayers in the *Historia* (see Barré 1963 pp 140–42). On the psalters, see **LITURGY, PSALTERS**.

For an exploration of the historical and cultural background to the work of Paul the Deacon of Naples, see Fuiano (1961 pp 131–52). For further bibliography on the Naples "school" of translators in the late ninth and tenth century, see Chiesa (1989/90 p 67).

The best edition of the text is that of Meersseman (1963) who includes variants from the Harley and Cotton Nero manuscripts in his apparatus, pointing out (p 15) that their texts of the *Historia* are very closely related. At least one variant, however, suggests that the Cotton Nero copy (mid-eleventh century, Worcester) does not derive directly from that in Harley (early eleventh century, Winchester: see Carley 1994 pp 277–79 and notes 66–67). Another later copy, for the same feast day, February 28, is in the early-twelfth-century Chester legendary, London, Gray's Inn 3 (Ker and Piper 1969–92 1.52).

Mary C. Clayton

Thomas. See **APOCRYPHA, PASSIO THOMAE**.

Thyrsus et Leucius, passio [ANON.Pas.Thyrs.Leuc.]: *BHL* 8280; *BSS* 12.501–02.
   ed.: *AS* Ian. 2.824–32.

MSS 1. London, BL Cotton Nero E. i: HG 344.
2. Salisbury, Cathedral Library 221 (formerly Oxford, Bodleian Library Fell 4): HG 754.5.
Lists – Refs none.

The only evidence for Anglo-Saxon knowledge of the cult of Thyrsus and his companions (feast day January 28), reputed martyrs of Nicomedia during the Decian persecution, is the pair of copies of their *passio* in the eleventh-century London and Salisbury manuscripts of the **COTTON-CORPUS LEGENDARY** (Jackson and Lapidge 1996 p 136; Webber 1992 p 155). According to Siegmund (1949 p 253) the Greek original of all the Latin versions of the *Passio Thyrsi* is *BHG* 1845. The Latin text in question here, designated Passio 3 in *BHL*, is of uncertain date but must be at least as early as the ninth century to judge from the surviving manuscripts (see Siegmund 1949 p 253).

Tiburtius. See **SEBASTIANUS** and **VALERIANUS ET TIBURTIUS**.

Timotheus Romae. See **SILVESTER**.

Torpes, passio [ANON.Pas.Torp.]: *BHL* 8307; *BSS* 12.627–28; *CPL* 2240.
ed.: *AS* Mai. 4.7–10.
MSS 1. London, BL Cotton Nero E. i: HG 344.
2. Salisbury, Cathedral Library 221 (formerly Oxford, Bodleian Library Fell 4): HG 754.5.
Lists – Refs none.

Torpes of Pisa (feast day May 17), whose cult was flourishing in Tuscany in the sixth–seventh centuries, is said to have been a Roman official martyred at the mouth of the Arno in the time of Nero after criticizing Nero's marvellous decorations of the temple of Diana at Pisa. The story told in the *passio* is said to have been dictated some years later than the martyrdom, after Nero's death, by an eye-witness named Artemius to a scribe named Audax, but the work is mainly fiction, composed possibly as early as the sixth century. The text in the eleventh-century London and Salisbury manuscripts of the **COTTON-CORPUS LEGENDARY** varies in numerous but minor readings from that in the *AS*. Another copy, which I have not seen, is in a Salisbury manuscript of the turn of the century (Salisbury, Cathedral Library 223, HG 754.7: see Webber 1992 p 170). An additional, even later English copy, slightly abridged and "corrected," occurs later in the London manuscript listed here, as part of a fragmentary thirteenth-century legendary bound in at the end of pt. 2 (fols 192–94).

In addition to the *AS* edition, see also that of Lazzarini (1968– 1.323–27), based on a twelfth–thirteenth century Lucca manuscript, along with an Italian translation and notes (pp 85–100).

Tranquilinus. See SEBASTIANUS.

Trudo, vita [DONAT.Vit.Trud.]: *BHL* 8321; *BLS* 4.413; *BSS* 12.683–85. ed.: *MGH* SRM 6.273–98.

MSS Cambridge, Corpus Christi College 9: HG 36.
Lists – Refs none.

The name of abbot Trudo or Trond (died 690, feast day November 23) survives in Saint-Trond, originally the monastery he founded near Louvain, where he was venerated as the missionary apostle of Hasbaye in Brabant, his native region. A copy of Vita 1, generally believed to have been composed in the eighth century by the deacon Donatus, is in the Cambridge manuscript of the **COTTON-CORPUS LEGENDARY** (Jackson and Lapidge 1996 p 142), but there are no other traces of Anglo-Saxon interest in the saint. The copy that existed in Salisbury, Cathedral Library 222, has been lost (Webber 1992 p 157 note 68). The mid-eleventh-century Cambridge copy, originally from Worcester, which lacks the author's prologue, is manuscript 5a in Levison's *MGH* edition, closely related to two later English manuscripts, now in Hereford and Salisbury, labeled by Levison 5b1 and 5b2. For manuscript families and affiliations, see his edition (pp 267–71). The textual history he worked out has been modified somewhat by Kesters (1955) in the light of a ninth-century manuscript that Levison initially overlooked (see *MGH* SRM 6.637–40).

Tryphon, passio [ANON.Pas.Tryph.]: *BHL* 8338; *BLS* 4.307–08; *BSS* 12.656–57.
 ed.: Bollandists 1889–93 1.284–92.
MSS 1. London, BL Cotton Nero E. i: HG 344.
 2. Salisbury, Cathedral Library 221 (formerly Oxford, Bodleian Library Fell 4): HG 754.5.
Lists – Refs none.

The relics of Tryphon (feast day February 3), a Phrygian gooseherd supposedly martyred at Nicea under Decius, appears in the Roman martyrology with saints Respicius and Nympha only because their relics were preserved together in one Roman location; otherwise they are unrelated (Delehaye et al. 1940 p 508, November 10). A joint legend (*BHL* 8340) was fabricated in the eleventh century by a monk of Fleury (see Siegmund 1949 p 273, and the bibliographical references in *BLS* 4.308) using earlier versions of the legend dealing with Trypho alone, including those designated in *BHL* as Passio 2 and Passio 3 (translated from *BHG* 1856). According to *BHL NS*, the oldest version is now thought to be Passio 3 (*BHL* 8339, printed by Delehaye, *AS* Nov. 4.357–65).

The next in chronological order, apparently, is the version at issue here, Passio 2, of which copies are preserved in the eleventh-century London and Salisbury manuscripts of the **COTTON-CORPUS LEGENDARY** (Jackson and Lapidge 1996 p 136). These may be somewhat better texts than the twelfth-century Paris manuscript on which the Bollandists base their edition in the Paris catalogue.

The oldest surviving manuscript of the *Passio Tryphonis* located by Siegmund (1949 p 273), and not included in Delehaye's list of manuscripts (*AS* Nov. 4.321), is a Turin manuscript, originally from Bobbio (tenth century). This has been identified by the Bollandists as a variant version (*BHL* 8338b) of Passio 2. The first part of the Turin manuscript (including the *Passio Tryphonis*), which also contains important versions of the legends of the Persian martyr **ANASTASIUS** and the virgins Anatolia and Victoria (see **ANATOLIA, VICTORIA, ET AUDAX**), is believed to represent a lost collection known to **ALDHELM** through the school of Archbishop **THEODORE OF CANTERBURY** (see Franklin 1995 and the entries for Anastasius). This (unprinted) version of the *passio* may thus be linked to early Anglo-Saxon traditions.

Tryphonia: *BSS* 3.1308, 12.657–58.

Tryphonia (feast day October 18) was the wife of the emperor Decius according to Part V (concerning **HIPPOLYTUS**) of the epic *passio* of **LAURENTIUS**, although the historical wife of Decius was Herennia Etruscilla (see Herzfeld, *EETS* OS 116.237). When Decius and his chief henchman died horribly as a result of their persecution and execution of Laurence and the others associated with him, Tryphonia and her daughter **CYRILLA** experienced conversion and were then baptized by the priest Justinus. Tryphonia died shortly afterwards but Cyrilla suffered martyrdom (feast day October 28) shortly after the Forty-Six Soldiers of Decius (**QUADRAGINTA SEX MILITES**), who had followed the example of Tryphonia and Cyrilla in converting to Christianity. See Delehaye's edition of the *Passio Laurentii* (1933b pp 96–98). The separate notices devoted to Tryphonia in **BEDE**'s **MARTYROLOGIUM** (ed. Dubois and Renaud 1976 p 189.11–15) and in the **OLD ENGLISH MARTYROLOGY** (*Mart*, B19.ia; ed. Kotzor 1981 2.231) are sourced by Quentin (1908 p 80) and Cross (1983a p 211) respectively. **ÆLFRIC**, in his homily on Laurence in **CATHOLIC HOMILIES**, I, 29, lines 279–91 (*ÆCHom* I, B1.1.31; ed. *EETS* SS 17; translation in Thorpe 1844–46 1.435), briefly recounts the conversion of Tryphonia and her daughter and its effect on the soldiers of Decius, but he does not mention the deaths of the two women.

On the manuscripts and recensions of the *passio* as a whole, see above, the entry for Laurentius.

Ursicinus. See **GERVASIUS ET PROTASIUS.**

Ursula: *BSS* 9.1254–55; *BLS* 4.165–68.

There is some evidence for Anglo-Saxon knowledge of the legend of the flotilla of British virgins (11 or 11,000) led by Ursula, the daughter of a British king, and their martyrdom at Cologne by the Huns. In the prologue to the earliest full *passio*, *BHL* 8427 (composed ca. 969–76, ed. Levison 1927 pp 142–57), the author (possibly Herricus, monk of Cologne, later of Saint-Bertin) claims that his informants, the nuns of St Mary's, Cologne, were told the story by a certain Count Hoolf, who in turn had learned it at Canterbury from **DUNSTANUS**, later archbishop, during negotiations for the marriage of the emperor Otto and the Anglo-Saxon princess Edith, daughter of Edward the Elder (ed. Levison 1927 p 144.1–15). Levison's work on the legend has been complemented and developed, with special reference to the English tradition, by Thiébaux (1992), whose discussion and bibliographical notes obviate the need for further commentary or references here. She is inclined to think (p 44) that Dunstan's knowledge of the legend, and his possible personal devotion to the virgin martyrs, would have resulted from his contacts with the Low Countries (where he was in exile in the mid-tenth century) rather than from older British or English traditions.

Valentinus Interamnensis, passio [ANON.Pas.Valent.Interamn.]: *BHL* 8460; *BLS* 1.332–34; *BSS* 12.899; *CPL* 2241.
    ed.: *AS* Feb. 2.756–57.

MSS 1. London, BL Cotton Nero E. i: HG 344.
      2. Salisbury, Cathedral Library 221 (formerly Oxford, Bodleian Library Fell 4): HG 754.5.
Lists none.
A-S Vers BEDA.Mart. 34.5–17.
Quots/Cits – Refs none.

In medieval calendars, two Valentines are commemorated on February 14, both reputedly martyred by being beheaded on the Flaminian Way in Rome. According to his legend, Valentine of Interamnes, modern Terni, 60 miles from Rome, was bishop of that town and suffered for his faith under a certain Furiosus Placidus, who has been identified with the historical consul of 273. The ancient *passio* of this Valentine, which exhibits surprisingly little textual variety (and which contains no hint of the secular customs associated with February 14 in the later Middle Ages and today), was known to **BEDE** who used it for his **MARTYROLOGIUM** notice (BEDA.Mart.; ed. Dubois and Quentin 1976, sourced by Quentin 1908 p 94); English copies are preserved in the eleventh-century London and Salisbury manuscripts of the **COTTON-CORPUS LEGENDARY**. It is likely that the lost February portion of the ninth-century **OLD ENGLISH MARTYROLOGY** also contained entries for each of these saints.

The martyrdom of the other Valentine, a priest of Rome, is part of the legend of **MARIUS ET MARTHA**. Delehaye (1933a pp 315–16) thinks the two Valentines were originally one and the same (see Amore 1966).

In addition to the *AS* edition, substantially the same text is printed in Mombritius (1910 2.623–25) and Rossi-Passavanti (1932–33 pp 257–61).

Valentinus Presbiter. See **MARIUS ET MARTHA**.

Valerianus et Tiburtius: *BLS* 2.91; *BSS* 12.466–69.

Valerianus, husband of **CAECILIA**, according to their legend in the *Passio Caeciliae* (*BHL* 1495), was martyred along with his brother, Tiburtius, on April 14, having been converted to the faith through the preaching and miracles of Cecilia. Maximus, a Roman military guard, befriended the brothers and, after affirming his belief in their sanctity at their execution, was immediately martyred himself. Delehaye (1936 p 80) argues that the three names and their feast day are those of genuine martyrs (about whom nothing is known) buried in the cemetary of Pretextatus on the Appian Way.

The April 14 feast day was important in its own right in Anglo-Saxon England. See, for example, the two graded late-tenth-century Anglo-Saxon calendars in F. Wormald (1934 pp 47, 61). For the three saints' extensive part in the legend, see Delehaye's edition of the *Passio Caeciliae* IV–XXIV (ed. Delehaye 1936 pp 196–214). Some legendaries, but no extant English manuscripts of our period, contain excerpted portions as a separate *passio* (*BHL* 8482–86). For English manuscripts, and **ÆLFRIC**'s account of the legend, see our entry for Caecilia.

The separate notice for these saints in **BEDE**'s **MARTYROLOGIUM** (ed. Dubois and Renaud 1976 p 61.2–5) is sourced by Quentin (1908 p 64); that in the **OLD ENGLISH MARTYROLOGY** (B19.bw: Kotzor 1981 2.53–54) by Herzfeld (*EETS* OS 116.xxxviii). The latter cites the excerpted text in *AS* Apr. 2.204 as the *Martyology*'s source and (p. xlii) that of Mombritius for Cecilia. J. E. Cross (private communication) suggests that a thorough sourcing would be based on Delehaye's complete text.

Valerianus Trenorchii, passio [ANON.Pas.Valerian.Tren.]: *BHL* 8488; *BLS* 3.483–84; *BSS* 12.914–15.
 ed.: *AS* Sept. 5.21–22.

MSS – Lists none.
A-S Vers Mart (B19.ha).
Quots/Cits – Refs none.

This Valerianus (feast day September 15), whose ancient cult site is Tournus near Autun in Burgundy, is traditionally the companion of Marcellus of Chalons (**MARCELLUS CABILLONENSIS**). The only evidence of Anglo-Saxon knowledge of Valerianus, as of Marcellus, is a notice in the **OLD ENGLISH MARTYROLOGY** (*Mart*; ed. Kotzor 1981 2.207) that has not been formally sourced, but J. E. Cross (personal communication) endorses Herzfeld (*EETS* OS 116.xii) in stipulating this often edited *passio*, formerly attributed to Baudry, archbishop of Dol (d. 1130), as the martyrologist's source. More recent dating of the *passio* as a tenth- or eleventh-century composition should be reexamined in the light of

Cross's and Herzfeld's sourcing of the ninth-century *Martyrology* passage; other evidence for an earlier date is the ninth-century martyrology of **ADO** (*PL* 123.357–58), which is surely based on the *passio*. In addition to the *AS* edition, see also *PL* 156.1209–12.

Vedastus, vita [ALCVUIN.Vit.Vedast.]: *BHL* 8508; *BLS* 1.263; *BSS* 12.965–68.
ed.: *MGH* SRM 3.416–27.
MSS Cambridge, Corpus Christi College 9: HG 36.
Lists – Refs none.

Vedast (Vaast) of Arras (feast day February 6) is remembered as one of the seminal figures in the Christianization of Merovingian Gaul. As a priest, he shared with Saint Rémy (**REMIGIUS**) the crucial task of initiating Clovis I into the faith (497), and he went on to become an energetic and successful bishop of Arras (499–539). His cult is widespread in the Arras-Cambrai region and in Flanders. Although there are no early Anglo-Saxon traces of Vedast's cult or hagiography, his February feast day shared with his co-worker, **AMANDUS**, and his translation day shared with Rémy (October 1) are well represented in Anglo-Saxon calendars of the eleventh century and in two earlier ones (F. Wormald 1934 pp 3, 11, 17, and 25), as well as in proper masses in later Anglo-Saxon service books (Ortenberg 1992 pp 34–35 and note 68). The *Vita Vedasti* preserved in the eleventh-century Cambridge manuscript of the **COTTON-CORPUS LEGENDARY** for the October 1 feast day, following the large collection of texts for Rémy, is not the early life by Jonas of Bobbio (*BHL* 8501–03), but **ALCUIN**'s later redaction (composed at the end of the eighth century), minus the epistle to Abbot Rado. The English copy is more closely identified by Levison (*MGH* SRM 7.573) as the later interpolated version (*BHL* 8508), which Krusch labels C1 (with two manuscripts from St Gall and Trier) in the classification of manuscripts for his edition (*MGH* SRM 3.404–05). Following the *vita* proper in the English manuscript is a liturgical, non-narrative homily (*PL* 101.678–81, *BHL* 8509), also by Alcuin. The Alcuinian life in its pristine form is discussed by I Deug-Su (1983 pp 73–114). On pertinent Anglo-Flemish relations in the tenth–eleventh centuries, see most recently Ortenberg (1992 pp 21–40).

Veronica: *BLS* 3.82–83; *BSS* 12.1044–48; *DACL* 15.2962–66; *RBMA* 180.

According to the early medieval apocryphal gospels, Veronica (Greek *Beronike*; feast day February 4) was a widow of Jerusalem who possessed a piece of cloth on which was painted a portrait of Christ's face while he was alive. She is first identified in the *Evangelium Nicodemi* (**APOCRYPHA, GOSPEL OF NICODEMUS**) with the woman in the canonical gospels whose hemhorrage was healed by touching the hem of Jesus' robe (Matt. 9.20–22; Marc. 5.25–34; see *Evangelium Nicodemi* VII, ed. Kim 1973 p 22). In her extended story, however, she is found in Jerusalem, years after Christ's death, by an imperial emissary, Volusianus, whom, after initial resistance, she accompanies to Rome so that the sacred "vultus" might be used to heal the emperor Tiberius's own ulcerous face when he looks at it. As a result, Veronica is rewarded with great riches, and the holy cloth is placed in a beautiful shrine after the emperor becomes a Christian. This story, which has been thought to be an adaptation of the Syrian legend of King Abgar of Edessa (Hall 1996 pp 60–62; see Apocrypha, **LETTER OF ABGAR AND JESUS**), appears first in an undated apocryphon (certainly eighth century or earlier) usually entitled *Cura sanitatis Tiberii* (*BHL* 4218), which includes legendary material concerning Pilate's exile and death and was often coupled in manuscripts with the Gospel of Nicodemus. It was later reworked into a longer legend that begins with a story of Titus and Vespasian and their destruction of Jerusalem as an act of vengeance for Christ's passion; hence the title **VINDICTA SALVATORIS** (*BHL* 4221; see Apocrypha). In the *Vindicta*, Veronica, instead of becoming rich in Rome, gives up her Jerusalem wealth to follow the holy "vultus" out of love for Christ.

There does not appear to have been a cult of Veronica herself in Anglo-Saxon England, although her name was invoked in certain Latin charms of the period and she is depicted more than once, with her curative cloth, in illuminated manuscripts (Cross et al. 1996 p 78), but the earliest editions of the Old English prose version of the *Vindicta* (Müller 1835 pp 5–18, Goodwin 1851 pp 26–47, and Assmann, *BaP* 3.181–92) use her name for the title of the work, doubtless in deference to her later medieval importance. This custom is followed also by Greenfield and Robinson in their bibliography (1980 p 377).

The Old English translation of the Latin *Vindicta Salvatoris* (B8.5.4; ed. Cross et al. 1996 pp 249–93, right-hand pages; for Veronica, see especially pp 271–73, 279–85, 291), appears to have been written in Exeter during the episcopacy of Leofric in the later eleventh century. It is preserved in full in two manuscripts, and partially in one other, which is a clumsily edited extract. While ultimately dependent on the same lost Exeter translation, each of the surviving texts is an independent recension. On the Old English manuscripts, and for further references, see Hall in Cross et al. (1996 pp 76–77). The Old English version alters its source, remarkably, to insist that the cloth only seemed to the faithful to have Christ's face on it, but that in fact its healing power derived from its being a piece of the garment worn by Christ himself, which Veronica had torn off when she grasped the hem (Cross et al. 1996 pp 273 and 281). On the origins and development of the Latin legend, see Hall's thorough discussion in the collaborative edition (Cross et al. 1996 pp 36–81). For the evidence that the Latin text in Saint-Omer, Bibliothèque Municipale 202, is the actual source manuscript of the Old English translations of the *Vindicta* and the *Evangelium*, see the detailed discussions in Cross et al. (1996 passim). The earlier edition of the *Vindicta* by Tischendorf (1876 pp 471–86, with variants from Goodwin's edition of the Old English version, in a Latin translation) is based on two Italian manuscripts of the fourteenth century, of the same type as that used by the Old English author but not as close to the Old English as the text in the Saint-Omer manuscript. This Latin text, with modern English translation, is printed by Cross et al., opposite the Old English version (1996 pp 248–92, left-hand pages). See also J. Elliott (1993 pp 213–16).

I am grateful to Thomas N. Hall for his help with this entry.

Victor et Corona, passio [ANON.Pas.Vict.Cor.1]: *BHL* 8559; *BSS* 12.1290–92; *DHGE* 13.911.
   ed.: *AS* Mai. 3.266–68.
MSS – Lists none.
A-S Vers 1. BEDA.Mart. 87.6–29.
   2. *Mart* (B19.cw).
Quots/Cits – Refs none.

Victor (feast day May 14) is said to have been a Cilician serving under the emperor Antoninus in the Roman army either in Egypt or Syria when he was arrested and tortured for his Christian faith by the governor of Egypt, Sebastianus. In his *passio*, a conventional sequence of sensational tortures culminates in an original episode in which Corona, the teenage wife of another soldier, witnesses Victor's faith and endurance and before he is executed encourages him by revealing her vision of two crowns descending from heaven. She is martyred by being pulled apart between two trees. The original Greek *passio* is probably more accurately mirrored in the surviving Latin translations than in the extant Greek manuscripts (e.g., *BHG* 1864: Siegmund 1949 p 254). The two saints have a complicated textual and calendar tradition, in that there are no less than eight entries for them (as Victor and Corona or Victor and Stephania) in the *Martyrologium Hieronymianum* (*AS* Nov. 2/2.253). Passio 1 of the version associated with May 14 seems to be that from which **BEDE** draws his detailed summary in his **MARTYROLOGIUM** (BEDA.Mart.; ed. Dubois and Renaud 1976, sourced by Quentin 1908 pp 94–95). Herzfeld (*EETS* OS 116.xxxviii) points to the same *passio* as the source for the notice in the ninth-century **OLD ENGLISH MARTYROLOGY** (*Mart*; ed. Kotzor 1981 2.103–04). J. E. Cross (private communication) confirms Herzfeld's opinion but expresses doubt about *BHL*'s classification of the texts. Siegmund (1949 p 254) mentions only one early medieval manuscript of Passio 1. The May 14 feast day is rarely found in the later Anglo-Saxon calendars (see F. Wormald 1934 pp 20, 48, 62, and 230, where it is uncertain if this Victor is meant).

In addition to the *AS* edition, this version of the *passio* is also printed in Mombritius (1910 2.641–44) and Zotto (1951) pp 9–14.

Victor et Corona, passio [ANON.Pas.Vict.Cor.3]: *BHL* 8561.
 ed.: unpublished.
MSS ?Dublin, Trinity College 174: HG 215.
Lists – Refs none.

According to Siegmund (1949 p 254), the version of the legend of Victor and Corona classified as Passio 3 in *BHL* occurs more frequently than Passio 1 in early manuscripts. Grosjean (1928 p 89) identifies the text in the Dublin manuscript cited here as Passio 3; it was copied by Webber's Group I scribes at Salisbury Cathedral in the late eleventh century (Webber 1992 p 142), perhaps because the **COTTON-CORPUS LEGENDARY**, of which there is a Salisbury set, does not include any text for Victor and Corona. Colker (1991 1.323) classifies the text as *BHL* 8559–61, however, implying that its precise identity is not settled. Another copy of *BHL* 8561 has been identified in the early-twelfth-century Chester legendary, London, Gray's Inn 3 (Ker and Piper 1969–92 1.53).

Victor Massiliensis, passio [ANON.Pas.Vict.Mass.]: *BHL* 8570; *BLS* 3.146–48; *BSS* 12.1261–73.
 ed.: Narbey 1899–1912 2.273–76.

MSS – Lists none.
A-S Vers Mart (B19.eu).
Quots/Cits – Refs none.

The cult of Victor of Marseilles (feast day July 21) was already famous in Gaul by the sixth century, but the various hagiographic traditions regarding him offer conflicting information as to whether the presumed fourth-century martyr was bishop, sailor, soldier, or merely "citizen," and they differ also as to the manner of his death and the names of his companions in martyrdom. Modern scholarship on Victor is neither plentiful nor very helpful, but it seems clear that Passio 1, printed by the Bollandists in *AS* and by Ruinart (*BHL* 8569), and Passio 2b, printed by Ehlers (1973 pp 181–83), which corresponds to *BHL* 8571, are both relatively late redactions, made in the eleventh and twelfth centuries, of older texts. Of the early versions, Passio 2a (*BHL* 8570) has been dated in the sixth century (Moulinier 1991), although it is not included in *CPL* and Quentin (1908 pp 198–99) repeats earlier claims that parts of this *passio* are culled from that of Saint **PHOCAS**.

It is Passio 2a, however, as edited by Narbey from a Spanish manuscript in Paris, not the text in *AS* indicated by Herzfeld (*EETS* OS 116.xl), that was used by the author of the ninth-century **OLD ENGLISH MARTYROLOGY** (*Mart*; ed. Kotzor 1981 2.155) for his brief, colorless notice for Victor. A similar version was used by another ninth-century martyrologist, **HRABANUS MAURUS** in his *Martyrologium* IVL. 211–31 (ed. *CCCM* 44.71). The principal sign that Passio 2a was the *Old English Martyrology*'s source is the names of the soldiers converted by Victor's miracles, viz., Alexander, Felicianus, and, crucially, Deuterius (*Martyrology*: "Theoderius"; cf. "Teoteri" in the *Martyrologium Hieronymianum*, manuscript B, *AS* Nov. 2/2.389). In other versions of the legend, either there are no soldier converts at all (as in Quentin's text of the late-eighth-century martyrology of Lyons, 1908 pp 193–94) or the soldier Deuterius is replaced by another named Longinus (as in *BHL* 8571), who in turn replaces Victor himself as father of the infant swimmer in a rather unusual posthumous miracle episode (cf. Passio 2a p 276 with Passio 2b ed. Ehlers 1973 p 185). This latter substitution had already been made by the ninth century also, as in the martyrology of **FLORUS OF LYONS** (Quentin 1908 p 285).

On the various versions of the *passio*, and their relations to one another, see the unsatisfactory survey by Moulinier (1991) who never identifies the text that he claims is the oldest of all and that he names only "le récit symbolique." A simpler and more forthright analysis (surprisingly not cited by Moulinier) is that of Quentin (1908 pp 193–200).

Along with Narbey's edition, see also that of the Bollandists (1883 pp 317–21).

Victor Maurus passio [ANON.Pas.Vict.Maur.]: *BHL* 8580; *BLS* 2.250; *BSS* 12.1274–75; *CPL* 2242.

ed.: *AS* Mai. 2.288–90.

MSS – Lists   none.
A-S Vers   Mart (B19.cs).
Quots/Cits – Refs   none.

Victor of Milan (feast day May 8), often known as Victor Maurus ("the Moor"), who was reputedly a veteran soldier martyred at Milan under Maximian, is another saint whose cult and hagiography were important and extensive in Christian Europe, but who did not achieve great fame in Anglo-Saxon England. Only a few of the earlier English calendars, of the late tenth/early eleventh century, record his feast day (F. Wormald 1934 pp 21, 34, 48, and 62), and the only firm witness to English knowledge of his *passio* is the substantial notice in the ninth-century **OLD ENGLISH MARTYROLOGY** (*Mart*; ed. Kotzor 1981 2.96–100). The passage has not been sourced in detail, but Cross (1981d p 485) provides some confirmation of Herzfeld's identification (*EETS* OS 116.xxxviii) of the *passio* printed by Mombritius as the source of the *Martyrology* passage. See also Kotzor (1981 2.312). The earliest English copy is the early-twelfth-century Chester legendary, London, Gray's Inn 3 (Ker and Piper 1969–92 1.53).

Victoria, passio [ANON.Pas.Victoriae]: *BHL* 8591. See **ANATOLIA, VICTORIA, ET AUDAX**.
   ed.: Bollandists 1883 pp 157–60.

MSS – Lists   none.
A-S Vers   ?BEDA.Mart. 228.2–8.
Quots/Cits – Refs   none.

BEDE in his **MARTYROLOGIUM** (BEDA.Mart.; ed. Dubois and Renaud 1976) devotes a separate notice to the virgin martyr Victoria (feast day December 23), sister of Anatolia, apparently drawing on a text similar to, but not identical with, the *Passio Victoriae* in question here. He may not have known the joint *Passio Anatoliae et Victoriae* used by **ALDHELM** for his celebrations of the two saints together in his prose and verse DE VIRGINITATE (see above, the entry for Anatolia, Victoria, et Audax). Victoria herself is unnoticed in later Anglo-Saxon sources.

In addition to the edition printed by the Bollandists from a Namur manuscript, see also Mara (1964 pp 172–92, left-hand pages only).

Vincentius Caesaraugustanus, passio [ANON.Pas.Vinc.]: *BHL* 8628, 8631, 8634; *BLS* 1.142–44; *BSS* 12.1149–55; *CPL* 2073a.
  ed.: Simonetti 1956 pp 231–41.
MSS 1. London, BL Cotton Nero E. i: HG 344.
  2. Paris, Bibliothèque Nationale lat. 10861: HG 898.
  3. Salisbury, Cathedral Library 221 (formerly Oxford, Bodleian Library Fell 4): HG 754.5.
Lists none.
A-S Vers 1. *Mart* (B19.aj).
  2. *ÆLS* Vincent (B1.3.35).
Quots/Cits – Refs none.

The early importance of the cult of Vincent the deacon, martyr of Saragossa (Spain) under the ubiquitous "Dacianus praeses" (see De Gaiffier 1954), is attested by **PRUDENTIUS, PERISTEPHANON** V (ed. *CCSL* 126), and **AUGUSTINE** in several sermons (e.g., **SERMONES** CCLXXVI, ed. *PL* 38.1255–57: see Saxer 1989b p 279). His relics were distributed widely throughout Gaul by the time of **GREGORY OF TOURS** (DE GLORIA MARTYRUM LXXXIX; ed. *MGH* SRM 1/2.547–48). The development of his hagiography, however, is unusually complex and, for reasons that will become obvious below, it is impossible to follow our usual practice of distinguishing different versions of the legend in separate entries for each *BHL* number.

The textual tradition of the *Passio Vincentii* has been the subject of much scholarly analysis since the Bollandists' initial classification in *BHL* (among others, see Dufourcq 1900–07 2.133–47; Narbey 1899–1912 2.221–24; Fábrega Grau 1953–55 1.92–107; Simonetti 1956; Zettel 1979 pp 59–61 and 126–36, and 1982 pp 27–31; Cross 1982c pp 51–58).

Unfortunately, the most recent of these studies, pursuing different goals, have been carried out largely independently of each other, without achieving an overall synthesis of the available evidence. Further complicating matters is the Bollandists' decision not to revise (in *BHL NS*) their original classification in the light of later scholarship but to adhere to their first analysis of the textual tradition, which implies, misleadingly, that the more modern editions of the *passio* contain essentially the same version as the old editions of *AS* and Mombritius.

The *Passio Vincentii* is represented in *BHL* as a three-part work existing in several variant forms and comprising *BHL* 8627–29 (variant preambles), *BHL* 8630–33 (variants of the *passio* proper), *BHL* 8634–36 (variants of an "additamentum" dealing with Vincent's cult in Gaul and Spain). But the "passion primitive" posited by modern scholarship as widely known in early medieval Europe, including Anglo-Saxon England (and probably very like the fifth-century text known to Prudentius and Augustine: Simonetti 1956 pp 220–26), is a simpler, shorter work, comprising simply Preamble 2, *Probabile satis* (Passio 1AII, *BHL* 8628), and Passio 1Bβ (*BHL* 8631). This is the text printed, with minor differences, by Simonetti, as cited above, and by Fábrega Grau (1953–55 2.187–96). The text in *AS* Ian. 2.394–97 (*BHL* 8627 plus 8630) is an expanded and considerably rewritten version of this ancient *passio*. It should be pointed out that Saxer has recently argued that there were apparently two versions of the ancient *passio*, one known to Augustine and a more developed text used by Prudentius. Saxer has in progress a comprehensive reevaluation of the manuscript traditions (1989b p 275).

With regard to Anglo-Saxon tradition, Cross (who independently confirms some of Simonetti's detailed arguments on the priority of the shorter *passio*) and Zettel have shown that the narrative notice for Vincent in the ninth-century **OLD ENGLISH MARTYROLOGY** (*Mart*; ed. Kotzor 1981 2.23–24) and **ÆLFRIC**'s account in **LIVES OF SAINTS** (*ÆLS*; ed. *EETS* OS 94 and 114; see below) are based on variant versions of the ancient *passio* rather than on the later reworking. In addition, all three of the English manuscripts listed here have copies of the ancient *passio*, although those in the **COTTON-CORPUS LEGENDARY** (the London and Salisbury manuscripts) also have the later Gallic "additamentum," *BHL* 8634. On the Canterbury (St Augustine's) provenance of the early-ninth-century Paris manuscript, see M. P. Brown (1986).

Despite the wide currency of the ancient *passio*, it is surprising that neither **BEDE** nor **ALDHELM** makes reference to Vincent, although they were doubtless familiar with his story through Prudentius's hymn and Augustine's sermons. Particularly surprising is Bede's omission of Vincent from his **MARTYROLOGIUM**.

The best edition of the *passio* is that of Simonetti, who collates four Parisian manuscripts (dating from the tenth to the early thirteenth century) originally singled out by Dufourcq (1900–07 2.144). Simonetti prints the "additamentum," *BHL* 8634, among his variants (p 241). Apparently he was unaware, however, of several much earlier copies consulted by Cross in his sourcing of the *Old English Martyrology* passage (including the Canterbury manuscript listed here), so Simonetti's edition cannot be considered definitive. Similarly Zettel's sourcing of Ælfric's *Vincent* in *Lives of Saints* does not take into account any of the early medieval manuscripts known to Cross, including the Canterbury passional, but relies on the printed edition of Fábrega Grau and the eleventh-century manuscripts of the Cotton-Corpus Legendary. S. Irvine's recent work on Ælfric's sources (1990 and *EETS* OS 302), developing that of Zettel, was also done without reference to the editions of Simonetti or the earlier manuscripts and may need refining as a result. For example, it is not certain, as she assumes (1990 pp 129–30), that Ælfric's source included, like the Cotton-Corpus Legendary, the "additamentum" (*BHL* 8634).

Although Ælfric's *Vincent* is printed in Skeat's edition of *Lives of Saints*, it does not occur in the most complete and authoritative manuscript and may well have been a later, separate commission. Irvine in her *EETS* edition of Ælfric's narrative (occurring uniquely in Cambridge, University Library Ii. 1. 33) prints it as part of the same text as a short gospel homily for a martyr's day, Belfour VIII (*ÆHomM* 9, B1.5.9; ed. *EETS* OS 137.74–76), accepting Clemoes's arguments (1959 p 236 note 1) that the homily was written to accompany the narrative piece. For her discussion of the links between the homily's gospel pericope (John 12.24–26) and the cults of **LAURENTIUS** and Vincent, see the introduction to her edition. See also, however, the independent objections of Nicholls (1991).

In her edition, below the Old English text, Irvine prints selected passages of the Latin *passio* from Fábrega Grau's edition, along with occasional variants from other texts, including the Cotton-Corpus Legendary and *AS*, since the latter version appears to be occasionally closer to Ælfric's source than the shorter, older texts. See Irvine on the sources (*EETS* OS 302.93–94) and on the cult of Vincent at Abingdon (pp 83–93); see also Thacker (1988 pp 60–61). There is a need for a thorough study of the textual tradition of the *Passio Vincentii* to coordinate and reconcile the data and arguments of the various studies cited above, especially in relation to the English texts. Particularly valuable would be a collation of the Cotton and Salisbury manuscripts with the Paris manuscript, in relation to the Vincent narratives in the *Old English Martyrology* and Ælfric.

Vitalis et Valeria: *BLS* 2.181; *BSS* 12.1229–31.

Vitalis, who may be merely a doublet of the martyr Vitalis of Bologna (*BHL* 8690–91, *CPL* 2244, *CPPM* IIA.28a), is the titular saint of the great basilica in Ravenna, but an important Roman church was also dedicated to him (feast day April 28), securing him a place in Roman service books and Western calendars, including those of later Anglo-Saxon England, whereas Vitalis of Bologna (with his companion, Agricola) is apparently unknown in our period. According to his legend, Vitalis of Ravenna was a government officer who encouraged the physician **URSICINUS** to persevere in his suffering for the faith and later buried his body. For this, Vitalis himself was punished by torture, then martyred by being buried in a pit. He and his wife, Valeria (who was later martyred by a pagan mob), are said to be the parents of **GERVASIUS ET PROTASIUS**. The story of Vitalis and Valeria always appears in extant Anglo-Saxon manuscripts as part of the *passio* of Gervasius and Protasius (*BHL* 3514), as in the *PL* edition of the *passio* (*PL* 17.744–45). In the early-twelfth-century Chester legendary (London, Gray's Inn 3), however, their story appears as a separate *passio, BHL* 8699, and also as part of the larger *Passio Gervasii et Protasii* (Ker and Piper 1969–92 1.52–53).

ALDHELM's account of Gervasius and Protasius, though derived from the *passio*, does not mention Vitalis and Valeria (doubtless because they were not virgins). Less discriminatory is the ninth-century **OLD ENGLISH MARTYROLOGY** (*Mart*, B19.ce; ed. Kotzor 1981 2.67–68). While the *Martyrology*'s source for Vitalis's story is almost certainly a recension of the *passio*, certain omissions and narrative details suggest that it was somewhat different from the printed edition: for example, the location of Vitalis's shrine at "Vicolongo" (p 67.10) and the statement that he converted "other people" to Christianity (p 67.13), although this last point may be a deliberate alteration, as in a similar detail of the *Martyrology*'s notice for Ursicinus (see the entry for Gervasius et Protasius).

The Exeter List of Relics (tenth and eleventh centuries) has a brief narrative notice (*Rec*.10.8, B16.10.8; ed. Förster 1943 pp 74–75; Conner 1993a pp 182–83) on Vitalis's burial in the pit. The Exeter notice, like the *Old English Martyrology* (but unlike the *passio*), mentions the fact that he was buried alive, "cucu" (doubtless a play on the meaning of Vitalis's name), but textual dependence of the Exeter text on the *Martyrology* seems unlikely (J. E. Cross, personal communication). Vitalis is one of only a small group, among the numerous saints in the relics list, to receive this sort of narrative tribute.

Vitus, Modestus, et Crescentia, passio [ANON.Pas.Vit.Mod.Cresc.]: *BHL* 8712; *BLS* 2.545–46; *BSS* 12.1244–46; *CPL* 2246.

ed.: unpublished.

MSS 1. London, BL Cotton Nero E. i: HG 344.
    2. Salisbury, Cathedral Library 222 (formerly Oxford, Bodleian Library Fell 1): HG 754.6.

Lists none.

A-S Vers Mart (B19.dm).

Quots/Cits – Refs none.

Vitus seems to have been a genuine martyr with a very early cult in southern Italy. His fanciful legend (dating from the seventh century?) describes him as a child convert who secretly left his wealthy pagan home in Sicily accompanied by his tutor, Modestus, and nurse, Crescentia, and, after numerous adventures at Lucania in southern Italy and a series of tortures in Rome, died with his companions in Lucania. Their feast day (June 15) figures in most Anglo-Saxon calendars. The *passio* had apparently reached England by the ninth century, in a distinctive form. Cross (1982c pp 58–62) finds that the long notice in the **OLD ENGLISH MARTYROLOGY** (*Mart*; ed. Kotzor 1981 2.119–21) depends not on Passio 3 (*BHL* 8714), the Mombritius text (1910 2.634–38), as indicated by Herzfeld (*EETS* OS 116.xxxix), or on Passio 1a (*BHL* 8711), the text in *AS* Iun. 2.1021–26, but on the unpublished Passio 2a; the same work is identified by Zettel (1979 p 22) in the eleventh-century London and Salisbury manuscripts of the **COTTON-CORPUS LEGENDARY** (see also Jackson and Lapidge 1996 p 138). See Cross (1982c p 59) for a list of early manuscripts in Continental libraries.

Walaricus, vita [ANON.Vit.Walaric.]: *BHL* 8762; *BLS* 2.1–2; *BSS* 12.920–24.
 ed.: *MGH* SRM 4.160–75.

MSS ?Boulogne, Bibliothèque Municipale 106: HG 804.
Lists ?Saewold: ML 8.23.
A-S Vers – Refs none.

Walaricus (Valéry), born ca. 565, was a monk under **COLUMBANUS** at Luxeuil, later abbot, then a hermit and missionary in the Somme region, where Saint-Valéry-sur-Somme is the site (formerly Luiconaus, Leuconaum) of his hermitage and later monastery. He is believed to have died in 619 (feast day April 1). The *vita* in question here purports to be a reworking of an ancient life by abbot Raginbertus, one of Walaric's immediate successors at his monastery, but Krusch, the *MGH* editor, doubts there was any ancient *vita* and regards the extant one as an eleventh-century fabrication. The Anglo-Saxons seem not to have had any special attachment to Walaric (see the calendar entries of the late tenth and early eleventh centuries in F. Wormald 1934 pp 19 and 61), but the evidence of the Boulogne manuscript and Saewold's booklist suggests that he was venerated perhaps by the Flemish monks from Saint-Bertin who migrated to Bath in the reign of Athelstan, bringing with them *vitae* of their honored saints. Over a century later, in the aftermath of the Norman Conquest, Abbot Saewold of Bath migrated as an exile in the opposite direction, presumably to Saint-Vaast, Arras, taking with him many books, including some that contained copies of the texts originally brought to England from the same region by the Saint-Bertin exiles (see **AICHARDUS, LUCIANUS BELLOVACENSIS, PHILIBERTUS**). These books were donated ca. 1070 to Saint-Vaast. Among the donations is a collection of saints' lives "in uno uolumine," the first of which is a life of Walaricus. The volume has not been identified with any surviving manuscripts (see Lapidge's note on ML 8.23), but the most important manuscript copy of the *Vita Walarici*, a copy that Krusch dates in the eleventh century (during the episcopacy of Archbishop Hugh of Besançon, 1031–66), is the first hagiographic item (fols 2–41) in the Boulogne manuscript cited above, which is partly of Anglo-Saxon provenance and closely related to one of the books definitely known to have been in Saewold's donation (Arras, Bibliothèque Municipale 1029 [812]: see ML 8.19, note). Van der Straeten (1971 p 137) says the Walaricus text in Boulogne 106 is copied "in three hands of the tenth and eleventh centuries." I am not suggesting that this is the same as the text mentioned in the donation list, but if Van der Straeten's paleography is correct it certainly contradicts Krusch's argument that the *Vita Walarici* was composed from whole cloth in the mid-eleventh century. A fresh codicological study of the Boulogne manuscript would seem to be called for to determine the origins and make-up of the Walaricus *vita* and its possible links with the supposedly lost life in the donation list.

Wandregisilus, vita [ANON.Vit.Wandreg.]: *BHL* 8805; *BLS* 3.164–65; *BSS* 12.944–47.

ed.: *AS* Iul. 5.272–81.

MSS London, BL Cotton Nero E. i: HG 344.
Lists – Refs none.

Wandrille (feast day July 22) was an Austrasian nobleman, born at Verdun early in the seventh century, who abandoned the secular life and a celibate marriage ca. 628 to begin a rather restless monastic career that culminated in the foundation of his own monastery at Fontanelle in Normandy (later Saint-Wandrille), the church of which was dedicated by his friend, Bishop Ouen (**AUDOENUS**), in 657. Wandrille died in 668. His cult center was initially in Normandy but his relics wandered considerably in the ninth and tenth centuries and were particularly important at St Peter's, Ghent, in the tenth. With such connections, one might expect him to be known in England in the reform era, but only a handful of Anglo-Saxon calendars list his feast day (F. Wormald 1934 pp 22, 64, and 162). There is an early *vita* (Vita 1, *BHL* 8804, *CPL* 2146) written at Fontanelle ca. 700 or earlier, but the text preserved (partially) in the eleventh-century London manuscript of the **COTTON-CORPUS LEGENDARY** is Vita 2 (Levison, *MGH* SRM 7.602; Zettel 1979 p 23 note 64, and p 34; Jackson and Lapidge 1996 p 139). Owing to loss of leaves after fol 48v of pt 2, the text breaks off near the end of chapter III, in the episode concerning Saints Hildemarchis and Sindardus, at "In quibus cellulis predictus uir domini" (see *AS* Iul. 5.277b.32–33). Vita 2 is a Carolingian reworking, much maligned by modern scholars, but more recently seen to be of greater interest in its own right (see Wood 1991). In the London manuscript listed here, from mid-eleventh century Worcester, this life of Wandrille is in its proper calendar position, but, in Zettel's opinion, in the Worcester scribe's exemplar the text was apparently at the end of the Legendary among a miscellaneous cluster of texts of various calendar dates, as is evident from the table of contents in the Salisbury recension of the Legendary. The life of Wandrille is therefore lost from Salisbury, Cathedral Library 222, along with many texts from the end of the Legendary (Webber 1992 p 157). It survives in this end position, however, in a twelfth-century recension of the Legendary in Oxford, Bodleian Library Bodley 354 (*SC* 2432). See Zettel (1979 p 34).

Wandregisilus, miracula [ANON.Mir.Wandreg.]: *BHL* 8807–09. ed.: *AS* Iul. 5.281–90 notes 1–8, 9–43, and 44–45.

MSS See below.

Lists – Refs none.

To judge from the elaborate set of *capitula* preceding its copy of the *Vita Wandregisili*, London, BL Cotton Nero E. i (HG 344) originally contained not only Vita 2, *BHL* 8805 (see previous entry) but also three sets of Wandrille's posthumous miracles (including the translation of the relics to Chartres in 885), but these are now missing owing to loss of leaves after fol 48v of volume 2.

Werburga: *BLS* 1.241–42; *BSS* 12.1027–28; Farmer (1987) p 434.

Werburg (feast day February 3) was one of the youngest members of the family of East Anglian and Kentish royal saints, including Æthelthryth and her sister Seaxburh (see **ÆTHELDRYTHA**, **SEXBURGA**), who were descended from the mid-seventh-century King Anna of East Anglia. Werburg herself, the daughter of King Wulfhere of Mercia and Queen Eormenild (daughter of Seaxburh), was apparently an important figure in the development of early Mercian monasticism (Tait 1920–23 1.vii–xiv). Her relics were venerated first at Hanbury in what is now Staffordshire, and later, in the late ninth or early tenth century, they were moved further north to Chester, possibly in connection with Mercian political and military responses to the Danish presence (see Rollason 1989a p 154 and note 72). Of her actual life, since she is not mentioned by **BEDE** and no pre-Conquest texts about her survive, most of what is said about her is derived from sources of the late eleventh and twelfth centuries, most notably a Latin life (*BHL* 8855, ed. *AS* Febr. 1.386–90, *PL* 155.97–110, and Horstmann in *EETS* OS 88.xix–xxvi), generally attributed (though not firmly) to the Flemish immigrant hagiographer, Goscelin (of Saint-Bertin and Canterbury), in the late eleventh century. This life survives in a few post-Anglo-Saxon manuscript copies, in various forms, of the twelfth century (see Blake 1962 p 52 notes 2 and 3) and is the basis of a later redaction by John of Tynemouth (*BHL* 8857; see Hardy, *RS* 26/1.422–23, number 953). In the opinion of Rollason (1982 pp 26–27; see also Thacker 1985 p 4), Goscelin's detailed life is based on a lost life of the saint, of the late ninth or early tenth century, composed at Hanbury after the Danish invasions but before the translation of Werburg's relics to Chester. Rollason's historical arguments are plausible, but literary history provides slight evidence of the composition of Latin narrative texts at this period (**ASSER**'s life of Alfred is an exception), nor have the *Vita Werburgae* and its manuscripts been subjected yet to the same kind of textual and stylistic analysis as has established **BYRHTFERTH**, for example, as the author of the *passio* of the murdered Kentish princes (**ÆTHELREDUS ET ÆTHELBERHTUS**), which also survives only in post-Conquest manuscripts. Oral tradition and literary invention are as likely sources as a lost *vita*, although the author of the *Vita Werburgae* does allude vaguely to Werburg's fame in "Anglicarum historiarum" (*PL* 155.97, bottom line). For Werburg's feast in Anglo-Saxon calendars, see F. Wormald (1934 pp 31, 59, and 255).

Other saints associated with the seventh-century East Anglian and Kentish royal lines whose hagiographies present problems and possibilities similar to those indicated here, and whose cults were promoted in the Anglo-Norman era, are Eormenild (Ermenilda), abbess of Ely (feast day February 13; cf. *BHL* 2611), and Witburg (Withburga), hermit and reputed founder of Deerham abbey in Norfolk (feast day March 17; cf. *BHL* 8979).

Wilfridus, vita [STEPH.HRYP.Vit.Wilfr.]: *BHL* 8889; *BLS* 4.96–100; *BSS* 12.1092–94; *CPL* 2151.
    ed.: Colgrave 1927 pp 2–148.
MSS 1. London, BL Cotton Vespasian D. vi: HG 390.
      2. Salisbury, Cathedral Library 223 (formerly Oxford, Bodleian Library Fell 3): HG 754.7.
Lists 1. Worcester II: ML 11.50.
      2. Peterborough: ML 13.41.

A-S Vers 1. BEDA.Hist.eccles. 296–308, 370–76, 516–28.
2. *Mart* (B19.ca).
3. FRITH.Breu.Vit.Wilf.
Quots/Cits – Refs none.

Few would disagree that Wilfrid (ca. 634–709, feast days April 24, October 12), Northumbrian nobleman, Lindisfarne alumnus, advocate of Roman Christianity at the Council of Whitby (663), abbot of Ripon, bishop of Northumbria, bishop of Hexham, bishop (and litigant) in exile, missionary, and founder of monasteries, was one of the most important and controversial figures in the early Anglo-Saxon church. His biography, written at Ripon probably before 721 by one of his followers, Stephen of Ripon (Eddius Stephanus), and dedicated to Tatberht and Acca, Wilfrid's successors at Ripon and Hexham, is one of the early classics of Anglo-Latin hagiography and an important, though unacknowledged, source of **BEDE**'s own life of Wilfrid scattered through various chapters of his **HISTORIA ECCLESIASTICA** (BEDA.Hist.eccles.; ed. Colgrave and Mynors 1969).

It was used by the author of the ninth-century **OLD ENGLISH MARTYROLOGY** (*Mart*; ed. Kotzor 1981 2.62–63; sourced 303–04), rendered into verse by **FRITHEGOD** (FRITH.Breu.Vit.Wilf.; ed. Campbell 1950 pp 1–62; see next entry), and rewritten by Eadmer of Canterbury in the early twelfth century (*BHL* 8893). These two last reworkings were prompted in part by the reputed presence of Wilfrid's relics at Canterbury, but the monks of Hexham would stoutly deny this in the future. According to Levison (*MGH* SRM 6.191), other adaptations of Stephen's life of Wilfrid are all from the later Middle Ages. It remains to be seen if other Anglo-Latin writers, especially of the tenth and eleventh centuries, made use of the *Vita Wilfridi*.

The surviving manuscripts listed here are late copies, independent of each other. The eleventh-century London manuscript (which has lost some leaves), although at Canterbury later in the Middle Ages, is of uncertain but possibly Northern English origin (Colgrave 1927 p xiii); the Salisbury manuscript was copied by Webber's Group II Salisbury scribes around the turn of the eleventh century or later (Webber 1992 p 170). This

Salisbury manuscript is the "lost" manuscript associated with Archbishop Ussher, Jean Mabillon, and Thomas Gale (see Levison, *MGH* SRM 6.184 and Colgrave 1927 pp xiv–xv). The references to the *Vita Wilfridi* in surviving booklists, respectively from Worcester (probably) and Peterborough, are likewise from the end of our period, although the copies they refer to could have been much older. Michael Lapidge is reediting Frithegod's verse life and will provide more information about the textual history of its prose source.

On the identity of "Stephen" or "Eddius Stephanus," see Colgrave (1927 pp ix–x). On Bede's use of Stephen's life, see Plummer's edition of Bede's *Historia ecclesiastica* (1896 2.315–29) and the recent studies by Kirby (1983) and especially Goffart (1988 pp 235–328). In addition to Colgrave's edition, see that of Levison (*MGH* SRM 6.193–263).

Wilfridus, vita metrica [FRITH.Breu.Vit.Wilf.]: *BHL* 8891–92.
    ed.: Campbell 1950 pp 1–62.
MSS   1. Leningrad, Public Library O.v.XIV.1: HG 843.
    2. London, BL Cotton Claudius A. i: HG 312.
    3. Paris, Bibliothèque Nationale lat. 8431.
    4. Boulogne, Bibliothèque Municipale 189: HG 805 (*BHL* 8891 only).
Lists – A-S Vers   none.
Quots/Cits   see below.
Refs   none.

By his own account, Oda, archbishop of Canterbury (942–58), participated in the removal of the relics of Wilfrid from Ripon during a West Saxon raid into Scandinavian Northumbria in 948, although a later account gave prominence to his nephew **OSWALDUS WIGORNIENSIS** (see Lapidge 1988a p 45 and note 2). Oda also commissioned the learned Frankish poet, **FRITHEGOD** (Fredegaud), to compose a poetical tour de force, modestly entitled **BREUILOQUIUM VITAE WILFRIDI** (*BHL* 8892), to complement the old Latin prose *Vita Wilfridi* by Stephen of Ripon (*BHL* 8889: see previous entry). An epistolary preface (*BHL* 8891), purportedly by Oda but probably also by Frithegod, was added some time after the completion of the body of the *Breuiloquium*, but both may be dated 948–58, the term of Oda's archiepiscopacy. The poem was copied and carefully glossed at Canterbury in the course of the tenth century, and it was used there in the early twelfth century by Eadmer in his version of the life of Wilfrid. Lapidge has also detected echoes of the poem in the Winchester writing of **LANTFRED** (see further in Lapidge 1988a p 57 note 54).

The Boulogne manuscript listed above (provenance Christ Church, Canterbury, ca. 1000), has only the verse epistle. For information on the three principal tenth-century manuscripts and for a recent expert introduction to the poem and what is known of its author, see Lapidge (1988a), who also has an edition and translation in progress. For a lost work of Frithegod, see also **AUDOENUS**.

Winnocus, vita [ANON.Vit.Winnoc.]: *BHL* 8952; *BLS* 4.276; *BSS* 12.1199–201.
ed.: *MGH* SRM 5.769–80.
MSS Cambridge, Corpus Christi College 9: HG 36.
Lists none.
A-S Vers Mart (B19.ir).
Quots/Cits – Refs none.

Winnoc (feast day November 6), who is believed to have been a Briton by birth and upbringing, is closely associated with the Flemish saints Bertin and Omer (**BERTINUS** and **AUDOMARUS**) in whose monastery at Saint-Omer he became a monk in the later seventh century. From Saint-Omer he was directed to establish a monastery himself, with his British companions, near Dunkirk at Wormhout. The latter was the initial center of his cult, until the relics were translated to Bergues-Saint-Winnoc. His ancient *vita* is not, properly speaking, an independent work, but forms part III of the collective *Vita Audomari, Bertini et Winnoci* (*BHL* 763). The three parts of the *vita prima* usually appear as separate lives in the surviving manuscripts, as here in the Cambridge manuscript (from eleventh-century Worcester) of the **COTTON-CORPUS LEG-ENDARY** (Zettel 1979 p 28; Jackson and Lapidge 1996 p 142). The collective text, however, seems to have been known to the ninth-century author of the **OLD ENGLISH MARTYROLOGY** (*Mart*; ed. Kotzor 1981 2.246–47), as is evident in the *Martyrology*'s notices for Ouen and Bertin. See the sourcing by Kotzor (pp 367–68), refining Herzfeld (*EETS* OS 116.xlii and 238), in relation to Levison's text and variants of the *vita prima*. In his *MGH* edition, Levison initially overlooks the Cambridge manuscript, but in his "Conspectus" (*MGH* SRM 7.573) he classifies the manuscript as a member of group 7, along with other, later English manuscripts in Oxford and London.

On Winnoc's possible Cornish origins, see Doble (1960–70 5.127–54).

Wistanus: *BLS* 3.440–41; *BSS* 12.1215–16.

A great deal is known archeologically about the cult of the Mercian prince Wigstan (Wistan), murdered ca. 850. His relics were the object of an important cult in the later ninth century at the old Mercian royal center at Repton and were removed to the abbey of Evesham in the early eleventh century. Unfortunately, the only written accounts of his supposed martyrdom, apart from the brief notice in a list of saints' shrines (see Rollason 1978 p 89), date from long after the Norman Conquest, such as that attributed in *BHL* to Thomas of Evesham (*BHL* 8975, ed. *RS* 29.325–32). Since this *passio* makes no specific mention of Evesham, however, it has been suggested that the basis of this and other later texts is a lost account, composed at Repton between 850 and 873–74, when Repton was overrun by Vikings (see Rollason's several studies for discussion and bibliography: 1981, 1982 pp 7–9, and 1989a pp 117–18; see also Thacker 1985 pp 12–14). It is equally possible that oral tradition in and around the cult sites was sufficient to perpetuate and elaborate on Wigstan's legend until the Anglo-Normans began writing it down. It was recently asserted (Hayward 1993 p 82 note 4) that Dominic of Evesham ca. 1100 wrote the life of Wigstan on which all the surviving recensions depend.

Wulfstanus II: *BLS* 1.121–23; *BSS* 12.1372–73.

Bishop Wulfstan II (so-called to distinguish him from his older kinsman, **WULFSTAN OF YORK** the homilist, bishop of Worcester 1002–16, archbishop of York 1002–23) was born in southwest Mercia ca. 1008. He was educated at Evesham and Peterborough before becoming a priest and then a monk at Worcester. He rose to be prior of Worcester (ca. 1050) and was elected bishop in 1062 in succession to Ealdred when the latter became Archbishop of York (see above, **LEO IX**). Wulfstan died in 1095 (feast day January 19). One of the few Anglo-Saxons to retain high office through and beyond the reign of the Conqueror, he was "the last surviving English bishop" (Mason 1990 p 286). His life is probably the best "documented" of all the English saints in this volume and was recently the subject of a detailed, thoroughly modern biography (Mason 1990).

The original life of Wulfstan was composed in Old English by Wulfstan's chaplain and chancellor, Coleman of Worcester, between 1095 and 1113 (the year of Coleman's death), but this text has disappeared (last heard of at Rome with Pope Innocent III, for Wulfstan's canonization in 1203: see Mason 1990 p 289). Coleman's Old English life was soon replaced at Worcester by a Latin translation (which is doubtless far from slavish) by William of Malmesbury (*BHL* 8756), the standard edition of which is still that of Darlington (1928). This remains the main witness to the contents of Coleman's work. Gransden (1974 pp 87–89) regards the life as modeled on the Latin lives of **ÆTHELWOLDUS**, but C. Jones (1978 p 143) suggests the influence of the hagiography of Saint Nicholas (see **NICOLAUS**). A further, equally late witness to Coleman's lost life, partly independent of William's Latin version, is the so-called *Chronicle of John of Worcester* (also known as "Florence of Worcester"), which was compiled mainly after Wulfstan's episcopacy by another Worcester monk, John, still working ca. 1140. The whole issue of John's sources is very complex (see the brief survey in Mason 1990 pp 296–98), but Darlington (1928 pp xi–xvi) studies John's lengthy annal for 1062 (ed. Darlington and McGurk 1995 pp 588–92) in relation to corresponding passages in William of Malmesbury's *Vita Wulfstani* I and concludes (Darlington

1928 p xi) that the "resemblances . . . are the kind that would be expected if each writer, the one summarizing and the other translating, had before him the same Old English original, namely Coleman's Life." On the Wulfstan sources in general, including the lives mentioned here and below, see the useful "Appendix" in Mason (1990 pp 286–307). Mason's book (1990) is itself a detailed commentary on the *vita*; see also her articles (1984, 1986) and an essay by Farmer (1967). On the historical and hagiographical writing of William of Malmesbury, see Rodney Thomson (1987 pp 11–38). On Coleman, see most recently Mason (1990 pp 286–89 and passim) and Jackson (1992). On the short life of Wulfstan by subprior Hemming, surviving in Old English and Latin, see next entry. The most recent modern English translation of William of Malmesbury's life of Wulfstan is that of Swanton (1984 pp 91–148).

Wulfstanus II, laudatio [HEMMING.laud.Wulf.]: *BHL* 8755.
   ed.: *PL* 150.1489–90.

MSS   London, BL Cotton Tiberius A. xiii: HG 366.
Lists   none.
A-S Vers   ?*StWulf* (B17.12).
Quots/Cits – Refs   none.

Hemming was subprior of Worcester during and after the episcopacy of Wulfstan II (see Mason 1990 pp 294–95 for a brief account of Hemming and further references). He is the main compiler of a late-eleventh-century Worcester cartulary, well-known to historians, preserved in the second part of the London manuscript listed here. Apparently the work was commissioned by Wulfstan himself but not completed until well after his death. In addition to the charters, Hemming's cartulary contains two consecutive versions of a brief biographical eulogy of Wulfstan, listing the successive stages of the saint's career and the principal landed estates acquired at each stage, with their donors. The first version is in Old English (*StWulf*; ed. Thorpe 1865 pp 445–47), the second in Latin. Both Mason (1990 p 294) and Atkins (1940 p 208) state that the Latin text is a "translation" of the Old English, implying the latter has priority. This seems at least debatable. The Latin version is more detailed and more elaborately written than the Old English. According to Mason, however, Wharton's edition of the Latin text (see below) is based on a different manuscript, now lost (?), of Hemming's *Chartularium*. A new study and edition of the two texts, Old English and Latin, is required, but it seems more likely that the Old English is abridged from the Latin, than that the Latin elaborates on the Old English.

The first edition of the Old English text was that of Hearne (1723 2.403–05). The most recent edition, by Thorpe, provides a facing modern English translation, not always accurate. Atkins (1940 pp 208–09) provides only a translation of the Old English, improving little on Thorpe's. There is no modern edition of the Latin text to my knowledge. The *PL* edition is a reprint of earlier editions by Wharton (1691 2.541) and Hickes (1705 1.175–76); see also Hearne (1723 2.405–08). For a brief appreciation and further references, see Gransden (1974 p 90; see also p 87 note 158).

Xystus. See SIXTUS II.

Yvo. See IVO.

Zoe. See SEBASTIANUS.

Bibliography

Abraham, Lenore. 1976. "Bede's Life of Cuthbert: A Reassessment." *Proceedings of the PMR Conference* 1: 23–32.

Adams, L. 1993. "St Patrick and Glastonbury: *nihil ex nihilo fit?*" In Dumville 1993 pp 233–42.

Algeo, John T. 1960. "The Forty Soldiers: An Edition." Ph.D. diss., University of Florida.

Altaner, Berthold, and Alfred Stuiber. 1980. *Patrologie: Leben, Schriften und Lehre der Kirchenväter.* 8th ed. Freiburg im Breisgau/Basel/Vienna.

Amore, A. 1965. "I santi Quattro Coronati." *Antonianum* 40: 177–243.

———. 1966. "S. Valentino di Roma e di Terni." *Antonianum* 41: 260–77.

Anderson, A. O., and M. O. Anderson, eds. 1991. *Adomnan's Life of Columba.* Rev. ed. Oxford.

Anderson, Earl R. 1983. *Cynewulf: Structure, Style, and Theme in His Poetry.* Rutherford, N.J.

Antropoff, Rurik von. 1965. *Die Entwicklung der Kenelm-Legende.* Bonn.

Arbellot, F. 1892. "Étude historique sur l'ancienne Vie de S. Martial." *Bulletin de la Société archéologique et historique du Limousin* 40: 213–60.

Arndt, W. 1874. "Passio Sancti Georgii." *Berichte über die Verhandlungen der Königlichen Sächsischen Gesellschaft der Wissenschaften zu Leipzig. Philologisch-Historische Klasse* 26: 49–70.

Arnold, John Charles. 2000. "Arcadia Becomes Jerusalem: Angelic Caverns and Shrine Conversion at Monte Gargano." *Speculum* 75: 567–88.
Atkins, I. 1940. "The Church of Worcester from the Eighth to the Twelfth Centuries, Part II." *The Antiquaries Journal* 20: 1–38 and 203–28.
Avril, François, and Patricia Danz Stirnemann. 1987. *Manuscrits enluminés d'origine insulaire viie–xxe siècle*. Paris.
Azevedo, E. de. 1752. *Vetus missale Romanum monasticum Lateranense*. Rome.
Backhaus, Oskar. 1899. *Über die Quelle der mittelenglischen Legende von der heiligen Juliane und ihr Verhältnis zu Cynewulfs "Juliana."* Halle.
Baker, E. P. 1937. "The Cult of St Alban of Cologne." *Archaeological Journal* 94: 207–56.
Baker, Peter S. 1982. "Byrhtferth's *Enchiridion* and the Computus in Oxford, St John's College 17." *Anglo-Saxon England* 10: 123–42.
Baluzius, S. 1678–1715. *Miscellaneorum libri VII. hoc est Collectio veterum monumentorum*. 7 vols. Paris.
Bandini, Angelo Maria. 1791–93. *Bibliotheca Leopoldina Laurentiana seu Catalogus manuscriptorum*. 3 vols. Florence.
Bannister, A. T. 1927. *A Descriptive Catalogue of the Manuscripts in the Hereford Cathedral Library*. Hereford.
Bardy, G., and Baudouin De Gaiffier. 1950. "Constance de Lyon, Biographe de Saint Germain d'Auxerre." In *Saint Germain d'Auxerre et Sons Temps. Congrès du XVe Centenaire de la Mort de Saint Germain*, 89–110. Auxerre.
Baring-Gould, Sabine, and John Fisher. 1907–13. *The Lives of the British Saints*. 4 vols. London.
Barlow, Frank. 1970. *Edward the Confessor*. London.
———. 1979. *The English Church 1000–1066*. 2nd ed. London.
———, ed. 1992. *The Life of King Edward Who Rests at Westminster*. 2nd ed. Oxford (1st ed., London, 1962).
Barré, H. 1963. *Prières anciennes de l'Occident à la Mère du Sauveur*. Paris.

Barringer, R. 1980. "The Pseudo-Amphilochian Life of St Basil: Ecclesiastical Penance and Byzantine Hagiography." *Theologia* 51: 49–61.
Bassett, S. R. 1985. "A Probable Mercian Royal Mausoleum at Winchcombe, Gloucestershire." *The Antiquaries Journal* 65: 82–100.
Bastiaensen, A. A. R., ed. 1975a. *Vita di Cipriano, Vita di Ambrogio, Vita di Agostino*. Rome.
———, ed. 1975b. *Vita di Martino, Vita di Ilarino, In memoria di Paola*. Rome.
———. 1994. "Jérome hagiographe." In Philippart 1994– 1.97–123.
Bately, Janet. 1988. "Old English Prose Before and During the Reign of Alfred." *Anglo-Saxon England* 17: 191–215.
Baudot, J., L. Chaussin, and J. Dubois. 1935–54. *Vies des saints et des bienheureux selon l'ordre du calendrier avec l'historique des fêtes*. 13 vols. Paris.
Bautier, Robert-Henri, ed. 1969. *André de Fleury, Vie de Gauzlin, Abbé de Fleury*. Paris.
Beau, A. 1980. "Les réliques de saint Benoît et de Scholastique." *Renaissance de Fleury* 29: 3–23.
Beaugrand, A. 1892. *Sainte Lucie*. Paris.
Beck, Edmund, ed. 1972. *Des Heiligen Ephraem des Syrers: Hymnen auf Abraham Kidunaya und Julianos Saba*. 2 vols. Louvain.
Beech, George. 1990. "England and Aquitaine in the Century before the Norman Conquest." *Anglo-Saxon England* 19: 81–101.
Bennett, J. A. W., and G. V. Smithers, eds. 1966. *Early Middle English Verse and Prose*. Oxford.
Benskin, Michael. 1994. "The Literary Structure of Ælfric's *Life of King Edmund*." In *Loyal Letters: Studies on Mediaeval Alliterative Poetry and Prose*, ed. L. A. J. R. Houwen and A. A. MacDonald, 1–27. Groningen.
Berchem, Denis van. 1956. *Le martyre de la Légion Thébaine. Essai sur la formation d'une légende*. Basel.
Bernt, Günter. 1971. "Die Quellen zu Walahfrids Mammes-Leben." In *Festschrift Bernhard Bischoff*, ed. Johanne Autenrieth and Franz Brunhölzl, 142–52. Stuttgart.

Berschin, Walter. 1973. "Zur lateinischen und deutschen Juliana-Legende." *Studi Medievali*, 3rd ser., 14: 1006–08.

———. 1974. "Die Anfänge der lateinischen Literatur unter den Alemannen." In Hübener 1974 pp 121–33.

———. 1980. *Griechisch-Lateinisches Mittelalter: Von Hieronymus zu Nikolaus von Kues*. Bern/Munich.

———. 1981. "Die älteste erreichbare Textgestalt der *Passio S. Afrae*." *Bayerische Vorgeschichtsblätter* 46: 217–24.

———. 1986–91. *Biographie und Epochenstil im lateinischen Mittelalter*. Vol. 1: *Von der Passio Perpetuae zu den Dialogi Gregors des Großen*. Vol. 2: *Merowingische Biographie. Italien, Spanien und die Inseln im frühen Mittelalter*. Vol. 3: *Karolingische Biographie 750–920*. Stuttgart.

———. 1989. "Opus deliberatum ac perfectum: Why Did the Venerable Bede Write a Second Prose Life of St Cuthbert?" In Bonner et al. 1989 pp 95–102.

Bestul, T. 1981. "Ephraim the Syrian and Old English Poetry." *Anglia* 99: 1–24.

Bethurum, Dorothy. 1932. "The Form of Ælfric's *Lives of Saints*." *Studies in Philology* 29: 515–33.

———, ed. 1957. *The Homilies of Wulfstan*. Oxford. Rev. ed., Oxford, 1971.

Bibliotheca Casinensis seu codicum manuscriptorum qui in tabulario Casinensi asservantur series. 1873–94. 5 vols. Monte Cassino.

Biddle, Martin. 1977. "Alban and the Anglo-Saxon Church." In *Cathedral and City*, ed. R. Runcie, 23–42. London.

Bieler, L., ed. 1952. *Libri epistolarum Sancti Patricii Episcopi*. Dublin. Reprint, 1993.

Biggs, Frederick M. 1996a. Review of Clayton and Magennis 1994. *Journal of English and Germanic Philology* 95: 223–25.

———. 1996b. "Ælfric as Historian: His Use of Alcuin's *Laudationes* and Sulpicius's *Dialogues* in His Two Lives of Martin." In Szarmach 1996b pp 289–315.

Biggs, Frederick M., Thomas D. Hill, and Paul E. Szarmach, eds. 1990. *Sources of Anglo-Saxon Literary Culture: A Trial Version*. Binghamton, N.Y.

Bishop, T. A. M. 1959–63. "Notes on Cambridge Manuscripts." *Transactions of the Cambridge Bibliographical Society* 3: 93–95 and 412–23.

Blair, John. 1989. "Frithuwold's Kingdom and the Origins of Surrey." In *The Origins of the Anglo-Saxon Kingdoms*, ed. S. R. Bassett, 97–107 and 263–65. Leicester.

Blaise, A. 1954. *Dictionnaire latin-francais des auteurs chrétiens*. Paris. Reprint, Turnhout, 1967.

Blake, E. O., ed. 1962. *Liber Eliensis*. London.

Bless-Grabher, Magdalen. 1978. *Cassian von Imola. Die Legende eines Lehrers und Märtyrers und ihre Entwicklung von der Spätantike bis zur Neuzeit*. Bern.

Bloch, Herbert. 1950. "The Schism of Anacletus II and the Glanfeuil Forgeries." *Traditio* 8: 159–221.

Bloch, Marc. 1923. "Vita beati ac gloriosi regis Anglorum Eadwardi." *Analecta Bollandiana* 41: 5–131.

Blokhuis, B. A. 1996. "Bede and Ælfric; the Sources of the Homily on St Cuthbert." In Houwen and MacDonald 1996 pp 107–38.

Bober, Harry. 1956–57. "An Illustrated Medieval School-Book of Bede's 'De Natura Rerum.'" *Journal of the Walters Art Gallery* 19–20: 65–97.

Bodden, Mary-Catherine. 1987. *The Old English Finding of the True Cross*. Cambridge.

Bollandists. 1882a. "Sancti Servatii Tungrensis episcopi vitae antiquiores." *Analecta Bollandiana* 1: 85–111.

———. 1882b. "Catalogus codicum hagiographicorum latinorum in bibliothecis publicis Namurci." Part 1. *Analecta Bollandiana* 1: 485–530, 609–32.

———. 1883. "Catalogus codicum hagiographicorum latinorum in bibliothecis publicis Namurci." Part 2. *Analecta Bollandiana* 2: 130–60 and 279–354.

———. 1885. "Appendix ad Catalogum Codd. Hagiog. Bibliothecae Academiae et Civitatis Gandavensis." *Analecta Bollandiana* 4: 157–206.

———. 1886–89. *Catalogus codicum hagiographicorum latinorum bibliothecae regiae Bruxellensis, Pars 1. Codices latini membranei.* 2 vols. Brussels.

———. 1889–93. *Catalogus codicum hagiographicorum latinorum in bibliotheca Nationali Parisiensi.* 3 vols. Brussels.

———. 1891. "Passio Christophori Martyris ex cod. Paris. signato num. 2179 inter noviter acquisitos." *Analecta Bollandiana* 10: 393–405.

———. 1892. "Catalogus codicum hagiographicorum latinorum Bibliothecae Ambrosianae Mediolanensis." *Analecta Bollandiana* 11: 205–368.

Bolton, W. F. 1959. "Latin Revisions of Felix's Vita Guthlaci." *Mediaeval Studies* 21: 36–52.

———. 1961. "The Manuscript Source of the Old English Prose Life of St. Guthlac." *Archiv* 197: 301–03.

Bond, W. H., and C. U. Faye. 1962. *Supplement to the Census of Medieval and Renaissance Manuscripts in the United States and Canada.* New York.

Bonfante, Larissa. 1979. *The Plays of Hrotswitha of Gandersheim.* New York.

Bonner, Gerald, David Rollason, and Clare Stancliffe, eds. 1989. *St Cuthbert, His Cult and His Community to AD 1200.* Woodbridge, Suff., and Wolfboro, N.H.

Bonser, Wilfrid. 1945. "The Seven Sleepers of Ephesus in Anglo-Saxon and Later Recipes." *Folklore* 46: 254–56.

Borgehammar, Stephan. 1991. *How the Holy Cross Was Found: From Event to Medieval Legend, with an Appendix of Texts.* Stockholm.

Bosquet, F. 1636. *Ecclesiae gallicanae historiarum tomus primus.* 2 vols. Paris.

Braswell, Laura. 1971. "St. Edburga of Winchester: A Study of Her Cult, A.D. 950–1500, with an Edition of the Fourteenth-Century Middle English and Latin Lives." *Mediaeval Studies* 33: 292–333.

Brett, Caroline. 1991. "A Breton Pilgrim in England in the Reign of King Æthelstan." In *France and the British Isles in the Middle Ages and the Renaissance. Essays by Members of Girton College, Cambridge in Memory of Ruth Morgan*, ed. Gillian Jondorf and David Dumville, 43–70. Woodbridge, Suff.

Brett, Martin. 1991. "The Use of Universal Chronicle at Worcester." In *L'historiographie médiévale en Europe*, ed. Jean-Philippe Genet, 277–85. Paris.

Brittain, F. 1928. *Saint Giles*. Cambridge.

Brooks, Nicholas. 1984. *The Early History of the Church at Canterbury: Christ Church from 597 to 1066*. Leicester and Atlantic Highlands, N.J.

Brooks, Nicholas, and Catherine Cubitt, eds. 1996. *St Oswald of Worcester: Life and Influence*. Leicester.

Brown, Mary Gifford. 1990. *An Illuminated Chronicle: Some Light on the Dark Ages of Saint Milburga's Lifetime*. Bath.

Brown, Michelle P. 1986. "Paris, Bibliothèque Nationale, lat. 10861 and the Scriptorium of Christ Church, Canterbury." *Anglo-Saxon England* 15: 119–37.

Brown, Peter. 1972. "The Patrons of Pelagius." In *Religion and Society in the Age of Augustine*, 208–26. London.

———. 1981. *The Cult of the Saints*. Chicago.

Brown, R., and David Yerkes. 1981. "A Sermon on the Birthday of St. Machutus." *Analecta Bollandiana* 99: 160–64.

Brunöhler, Ernst. 1912. *Über einige lateinische, englische, französische und deutsche Fassungen der Julianenlegende*. Bonn.

Brusa, Luciana. 1959. "Gli atti dei martirio di S. Agata." *Rivista di Cultura Classica e Mediavale* 1: 342–67.

Bubnov, Nicolaus, ed. 1899. *Gerberti opera mathematica*. Hildesheim.

Bullough, Donald A. 1998. "A Neglected Early-Ninth-Century Manuscript of the Lindisfarne *Vita S. Cuthberti*." *Anglo-Saxon England* 27: 105–37.

Calder, Daniel G., and Michael J. B. Allen. 1976. *Sources and Analogues of Old English Poetry*. Cambridge and Totowa, N.J.

Campbell, Alistair, ed. 1950. *Frithigodi monachi breviloquium vitae beati Wilfredi et Wulfstani cantoris narratio metrica de Sancto Swithuno.* Zurich.

———, ed. 1967. *Æthelwulf De Abbatibus.* Oxford.

Campbell, James, Eric John, and Patrick Wormald. 1982. *The Anglo-Saxons.* Ithaca, N.Y.

Canart, Paul. 1966. "Le nouveau-né qui dénonce son père. Les avatars d'un conte populaire dans la littérature hagiographique." *Analecta Bollandiana* 84: 309–33.

Caporale, G. 1885. *Il martirio e culto dei SS. Conone e figlio protettori della città di Acerra.* Naples.

Carley, James P. (with David Townsend). 1985. *The Chronicle of Glastonbury Abbey. An Edition, Translation and Study of John of Glastonbury's Cronica sive Antiquitates Glastoniensis Ecclesie.* Woodbridge, Suff.

Carley, James P. 1994. "More Pre-Conquest Manuscripts from Glastonbury Abbey." *Anglo-Saxon England* 23: 265–81.

Carnicelli, Thomas A., ed. 1969. *King Alfred's Version of St. Augustine's Soliloquies.* Cambridge, Mass.

Cassidy, Frederick J., and Richard Ringler, eds. 1971. *Bright's Old English Grammar and Reader.* 3rd ed. New York.

Catalogue of Manuscripts in the British Museum. New Series (by J. Forshall). 1834–40. 3 pts. in 1. London. [Pt. 1: Arundel MSS. Pt. 2: Burney MSS. Pt. 3: Index.]

Cavallin, C. 1945. "Saint Genèse le notaire." *Eranos* 43: 150–75.

Cazzaniga, E., ed. 1948. *S. Ambrosii Mediolanensis episcopi de virginibus libri tres.* Turin.

Chadwick, H. M., and N. K. Chadwick. 1954. "Vortigern." In *Studies in Early British History,* ed. N. K. Chadwick, 21–33. Cambridge.

Chadwick, N. K. 1955. *Poetry and Letters in Early Christian Gaul.* London.

———. 1958. "Early Culture and Learning in North Wales." In *Studies in the Early British Church,* ed. N. K. Chadwick, 29–110. Cambridge.

Chase, C. 1986. "Source Study as a Trick with Mirrors: Annihilation of Meaning in the Old English 'Mary of Egypt.'" In *Sources of Anglo-Saxon Culture*, ed. Paul E. Szarmach and Robin Oggins, 23–33. Kalamazoo, Mich.

Chastel, Guy. 1939. *Sainte Colombe de Sens*. Paris.

Chavasse, Antoine. 1958. *Le sacramentaire gélasien, Vaticanus Reginensis 316, sacramentaire presbytéral en usage dans les titres romains au VIIe siècle*. Tournai.

Chiesa, Paolo. 1989/90. "Le traduzioni dal greco: l'evoluzione della scuola napoletana ne X secolo." *Mittellateinisches Jahrbuch* 24/25: 67–86.

Ciccarese, Maria P. 1981–82. "La Visio Baronti nella tradizione letteraria delle visiones dell'aldilá." *Romanobarbarica* 6: 28–52.

———. 1982. "Osservazioni sulli fonti e i modelli della 'Vita Guthlaci' di Felice." *Studi storico-religiosi* 6: 135–42.

———. 1984–85. "Le visioni di S. Fursa." *Romanobarbarica* 8: 231–303.

———, ed. 1987. *Visioni dell'aldilá in occidente: fonti, modelli, testi*. Florence.

Clark, Cecily. 1968. "Ælfric and Abbo." *English Studies* 49: 30–36.

———. 1979. "Notes on a Life of Three Thorney Saints: Thancred, Torhtred and Tova." *Proceedings of the Cambridge Antiquarians' Society* 69: 45–52.

Classen, G., and F. G. Harmer. 1926. *An Anglo-Saxon Chronicle*. Manchester.

Clayton, Mary. 1990. *The Cult of the Virgin Mary in Anglo-Saxon England*. Cambridge.

———. 1994. "Ælfric's *Judith*: Manipulative or Manipulated?" *Anglo-Saxon England* 23: 215–27.

Clayton, Mary, and Hugh Magennis, eds. 1994. *The Old English Lives of St Margaret*. Cambridge.

Clemoes, Peter. 1959. "The Chronology of Ælfric's Works." In *The Anglo-Saxons: Studies in Some Aspects of their History and Culture Presented to Bruce Dickins*, ed. Clemoes, 212–47. London.

———. 1960. "The Old English Benedictine Office, Corpus Christi College, Cambridge MS 190, and the Relations between Ælfric and Wulfstan: A Reconsideration," *Anglia* 78: 265–83.

———. 1984. *The Cult of St Oswald on the Continent*. Jarrow.

Cockayne, T. O. 1861. *Narratiunculae Anglice Conscriptae*. London.

Coens, M. 1885. "Un sermon inconnu de Rupert, Abbé de Deutz." *Analecta Bollandiana* 4: 254–67.

———. 1956. "Aux origines de la céphalophorie: un fragment retrouvé d'une ancienne Passion de S. Juste, martyr de Beauvais." *Analecta Bollandiana* 74: 86–114.

Coleiro, E. 1957. "St Jerome's Lives of the Hermits." *Vigiliae Christianae* 11: 161–78.

Colgrave, Bertram. 1927. *The Life of Bishop Wilfrid by Eddius Stephanus*. Cambridge. Reprint, 1985.

———, ed. 1940. *Two Lives of Saint Cuthbert. A Life by an Anonymous Monk of Lindisfarne and Bede's Prose Life*. Cambridge. Reprint, 1985.

———. 1950. "The Post-Bedan Miracles and Translations of St Cuthbert." In *The Early Cultures of North-West Europe*, ed. Cyril Fox and Bruce Dickins, 307–32. Oxford.

———, ed. 1956. *Felix's Life of Saint Guthlac*. Cambridge. Reprint, 1985.

———. 1958. "The Earliest Saints' Lives Written in England." *Proceedings of the British Academy* 44: 35–60.

———, ed. 1968. *The Earliest Life of Gregory the Great*. Cambridge. Reprint, 1985.

Colgrave, Bertram, and R. A. B. Mynors, eds. 1969. *Bede's Ecclesiastical History of the English People*. Oxford.

Colker, Marvin. 1965. "Texts of Jocelyn of Canterbury which Relate to the History of Barking Abbey." *Studia Monastica* 7: 383–460.

———. 1977. "A Hagiographic Polemic." *Mediaeval Studies* 39: 60–108.

———. 1991. *Trinity College, Dublin. Descriptive Catalogue of the Medieval and Renaissance Latin Manuscripts*. 2 vols. Brookfield, Vt.

Collins, Marie, Jocelyn Price, and Andrew Hamer, eds. 1985. *Sources and Relations: Studies in Honour of J. E. Cross*. Special Issue: *Leeds Studies in English*, n.s., 16.

Collins, Roger. 1980. "Merida and Toledo: 550–585." In *Visigothic Spain: New Approaches*, ed. Edward James, 189–219. Oxford.

Collins, Rowland. 1981. Review of Le Duc 1979. *Old English Newsletter* 15/1 (Fall): 103.

Combefis, F., ed. 1644. *Sanctorum patrum Amphilochii Iconiensis, Methodii Patarensis et Andreae Cretensis opera omnia quae supersunt.* Paris.

Conner, Patrick W. 1993a. *Anglo-Saxon Exeter: A Tenth-Century Cultural History*. Woodbridge, Suff., and Rochester, N.Y.

———. 1993b. "Source Studies, the Old English Guthlac A and the English Benedictine Reformation." *Revue Bénédictine* 103: 380–413.

Connolly, Sean, and Jean-Michel Picard. 1988. "Cogitosus's Life of St Brigit: Content and Value." *Journal of the Royal Society of Antiquaries of Ireland* 117 (for 1987): 5–27.

Connolly, T. H. 1979. "The Legend of St. Cecilia: I, The Origins of the Cult." *Studi Musicali* 7: 3–37.

———. 1980. "The Legend of St. Cecilia: II, Music and the Symbols of Virginity." *Studi Musicali* 9: 3–44.

Cook, A. S. 1903. *Biblical Quotations in Old English Prose Writers. Second Series*. New York.

Corbet, P. 1980. "La diffusion du culte de Saint-Gilles au Moyen Age (Champagne, Lorraine, Nord de la Bourgogne)." *Annales d'Est* 32: 3–42.

Corrêa, Alicia. 1993. "A Mass for St Patrick in an Anglo-Saxon Sacramentary." In Dumville 1993 pp 245–52.

———. 1996. "The Liturgical Manuscripts of Oswald's Houses." In Brooks and Cubbitt 1996 pp 285–324.

Corsi, Pasquale. 1979. "La 'Vita' di san Nicolo e un codice della versione di Giovanni diacono." *Nicolaus. Rivista di teologia ecumenico-patristica* 7: 359–80.

Corssen, P. 1914. "Das Martyrium des Bischofs Cyprian." *Zeitschrift für die neutestamentliche Wissenschaft* 15: 221–33.

Cousin, Patrice. 1954. *Abbon de Fleury-sur-Loire*. Paris.

Cownie, Emma. 1998. "The Cult of St Edmund in the Eleventh and Twelfth Centuries." *Neuphilologische Mitteilungen* 99: 177–97.

Coxe, H. O. 1852. *Catalogus codicum mss. qui in Collegiis aulisque Oxoniensibus hodie adservantur*. 2 vols. Oxford.

Craster, H. H. E. 1925. "The Red Book of Durham." *English Historical Review* 40: 504–32.

———. 1954. "The Patrimony of St. Cuthbert." *English Historical Review* 69: 177–99.

Crawford, S. J. 1929. "Byrhtferth of Ramsey and the Anonymous Life of St Oswald." In *Speculum Religionis, Being Essays and Studies in Religion and Literature from Plato to Von Hugel*, ed. F. C. Burkitt, 99–111. Oxford.

Crosby, S. McKnight. 1987. *The Royal Abbey of Saint-Denis From Its Beginnings to the Death of Suger, 475–1151*. Ed. Pamela Z. Blum. Yale.

Cross, J. E. 1965a. "Oswald and Byrhtnoth: A Christian Saint and a Hero Who Is Christian." *English Studies* 46: 93–109.

———. 1965b. "Gregory, Blickling Homily X, and Ælfric's Passio S. Mauricii on the World's Youth and Age." *Neuphilologische Mitteilungen* 66: 327–30.

———. 1971a. "Sources and Analysis of Some Ælfrician Passages." *Neuphilologische Mitteilungen* 72: 446–53.

———. 1971b. "Lexicographical Notes on the Old English 'Life of St. Giles' and the 'Life of St. Nicholas.'" *Notes and Queries*, n.s., 18: 369–72.

———. 1975. "Blickling Homily XIV and the Old English Martyrology on John the Baptist." *Anglia* 93: 145–60.

———. 1977a. "Two Saints in the *Old English Martyrology*." *Neuphilologische Mitteilungen* 78: 101–07.

———. 1977b. "Ælfric's 'Life of St. George.'" *Notes and Queries*, n.s., 24: 195–96.

———. 1977c. "'Legimus in ecclesiasticis historiis' — a Sermon for All Saints, and Its Use in Old English Prose." *Traditio* 33: 101–35.

———. 1978. "Mary Magdalen in the *Old English Martyrology*: The Earliest Extant 'Narrat Josephus' Variant of Her Legend." *Speculum* 53: 16–25.

———. 1979. "Popes of Rome in the *Old English Martyrology*." In *Papers of the Liverpool Latin Seminar*, vol. 2, ed. Francis Cairns, 191–211. Liverpool.

———. 1981a. "*Passio Symphoriani* and Old English *cun(d)*." *Neuphilologische Mitteilungen* 82: 269–75.

———. 1981b. "An Unrecorded Tradition of St. Michael in Old English Texts." *Notes and Queries*, n.s., 28: 11–13.

———. 1981c. "Eulalia of Barcelona: A Notice without Source in the *Old English Martyrology*." *Notes and Queries*, n.s., 28: 483–84.

———. 1981d. "Old English *Leasere*." *Notes and Queries*, n.s., 28: 484–86.

———. 1981e. "The Influence of Irish Texts and Traditions on the *Old English Martyrology*." *Proceedings of the Royal Irish Academy. Section C.* 81: 173–92.

———. 1982a. "A *Virgo* in the *Old English Martyrology*." *Notes and Queries*, n.s., 29: 102–06.

———. 1982b. "Passio S. Eugeniae et Comitum and the *Old English Martyrology*." *Notes and Queries*, n.s., 29: 392–97.

———. 1982c. "Saints' Lives in Old English: Latin Manuscripts and Vernacular Accounts: The *Old English Martyrology*." *Peritia* 1: 38–62.

———. 1982d. "A Lost Life of Hilda of Whitby: The Evidence of the *Old English Martyrology*." In *The Early Middle Ages*, ed. W. Snyder and Paul E. Szarmach, 21–43. Binghamton, N.Y., for 1979.

———. 1983a. "The *Passio S. Laurentii et Aliorum*: Latin Manuscripts and the *Old English Martyrology*." *Mediaeval Studies* 45: 200–13.

———. 1983b. "Cosmas and Damian in the *Old English Martyrology*." *Notes and Queries*, n.s., 30: 15–18.

———. 1983c. "Euphemia and the Ambrosian Missal." *Notes and Queries*, n.s., 30: 18–22.

———. 1983d. "Columba of Sens in the *Old English Martyrology*." *Notes and Queries*, n.s., 30: 195–98.

———. 1984a. "Source, Lexis, and Edition." *Bonner Beiträge zur englischen Wissenschaft* 15: 25–36.

———. 1984b. "Antoninus of Apamea and an Image in the *Old English Martyrology*." *Notes and Queries*, n.s., 31: 18–22.

———. 1984c. "Genesius of Rome and Genesius of Arles." *Notes and Queries*, n.s., 31: 149–52.

———. 1984d. "Pelagia in Mediaeval England." In Petitmengin 1981–84 2.281–93.

———. 1985a. "The Use of Patristic Homilies in the Old English Martyrology." *Anglo-Saxon England* 14: 107–28.

———. 1985b. "On the Library of the Old English Martyrologist." In Lapidge and Gneuss 1985 pp 227–49.

———. 1986a. "Identification: Towards Criticism." In *Modes of Interpretation in Old English Literature: Essays in Honor of Stanley B. Greenfield*, ed. Phyllis Rugg Brown, Georgia Ronan Crampton, and Fred C. Robinson, 229–46. Buffalo and London.

———. 1986b. "The Latinity of the Ninth-Century Old English Martyrologist." In Szarmach 1986 pp 275–99.

———. 1988. "The Use of a *Passio S. Sebastiani* in the Old English Martyrology." *Mediaevalia* 14: 39–50.

———, ed. (with Denis Brearley, Julia Crick, Thomas N. Hall, and Andy Orchard). 1996. *Two Old English Apocrypha and Their Manuscript Source: "The Gospel of Nichodemus" and "The Avenging of the Saviour."* Cambridge.

———. 2000. "The Notice on Marina (7 July) and *Passiones S. Margaritae*." In Szarmach 2000 pp 419–32.

Cross, J. E., and Alan Brown. 1989. "Literary Impetus for Wulfstan's *Sermo Lupi*." *Leeds Studies in English* 20: 271–87.

———. 1993. "Wulfstan and Abbo of Saint-Germain-des-Prés." *Mediaevalia* 15 (for 1989): 71–91.

Cross, J. E., and Thomas N. Hall. 1993. "The Fragments of Homiliaries in Canterbury Cathedral Library MS. Addit. 127/1 and in Kent, County Archives Office, Maidstone, MS. PRC 49/2." *Scriptorium* 47: 186–92.

Cross, J. E., and Jennifer Morrish Tunberg. 1993. *The Copenhagen Wulfstan Collection: Copenhagen Kongelige Bibliotek GL.KGL.SAM. 1595)*. Copenhagen.

Cross, J. E., and C. J. Tuplin. 1980. "An Unrecorded Variant of the 'Passio S. Christinae' and the 'Old English Martyrology.'" *Traditio* 36: 161–236.

Cureton, W. 1861. *History of the Martyrs in Palestine by Eusebius, Bishop of Caesarea*. London and Edinburgh

Dagron, G., ed. 1978. *Vie et Miracles de sainte Thècle*. Brussels.

Darlington, Reginald P., ed. 1928. *The Vita Wulfstani of William of Malmesbury*. London.

Darlington, Reginald P., and P. McGurk, eds. 1995. *The Chronicle of John of Worcester*. Vol. 2: *The Annals from 450 to 1066* (trans. Jennifer Bray and P. McGurk). Oxford.

D'Arrigo, S., ed. 1988. *Il martirio di sant'Agata nel quadro storico del suo tempo*. 2 vols. Catania.

Dassman, E. 1975. "Ambrosius und die Märtyrer." *Jahrbuch für Antike und Christentum* 18: 49–68.

De Certain, E. 1858. *Les miracles de S. Benoît*. Paris.

Declerck, José. 1987. "Les recensions grècques de la passion de S. Pancrace, martyr à Rome (*BHG* 1408–09)." *Analecta Bollandiana* 105: 65–85.

De Gaiffier, Baudouin. 1943. "S. Marcel de Tanger ou de Leon? Évolution d'une légende." *Analecta Bollandiana* 61: 116–39.

———. 1947. "Intactam sponsam relinquens. À propos de la Vie de S. Alexis BHL 289." *Analecta Bollandiana* 65: 157–95.

———. 1948. "Les sources de la vie de S. Cassien, évêque d'Autun." *Analecta Bollandiana* 66: 33–52.

———. 1954. "*Sub Daciano praeside*. Étude de quelques Passions espagnoles." *Analecta Bollandiana* 72: 378–96.

———. 1956. "'Sub Iuliano Apostate,' dans le martyrologe romain." *Analecta Bollandiana* 74: 5–49.
———. 1959. "Hispana et Lusitana." *Analecta Bollandiana* 77: 188–217.
———. 1963. "Les notices des papes Félix dans le martyrologe romain." *Analecta Bollandiana* 81: 336–46.
———. 1979. "Isembard de Fleury-sur-Loire auteur de la *Vita S. Iudoci* (*BHL* 4505–4510)." *Jahrbuch der Gesellschaft für niedersächsische Kirchengeschichte* 77: 9–12.
Delehaye, Hippolyte. 1897a. "Les saints du cimitière de Commodille." *Analecta Bollandiana* 16: 22–23.
———. 1897b. "Eusebii Caesariensis De martyribus Palaestinae longioris libelli fragmenta." *Analecta Bollandiana* 16: 113–39.
———. 1909. *Les légendes grecques des saints militaires*. Brussels.
———. 1920. "Saint Martin et Sulpice Sévère." *Analecta Bollandiana* 38: 5–136.
———. 1921a. "La Passion de S. Félix de Thibiuca." *Analecta Bollandiana* 39: 241–76.
———. 1921b. "Cyprien d'Antioche et Cyprien de Carthage." *Analecta Bollandiana* 39: 314–32.
———. 1923a. "Les actes de S. Marcel le centurion." *Analecta Bollandiana* 41: 257–87.
———. 1923b. *Les saints stylites*. Brussels.
———. 1927. *Sanctus. Essai sur le culte des saints dans l'antiquité*. Brussels.
———. 1929. "L'hagiographie ancienne de Ravenne." *Analecta Bollandiana* 47: 5–30.
———. 1933a. *Les origines du culte des martyrs*. 2nd ed. Brussels.
———. 1933b. "Recherches sur le légendier Romain." *Analecta Bollandiana* 51: 34–98.
———. 1935. "Saints et réliquaires d'Apamée." *Analecta Bollandiana* 53: 225–44.
———. 1936. *Étude sur le légendier Romain: les Saints de novembre et de décembre*. Brussels. Reprint, 1968.
———. 1937. "Sainte Théodote de Nicée." *Analecta Bollandiana* 55: 201–25.

———. 1940. "Passio Sancti Mammetis." *Analecta Bollandiana* 58: 126–41.

———. 1955. *Les légendes hagiographiques*. 4th ed. Brussels.

———. 1966. *Les passions des martyrs et les genres littéraires*. 2nd ed. Brussels.

Delehaye, Hippolyte, et al., eds. 1940. *Propylaeum ad Acta Sanctorum Decembris. Martyrologium Romanum*. Brussels.

Denomy, A. 1938. *The Old French Lives of St. Agnes and Other Vernacular Versions*. Cambridge.

De Rossi, G. B., and A. Ferrua. 1983. *Inscriptiones Christianae urbis Romae, septimo seculo antiquiores. Nova series*. Vol. 8, *Coemetria viarum Nomentanae et Salariae*. Rome.

Deshusses, J., and Jacques Hourlier. 1979. "S. Benoît dans les livres liturgiques." *Studia Monastica* 21: 143–204.

Devic, C., and J. Vaissette. 1872–1905. *Histoire générale de Languedoc par deux réligieux Bénédictins de la Congrégation de S. Maur*. Nouv. ed. 16 vols. Toulouse.

Devisse, Jean. 1975–76. *Hincmar, archevêque de Reims, 845–882*. 3 vols. Geneva.

De Vogüé, A. 1981. "La rencontre de Benoît et de Scholastique: essai d'interpretation." In De Vogüé, *Saint Benoît, sa vie et sa règle. Études choisies*, 45–59. Abbeye de Bellefontaine.

———. 1983. "The Meeting of Benedict and Scholastica: An Interpretation." *Cistercian Studies* 18: 167–83 (trans. of De Vogüé 1981).

———. 1991. "La 'vita Pauli' de saint Jérôme et sa datation." In *Eulogia. Mélanges offerts à Antoon A. R. Bastiaensen à l'occasion de son soixante-cinquième anniversaire*, ed. G. J. M. Bartelink et al., 395–406. Steenbrugge.

———. 1991–93. *Histoire littéraire du mouvement monastique dans l'antiquité. Première partie, le monachisme latin*. 2 vols. Paris.

Devos, Paul. 1965. "Une passion grècque inédit de S. Pierre d'Alexandrie et sa traduction par Anastase le Bibliothecaire." *Analecta Bollandiana* 83: 157–87.

Doble, G. H. S. 1929. *Neot, Patron of St. Neot, Cornwall, and St. Neot's, Huntingdonshire*. Exeter.

———. 1931. *Saint Symphorian, Martyr, Patron of Veryan*. Truro.

———. 1934. "St. Ivo, Bishop and Confessor, Patron of the Town of St. Ives." *Laudate* 12: 149–56.

———. 1942. "Saint Indract and Saint Dominic." *Somerset Record Society Publications* 57: 1–24.

———. 1960–70. *The Saints of Cornwall*. 5 pts. Ed. Donald Attwater. Truro.

Dobschütz, Ernst von. 1899. *Christusbilder. Untersuchungen zur christlichen Legende*. TU, n.f., 3. Leipzig.

Dolbeau, François. 1981. "La traduction latine 'sacratissimus' ou A." In Petitmengin 1981–84 1.161–216.

———. 1983a. Review of Le Duc 1979. *Analecta Bollandiana* 101: 194–96.

———. 1983b. "Les sources d'un sermon en l'honneur de Saint Malo." *Analecta Bollandiana* 101: 417–19.

———. 1995. "Un sermon inédit d'origine Africaine pour la fête des saintes Perpètue et Félicité." *Analecta Bollandiana* 113: 89–106.

Dölger, F. J. 1933. "Die Blutsalbung des Soldaten mit der Lanze im Passionspiel *Christus Patiens*." *Antike und Christentum: Kultur- und Religionsgeschichtliche Studien* 4: 81–94.

Drobner, Hubertus K. 1988. "Die Anfänge der Verehrung des römischen Märtyrers Pankratius in Deutschland." *Römische Quartalschrift* 83: 76–98.

Dubois, Jacques. 1961. "Le martyrologe métrique de Wandelbert. Ses sources, son originalité, son influence sur Usuard." *Analecta Bollandiana* 79: 257–93.

Dubois, Jacques, and Jean-Loup Lemaitre. 1993. *Sources et méthodes de l'hagiographie médiévale*. Paris.

Dubois, Jacques, and Geneviève Renaud. 1976. *Edition pratique des martyrologes de Bède, de l'Anonyme lyonnais et de Florus*. Paris.

———. 1984. *Le martyrologe d'Adon: ses deux familles, ses trois recensions: texte et commentaire*. Paris.

Duby, G., ed. 1990. *La femme au moyen âge*. Paris.

Duchesne, L., ed. 1955. *Liber Pontificalis*. 2nd ed. 2 vols. Paris.

Dufourcq, A. 1900–07. *Étude sur les Gesta Martyrum romains*. 3 vols. Paris.
Dumville, David N. 1985. *Historia Brittonum*. Vol. 3: *The "Vatican" Recension*. Cambridge and Dover, N.H.
———. 1987. "English Square Minuscule Script: The Background and Earliest Phases." *Anglo-Saxon England* 16: 147–79.
———. 1992. *Liturgy and the Ecclesiastical History of Late Anglo-Saxon England*. Woodbridge, Suff.
———. 1993. *Saint Patrick, A.D. 493–1993*. Woodbridge, Suff.
Dumville, David N., and Michael Lapidge, eds. 1985. *The Anglo-Saxon Chronicle: A Collaborative Edition*. Vol. 17: *The Annals of St. Neots with Vita prima Sancti Neoti*. Cambridge.
Dupraz, L. 1961. *Les passions de S. Maurice d'Agaune: essai sur l'historicité de la tradition et contribution a l'étude de l'armée prédioclétienne (260–286) et des canonisations tardives de la fin du IVe siècle*. Fribourg.
Edwards, A. J. M. 1960. "Odo of Ostia's History of the Translation of Saint Milburga and Its Connections with the Early History of Much Wenlock Abbey." M.A. thesis, London University.
Ehlers, J. 1973. *Hugo von St. Viktor. Studien zum Geschichtsdenken und zur Geschichtsschreibung des 12. Jahrhunderts*. Wiesbaden.
Elfassi, Jacques. 1998. "Germain d'Auxerre, figure d'Augustin de Cantorbéry. La réécriture par Bède de la 'Vie de saint Germain d'Auxerre.'" *Hagiographica* 5: 37–47.
Elliott, Dyan. 1993. *Spiritual Marriage: Sexual Abstinence in Medieval Wedlock*. Princeton.
Elliott, J. K. 1993. *The Apocryphal New Testament*. Oxford.
Engelen, Eva-Maria. 1993. *Zeit, Zahl und Bild: Studien zur Verbindung von Philosophie und Wissenschaft bei Abbo von Fleury*. Berlin and New York.
Esposito, M. 1912/13. "On the Earliest Latin Life of St. Brigid of Kildare." *Proceedings of the Royal Irish Academy. Section C*. 30: 307–26.
Evans, Gillian R. 1979. "Schools and Scholars: The Study of the Abacus in English Schools c. 980–c. 1150." *English Historical Review* 94: 71–89.

Evans, Gillian R., and A. M. Peden. 1985. "Natural Science and the Liberal Arts in Abbo of Fleury's Commentary on the Calculus of Victorius of Aquitaine." *Viator* 16: 109–27.

Ewig, Eugen. 1978. "Bemerkungen zur Vita des Bischofs Lupus von Troyes." In Hauck and Mordek 1978 pp 14–26.

Fábrega Grau, Angelo. 1953–55. *Pasionario Hispánico*. 2 vols. Madrid/Barcelona.

Falconi, Niccolo Carminio. 1751. *Sancti confessoris Pontificis et Celeberrimi Thaumaturgi Nicolai Acta Primagenua nuper Detecta*. Naples.

Faral, Edmond. 1920. "D'un 'passionaire' latin à un roman français. Quelque sources immédiates du roman d'Éracle." *Romania* 46: 512–36.

Farmer, D. H. 1967. "Two Biographies by William of Malmesbury." In *Latin Biography*, ed. T. A. Dorey, 165–74. London.

———. 1987. *The Oxford Dictionary of Saints*. 2nd ed. Oxford.

Fasola, Umberto. 1967. *La basilica dei SS. Nerei e Achilleo e la catacomba di Domitilla*. Rome.

Fell, Christine. 1971. *Edward King and Martyr*. Leeds.

———. 1978. "Edward King and Martyr and the Anglo-Saxon Hagiographic Tradition." In *Ethelred the Unready, Papers from the Millenary Conference*, ed. D. Hill, 1–13. Oxford.

Fell, John, ed. 1680. *Lucii Caecilii Firmiani Lactantii De mortibus persecutorum liber*. Oxford.

Ferrari, Guy. 1957. *Early Roman Monasteries*. Vatican.

Ferrua, A. 1942. *Epigrammata Damasiana*. Vatican.

Finberg, H. P. R. 1967. "St Patrick at Glastonbury." *Irish Ecclesiastical Record*, 5th ser., 108: 345–61.

———. 1972. *The Early Charters of the West Midlands*. 2nd ed. Leicester.

Floyer, John Kestell, and Sidney Graves Hamilton. 1906. *Catalogue of Manuscripts Preserved in the Chapter Library of Worcester Cathedral*. Oxford.

Flusin, Bernard, ed. 1992. *Saint Anastase le Perse et l'histoire de la Palestine au début du VIIe siècle*. 2 vols. Paris.

Folz, R. 1975. "Tradition hagiographique et culte de sainte Balthilde, reine des Francs." *Comptes-rendus de l'Académie des Inscriptions et Belles-lettres*: 369–84.

———. 1978. "Naissance et manifestation d'un culte royal: saint Édmond, roi d'Est-Anglie." In Hauck and Mordek 1978 pp 226–46.

———. 1980. "Trois saints rois 'souffre-passion' en Angleterre: Oswin de Deira, Ethelbert d'Est-Anglie, Edouard le Martyr." *Comptes-rendus de l'Académie des Inscriptions et Belles-lettres*: 36–49.

———. 1984. *Les saints rois du moyen âge en occident (VIe – XIIIe siecles)*. Brussels.

Forman, Mary. 1990. "Three Songs about St. Scholastica by Aldhelm and Paul the Deacon." *Vox Benedictina* 7: 229–52.

Formige, Jules. 1960. *L'Abbaye Royale de Saint-Denis; recherches nouvelles*. Paris.

Forsey, George Frank. 1928. "Byrhtferth's *Preface*." *Speculum* 3: 505–22.

Förster, Max. 1892. *Über die Quellen von Aelfrics Homiliae Catholicae: I. Legenden*. Berlin.

———. 1893. "Zu den Blickling Homilies." *Archiv* 91: 179–206.

———. 1894. "Über die Quellen von Aelfrics exegetischen *Homiliae Catholicae*." *Anglia* 16: 1–61.

———. 1901. "Zur altenglischen Quintinus-Legende." *Archiv* 106: 258–59.

———. 1914. "Die altenglische Beigaben des Lambeth-Psalters." *Archiv* 132: 333–35.

———. 1943. *Zur Geschichte des Reliquienkultus in Altengland*. Munich.

Fouracre, Paul. 1990. "Merovingian History and Merovingian Hagiography." *Past and Present* 127 (May): 1–38.

Fourrier, Anthime. 1960. *Le courant réaliste dans le roman courtois en France au moyen-âge, 1. Les débuts (XIIe siècle)*. Paris.

Fowler, J. T., ed. 1891, 1893. *The Coucher Book of Selby*. 2 vols. Durham.

Franchi de' Cavalieri, P. 1899. *S. Agnese nella tradizione e nella leggenda*. Rome. Reprint, *Scritti agiografichi*, 2 vols., Vatican, 1962, 1:293–379.

———. 1902. "Di una probabile fonte della leggenda dei SS. Giovanni e Paulo." In *Nuove note agiografiche*, 55–65. Vatican.
———. 1903. "S. Martina." *Römische Quartalschrift* 17: 222–36.
———. 1908. "Della leggenda di S. Pancrazio Romano." *Studi e Testi* 19: 77–120.
———. 1912. "La Passio S. Theagenis." In *Note agiografiche. Fascicolo 4*, 161–85. Vatican.
———. 1920. "S. Teodoreto di Antiochia." In *Note agiografiche. Fascicolo 6*, 57–101. Vatican.
———. 1928. "S. Euplo. Appendici: I. II. III. IV. Passio S. Eupli sacerdotis et martyris ex cod. vat. lat. 1190." In *Note agiografiche. Fascicolo 7*, 1–54. Vatican.
———. 1935. "Gli atti di S. Fruttuoso di Taragona." In *Note agiografiche. Fascicolo 8*, 129–99. Vatican.
———. 1953. "Della 'custodia Mamertini' e della 'Passio SS. Processi et Martininani.' " In *Note agiografiche. Fascicolo 9*, 1–52. Vatican.
Francis, Elizabeth A. 1927. "A Hitherto Unprinted Version of the Passio Sanctae Margaritae with Some Observations on Vernacular Derivatives." *PMLA* 42: 87–105.
Franklin, Carmela. 1995. "Theodore and the *Passio S. Anastasii*." In Lapidge 1995 pp 175–203.
Franklin, Carmela, and Paul Meyvaert. 1982. "Has Bede's Version of the 'Passio S. Anastasii' Come Down to Us in 'BHL' 408?" *Analecta Bollandiana* 100: 373–400.
Frederick, Jill. 1989. " 'His ansyn wæs swylce rosan blostma': A Reading of the Old English *Life of St. Christopher*." *Proceedings of the PMR Conference* 12–13 (for 1987–88): 137–48.
Freire, J. Geraldes. 1971. *A versáo latino por Pascasio di Dume dos Apophthegmata Patrum*. 2 vols. Coimbra.
Fritzsche, C. 1886. "Die lateinischen Visionen des Mittelalters bis zur Mitte des 12. Jahrhunderts. Ein Beitrag zur Culturgeschichte." *Romanische Forschungen* 2: 247–79.
Frolow, A. 1953. "La vraie croix et les expéditions d'Héraclius en Perse." *Revue des Études Byzantines* 11: 88–105.

Fuiano, M. 1961. *La cultura a Napoli nell'alto medioevo.* Naples.
Funk, F. X., and F. Diekamp, eds. 1913. *Patres Apostolici.* 3rd ed. Tübingen.
Gameson, Richard. 1996. "Book Production and Decoration at Worcester in the Tenth and Eleventh Centuries." In Brooks and Cubitt 1996 pp 194–243.
García Rodríguez, C. 1966. *El culto de los santos en la España romaña y visigoda.* Madrid.
Garnett, James M. 1899. "The Latin and the Anglo-Saxon *Juliana.*" *PMLA* 14: 279–98.
Garrison, Christine Wille. 1990. "The Lives of St. Ætheldreda. Representation of Female Sanctity from 700 to 1300." Ph.D. diss., University of Rochester.
Gärtner, H. A. 1989. "Die Acta Scillitani: eine literarische Interpretation." *Wiener Studien* 102: 149–67.
Gatch, M. McC. 1977. *Preaching and Theology in Anglo-Saxon England: Ælfric and Wulfstan.* Toronto/Buffalo.
Geary, Patrick. 1990. *Furta Sacra: The Theft of Relics in the Central Middle Ages.* Rev. ed. Princeton.
Geith, Karl-Ernst. 1965. *Priester Arnolts Legende von der Heiligen Juliana. Untersuchungen zur lateinischen Juliana-Legende und zum Text des deutschen Gedichtes.* Freiburg.
Gelzer, H. 1893. *Leontios' von Neapolis Leben des Heiligen Iohannes des Barmherzigen Eerzbischofs von Alexandrien.* Freiburg/Leipzig.
Gerould, Gordon Hall. 1916. *Saints' Legends.* Boston/New York. Reprint, 1969.
———. 1924–25. "Abbot Ælfric's Rhythmic Prose." *Modern Philology* 22: 353–66.
———. 1925. "Ælfric's Lives of St. Martin of Tours." *Journal of English and Germanic Philology* 24: 206–10.
Gibson, Margaret, T. A. Heslop, and Richard W. Pfaff, eds. 1992. *The Eadwine Psalter: Text, Image, and Monastic Culture in Twelfth-Century Canterbury.* London/University Park, Pa.
Giles, J. 1854. *Vita quorundam Anglo-Saxonum.* London.

Gilles, Anne-Veronique. 1982. "L'evolution de l'hagiographie de saint Saturnin de Toulouse et son influence sur la liturgie." *Cahiers de Fanjeaux* 17: 359–79.

Glöde, Otto. 1889. "Cynewulf's *Juliana* und ihre Quelle." *Anglia* 11: 146–58.

Gneuss, Helmut. 1968. *Hymnar und Hymnen im englischen Mittelalter.* Tübingen.

———. 1978. "Dunstan und Hrabanus Maurus: zur Hs. Bodleian Auctarium F.4.32." *Anglia* 96: 136–48.

———. 1985. "Liturgical Books in Anglo-Saxon England and their Old English Terminology." In Lapidge and Gneuss 1985 pp 91–141.

Godden, Malcolm. 1968. "The Sources for Ælfric's Homily on St. Gregory." *Anglia* 86: 79–88.

———. 1996. "Experiments in Genre: The Saints' Lives in Ælfric's *Catholic Homilies.*" In Szarmach 1996b pp 261–87.

Godman, Peter. 1982. *Alcuin. The Bishops, Kings and Saints of York.* Oxford.

Goffart, Walter. 1967. "Le Mans, St. Scholastica, and the Literary Tradition of the Translation of St. Benedict." *Revue Bénédictine* 77: 107–41.

———. 1988. *Narrators of Barbarian History (A.D. 550–800). Jordanes, Gregory of Tours, Bede, and Paul the Deacon.* Princeton.

Gonser, Paul, ed. 1909. *Das angelsächsische Prosa-Leben des heiligen Guthlac.* Heidelberg.

Gonsette, M. 1933. "Les directeurs spirituels de Demetriade." *Nouvelle revue théologique* 60: 783–801.

Goodwin, Charles W. 1851. *The Anglo-Saxon Legends of St. Andrew and St. Veronica.* Cambridge.

Gradon, P. O. E., ed. 1958. *Cynewulf's Elene.* London. Reprint, Exeter, 1977.

Graesse, T., ed. 1890. *Jacobi a Voragine legenda aurea vulgo historia Lombardica dicta.* 3rd ed. Dresden and Leipzig. Reprint, Osnabrück, 1969.

Gransden, Antonia. 1974. *Historical Writing in England c.550 to c.1307.* Ithaca, N.Y.

———. 1982. "Baldwin, Abbot of Bury St Edmunds, 1065–1097." In *Proceedings of the Battle Conference on Anglo-Norman Studies IV, 1981*, ed. R. Allen Brown, 65–76 and 187–95. Woodbridge, Suff., and Totowa, N.J.

———. 1985. "The Legends and Traditions Concerning the Origins of the Abbey of Bury St Edmunds." *English Historical Review* 100: 1–24.

———. 1995. "Abbo of Fleury's *Passio Sancti Edmundi.*" *Revue Bénédictine* 105: 20–78.

Grant, Judith. 1978. "A New *Passio Beati Edmundi Regis [et] Martyris.*" *Mediaeval Studies* 40: 81–95.

Grant, Raymond S., ed. 1982. *Three Homilies from Cambridge, Corpus Christi College, 41*. Ottawa.

Greenfield, Stanley B., and Fred C. Robinson. 1980. *A Bibliography of Publications on Old English Literature to the End of 1972*. Toronto.

Greenwell, W., ed. 1853. *The Pontifical of Egbert, Archbishop of York, A.D. 732–766*. Durham.

Grégoire, H., and P. Orgels. 1954. "S. Galicanus, consul et martyr dans le passion des SS. Jean et Paul et sa vision 'constantinienne' du crucifié." *Byzantion* 24: 579–605.

———. 1957. "S. Gallicanus et S. Hilarinus." *Studi byzantini e neoellenici* 9: 171–75.

Grégoire, R. 1986. *Manuale d'Agiologia*. S. Silvestro.

Grelier, A. 1952. *S. Symphorien d'Autun*. Challans.

———. 1953. *Le culte de saint Symphorien d'Autun en France et à l'étranger*. Paris.

Grennen, Joseph. 1966. "St. Cecilia's 'Chemical Wedding': The Unity of the Canterbury Tales, Fragment VIII." *Journal of English and Germanic Philology* 65: 466–81.

Grierson, Philip. 1940. "Les livres de l'abbé Seiwold de Bath." *Revue Bénédictine* 52: 96–116.

Griffe, E. 1964–66. *La Gaule Chrétienne à l'Epoque Romaine*. Rev. ed. 3 vols. Paris.

———. 1965. "L'hagiographie gauloise au Ve s. La vie de saint Germain d'Auxerre." *Bulletin de littérature ecclésiastique* 66: 289–94.

Grisar, H. 1887. "Die Gregorbiographie des Paulus Diakonus in ihrer ursprünglichen Gestalt nach italienischen Handschriften." *Zeitschrift für katholische Theologie* 11: 158–73.

Grosjean, P. 1928. "Catalogus codicum hagiographicorum latinorum bibliothecarum Dubliniensium." *Analecta Bollandiana* 46: 81–148.

———. 1938. "Vita S. Roberti Nova Monasterii in Anglia abbatis." *Analecta Bollandiana* 56: 334–60.

———. 1940. "De codice hagiographico Gothano." *Analecta Bollandiana* 58: 90–103; "Codicis Gothani appendix," 177–204.

———. 1942. Review of Huisman 1939. *Analecta Bollandiana* 60: 258–61.

Guerreau-Jalabert, Anita, ed. 1982. *Abbon de Fleury. Questions grammaticales*. Paris.

Gwara, Scott. 1992. "Three Acrostic Poems by Abbo of Fleury." *The Journal of Medieval Latin* 2: 203–35.

Halkin, F. 1965. *Euphémie de Chalcedoine. Légendes Byzantines*. Brussels.

———. 1980a. "La passion ancienne des saints Julien et Basilisse (BHG 970–971)." *Analecta Bollandiana* 98: 241–96.

———. 1980b. Review of Gelasio Zucconi, *La fanciulla del lago, Cristina di Bolsena v. e m.* (1979). *Analecta Bollandiana* 98: 447.

———. 1983. "La légende grècque de saint Érasme." *Analecta Bollandiana* 101: 5–17.

———. 1985. Review of Vogt 1984. *Analecta Bollandiana* 103: 180.

Hall, Thomas N. 1996. "The *Euangelium Nichodemi* and *Vindicta saluatoris* in Anglo-Saxon England." In Cross 1996 pp 36–81.

Hamilton, B. 1965. "The Monastery of S. Alessio and the Religious and Intellectual Renaissance of Tenth Century Rome." *Studies in Medieval and Renaissance History* 2: 265–310.

Handley, Rima. 1974. "British Museum MS. Cotton Vespasian D. xiv." *Notes and Queries*, n.s., 21: 243–50.

Harnack, A. 1878. *Die Zeit des Ignatius*. Leipzig.

Hart, Cyril R. 1953. *Early Charters of Barking Abbey*. Colchester.

———. 1966. *The Early Charters of Eastern England*. Leicester.

———. 1970. "The Ramsey *Computus.*" *English Historical Review* 85: 29–44.

———. 1982. "Byrhtferth's Northumbrian Chronicle." *English Historical Review* 97: 558–82.

Hartzell, K. D. 1975. "A St. Albans Miscellany in New York." *Mittellateinisches Jahrbuch* 10: 20–61.

Haubrichs, Wolfgang. 1979. *Georgslied und Georgslegende im frühen Mittelalter. Text und Rekonstruktion.* Königstein.

Hauck, Karl, and Hubert Mordek, eds. 1978. *Geschichtsschreibung und geistiges Leben im Mittelalter: Festschrift fur Heinz Löwe zum 65. Geburtstag.* Cologne.

Hayes, R. J. 1965. *Manuscript Sources for the History of Irish Civilization.* 11 vols. Boston.

———. 1979. *Manuscript Sources for the History of Irish Civilization. First Supplement.* Boston.

Hayward, Paul A. 1993. "The Idea of Innocent Martyrdom in Late Tenth- and Eleventh-Century English Hagiology." In *Martyrs and Martyrologies*, ed. Diana Wood, 81–92. Oxford.

Head, Thomas. 1990. *Hagiography and the Cult of the Saints: The Diocese of Orléans, 800–1200.* Cambridge.

Hearne, Thomas, ed. 1723. *Hemingi Chartularium ecclesiae Wigorniensis.* 2 vols. Oxford.

Heffernan, Thomas J. 1973. "An Analysis of the Narrative Motifs in the Legend of St Eustace." *Medievalia et Humanistica*, n.s., 6: 63–89.

———. 1988. *Sacred Biography: Saints and Their Biographers in the Middle Ages.* Oxford.

Heinzelmann, Martin. 1979. *Translationsberichte und andere Quellen des Reliquienkultes.* Turnhout.

———, ed. 1992. *Manuscrits hagiographiques et travail des hagiographes.* Sigmaringen.

Henel, H. 1934. "Ein altenglisches Prosa-Menologium." In *Studien zum altenglischen Computus*, 71–91. Leipzig.

Heningham, E. K. 1946. "The Genuineness of the *Vita Æduuardi Regis.*" *Speculum* 21: 419–56.

———. 1975. "The Literary Unity, the Date, and the Purpose of Lady Edith's Book: 'The Life of King Edward Who Rests at Westminster.'" *Albion* 7: 24–40.
Herbst, Lenore, ed. 1976. *Die altenglische Margareten-Legende in der Hs. Cotton Tiberius A. III.* Göttingen.
Hervey, Francis. 1907. *Corolla Sancti Eadmundi. The Garland of Saint Edmund King and Martyr.* London.
Hesbert, Réné-Jean. 1935. *Antiphonale missarum sextuplex.* Brussels.
———. 1963–79. *Corpus antiphonalium officii.* 6 vols. Rome.
Heuclin, J. 1986. "Eremitisme et évangelisation: recherche sur l'influence de la Vie d'Abraham de Quiduna dans les courants eremitiques de la Gaule du Nord." *Revue du Nord* 68: 415–32.
Hicks, C., ed. 1992. *England in the Eleventh Century: Proceedings of the 1990 Harlaxton Symposium.* Stamford, Lincs.
Hill, Joyce. 1985–86. "Saint George before the Conquest." *Report of the Society of the Friends of St George and the Descendants of the Knights of the Garter (Windsor Castle)* 6/7: 284–95.
———. 1989. "Ælfric, Gelasius and St. George." *Mediaevalia* 11 (for 1985): 1–17.
———. 1996. "The Dissemination of Ælfric's *Lives of Saints*: A Preliminary Survey." In Szarmach 1996b pp 235–59.
Hill, Thomas D. 1979. "The Middle Way: *Idel-wuldor* and *Egesa* in the Old English *Guthlac A*." *Review of English Studies* 30: 182–87.
———. 1996. "*Imago Dei*: Genre, Symbolism, and Anglo-Saxon Hagiography." In Szarmach 1996b pp 35–50.
Hillgarth, J. N., ed. 1986. *Christianity and Paganism, 350–750. The Conversion of Western Europe.* Rev. ed. Philadelphia.
Hoare, D. C. 1978. "The Cult of St Denys in England in the Middle Ages." M.Phil. thesis, Nottingham University.
Hoare, Frederick R. 1954. *The Western Fathers.* New York.
Hofstetter, Walter. 1987. *Winchester und der spätaltenglische Sprachgebrauch: Untersuchungen zur geographischen und zeitlichen Verbreitung altenglischer Synonyme.* Munich.

Hohler, Christopher. 1967. "The Proper Office of St. Nicholas and Related Matters With Reference to a Recent Book." *Medium Ævum* 36: 40–48.

———. 1995. "Theodore and the Liturgy." In Lapidge 1995 pp 222–35.

Holder, A. 1889. *Inventio Sanctae Crucis*. Leipzig.

———. 1914. *Die Reichenauer Handschriften* 2. Leipzig. Reprint, *Die Handschriften der Badischen Landesbibliothek in Karlsruhe* 6, Wiesbaden, 1971.

Hollis, Stephanie. 1992. *Anglo-Saxon Women and the Church: Sharing a Common Fate*. Woodbridge, Suff., and Rochester, N.Y.

———. 1993. "The OE *Mildrith* Fragments and their Social Context." *Old English Newsletter* 26/3 (Spring): A-53 (abstract of conference paper).

Homeyer, H., ed. 1970. *Hrotsvithae opera*. Munich/Paderborn/Vienna.

Horstmann, Carl, ed. 1901. *Nova Legenda Anglie*. 2 vols. Oxford.

Hourlier, Jacques. 1971. "Sainte Scholastique au Mans." *Revue historique et archéologique du Maine*, 2nd ser., 51: 41–58.

———. 1979a. "La translation d'après les sources narratives." *Studia Monastica* 21: 213–39.

———. 1979b. "La translation de Sainte Scholastique au Mans." *Studia Monastica* 21: 313–33.

Houwen, L. A. J. R., and A. A. MacDonald, eds. 1996. *Beda Venerabilis: Historian, Monk & Northumbrian*. Groningen.

Hübener, W., ed. 1974. *Die Alemannen in der Frühzeit*. Bühl.

Huber, P. M. 1902–05. *Beitrag zur Visionsliteratur und Siebenschläferlegende des Mittelalters, 1. Teil*. Landschut.

———. 1906. "Zur Georgslegende." In *Festschrift zum XII Allgemeinen Deutschen Neuphilologentage in München, Pfingsten 1906*, ed. E. Stollreither, 175–235. Erlangen.

———. 1910. *Die Wanderlegende von den Siebenschläfern: eine literargeschichtliche Untersuchung*. Leipzig.

Huisman, A. Z. 1939. *Die Verehrung des heiligen Pancratius in West- und Mitteleuropa*. Haarlem.

I Deug-Su. 1983. *L'opera agiografica di Alcuino*. Spoleto.

Irvine, Martin. 1986. "Anglo-Saxon Literary Theory Exemplified in Old English Poems: Interpreting the Cross in *The Dream of the Rood* and *Elene*." *Style* 20: 157–81.

Irvine, Susan E. 1990. "Bones of Contention: The Context of Ælfric's Homily on St Vincent." *Anglo-Saxon England* 19: 117–32.

Jaager, W., ed. 1935. *Bedas Metrische Vita Sancti Cuthberti*. Leipzig.

Jackson, Peter. 1992. "The *Vitas Patrum* in Eleventh-Century Worcester." In Hicks 1992 pp 119–34.

———. 2000. "Ælfric and the Purpose of Christian Marriage: A Reconsideration of the *Life of Æthelthryth*, Lines 120–30." *Anglo-Saxon England* 29: 235–60.

Jackson, Peter, and Michael Lapidge. 1996. "The Contents of the Cotton-Corpus Legendary." In Szarmach 1996b pp 131–46.

James, M. R. 1907. *A Descriptive Catalogue of the Manuscripts in the Library of Trinity Hall*. Cambridge.

———. 1911–12. *A Descriptive Catalogue of the Manuscripts in the Library of Corpus Christi College Cambridge*. 2 vols. Cambridge.

———. 1913. *A Descriptive Catalogue of the Manuscripts in the Library of St. John's College, Cambridge*. Cambridge.

———. 1917. "Two Lives of St. Ethelbert, King and Martyr." *English Historical Review* 32: 214–44.

———. 1924. *The Apocryphal New Testament*. Oxford. Corrected ed., 1953.

———. 1926. *Lists of Manuscripts formerly in Peterborough Abbey Library*. Oxford.

James, M. R., and Claude Jenkins. 1930–32. *A Descriptive Catalogue of the Manuscripts in the Library of Lambeth Palace*. 5 pts. Cambridge. Reprint, one volume, 1955.

Jameson, Harriet C. 1943. "The Latin MS Tradition of Jerome's *Vita Sancti Malchi*." In Oldfather 1943 pp 449–511.

Jansen, A. M. 1996. "Bede and the Legends of St Oswald." In Houwen and MacDonald 1996 pp 167–78.

John, Eric. 1983. "The World of Abbot Ælfric." In *Ideal and Reality in Frankish and Anglo-Saxon Society*, ed. Patrick Wormald, 300–16. Oxford.

Johnson, Richard. 1998a. "Archangel in the Margins: St. Michael in the Homilies of Cambridge, Corpus Christi College MS 41." *Traditio* 53: 63–91.

———. 1998b. "The Cult of St. Michael the Archangel in Anglo-Saxon England." Ph.D. diss., Northwestern University.

Johnson-South, T. 1990. "The *Historia de Sancto Cuthberto*: A New Edition and Translation, with Discussions of the Surviving Manuscripts, the Text, and Northumbrian Estate Structure." Ph.D. diss., Cornell University.

———. 1991. "Competition for King Alfred's Aura in the Last Century of Anglo-Saxon England." *Albion* 23: 613–26.

Jones, Charles W. 1939. *Bedae Pseudepigrapha: Scientific Writings Falsely Attributed to Bede*. Ithaca.

———. 1963. *The Saint Nicholas Liturgy and its Literary Relationships. With an Essay on Music by Gilbert Reaney*. Berkeley and Los Angeles.

———. 1978. *Saint Nicholas of Myra, Bari, and Manhattan. Biography of a Legend*. Chicago.

Jones, E. C. 1914. *Saint Gilles, essai d'histoire littéraire*. Paris.

Jonsson, Ritva. 1968. *Historia. Études sur la genèse des offices versifiés*. Lund.

Jubaru, Florian. 1907. *Sainte Agnès*. Paris.

Julien, Pierre, and François Ledermann, eds. 1985. *Saint Côme et Saint Damien. Culte et Iconographie*. Zurich.

Karlin-Hayter, P. 1991. "Passio of the XL Martyrs of Sebasteia. The Greek Tradition: The Earliest Account (BHG 1201)." *Analecta Bollandiana* 109: 249–304.

Karras, Ruth M. 1990. "Holy Harlots: Prostitute Saints in Medieval Legend." *Journal of the History of Sexuality* 1: 3–32.

Kellner, A. 1930. "Der hl. Agapitus von Praeneste, Patron des Stiftes Kremsmünster." *Studien und Mitteilungen zur Geschichte des Benediktiner-Ordens und seiner Zweige* 17: 404–32.

Kelly, J. N. D. 1986. *Oxford Dictionary of the Popes*. Oxford/New York.

Kennedy, V. L. 1938. *The Saints of the Canon of the Mass*. Rome.

Ker, N. R. 1964. *Medieval Libraries of Great Britain: A List of Surviving Books.* 2nd ed. London.

———. 1985. "A Palimpsest in the National Library of Scotland: Early Fragments of Augustine 'De Trinitate,' the 'Passio S. Laurentii' and Other Texts." In *Books, Collectors, and Libraries: Studies in the Medieval Heritage,* ed. Andrew G. Watson, 121–30. London and Ronceverte, W. Va. Reprint from *Edinburgh Bibliographical Society Transactions* 3 (1948–55): 169–78.

Ker, N. R., and A. J. Piper. 1969–92. *Medieval Manuscripts in British Libraries.* 4 vols. Oxford.

Kesters, H. 1955. "Notes sur la Vita Trudonis." *Bulletin de la Société d'art et d'histoire du diocèse de Liège* 39: 187–204.

Keynes, Simon. 1980. *The Diplomas of Æthelred 'the Unready' 978–1016.* Cambridge.

Keynes, Simon, and Michael Lapidge. 1983. *Alfred the Great.* Harmondsworth.

Kiernan, Kevin S. 1981. *Beowulf and the Beowulf Manuscript.* New Brunswick, N.J.

Kim, H. C., ed. 1973. *The Gospel of Nicodemus / Gesta Salvatoris.* Toronto.

Kirby, D. P. 1983. "Bede, Eddius Stephanius, and the *Life of Wilfrid*." *English Historical Review* 98: 101–14.

Kirsch, J. P. 1910. *Die heilige Cecilia in der römischen Kirche des Altertums.* Paderborn.

Knowles, David. 1963. *The Monastic Order in England; a History of Its Development from the Times of St. Dunstan to the Fourth Lateran Council, 940–1216.* 2nd ed. Cambridge.

Knowles, David, and R. N. Hadcock. 1972. *Medieval Religious Houses: England and Wales.* Rev. ed. London and New York.

Kotzor, Günter, ed. 1981. *Das altenglische Martyrologium.* 2 vols. Munich.

———. 1986. "The Latin Tradition of Martyrologies and the *Old English Martyrology*." In Szarmach 1986 pp 301–33.

Kozik, Ignatius S., ed. 1968. *The First Desert Hero: St. Jerome's Vita Pauli.* Mount Vernon, N.Y.

Krusch, Bruno. 1891. "Die älteste Vita Leudegarii." *Neues Archiv* 16: 565–96.

———. 1904. "Die älteste Vita Richarii." *Neues Archiv* 29: 15–48.

Künstle, C. 1910. *Vita S. Genouefae*. Leipzig.

Künstle, K. 1894. *Hagiographische Studien über die Passio Felicitatis*. Paderborn.

Kunze, K. 1969. *Studien zur Legende der heiligen Maria Aegyptiaca im deutschen Sprachgebiet*. Berlin.

Kupper, J. L. 1984. "Saint Lambert: de l'histoire à la légende." *Revue d'histoire ecclésiastique* 79: 5–49.

Kurtz, B. P. 1926. "From St Antony to St Guthlac." *University of California Publications in Modern Philology* 12, 2: 104–46.

Laehr, G. 1928. "Briefe und Prologe des Bibliothekars Anastasius." *Neues Archiv* 47: 416–68.

Laistner, M. L. W. 1924. "Abbo of St-Germain-des-Prés." *Archivum Latinitatis Medii Aevi* 1: 27–31.

Lambert, B. 1969–72. *Bibliotheca Hieronymiana Manuscripta*. 4 vols. in 7. Steenbrugge.

Lamirande, Emilien. 1983. *Paulin de Milan et la "Vita Ambrosii." Aspectes de la religion sous le Bas-Empire*. Montreal and Paris.

Lanzoni, Francisco. 1903. "La 'Passio S. Sabini' o 'Savini.'" *Römische Quartalschrift* 17: 1–26.

———. 1923. *Le origini delle diocesi antiche d'Italia*. Vatican.

Lapidge, Michael. 1975a. "The Hermeneutic Style in Tenth-Century Anglo-Latin Literature." *Anglo-Saxon England* 4: 67–111.

———. 1975b. "Some Remnants of Bede's Lost *Liber Epigrammatum*." *English Historical Review* 90: 798–820.

———. 1977. "The Medieval Hagiography of St. Ecgwine." *Vale of Evesham Historical Society Research Papers* 6: 77–93.

———. 1978. "Dominic of Evesham, 'Vita S. Ecgwini episcopi et confessoris.'" *Analecta Bollandiana* 96: 65–104.

———. 1979. "Byrhtferth and the Vita S. Ecgwini." *Mediaeval Studies* 41: 331–53.

———. 1982a. "Byrhtferth of Ramsey and the Early Sections of the *Historia Regum* Attributed to Symeon of Durham." *Anglo-Saxon England* 10: 97–122.

———. 1982b. "The Cult of St Indract at Glastonbury." In *Ireland in Early Medieval Europe*, ed. Dorothy Whitelock and Rosamund McKitterick, 179–212. Cambridge.

———. 1983. "Ealdred of York and MS. Cotton Vitellius E. XII." *Yorkshire Archaeological Journal* 55: 11–25.

———. 1984. "A Tenth-Century Metrical Calendar from Ramsey." *Revue Bénédictine* 94: 326–69.

———, ed. 1985. *Vita Primi Sancti Neoti*. In Dumville and Lapidge 1985 pp lxxv–cxxiv and 111–42.

———. 1986a. "The School of Theodore and Hadrian." *Anglo-Saxon England* 15: 45–72.

———. 1986b. "The Anglo-Latin Background." In Stanley B. Greenfield and Daniel G. Calder, *A New Critical History of Old English Literature*, 5–37. New York.

———. 1987. "The Lost 'Passio Metrica S. Dionysii' by Hilduin of Saint-Denis." *Mittellateinisches Jahrbuch* 22: 56–79.

———. 1988a. "A Frankish Scholar in Tenth-Century England: Frithegod of Canterbury/Fredegaud of Brioude." *Anglo-Saxon England* 17: 45–65.

———. 1988b. "Æthelwold and the *Vita S. Eustachii*." In *Scire litteras: Forschungen zum mittelalterlichen Geistesleben*, ed. Sigrid Krämer and Michael Bernhard, 255–65. Munich.

———. 1989a. "Bede's Metrical *Vita S. Cuthberti*." In Bonner et al. 1989 pp 77–93.

———. 1989b. "Ædiluulf and the School of York." In *Lateinische Kultur im VIII. Jahrhundert. Traube-Gedenkschrift*, ed. Albert Lehner and Walter Berschin, 161–78. St. Ottilien.

———. 1989/90. "Tenth-Century Anglo-Latin Verse Hagiography." *Mittellateinisches Jahrbuch* 24/25: 249–60.

———. 1991a. "The Saintly Life in Anglo-Saxon England." In *The Cambridge Companion to Old English Literature*, ed. Malcolm Godden and Michael Lapidge, 243–63. Cambridge.

———. 1991b. "The *Life of St Oswald.*" In *The Battle of Maldon AD 991*, ed. D. G. Scragg, 51–58. Oxford/Cambridge, Mass.

———. 1992a. "Abbot Germanus, Winchcombe, Ramsey and the Cambridge Psalter." In *Words, Texts and Manuscripts. Studies in Anglo-Saxon Culture Presented to Helmut Gneuss on the Occasion of his Sixty-Fifth Birthday*, ed. Michael Korhammer, 99–129. Cambridge and Rochester, N.Y.

———. 1992b. "B. and the Vita S. Dunstani." In Ramsay and Sparks 1992a pp 247–59.

———, ed. 1995. *Archbishop Theodore. Commemorative Studies on his Life and Influence.* Cambridge.

———. 1996a. "Byrhtferth and Oswald." In Brooks and Cubitt 1996 pp 64–83.

———. 1996b. "Ælfric's Sanctorale." In Szarmach 1996b pp 115–29.

———. Forthcoming a. *The Cult of St. Swithun.* Winchester Studies 4.2.

———, ed. Forthcoming b. *Byrhtferth of Ramsey: The Lives of Oswald and Ecgwine.* Oxford.

Lapidge, Michael, and Peter S. Baker. 1997. "More Acrostic Verse by Abbo of Fleury." *The Journal of Medieval Latin* 7: 1–27.

Lapidge, Michael, and Helmut Gneuss, eds. 1985. *Learning and Literature in Anglo-Saxon England.* Cambridge.

Lapidge, Michael, and Michael Herren. 1979. *Aldhelm the Prose Works.* Cambridge and Totowa, N.J.

Lapidge, Michael, and Richard Sharpe. 1985. *A Bibliography of Celtic-Latin Literature 400-1200.* Dublin.

Lapidge, Michael, and Michael Winterbottom, eds. 1991. *Wulfstan of Winchester: The Life of St Æthelwold.* Oxford.

———, eds. Forthcoming. *The Early Lives of St Dunstan.* Oxford.

Laporte, J.-P. 1990. "La reine Balthilde ou l'ascension sociale d'une esclave." In Duby 1990 pp 147–67.

Laugardière, Maurice de. 1951. *L'Église de Bourges avant Charlemagne.* Paris/Bourges.

Lazzari, Loredana. 1997. *La versione anglo-sassone della 'Vita Sancti Nicolai' (Cambridge, Corpus Christi College, MS 303).* Rome.

Lazzarini, Pietro. 1968. *Storia della chiesa di Lucca*. Lucca.
Lazzeri, C. 1938. *La donazione del tribuno romano Zenobio al vescovo d'Arezzo San Donato*. Arezzo.
Le Bourdellès, Hubert. 1993. "Vie de St Josse avec commentaire historique et spirituel." *Studi Medievali*, 3rd ser., 34: 861–958.
Lechat, R. 1929. "Catalogus codicum hagiographicorum bibliothecae publicae Audomaropolitanae." *Analecta Bollandiana* 47: 241–306.
Lecler, P. 1988. "Antoine et Paul: metamorphose d'un héros." In *Jérôme entre l'occident et l'orient*, ed. Yves-Marie Duval, 257–65. Paris.
Lecouteux, C. 1981. "Les Cynocéphales. Étude d'une tradition teratologique de l'antiquité au XIIe siècle." *Cahiers de Civilisation Médiévale* 24: 117–28.
Le Duc, Gwenaël. 1979. *Vie de Saint Malo, évèque d'Alet: Version écrite par le diacre Bili*. Rennes.
Lee, S. D. 1995. "Ælfric's Treatment of Source Material in his Homily on the Books of the Maccabees." *Bulletin of the John Rylands University Library of Manchester* 77/3: 165–76.
Leinbaugh, Theodore H. 1985. "St Christopher and the *Old English Martyrology*: Latin Sources and the Phrase *hwaes gneaðes*." *Notes and Queries*, n.s., 32: 434–37.
Lendinara, Patrizia. 1986. "The Third Book of the *Bella Parisiacae Urbis* by Abbo of Saint-Germain-des-Prés and Its Old English Gloss." *Anglo-Saxon England* 15: 73–89. Reprint, Lendinara 1999 pp 157–75.
———. 1988. "Una nuova versione del *Quid suum virtutis*." *Schede Medievali* 14–15: 15–28.
———. 1990. "The Abbo Glossary in London, British Library, Cotton Domitian i." *Anglo-Saxon England* 19: 133–49.
———. 1996. "L'attività glossatoria del periodo anglosassone." In *Les manuscrits des lexiques et glossaires de l'antiquité tardive à la fin du moyen âge: actes du colloque international organisé par le "Ettore Majorana Centre for Scientific Culture" (Erice 23–30 septembre 1994)*, ed. Jacqueline Hamesse, 615–55. Louvain-la-neuve. Reprint, Lendinara 1999 pp 289–328.
———. 1999. *Anglo-Saxon Glosses and Glossaries*. Aldershot, Hamp.

Leonardi, Claudio. 1977. "La 'Vita Gregorii' di Giovanni Diacono." *Renovatio* 12: 51–66.
Levison, Wilhelm, ed. 1905. *Vitae Sancti Bonifatii Archiepiscopi Moguntini*. Hannover and Leipzig.
———. 1924. "Konstantinische Schenkung und Silvesterlegende." In *Miscellanea Francesco Ehrle. Scritti di Storia e Paleografia*, vol. 2: *Per la Storia di Roma*, 159–247. Vatican.
———. 1927. "Das Werden der Ursula-Legende." *Bonner Jahrbücher* 132: 1–162.
———. 1940. "An Eighth-Century Poem on St. Ninian." *Antiquity* 14: 280–91.
———. 1941. "St. Alban and St. Albans." *Antiquity* 15: 337–59.
———. 1946. *England and the Continent in the Eighth Century*. Oxford.
Levy, Carlos, P. Petitmengin, J.-P. Rothschild, and J. Y. Tilliette, eds. 1981. "La réfection latine B." In Petitmengin 1981–84 1.217–49.
Lexikon des Mittelalters. 1977– . Ed. Robert Auty et al. Munich/Zürich.
Liebermann, Felix. 1889. *Die Heiligen Englands, lateinische und angelsächsische*. Hannover.
———. 1900. "Zum Old English martyrology." *Archiv* 105: 86–87.
Limone, Oronzo. 1978. "La vita di Gregorio Magno dell'Anonimo di Whitby." *Studi Medievali*, 3rd ser., 19: 37–67.
———. 1988. "La tradizione manoscritta della 'Vita Gregorii Magni' di Paolo Diacono (B.H.L. 3639). Censimento dei testimoni." *Studi Medievali*, 3rd ser., 29: 887–953.
Llewellyn, P. A. B. 1976. "The Passion of St. Alexander and His Companions, St. Hermes and St. Quirinus: A Suggested Date and Author." *Vetera Christianorum* 13: 289–96.
Loenertz, Raymond J. 1951. "La légende parisienne de S. Denys l'Aréopagite: sa genèse et son premier témoin." *Analecta Bollandiana* 69: 217–37.
———. 1975. "Actus Sylvestri. Genèse d'une légende." *Revue d'histoire ecclésiastique* 70: 426–39.
Löfstedt, Bengt. 1990. "Zur 'Vita Gregorii Magni' des Mönchs von Whitby." *Orpheus*, n.s., 11: 331–36.

Loomis, C. G. 1931. "Further Sources of Ælfric's Saints' Lives." *Harvard Studies and Notes in Philology and Literature* 13: 1–8.
———. 1932. "The Growth of the Saint Edmund Legend." *Harvard Studies and Notes in Philology and Literature* 14: 83–113.
———. 1933. "St Edmund and the Lodbrok (Lothbroc) Legend." *Harvard Studies and Notes in Philology and Literature* 15: 1–23.
Loomis, L. H. 1949. "The Saint Mercurius Legend in Medieval England and in Norse Saga." In *Philologica: The Malone Anniversary Studies*, ed. T. A. Kirby and H. B. Woolf, 132–43. Baltimore.
Lot, Ferdinand. 1907. *Mélanges d'Histoire bretonne (VIe–XIe siècle)*. Paris.
Love, Rosalind, ed. 1996. *Three Eleventh-Century Anglo-Latin Saints' Lives*. Oxford.
Lowe, E. A. 1960. *English Uncial*. Oxford.
Luiselli Fadda, Anna M. 1982. "Un esempio di diffrazione nella tradizione manoscritta diretta e indiretta della 'Vita Sancti Aegidii abbatis.'" *AION-Filologia germanica* 25: 57–60.
———. 1982–83. "La versione anglosassone della *Vita sancti Aegidi abbatis*." *Romanobarbarica* 7: 273–352.
———. 1984. "Sulle traduzioni altomedievali di testi agiografici: considerazioni in margine alla versione anglosassone della 'Vita' di sant'Egidio abbate." In *Culto dei santi, instituzioni e società in età pre-industriale*, ed. Sofia Boesch Gajano and Lucia Sebastiani, 2 vols., 1.13–35. L'Aquila.
Luscombe, D. 1985. "The Reception of the Writings of Denis the Pseudo-Areopagite into England." In *Tradition and Change: Essays in Honour of Marjorie Chibnall*, ed. D. Greenaway, C. Holdsworth, and J. Sayers, 115–43. Cambridge.
———. 1988. "Denis the Pseudo-Areopagite in the Middle Ages from Hilduin to Lorenzo Valla." In *Fälschungen im Mittelalter: internationaler Kongress der Monumenta Germaniae Historica, München, 16.–19. September 1986*, 6 vols., 1.133–52. Hannover.
Lysaght, G. 1984. "Fleury and Saint Benedict: Monastery and Patron Saint (640–877)." Ph.D. diss., Oxford University.

MacQueen, J. 1961. *St Nynia*. Edinburgh/London.
——. 1962. "History and Miracle. Stories in the Biography of Nynia." *Innes Review* 13: 115–29.
——. 1980. "Myths and Legends of Lowland Scottish Saints." *Scottish Studies* 24: 1–21.
Macray, W. D. 1883. *Catalogi codicum manuscriptorum Bibliothecae Bodleianae pars nona*. Oxford.
Magennis, Hugh. 1985a. "On the Sources of the Non-Ælfrician Lives in the Old English *Lives of the Saints*, with Reference to the Cotton-Corpus Legendary." *Notes and Queries*, n.s., 32: 292–99.
——. 1985b. "Style and Method in the Old English Version of the Legend of the Seven Sleepers." *English Studies* 66: 285–95.
——. 1986. "Contrasting Features in the Non-Ælfrician Lives in the Old English *Lives of the Saints*." *Anglia* 104: 316–48.
——. 1991. "The Anonymous Old English Legend of the Seven Sleepers and its Latin Source." *Leeds Studies in English*, n.s., 22: 43–56.
——, ed. 1994. *The Anonymous Old English Legend of the Seven Sleepers*. Durham.
——. 1996a. "Ælfric and the Legend of the Seven Sleepers." In Szarmach 1996b pp 317–31.
——. 1996b. "St Mary of Egypt and Ælfric: Unlikely Bedfellows in Cotton Julius E. vii?" In Poppe and Ross 1996 pp 99–112.
Maior, G., ed. 1544. *Vitae patrum in usum ministrorum verbi*. Wittenburg.
Mallardo, Domenico. 1940. "S. Gennaro e compagni nei più antichi testi e monumenti." *Rendiconti della Reale Accademia di archeologia, lettere, e belle arti*, n.s., 20: 163–267.
Manitius, Max. 1911–31. *Geschichte der lateinischen Literatur des Mittelalters*. 3 vols. Munich.
Mara, Grazia M., ed. 1964. *I martiri della Via Salaria*. Rome.
Mason, Emma. 1984. "St. Wulfstan's Staff: A Legend and Its Uses." *Medium Ævum* 53: 157–79.
——. 1986. "Change and Continuity in Eleventh-Century Mercia: The Experience of St Wulfstan of Worcester." In *Anglo-Norman Studies*

VIII: Proceedings of the Battle Conference 1985, 154–76. Woodbridge, Suff.
———. 1990. *St Wulfstan of Worcester c.1008–1095*. Oxford/Cambridge, Mass.
Massmann, H. F. 1843. *Sanct Alexius Leben in acht gereimten mittelhochdeutschen Behandlungen*. Quedlinburg/Leipzig.
Matthews, P. M. 1966. "The Old English Life of Saint Pantaleon." M.A. thesis, University College, London.
Matzke, R. 1902. "Contributions to the History of the Legend of Saint George, with Special Reference to the Sources of the French, German, and Anglo-Saxon Metrical Versions I." *PMLA* 17: 464–535.
McClure, Judith. 1984. "Bede and the Life of Ceolfrid." *Peritia* 3: 71–84.
McClure, Robert. 1971. "Studies in the Text of the Vita Ambrosii of Paulinus of Milan." Ph.D. diss., University of California at Los Angeles.
———. 1973. "The Pellegrino Edition of the 'Vita Ambrosii' of Paulinus of Milan." *Symbolae Osloenses* 48: 117–30.
McCrea, C. 1976. "Ælfric: His Sources and Style in the Lives of Æthelthryth, Oswald, and Edmund." Ph.D. diss., Fordham University.
McGurk, Patrick. 1974. "Computus Helperici: Its Transmission in England in the Eleventh and Twelfth Centuries." *Medium Ævum* 43: 1–5.
McNamara, Jo Ann, and John E. Halborg (with E. Gordon Whatley). 1992. *Sainted Women of the Dark Ages*. Durham, N.C.
McNamara, Martin. 1975. *The Apocrypha in the Irish Church*. Dublin.
Meaney, Audrey L. 1985. "Ælfric's Use of His Sources in His Homily on Auguries." *English Studies* 66: 477–95.
Meersseman, G. G. 1963. *Kritische Glossen op de Griekse Theophilus-Legende (7 eeuw) en haar latijnse Vertaling (9 eeuw)*. Brussels.
Meinardus, Otto. 1965. *Christian Egypt Ancient and Modern*. Cairo.
Meisen, Karl. 1931. *Nikolauskult und Nikolausbrauch im Abendlande*. Düsseldorf.
Meyer, H. B., et al., eds. 1983– . *Gottesdienst der Kirche. Handbuch der Liturgiewissenschaft*. Regensburg.
Meyer, Wilhelm. 1904. "Die Legende des heiligen Albanus des Protomartyr Angliae in Texten vor Beda." *Abhandlungen der königlichen*

Gesellschaft der Wissenschaften zu Göttingen. Philologisch-historische Klasse, Neue Folge (= Nachrichten Göttingen) 8, 1: 35–62.

Meyvaert, Paul. 1992. "A New Perspective on the Ruthwell Cross: Ecclesia and the Vita Monastica." In *The Ruthwell Cross: Papers from the Colloquium Sponsored by the Index of Christian Art, Princeton University, 8 December 1987*, ed. Brendan Cassidy, 95–166. Princeton.

Miedema, R. 1913. *De heilige Menas*. Rotterdam.

Mierow, C. C. 1945. "The 35 Vatican MSS of St. Jerome's Vita Malchi. Prolegomena to an Edition." *Speculum* 20: 468–81.

———. 1946. "Sancti Eusebii Hieronymi vita Malchi monachi captivi." In *Classical Essays presented to J. A. Kleist*, ed. R. E. Arnold, 31–60. St. Louis.

Millinger, Susan. 1979. "Liturgical Devotion in the Vita Oswaldi." In *Saints, Scholars, and Heroes: Studies in Medieval Culture in Honor of Charles W. Jones*, ed. Margot King and Wesley Stevens, 2 vols., 2.239–64. Collegeville, Minn.

Mölk, U. 1976. "Die älteste lateinische Alexiusvita (9/10 Jahrhundert). Kritischer Text und Kommentar." *Romanistisches Jahrbuch* 27: 293–315.

Moloney, Bernadette. 1982. "Another Look at Ælfric's Use of Discourse in Some Saints' Lives." *English Studies* 63: 13–19.

———. 1984. "Be Godes Halgum: Ælfric's Hagiography and the Cult of the Saints in England in the Tenth Century." In *Learning and Literature in Medieval and Renaissance England. Essays Presented to Fitzroy Pyle*, ed. J. Scattergood, 25–40. Dublin.

Mombritius, B. N.d.(?1480). *Sanctuarium seu vitae sanctorum*. 2 vols. Milan.

———. 1910. *Sanctuarium seu vitae sanctorum*. 2nd ed. 2 vols. Paris.

Monteverdi, A. 1908–11. "I testi della leggenda di S. Eustachio." *Studi Medievali* 3: 393–498.

Moreau, E. de. 1949. "La *Vita Amandi Prima* et les fondations monastiques de S. Amand." *Analecta Bollandiana* 67: 447–64.

Moretus Plantin, H. 1948. "Les passions de Saint Denys." In *Mélanges offerts au R. P. Ferdinand Cavallera*, 215–30. Toulouse.

———. 1953. *Les passions de saint Lucien et leurs derivés céphalophoriques*. Namur/Louvain/Paris.
Morini, Carla. 1988. "I Manoscritti Inglesi e Scandinavi della Passio di S. Agata." In D'Arrigo 1988 1.379–87.
———. 1990. "Pascasio, il fidanzato di Lucia: il reflesso di una 'varia lectio' nella S. Lucia di Ælfric." *Le Forme e la Storia*, n.s., 2: 315–23.
———. 1991a. "Le Fonti della *Passio S. Agathae*." *AION-Filologia germanica* 30–31 (for 1987–88): 83–94.
———. 1991b. "Una redazione sconosciuta della Passio S. Agathæ: Ms. Auxerre, Bibl. Mun., 127 (s. XII in.), f. 17^r–19^r." *Analecta Bollandiana* 109: 305–30.
———, ed. 1993. *La passione di S. Agata di Ælfric di Eynsham*. Alessandria.
Morris, John. 1980. *Nennius, British History and the Welsh Annals*. London/Chichester/Totowa, N.J.
Morris, Lewis. 1892. *A Vision of Saints*. London.
Morrisey, Jane. 1990. "Scholastica and Benedict: A Picnic, a Paradigm." In *Equally in God's Image. Women in the Middle Ages*, ed. Julia B. Holloway, Constance S. Wright, and Joan Bechthold, 251–57. New York.
Mosford, S. 1988. "A Critical Edition of the Vita Gregorii Magni by an Anonymous Member of the Community of Whitby." Ph.D. diss., Oxford University.
Mostert, Marco. 1986. "Le séjour d'Abbon de Fleury à Ramsey." *Bibliothèque de l'École des Chartes* 144: 199–208.
———. 1987. *The Political Theology of Abbo of Fleury: A Study of the Ideas about Society and Law of the Tenth-Century Monastic Reform Movement*. Hilversum.
Mostert, W., and E. Stengel. 1895. *L'Ystoyre et la vie de Saint Genis*. Marburg.
Moulinier, Jean-Claude. 1991. "Saint Victor de Marseille. De l'histoire à la légende." In *L'abbaye parisienne de Saint-Victor au moyen âge*, ed. Jean Longère, 13–21. Paris and Turnhout.
Müller, L. C. 1835. *Collectanea Anglo-Saxonica Maximam Partem nunc Primum Edita et Vocabulario Illustrata*. Copenhagen.

Musurillo, Herbert, ed. 1972. *The Acts of the Christian Martyrs*. Oxford.
Mynors, R. A. B. 1939. *Durham Cathedral Manuscripts to the End of the Twelfth Century*. Oxford.
Mynors, R. A. B., and Rodney Thomson. 1993. *Catalogue of the Manuscripts of Hereford Cathedral Library*. Woodbridge, Suff./Rochester, N.Y.
Napier, Arthur, ed. 1883. *Wulfstan. Sammlung der ihm zugeschriebenen Homilien nebst Untersuchungen über ihre Echtheit. I. Text und Varianten*. Berlin.
Narbey, C. A. 1899–1912. *Supplément aux Acta Sanctorum pour des vies de saints de l'époque mérovingienne*. 2 vols. Paris.
Nau, F. 1903. "Histoire de Thaïs. Publication des textes grecs inédits et de divers autres textes et versions." *Annales du Musée Guimet* 30, 3: 51–112.
Needham, Geoffrey I. 1958. "Additions and Alterations in Cotton MS. Julius E VII." *Review of English Studies*, n.s., 9: 160–64.
——, ed. 1966. *Ælfric. Lives of Three English Saints*. London.
Nelson, Janet. 1978. "Queens as Jezebels." In *Medieval Women*, ed. Derek Baker, 31–77. London.
Nicholls, A. 1991. "Ælfric's 'Life of Vincent': The Question of Form and Function." *Notes and Queries*, n.s., 38: 445–50.
——. 1993. "The Corpus of Prose Saints' Lives and Hagiographic Pieces in Old English and Its Manuscript Distribution." Part 1. *Reading Medieval Studies* 19: 73–96.
——. 1994. "The Corpus of Prose Saints' Lives and Hagiographic Pieces in Old English and its Manuscript Distribution." Part 2. *Reading Medieval Studies* 20: 51–87.
Nitti di Vito, Francesco. 1937. "Leggenda del monaco Niceforo." *Japigia*, n.s., 8: 336–66.
Noret, Jacques. 1972. "La Passion des SS. Chrysanthus et Daria: fut-elle écrit en Grec ou Latin?" *Analecta Bollandiana* 90: 109–17.
O'Neill, Patrick P. 1991. "Latin Learning at Winchester in the Early Eleventh Century: The Evidence of the Lambeth Psalter." *Anglo-Saxon England* 20: 143–66.

Ó Riain, Pádraig. 1986. "Les vies de S. Fursey: les sources irlandaises." *Revue du Nord* 68: 405–13.
———. 1990. "Sainte Brigitte, paradigme de l'abbesse celtique?" In Duby 1990 pp 27–32.
Oldfather, W. A., et al. 1943. *Studies in the Text Tradition of St. Jerome's Vitae Patrum.* Urbana, Ill.
Olsen, Alexandra Hennessey. 1981. *Guthlac of Croyland: A Study of Heroic Hagiography.* Washington, D.C.
———. 1983. "Old English Poetry and Latin Prose." *Classica et Mediaevalia* 34: 273–82.
Önnerfors, Ute. 1985. *Abbo von Saint-Germain-des-Prés, 22 Predigten: kritische Ausgabe und Kommentar.* Frankfurt am Main, Bern, New York, and Nancy.
Orchard, Andy. 1994. *The Poetic Art of Aldhelm.* Cambridge.
———. 1995. *Pride and Prodigies: Studies in the Monsters of the Beowulf-Manuscript.* Woodbridge, Suff.
Ortenberg, Veronica. 1992. *The English Church and the Continent in the Tenth and Eleventh Centuries.* Oxford.
Otranto, Giorgio. 1981. "Il 'Liber de apparitione' e il culto di san Michele sul Gargano nella documentazione liturgica alto medievale." *Vetera Christianorum* 18: 423–42.
———. 1988. "Per una metodologia della ricerca storico-agiografica, il santuario micaelico del Gargano tra Bizantini e Langobardi." *Vetera Christianorum* 25: 381–405.
Ott, J. Heinrich. 1892. *Über die Quellen der Heiligenleben in Ælfrics Lives of the Saints I.* Halle.
Pächt, Otto, C. R. Dodwell, and F. Wormald. 1960. *The St. Albans Psalter.* London.
Paredi, A. 1937. *I prefazi ambrosiani.* Milan.
———, ed. 1964. *Vita e meriti di S. Ambrogio. Testo inedito del secolo nono.* Milan.
Paschini, P. 1919. *La passio delle martiri sabine Vittoria ed Anatolia.* Vatican.
Patch, Howard R. 1919. "Liturgical Influence in the *Dream of the Rood.*" *PMLA* 34: 233–57.

Patlagean, Evelyne. 1976. "L'histoire de la femme déguisée en moine et l'évolution de la sainteté féminine à Byzance." *Studi Medievali*, 3rd ser., 17: 597–623.

Peebles, R. J. 1911. *The Legend of Longinus in Ecclesiastical Tradition and English Literature*. Bryn Mawr, Pa.

Peeters, P. 1943. "S. Simeon Stylites et ses premiers biographes." *Analecta Bollandiana* 61: 29–71.

Pellegrin, Élisabeth. 1984–85. "La tradition des textes classiques latins à l'abbaye de Fleury-sur-Loire." *Revue d'Histoire des Textes* 14–15: 155–67.

Pellegrino, M., ed. 1955. *Possidio. Vita di S. Agostino*. Alba.

———. 1956. "Intorno al testo della vita di S. Agostino scritta da Possidio." *Revue des Études Augustiniennes* 2: 195–229.

———, ed. 1961. *Paulinus Mediolanus Vita S. Ambrosii*. Rome.

Pesci, B. 1945. "Il Culto di S. Sebastiano a Roma nell'antichita e nel medioevo." *Antonianum* 20: 177–200.

Petitmengin, P., ed. 1981–84. *Pélagie la Pénitente: metamorphoses d'une légende*. 2 vols. Paris.

Petitmengin, P., et al. 1977. "Les Vies latines de sainte Pélagie. Inventaire des textes publiés et inédites." *Recherches Augustiniennes* 12: 279–305.

———. 1980. "Les Vies latines de sainte Pélagie, II. Complément à l'inventaire et classement des manuscrits du texte B." *Recherches Augustiniennes* 15: 265–304.

Pfaff, Richard W., ed. 1995. *The Liturgical Books of Anglo-Saxon England*. Old English Newsletter *Subsidia* 23. Kalamazoo, Mich.

———. 1998. "The Hagiographical Peculiarity of Martha's Companion(s)." In *Liturgical Calendars, Saints, and Services in Medieval England*, chapter IV. Aldershot.

Pheifer, J. D. 1987. "Early Anglo-Saxon Glossaries and the School of Canterbury." *Anglo-Saxon England* 16: 17–44.

Philippart, Guy. 1977. *Les légendiers latins et autres manuscrits hagiographiques*. Turnhout.

———. 1992. "Le manuscrit hagiographique latin comme gisement documentaire." In Heinzelmann 1992 pp 17–48.

———, ed. 1994– . *Hagiographies. Histoire internationale de la littérature hagiographique, latine et vernaculaire, des origines à 1550.* 2 vols. Turnhout.
Picard, Barbara. 1980. *Das altenglische Aegidiusleben in Ms CCCC 303. Textedition mit Einleitung und Anmerkungen.* Freiburg.
Pickles, J. D. 1971. "Studies in the Prose Texts of the *Beowulf* Manuscript." Ph.D. diss., Cambridge University.
Pietri, C. 1976. *Roma christiana. Recherches sur l'église de Rome, son organisation, sa politique, son ideologique de Miltiade à Sixte III (311–440).* Rome.
Pigoulewsky, N. 1927–28. "Le martyre de Saint Cyriaque de Jérusalem." *Revue de l'Orient Chrétien* 26: 305–56.
Platts, C. 1921–23. "The Martyrdom of Indract." *Notes and Queries for Somerset and Dorset* 17: 18–23.
Plummer, Charles, ed. 1892–99. *Two of the Saxon Chronicles Parallel.* 2 vols. Oxford.
———. 1896. *Venerabilis Baedae Opera Historica.* 2 vols. Oxford.
Pohlkamp, Wilhelm. 1983. "Tradition und Topographie: Papst Silvester I (314–335) und der Drache vom Forum Romanum." *Römische Quartalschrift* 78: 1–100.
———. 1984. "Kaiser Konstantin, der heidnische und der christliche Kult in der Actus Silvestri." *Frühmittelalterliche Studien* 18: 357–400.
Poncelet, A. 1901. "Carmen de S. Quintino." *Analecta Bollandiana* 20: 5–44.
———. 1903. "La plus ancienne vie de S. Riquier." *Analecta Bollandiana* 22: 173–94.
———. 1909. *Catalogus codicum hagiographicorum bibliothecarum Romanarum praeter quam Vaticanae.* Brussels.
———. 1910. *Catalogus codicum hagiographicorum latinorum bibliothecae Vaticanae.* Brussels.
———. 1912. "Les biographes de Ste Amalberge." *Analecta Bollandiana* 31: 401–09.
Poppe, Erich, and Bianca Ross, eds. 1996. *The Legend of Mary of Egypt in Medieval Insular Hagiography.* Dublin/Portland, Ore.

Poulin, Joseph-Claude. 1977–78. "S. Léger d'Autun et ses premiers biographes." *Bulletin de la Société des Antiquaires de l'Ouest (Poitiers)* 14: 167–200.

———. 1983. "Les cinq premières Vitae de Sainte Geneviève, Analyse formelle, comparaison, essai de datation." *Journal des Savants*: 81–150.

———. 1990. "Les dossiers de S. Magloire de Dol et de S. Malo d'Alet (province de Bretagne)." *Francia* 17, 1: 159–209.

Poulin, Joseph-Claude, and Martin Heinzelmann. 1986. *Les vies anciennes de Sainte Geneviève de Paris. Études critiques*. Paris.

Prago, G. 1938. "La Legenda di S. Ilarione a Epidauro in Adelmo scrittore anglosassone." *Archivio storico di Dalmazia* 25: 83–91.

Price, Jocelyn G. 1985. "The Virgin and the Dragon: The Demonology of Seinte Margarete." In Collins, Price, and Hamer 1985 pp 337–57.

———. 1986. "The *Liflade of Seinte Iuliene* and Hagiographic Convention." *Medievalia et Humanistica*, n.s., 14: 37–58.

Prinz, Friedrich. 1981. "Die heilige Afra." *Bayerische Vorgeschichtsblätter* 46: 211–16.

Proud, Joanna. 1997. "The Old English Life of Saint Pantaleon and Its Manuscript Context." *Bulletin of the John Rylands University Library of Manchester* 79/3: 119–32.

Pulsiano, Phillip. Forthcoming. "The Old English Life of Saint Pantaleon." In *Via Crucis: Essays on Sources and Ideas in Memory of J. E. Cross*, ed. Thomas N. Hall, Charles D. Wright, and Thomas D. Hill. Morgantown, W. Va.

Quasten, J. 1950–66. *Patrology*. 3 vols. Utrecht.

Quentin, H. 1908. *Les martyrologes historiques du Moyen Age*. Paris.

Ramsay, Nigel, and Margaret Sparks, eds. 1992a. *St Dunstan: His Life, Times, and Cult*. Woodbridge, Suff., and Rochester, N.Y.

———. 1992b. "The Cult of St Dunstan at Christ Church, Canterbury." In Ramsay and Sparks 1992a pp 311–24.

Rau, Reinhold, ed. 1968. *Briefe des Bonifatius. Willibalds Leben des Bonifatius nebst einigen zeitgenössischen Dokumenten*. Darmstadt.

Reames, Sherry L. 1980. "The Cecilia Legend as Chaucer Inherited It and Retold It: The Disappearance of an Augustinian Ideal." *Speculum* 55: 38–57.

Rees, B. R. 1991. *The Letters of Pelagius and His Followers*. Woodbridge, Suff.

Reitzenstein, R. 1913. *Die Nachrichten über den Tod Cyprians ein philologischer Beitrag zur Geschichte der Märtyrerliteratur*. Heidelberg.

———. 1919. "Bemerkungen zur Märtyrerliteratur. II. Nachträge zu den Akten Cyprians." In *Nachrichten von der königlichen Gesellschaft der Wissenschaften zu Göttingen, Philologisch-historische Klasse*, 177–219. Göttingen.

Renaud, G. 1978. "Saint Aignan et sa légende, les 'vies' et les 'miracles.'" *Bulletin de la Société archéologique et historique de l'Orléanais* 49: 83–109.

———. 1979. "La dévotion à Saint Aignan." *Bulletin de la Société archéologique et historique de l'Orléanais* 50: 17–32.

Rice, Eugene F. 1985. *Saint Jerome in the Renaissance*. Baltimore.

Richards, Mary P. 1981. "The Medieval Hagiography of St. Neot." *Analecta Bollandiana* 99: 259–78.

Richter, Michael. 1984. "Bede's *Angli*: Angles or English?" *Peritia* 3: 99–114.

Ridyard, Susan J. 1988. *The Royal Saints of Anglo-Saxon England: A Study of West Saxon and East Anglian Cults*. Cambridge.

Rigg, A. G. 1996. "A Latin Poem on St. Hilda and Whitby Abbey." *Journal of Medieval Latin* 6: 12–43.

Roberts, Jane. 1967. "Guthlac: An Edition of the Old English Prose Life, Together With the Poems in the Exeter Book." Ph.D. diss., Oxford University.

———. 1970. "An Inventory of Early Guthlac Materials." *Mediaeval Studies* 32: 193–233.

———, ed. 1979. *The Guthlac Poems of the Exeter Book*. Oxford.

———. 1986. "The Old English Prose Translation of Felix's *Vita sancti Guthlaci*." In Szarmach 1986 pp 363–79.

———. 1988. "Guthlac A: Sources and Source Hunting." In *Medieval Studies Presented to George Kane*, ed. E. D. Kennedy, R. Waldron, and J. S. Wittig, 1–18. Wolfeboro, N.H.

———. 2000. "The English Saints Remembered in Old English Anonymous Homilies." In Szarmach 2000 pp 433–61.

Rollason, David W. 1978. "Lists of Saints' Resting Places in Anglo-Saxon England." *Anglo-Saxon England* 7: 61–93.

———. 1981. *The Search for St. Wigstan, Prince-Martyr of the Kingdom of Mercia*. Leicester.

———. 1982. *The Mildrith Legend: A Study in Early Medieval Hagiography in England*. Leicester.

———. 1983. "The Cults of Murdered Royal Saints in Anglo-Saxon England." *Anglo-Saxon England* 11 (for 1982): 1–22.

———. 1985. "The Miracles of St Benedict: A Window on Early Medieval France." In *Studies in Medieval History Presented to R.H.C. Davis*, ed. Henry Mayr-Harting and R. I. Moore, 73–90. London.

———. 1986. "Goscelin of Canterbury's Account of the Translation and Miracles of St. Mildrith." *Mediaeval Studies* 48: 139–210.

———. 1989a. *Saints and Relics in Anglo-Saxon England*. Oxford.

———. 1989b. "Saint Cuthbert and Wessex: The Evidence of Cambridge, Corpus Christi College 183." In Bonner et al. 1989 pp 413–24.

———. 1992. "The Concept of Sanctity in the Early Lives of St Dunstan." In Ramsay and Sparks 1992a pp 261–72.

Römer, F. 1972. *Die handschriftliche Überlieferung der Werke des Heiligen Augustinus*, ed. M. Oberleitner, F. Römer, et al., 1969– . Vol. II/1: *Grossbritannien und Irland: Werkverzeichnis*. Vol. II/2: *Grossbritannien und Irland: Verzeichnis nach Bibliotheken*. Vienna.

Rordorf, W. 1984. "Sainte Thècle dans la tradition hagiographique occidentale." *Augustinianum* 24: 73–81.

Rosenfeld, H.-F. 1937. *Der heilige Christophorus, Seine Verehrung und seine Legende. Eine Untersuchung zur Kultgeographie und Legendenbildung des Mittelalters*. Helsingfors.

Rosenthal, Constance. 1936. *The "Vitae Patrum" in Old and Middle English Literature*. Philadelphia.

Rossi-Passavanti, E. 1932–33. *Interamna Nahars: storia di Terni dalle origini al medio-evo*. 2 vols. Rome.
Rosweyde, H., ed. 1615. *Vitae patrum*. Antwerp.
Roy, Gopa. 1992. "A Virgin Acts Manfully: Ælfric's *Life of St Eugenia* and the Latin Versions." *Leeds Studies in English* 23: 1–27.
Rubenstein, Jay. 1995. "The Life and Writings of Osbern of Canterbury." In *Canterbury and the Norman Conquest. Churches, Saints, and Scholars 1066–1109*, ed. Richard Eales and Richard Sharpe, 27–40. London and Rio Grande.
Ruggiero, F. 1991. *Atti dei Martiri Scilitani*. Rome.
Ruggini, Lelia Cracco. 1992. "Roma alla confluenza di due tradizione agiografiche. Pancrazio martire 'urbano' e Pancrazio vescovo-martire di Taormina." *Rivista di storia e letteratura religiosa* 28: 35–52.
Ruinart, Theodoric, ed. 1859. *Acta martyrum*. Ratisbon.
Ruiz Bueno, Daniel. 1968. *Actas de los mártires: texto bilingüe*. 2nd ed. Madrid.
Rushing, Dorothy B. 1949. "The St. Michael legends in Anglo-Saxon and Middle English." Ph.D. diss., University of Illinois, Champaign/Urbana.
Russell, Norman, and Benedicta Ward. 1980. *The Lives of the Desert Fathers. The Historia Monachorum in Aegypto*. London and Oxford.
Salmon, P. 1944–53. *Le lectionnaire de Luxeuil (Paris, ms. lat. 9427)*. Vol. 1: *Edition et étude comparative*. Vol. 2: *Étude paléographique et liturgique*. Rome/Vatican City.
Sanders, G. 1982. "Le remaniement Carolingien de la 'Vita Balthildis' Merovingienne." *Analecta Bollandiana* 100: 411–28.
Sauvage, P. 1885. "Sancti Swithuni Wint. ep. translatio et miracula auctore Lantfredo monacho wintoniensi." *Analecta Bollandiana* 4: 367–410.
Saxer, Victor. 1959. *Le culte de Marie-Madeleine en Occident des origines à la fin du moyen age*. Paris.
———. 1979. *Saints anciens d'Afrique du Nord*. Vatican.
———. 1986. "Santa Maria Maddalena dalla storia evangelica alla legenda e all'arte." In *La Maddalena tra sacra e profana*, ed. Marilena Mosco, 24–28. Florence.

———. 1989a. "Les Origines du culte de Sainte Marie Madeleine en Occident." In *Marie Madeleine dans la mystique, les arts et les lettres*, ed. E. Duperray, 34–47. Paris.

———. 1989b. "La passion primitive de S. Vincent diacre dans la première moitié du Ve siècle. Essai de réconstitution." *Revue des Études Augustiniennes* 35: 275–97.

———. 1994. "Afrique latin." In Philippart 1994– 1.25–95.

———. 1995. "La *Vita Cypriani* de Pontius, 'Première Biographie Chretienne.' " In *Orbis Romanus Christianusque ab Diocletiani aetate usque ad Heraclium. Travaux sur l'Antiquité Tardive rassemblés autour des recherches de Noël Duval*, ed. T. Baratte, J.-P. Caillet, and C. Metzger, 237–51. Paris.

Saxl, Fritz, and Hans Meier. 1953. *Verzeichnis astrologischer und mythologischer illustrierten Handschriften des lateinischen Mittelalters. III. Handschriften in englischen Bibliotheken.* 2 vols. London.

Scarfe, Norman. 1984. "The Historical Evidence Reviewed." In West, Scarfe, and Cramp 1984 pp 293–300.

Schatkin, Margaret. 1974. "The Maccabean Martyrs." *Vigiliae Christianae* 28: 97–113.

Scheibelreiter, George. 1989. "Audoin von Rouen. Ein Versuch über den Charakter des 7. Jahrhunderts." In *La Neustrie. Les pays du Nord de la Loire de 650 à 850*, ed. Hartmut Atsma, 195–216. Sigmaringen.

Schelstrate, Emmanuel. 1692–97. *Antiquitas ecclesiae dissertationibus monimentis ac notis illustrata.* 2 vols. Rome.

Schipper, William. 1986. "The Normans and the Old English Lives of Saint Giles and Saint Nicholas." *International Christian University Language Research Bulletin* (Mitaka, Tokyo) 1: 97–108.

Schneider, A. M. 1951. "Sankt Euphemia und das Konzil von Chalkedon." In *Das Konzil von Chalkedon: Geschichte und Gegenwart*, ed. A. Grillmeier and H. Bacht, 3 vols., 1.291–302. Würzburg.

Schoenen, H. G., ed. 1981. *Der Mann mit den glühenden Kohlen. Leben und Verehrung des heiligen Briktius. L'homme aux charbons ardents. Vie et culte de Saint Brice. Edition bilingue pro manuscripto.* Rommerskirchen-Oekoven.

Schrier, O. J. 1984. "À propos d'une donnée negligée sur la mort de Ste Euphémie." *Analecta Bollandiana* 102: 329–53.

Schulz-Flügel, E., ed. 1990. *Tyrannus Rufinus, Historia monachorum*. Berlin/New York.

Schupp, Franz, ed. 1997. *Abbo von Fleury. De Syllogismis Hypotheticis*. Leiden.

Scott, John, ed. 1981. *The Early History of Glastonbury. An Edition, Translation and Study of William of Malmesbury's De antiquitate Glastonie ecclesie*. Woodbridge, Suff.

Scragg, D. G. 1979. "The Corpus of Vernacular Homilies and Prose Saints' Lives Before Ælfric." *Anglo-Saxon England* 8: 223–77.

———. 1996. "The Corpus of Anonymous Lives and Their Manuscript Context." In Szarmach 1996b pp 209–30.

Scragg, D. G., and Elaine Treharne. 1996. "Appendix: The Three Anonymous Lives in Cambridge, Corpus Christi College 303." In Szarmach 1996b pp 231–34.

Sharpe, Richard. 1990a. "Some Medieval *miracula* from Llandegly (Lambeth Palace Library, MS. 94 fols. 153v–155r)." *Bulletin of the Board of Celtic Studies* 37: 166–76.

———. 1990b. "Goscelin's St. Augustine and St. Mildreth: Hagiography and Liturgy in Context." *Journal of Theological Studies* 41: 502–16.

Siegmund, A. 1949. *Die Überlieferung der griechischen christlichen Literatur in der lateinischen Kirche bis zum zwölften Jahrhundert*. Munich.

Silk, Edmund T. 1935. *Saeculi noni auctoris in Boetii Consolationem philosophiae commentarius*. Rome.

Simonetti, M. 1956. "Una redazione poco conosciuta della passione di S. Vincenzo." *Rivista di archeologia cristiana* 32: 219–41.

Simpson, Luisella. 1989. "The King Alfred/St Cuthbert Episode in the *Historia de sancto Cuthberto*: Its Significance for Mid-Tenth-Century English History." In Bonner et al. 1989 pp 397–411.

Sims-Williams, P. 1990. *Religion and Literature in Western England 600–800*. Cambridge.

Sisam, Kenneth. 1953. *Studies in the History of Old English Literature*. Oxford.

Smetana, C. 1959. "Ælfric and the Early Medieval Homiliary." *Traditio* 15: 163–204.

Smith, John, ed. 1722. *Historia Ecclesiastica Gentis Anglorum*. Cambridge.

Smith, Julia H. 1990. "Oral and Written: Saints, Miracles, and Relics in Britanny c. 850–1250." *Speculum* 65: 309–43.

Smith, Thomas. 1984. *Catalogue of the Manuscripts in the Cottonian Library 1696 (Catalogus librorum manuscriptorum bibliothecae Cottonianae)*. Ed. C. G. C. Tite. Cambridge.

Southern, R. W. 1963. *Anselm and His Biographer: A Study of Monastic Life and Thought 1059 – c. 1130*. Cambridge.

Spiegel, Gabrielle M. 1983. "The Cult of St Denis and Capetian Kingship." In *Saints and Their Cults*, ed. Stephen Wilson, 141–68. Cambridge.

Sprissler, M. 1966. *Das rhythmische Gedicht 'Pater deus unigenite' (11 Jh.) und das altfranzösische Alexiuslied*. Münster.

Stancliffe, Clare. 1989. "Cuthbert and the Polarity between Pastor and Solitary." In Bonner et al. 1989 pp 21–44.

Stenton, F. M. 1971. *Anglo-Saxon England*. 3rd ed. Oxford.

Stevens, W. O. 1904. *The Cross in the Life and Literature of the Anglo-Saxons*. New York. Reprint (with new preface by Thomas D. Hill), *The Anglo-Saxon Cross*, Hamden, Conn., 1977.

Stevenson, Jane. 1996a. "The Holy Sinner: The Life of Mary of Egypt." In Poppe and Ross 1996 pp 19–50.

———. 1996b. "*Vitae Sanctae Mariae Egiptiacae*." In Poppe and Ross 1996 pp 51–98.

Stevenson, Joseph. 1853. *The Church Historians of England*. 5 vols. in 8. Vol. 1, pt. 2: *The Historical Works of the Venerable Beda*. London.

Stevenson, W. H., ed. 1904. *Asser's Life of King Alfred*. Oxford.

Stevenson, W. H., and W. M. Lindsay. 1929. *Early Scholastic Colloquies*. Oxford.

Stokes, Whitley. 1891. "Glosses from Turin and Rome." *Beiträge zur Kunde der indogermanischen Sprachen* 17: 133–46.

Strecker, K. 1922. "Zu den Quellen für das Leben des hl. Ninian." *Neues Archiv* 43: 1–26.

Strunk, William, ed. 1904. *Juliana*. Boston.
Surius, Laurentius. 1570–75. *De probatis sanctorum historiis*. 6 vols. Cologne. 2nd ed., 7 vols., Cologne, 1576–81.
———. 1875–80. *Historiae, seu Vitae sanctorum, juxta optimam Coloniensem editionem*. 13 vols. Turin.
Swanton, Michael J. 1975. "A Fragmentary Life of St Mildred and other Kentish Royal Saints." *Archaeologia Cantiana* 91: 15–27.
———. 1984. *Three Lives of the Last Englishmen*. New York.
Symons, Thomas, and Sigrid Spath, eds. 1984. *Regularis Concordia Anglicae Nationis*. In Corpus Consuetudinum Monasticarum. 7/3. Consuetudinum saeculi X/XI/XIII. Monumenta non-Cluniaciensia, ed. Kassius Hallinger. Siegburg.
Szarmach, Paul E., ed. 1981. *Vercelli Homilies IX–XXIII*. Toronto.
———, ed. 1986. *Studies in Earlier Old English Prose*. Albany, N.Y.
———. 1987. "Ælfric, the Prose Vision, and the Dream of the Rood." In *Studies in Honour of René Derolez*, ed. A. M. Simon-Vandenbergen, 592–602. Ghent.
———. 1990. "Ælfric's Women Saints: Eugenia." In *New Readings on Women in Old English Literature*, ed. Helen Damico and Alexandra H. Olsen, 146–57. Bloomington/Indianapolis.
———. 1996a. "Saint Euphrosyne: Holy Transvestite." In Szarmach 1996b pp 353–65.
———, ed. 1996b. *Holy Men and Holy Women: Old English Prose Saints' Lives and Their Contexts*. Albany, N.Y.
———, ed. (with the assistance of Deborah A. Oosterhouse). 2000. *Old English Prose: Basic Readings*. New York and London.
Tait, James, ed. 1920–23. *The Chartulary or Register of the Abbey of St. Werburgh, Chester*. 2 pts. Manchester.
Teviotdale, Elizabeth Cover. 1991. "The Cotton Troper (London, British Library, Cotton MS Caligula A.xiv, ff. 1–36): A Study of an Illustrated English Troper of the Eleventh Century." Ph.D. diss., University of North Carolina.
Thacker, Alan T. 1976. "The Social and Continental Background to Early Anglo-Saxon Hagiography." Ph.D. diss., Oxford University.

———. 1985. "Kings, Saints, and Monasteries in Pre-Viking Mercia." *Midland History* 10: 1–25.

———. 1988. "Æthelwold and Abingdon." In Yorke 1988 pp 43–64.

———. 1989. "Lindisfarne and the Origins of the Cult of St Cuthbert." In Bonner et al. 1989 pp 103–22.

———. 1992. "Cults at Canterbury: Relics and Reform under Dunstan and His Successors." In Ramsay and Sparks 1992 pp 221–46.

———. 1996a. "Saint-making and Relic Collecting by Oswald and His Communities." In Brooks and Cubbitt 1996 pp 243–68.

———. 1996b. "Membra Disjecta: The Division of the Body and the Diffusion of the Cult." In *Oswald: Northumbrian King to European Saint*, ed. Clare Stancliffe and Eric Cambridge, 97–127. Stamford, Lincs.

———. 1998. "Memorializing Gregory the Great: The Origin and Transmission of a Papal Cult in the Seventh and Early Eighth Centuries." *Early Medieval Europe* 7: 59–84.

Thiébaux, Marcelle. 1992. "'Dameisele' Ursula: Traditions of Hagiography and History in the *South English Legendary* and Lazamon's *Brut*." In *The South English Legendary. A Critical Assessment*, ed. Klaus P. Jankofsky, 29–48. Tübingen.

Thomas, Charles. 1981. *Christianity in Roman Britain to AD 500*. Berkeley and Los Angeles.

Thompson, E. A. 1984. *Saint Germanus of Auxerre and the End of Roman Britain*. Woodbridge, Suff.

Thompson, Pauline A. 1996. "St Æthelthryth: The Making of History from Hagiography." In *Studies in English Language and Literature: 'Doubt Wisely' Papers in Honour of E.G. Stanley*, ed. M. J. Toswell and E. M. Tyler, 475–92. London/New York.

Thomson, Rodney. 1974. "Two Versions of a Saint's Life from St Edmund's Abbey: Changing Currents in a XIIth Century Monastic Style." *Revue Bénédictine* 84: 383–408.

———. 1987. *William of Malmesbury*. Woodbridge, Suff.

Thomson, Ron B. 1985. "Two Astronomical Tractates of Abbo of Fleury." In *The Light of Nature: Essays in the History and Philosophy of Science presented to A. C. Crombie*, ed. J. D. North and J. J. Roche, 113–33. Dordrecht, Boston, Lancaster.

———. 1988. "Further Astronomical Material of Abbo of Fleury." *Mediaeval Studies* 50: 671–73.

Thorndike, Lynn, and Pearl Kibre. 1963. *A Catalogue of Incipits of Mediaeval Scientific Writings in Latin*. Rev. ed. London.

Thorpe, Benjamin, ed. 1844–46. *The Sermones Catholici or Homilies of Ælfric*. 2 vols. London.

———. 1865. *Diplomatarium Anglicum Ævi Saxonici*. London.

Tischendorf, C. 1876. *Evangelia apocrypha*. 2nd ed. Leipzig.

Townsend, David. 1989. "An Eleventh-Century Life of Birinus of Wessex." *Analecta Bollandiana* 107: 129–59.

———. 1991. "Anglo-Latin Hagiography and the Norman Transition." *Exemplaria* 3: 385–433.

Treharne, Elaine M., ed. 1997. *The Old English Life of St Nicholas with the Old English Life of St Giles*. Leeds.

Trier, J. 1924. *Der heilige Jodocus*. Breslau.

Tristram, Hildegard L. C. 1970. *Vier altenglische Predigten aus der heterodoxen Tradition*. Freiburg.

Tritz, H. 1952. "Die hagiographischen Quellen zur Geschichte Papst Leo IX. Eine Untersuchungs- und Entstehungsgeschichte." *Studi Gregoriani* 4: 191–364.

Ughelli, F. 1644–62. *Italia sacra sive de episcopis Italiae*. 9 vols. Rome. 2nd ed., ed. N. Colet, 10 vols., Venice, 1717–22.

Usener, H., ed. 1886. "Acta S. Marinae et S. Christophori." In *Festschrift zur fünften Säcularfeier der Carl-Ruprechts-Universität zu Heildelberg überreicht von Rector und Senat der Rheinischen Friedrich-Wilhelms-Universität*, 1–80. Bonn.

Ussher [Usserius], James, ed. 1647. *Appendix Ignatiana*. [2 parts in 1]. [Part 2:] *Ignatii Antiocheni et Polycarpi Smyrnensis episcopi martyria*. London.

Vaccari, A. 1958. "Le antiche vite di S. Girolamo." In *Scritti di erudizione e di filologia*, vol. 2: *Per la storia de testo e dell'esegesi biblica*, 31–51. Rome.

Van Beek, C. J. M. J., ed. 1936. *Passio Sanctarum Perpetuae et Felicitatis: Latine et Graece*. Nijmegen.
Van Dam, Raymond. 1988. *Gregory of Tours: Glory of the Martyrs*. Liverpool.
Vanderlinden, S. 1946. "Revelatio Sancti Stephani (B.H.L. 7850–6)." *Revue des Études Byzantines* 4: 178–217.
Van der Straeten, Joseph. 1960. "La passion de S. Patrocle de Troyes. Ses sources." *Analecta Bollandiana* 78: 145–53.
———. 1961. "Les Actes des Martyrs d'Aurélien en Bourgogne. Étude littéraire." *Analecta Bollandiana* 79: 114–44; "Le texte de Farfa," pp 447–68.
———. 1962. "Actes des Martyrs d'Aurélien en Gaule." *Analecta Bollandiana* 80: 116–41.
———. 1971. *Les manuscrits hagiographiques d'Arras et de Boulogne-sur-Mer*. Brussels.
———. 1982. *Les manuscrits hagiographiques d'Orléans, Tours et Angers*. Brussels.
Van de Vyver, A. 1935. "Les oeuvres inédites d'Abbon de Fleury." *Revue Bénédictine* 47: 127–69.
———, ed. 1966. *Abbonis Floriacensis opera inedita. I. Syllogismorum Categoricorum et Hypotheticorum Enodatio*. Brugge.
Vanmaele, Basile. 1965. *L'église Pudentienne de Rome*. Averbode.
Van Ortroy, F. 1892. "Catalogus codicum hagiographicorum latinorum Bibliothecae Ambrosianae Mediolanensis." *Analecta Bollandiana* 11: 205–368.
Varnhagen, H. 1881. "Zwei lateinische metrische Versionen der Legende von Placidius-Eustachius II. Eine Version in Hexametern." *Zeitschrift für deutsches Altertum* 25: 1–25.
Verrando, Giovanni Nino. 1982. "Le numerose recensioni della Passio Pancratii." *Vetera Christianorum* 19: 105–29.
———. 1983. "Osservazioni sulla Collocazione Cronologica degli Apocrifi Atti di Pietro dello Pseudo-Lino." *Vetera Christianorum* 20: 391–426.
———. 1984. "La *Passio Callisti* e il santuario della via Aurelia." *Mélanges d'École Français de Rome, Antiquité* 96, 2: 1039–83.

———. 1987. "Note sulle tradizione agiografiche su Processo, Martiniano e Lucina." *Vetera Christianorum* 24: 353–73.

Vezin, Jean. 1977. "Leofnoth. Un scribe anglais à Saint-Bénoit-sur-Loire." *Codices Manuscripti* 3: 109–20.

Vidier, A. 1965. *L'historiographie à Saint Benoît-sur-Loire et les miracles de Saint Benoît*. Paris.

Vieillard-Troiekouroff, M. 1976. *Les monuments réligieux de la Gaule d'après les oeuvres de Grégoire de Tours*. Paris.

Villamor, M. C. Solana. 1980. "El culto a Santo Iñes y su difusion en Occidente." *Ephemerides Liturgicae* 94: 411–30.

Violet, B. 1896. *Die Palästinischen Märtyrer des Eusebius*. Leipzig.

Vleeskruyer, Rudolf, ed. 1953. *The Life of St. Chad. An Old English Homily*. Amsterdam.

Vogt, G. 1984. *Felizitas, Martyrium und Verherrlichung der römischen Blutzeugin*. Münsterschwarzach.

Waddell, Helen. 1936. *The Desert Fathers*. London.

Waitz, G., ed. 1878. *Scriptores rerum Langobardicarum et Italicarum saec. VI–IX*. Hannover.

Wallace-Hadrill, J. M. 1983. *The Frankish Church*. Oxford.

———. 1988. *Bede's Ecclesiastical History of the English People: A Historical Commentary*. Oxford.

Ward, Benedicta. 1987. *Harlots of the Desert: A Study of Repentance in Early Monastic Sources*. Kalamazoo, Mich.

Warren, F. E., ed. 1883. *The Leofric Missal*. Oxford.

Watson, A. G. 1984. *Catalogue of Dated and Datable Manuscripts c. 435–1600 in Oxford Libraries*. 2 vols. Oxford.

Webb, J. F., and David Farmer. 1983. *The Age of Bede*. Harmondsworth.

Webber, Teresa. 1992. *Scribes and Scholars at Salisbury Cathedral c. 1075–c. 1125*. Oxford.

Weiskotten, Herbert, ed. 1919. *Sancti Augustini Vita Scripta a Possidio Episcopo*. Princeton/London.

Weismann, Werner. 1975. "Gelasinos von Helopolis, ein Schauspieler-Märtyrer." *Analecta Bollandiana* 93: 39–66.

———. 1977. "Die 'Passio Genesii mimi,' BHL 3320." *Mittellateinisches Jahrbuch* 12: 22–43.

Wendell, Barrett. 1926. *The History of the Translation of the Blessed Martyrs of Christ, Marcellinus and Peter*. Cambridge, Mass.

Wenisch, F. 1979. *Spezifisch anglisches Wortgut in den nordhumbrischen Interlinearglossierungen des Lukasevangeliums*. Heidelberg,

West, S. E., Norman Scarfe, and R. Cramp. 1984. "Iken, St Botolph and the Coming of East Anglian Christianity." *Proceedings of the Suffolk Institute of Archeology and History* 35: 279–301

Wharton, Thomas. 1691. *Anglia Sacra*. 2 vols. London.

Whatley, E. Gordon. 1981. "Vita Erkenwaldi: An Anglo-Norman's Life of an Anglo-Saxon Saint." *Manuscripta* 27: 67–81.

———, ed. 1989. *The Saint of London: The Life and Miracles of St. Erkenwald*. Binghamton, N.Y.

———. 1993. "An Early Literary Quotation from the *Inventio S.Crucis*: A Note on Baudonivia's *Vita S. Radegundis* (*BHL* 7049)." *Analecta Bollandiana* 111: 81–91.

———. 1996a. "Hagiography in England, ca. 950–1150." In Philippart 1994– 2.429–99.

———. 1996b. "An Introduction to the Study of Old English Prose Hagiography: Sources and Resources." In Szarmach 1996b pp 3–32.

———. 1997. "Lost in Translation: Omission of Episodes in Some Old English Prose Saints' Legends." *Anglo-Saxon England* 26: 187–208.

———. 2000. "Constantine the Great, the Empress Helena and the Relics of the Holy Cross." In *Medieval Hagiography: An Anthology*, ed. Thomas Head, 77–95. New York/London.

White, Carolinne. 1998. *Early Christian Lives*. Harmondsworth, Middlesex.

Whitelock, Dorothy. 1961. "The Numismatic Interest of an OE Version of the Legend of the Seven Sleepers." In *Anglo-Saxon Coins: Studies Presented to F. M. Stenton on the Occasion of his 80th Birthday, 12 May, 1960*, ed. R. H. M. Dolley, 188–94. London.

———, ed. 1963. *Sermo Lupi ad Anglos*. 3rd ed. London.

———, ed. 1967. *Sweet's Anglo-Saxon Reader in Prose and Verse*. 15th ed. Oxford. Reprint, 1988.

———. 1970. "Fact and Fiction in the Legend of St Edmund." *Proceedings of the Suffolk Institute of Archaeology* 31: 217–33.

———. 1972. "The Pre-Viking Age Church in East Anglia." *Anglo-Saxon England* 1: 1–22.

Whiting, C. E. 1936. "Bede in After History." *Transactions of the Architectural and Archaeological Society of Durham and Northumberland* 7: 178–99.

Whitney, K. P. 1984. "The Kentish Royal Saints: An Enquiry into the Facts behind the Legend." *Archaeologia Cantiana* 101: 1–21.

Wilcox, Jonathan. 1991. "The Dissemination of Wulfstan's Homilies: The Wulfstan Tradition in Eleventh-Century Vernacular Preaching." In Hicks 1992 pp 199–217.

———. 1994. "A Reluctant Translator in Late Anglo-Saxon England: Ælfric and Maccabees." *Proceedings of the Medieval Association of the Midwest* 2: 1–18.

Wilmart, A. 1934. "Un témoin Anglo-Saxon du calendrier métrique d'York." *Revue Bénédictine* 46: 41–69.

———. 1938a. "Les rédactions latines de la vie de Abraham eremite." *Revue Bénédictine* 50: 222–45.

———. 1938b. "La légende de Ste Édith en prose et vers par le moine Goscelin." *Analecta Bollandiana* 56: 5–101 and 265–307.

Wilson, R. M. 1970. *The Lost Literature of Medieval England*. 2nd ed. London.

Winterbottom, Michael, ed. 1972. *Three Lives of English Saints*. Toronto.

———. 2000. "The Earliest Life of St Dunstan." *Scripta Classica Israelitica* 19: 163–79.

Wolpers, Theodor. 1964. *Die englische Heiligenlegende des Mittelalters. Eine Formgeschichte des Legendenerzählens von der spätantiken lateinischen Tradition bis zur Mitte des 16. Jahrhunderts*. Tübingen.

Wood, Ian. 1984. "The End of Roman Britain: Continental Evidence and Parallels." In *Gildas: New Approaches*, ed. Michael Lapidge and David Dumville, 1–26. Woodbridge, Suff.

———. 1991. "Saint-Wandrille and its Hagiography." In *Church and Chronicle in the Middle Ages*, ed. Wood and G. A. Loud, 1–14. London and Rio Grande, Ohio.

———. 1994. "The Mission of Augustine of Canterbury to the English." *Speculum* 69: 1–17.

Woolf, Rosemary. 1966a. *Juliana.* 2nd ed. London. Reprint, Exeter, 1977.
———. 1966b. "Saints' Lives." In *Continuations and Beginnings,* ed. E. G. Stanley, 37–66. London.
Wormald, Francis, ed. 1934. *English Kalendars before A.D. 1100.* HBS 72. London.
Wormald, Patrick. 1976. "Bede and Benedict Biscop." In *Famulus Christi. Essays in Commemoration of the Thirteenth Centenary of the Birth of the Venerable Bede,* ed. Gerald Bonner, 141–69. London.
———. 1985. *Bede and the Conversion. The Charter Evidence.* Jarrow.
Wortley, John. 1980. "The Pseudo-Amphilochian Vita Basilii: An Apocryphal Life of Saint Basil the Great." *Florilegium* 2: 217–39.
Wright, Neil. 1995. "Alfred Burns the Cakes: The *Vita prima Sancti Neoti, telesinus,* and Juvenal." *History and Literature in Late Antiquity and the Early Medieval West: Studies in Intertextuality,* chapter XV, 1–8. Aldershot, Hants., and Brookfield, Vt.
Wright, Thomas, and J. O. Halliwell, eds. 1841–43. *Reliquae Antiquae.* 2 vols. London.
Yerkes, David. 1982. "British Library, Cotton Otho A.viii, fols. 1–6." *Old English Newsletter* 16/1: 28–29.
———, ed. 1984. *The Old English Life of Machutus.* Toronto.
———. 1986. "The Provenance of the Unique Copy of the Old English Translation of Bili, Vita Sancti Machuti." *Manuscripta* 30: 108–11.
Yorke, Barbara. 1985. "The Kingdom of the East Saxons." *Anglo-Saxon England* 14: 1–36.
———, ed. 1988. *Bishop Æthelwold. His Career and Influence.* Woodbridge, Suff.
———. 1990. *Kings and Kingdoms of Early Anglo-Saxon England.* London.
Zahn, T., ed. 1876. *Ignatii et Polycarpi epistolae martyria fragmenta.* Vol. 2 of *Patrum apostolicorum opera,* ed. O. von Gebhardt, A. Harnack, and Zahn, 3rd ed., 3 vols. Leipzig, 1875–77.
———. 1882. *Cyprian von Antiochien und die deutsche Faustsage.* Erlangen.
Zaleski, Carol. 1987. *Otherworld Journeys: Accounts of Near-Death Experience in Medieval and Modern Times.* New York/London.

Zanetti, U. 1979. "Les passions des SS. Nazaire, Gervais, Protais et Celse." *Analecta Bollandiana* 97: 69–88.

Zettel, Patrick. 1979. "Ælfric's Hagiographic Sources and the Latin Legendary Preserved in B.L. MS Cotton Nero E. i + CCCC MS 9 and Other Manuscripts." Ph.D. diss., Oxford University.

———. 1982. "Saints' Lives in Old English: Latin Manuscripts and Vernacular Accounts: Ælfric." *Peritia* 1: 17–37.

Zotto, A. Dal. 1951. *La traslazione da Alessendria d'Egitio dei SS. Vitore e Corona*. Padua.

Zufferey, Maurice. 1983. "Le dossier hagiographique de Saint Maurice." *Zeitschrift für schweizerische Kirchengeschichte* 77: 2–46.

Zupitza, Julius. 1887. "Altenglische Glossen zu Abbos Clericorum Decus." *Zeitschrift für deutsches Altertum und deutsche Literatur* 31: 1–27.